—

Means-Tested Transfer Programs in the United States

**A National Bureau
of Economic Research
Conference Report**

Means-Tested Transfer Programs in the United States

Edited by **Robert A. Moffitt**

The University of Chicago Press

Chicago and London

362.582

M483

ROBERT A. MOFFITT is professor of economics at Johns Hopkins University and a research associate of the National Bureau of Economic Research.

The University of Chicago Press, Chicago 60637
The University of Chicago Press, Ltd., London
© 2003 by the National Bureau of Economic Research
All rights reserved. Published 2003
Printed in the United States of America

MIC 12 11 10 09 08 07 06 05 04 03   1 2 3 4 5
ISBN: 0-226-53356-5 (cloth)

Library of Congress Cataloging-in-Publication Data

Means-tested transfer programs in the United States / edited by
    Robert A. Moffitt.
        p.   cm.
    Papers presented at a conference sponsored by the National Bureau
    of Economic Research and held in Cambridge, Mass. on May 11–12,
    2000.
    Includes bibliographical references and index.
    ISBN 0-226-53356-5 (cloth : alk. paper)
    1. Income maintenance programs—United States—Congresses.
    2. Public welfare—United States—Congresses. I. Moffitt, Robert.
    II. National Bureau of Economic Research.
    HC110.I5 .M378 2003
    362.5'82—dc21

                                                        2002043563

Contents

Acknowledgments

This volume contains revised versions of papers that were presented in Cambridge, Massachusetts on 11–12 May 2000 at an NBER conference. The idea of a conference and volume on this topic came from suggestions by Martin Feldstein and James Poterba, who were involved at all stages of the planning and who were active participants at the conference. Financial support was also generously provided by the Smith-Richardson Foundation.

Kirsten Foss Davis and Brett Maranjian assisted in the logistical and local arrangements, for which I am grateful. Helena Fitz-Patrick ably shepherded the papers through the revision process and on to final publication. Anonymous reviewers from the University of Chicago Press and the NBER improved the papers as well.

All those involved performed at a high level of professionalism and have helped make the final product as useful a volume as I hope it to be.

Introduction

Robert A. Moffitt

The system of means-tested transfers in the United States continues to be an important area of research by economists as well as a topic of intense policy interest. Significant transformations in that system have occurred over the last decade, as the Aid to Families with Dependent Children (AFDC) program has been replaced by the Temporary Assistance to Needy Families (TANF) program, as the Earned Income Tax Credit (EITC) has grown from a minor program to one of the most important transfers to low-income families, and as the Medicaid program has greatly expanded eligibility to new groups. Significant caseload and expenditure growth in the Supplementary Security Income (SSI) program has also gathered public attention, and there continue to be important issues debated in the Food Stamp Program, housing programs, and other means-tested transfer programs.

Current policy developments surrounding the major means-tested programs are difficult to follow for those who are not specialists in the area, and even those who are specialists tend to follow developments in one program and not others. In addition, a considerable body of research has grown up around each of the major programs, and new contributions have been made in the last ten years, so most have difficulty keeping up with this evolving body of research as well. To assist economists and other researchers, as well as policy analysts, in learning about recent developments in the programs and in research surrounding them, the National Bureau of

Robert A. Moffitt is professor of economics at Johns Hopkins University and a research associate of the National Bureau of Economic Research.

The author would like to thank the Smith-Richardson Foundation for support for the conference and National Bureau of Economic Research volume upon which this paper is based, and the authors of the individual chapters for their work on the volume.

Economic Research (NBER) convened a conference in Cambridge, Massachusetts on 11–12 May 2000 to hear papers delivered on the major transfer programs in the United States. Sponsored by the Smith-Richardson Foundation, the conference included papers on each major program in the country. Each served the triple purpose of explicating the institutional history and current rules of the program; describing its current caseloads, expenditures, and recipient characteristics; and summarizing recent research on each program. Relative to most literature reviews, these papers were intended to provide more institutional detail on each program, but, relative to most government publications, which describe only the institutional details, the papers provide much more discussion of research evidence. In the end, the papers were intended to provide a succinct introduction to each program for those interested in learning about both history and current policy issues and rules as well as recent research evidence.

This volume contains revised papers from that conference. The nine chapters cover the major means-tested transfer programs in the United States: the Medicaid program, the SSI program, the EITC, food and nutrition programs, the TANF program, housing programs, programs that subsidize child care, employment and training programs, and the child support enforcement program. Taken as a whole, the volume furnishes a picture of the current state of U.S. means-tested programs, and research on those programs, at the turn of the century.

This introduction has two remaining sections. The first provides an overview of trends in expenditures in means-tested transfers in the United States over the last three decades. The second provides a brief summary of each of the chapters.

Overall Trends in Expenditures in Means-Tested Transfer Programs

Figure 1 shows trends since 1968 in per capita expenditures in the eighty largest means-tested transfer programs in the country.[1] The figure reveals that there have been four phases of spending growth: an expansionary phase beginning in the 1960s and running through the early or mid-1970s; a contractionary (or stationary) phase beginning in the mid-1970s and running until the mid-1980s; another expansionary phase running from the late 1980s to the mid 1990s; and another contractionary (or stationary) phase beginning in the mid-1990s.

The first phase saw an increase in AFDC benefits; enactment of a major piece of welfare legislation—the 1967 Social Security Amendments— which raised earnings disregards in the program (i.e., it lowered the tax rate

---

1. These eighty are those included in the useful volumes by Burke (1993, 1999, 2001). The majority of these programs are very small. Consequently, the volume captures virtually all programs in the United States.

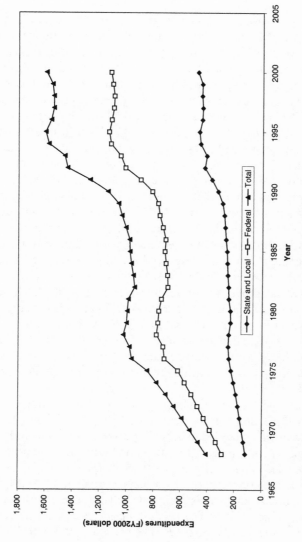

Fig. 1   Real per capita expenditures on means-tested transfers, 1968–2000

Sources: Burke (2001, tables 3 and 4); U.S. Department of Commerce (2002, table 2, Population).

on earnings); and witnessed the creation of the Food Stamp and Medicaid programs and, later in the period, the SSI program. Caseloads grew rapidly in all four of these programs. This period was later termed the era of the "welfare explosion" and set the modern framework of means-tested transfers.

The second phase saw a steady decline in real AFDC benefits; enactment of a major piece of AFDC legislation—the 1981 Omnibus Budget Reconciliation Act—which effectively eliminated the earnings disregards enacted in 1967 and consequently cut thousands of families with earnings from the rolls; and an increasing interest in work requirements and mandatory training programs for welfare recipients among federal policymakers. Declining real AFDC benefits were accompanied by slow but steady growth in the number of single-mother families, and the offsetting effects of these two forces left AFDC expenditures more or less unchanged in real terms.

The third phase—which is not always recognized, for it is often presumed that the system has been in steady contraction since the 1970s—saw a dramatic expansion of the EITC; major expansions of eligibility in the Medicaid program, primarily to non-AFDC families; and sizable expansions of the caseload in the SSI program, arising mostly from increased numbers of disabled adults and children. The Family Support Act of 1988, although occurring in the third phase and seemingly contractionary—it mandated work and training for AFDC recipients more heavily than in the past—is best viewed as neutral, for not only was it never effectively implemented, but it also could be interpreted as expansionary inasmuch as it required new expenditures on work programs for AFDC recipients. The runup of expenditures in this period, although not quite as large in magnitude as that in the welfare explosion of the late 1960s and early 1970s, occurred much more quickly—essentially all taking place in a five-year period between 1990 and 1995.

A fourth phase, which is continuing at this writing, is a combined result of 1996 welfare legislation that contracted the AFDC-TANF program and a robust economy, which has led to declining caseloads in many programs, thereby slowing expenditure growth. The Food Stamp and Medicaid programs have seen declining caseloads as well as AFDC-TANF.[2]

Table 1 shows the composition of this expenditure by general type of benefit at the approximate turning points of each of the major phases, and at the most recent date (2000). The 1968–78 period saw major percentage expansions across the board in all types of benefits, demonstrating that this was the period in which most of the major programs were introduced or expanded significantly. The 1978–88 period saw continued major growth in

2. The unemployment rate appears to have started to increase in late 2000 or 2001, indicating the beginning of a recession. Whether this will signal the beginning of a fifth phase or a modification of the fourth remains to be seen, and will depend on legislative developments and on the course of expenditure growth over the next few years.

Table 1   **Composition of Real Expenditures on Means-Tested Transfers, 1968–2000 (millions of fiscal year (FY) 2000 dollars)**

	Medical	Cash	Food	Housing	Education	Jobs/Training	Services	Energy
1968	24,122	37,810	4,486	3,933	4,320	3,777	2,507	0
1978	65,080	65,406	25,099	20,650	11,514	26,119	11,439	730
1988	96,029	66,729	31,177	23,173	17,068	5,577	9,620	2,921
1995	196,922	103,291	43,558	35,764	18,146	6,132	12,775	1,896
2000	225,858	91,703	34,347	34,906	20,385	7,347	20,724	1,715
Share of total (%)	57	15	8	9	5	1	5	1

Source: Burke (2001, tables 3 and 4).

Note: Combined federal and state and local.

Table 2   **Change in Real Expenditures in Six Major Programs, FY 1990 to FY 1996 (in millions of 1996 dollars)**

	AFDC	Food Stamps	Medicaid	EITC	Housing	SSI
1990	24,758	20,654	84,658	8,092	16,922	20,125
1996	23,677	27,344	159,357	24,088	19,877	32,065
Change from 1990 (%)	−4	42	88	198	17	59
Share of growth (%)	−1	7	60	13	4	10

Sources: Burke (1993, table 15); Burke (1999, tables 3 and 12).

Notes: EITC amounts include reduction in tax liability, not just refundable portion. Housing is the sum of expenditures on public and Section 8 housing. Federal and state combined totals are shown.

medical benefits; modest growth in food, housing, education, and energy programs; and slow or negative growth in cash, jobs and training, and services benefits. The 1988–95 period witnessed even greater growth in medical benefits; renewed growth in cash, housing, food, and services programs; and slow but continued growth in the other benefit types. Since 1995, although total expenditures have been very flat, the composition has changed, as medical benefits have continued to rise but cash and food benefit expenditures have declined as caseloads in those programs have fallen. Service expenditures, primarily child care subsidies, have also risen over this period as the government has sought to assist women moving into the workforce. Over the entire period 1968 to 2000, the growth of medical expenditures dominated overall growth (57 percent of the total), growth of cash benefits accounted for a much smaller amount (15 percent), and the other programs accounted for varying amounts of the remainder, with jobs and training, and energy programs, accounting for the least.

The most important recent era of expenditure growth is the third phase noted previously. Table 2 shows the sources of expenditure growth from

1990 to 1996 for the six most important programs over this period. Real AFDC expenditures actually declined, presaging the further decline that has occurred subsequent to the 1996 legislation. The Food Stamp Program expanded by 42 percent, however, indicating robust growth. A very large percentage expansion occurred in the Medicaid program, which grew by 88 percent. As will be discussed further, the Medicaid program covers different types of recipients, and the growth over this period came not only from expansions of expenditures for single mothers and their children, but also from increased expenditures on the disabled. While single mothers and their children represent the largest fraction of the Medicaid caseload, expenditures are greater for the disabled because of their greater medical needs. The largest percentage expansion in table 2, however, occurred in the EITC program, whose expenditures almost tripled over the period. As will be discussed presently, major expansions of the size of the credit resulted in this growth. Housing programs grew modestly during the period but the SSI program grew by a large amount, 59 percent, reflecting, as in Medicaid, increases in expenditures on the disabled.[3] Table 2 shows that the growth in cash benefits in the 1990s, which was shown to be significant in table 1, was entirely the result of growth in EITC and SSI expenditures, not AFDC-TANF.

The last row of table 2 shows the shares of total expenditure growth in the largest eighty means-tested transfers from 1990 to 1996 accounted for by each of these six programs. Medicaid expenditure growth, although not the largest in percentage terms, is the largest in dollar terms and accounts for the largest fraction, 60 percent. The EITC and SSI together account for another 23 percent. Altogether, these six programs accounted for 93 percent of the overall increase in means-tested expenditures in the 1990–96 expansionary phase.

Table 3 shows the expenditures and caseloads in the nine means-tested transfer programs covered in this volume.[4] The largest is Medicaid, as expected, and the next five—SSI, EITC, subsidized housing, child care, and food stamps—are of the same general magnitude but at a large distance from Medicaid. The TANF program, which in the 1960s was the largest of the programs, is now a distant seventh in rank.

The evolution of means-tested transfers that has led to the developments shown in these tables reflects several trends. One is the gradual decline of cash transfers like AFDC relative to in-kind transfers like Medicaid, food

3. If medical care prices are used to deflate Medicaid expenditures instead of a general price index, Medicaid expenditure growth amounted to only 34 percent. Which index should be used depends on whether the goal is to value expenditures from the point of view of the taxpayer or the recipient.

4. The child care and job-training entries in the table actually represent expenditures on a collection of programs, and are consequently slightly noncomparable with the other entries. Also, it should be noted that some of the chapters in the volume (e.g., on housing and food) cover more programs than those whose expenditures are shown in the table.

Table 3   **Annual Expenditures and Caseloads in the Programs in This Volume, FY 2000**

	Expenditures ($ millions)	Caseloads ($ thousands)	Expenditures per Recipient
Medicaid	207,195	42,020[a]	4,931
SSI	35,066	6,609	5,306
EITC	25,800	55,320	466
Subsidized housing[b]	22,498	26,961	834
Child care	20,580[c]	11,447[d]	1,798
Food stamps	20,341	18,200	1,118
TANF	14,490	6,035	2,401
Jobs and training	7,347	2,028	3,623
Child support enforcement	3,255[e]	11,900[f]	274

Sources: Burke (2001, table 11); Blau (chap. 7 in this volume, table 7.2); Lerman and Sorensen (chap. 9 in this volume, table 9.6).
Note: Last column equals the ratio of the second to the third, multiplied by 1,000.
[a]FY 1999.
[b]Section 8 and public housing.
[c]FY 1999–2001.
[d]FY 1998–2001, children served (incomplete list).
[e]FY 1997.
[f]FY 1997, custodial mothers.

stamps, housing, and child care. Voters and legislators appear to prefer to make transfers tied to specific consumption items rather than open-ended cash transfers. A second is the increasing narrowness of the targeting of transfers, because the programs that have seen the largest growth in the last decade are tied to specific eligibility groups. The EITC is specifically targeted to families with earnings, the SSI program is targeted to the disabled and elderly, and Medicaid is targeted to the disabled and—in the expansions that have occurred—mainly to single mothers and their children off TANF. This development represents a continued, if not increased, categorization of the nation's welfare population into a system in which different demographic groups are judged to be needy not just on the basis of income but on the basis of some other specific characteristic that leads them to be deserving in the eyes of the public. This also explains why the EITC and SSI programs, which provide cash transfers, have expanded while the AFDC-TANF program has not. As a consequence of these developments, the great expenditure expansion of the late 1980s and early 1990s increased total transfers to the low-income population but also changed the distribution of those transfers. The disabled as well as families off welfare with earnings gained, for example, relative to low-income single-mother families as a whole, especially those on welfare or not working.

The nine chapters in the volume are ordered roughly by their total expenditures and will be summarized in that order as well.

Summaries of the Chapters

As described by Jonathan Gruber, the Medicaid program is really four separate programs rolled into one. One supports the medical expenses of low-income single mothers and their children, while the other three provide public insurance for portions of medical expenditures not covered by Medicare for the low-income elderly, support medical expenses for the low-income disabled, and provide coverage of nursing home expenditures of the institutionalized elderly. The large enrollment and expenditure growth that has recently occurred has arisen primarily among the disabled and children under twenty-one. While the program was originally focused on traditional welfare populations, over time eligibility has been expanded to children in low-income two-parent and one-parent families, sometimes those fairly high up the income distribution. Recent expansions accompanying the Children's Health Insurance Program have occurred as well.

The research reviewed by Gruber primarily focuses on the single-mother and low-income-children portion of the program. Research has been conducted that calculates participation rates of eligibles, showing a declining rate among children; on the extent of Medicaid "crowdout," which occurs when Medicaid expansions displace private insurance coverage; and on the effect of Medicaid expansions on health outcomes, where many favorable effects have been found. Research on the labor supply disincentives of the program has demonstrated that those disincentives were stronger when Medicaid eligibility was closely tied to AFDC receipt but have weakened as that tie has loosened. A final area of research, not on single mothers and children, has concerned the effects of physician reimbursement rates, and how Medicaid affects the quality of long-term care and nursing homes.

Mary C. Daly and Richard V. Burkhauser discuss SSI, a federal program that pays cash benefits to low-income individuals who are sixty-five or older, or who are blind or disabled. The high caseload growth in the 1990s primarily occurred among the blind and disabled, children, and noncitizens. Eligibility requires not only low income and assets but also, for the blind and disabled, a medical test that is quite complex and stringent and which denies benefits to 63 percent of applicants. The medical test for children is less onerous and has fluctuated over time in its stringency; it was relaxed in 1990 but tightened up again in 1996. The program also has work incentives in the familiar negative income form, by reducing benefits by only fifty cents for every dollar of earnings.

Research on the SSI program has focused on several issues. One is the reason for the high caseload growth in the program. The most common factor identified is variation in the stringency of the medical tests, which has fluctuated greatly over time, but the business cycle has caused considerable fluctuation in caseloads as well. Yet another reason identified is an incentive for disabled children on AFDC to move to SSI. Another area of research is on work incentives, where the major issue has been the encouragement of work in light of the fact that only about 4 percent of recipients take advantage of the 50 percent tax rate in the program. Several SSI innovations have been attempted that seek to increase financial and other work incentives but have found recipient labor supply to be rather unresponsive. This therefore remains as one of the major issues in the program.

The EITC, as V. Joseph Hotz and John Karl Scholz note, has been one of the fastest-growing means-tested programs in the country. Its popularity stems from its emphasis on rewarding families that have significant levels of employment and earnings. The program provides a refundable tax credit to families with earnings that can be as high as $3,800 a year (1999). The program was introduced into the tax code in 1975 but did not see significant expansion in terms of generosity until the 1980s, when the size of the subsidy was increased and then indexed to inflation. Tax bills in 1990 and 1993 increased the amount of subsidy greatly and have led to the sizable growth in expenditures in the 1990s. The size of the tax credit is proportional to earnings up to some maximum level, and then it is phased out as earnings increase; it is possible for families with incomes up to $30,580 to still be eligible for the credit. An important administrative issue in the program has been overpayment of subsidies, which in 1995 were estimated to be 25 percent of tax expenditures, most of which results from inaccuracies in the claim for qualifying children.

Research on the EITC has concerned several issues, but its effects on work incentives has been one of the most important since this is one of the main appeals of the program. Most studies have indicated that there is a strong and significant positive effect of the EITC on the labor force participation rates of single-mother households. But research has also suggested that the program may have had a slight negative effect on the employment rates of married women, for many women are married to men who earn sufficiently high wages that additional earnings from the wife fall into the phaseout region of the EITC. In addition, there is some evidence that, while increasing employment rates overall, the EITC may have dampened hours of work of men and women in two-earner families. Research has also been directed at the effect of the credit on marriage, for there has been some concern that it may discourage marriage because men and women in certain earnings ranges can receive a greater EITC sum by not marrying and filing separate returns than by marrying and filing joint returns. The empirical evidence to date, however, suggests little effect of this incentive on actual patterns of marriage. A third area of research has been on the advance payment option, under which recipients can receive their credit over the tax year in question, as they earn wages, rather than in a lump sum at the end of the year or in the following spring. The high administrative costs of this option as well as the potential for fraud and noncompliance constitute significant barriers to its adoption.

Janet Currie surveys several programs that support food expenditure and nutrition among low-income families. The Food Stamp Program (FSP) is the largest, but also important are the Special Supplemental Nutrition Program for Women, Infants, and Children (WIC), the National School Lunch Program (NLSP), and the School Breakfast Program (SBP). Expenditures on the latter three programs are over 50 percent of those of the FSP, thus constituting a sizable additional amount of spending. All of these programs are federally financed and uniform across the states. The FSP provides food assistance to individuals and families, regardless of family structure, who meet income and asset conditions; has benefits that are indexed to inflation; and has a 30 percent nominal tax rate on earnings. The WIC, NSLP, and SBP are quite different. The WIC program provides financial assistance for the purchase of nutritious foods, nutrition education, and access to health services for pregnant or lactating women and children under five and requires for eligibility not only low income and assets but also that the women and children be at "nutritional risk." The NLSP and SBP allow children in low-income families to receive reduced-price or free school lunches or breakfasts. The NLSP is the far larger program of the two, having almost five times larger expenditure than the SBP.

There has been a considerable amount of research on the FSP, WIC, and NLSP programs. One area of research has focused on the effects of these programs on food expenditures, nutrient availability, and nutrient intake, showing that the FSP increases food expenditures (although not dollar for dollar) and increases the nutritional content of the foods purchased or brought into the home, but not necessarily nutritional intake (i.e., taking account of wastage and food eaten away from home). Evidence on the WIC program generally indicates favorable effects on child birth weight but also that the program tends to discourage breastfeeding, which is generally preferable to using infant formula. The effect of WIC on infant outcomes is more variable, but the evidence does indicate increases in nutrient consumption and reductions in the incidence of anemia. Research on the NLSP indicates that it improves nutrient intake. Other topics of research have concerned the reasons for relatively modest rates of participation of eligibles in the FSP (approximately 60 percent), the effects of converting the FSP to a cash program, and the work disincentives of the FSP.

In his survey of the TANF program and its precursor, AFDC, Robert A. Moffitt describes the major restructuring that followed 1996 Congressional legislation. In replacing the AFDC program with TANF, the legislation changed the program in fundamental ways by devolving the responsibility of major program design elements as well as financing to the individual states, converting a matching grant to a block grant, imposing strict work requirements on recipients and requiring that significant benefit penalties (or "sanctions") be assessed on those who do not comply, and imposing a lifetime limit of five years of benefit receipt that could be paid to a parent out of federal funds. The entitlement nature of the program was eliminated, and states were given the freedom to provide in-kind services instead of benefits and to set eligibility rules, benefit levels, tax rates, and family composition requirements at their discretion. States have vigorously pursued their options by modifying their programs in many ways, with a consequent proliferation of different programs around the country.

Research on the AFDC and TANF programs is large in volume. The most heavily researched issue relates to work incentives and programs that seek to improve employment and training outcomes. Most research indicates that the overall effect of lowering the tax rate on earnings in the program, a familiar reform since the discussion of the negative income tax in the 1960s, is likely to be small or zero, contrary to expectations of many economists. However, work requirements have a more positive effect although they come at the cost of requiring a categorization of the caseload into those who can and cannot work, which may be difficult to implement. Research comparing the TANF philosophy of encouraging recipients to enter the workforce immediately rather than undergoing education and training has shown it to have superior short-run payoffs but possibly lower long-run returns. Other research has shown that the TANF program, taken as a whole, has almost certainly increased employment and earnings and reduced the caseload, although its effects on income have been more mixed because increased earnings are often offset by reduced benefits. Findings from studies of the effect of welfare reform on demographic outcomes such as marriage and nonmarital fertility fail to show strong evidence of major effects. In addition, little is known about the separate and independent effects of time limits, work requirements, and other individual components of the TANF program or about their relative contributions to the overall effects of reform.

Edgar O. Olsen reviews the complex mix of housing programs for low-income families in the United States. Programs divide into those that are project-based, either owned by the government or by private contractors who are subsidized by the government, and tenant-based programs, in which eligible families receive subsidies to defray the rent in private housing. The public housing program, begun in the 1930s, is the best-known project-based program, consisting of units owned and operated by the government. Housing projects that are instead built by contracting with private parties to construct low-income housing or to rehabilitate existing housing were begun in 1954 but were largely terminated in 1983. The largest housing subsidy program today is tenant-based and uses vouchers to pay a portion of the rent of eligible low-income households who locate housing in the private market that meets the program's minimum housing standards. Eligibility for the programs is generally based on income, but space is not guaranteed and there are waiting lists for units and vouchers. The nominal tax rate on income varies but is most commonly 30 percent.

Research on housing programs has concerned a number of issues. One is cost-effectiveness, with research showing that tenant-based assistance provides housing equal in quality to that of project-based assistance but at a lower cost. Housing assistance has been shown by research to increase the consumption of housing by recipients and to do so more than would a cash grant. Supply effects have been studied as well, showing that an entitlement program of housing assistance would call forth a new supply of housing units but would have little effect on rent levels. Other topics that have received research attention are the work disincentives of housing programs and the effect of subsidized housing on constraining neighborhood location of recipients.

Means-tested child care programs are reviewed by David M. Blau. One of the most important is the Child Care and Development Fund (CCDF), a block grant intended to support child care services both for the TANF population and for nonwelfare poor families. States have some discretion in eligibility rules and much discretion in setting the subsidy mechanisms in their programs. A second is the Title XX Social Services Block Grant, which is again a block grant to the state for social services in general but of which 15 percent is spent on child care for low-income families. A third is the Dependent Care Tax Credit, a nonrefundable tax credit in the federal income tax. The Head Start and Title I-A programs, which are not tied to parental employment but are intended to improve child development for children in low-income families, are a final set of child-care-related programs.

Research on the effects of child care programs has been concentrated on a few selected issues. One is whether child care subsidies in general increase the employment of mothers, where the evidence strongly suggests that they do even though the magnitude of the effect is quite uncertain. Price elasticities of employment response are relatively low but are still statistically significant. Research on the effect of price on the quality of care chosen by parents using formal day care centers shows that child care subsidies may lead parents to use more care but at lower-quality centers, as measured by child-staff ratios and staff training. Yet other research shows that child care subsidies lower the probability that a single mother would be on AFDC. There is also a large literature on the effect of early childhood education on child outcomes, where the evidence supports an effect of such education on some outcomes for some programs. Whether the effects fade out over time or persist is more controversial, although some studies do show persistent effects.

As discussed by Robert J. LaLonde, the main omnibus employment and training program in the United States at the present time is the set of programs created by the Workforce Investment Act (WIA). The WIA provides block grants to the states to fund employment and training programs for adults and youth and has several titles with different programs and different services, including titles that cover adults, youth, and the Job Corps, a high-cost training program for disadvantaged youth. Except for the Job Corps program, states have great freedom to design their own WIA-funded programs. Training is primarily provided through "individual training accounts" that allow the individual to choose from a list of acceptable providers, and thus retains some features of a voucher. Training is typically provided in one of three types: one aimed at enhancing skill development, and which includes both classroom training and on-the-job training; a second called "work experience," which involves temporary placement in an actual job; and a third called "employability development," which includes job search assistance and career counseling.

There is no research on the WIA program because it has been put in place very recently (2000) but there is a large body of research on its predecessor, the Job Training Partnership Act (JTPA), which should still be quite relevant to WIA given that the basic types of programs are unlikely to change markedly. For adult women, the research shows that low-cost training programs have a fairly large impact relative to cost and constitute what appears to be a worthwhile investment. Higher-cost programs may be cost-effective as well, but this depends on the size of their long-term impact, about which little is known. For youth, it appears that only high-cost comprehensive training programs are likely to be productive social investments, the best example being the Job Corps. For adult men, however, most evaluations show essentially little impact on employment and earnings overall. Some programs appear to have positive impacts for certain subgroups of men, but the pattern does not have any clear explanation.

Robert I. Lerman and Elaine Sorensen review the Child Support Enforcement (CSE) system, the governmental program aimed at enforcing private child support obligations, particularly for the low-income population. The CSE program was established by Congress in 1975 to provide matching funds to states to collect child support obligations, establish paternity, and obtain support awards. Reducing welfare costs as well as increasing child support were both goals of the system. Since 1975 Congress has steadily increased pressure on the states to strengthen the CSE system by setting numeric goals for paternity establishment, increasing pressure on states to require judges to adhere to state child support guidelines governing the setting of child support awards, and increasing requirements to use wage withholding to obtain payments from noncustodial parents. Despite these increased efforts, only 24 percent of low-income custodial mothers received any child support at all in 1997, and even fewer received the full amount that has been awarded by the court. However, only 17 percent of mothers received support twenty years ago, when enforcement was much weaker, suggesting that CSE has had some impact. Much of that impact is thought to be from increased paternity establishment per se.

Research on child support issues has focused on several issues. One is aimed at determining the income levels of poor noncustodial fathers in order to determine how much they are capable of paying, a difficult task because there is no ready data set to identify noncustodial fathers and their incomes. Estimates indicate that, overall, noncustodial fathers could pay three to four times more than they are actually paying, given their incomes and given customary guidelines for how child support awards are based on income, although no estimates are available for low-income fathers alone. Other research indicates that strengthened CSE reduces AFDC caseloads and that increases in child support reduce rates of AFDC participation and increase employment rates. Another body of research focuses on the effect of CSE on absent fathers, indicating that CSE tends to drive many men into the underground economy, where income is not reported, and that the AFDC policy of capturing all child support payments to the custodial mother and using them to reduce AFDC expenditures instead of to increase her and her child's income results in a lack of incentive for the noncustodial father to pay support.

References

Burke, V. 1993. Cash and noncash benefits for persons with limited income: Eligibility rules, recipient and expenditure data, FY 1990–92. Washington, D.C.: Congressional Research Service.

———. 1999. Cash and noncash benefits for persons with limited income: Eligibility rules, recipient and expenditure data, FY 1996–FY 1998. Washington, D.C.: Congressional Research Service.

———. 2001. Cash and noncash benefits for persons with limited income: Eligibility rules, recipient and expenditure data, FY 1998–FY 2000. Washington, D.C.: Congressional Research Service.

U.S. Department of Commerce, Bureau of the Census. 2002. *Statistical abstract of the U.S.: 2001.* Washington, D.C.: Government Printing Office.

1

Medicaid

Jonathan Gruber

The largest growth in entitlement program spending in the United States over the past fifteen years has been in the Medicaid program, which provides health insurance to low-income populations. In 1984, the Medicaid program spent $38 billion, which was 4.4 percent of the federal budget in that year and 0.97 percent of gross domestic product (GDP) and covered 22 million persons. By 2001, the program was projected to spend $219 billion, which is 10.8 percent of the federal budget and 2.3 percent of GDP, and to cover 40 million persons. This astronomical growth is particularly striking in light of another important trend over the past fifteen years: a continued steady rise in the fraction of the nonelderly population without health insurance. From 1988 through 1998, this share rose by almost 20 percent, before leveling out in recent years (Employee Benefits Research Institute [EBRI] 2000).

These facts raise a number of interesting and important questions about the purpose and structure of the third largest entitlement program in the United States (trailing only Social Security and Medicare). Medicaid is in fact really four public insurance programs in one. The first provides coverage of most medical expenses for low-income women and children families; this function absorbs only about one-quarter of program dollars but encompasses two-thirds of program enrollees. The second is a program that provides public insurance for the portions of medical expenditures not covered by the Medicare program for the low-income elderly. The third is a program that covers most medical expenses for the low-income disabled.

Jonathan Gruber is professor of economics at the Massachusetts Institute of Technology and a research associate of the National Bureau of Economic Research.

The author is grateful to Jeff Hoffner and Becky Neuschatz for research assistance and to Robert Moffitt for helpful comments.

The last is a program that pays the nursing home expenditures of many of the institutionalized elderly. These last three functions apply to only one-third of beneficiaries but use three-quarters of program dollars. This panoply of functions has led to uneven program growth and some confusion about the mission of the program and how it integrates with other public insurance institutions.

In this chapter, I will review the structure of the Medicaid program and its economic impact. I start in part 1.1 by reviewing program history, and discussing the evolution and current structure of program rules. In part 1.2, I then turn to a more detailed discussion of the program as it currently exists, presenting a variety of statistics on enrollment and expenditures. Part 1.3 then provides a heuristic overview of the economic impacts of the Medicaid program, and part 1.4 reviews the large empirical literature on the Medicaid program and its impacts on health care utilization, health, labor supply, family structure, and other behaviors. Part 1.5 then discusses current policy issues and how they are informed (or not informed) by the existing literature. Part 1.6 concludes.

1.1   Program History, Rules, and Goals

In this section, I will review the historical evolution and current structure of program rules. In doing so, I will draw primarily on two invaluable sources. The first is the *Green Book* (U.S. Congress, Committee on Ways and Means 2000; hereafter GB), a generally invaluable source for understanding the current operation of this program (and most other social programs as well). The second is the *Yellow Book* (Congressional Research Service 1993; hereafter YB), a source that provides a more detailed investigation of the Medicaid program itself.

1.1.1   Origin and Goals of the Medicaid Program

The Medicaid program was created by the Social Security Amendments of 1965, the same legislation that created the Medicare program of health insurance for the elderly. Medicaid and Medicare replaced two earlier programs of federal grants to states to provide medical care to low-income persons, one for welfare recipients, and the other for the aged. Combined spending on these programs was $1.3 billion in 1965.

The new Medicaid program continued the tradition of allowing states substantial latitude to design their own programs, subject to federal minimum standards. Eligibility was largely confined to the populations traditionally eligible for welfare—single-parent families, and the aged, blind, and disabled. But there were two important early exceptions, foreshadowing larger exceptions to arise in the 1980s. The first was the "Ribicoff children": States could choose to cover children who met the financial standards of welfare programs but not the categorical standards (e.g., because

Table 1.1   **The Introduction of Medicaid by State**

	State(s)
1966	
January	HI, IL, MN, ND, OK, PA
March	CA
July	CT, ID, KY, LA, ME, MD, OH, RI, UT, VT, WA, WV, WI
September	MA
October	DE, MI, NY
November	NE
December	NM
1967	
July	IA, KS, MT, NV, NY, OR, WY
September	TX
October	GA, MO, SD
1968	
July	DC, SC
1969	
January	CO, TN
July	VA
1970	
January	AL, AR, FL, IN, MS, NJ, NC
1972	
September	AK

Note: Arizona began a special managed-care Medicaid program in the early 1980s.

they were in a two-parent family). The second was the "medically needy," populations whose income was above the eligibility standards but who had very high medical bills. States were initially given no upper limit for eligible incomes. States were also given latitude about when to join the program. As table 1.1, from Decker (1994) shows, although a number of states joined immediately in January 1966, states phased in steadily over the next four years, and the last state, Arizona, did not join the Medicaid program until 1982.

The history of federal Medicaid legislation is presented in table 1.2, from YB. This history presents a striking profile of continuous expansions and contractions in program generosity, sometimes within the same legislation. This is exemplified by the 1967 legislation that limited how generous states could be within their medically needy programs, but at the same time established one of the most important features of the Medicaid benefits package, the Early and Periodic Screening, Diagnostic, and Treatment Program (EPSDT) to improve child health. Another feature of this legislation was a move away from state restrictions on who Medicaid patients could see for their care, toward allowing those patients to use any provider of their choice (if the provider was willing to take Medicaid patients). This is striking because it was roughly thirty years later that states began to

Table 1.2	Major Medicaid Legislation, 1965 to 1997
	Description
Social Security of 1965	Established the Medicaid program
Social Security Amendments of 1967	Limited financial standards for the medically needy; established the EPSDT program to improve child health; permitted Medicaid beneficiaries to use providers of their choice
Act of 14 December 1971	Allowed states to cover services in ICFs and ICFs for the mentally retarded
Social Security Amendments of 1972	Repealed 1965 provision requiring states to move toward comprehensive Medicaid coverage; allowed states to cover care for beneficiaries under age twenty-two in psychiatric hospitals
Medicare-Medicaid Anti-Fraud and Abuse Amendments of 1977	Established Medicaid Fraud Control Units
Mental Health Systems Act, 1980	Required most states to develop a computerized Medicaid Management Information System
Omnibus Reconciliation Act of 1980	Boren amendment permitted states to establish payment systems for nursing home care in lieu of Medicare's rules
Omnibus Budget Reconciliation Act of 1981	Enacted three-year reductions in federal matching percentages for states whose spending exceeded growth targets; established Section 1915(b) and 1915(c) waiver programs; extended the Boren amendment to inpatient hospital services; eliminated special penalties for noncompliance with EPSDT requirements and gave states with Medically Needy programs broader authority to limit coverage
Deficit Reduction Act of 1984	Eliminated categorical test for certain pregnant women and young children
Consolidated Omnibus Budget Reconciliation Act of 1985	Extended coverage to all pregnant women meeting AFDC financial standards
Omnibus Budget Reconciliation Act of 1986	Allowed coverage of pregnant women and young children to 100 percent of poverty; established a new optional category of QMBs
Medicare and Medicaid Patient and Program Protection Act of 1987	Strengthened authorities to sanction and exclude providers
Omnibus Budget Reconciliation Act of 1987	Allowed coverage of pregnant women and infants to 185 percent of poverty; strengthened quality-of-care standards and monitoring of nursing homes; strengthened OBRA 1981 requirements that states provide additional payment to hospitals treating a disproportionate share of low-income patients
Medicare Catastrophic Coverage Act of 1988	Mandated coverage of pregnant women and infants to 100 percent of poverty; expanded coverage of low-income Medicare beneficiaries; established special eligibility rules for institutionalized persons whose spouse remained in the community to prevent "spousal impoverishment"
Family Support Act of 1988	Extended work transition coverage for families losing AFDC because of increased earnings and expanded coverage for two-parent families whose principal earner was unemployed
Omnibus Budget Reconciliation Act of 1989	Mandated coverage of pregnant women and children under age six to 133 percent of poverty; expanded EPSDT program requirements; mandated coverage and full-cost reimbursement of federally qualified health centers (FQHCs)

Table 1.2 (continued)

	Description
Omnibus Budget Reconciliation Act of 1990	Phased in coverage of children ages six through eighteen to 100 percent of poverty; expanded coverage of low-income Medicare beneficiaries; established Medicaid prescription drug rebate program
Medicaid Voluntary Contribution and Provider-Specific Tax Amendments of 1991	Restricted use of provider donations and taxes as state share of Medicaid spending; limited disproportionate share hospital payments
Omnibus Budget Reconciliation Act of 1993	Mandated that individuals must spend their assets down to a state-established level before Medicaid pays for nursing facilities and other medical care; established designation of disproportionate share hospitals to facilities in which Medicaid beneficiaries account for at least 1 percent of the hospital's inpatient days
Personal Responsibility and Work Opportunity Act of 1996	Introduced TANF, a cash welfare block grant to states that used the same application as Medicaid; severed the automatic link between AFDC and Medicaid; narrowed the eligibility criteria for disabled children
Balanced Budget Act of 1997	Guaranteed continued Medicaid eligibility for children with disabilities who are expected to lose their SSI eligibility as a result of restrictions enacted in 1996; permitted states to create a new category (with a sliding scale premium) for individuals with incomes up to 250 percent of poverty who would, but for income, be eligible for SSI

move back to this pre-1967 system through the use of managed care contracting. This legislation also highlights directly the three policy levers that are available to policymakers to change the generosity of the Medicaid program: eligibility, the construction of the benefits package, and reimbursement of providers.

1.1.2 Eligibility for Nonelderly and Nondisabled

Eligibility for the Medicaid program has evolved substantially over time. As noted above, eligibility was originally restricted to those receiving cash welfare payments, along with Ribicoff children and the medically needy. These base populations of eligibles are still in place, and they were the main populations covered until the mid-1980s; there were some other special options to cover women without children who met the Aid to Families with Dependent Children (AFDC) income criteria for the expenses of their pregnancy only (Currie and Gruber 1996b), but these groups were very small.

Beginning in 1984, however, the program began to expand eligibility for all children and for pregnant women; that is, among women these expansions applied only to the expenses of pregnancy. Changes in Medicaid policy since 1984 can be broadly categorized into two eras. The first, from 1984 to mid-1987, was a period of incremental increases in Medicaid eligibility for populations that had similar financial circumstances to AFDC families but did not meet the eligibility criterion for other reasons. This began a gradual weakening of the linkage between AFDC coverage and eligibility for Medicaid. This occurred both at the state level—for example, through expansions of the Ribicoff option[1]—and at the federal level, through the 1984 Department for Environment, Food, and Rural Affairs (DEFRA) and 1985 Consolidated Omnibus Reconciliation Act (COBRA) legislation.

The second era, from mid-1987 to the present, saw a more dramatic de-coupling of Medicaid and AFDC through substantial increases in the income cutoff for Medicaid eligibility. These expansions substantially increased (in most states) the income that a family could have and still qualify for Medicaid, while providing these higher eligibility levels to all family structures, not just to single-parent families. By 1992, states were required to cover all pregnant women and children under the age of six up to 133 percent of poverty (independent of family composition), and were allowed to expand coverage up to 185 percent of poverty. In addition, children born after 30 September 1983 were mandatorily covered up to 100 percent of poverty (once again independent of family composition). Income for these purposes is defined similarly to the AFDC or Temporary Assistance for Needy Families (TANF) program, including all sources of cash income.

The pattern of legislative action over this period was one of initial federal permission for states to expand their programs, followed within a period of several years by federal mandates for all states to cover these groups. This pattern of laws generated substantial variation across the states in eligibility changes, since states initially had different qualification limits through AFDC and other optional programs (such as Ribicoff children), and they took up the new options at different rates. There was also variation within states in the eligibility of children of different ages for the Medicaid expansions, due to different age thresholds in the laws. This variation is illustrated in table 1.3, from Gruber and Yelowitz (1999). This shows the age and percent of poverty cutoffs for expansions to the youngest group of children in each state at three different points in time.[2] In January 1988, only some states had expanded eligibility, and the income and age cutoffs varied. By December 1989, all states had some expansion in place since federal law mandated coverage of infants up to 75 percent of the poverty line; but some states had expanded coverage up to age seven or

1. In 1984, only twenty-three states offered the Ribicoff program; by 1987, this had expanded to thirty-two states, although some states limited eligibility to somewhat younger children (less than age seventeen, eighteen, or nineteen, instead of the traditional cutoff of age twenty-one).

2. There were also differential expansions to older children as well, adding further richness to the variation in legislation across the states. The age restrictions were couched in terms of either date of birth or calendar date, or both, giving rise to the fractional ages of eligibility in some states at a given point in time.

Table 1.3   State Medicaid Age and Income Eligibility Thresholds for Children

State	January 1988 Age	Medicaid	December 1989 Age	Medicaid	December 1991 Age	Medicaid	December 1993 Age	Medicaid
Alabama			1	185	8	133	10	133
Alaska			2	100	8	133	10	133
Arizona	1	100	2	100	8	140	12	140
Arkansas	2	75	7	100	8	185	10	133
California			5	185	8	185	10	200
Colorado			1	75	8	133	10	133
Connecticut	0.5	100	2.5	185	8	185	10	185
Delaware	0.5	100	2.5	100	8	160	18	185
District of Columbia	1	100	2	100	8	185	10	185
Florida	1.5	100	5	100	8	150	10	185
Georgia	0.5	100	3	100	8	133	18	185
Hawaii			4	100	8	185	10	185
Idaho			1	75	8	133	10	133
Illinois			1	100	8	133	10	133
Indiana			3	100	8	150	10	150
Iowa	0.5	100	5.5	185	8	185	10	185
Kansas			5	150	8	150	10	150
Kentucky	1.5	100	2	125	8	185	10	185
Louisiana			6	100	8	133	10	133
Maine			5	185	8	185	18	185
Maryland	0.5	100	6	185	8	185	10	185
Massachusetts	0.5	100	5	185	8	185	10	200
Michigan	1	100	3	185	8	185	10	185
Minnesota			6	185	8	185	18	275
Mississippi	1.5	100	5	185	8	185	10	185
Missouri	0.5	100	3	100	8	133	18	185
Montana			1	100	8	133	10	133
Nebraska			5	100	8	133	10	133
Nevada			1	75	8	133	10	133
New Hampshire			1	75	8	133	10	170
New Jersey	1	100	2	100	8	185	10	300
New Mexico	1	100	3	100	8	185	10	185
New York			1	185	8	185	12	185
North Carolina	1.5	100	7	100	8	185	10	185
North Dakota			1	75	8	133	10	133
Ohio			1	100	8	133	10	133
Oklahoma	1	100	3	100	8	133	10	150
Oregon	1.5	85	3	100	8	133	10	133
Pennsylvania	1.5	100	6	100	8	133	10	185
Rhode Island	1.5	100	6	185	8	185	10	185
South Carolina	1.5	100	6	185	8	185	10	185
South Dakota			1	100	8	133	10	133
Tennessee	1.5	100	6	100	8	185	10	185
Texas			3	130	8	185	10	185
Utah			1	100	8	133	10	133
Vermont	1.5	100	6	225	8	225	17	225

(*continued*)

Table 1.3   (continued)

State	January 1988		December 1989		December 1991		December 1993	
	Age	Medicaid	Age	Medicaid	Age	Medicaid	Age	Medicaid
Virginia			1	100	8	133	18	133
Washington	1.5	100	8	185	8	185	18	185
West Virginia	0.5	100	6	150	8	150	18	150
Wisconsin			1	130	8	155	10	155
Wyoming			1	100	8	133	10	133

Sources: Yelowitz (1995) and Intergovernmental Health Policy Project (various editions).

Notes: The age limit represents the oldest that a child could be (at a given point in time) and still be eligible. Medicaid column represents the Medicaid income limit for an infant (the maximum for an older child is less).

eight, and coverage ranged as high as 185 percent of the poverty line. By December 1991, state policies were more uniform because the most restrictive federal mandates had taken place, but some variation in poverty cutoffs remained. In the subsequent years, several states expanded the age limits even further, using state-only funds.

Most states continue to base eligibility, even for expansion populations, on the income definitions used for cash welfare programs, formerly known as AFDC and currently as TANF. In order to qualify for welfare, a family must pass three tests: Their gross income must be below a multiple of the state's *needs* standard (this test was applied from 1982 onward only);[3] their gross income less certain disregards for work expenses and child care must be below the state's needs standard; and their gross income less certain disregards less a portion of their earnings must be below the state's *payment* standard. The precise structure of these rules is described in the appendix to Currie and Gruber (1994). States are also mandated to extend Medicaid coverage for an additional twelve months to those families whose income rises above TANF cutoffs, although states can impose premiums or other restrictions after six months.

Although these broad rules describe eligibility, there is some state discretion, and increasingly so since the mid-1990s through state waivers to AFDC, and then through the decentralization of welfare with the transition to the TANF program. The current panoply of rules is described in more detail in Ku, Ullman, and Almeida (1999). It is worth noting that, even if states tighten eligibility for cash assistance using their new discretion under TANF, states are required to continue to provide Medicaid to those who meet the AFDC criteria for eligibility in place in July 1996 (although the enforceability of this requirement is unclear). Categorical eligibility for AFDC/TANF and the expansions for pregnant women and chil-

---

3. From 1982 to 1984, this multiple was 1.5; from 1985 onward, the multiple was 1.85.

dren provide the vast majority of eligibility for Medicaid for those who are not elderly or disabled; there are a few other minor optional state programs described in YB.

Traditionally, eligibility for AFDC (and hence Medicaid) was conditioned on asset holdings of less than $1,000 per family. As part of the legislation that allowed states to expand their income cutoffs for Medicaid eligibility, the federal government also authorized states to remove their asset tests for determining eligibility. States were quick to drop asset testing once they had the chance, so that by the middle of 1989 fewer than ten states still had asset tests.

1.1.3   Eligibility for the Elderly and Disabled

For the elderly and disabled, there are four primary routes to Medicaid eligibility. The first is through the Supplemental Security Income (SSI) program. The SSI program is a purely means-tested transfer program to the elderly with countable income (which excludes income elements such as the first $20 of Social Security payments per month) below a certain threshold ($545 for an individual and $817 for a couple, in 2002), and with countable assets (which exclude the value of the home, automobiles, and substantial personal effects) below $2,000 for an individual and $3,000 for a couple. States are generally required to make all those elderly who qualify for SSI eligible for Medicaid, unless they had more restrictive rules in place for eligibility before 1972; in that case, they can apply these more restrictive rules rather than the federal SSI cutoffs. States can also extend eligibility to somewhat higher-income groups if they make supplemental payments under their state SSI programs.

The second route to eligibility for the elderly is the Medically Needy program, which is designed to cover individuals who meet the family structure requirements for welfare and whose gross resources are above welfare levels, but whose high medical expenditures bring their net resources below some certain minimal level. States who take up this option may establish Medically Needy thresholds that are no more than 133 percent of the state's needs standard; states may also include asset limits that are no more restrictive than those used for cash welfare (generally the asset limit for SSI is used). Individuals can then "spend down" to these thresholds by subtracting their medical expenditures from their gross income; if they do, Medicaid will pay the remainder of their expenditures.[4] Currently, thirty-five states have a Medically Needy program (GB). Although this option is available to all populations, it is used rarely by the nonelderly and nondisabled, but very frequently by the elderly, for whom the large costs of nursing home care can easily cause low countable incomes.

---

4. The time frame over which such spend-down occurs varies across the states. See Norton (1995, 2000) for a richer discussion of spend-down rules.

A third route to eligibility is the "300 percent rule", which allows states to cover those who have low assets and income that does not exceed 300 percent of the SSI payment level. In states for which this is the only route to Medicaid coverage of nursing home costs (seventeen states as of 1993, according to YB), this means that if income exceeds this limit, these costs are not covered regardless of their level.

A fourth route to eligibility for home- and community-based services (HCBS; as opposed to institutionally provided care) is through the rapidly growing number of state waivers in this area. As described in detail for each state at www.hcfa.gov/medicaid/hpg4.htm, these waivers provide mechanisms for states to experiment with alternatives to institutional care, in an effort to reduce spending on caring for the elderly and disabled. There are seven explicit services that may be provided in HCBS waiver programs (case management, homemaker/home health aide services, personal care services, adult day health, habilitation, and respite care), and other services may be requested by states (such as nonmedical transportation, in-home support services, special communication services, minor home modifications, and adult day care). To receive approval to implement HCBS waiver programs, state Medicaid agencies must assure the Health Care Financing Administration (HCFA) that, on an average per capita basis, the cost of providing home- and community-based services will not exceed the cost of care for the identical population in an institution; but to date there is little evaluation of the net impact of these waivers on either noninstitutional or (more relevantly) total program costs. There are currently 240 such waivers in effect, with all states having at least one.

For all of these routes, for the elderly, there are complicated rules corresponding to the treatment of income at the point of application versus ongoing enrollment. In particular, since 1988, there has been a detailed set of rules in place to protect against spousal impoverishment for those elderly who have a spouse remaining in the community. These rules, which are described in detail in YB, essentially allow those with spouses in the community to disregard substantial sums of income in considering eligibility for Medicaid.

For the disabled, an additional element is that Medicaid coverage has been extended to those who work their way off the SSI rolls. This coverage is available for a limited period of time and up to a limited income level.

Finally, there is an additional category of *partial* Medicaid eligibility for other groups of elderly and the disabled. The Qualified Medicare Beneficiary (QMB, or "quimbee") program provides that for those aged and disabled persons who are receiving Medicare whose incomes are below the federal poverty level, and whose assets do not exceed twice the allowable amount under SSI, states must pay Medicare part B premiums (the payment, currently $45.50 [1999] per month, that finances part of the cost of physician care for the elderly) and any required Medicare coinsurance and deductible amounts. The Specified Low-Income Medicare Beneficiaries (SLMB, or "slimbees") program mandates payment of part B premiums only for those elderly/disabled with incomes between 100 and 135 percent of the poverty line, and a portion of these premiums for those between 135 and 175 percent of the poverty line. Expansions to this program were phased in along with the expansions to younger populations in the late 1980s and early 1990s, as described in more detail by Yelowitz (2000a). Other groups of former disability recipients are also entitled to Medicaid payment of their Medicare costs; see GB and YB for more details.

A group of particular interest, particularly in the wake of the 1996 welfare reform legislation, is legal immigrants. Current law stipulates that legal immigrants arriving in the United States after 22 August 1996 are ineligible for Medicaid benefits for five years; after that period, coverage is a state option. Coverage is mandated for those arriving earlier than that date who became disabled since arriving.

1.1.4   Services

Although states have substantial leeway along the two other key dimensions of Medicaid policy, eligibility and reimbursement, they have much less discretion when it comes to covered services, at least traditionally. All categorically needy (as opposed to medically needy) enrollees are mandatorily entitled to

- inpatient hospital services
- outpatient hospital services
- rural health clinic services
- federally qualified health center services
- other laboratory and X-ray services
- nursing facility services for individuals twenty-one or older
- EPSDT services for individuals under age twenty-one
- family planning services
- physicians' services
- home health services for any individual entitled to nursing facility (NF) care
- nurse-midwife services
- services of certified nurse practitioners and certified family nurse practitioners

States do have the option of providing a more restrictive package of benefits to the medically needy, with the minimum standards including only prenatal and delivery services for pregnant women; ambulatory services for individuals under age eighteen and those entitled to institutional services; home health services for individuals entitled to NF services; and, if the state covers the mentally disabled in intermediate care facilities (ICFs), they must cover all the services provided to the categorically eligible.

There is also a wide range of optional services, although they in general do not amount to a very large share of total medical spending. The most important of these (in terms of total program costs) are prescription drugs, which are covered in every state, although a minority of states cover them only for the categorically needy and not the medically needy (YB). Other services covered by all or virtually all states include clinic services, optometrists' services and eyeglasses, dental services, prosthetic devices, eyeglasses, nursing facility services for those under age twenty-one, intermediate care facility/mentally retarded services, and transportation services. Although there is a long list of optional services, the fact that the most expensive ones are covered by virtually every state implies that there is substantial uniformity of the package of services covered from state to state.

There is some state leeway on services through utilization controls and service limitations. States can impose limits on length of inpatient hospital stay, on the number of visits to various sites of outpatient care, and on the number of prescriptions and quantity of drugs per prescription, and many states take advantage of these limitations (although with fairly high limits that are likely to be infrequently binding). States also have some limited discretion to impose cost sharing on enrollees, with some major exceptions: those under age eighteen, services related to pregnancy; hospital, NF, and ICF services if the individual is required to spend all his or her income (aside from a personal needs allowance) on the service; emergency, family planning, or hospice services; and those enrolled in health maintenance organizations (HMOs). These cost-sharing amounts are nominal, however.

1.1.5   Reimbursement

States do have substantial discretion along the third major dimension of Medicaid policy-making, provider reimbursement. States have always had discretion in setting physician reimbursement. Before 1980, however, states were required to use Medicare rules for reimbursing hospitals and nursing facilities. The Boren amendment of 1980 allowed states to move to their own methodologies for reimbursing these providers, so long as rates were "reasonable and adequate." In the wake of a long history of lawsuits brought under the Boren amendment that reimbursement rates were not reasonable, the amendment was repealed as part of the Balanced Budget Act of 1997, which mandated only that states must provide public notice of their proposed rates for reimbursing hospitals, nursing facilities, and ICFs and the methods used to establish those rates.

For hospitals, almost all states used the freedom conferred on them by the Boren amendment to move away from traditional retrospective, cost-based reimbursement (a move made by the Medicare program itself under the Prospective Payment System implemented in 1983). Most states moved to a purely prospective system of rates that either pay a fixed amount per day or pay for the entire stay for a given diagnosis, while some states use a hybrid of retrospective and prospective reimbursement. Some states also negotiate rates with hospitals through a bidding process, whereby the states restrict enrollees' choice of hospital and negotiate with hospitals for the right to provide services to Medicaid enrollees. In 1990, the American Hospital Association estimated that, on average, Medicaid reimburses hospitals for roughly 80 percent of their costs (YB).

Another important component of hospital reimbursement policy is Disproportionate Share payments (DSH). The Omnibus Budget Reconciliation Act (OBRA) of 1981 mandated that states Medicaid reimbursement systems "take into account the situation of hospitals which serve a disproportionate number of low-income patients with special needs." This definition was state-determined until 1988, and then federally mandated as relating to a hospital's load of both Medicaid and other low-income patients. As discussed in more detail presently, this program provided a loophole that allowed states to effectively increase the federal share of financing of hospital payments, and starting in 1992 state DSH payments were capped.

Nursing facility reimbursement is also done on a largely prospective basis, usually using per diem rates; once again, states have substantial discretion here, and there are wide variations in reimbursement rates. Some states also adjust payments for the case mix of patients residing in the facility. Medicaid reimbursement rates appear to be roughly 80 percent as generous as those of the private sector (YB). For an excellent review of Medicaid policy and other issues in long-term care, see Norton (2000).

Physician reimbursement is also largely determined by the states, and, as a rule, reimbursement is fairly low relative to private plans and to Medicare. States generally use a fee schedule, whereby physicians are reimbursed for their charges up to a set amount, based on diagnosis and treatment. Fees vary enormously for individual services, as well as (although to a lesser extent) for the overall package of services: In 1989, the range of fees across states for an office visit was from $10 to $104, and for total obstetric care with a vaginal delivery the range was from $344 to $1,316; the range for the value of the total package of services was a factor of 3.3 (YB). The average state pays roughly 70 percent of what is paid under the Medicare program for comparable treatments. The gap with private payers is even larger; for vaginal childbirth, for example, Medicaid paid 43 percent of the amount paid by private payers, and the increment for cesarean delivery was only 23 percent as large (Gruber, Kim, and Mayzlin 1998).

The method of reimbursing the other primary source of ambulatory care, hospital outpatient departments, is varied as well, with most states using prospective systems but with a larger component of retrospective cost-based reimbursement than is used on the inpatient side. Importantly, all providers are required to accept Medicaid payment rates as payments in full, except where the nominal cost-sharing noted above is allowed.

Finally, an important and complicated area of Medicaid reimbursement policy is for prescription drugs. As described in Scott-Morton (1997), under OBRA 1990 the Medicaid program established a "most-favored-nation" provision under which pharmaceutical producers could charge Medicaid no more than they charged to other payers. As predicted by theory, this led to a rise in pharmaceutical prices by weakening the incentives for price competition. Other specific details of Medicaid state reimbursement policy for drugs are provided in YB.

States are also entitled to "buy into" private coverage for Medicaid when it is cost-effective to do so. This situation might arise, for example, if a person eligible for Medicaid is provided group health insurance; Medicaid could in principle pay the employee's share of the group premiums in that case, lowering costs below the total cost of Medicaid coverage.

1.1.6   Waiver Options/Managed Care

An area of growing importance for state Medicaid policy is that of waiver options, which allow states to experiment in limited ways outside of the structure provided by federal guidelines. Since the early stages of Medicaid, states have been allowed to enroll their caseload in managed care organizations such as HMOs. OBRA 1981 established two new options, "freedom of choice" and "home- and community-based care" waivers. The former allows states to place some restrictions on the provider choice set for enrollees, such as using primary care case management programs through which enrollees must see a gatekeeper physician before seeking specialty services, or using selective contracting of the type noted above with hospitals. The latter option allows states to innovate with alternatives to institutionally based care; originally, these innovations had to be demonstrated to be cost-neutral, but since OBRA 1990 there are limited funds available for waivers that increase costs. Of course, projections of cost neutrality are tenuous at best, and to date there is little retrospective evidence on the actual cost efficacy of these alternatives.

The past decade has seen an explosion in state use of managed care as a means of controlling Medicaid program costs. Between 1993 and 2001, enrollment in Medicaid managed care increased by over 450 percent, and by 2001, 58 percent of Medicaid beneficiaries were enrolled in some form of managed care. Medicaid managed care programs generally fall into two categories: those where the health plan assumes full financial risk for the services that it provides to enrollees ("risk-based" programs), and those where an individual health provider is paid a monthly amount by the state for managing health care services (the gatekeeper approach previously noted). The Balanced Budget Act of 1997 further increased use of managed care by removing the requirement of a federal waiver for enrolling the majority of Medicare beneficiaries in managed care, allowing states to contract with "Medicaid only" HMOs, and allowing states to lock beneficiaries in the same plan for up to twelve months (GB).

Despite its phenomenal growth, there has been relatively little work on managed care in Medicare. Currie and Fahr (2000) nicely review the literature in this area. There are conjectures that the impacts of managed care on health might be positive (through increased gatekeeping and facilitation of primary care) or negative (through supply limits on care), but there is little evidence to support either view. The best work here is probably Levinson and Ullman's (1998) study of managed care on birth outcomes in Wisconsin. They found that enrollment in managed care by Medicaid mothers was associated with increased use of prenatal care but no changes in birth outcomes. A more general finding of past work is that Medicaid managed care organizations (MCOs) select on health in their enrollment decisions. Consistent with this, Currie and Fahr find that areas with higher managed care penetration have higher enrollment of low-cost groups (whites and older children) and lower penetration of high-cost groups (blacks and younger children). The impact of managed care on the Medicaid program is clearly an area deserving of further work.

1.1.7   Administration and Financing

The Medicaid program is administered by state agencies under the general oversight of the HCFA, Department of Health and Human Services (DHHS). Within HCFA, Medicaid operations have been centered since 1990 in a separate Medicaid Bureau. States must designate a single administrative agency for program operations. This can be either the welfare or social services department, the health department, a combination health/ social services department, or a separate entity that is Medicaid-specific.

A key component of Medicaid enrollment is the application process for determining eligibility. Medicaid applications can be lengthy and cumbersome. As a result, a number of states have established streamlined application processes for pregnant women and children, along several dimensions. The most important is "presumptive eligibility," which allows potential enrollees to receive services after an interim determination by providers that the woman or child is eligible. States have also shortened applications, expedited eligibility processes, and outstationed case workers in health care sites to ease the application process. By early 1998, forty states had dropped asset tests for eligibility, forty-four had shortened application forms, and twenty-seven had presumptive eligibility for pregnant women (National Governors Association [NGA] 1998).

Medicaid also has a significant quality control component that is described in great detail in YB. There are also detailed certification processes for providers, particularly for nursing homes, to ensure quality care, as described in YB.

Medicaid services and associated administrative costs are jointly financed by the federal government and the states. The federal share of state payments for services is an uncapped entitlement that is determined through the federal medical assistance percentage (FMAP), which is calculated annually based on a formula designed to provide a higher percentage of federal matching payments to states with lower per capita incomes. On average, the federal government pays roughly 57 percent of the costs of the Medicaid program, with the percentage varying between 50 and 83 percent across states. One source of controversy is whether state per capita income is the right measure of state need in determining the federal cost share; in a series of studies, the Government Accounting Office (GAO) concluded that a measure based on state property values and the share of the population in poverty would better capture both need and the state's own ability to finance care (YB). Federal funding for Medicaid is an entitlement, created by Title XIX of the Social Security Act, and so does not require reauthorization by the Congress.

State Medicaid spending has been rising very rapidly since the late 1980s, as is documented in more detail presently. One controversial source of this spending increase has been provider donations or taxes to the state. Essentially, states had providers of Medicaid services either pay taxes or donations to the state, and then bill the cost of these actions to the Medicaid program by selectively raising reimbursement through DSH. Since the donations or taxes accrue 100 percent to the state, but increased DSH costs are borne partially by the federal government (according to the FMAP for that state), this mechanism caused a net transfer from federal to state governments. The exact mechanics of these schemes is described in more detail in YB. This became a very popular source of funding for the Medicaid program in the early 1990s, a period when the federal government was mandating expanded eligibility for pregnant women and children, and contributed to an explosion of both DSH and overall program costs. Subsequent legislation has limited the use of these mechanisms, both by directly ruling out some types of structures and by capping the magnitude of DSH payments.

1.1.8   Children's Health Insurance Program

The largest single expansion of insurance entitlement since the establishment of the Medicaid program was the Children's Health Insurance Program (CHIP) in the Balanced Budget Act of 1997. This program allows states to extend eligibility to children with incomes above Medicaid limits, either through further expansions of Medicaid or through newer, more flexible programs. The ultimate structure of the program represents an interesting compromise between groups that advocated expansion of the existing Medicaid program and those that wanted simple lump-sum grants to the states to spend on health care.

This program is a capped federal expenditure, amounting to $4.3 billion in each of its first four years, and a total of $40 billion over ten years. These funds are allotted to states initially in proportion to their share of the low-income uninsured population, and eventually in proportion to both this and the total number of low-income children (so as to not penalize states that make progress on increasing insurance coverage). The FMAP for this program is equal to 1.3 times the states' FMAP for Medicaid, to entice states to expand coverage through this option.

State benefits packages under CHIP can be more limited than under Medicaid, but they must meet (or be actuarially equivalent to) the coverage standards through either the Blue Cross/Blue Shield option of the Federal Employees Health Benefits Program (FEHBP), a health benefits plan that is offered to state employees, or the HMO plan with the largest commercial enrollment in the state. States with existing "state only" programs that expanded beyond Medicaid limits using state funds could continue to use their existing benefit packages. Cost sharing must remain nominal below 150 percent of the poverty line, but above that point copayments and premiums can amount to as much as 5 percent of family income.

This program leaves a substantial amount of discretion for the states in how to spend their allotment, reflecting the compromise previously noted. States were required to submit state plans to be reviewed by HCFA before they could receive their initial allotments. As of 1 August 1999, all fifty states and the District of Columbia had developed plans for children's health insurance expansions under CHIP—and all but three had received federal approval (Ullman, Hill, and Almeida 1999). CHIP will in principle dramatically increase eligibility for children; the average income threshold for children across the states will rise from 121 percent of the federal poverty line to 206 percent. Of the fifty-one CHIP plans submitted, eighteen expand Medicaid, seventeen create programs separate from Medicaid, and sixteen do both; ten of the states with "new" programs actually have Medicaid look-alike programs that cap enrollment, impose expanded cost-sharing requirements, or both (Ullman, Hill, and Almeida).

1.2   Program Statistics

1.2.1   Expenditures and Enrollment

Medicaid expenditures over time are shown in table 1.4. Expenditures in 1966 totaled $1.7 billion and by 2001 were expected to rise to over $219 billion. Program growth was fastest from 1988 through 1994, when the program virtually tripled over a seven-year period; as previously noted, this is a period marked by both substantial eligibility expansions and state gaming of the DSH system to pay for the expansions. There has been a slight rise in the federal share since the early years of the program; the federal share rose from 54 percent on average in 1970 to 57 percent in 2001.

Enrollment growth has also been rapid, as shown in table 1.5. The total number of recipients has risen from 17.6 million in 1972 to 37.9 billion in 2001. The most rapid growth has been in the disabled, and the largest absolute growth has been in dependent children under age twenty-one. The current division of spending across these groups is shown as well at the bottom of table 1.5.

Table 1.4   **Medicaid Expenditures**

Fiscal Year	Total ($ millions)	Total % Increase	Federal ($ millions)	Federal % Increase	State ($ millions)	State % Increase
1966[a]	1,658	—	789	—	869	—
1967[a]	2,368	42.8	1,209	53.2	1,159	33.4
1968[a]	3,686	55.7	1,837	51.9	1,849	59.5
1969[a]	4,166	13.0	2,276	23.9	1,890	2.2
1970[a]	4,852	16.5	2,617	15.0	2,235	18.3
1971	6,176	27.3	4,361	29.3	4,074	45.4
1972[b]	8,434	36.6	4,361	29.3	4,074	45.4
1973	9,111	8.0	4,998	14.6	4,113	1.0
1974	10,229	12.3	5,833	16.7	4,396	6.9
1975	12,637	23.5	7,060	21.0	5,578	26.9
1976	14,644	15.9	8,312	17.7	6,332	13.5
TQ[c]	4,106	n.a.	2,354	n.a.	1,752	n.a.
1977	17,103	16.8[d]	9,713	16.9[d]	7,389	16.7[d]
1978	18,949	10.8	10,680	10.0	8,269	11.9
1979	21,755	14.8	12,267	14.9	9,489	14.8
1980	25,781	18.5	14,550	18.6	11,231	18.4
1981	30,377	17.8	17,074	17.3	13,303	18.4
1982	32,446	6.8	17,514	2.6	14,931	12.2
1983	34,956	7.7	18,985	8.4	15,971	7.0
1984	37,568	7.5	20,061	5.7	17,508	9.6
1985[e]	40,917	8.9	22,655[f]	12.9	18,262[f]	4.3
1986	44,851	9.6	24,995	10.3	19,856	8.7
1987	49,344	10.0	27,435	9.8	21,909	10.3
1988	54,116	9.7	30,462	11.0	23,654	8.0
1989	61,246	13.2	34,604	13.6	26,642	12.6
1990	72,492	18.4	41,103	18.8	31,389	17.8
1991	91,519	26.2	52,532	27.8	38,987	24.2
1992	118,166	29.1	67,827	29.1	50,339	29.1
1993	131,775	11.5	75,774	11.7	56,001	11.2
1994	143,204	8.7	82,034	8.3	61,170	9.2
1995	156,395	9.2	89,070	8.6	67,325	10.1
1996	161,963	3.6	91,990	3.3	69,973	3.9
1997	167,635	3.5	95,552	3.8	72,083	3.1
1998	177,364	5.8	100,177	4.8	77,187	7.1
1999[g]	189,547	6.9	108,042	7.9	81,505	5.6
2000[g]	203,714	7.5	116,117	7.5	87,597	7.5
2001[g]	219,014	7.5	124,838	7.5	94,176	7.6

Source: Budget of the U.S. Government, fiscal years 1969–2001, and HCFA.

Notes: n.a. indicates not available. Totals may not add due to rounding.

[a]Includes related programs that are not separately identified, although for each successive year a larger portion of the total represents Medicaid expenditure. As of 1 January 1970, federal matching was only available under Medicaid.

[b]Intermediate care facilities (ICFs) transferred from the cash assistance programs to Medicaid effective 1 January 1972. Data for prior periods do not include these costs.

[c]Transitional quarter (beginning of federal fiscal year moved from July 1 to October 11).

[d]Represents increase over fiscal year 1976 (i.e., five calendar quarters).

[e]Includes transfer of function of state fraud control units to Medicaid from Office of Inspector General.

[f]Temporary reductions in federal payments authorized for fiscal years 1982–84 were discontinued in fiscal year 1985.

[g]Current law estimate.

Table 1.5   **Unduplicated Number of Medicaid Recipients by Eligibility Category, Fiscal Years 1972–95 (in thousands)**

Fiscal Year	Total	Age 65	Blindness	Disabled	Dependent Children	Adults with Dependent Children	Other Title XIX[a]
1972	17,606	3,318	108	1,625	7,841	3,137	1,576
1973	19,622	3,496	101	1,804	8,659	4,066	1,495
1974	21,462	3,732	135	2,222	9,478	4,392	1,502
1975	22,007	3,615	109	2,355	9,598	4,529	1,800
1976	22,815	3,612	97	2,572	9,924	4,774	1,836
1977	22,832	3,676	82	2,636	9,651	4,785	1,852
1978	21,965	3,376	82	2,636	9,376	4,643	1,852
1979	21,520	3,364	79	2,674	9,106	4,570	1,727
1980	21,605[b]	3,440	92	2,817	9,333	4,877	1,499
1981	21,980	3,367	86	2,993	9,581	5,187	1,364
1982	21,603	3,240	84	2,806	9,563	5,356	1,434
1983	21,554	3,371	77	2,844	9,535	5,592	1,129
1984	21,607	3,238	79	2,834	9,684	5,600	1,187
1985	21,814	3,061	80	2,937	9,757	5,518	1,214
1986	22,515	3,140	82	3,100	10,029	5,647	1,362
1987	23,109	3,224	85	3,296	10,168	5,599	1,418
1988	22,907	3,159	86	3,401	10,037	5,503	1,343
1989	23,511	3,132	95	3,496	10,318	5,717	1,175
1990	25,255	3,202	83	3,635	11,220	6,010	1,105
1991	28,280	3,359	85	3,983	13,415	6,778	658
1992	30,926	3,742	84	4,378	15,104	6,954	664
1993	33,432	3,863	84	4,932	16,285	7,505	763
1994	35,053	4,053	87	5,372	17,194	7,586	763
1995	36,282	4,119	92	5,767	17,164	7,605	1,537
1996	36,118	4,285	95	6,126	16,739	7,127	652
1997[c]	34,872	3,955	6,129[d]		15,266	6,803	524
1998	40,649	3,964	6,638		18,309	7,908	655
1999	37,500	4,700	7,000		17,500	7,600	700

Source: Health Care Financing Administration, U.S. Department of Health and Human Services; [http://www.hcfa.gov/stats/hstats98/blusta98.htm#Table 11] and [http://www.hcfa.gov/medicaid/MCD97T09.htm].

[a]This category is composed predominantly of children not meeting the definition of "dependent" children, that is, "Ribicoff children."

[b]Beginning in fiscal year 1980, recipients categories do not add to the unduplicated total due to the small number of recipients that are in more than category during the year.

[c]Fiscal year 1977 began in October 1976 and was the first year of the new federal fiscal cycle. Before 1977, the fiscal year began in July.

[d]For fiscal years 1997–99, blind and disabled categories are combined.

In recent years, enrollment growth has slowed for nonelderly or disabled adults and their dependents. This slowdown has been noticeable because of the correspondence in timing with the enormous reduction in welfare caseloads of recent years, leading to the possibility that a costly side effect of welfare reform is reduced health insurance coverage. Ku and Garrett (2000) investigate the determinants of Medicaid caseloads over time and conclude

Table 1.6   Medicaid Payments by Eligibility Category, Fiscal Years 1975, 1980, 1985, 1990, 1995, and 1998 (in billions of constant 1998 dollars)

	Age 65 and Older	Blind or Disabled	Children	Adults	Other	Total
1975	13.7	9.9	6.9	6.5	1.5	38.4
1980	17.7	15.4	6.3	6.6	1.2	47.3
1985	21.4	20.4	6.7	7.2	1.2	57.0
1990	27.1	30.7	11.5	10.8	1.3	81.7
1995	39.1	52.9	19.2	14.5	1.6	128.6
1998	40.6	60.4	20.5	14.8	6.0	142.3
Average annual % change 1975–98	5.1	8.6	5.1	3.8	6.4	6.1

Source: U.S. Congress, Committee on Ways and Means (2000).

that the recent declines are primarily attributable to both the improved economy and welfare reforms. Garrett and Holahan (2000) show that many welfare leavers lose their Medicaid coverage despite laws that allow them to extend Medicaid for one year after exiting welfare. In particular, they find that, among children whose families have been off welfare for six months, only one-fifth are uninsured. Of the children whose families have been off welfare for a year or more, however, almost one-third are uninsured.

Table 1.6 shows the division of Medicaid program spending by enrollment category, in 1998 and over time. Spending rose most rapidly for the blind and disabled, and least rapidly for adults. In recent years, spending growth has also been particularly rapid for children.

Table 1.7 shows the division of Medicaid program spending by service category, in 1997 and over time. Roughly one-fifth of program spending is on inpatient hospital expenses, and roughly another quarter is on skilled nursing facilities. Another 8 percent is on intermediate care facilities for the mentally retarded. Only 6 percent of program spending is on physicians' services, and another 5 percent is spent on other ambulatory care delivered in hospital outpatient departments and in clinics. The other major categories of spending are home health care and prescription drugs, each with 10 percent of program spending.

In terms of spending growth, the most rapidly growing categories since 1975 have been outpatient hospital expenses and home health expenses. In the 1990s in particular, home health, skilled nursing facility, and prescribed drug expenditures have grown the most rapidly, while hospital inpatient expenditures have been kept relatively in check, perhaps due to increasing use of prospective reimbursement strategies.

1.2.2   Eligibility and Takeup

A key issue with all social insurance programs is limited takeup among those eligible, and Medicaid is no exception, an issue discussed at length

Table 1.7   Medicaid Payments by Service Category, Fiscal years 1975, 1981, 1990, 1995, and 1997 (in billions of constant 1997 dollars)

Service Category	1975 Amount	1975 %	1981 Amount	1981 %	1990 Amount	1990 %	1995 Amount	1995 %	1997 Amount	1997 %	Average Annual % Change 1975–97
Inpatient hospital	11.4	31	14.5	30	22.8	28	30.4	24	25.1	20	3.8
General	10.2	28	12.9	26	20.6	26	27.7	22	23.1	18	4.0
Mental	1.2	3	1.6	3	2.1	3	2.6	2	2.0	2	2.4
Skilled nursing facilities	7.3	20	7.2	15	9.9	12	30.6	24	31.9	26	7.2
Intermediate care facilities	1.1	3	5.4	11	9.1	11	10.9	9	9.8	8	10.8
Other	5.7	15	8.1	17	12.0	15	n.a.	n.a.	n.a	n.a.	n.a.
Physician	3.7	10	3.8	8	5.0	6	7.8	6	7.0	6	3.1
Dental	1.0	3	1.0	2	0.7	1	1.1	1	1.0	1	−0.1
Other practitioner	0.4	1	0.4	1	0.5	1	1.0	1	1.0	1	4.7
Outpatient hospital	1.1	3	2.5	5	4.1	5	7.0	6	6.2	5	8.5
Clinic	1.2	3	0.7	1	2.1	3	4.5	4	4.3	3	6.4
Lab and X ray	0.4	1	0.3	1	0.9	1	1.2	1	1.0	1	4.7
Home health	0.2	1	0.8	2	4.2	5	9.9	8	12.2	10	21.3
Prescribed drugs	2.5	7	2.8	6	5.5	7	10.3	8	12.0	10	7.8
Family planning	0.2	1	0.2	1	0.3	0	0.5	0	0.4	0	3.3
Early and periodic screening	n.a.	n.a.	0.1	0	0.2	0	1.2	1	1.6	1	n.a.
Rural health clinic	n.a.	n.a.	0.0	0	0.0	0	0.2	0	0.3	0	n.a.
Other care	0.7	2	1.1	2	3.0	4	9.7	8	11.0	9	14.0
Total	37.8	100	46.6	100	80.4	100	126.5	100	124.9	100	5.9

Source: www.hcfa.gov/medicaid/msis/2082-5.htm.

Note: N.a. indicates data not available.

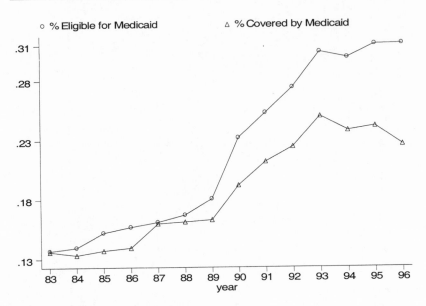

Fig. 1.1   Eligibility and coverage of children 0–15

presently. Eligibility, as described above, is determined through a complicated set of screens on income, family structure, and in some cases assets.
In a series of papers with Janet Currie and Aaron Yelowitz, I have developed an eligibility calculator for children and pregnant women for the
Medicaid program based on data from the Current Population Survey
(CPS). This program has been recently updated to 1996 and improved for
children in Dafny and Gruber (2000).[5]

Figure 1.1 graphs our estimates of national eligibility, and Medicaid coverage rates, for children aged zero to fifteen; these data are from the CPS as
well. Take-up is close to full in the early 1980s, before the expansions of
Medicaid, but falls considerably over time as Medicaid expands.[6] By 1996,
31 percent of children are eligible for Medicaid, but only 22.6 percent are
enrolled, for an average take-up rate of 73 percent. But the falling take-up
rate over time highlights the difference between average and marginal take-
up rates of expansions, which is discussed in more detail presently.

This figure masks enormous state heterogeneity in eligibility policy,
which is illustrated in table 1.8, which shows estimated eligibility by state

5. In particular, we make two major limitations to eligibility relative to the approach used
in the model previously. First, we do not assume that children can avail themselves of the medically needy option, since this requires extensive medical spending over several consecutive
months and is unlikely to be a realistic consideration for the typical child. Second, we incorporate in only a limited way the child care deduction for earned income, reflecting the limited
take-up of this deduction in practice.

6. The large jump in coverage in 1987 is due to a CPS redesign in March 1988 (which collected the coverage data for 1987).

Table 1.8 **Estimated Eligibility by State (average among children up to age fifteen)**

State	1983 Eligibility	1996 Eligibility	Difference
United States	0.131	0.292	0.161
Alabama	0.084	0.284	0.200
Alaska	0.173	0.150	−0.023
Arizona	0.087	0.472	0.385
Arkansas	0.084	0.289	0.205
California	0.223	0.22	0.099
Colorado	0.076	0.192	0.116
Connecticut	0.124	0.309	0.185
Delaware	0.070	0.188	0.118
District of Columbia	0.304	0.473	0.169
Florida	0.102	0.323	0.221
Georgia	0.095	0.287	0.192
Hawaii	0.213	0.672	0.459
Idaho	0.0455	0.225	0.1795
Illinois	0.148	0.231	0.083
Indiana	0.090	0.153	0.063
Iowa	0.161	0.200	0.039
Kansas	0.073	0.228	0.155
Kentucky	0.103	0.346	0.243
Louisiana	0.087	0.345	0.258
Maine	0.134	0.267	0.133
Maryland	0.104	0.318	0.214
Massachusetts	0.109	0.214	0.105
Michigan	0.226	0.304	0.078
Minnesota	0.107	0.514	0.407
Mississippi	0.113	0.319	0.206
Missouri	0.123	0.232	0.109
Montana	0.045	0.338	0.293
Nebraska	0.051	0.225	0.174
Nevada	0.043	0.157	0.114
New Hampshire	0.037	0.267	0.23
New Jersey	0.135	0.221	0.086
New Mexico	0.060	0.589	0.529
New York	0.204	0.321	0.117
North Carolina	0.054	0.243	0.189
North Dakota	0.097	0.148	0.051
Ohio	0.129	0.220	0.091
Oklahoma	0.115	0.305	0.190
Oregon	0.101	0.298	0.197
Pennsylvania	0.164	0.314	0.150
Rhode Island	0.149	0.209	0.060
South Carolina	0.131	0.251	0.120
South Dakota	0.054	0.212	0.158
Tennessee	0.112	0.266	0.154
Texas	0.063	0.283	0.220
Utah	0.168	0.178	0.010
Vermont	0.183	0.458	0.275
Virginia	0.083	0.256	0.173
Washington	0.058	0.434	0.376
West Virginia	0.120	0.494	0.374
Wisconsin	0.146	0.210	0.064
Wyoming	0.023	0.202	0.179

for 1983 and 1996, on average among children aged zero to fifteen. Eligibility varied substantially across the states in both 1983 and 1996, and there were quite differential changes in eligibility across states as well. For example, over this period, eligibility rose by over 50 percent in New Mexico, by 45 percent in Hawaii, and by 39 percent in Arizona; but eligibility rose by only 1 percent in Utah and 6 percent in Rhode Island, and actually fell by 2.3 percent in Alaska.

Unfortunately, there are no estimates of eligibility for Medicaid and take-up of the program by the elderly and disabled. These would be complicated dynamic calculations, because many elderly or disabled who are not currently eligible could become so by spending down enough of their resources to qualify.

1.3   Review of Issues

1.3.1   How Does Public Health Insurance Affect Health?[7]

Ultimately, the question of most interest for analysis of the Medicaid program is how it affects the health of the target population, and at what cost. To understand the effects of Medicaid policy on health, however, it is important to trace through the channels by which these legislative rules are translated to actual health improvements. In this section I provide a brief overview of these channels through a general structure that applies to all elements of the Medicaid program. In the next section, I review what we know about each of them, within the context of each of the different functions of the Medicaid program.

The process by which Medicaid determines health is depicted in figure 1.2. The first step in evaluating the effect of Medicaid policy on outcomes of interest, such as health, is to examine the effects on the eligibility of persons for the Medicaid program. How rules get translated to actual eligible populations is a function of where the eligibility levels cut in the distribution of income and other characteristics such as family structure. Determining population eligibility is particularly difficult for the disabled, since disability is a somewhat ambiguous concept in this context.

The next step is the translation of Medicaid eligibility into Medicaid coverage. An important feature of social insurance programs is that individuals do not always take up the benefits for which they are eligible. For example, Blank and Card (1991) estimate that take-up of unemployment insurance benefits only about two-thirds, and Blank and Ruggles (1996) find similar take-up rates for the AFDC and Food Stamps programs. Thus, only some of the previously uninsured will take-up the benefits to which they are entitled.

---

7. This discussion parallels and draws extensively on Gruber (1997).

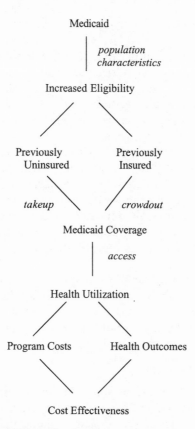

Fig. 1.2   How Medicaid determines health

The previously uninsured are not the only group that takes up benefits, however. In fact, the majority of those made eligible for the expansions actually had private insurance already. Some of those individuals will find it attractive to drop that private insurance and join the Medicaid program, "crowding out" their private insurance coverage.

Moreover, once covered by Medicaid, individuals will not automatically increase their utilization of medical care. Many physicians do not treat publicly insured patients, possibly because public insurance programs generally reimburse at rates far below private fee levels. A number of observers have alleged that there is a shortfall in the supply of physicians willing to serve Medicaid patients. The American Medical Association (AMA; 1991) reports that 26 percent of physicians described themselves as "non-participants" in the Medicaid program, and only 34 percent reported that they participated "fully" and were accepting new Medicaid patients. This problem is exacerbated by the fact that many of the patients who would be made eligible for public insurance are concentrated in areas that are underserved by physicians (Fossett and Peterson 1989; Fossett et al. 1992).[8]

Finally, increases in the utilization of care will not necessarily improve health. Many economists emphasize that medical care may actually be of limited relevance for health, relative to the other behavioral and environmental factors affecting the health of low-income persons. A number of studies suggest that much of the medical care provided to both adults and children is inappropriate and may have little health benefit. There is a large literature that suggests that insured persons are in better health than the uninsured, but this literature has generally failed to fully surmount the problem of omitted joint determinants of insurance and health status. Clever studies that use exogenous variation in insurance coverage or medical access (Lurie et al. 1984; Bindman et al. 1991) document positive effects of insurance on adult health, but a randomized trial (Newhouse 1993) suggested that increasing the generosity of insurance coverage had little health benefit.

Whether or not increases in utilization improve health outcomes, there is a definite link between increased utilization and increases in Medicaid program costs. Thus, the final step in assessing the efficacy of Medicaid policy is to compare the costs of utilization increases to any health benefits, to compute the cost-effectiveness of the program.

1.3.2   Take-up and Crowdout

Given the importance of translating Medicaid eligibility into participation, it is worth reviewing in some more detail the mechanics of this step. The economics of program participation among the existing uninsured parallels a number of analyses of take-up of programs such as AFDC. Moffitt (1983) provides an excellent exposition of the economics of that take-up decision. To summarize, in this model, individuals are trading off the income gained from participation against the stigma costs of participating. They must also incorporate the high implicit taxes on working in the range of program eligibility, so that the underlying wage rate is a key determinant of participation. If the return to work is high enough, or stigma is high enough, eligibles will not participate.

Cutler and Gruber (1996a) lay out the economics of crowdout, following Peltzman's (1973) seminal analysis of crowdout of private education by public education expenditures. Consider a person or family eligible for Medicaid, deciding on their insurance choice. For simplicity, they assume that insurance is sold individually and that policies differ only in the comprehensiveness of medical care that is covered. For example, more gener-

---

8. For example, Fossett et al. (1992) compared Chicago neighborhoods with 50 percent of the population on welfare to neighborhoods with 10 percent of the population on welfare and found that there were twice as many physicians practicing in the wealthier areas (on a per child basis).

ous plans offer a greater range of providers or cover a wider set of medical services. People choose between more generous insurance and other goods, as shown in figure 1.3. People valuing insurance highly (i.e., those demanding the highest quality providers) will choose a policy such as D, whereas those valuing insurance less highly will choose a point such as E.

Now the government introduces free public insurance with generosity M. On paper, Medicaid is a very valuable policy—almost everything is covered, and there is little or no cost sharing. For many reasons, however, the value of Medicaid is below that of private policies. Because of low Medicaid reimbursement rates, providers are often reluctant to treat Medicaid patients, thus reducing the value of coverage. In addition, individuals may not want to be enrolled in public programs because of the stigma associated with public programs or the difficulty in enrolling. Finally, the value of Medicaid may be low because individuals may have difficulty shifting from Medicaid back into private coverage if they have preexisting medical conditions. We thus show the value of the Medicaid package as below the value of most private policies.

Individuals cannot purchase a supplement to Medicaid (for example, an

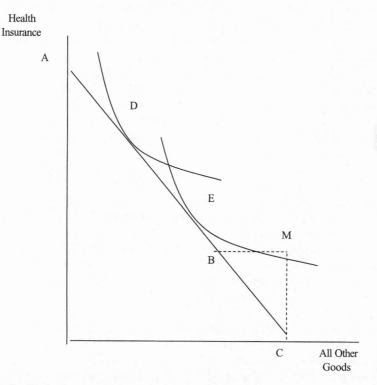

Fig. 1.3   Choice between insurance coverage and other goods

option to see higher-quality doctors by paying more on the margin). Thus, individuals who choose the public sector must consume insurance of exactly the amount M; if they want any higher-quality insurance, they return to the original budget constraint. The budget constraint with Medicaid is therefore ABMC. In response to this public coverage, people with low values of private insurance (such as E) will choose to enroll in the public sector, while individuals with a high valuation of insurance (such as D) will choose to retain their private insurance.

The key empirical prediction of this model is readily apparent in figure 1.3: As the value of public coverage rises, relative to the underlying demand for insurance quality, then individuals will be more likely to drop their private insurance and enroll in Medicaid. Given the absence of information on desired insurance coverage for individuals, most work in this area tests a weaker prediction of this model: On average, individuals made eligible for public insurance will reduce their private insurance coverage, relative to groups not eligible for public insurance. A complication to this analysis is that most private health insurance is provided through employment, rather than being purchased individually, so that workers may not receive the savings from forgoing employer-provided coverage. Although empirical evidence suggests that health insurance costs are passed back to workers (Gruber 1994; Sheiner 1994), this research has not established whether this passback occurs in response to individual or group choices of insurance. If individual workers do not receive the savings from choosing not to purchase insurance, they will perceive moving to Medicaid as a reduction in health insurance but not as an increase in other consumption. Fewer people will drop private insurance coverage in this case.

In the absence of complete wage shifting, employers may encourage workers to drop coverage in other ways. One way to do this is to reduce the generosity of the benefits offered, or in the limit, to simply stop offering insurance to the workers; in either case, these limitations on the private option will make the public option relatively more attractive. Alternatively, employers can reduce the share of the premium that they pay. When employees pay more of the premium, the link between Medicaid receipt and additional income may be more direct (since it does not operate through the veil of shifting to wages). In addition, because there is a tax subsidy for employer spending on insurance but not for individual spending, increasing the share of the premium that employees pay directly effectively raises the price of private insurance relative to Medicaid.

Because of IRS nondiscrimination rules, however, neither of these actions can be used selectively for those workers eligible for public insurance. If insurance is offered, it must be offered to all full-time workers (Cutler and Madrian 1998). As a result, all of these actions increase the total cost of insurance for employees that do not qualify for public coverage, since they lose the tax subsidy for some insurance purchases, or (if employers drop coverage) they must purchase insurance in the more expensive individual market.

On net, therefore, the link between health insurance and employment may increase or decrease the amount of crowdout. If worker-specific shifting is not possible, then crowdout may be reduced, as employees do not realize the savings from moving to the public sector. If employers increase cost sharing or reduce coverage for all workers, however, more workers may decide to drop coverage than are immediately eligible for Medicaid.

A key issue for thinking about take-up and crowdout is the cash equivalent value of Medicaid coverage. Estimating this value is a daunting challenge, and there has been little work in this area since the important study of Smeeding (1982). He summarizes the various approaches to valuing in-kind benefits such as Medicaid and concludes that the economic value of Medicaid benefits to recipients is less than half of the market value. But this conclusion is based on a number of assumptions about preferences for medical care that are difficult to verify empirically. There is clearly no consensus at this point on the value of Medicaid to recipients in dollar terms.

1.3.3   Medicaid and Labor Supply

The impact of the Medicaid program on labor supply is also potentially important, as is illustrated by the excellent exposition in Yelowitz (1995). As noted earlier, a key feature of several public assistance plans is that, in addition to cash benefits, individuals qualify for Medicaid coverage of their medical expenses. This coverage can amount to quite a valuable benefit, particularly since the work opportunities available to potential AFDC and SSI participants are low-wage, low-skilled jobs without health coverage.[9] As a result, the linkage of Medicaid to public assistance participation both encourages nonworkers to sign up for the programs and taxes work among potential recipients. That is, there is a form of "welfare lock": Individuals are reluctant to leave government programs because they will lose their health insurance.

This effect is illustrated in figure 1.4, from Yelowitz (1995); see also Winkler (1991). This figure shows the welfare receipt and work decisions of a single woman with children, who can receive AFDC if her income is below $H_{breakeven}$. This woman trades off utility from leisure and from consumption of goods that is financed from wage income or from welfare payments. The recipient faces a constant post-tax wage w^0. However, she is assumed to be unable to obtain a job with health insurance.[10]

At zero income, this woman receives a certain amount of cash welfare income from AFDC, as well as in-kind benefits, such as food stamps and

9. I use AFDC to summarize the effects of AFDC/TANF, since all of the work cited in this area refers to the older program.

10. Equivalently, she may be able to obtain a job with insurance, but only at a compensating differential that exactly equals her valuation of that insurance. Short, Cantor, and Monheit (1988) find that 43 percent of people who left welfare were covered by private health insurance. Since only those with the best opportunities leave welfare, the likelihood of finding a job with insurance for the average welfare recipient, should he or she leave the program, is quite low.

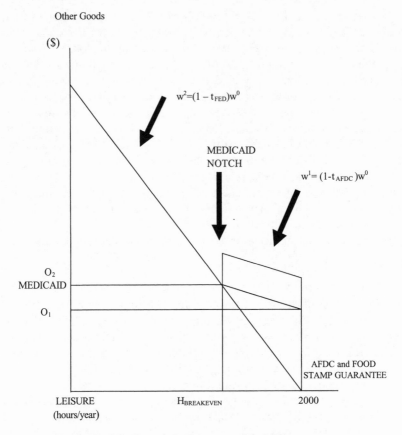

Other Goods

($)

$w^2 = (1 - t_{FED})w^0$

MEDICAID
NOTCH

$w^1 = (1 - t_{AFDC})w^0$

O_2
MEDICAID

O_1

AFDC and FOOD
STAMP GUARANTEE

LEISURE $H_{BREAKEVEN}$ 2000
(hours/year)

Fig. 1.4   "Welfare lock" effect on single women with children

Medicaid. As she earns labor income, her AFDC and non-Medicaid in-
kind benefits are taxed away at a high marginal rate, so that her after-tax
wage is $w^1 = (1 - \tau_{AFDC}) \cdot w^0$.[11] Once she works more than $H_{breakeven}$, the
hours of work where the entire welfare benefit is taxed away, she loses her
AFDC eligibility and hence her Medicaid benefits. This creates a dominated part of the budget set, known as the "Medicaid notch." This notch
provides a major disincentive to working her way off welfare. As Yelowitz
documents, for a mother with two children in Pennsylvania in January
1991, the woman would have to earn more than $5,000 additional dollars
off welfare to break even with her income on AFDC at point $H_{breakeven}$. Of
course, although removing the notch (e.g., by allowing those to keep Medicaid if they leave the welfare rolls) will improve incentives to leave welfare,

11. This marginal rate is 67 percent for the first four months, and 100 percent thereafter (after a basic exemption and some deductions for work and child care expenses).

this could reduce incentives for work among those with incomes slightly above this notch, so the net effect of the notch on total labor supply is unclear.

Reducing welfare lock through public insurance expansions can also have additional effects on labor market equilibrium, through adjustments of private insurance coverage and wages. If there is crowdout of private insurance through Medicaid expansions, then public insurance expansions will not only reduce welfare lock, but will also potentially reduce "job lock" (insurance-induced immobility across private-sector jobs) as well. By providing extra-workplace insurance coverage for workers or their dependents, Medicaid frees up workers to move to more productive positions. In addition, there may also be effects on wages and hiring, since employer insurance costs have been shifted to the government. If the costs of insurance are not shifted to wages, then the expansions provide a subsidy to the hiring of the low-wage workers who are likely to be eligible for the program and who will therefore not take up costly employer-provided insurance.

1.3.4   Medicaid and Family Structure

Another potentially important set of impacts of the Medicaid program for families is on family structure, along at least two dimensions. The first is the marriage decision, as described in Yelowitz (1998b). Traditionally, in order to qualify for Medicaid, women had to be single mothers on the AFDC program. Given that the potential marriage partners for many welfare mothers may not have health insurance to provide for the woman and her children, this could result in the woman's remaining single in order to qualify for Medicaid.

The second is for fertility, through two channels. First, Medicaid coverage of pregnancy may lower the financial barriers to childbirth. Unless discount rates are incredibly high, it seems unlikely that coverage for pregnancy could actually cause women to have more children. But Leibowitz (1990) did find that more generous insurance coverage in the RAND Health Insurance Experiment led to shifts in the timing of childbirth. Second, by covering the costs of children's medical care, Medicaid may lower the present discounted value costs of having a child. Of course, this analysis is complicated because the both the family's financial situation and the restrictions and benefits of the Medicaid program may change substantially over the eighteen years that the child may be covered by Medicaid, so it may be difficult to project the actual value of the program in lowering future medical costs.

1.3.5   Medicaid and Saving

As discussed in Gruber and Yelowitz (1999), there are three channels through which increased Medicaid generosity might affect saving and consumption decisions: precautionary accumulation, redistribution, and asset testing. First, by reducing medical expenditure risk for eligible families, the Medicaid program lowers their need for precautionary saving. This will raise consumption and lower wealth holdings. This point is explicitly demonstrated by Kotlikoff (1988). He presents simulations of a life-cycle model with uncertainty that demonstrate that asset accumulation will be much lower in an economy with public insurance available than in one where individuals self-insure their medical expenses through savings.

This negative effect on wealth holdings may be offset, however, by the second effect: Medicaid is explicitly redistributive and consequently increases the resources of persons who become eligible for the program. For those who were previously uninsured, this increase occurs through a reduction in their expected medical outlays. For those who had private insurance but chose to drop it in order to sign up for the Medicaid program, there is a reduction in expected outlays for both out-of-pocket spending and insurance payments. This redistributive transfer is transitory; it only lasts as long as the family is eligible for Medicaid, on both income and demographic grounds. Thus, to the extent that families are operating in a forward-looking life-cycle framework, the transfer will be saved and spread over future periods when there is higher out-of-pocket medical spending risk, offsetting the precautionary saving effect. On the other hand, to the extent that families are not perfectly forward-looking or that they are qualifying for Medicaid because they are transitorily poor, some of this transfer will be spent today.

The third and final channel is one that is highlighted by Hubbard, Skinner, and Zeldes (1995): asset testing. Over the entire population, asset tests should lower savings; but this effect might be expected to be small, to the extent that a large share of the population does not consider Medicaid to be a relevant option. Of potentially more interest is the interaction of asset tests with eligibility. On the one hand, following the Hubbard-Skinner-Zeldes logic, in a world with an asset test individuals who are made eligible on income grounds but not on asset grounds may reduce their savings to qualify for the program. In this case the presence of an asset test will exacerbate the savings reduction (and consumption increase) from expanding Medicaid, since the newly eligible individuals must reduce their savings to qualify (on top of the precautionary effect discussed earlier).

On the other hand, if an asset test is in place, newly eligible individuals with reasonably high savings may not consider this program a realistic option, so that the expansions will not affect their savings. Under this model, asset tests may mitigate the savings and consumption effects of expansions, since there is no precautionary saving effect or redistributive effect for newly eligible persons who are high savers (and who consider the program irrelevant). Finally, asset tests may have no effect, in that they are not binding or difficult to enforce. Thus, the net interactive effect of asset tests and eligibility is unclear. As a result, on net across these three effects, there is an ambiguous prediction for the effect of Medicaid eligibility on saving.

For the elderly, the impact of Medicaid on saving operates in a similar way, with all three effects. Here, however, we might expect the impact to be heightened since the potential spending risk on nursing homes is so much larger, and since even low-income elderly families can have substantial financial assets.

1.4   Evidence on Medicaid's Impacts

There is a large empirical literature that investigates the impact of Medicaid on insurance coverage, health care utilization and outcomes, labor supply, family structure, saving, and long-term care utilization and quality. I will review each of these literatures in turn.

1.4.1   Introduction: Identification of Medicaid Impacts

To introduce these literatures, it is worth reviewing the key issue in evaluating empirically the effects of Medicaid on behavior: how to separate (or identify) Medicaid's effects relative to confounding influences that might be correlated with changes in Medicaid. Consider, for example, a simple regression in a cross section of individuals of some behavior (e.g., health care utilization) on a dummy for whether the individual is covered by Medicaid. There are three confounding influences on a causal interpretation of the Medicaid coefficient in this type of regression. First, as highlighted earlier, take-up of Medicaid among eligibles is an individual decision that could be correlated with other behaviors, such as tastes for medical intervention. For example, individuals who are in poorer health will use more medical care and will be more likely to enroll in Medicaid. Thus, the exogenous regressor here is Medicaid eligibility, not Medicaid coverage, since the latter will produce estimates that suffer from selection bias.

Second, however, an individual indicator for Medicaid eligibility may itself lead to biased estimates, for three reasons. One is omitted variables bias. Eligibility is a function of a variety of factors about individuals that might also be correlated with their underlying behavior, such as income, family structure, or age. In principle, these factors can be controlled for in multivariate regression. But, in practice, eligibility is a complicated nonlinear function of these factors and how they interact with a state's policy regime, so it will be difficult to fully control for their influence. Moreover, differences in the financial circumstances of particular places and times (e.g., a recession in a particular state) might be correlated with both aggregate eligibility and the outcome variables of interest. Another factor is endogeneity: A sick child may cause lower parental income (if a parent is forced to leave work to care for the child, for example), leading to a spurious positive correlation between Medicaid eligibility and utilization. Finally, there may be substantial measurement error in the eligibility indicator, given the limitations of standard survey data sets (e.g., the reporting of only annual income instead of the monthly income used by program administrators to assess eligibility).

A solution to this second class of confounding influences is to find an instrument that is correlated with individual eligibility for Medicaid but not otherwise correlated with the outcome variables of interest. A natural instrument that meets these conditions is one that varies only with the legislative environment in the state and year in which the individual lives. In a series of articles on the impacts of Medicaid expansions for pregnant women and children on utilization and health, Janet Currie and I introduced an instrument to serve this purpose, which we called *simulated eligibility*. To create this instrument, we first select a *national* random sample of children of each age and of women of childbearing age in each year. We then assign that same sample to each state in that year and use the eligibility program described earlier to compute average state-level eligibility measures for this sample. This measure can be thought of as a convenient parameterization of legislative differences affecting children in different state, year, and age groups—a natural way to summarize the generosity of state Medicaid policy as it affects each group is in terms of the effect it would have on a given, nationally representative, population.

This instrumental variables strategy addresses the econometric difficulties noted above. First, by using instruments that are arguably exogenous to the dependent variable, it purges the model of endogeneity bias. Second, by using the fraction of the nationally representative population eligible in each woman or child's state/year/age group, this approach abstracts from any individual-level omitted variables correlated with both eligibility and outcomes. Third, to the extent that the measurement error in the instrument is uncorrelated with the measurement error in the individual eligibility measure, this also surmounts the measurement error problem. Finally, by using a national random sample to construct the instrument, the instrument is purged of any effects of state- and year-specific economic conditions that might be correlated with both eligibility and utilization.

Even with this careful econometric approach, however, there is a third major concern: legislative endogeneity. That is, the state policy parameters themselves may be a function of the dependent variable, leading to a correlation between even simulated (legislated) eligibility and outcomes. This problem is fundamentally impossible to solve, but it can be addressed in two ways. First, by including state and year fixed effects, models can control for any correlated fixed differences across places or over time in legislative tastes and in outcomes. Second, for the case of the children's expansions, it is actually possible to include as well as full set of state · year interactions, controlling for year-specific differences in tastes across states, since the children's expansions covered different groups of children very differently across the states. Moreover, this "endogenous legislation" scenario is unlikely to be very problematic in the context of the Medicaid expansions in that much of the permanent variation in eligibility is coming from federal mandates on states of differing initial eligibility generosity, rather than state-specific expansions beyond the federal mandates. As Cutler and Gruber (1996a) note, 90 percent of the children and 70 percent of the pregnant women made eligible between 1987 and 1992 qualified for Medicaid under federally imposed minimum guidelines.

An alternative identification strategy, pursued by Currie and Thomas (1995), is to use fixed effects, examining the impact of Medicaid on medical care for children who gain and lose coverage. This approach has the advantage of not relying on legislative exogeneity, but the disadvantage that the changes in circumstances that lead children on and off the Medicaid rolls may also be correlated with their health and tastes for health care utilization. Interestingly, their findings mirror the instrumental variables findings discussed below.

1.4.2 Medicaid and Public Insurance Coverage

As noted earlier, take-up of Medicaid by program eligibles is much less than full. This is not surprising, given the large literature that documents partial take-up of other social insurance programs (e.g., Blank and Card 1991; Blank and Ruggles 1996). Indeed, the average take-up rate for Medicaid is comparable to the take-up rates of two-thirds found for other social insurance programs.

For thinking about the impact of expanding Medicaid, however, what is relevant is not just the *average* take-up rate, but also the *marginal* take-up rate among the newly eligible. In fact, take-up problems are likely to be even larger for the Medicaid expansions, relative to other social insurance programs, due to the nature of the population that is being newly covered. This point is highlighted in table 1.9, from Gruber (1997). This table presents data for the 1984 population of children and women age fifteen to forty-four. I divide this population into three groups: those eligible for Medicaid in 1984; those who were not eligible in 1984, but who would be eligible by 1992 rules; and those who would not be eligible by 1992 rules. When I project future eligibility, I inflate 1984 incomes to 1992 levels using the CPI.

Table 1.9 shows two reasons why we might expect relatively low take-up of the Medicaid expansions. First, the population covered by the expansions was much less disadvantaged than was the population already eligible for Medicaid at the start of the period. Most important, they were relatively unlikely to be receiving public assistance through AFDC. Limited contacts with the social welfare system may make these persons unaware of the benefits to which they were newly entitled. Second, much of the population that was covered by the expansions already had insurance coverage from other sources before being made eligible for Medicaid. Indeed, *two-*

Table 1.9   Characteristics of Medicaid Eligibles

Characteristic	Eligible in 1984	Made Eligible between between 1984 and 1992	Not Eligible in 1992
Share of population (%)	16	28	56
Demographics			
Female headed (%)	63	30	13
Head is high school dropout (%)	45	25	12
Head works (%)	51	88	95
Family in poverty (%)	79	19	2
Mean family income ($)	10,276	18,517	38,263
Family receives AFDC (%)	47	5	1
Insurance coverage (%)			
Private	23	69	88
Public	52	7	2
Uninsured	29	26	11

thirds of those made eligible for Medicaid already had private insurance coverage. Thus, the demand for taking up Medicaid may be much lower even when it is conditional on being aware of one's eligibility.

In fact, previous research documents quite low take-up rates for Medicaid. Cutler and Gruber (1996a), for example, find a take-up rate of only 23 percent for children; Currie and Gruber (1996a,b) estimate take-up rates of 23 percent for children and 34 percent for women of childbearing age. This finding suggests that there is only weak translation of the tremendous eligibility expansions into Medicaid coverage. Of course, take-up findings are more difficult to interpret in the context of Medicaid than of other programs, since some of those who don't take up coverage are actually simply in good health and will take it up when they get sick. But this is still to some extent a failure of take-up, to the extent that those families do not take their children for well-child visits. This issue is discussed further below when computing the extent of Medicaid crowdout.

A recent paper by Currie and Grogger (2000) explores the implications of policies that might affect take-up for use of medical care, in particular prenatal care for pregnant women. They find that state administrative efforts to increase the ease of enrollment in Medicaid have had little impact on use of medical care. This suggests either than enrollment barriers are not the cause of low take-up or that state efforts to mitigate those barriers have not been sufficient to date.

1.4.3   Medicaid and Crowdout

The fact that such a large share of the newly eligible population under the Medicaid expansions had access to private insurance raises the prospect that many of the new enrollees on the program may have been crowded out of private insurance purchases. The crowdout of private insurance mechanisms by public interventions has been the subject of a long literature, but the first paper to specifically consider the interaction of private and public health insurance was by Cutler and Gruber (1996a).

The approach used by Cutler and Gruber is to exploit the tremendous variation in Medicaid eligibility across states, within states over time, and even within states at a point in time (from age notches in eligibility). They use the CPS data and eligibility imputations previously described to estimate models of the effect of Medicaid eligibility on private insurance coverage over the 1987–92 period. They control for state and time fixed effects, thereby using only within-state changes in policy to identify the effects of Medicaid on private insurance, and they use the simulated instruments approach described above.

A key feature of their approach is the recognition that there may be *within-family spillovers* in insurance coverage decisions. That is, it may be inappropriate to model a child's private insurance coverage as a function of that child's eligibility only. This is because private health insurance is generally sold only for individuals or families, without gradations among types of dependents. Thus, a family that wants to cover both parents but not the children (because the children may qualify for Medicaid) may find it impossible to do so with only one policy. Similarly, there is often no saving from enrolling some dependents in a policy but not others. This lack of distinction among dependents may increase or decrease the amount of crowdout. To the extent that families value coverage of all members and some members cannot qualify for public coverage, crowdout is likely to be smaller than an individual-by-individual calculation would suggest. On the other hand, if the Medicaid subsidy is large, families may drop coverage of all members, even those who do not qualify for public insurance directly. In either case, accounting for within-family spillovers is key.

Cutler and Gruber account for the effect of Medicaid eligibility on the family's insurance coverage decisions by modeling each family member's insurance coverage as a function of the "Medicaid replacement rate": the share of expected family medical spending that is made eligible for Medicaid. The results of this exercise are summarized in table 1.10, from Cutler and Gruber (1996a). They estimate that the Medicaid expansions brought 1.5 million children and 700,000 women onto the Medicaid rolls. At the same time, they were responsible for 600,000 children, 800,000 women, and 300,000 other family members dropping their private insurance coverage in order to take advantage of free Medicaid coverage. The greater than 100 percent crowdout for women, and the effect on other family members, is a by-product of within-family spillovers.

But the estimated increase in the Medicaid rolls is an underestimate of the true increase in the availability of Medicaid to these populations. The Medicaid expansions explicitly *did not* give continuous coverage to women. Rather, they created a form of conditional coverage: Women are

Table 1.10   Effect of Medicaid Expansions on Insurance Coverage

	Change in Coverage (millions)	
Type of Coverage	Medicaid	Private
Children	1.5	−0.6
Women 15–44	0.7	−0.8
Other adults	n.a.	−0.3
Total	2.2	−1.7 (−77%)
Conditional coverage of women	0.9	n.a.
Conditional coverage of children	0.4	n.a.
Total	3.5	−1.7 (−49%)

Source: Cutler and Gruber (1996a).

Notes: N.a. indicates data not available. Shows change in Medicaid and private coverage of women and children due to the expansions. Each cell is number of persons (in millions).

covered, but only for some expenses. As a result, women who are eligible for Medicaid in the event of pregnancy but who report themselves to be uninsured actually have some partial (conditional) insurance coverage. In particular, these women will have their hospital bills for delivery covered, since hospitals have developed detailed systems to insure that uninsured persons who are eligible for Medicaid get signed up for the program.

In the same vein, Medicaid also provides a form of conditional coverage for uninsured children. The fact that these children are not continuously covered by Medicaid suggests that they are not availing themselves of the insurance for the purpose of their primary medical care. Once again, however, when these children need hospital services, they may be signed up for Medicaid, so that they have conditional coverage for their hospital spending.

Cutler and Gruber value conditional coverage for women as the share of average annual medical spending that is accounted for by hospital expenses for pregnancy (25 percent), and for children as the share of annual total spending that is at the hospital (44 percent). Doing so, shown in the next set of rows in table 1.10, increases the estimated coverage increase to 3.5 million people. Accounting for conditional coverage, the bottom-line estimate is that 50 percent of the increase in Medicaid eligibility was associated with a reduction in private insurance coverage.

This is a sizable effect, suggesting the importance of this issue for Medicaid policy design. Nevertheless, these results also suggest that at least half of those enrolling in Medicaid were previously uninsured, so that there was a large net improvement in health insurance coverage in the United States as a result of the expansions.[12]

12. Cutler and Gruber (1996b) estimate that in fact as much as 80 percent of the newly enrolled Medicaid population was previously uninsured. The difference between the 50 percent and 80 percent figures is the population that dropped private insurance due to the expansions but did not enroll in Medicaid (e.g., women who are waiting for pregnancy to enroll).

This article has led to a fairly sizable literature on crowdout. Subsequent papers have attempted a variety of different approaches to identifying the impacts of Medicaid on private insurance coverage, and have generally produced much more mixed evidence on the importance of crowdout. Dubay and Kenney (1997) used an alternative strategy of examining how the coverage of low-income women and children changed over time, relative to control groups such as single men. They estimate much smaller crowdout effects. However, this approach to controlling for omitted time series imposes the assumption that there is no other reason why private coverage might be independently falling more for single men than these other groups, such as group-specific impacts of the early 1990s recession. This seems a much stronger restriction than Cutler and Gruber's implicit restriction that within-state changes in policy are not correlated with within-state changes in underlying insurance coverage. Three other articles that use a similar identification strategy to Cutler and Gruber (Rask and Rask 2000; Currie 1996; and Shore-Sheppard, 1999) also find large crowdout effects.

Another criticism of the Cutler and Gruber approach has been that crowdout is fundamentally a longitudinal phenomenon, yet Cutler and Gruber use repeated cross-sections to assess its presence. Several recent articles use longitudinal data to assess crowdout, looking at the private insurance coverage of the same children before and after they become Medicaid eligible by legislation (Yazici and Kaestner, 1998; Thorpe and Florence 1999; Blumberg, Dubay, and Norton 2000). These articles find little evidence of crowdout. This alternative approach also has its limitations: The samples used are often much smaller than with repeated cross sections, leading to much less precision (and the resultant inability to rule out large crowdout effects); these studies do not consider the impact of within-family spillovers, which Cutler and Gruber found to be important; and they consider only the short-run impacts of becoming eligible, whereas repeated cross sections assess the steady-state effects. Nevertheless, these longitudinal studies pose a fundamental challenge to the notion of very large crowdout effects and suggest the value of further work in this area, particularly with large longitudinal samples.

There are also a variety of questions about the *mechanisms* of crowdout that are yet to be addressed by the literature. For example, does crowdout result from firms' deciding not to offer insurance, or from workers' opting not to take up coverage for which they are being charged (and to use free Medicaid instead)? Cutler and Gruber find no evidence of an effect of Medicaid eligibility on employer decisions to offer insurance, however; all of the crowdout effect appears to come through employee take-up decisions. At the same time, they find some suggestive evidence that employers are increasing premium sharing in response to the expansions, in order to induce lower take-up of workplace coverage and a shift to the public program. Shore-Sheppard, Buchmueller, and Jensen (2000) also find no impact on employers' offering decisions, and they find some evidence that the crowdout is occurring through employee take-up.

At the most fundamental level, understanding crowdout requires understanding the process by which firms set wages, and in particular how finely firms could increase the wages of particular workers who leave the firm to join the Medicaid program. Gruber (2000) reviews the literature on wage shifting and concludes that there is strong evidence of full shifting of insurance costs to wages on average, but little evidence on this critical question of how *finely* shifting can be done.

1.4.4   Effects of Medicaid Entitlement on Utilization of Health Care and Health Outcomes[13]

A natural motivation for increasing the eligibility of the low-income population for public insurance is to improve their health. But, as highlighted above, there are a number of reasons why increased health *insurance* does not guarantee improved health *outcomes*. Thus, simply documenting that the Medicaid expansions increased insurance coverage is not enough to prove that they improved health. In this section, I therefore review studies that focus directly on the effects of the expansions on medical care utilization and health outcomes. These studies focus in particular on use of preventative care and on directly measurable outcomes such as mortality and fetal health (e.g., low birthweight).[14]

A number of studies have assessed the effects of Medicaid by comparing the utilization and health of persons with Medicaid coverage to those of the uninsured. These studies have shown that uninsured persons have lower utilization levels, a less efficient distribution of utilization across sites of care, and worse health outcomes (e.g., Kasper 1986; Short and Lefkowitz 1992; Mullahy 1994). But since the uninsured are likely to differ from the insured in both observable and unobservable respects, it is difficult to draw causal inferences from these types of comparisons. Furthermore, insurance coverage itself may be a function of health status, leading to endogeneity bias in estimates of the effects of insurance on health and on the utilization of medical care.

A natural alternative approach to analyzing the effect of Medicaid on utilization and health is to contrast the experience of a single state before and after a Medicaid program expansion. This approach has been the focus of three important studies of prenatal care use and infant outcomes: Piper, Riley, and Griffin (1990), Hass et al. (1993), and Epstein and New-

---

13. This subsection draws heavily on Gruber (1997).

14. This focus is dictated by the empirical difficulties with using measures of acute care (since, if Medicaid affects health, it will have a feedback effect on use of acute care) and self-reported health (since increased contacts with the medical system may worsen perceptions of health through improved medical information). See Currie and Gruber (1996b) for a more detailed discussion of these issues.

house (1998). Piper, Riley, and Griffin analyzed the effect of the extension of Medicaid coverage to low-income married women in Tennessee in 1985; Hass et al. examined the effect of expanding insurance to women with incomes under 185 percent of the poverty line in Massachusetts in 1985; and Epstein and Newhouse look at expansions from the poverty line to 185 percent of the poverty line in Medicaid eligibility among women in South Carolina and California.[15]

All of these studies have a common finding: There was no consistent effect of insurance expansions on either use of prenatal care or infant outcomes. Piper, Riley, and Griffin (1990) suggest one reason for this finding: More than two-thirds of the women who were eligible for Medicaid enrolled after the first trimester of pregnancy; almost 30 percent enrolled in the last thirty days before birth.[16] The extent of late enrollment grew after the expansion of Medicaid, suggesting that the newly eligible were enrolling even later. Ellwood and Kenney (1995) use more recent data to refute this contention, however, finding that, among women who were newly enrolled for their pregnancy, the expansion population was as successful as the AFDC population in enrolling the first trimester. Even in the Ellwood and Kenney data, however, only about one-half of the newly enrolling women were enrolled during the first trimester. A large literature on the effectiveness of prenatal care suggests that it is receipt of care in the first trimester that is key for improving fetal health (Institute of Medicine 1985). Thus, it is perhaps unsurprising that there was no effect on outcomes of these expansions.

While informative, these studies suffer from two potentially important problems. First, they are unable to control for correlated time series trends in the use of prenatal care and birth outcomes. There are a number of other changes in the circumstances of low-income households in the 1980s that might lead to lower use of prenatal care or worse outcomes, such as the erosion of the real earnings of low wage earners (Katz and Murphy 1992). These could interfere with uncovering the true effect of the Medicaid expansion. Second, the experience of one state's program may not be broadly prescriptive for the effects of national Medicaid policy.

An alternative approach involves using the experience of not just one or two states, but all of the states, to assess the effects of changing Medicaid policy. By comparing more broadly states that do and do not increase Medicaid generosity over time, one can also control for correlated time series trends. This is the approach taken by Currie and Gruber (1996b) for the case of prenatal care utilization and infant outcomes, and Currie and

15. The Massachusetts expansion was not technically a Medicaid policy, but rather a state-only program for the uninsured; but it foreshadowed the expansions that would be implemented under the Medicaid programs several years later.

16. Howell and Ellwood (1991) study this question for an earlier period (1983), and they find that roughly 50–60 percent of women whose deliveries were paid for by Medicaid were enrolled in Medicaid in the first trimester.

Gruber (1996a) for the case of child health care utilization and health outcomes. In both cases, the authors use individual-level data on health care utilization, either from the National Longitudinal Survey of Youth (NLSY) on prenatal care utilization, or from the National Health Interview Survey (NHIS) on child health care utilization. They combine this with aggregate data on mortality outcomes from the *Vital Statistics*. In all cases, the data are a time series of national cross sections, providing information on a number of states over time.

The measure of utilization for pregnant women is whether these women delayed their prenatal care until after the first trimester of pregnancy. In fact, in contrast to the pre-post studies described earlier, there is a large improvement in prenatal care utilization associated with Medicaid eligibility. Making someone eligible for Medicaid lowers the odds of her delaying prenatal care by almost 50 percentage points, which is essentially a 100 reduction in the odds of delaying care. Currie and Gruber (1996a) also find a sizable effect of Medicaid on use of preventive care by children: Being made eligible for Medicaid is associated with a drop in the probability of going without a visit over a year of almost 10 percent; this is almost one-half of the baseline probability of going without a visit.

Dubay et al. (2000) take a somewhat different approach from that of Currie and Gruber, examining time series trends in prenatal care utilization by socioeconomic groups more and less likely to be affected by the expansions. But they also find significant impacts of the expansions in terms of reducing the extent of delayed initiation of prenatal care. Thus, there appears to be clear evidence of benefits of the expansions in terms of medical care utilization.

Kaestner, Joyce, and Racine (1999) and Dafny and Gruber (2000) explore the impact of the Medicaid expansions not just on the level of hospitalizations of children, but also on the nature of those hospitalizations. Dafny and Gruber find, like Currie and Gruber (1996a), that increased Medicaid eligibility of children leads to more hospitalizations overall. But both articles find that eligibility leads to fewer "avoidable" hospitalizations, or those hospitalizations that are likely to be avoided by early contact with a primary care physician. This suggests that Medicaid coverage increases not just utilization but also the efficiency with which care is used.

One interesting feature of the expansions is their effect not only on mean utilization but also on the distribution of utilization. Currie and Gruber (1996a) and Currie (1996) explore the differential impact of the expansions by race, education, and immigrant status. In all cases there are some equalization impacts, with the utilization effects being particularly large for blacks, low-education groups, and immigrants.

Currie and Gruber (2001) further investigate the impact of the Medicaid expansions on the treatment of women at childbirth. They use information from birth certificate data on utilization of obstetric procedures during childbirth, such as fetal monitoring and cesarean section delivery. They divide the population of women into two groups: teen mothers and high school dropouts ("low education") and all others ("high education"). Mothers in the former group are quite likely to have been uninsured before enrolling in Medicaid, whereas mothers in the latter group were much more likely to have been privately insured. For the low-education mothers, they find sizable and significant positive effects of eligibility for Medicaid on the treatment of childbirth for the lower-education group; there is a uniform increase in the likelihood that women receive each of the procedures documented on birth certificates.[17]

But they also note that even if there is little net increase in insurance coverage for other mothers, this does not mean that there is no effect on their procedure use. Medicaid reimburses hospitals at a much lower level than do most private insurance plans. Thus, crowdout represents a shift from more to less generous insurance coverage for women, which may affect their procedure use even as their overall insurance coverage status does not change. Indeed, for these mothers, they find the effect opposite to that for low-education mothers: a significant reduction in the use of three of the five obstetrical procedures studied, and no effect on the other two. Overall, in fact, procedure use was basically unchanged in every case. That is, while Medicaid costs were rising substantially, social costs of treatment were unchanged: Women were obtaining the same treatment as before on average, with an equalizing trend toward more intensive treatment for low-education groups and less intensive treatment for higher-education groups.

Currie and Gruber (1996b) also find significant improvements in infant health from the Medicaid expansions. They estimate that each 10 percentage point increase in Medicaid eligibility lowered infant mortality by 0.03 percentage points, so that the 30 percent rise in eligibility over the 1979 to 1992 period was associated with a 8.5 percent decline in the infant mortality rate. There is a smaller and marginally significant effect on low birth weight. The authors go on to draw a distinction between two types of Medicaid policies during the 1979–92 period: "targeted" eligibility changes through 1987, which were addressed to very low-income populations including AFDC recipients; and the "broad" expansions after 1987, which were addressed to somewhat higher-income groups. As that paper highlights, these different types of policies affected quite different populations; in particular, the persons covered by the broad expansions had higher incomes and were more likely to be privately insured. As a result, the take-up of the targeted expansions was three times as high as take-up of the broad expansions.

17. This echoes findings for the state of Massachusetts expansions in Hass, Udarhelyi, and Epstein (1993), who showed that this eligibility increase was associated with a rise in the rate of cesarean section delivery. On the other hand, Epstein and Newhouse (1998) do not find consistent effects of expansions in California and South Carolina on cesarean section rates.

The authors then note that there were correspondingly different effects on outcomes from these two types of policies. There were very sizable effects of the targeted expansions on mortality, but only an insignificant effect of broad expansions: A 30 percentage point increase in targeted eligibility would have been associated with a 11.5 percent decline in infant mortality, compared to a 2.9 percent decline under the broad policy changes. There is also a very sizable reduction in the incidence of low birth weight associated with the targeted expansions (7.8 percent for a 30 percentage point eligibility increase), but there is no effect on low birth weight from the broad expansions.

Medicaid reduces the mortality of older children as well. Currie and Gruber (1996a) find that for every 10 percentage point increase in the fraction of children eligible for Medicaid, mortality drops by 0.013 percentage points; the 15.1 percentage point rise in eligibility between 1984 and 1992 is therefore estimated to have decreased child mortality by 5.1 percent.

There is less consistency in the literature, however, on the health benefits of the Medicaid expansions. Kaestner, Joyce, and Racine (1999) find no impact of Medicaid on self-reported health status and bed days, comparing income groups more and less likely to be eligible for expansion-based eligibility across states. One difficulty with this approach is that changes in subjective measures of health are hard to evaluate when access to care is changing; if insurance coverage leads to more contacts with physicians that reveal underlying health problems, this can lead to both worse self-assessed health status and more bed days. Dubay et al. (2000) do use objective data on birth weight, and they find little impact of the expansions on the incidence of low birth weight, despite the improvements in prenatal care adequacy noted above. These findings are consistent with the conclusion that the broader Medicaid expansions to pregnant women higher up the income scale of the late 1980s and early 1990s had minimal measured impacts on health.

A natural means of evaluating these findings is to consider the cost to the Medicaid program per life saved. This can be calculated by modeling administrative spending for each state or year on the Medicaid program as a function of changes in eligibility, and comparing these cost changes to any outcome improvements. For infants, the cost is roughly $1 million; in fact, when Currie and Gruber once again disaggregate into the targeted and broad policy changes, they find that the cost under the targeted changes ($840,000) was much lower than under the broad expansions ($4 million). For children, the cost per life saved is $1.6 million. As Currie and Gruber (1996b) discuss, these costs are low relative to typical estimates of the value of an adult life ($3–7 million) and relative to what the government spends to save child lives in other contexts.

A final area of interest with respect to the Medicaid entitlement is the impact of restrictions on services. As discussed earlier, most of the major health care services are covered by virtually all states. But there is some interesting variation in copayments and limits on the availability of prescription drugs. Stuart and Zacker (1999) find that elderly and disabled Medicaid recipients who reside in states with copayments for drugs have significantly lower rates of drug use than their counterparts in states without copayments; the primary channel for this effect appears to be through the likelihood of filling any prescription during the year, not the conditional number filled. Soumerai et al. (1994) found that limits on the use of antipsychotic drugs in New Hampshire lead to less use of these drugs and more spending on acute mental health services. These sets of results are provocative and suggest the value of additional work that carefully assesses the costs and benefits of prescription drug limitations under Medicaid.

1.4.5 Impact of Medicaid Reimbursement Policy on Utilization and Health Outcomes

The discussion thus far has focused on policies that increase the demand for medical care. But for a number of reasons it may be supply side policies that are more effective. As noted above, there is a shortage of physicians willing to serve the Medicaid population. This suggests that increased demand for services generated by expansions of the Medicaid program could go largely unmet, undercutting any potential gains.

One natural supply side tool is Medicaid fee policy. The low fees paid by state Medicaid programs represent a major potential deterrent to physician willingness to see Medicaid patients. Holahan (1991) reports that the ratio of Medicaid fees to private fees was approximately 0.5 for most procedures surveyed, and 0.56 for total obstetrical care with vaginal delivery. And the Physician Payment Review Commission (1991) found that thirty-eight states identified low fees as the major cause of low physician participation rates. A large body of research suggests that increasing the ratio of Medicaid fees relative to private-sector fees will increase physician participation in the Medicaid program (Hadley 1979; Sloan, Mitchell, and Cromwell 1978; Held and Holahan 1985; Mitchell 1991). Mitchell and Schurman (1984) and Adams (1994) find that the participation of OB/ GYNs is especially responsive to fee increases.

More recent work, however, suggests that physician responsiveness to fees may be somewhat more limited than was implied by the previous literature. Baker (1997) finds that higher fees are associated with more access to public and hospital clinics, but not to physician's offices. Decker (1992) finds that higher fees are not associated with increased physician willingness to see Medicaid patients but are associated with a shift from general practitioner to specialist visits. These findings do not forcefully dispute the raw contention that Medicaid fee increases raise access to ambulatory care, but they do suggest that more work is needed on the mechanisms by which higher fees have these impacts.

Of course, higher physician fees are not guaranteed to improve outcomes, due to the physician segregation noted above; only if fee increases generate improvements in access in the places where Medicaid recipients live will there be health improvements. Direct evidence on this question is provided by Gruber, Adams, and Newhouse (1996), who examined access to physicians after a large fee increase in Tennessee. They find that there was a sizable, but insignificant, fall in the average distance of Medicaid patients from a physician. Decker (1992) also finds that higher fees lead physicians to spend more time with their Medicaid patients.

Currie, Gruber, and Fischer (1995) examine directly the effect of the relative fees paid to physicians by the Medicaid program on infant mortality, using matched measures of state/year infant mortality rates, physician fee indexes, and physician and total medical spending. They find that, over the entire 1979–92 period, there is a significant but small impact of higher fees in terms of lowering infant mortality; doubling the fee ratio would lower mortality by 5.2 to 7 percent. But they find that the cost was low as well, with the physician cost per life saved ranging from $260,000 to $1.3 million depending on the specification. They also find some evidence of a countervailing "offset" effect on hospital spending, with hospital spending falling by a substantial amount to offset the increased physician costs. This is consistent with the findings in Gruber, Adams, and Newhouse (1996), who find that after the state of Tennessee increased its physician fees, physician spending rose, but hospital spending fell. Gray (1999), using microdata on birth outcomes matched to physician fee information, produces an even larger effect of fees on outcomes. Overall, raising physician fees seems a much more efficient route to improved outcomes than the broad expansions.

Higher physician fees can affect not only the access of Medicaid patients to the physician, but also how patients are treated by physicians. A large literature on the impact of Medicare reimbursement on treatment intensity suggests that higher Medicare reimbursement leads to *lower* intensity, as physician income effects dominate substitution effects. But the typical doctor who sees Medicaid patients has a relatively small share of his practice made up of Medicaid patients, so it is plausible that income effects might be weaker in this context. Indeed, Gruber, Kim, and Mayzlin (1999) find that higher Medicaid fee differentials for cesarean section delivery are associated with higher rates of cesarean delivery among Medicaid patients; they estimate that as much as one-half of the sizable differential in cesarean delivery rates between Medicaid and private-pay patients is due to lower Medicaid reimbursement levels.

Of course, physicians are not the only health care providers reimbursed by Medicaid. However, the literature on Medicaid reimbursement in other arenas is much more sparse. There was some work in the late 1980s on Medicaid hospital reimbursement, but virtually no work since. These studies (Holahan 1988; Zuckerman 1987) found that Medicaid-only prospective payment systems were successful in lowering costs in the short run but not in the long run. Rather, to control costs in the long run, it was important to embed Medicaid reimbursement within a systemwide reimbursement structure that regulates all payers. Holahan also reports some evidence that states with lower per diem reimbursements under Medicaid feature lower access of Medicaid patients to hospitals, particularly among nongovernmental hospitals, so that lower rates led to a net shift of Medicaid patients to government hospitals. He also finds sharp one-time gains from the selective contracting program in California that negotiated rates with hospitals, but he once again raises questions about whether price negotiation will continue to work over the long term.

A provocative recent study by Duggan (1999) examines the impact of DSH payments on hospital behavior in California. He finds that these transfers have little impact on the treatment of low-income populations: Private hospitals simply absorb the payments in higher profits (for for-profits hospitals) or higher retained net worth (for not-for-profit hospitals); and public hospitals saw no net increase in available funds because local governments cut their public subsidies one for one with the rise in federal subsidies. Consistent with these results, he finds no impact of larger DSH payments on the birth outcomes of women in California.

The lack of work on Medicaid hospital reimbursement, given the enormous volume of literature on Medicare hospital reimbursement, is striking. Variations across states, and within states over time, in Medicaid reimbursement policies offer the potential for rich investigation of how hospitals respond to reimbursement differences. Moreover, there is no work on the health impacts of these hospital responses. Although state reimbursement rules may be difficult to obtain, this is clearly an interesting area for future work.

1.4.6   Medicaid and Long-Term Care

Another literature of particular interest is the work on Medicaid reimbursement of nursing homes, access to care by Medicaid patients, and quality of care delivered. This literature is nicely reviewed in Norton (2000).

There are two important issues raised in this literature. The first is how Medicaid policy affects access to, and demand for, nursing home stays by the elderly. A key issue here is that the market for nursing home stays may not be in equilibrium. A number of articles argue that due to government regulation, nursing homes are at full capacity and face excess demand from Medicaid patients who pay nothing out of pocket for care (Scanlon 1980; Nyman 1989). Other research has also found that Medicaid patients have less access to nursing homes than their private-pay counterparts, which is consistent with the excess demand interpretation. This also has the important implication that the frail elderly may spend more time in hospitals when they are Medicaid financed, offsetting some of the savings to the Medicaid program from lower nursing home reimbursement rates. Gruenberg and Willemain (1982) found that the length of stay in Massachusetts hospitals was longer for Medicaid patients waiting for placement in a nursing home, and Ettner (1993) also found evidence that Medicaid patients have more nursing home access problems than private patients. She found that Medicaid patients in areas with relatively low bed supply and in areas with greater demand from private patients were more likely to be on a waiting list for admission to a nursing home.

On the other hand, some work finds that more generous Medicaid subsidies to nursing home care increase overall nursing home utilization (not just relative utilization of those on Medicaid), which is not consistent with excess demand. Hoerger, Picone, and Sloan (1996) and Cutler and Sheiner (1994) both find that elderly persons are more likely to use a nursing home when Medicaid eligibility is looser and Medicaid reimbursement is more generous. Cutler and Sheiner also find that these state policies appear to draw persons into nursing homes who would otherwise live with their children; this suggests that the benefits of more generous Medicaid systems may largely accrue to children who would otherwise have to support their elderly parents. And Hoerger, Picone, and Sloan find that increased Medicaid home health expenditures are not associated with reduced use of institutional care, but simply with reduced use of care from other family members; this is consistent with the experimental evidence from the chanelling experiment of the 1970s, which found that more generous home care did not reduce the use of institutional care (Norton 2000).

The second issue is how Medicaid reimbursement affects the quality of nursing home care. Gertler (1989) and Nyman (1985) make an important theoretical observation about Medicaid fee policy toward nursing homes. Nursing homes compete for private patients over both price and quality, and Medicaid patients will accept minimum quality since the care is free. Common quality is assumed to be provided across patient types; that is, quality is a "public good."[18] Moreover, as noted above, nursing homes are assumed to be at full capacity and face excess demand from Medicaid patients who pay nothing out of pocket for care. As Medicaid raises its reimbursement in this model, nursing homes on the margin will want more Medicaid patients, which means they will need fewer private-pay patients. They therefore raise price and lower quality to their private-pay patients to reach equilibrium. As a result, since common quality is provided, higher Medicaid reimbursement leads to lower quality care.

Gertler (1989) provides evidence to support this hypothesis, using an in-

18. This is the key assumption of the model, and an interesting question for future investigation is whether this assumption is truly warranted in the nursing home setting; there is substantial evidence from physician and hospital settings that patients with different payer sources are treated differently.

put-based measure of quality across a sample of nursing homes. He finds that higher Medicaid reimbursement is indeed associated with lower quality of care along this metric. Gertler (1992) uses data for New York state to estimate that a 10 percent increase in Medicaid expenditures leads to 4.1 percent increase in Medicaid patient care and a 3.4 percent reduction in nursing home expenditures on services provided to patients. This suggests both substantial public-sector costs and private quality costs to attempting to improve the access of low-income patients to nursing homes.

This test has been recently updated in Grabowski (2001). This study improves on previous tests along three dimensions: by using national, rather than state-specific data; by using the substantial and exogenous variation in average Medicaid reimbursement available across the states; and by using an outcome-based measure of quality (facility-acquired pressure sores). In fact, Grabowski finds that Medicaid reimbursement is *positively* associated with quality, in contrast to previous evidence and to the theory laid out above. Moreover, this positive association is found both in the early 1980s and in more recent years, and in both a sample of New York homes and the national sample. These findings cast significant doubt on the validity of the previous empirical literature and suggest the value in understanding where this model breaks down; a natural candidate may be the untested assumption that quality is a common good in nursing homes.

1.4.7 Medicaid, Labor Force Participation, and Welfare Participation

As discussed earlier, the fact that low-income households can obtain fairly high-quality insurance through the Medicaid program by being on cash welfare, but are unlikely to obtain that coverage in the low-wage labor market, provides a substantial disincentive to leaving welfare ("welfare lock"). Given the existence of welfare lock, one potential advantage of decoupling Medicaid from the AFDC program is that it could allow individuals to leave AFDC without fear of losing insurance for their children or for the costs of pregnancy. The result would be lower costs of the AFDC program, as well as potential tax revenues from the earnings of these new workers. The magnitude of the welfare lock problem, however, is uncertain: Given the harsh job prospects for low-income populations, even with health insurance they may be reluctant to leave the welfare rolls.

The magnitude of welfare lock has been the subject of a number of studies, as reviewed in Gruber (2000). There have been three basic empirical approaches used in this literature. The first is to use differences in individual characteristics to predict who is likely to be "locked" into the AFDC program by Medicaid due to high medical spending, and then to assess differential participation rates by this imputed value of Medicaid. Ellwood and Adams (1990) follow this approach using administrative Medicaid claims data to examine exits from AFDC, and Moffitt and Wolfe (1992) model participation as a function of imputed value in the SIPP. The results are fairly similar, showing sizable decreases in the likelihood of exiting AFDC as the imputed value of Medicaid rises.

The second approach is to abstract from individual health and to use variation in the characteristics of state Medicaid programs to identify the value of Medicaid to the potential AFDC participant.[19] Blank (1989) was the first to pursue this approach, estimating models of AFDC participation and hours of work on average state Medicaid expenditures and the presence of a state Medically Needy program, which provides Medicaid to non-AFDC families if their income net of medical expenditures falls below a certain floor. She finds no effect of either policy variable on AFDC participation. Winkler (1991) also finds no effect of average expenditures on AFDC participation, but he does find an effect of average expenditures on labor force participation, a finding echoed by Montgomery and Navin (1996), albeit with a much smaller estimate. But there is no effect of Medicaid expenditures on participation in Montgomery and Navin's work after state fixed effects are included in the regression models.

The third approach that has been taken to this question extends the notion of using state parameters by exploiting the variation that comes from the Medicaid expansions. As Yelowitz (1995) notes, these expansions served to decouple Medicaid eligibility from AFDC receipt, thereby providing precisely the variation needed to separately identify the role of Medicaid from that of other factors in determining welfare participation. A key feature of these expansions was variation across the states in the timing and generosity of increased income limits. Indeed, there was even variation within states at a point in time, due to different age cutoffs for eligibility of children across the states. This allows Yelowitz to form plausibly identical groups of families, some of which (the "treatments") were able to leave AFDC and retain their Medicaid coverage, and others of which (the "controls") were not. And he finds significant effects of being in the treatment group on both AFDC participation and labor force participation: He estimates that increasing the income cutoff for eligibility by 25 percent of the poverty line decreases AFDC participation by 4.6 percent and increases labor force participation by 3.3 percent. More recent work by Meyer and Rosenbaum (1999), however, suggests that the Yelowitz findings may be fragile, as they find no large effects from a different specification over a later set of years. Ham and Shore-Sheppard (1999) also find small effects of Medicaid entitlement on transitions both off and on to welfare.

A related approach is taken by Decker (1994). She examines the effect of the introduction of the Medicaid program in the late 1960s and early 1970s on AFDC participation in that era. Since the Medicaid program was phased

---

19. Features of the state Medicaid program are included in the set of variables used to predict Moffitt and Wolfe's (1992) index, but the papers discussed here use *only* state features for identification.

in across the states over a period of several years, she is able to assess whether states that adopted Medicaid saw a subsequent increase in their AFDC rolls, relative to states that did not. In fact, she finds a very strong effect, with the introduction of Medicaid leading to a 6.4 percentage point (24 percent) rise in the odds that a single female head participates in AFDC.[20]

In a series of subsequent studies, Yelowitz has explored the effect of Medicaid on participation in other public assistance programs. The first is SSI; as Yelowitz emphasizes, this program is actually larger in dollar terms than is AFDC, and the same type of welfare lock problem arises in this context. For elderly SSI recipients, this problem arises because the Medicaid coverage that they receive on SSI pays for their noncovered Medicare expenditures. Using an expansion of Medicaid for the elderly, Yelowitz (2000b) finds a nontrivial welfare lock for this population as well. For the disabled, who get Medicaid if on SSI, Yelowitz (1998a) follows the second approach noted above, using variation across states in the Medicaid spending to proxy for the program's generosity. He finds that the growth in Medicaid generosity over 1987–93 can explain almost all of the substantial growth in the SSI disabled caseload. Finally, Yelowitz (1996) asks whether increased eligibility for Medicaid raises utilization of the food stamps program, both through reducing labor supply and increasing awareness of public assistance programs. Using the same estimation approach as Yelowitz (1995), he finds that Medicaid eligibility does increase food stamp participation and that this increase occurs through both channels.

Thus, to summarize, this literature suggests that health insurance is a very important determinant of public assistance participation. This has two important welfare implications. First, it suggests that reduced public assistance expenditures may offset a share of the increased costs of expanding health insurance availability. Yelowitz (1995) estimates that expanding eligibility for Medicaid to all women and children with incomes below 185 percent of the poverty line in 1989 would have saved the government $410 in expenditures per female-headed household per year. Second, there may be nonfinancial costs to the increase in welfare dependence that results from welfare lock. A number of analysts have suggested a hysteresis-type model of welfare behavior, with exposure to the welfare system increasing future utilization by both a mother and her children as adults (Murray 1984). Existing evidence on welfare dependence is mixed, with some recent studies concluding that there is little intergenerational transmission of welfare (Zimmerman and Levine 1993). But this possibility highlights the benefits of moving welfare recipients off the public assistance rolls through reducing welfare lock.

---

20. For this era, however, her results indicate that this increase is primarily due to increased take-up among those already eligible for AFDC, *not* to reduced labor supply in order to make oneself eligible; the labor supply effects are imprecisely estimated, however.

Reducing welfare lock through public insurance expansions can also have additional effects on labor market equilibrium, through adjustments of private insurance coverage and wages, as discussed earlier. But there is no empirical work to date on the effect of the expansions on job mobility, wages, or employment determination.

1.4.8   Medicaid and Family Structure

As discussed earlier, Medicaid can also have effects on family structure, along two channels. The first is marriage: By tying receipt of Medicaid to receipt of cash welfare that requires being nonmarried (in the main), public policy provides a disincentive to marriage. Yelowitz (1995) once again uses the structure of the Medicaid expansions of the 1988–91 period to explore this issue, by assessing whether women who were made eligible for the insurance in the state of marriage were then more likely to get married. He finds a small but significant effect on marriage propensities from the Medicaid expansions through this channel.[21]

The second is fertility: As noted above, Medicaid expansions can in principle increase fertility by lowering the cost of bearing and raising children. Indeed, Joyce, Kaestner, and Kwan (1998) do find that Medicaid entitlement for pregnancy expenses for low-education women was associated with a 5 percent increase in the fertility rate for white women; this arises partly through reduced abortions (see the discussion that follows). This is a striking finding and provides confirmation that insurance coverage can matter for fertility decisions. This paper does not, however, address two important questions about this finding. First, does this represent a permanent upward shift in fertility rates, or simply a shift in the timing of when children are born (i.e., children are born earlier than they otherwise would, which appears to be a rise in the fertility rate in a cross section)? Second, how much of this impact is due to coverage of pregnancy per se, as opposed to correlated expansions in the coverage of children that may have a larger impact on the net cost of raising a child?

Another channel through which Medicaid can affect fertility is abortion decisions. Medicaid financing of abortion has been a contentious issue for many years, and there has been significant variation in reimbursement policy. Several recent papers (Haas-Wilson 1994; Blank, George, and London 1996; Levine, Trainor, and Zimmerman 1996; Kane and Staiger 1996) have found that restricting Medicaid funding of abortions significantly reduces teen and aggregate abortion rates. At the same time, the last two of these

---

21. As Yelowitz notes, there is in fact a countervailing influence here. For some women who were married to their husbands just to get health insurance, the increased income cutoffs would allow them to divorce their husbands but maintain coverage. He is able to distinguish this effect from the marriage incentive effect described above by separating changes in income cutoffs from changes in coverage of traditional families. He finds that both effects are present but that the positive marriage incentive effect predominates.

papers also find little impact on teen births. This suggests that restrictions on abortion access lead to fewer pregnancies (through more preventative measures by teens), offsetting the reduction in abortion access. Joyce and Kaestner (1996) find that Medicaid eligibility itself is associated with reductions in the abortion rate among white women, which is consistent with the impacts on fertility documented above.

1.4.9   Medicaid and Saving

The final area of work on Medicaid and economic behavior is on saving, in two areas. Gruber and Yelowitz (1999) explore the impact of the Medicaid expansions for children and pregnant women on saving and consumption. They find that the expansions led to both lower saving and higher consumption, confirming in two data sets that the type of precautionary saving effects discussed in Kotlikoff (1988) or Hubbard, Skinner, and Zeldes (1995) are empirically important. In particular, they find that in 1993 the Medicaid program lowered the wealth holdings of eligible households by 16.3 percent. They also find that the expansions of this program over the 1984–93 period lowered wealth holdings by 7.2 percent. And they use the fact that the expansions were accompanied by the removal of asset testing for Medicaid eligibility in many states to document that asset testing is also an important determinant of savings: The reduction in savings for those becoming eligible for Medicaid in a regime where there is asset testing is twice as large as for those becoming eligible in a regime without asset testing.

The other area in which the impacts of Medicaid on saving have been investigated is in terms of nursing home coverage. Theory would suggest that there could be potentially quite large impacts on savings of Medicaid entitlement to nursing home coverage, since nursing home care is very expensive, so that precautionary savings may be large. Norton and Kumar (1998) investigate whether the spousal impoverishment provisions of the Medicare Catastrophic Care Act of 1988, which (as noted earlier) allowed families to shield significant assets with a community-based spouse, led to higher savings. Using data on community or institutionally based chronically impaired couples, they find no higher savings after this act among couples with a community-based spouse and singles without such a spouse.

Moreover, very few persons spend down to Medicaid eligibility after entering the nursing home. Although roughly 40 percent of new admissions are covered by Medicaid, and there is a perception in the popular press that spend-down is widespread, less than 20 percent of persons who are private-pay at admission actually spend down after admission (Norton 2000).

Evidence on whether the elderly transfer assets to others to avoid the implicit Medicaid "tax" is mixed. Norton (1995) uses data from two different samples of the elderly to predict the distribution of time until spend-down according to a model of spend-down absent of behavioral effects. These distributions were then compared to the actual distribution of the time until spend-down for nursing home residents. Contrary to expectations, it appears that the elderly avoid Medicaid eligibility. This result cannot be explained away by sample selection, demographics, or uncertainty about prices.

1.5   Implications and Unanswered Questions

As is clear from the foregoing discussion, there is a large and rich literature exploring the impacts of Medicaid on individual behavior and outcomes. This literature has a number of important policy implications. But, in thinking through policy directions, it also becomes apparent that there are a number of unanswered questions about Medicaid's impacts as well.

1.5.1   Eligibility Policy

The first area of policy that is informed by this literature is Medicaid eligibility policy as a tool for dealing with the large and growing number of uninsured individuals in the United States. One straightforward alternative for increasing insurance coverage is to continue to expand our public insurance safety net. This was the approach taken by the CHIP expansion. The problem with this approach is that the CHIP program will be spending its dollars primarily on those children around 200 percent of poverty, and this is a population that is heavily privately insured already. For example, among those children between 200 and 250 percent of poverty, only 14 percent are uninsured, and almost 80 percent already have private health insurance. A key lesson from the recent literature on Medicaid is that crowd-out may be a significant concern under these types of conditions. As a result, there could be relatively low "bang for the buck," with most public dollars going to those already insured and switching to the public program.

On the other hand, the flexibilities built into CHIP are likely to help mitigate crowdout. By making the benefits package less generous than Medicaid, and by introducing premiums and copayments for services, state CHIP programs make it less attractive to drop one's private health insurance to join the public program. Clearly, as public insurance is expanded further and further up the income scale, given the strong correlation between income and private insurance coverage, more and more limitation of this form is called for.

An important priority for research is to assess whether the flexibilities in CHIP have a real impact on crowdout. Some casual evidence suggests that they might. Before CHIP, the states of Florida and Minnesota had public insurance programs for children funded out of state monies only, and these programs provided insurance that was much more restrictive than Medicaid, particularly with regard to premiums for enrollment, where were nontrivial. Two evaluations of these programs suggested much lower crowdout than the estimates for the national program, in that fewer than 10 percent of the enrollees had private insurance before joining the program.[22] While only suggestive, these findings may provide a key insight into how to combat crowdout, which is to make the public option less attractive. Of course, what is missing from these analyses is any information on the impact of these policies on the take-up of the plan by those who were previously uninsured. If such policies reduce crowdout but reduce take-up by the previously uninsured even more, they may not be an attractive barrier for combating crowdout. Clearly, more research is needed on how the structure of public insurance programs influences both take-up and crowdout.

Although expansions of insurance up the income scale seems an obvious way to reach more uninsured, the CHIP legislation largely ignored a more needy and obvious population: those who are already eligible for Medicaid but do not take it up. Indeed, most estimates suggest that there are on the order of 4 million children who are eligible for Medicaid but do not take up coverage. Moreover, as previously noted, there is tremendous underuse of prenatal care services by women who are Medicaid eligible, particularly during the first trimester. The reasons for this limited take-up are unclear and reflect some mix of poor information about eligibility and stigma about enrollment in a public insurance program.

Regardless of the cause, however, this is a very high bang-for-the-buck population. Of those children not on Medicaid already, but with incomes below 150 percent of the poverty line, 53 percent are uninsured. This suggests that the highest priority for government policy is to expand coverage of this group through outreach initiatives, even if they are somewhat costly. In other words, in thinking about expanding insurance coverage in the low-income population, it is probably best to think about filling the cup from the bottom: Start by maximizing the coverage of the lowest-income population with few other insurance alternatives, and then move to higher-income groups that often have access to private coverage.

For largely political reasons, the expansions of health insurance through both Medicaid and CHIP have focused on children and pregnant women. But there is little coherent argument for covering an eighteen-year-old woman up to 200 percent of poverty, while a nineteen-year-old woman receives no public coverage unless she is pregnant or on welfare. This is particularly true given the low use of prenatal care by lower-income women; if they had continuous insurance coverage, they would perhaps be more likely to seek care as soon as they got pregnant.

One particularly helpful approach that has been proposed is to extend

22. It is important to note that this does *not* imply crowdout of less than 10 percent, since some of those crowded out may not join the program (e.g., through within-family spillovers), and since some of those joining the program might have lost their private insurance even if there were no crowdout (e.g., through natural turnover).

coverage to the parents of Medicaid and CHIP children. This would have the additional advantage of increasing take-up by these children, since once the parents are eligible it might increase their awareness of the entire family's entitlement.

In summary, public insurance remains a powerful tool for reducing high and rising numbers of uninsured in the United States. But the efficiency of different public insurance routes may differ dramatically. Public policy could most usefully focus on the neediest populations first, such as those eligible for and not taking up coverage and other demographically noneligible groups, before moving on to higher-income groups of traditionally eligible populations where private coverage is fairly common.

1.5.2   Supply Side

An area that has received less attention, but which may be equally important, is Medicaid reimbursement policy. Work on physician reimbursement suggests that more generous fee schedules can lead to more access to physicians for Medicaid patients, and ultimately to better health outcomes.

Of particular interest within the reimbursement arena is an assessment of the trade-offs between physician and hospital reimbursement levels. Although the evidence cited earlier suggests real costs to low physician reimbursement, there is much less evidence suggesting significant costs to lower Medicaid reimbursement of hospitals. Clearly, an important priority for future work is to think about the trade-offs between the reimbursement levels set for these different types of providers.

1.5.3   Long-Term Care

In terms of government spending, the most important area for Medicaid reform is long-term care. This is the largest share of Medicaid program spending, and it will clearly grow rapidly with the aging of the population. The literature on Medicaid long-term care, while limited, suggests three policy-relevant conclusions. First, if policymakers attempt to control costs by reducing Medicaid reimbursement levels, they may not sacrifice quality of care (and indeed may actually raise quality). Second, however, lower reimbursement levels will lower the access of Medicaid patients to nursing home care. Third, the beneficiaries of more access of Medicaid patients to nursing home care appear to be the children of these patients with whom they were living before admission.

These findings suggest that there is a crowdout-like effect of increasing Medicaid reimbursement: It raises access for Medicaid patients, but at the cost of lower quality for private patients. The recent removal of the Boren amendment, and the resultant flexibility for states to experiment more with nursing home reimbursement, may provide more evidence on this front. The last finding also suggests that if children are the beneficiaries of Medicaid entitlement, perhaps they should bear more of the costs. As Cutler and Sheiner (1994) note, in Germany, the income of children is counted toward the resource base for paying for nursing home care for elderly parents. Such a system in the United States may more tightly tie the costs of Medicaid entitlement to the beneficiaries.

But there is clearly room for much more work on this important area, as a host of unanswered questions remain. First, the importance of excess demand for nursing homes remains unclear; whereas some studies find evidence of excess demand, others find that Medicaid generosity increases lead to more total nursing home care, which is inconsistent with excess demand. Second, more work is needed on the substitutability of home and community care for institutional care of the elderly. The available research, mostly from a social experiment run in the 1970s, suggests that there is little substitutability; more generous home care does not reduce the incidence of institutional care. But this evidence is old and may no longer be relevant in the rapidly changing world of home care. More work in this area would be very useful as Medicaid assesses its spending priorities. Third, it is important to assess how states are reacting to their new freedoms with respect to nursing home reimbursement, and what impacts this has on Medicaid patient access. Finally, there is almost no work on the impact of policies on the actual outcomes of the institutionalized elderly. Can Medicaid improve the health or well-being of the elderly through subsidizing institutionalization, or is the program simply taking the elderly off their children's hands and warehousing them in an institution until death?

1.6 Conclusions

The rapid growth of Medicaid, in the face of a continuing rise in the number of uninsured, suggests that changes to this program, and related eligibility expansions such as CHIP, will continue to be a dominant policy issue in the coming years. These changes can be well informed by the large and growing literature on the Medicaid program. But many unanswered questions remain. The significant advantage of the Medicaid program for future research is the exciting natural laboratory provided by variation across states in their program provisions, particularly along the lines of eligibility and provider reimbursement. Future work can usefully continue to exploit this laboratory in answering the remaining questions needed to intelligently move forward with Medicaid policy.

References

Adams, Kathleen. 1994. The effect of increased Medicaid fees on physician participation and enrollee service utilization in Tennessee. *Inquiry* 31:173–89.

American Medical Association (AMA). 1991. *Physician marketplace update, July 1991*. Chicago: AMA.

Baker, Laurence. 1997. Medicaid policy, physician behavior, and health care for low-income populations. Stanford University Medical School. Mimeograph.

Bindman, A., K. Grumbach, D. Keane, L. Rauch, and J. M. Luce. 1991. A public hospital closes: Impact on patients' access to care and health status. *Journal of the American Medical Association* 264:2899–904.

Blank, Rebecca, and David Card. 1991. Recent trends in insured and uninsured unemployment: Is there an explanation? *Quarterly Journal of Economics* 106:1157–90.

Blank, Rebecca M., Christine C. George, and Rebecca A. London. 1996. State abortion rates: The impact of policy, provider availability, political climate, demography, and economics. *Journal of Health Economics* 15:513–53.

Blank, Rebecca, and Patricia Ruggles. 1996. When do women use AFDC and food stamps? The dynamics of eligibility vs. participation. *Journal of Human Resources* 31:57–89.

Blumberg, Linda, Lisa Dubay, and Stephen Norton. 2000. Did the Medicaid expansions displace private insurance? An analysis using the SIPP. *Journal of Health Economics* 19 (1): 33–60.

Congressional Research Service. 1993. *Medicaid source book: Background data and analysis.* Washington, D.C.: Government Printing Office.

Currie, Janet. 1996. Do children of immigrants make differential use of public health insurance? University of California–Los Angeles, Department of Economics. Mimeograph.

Currie, Janet, and John Fahr. 2000. Medicaid managed care: Effects on children's Medicaid coverage and utilization. University of California–Los Angeles.

Currie, Janet, and Jeffrey Grogger. 2000. Medicaid expansions and welfare contractions: Offsetting effects on prenatal care and infant health? NBER Working Paper no. 7667. Cambridge, Mass.: National Bureau of Economic Research, April.

Currie, Janet, and Jonathan Gruber. 1994. Saving babies: The efficacy and cost of recent expansions of Medicaid eligibility for pregnant women. NBER Working Paper no. 4644. Cambridge, Mass.: National Bureau of Economic Research.

———. 1996a. Health insurance eligibility, utilization of medical care, and child health. *Quarterly Journal of Economics* 111:431–66.

———. 1996b. Saving babies: The efficacy and cost of recent expansions of Medicaid eligibility for pregnant women. *Journal of Political Economy* 104:1263–96.

———. 2001. Public health insurance and medical treatment: The equalizing impact of the Medicaid expansions. *Journal of Public Economics* 82 (1): 63–89.

Currie, Janet, Jonathan Gruber, and Michael Fischer. 1995. Physician payments and infant mortality: Evidence from Medicaid fee policy. *American Economic Review* 85:106–11.

Currie, Janet, and Duncan Thomas. 1995. Medical care for children: Public insurance, private insurance, and racial differences in utilization. *Journal of Human Resources* 30:131–62.

Cutler, David, and Brigitte Madrian. 1998. Labor market responses to rising health care costs. *RAND Journal of Economics* 29:509–23.

Cutler, David, and Jonathan Gruber. 1996a. Does public insurance crowd out private insurance? *Quarterly Journal of Economics* 111:391–430.

———. 1996b. The effect of expanding the Medicaid program on public insurance, private insurance, and redistribution. *American Economic Review* 86:368–73.

Cutler, David, and Louise Sheiner. 1994. Policy options for long-term care. In *Studies in the economics of aging,* ed. David Wise, 395–434. Chicago: University of Chicago Press.

Dafny, Leemore, and Jonathan Gruber. 2000. Does public insurance improve the efficiency of medical care? Medicaid expansions and child hospitalizations. MIT, Department of Economics. Mimeograph.

Decker, Sandra. 1992. The effect of physician reimbursement levels on the primary care of Medicaid patients. Harvard University, Department of Economics. Mimeograph.

———. 1994. The effect of Medicaid on participation in the AFDC program: Evidence from the initial introduction of Medicaid. New York University. Mimeograph.

Dubay, Lisa, Theodore Joyce, Robert Kaestner, and Genevieve Kenney. 2000. Changes in prenatal care timing and low birth weight by race and socioeconomic status: Implications for the Medicaid expansions for pregnant women. *Health Services Research,* forthcoming.

Dubay, Lisa, and Genevieve Kenney. 1997. Did Medicaid expansions for pregnant women crowd out private insurance? *Health Affairs* 16:185–193.

Duggan, Mark. 1999. Hospital ownership and public medical spending. Harvard University, Department of Economics. Mimeograph.

Ellwood, D., and K. Adams. 1990. Medicaid mysteries: Transitional benefits, Medicaid coverage, and welfare exits. *Health Care Financing Review* 1990 Annual Supplement: 119–31.

Ellwood, Marilyn R., and Genevieve Kenney. 1995. Medicaid and pregnant women: Who is being enrolled and when? *Health Care Financing Review* 17 (winter): 7–28.

Employee Benefits Research Institute (EBRI). 1995. *EBRI databook of employee benefits.* Washington, D.C.: EBRI.

———. 2000. *Sources of health insurance and characteristics of the uninsured.* Washington, D.C.: EBRI.

Epstein, Arnold, and Joseph Newhouse. 1998. Impact of Medicaid expansion on early prenatal care and health outcomes. *Health Care Financing Review* 19 (4): 85–99.

Ettner, Susan L. 1993. Do elderly Medicaid patients experience reduced access to nursing home care? *Journal of Health Economics* 12:259–80.

Fossett, James W., Janet D. Perloff, Phillip R. Kletke, and John A. Peterson. 1992. Medicaid and access to child health care in Chicago. *Journal of Health Politics, Policy, and Law* 17:273–98.

Fossett, James W., and John A. Peterson. 1989. Physician supply and Medicaid participation: The causes of market failure. *Medical Care* 27:386–96.

Garrett, Bowen, and John Holahan. 2000. Welfare leavers, Medicaid coverage, and private health insurance. Urban Institute Report no. B-13. Washington, D.C.: The Urban Institute, March.

Gertler, Paul J. 1989. Subsidies, quality, and the regulation of nursing homes. *Journal of Public Economics* 38:33–52.

———. 1992. Medicaid and the cost of improving access to nursing home care. *Review of Economics and Statistics* 74:338–45.

Grabowski, David. 2001. Medicaid reimbursement and the quality of nursing home care. *Journal of Health Economics* 20:549–69.

Gray, Bradley. 1999. Do Medicaid physician fees for prenatal services affect birth outcomes? Tulane University, Department of Economics. Mimeograph.

Green Book (GB). *See* U.S. Congress, Committee on Ways and Means

Gruber, Jonathan. 1994. The incidence of mandated maternity benefits. *American Economic Review* 84:622–41.

———. 1997. Health insurance for poor women and children in the U.S.: Lessons from the past decade. In *Tax policy and the economy 11,* ed. James Poterba, 169–211. Cambridge: MIT Press.

————. 2000. Health insurance and the labor market. In *Handbook of health economics,* ed. Joseph Newhouse and Anthony Culyer. Forthcoming.

Gruber, Jonathan, Kathleen Adams, and Joseph Newhouse. 1996. Physician fee policy and Medicaid program costs. MIT, Department of Economics. Mimeograph.

Gruber, Jonathan, John Kim, and Dina Mayzlin. 1999. Physician fees and procedure intensity: The case of cesarean delivery. *Journal of Health Economics* 18:473–90.

Gruber, Jonathan, and Aaron Yelowitz. 1999. Public health insurance and private savings. *Journal of Political Economy* 107 (6): 1249–74.

Gruenberg, L. W., and T. R. Willemain. 1982. Hospital discharge queues in Massachusetts. *Medical Care* 20:188–200.

Hadley, Jack. 1979. Physician participation in Medicaid: Evidence from California. *Health Services Research* 14:266–80.

Ham, John, and Lara Shore-Sheppard. 1999. The impact of public health insurance on labor market transitions. Ohio State University, Department of Economics. Mimeograph.

Hass, Jennifer S., Seven Udarhelyi, and Arnold M. Epstein. 1993. The effect of health coverage for uninsured pregnant women on maternal health and the use of cesarean section. *Journal of the American Medical Association* 270:61–64.

Hass, Jennifer S., Seven Udarhelyi, Carl N. Morris, and Arnold M. Epstein. 1993. The effect of providing health coverage to poor uninsured pregnant women in Massachusetts. *Journal of the American Medical Association* 269:87–91.

Haas-Wilson, Deborah. 1994. The impact of state abortion restrictions on minors' demand for abortions. *Journal of Human Resources* 31:140–58.

Held, Philip J., and John Holahan. 1985. Containing Medicaid costs in an era of growing physician supply. *Health Care Financing Review* 7 (1): 49–60.

Hoerger, Thomas J., Gabriel Picone, and Frank A. Sloan. 1996. Public subsidies, private provision of care, and living arrangements. *Review of Economics and Statistics* 78:428–40.

Holahan, John. 1988. The impact of alternative hospital payment systems on Medicaid costs. *Inquiry* 25:517–32.

————. 1991. Medicaid physician fees, 1990: The results of a new survey. Urban Institute Working Paper no. 6110–01. Washington, D.C.: The Urban Institute.

Howell, E. M., and Marilyn Ellwood. 1991. Medicaid and pregnancy: Issues in expanding eligibility. *Family Planning Perspectives* 23:123–28.

Hubbard, R. Glenn, Jonathan Skinner, and Stephen P. Zeldes. 1995. Precautionary saving and social insurance. *Journal of Political Economy* 103:360–99.

Institute of Medicine. 1985. *Preventing low birthweight.* Washington, D.C.: National Academy Press.

Joyce, Theodore, and Robert Kaestner. 1996. The effect of expansions in Medicaid income eligibility on abortion. *Demography* 33:181–92.

Joyce, Theodore, Robert Kaestner, and Florence Kwan. 1998. Is Medicaid pronatalist: The effect of eligibility expansions on abortions and births. *Family Planning Perspectives* 30:108–13.

Kaestner, Robert, Theodore Joyce, and Andrew Racine. 1999. Does publicly provided health insurance improve the health of low-income children in the United States? NBER Working Paper no. 6887. Cambridge, Mass.: National Bureau of Economic Research.

Kane, Thomas J., and Douglas Staiger. 1996. Teen motherhood and abortion access. *Quarterly Journal of Economics* 111:467–506.

Kasper, Judith. 1986. Health status and utilization: Differences by Medicaid coverage and income. *Health Care Financing Review* 7:1–17.

Katz, Lawrence, and Kevin M. Murphy. 1992. Changes in relative wages, 1963–1987: Supply and demand factors. *Quarterly Journal of Economics* 107:37–78.

Kotlikoff, Laurence J. 1988. Health expenditures and precautionary saving. In *What determines saving?* ed. L. Kotlikoff, 141–62. Cambridge: MIT Press.

Ku, Leighton, and Bowen Garrett. 2000. How welfare reform and economic factors affected Medicaid participation: 1984–1996. Urban Institute Discussion Paper no. 00–01. Washington, D.C.: The Urban Institute, February.

Ku, Leighton, Frank Ullman, and Ruth Almeida. 1999. What counts? Determining Medicaid and CHIP eligibility for children. Urban Institute Discussion Paper no. 99–05. Washington, D.C.: The Urban Institute.

Leibowitz, Arleen. 1990. The response of births to changes in health care costs. *Journal of Human Resources* 25:671–97.

Levine, Phillip B., Amy B. Trainor, and David J. Zimmerman. 1996. The effect of Medicaid abortion funding restrictions on abortions, pregnancies, and births. *Journal of Health Economics* 15:555–78.

Levinson, Arik, and Frank Ullman. 1998. Medicaid managed care and infant health. *Journal of Health Economics* 17:351–68.

Lurie, N., N. B. Ward, M. F. Shapiro, and N. H. Brook. 1984. Termination from Medi-Cal: Does it affect health? *New England Journal of Medicine* 111:480–84.

Madrian, Brigitte C. 1994. Employment-based health insurance and job mobility: Is there evidence of job-lock? *Quarterly Journal of Economics* 109:27–51.

Meyer, Bruce, and Dan Rosenbaum. 1999. Welfare, the earned income tax credit, and the labor supply of single mothers. Northwestern University, Department of Economics. Mimeograph.

Mitchell, Janet B. 1991. Physician participation in Medicaid revisited. *Medical Care* 29:645–53.

Mitchell, Janet B., and Rachel Schurman. 1984. Access to private obstetrics/gynecology services under Medicaid. *Medical Care* 22:1026–37.

Moffitt, Robert. 1983. An economic model of welfare stigma. *American Economic Review* 73:1023–35.

Moffitt, Robert, and B. Wolfe. 1992. The effect of the Medicaid program on welfare participation and labor supply. *Review of Economics and Statistics* 64:615–26.

Montgomery, E., and J. Navin. 1996. Cross-state variation in Medicaid program and female labor supply. NBER Working Paper no. 5492. Cambridge, Mass.: National Bureau of Economic Research.

Mullahy, John. 1994. Medicaid and the timing of preventive health care for young children. Trinity College, Department of Economics. Mimeograph.

Murray, Charles. 1984. *Losing ground.* New York: Basic Books.

National Governors Association (NGA). 1998. *Maternal and child health update.* Washington, D.C.: NGA.

Newhouse, Joseph. 1993. *Free for all? Lessons from the RAND health insurance experiment.* Santa Monica, Calif.: RAND.

Norton, Edward C. 1995. Elderly assets, Medicaid policy, and spend-down in nursing homes. *Review of Income and Wealth* 41:309–29.

———. 2000. Long term care. In *Handbook of health economics,* vol. 1B, ed. Anthony Culyer and Joseph Newhouse. 956–94. Amsterdam: Elsevier Science.

Norton, Edward C., and V. Kumar. 1998. Medicaid moral hazard: Evidence from the Medicare catastrophic coverage act. University of North Carolina at Chapel Hill, Department of Economics. Working Paper.

Nyman, J. A. 1985. Prospective and cost-plus Medicaid reimbursement, excess Medicaid demand, and the quality of nursing home care. *Journal of Health Economics* 4:237–59.

———. 1989. The private demand for nursing home care. *Journal of Health Economics* 8:209–31.

Peltzman, Sam. 1973. The effect of government subsidies-in-kind on private expenditures: The case of higher education. *Journal of Political Economy* 81:1–27.

Physician Payment Review Commission. 1991. Annual report to Congress. Washington, D.C.: Physician Payment Review Commission.

Piper, Joyce, Wayne Riley, and Marie Griffin. 1990. Effects of Medicaid eligibility expansion on prenatal care and pregnancy outcome in Tennessee. *Journal of the American Medical Association* 264:2219–23.

Rask, Kevin, and Kimberly Rask. 2000. Public insurance substituting for private insurance: New evidence regarding public hospitals, uncompensated care funds, and Medicaid. *Journal of Health Economics* 19:1–31.

Scanlon, William J. 1980. A theory of the nursing home market. *Inquiry* 17:25–41.

Scott-Morton, Fiona. 1997. The strategic response by pharmaceutical firms to the Medicaid most-favored-customer rules. *RAND Journal of Economics* 28:269–90.

Sheiner, L. 1994. Health care costs, wages, and aging: Assessing the impact of community rating. Washington, D.C.: Federal Reserve Board. Mimeograph.

Shore-Sheppard, Lara. 1999. Stemming the tide? The effect of expanding Medicaid eligibility on health insurance coverage. University of Pittsburgh, Department of Economics. Mimeograph.

Shore-Sheppard, Lara, Thomas Buchmueller, and Gail Jensen. 2000. Medicaid and crowding out of private insurance: A re-examination using firm-level data. *Journal of Health Economics* 19:61–91.

Short, Pamela, J. Cantor, and A. Monheit. 1988. The dynamics of Medicaid enrollment. *Inquiry* 25:504–16.

Short, Pamela, and Doris Lefkowitz. 1992. Encouraging preventive services for low-income children: The effect of expanding Medicaid. *Medical Care* 30:766–80.

Sloan, Frank, Janet Mitchell, and Jerry Cromwell. 1978. Physician participation in state Medicaid programs. *Journal of Human Resources* 8:212–45.

Smeeding, Timothy. 1982. Alternative methods for valuing selected in-kind transfer benefits and measuring their effect on poverty. Census Technical Paper no. 50. Washington, D.C.: U.S. Bureau of the Census.

Soumerai, Stephen, T. J. McLaughlin, D. Ross-Degnan, C. S. Casteris, and P. Bollini. 1994. Effects of limiting Medicaid drug-reimbursement benefits on the use of psychotropic agents and acute mental health services by patients with schizophrenia. *New England Journal of Medicine* 331:650–55.

Stewart, Anne. 1992. Head Start: Funding, eligibility, and participation. Congressional Research Service report for Congress, 22 July. Washington, D.C.: Congressional Research Service.

Stuart, Bruce, and Christopher Zacker. 1999. Who bears the burden of Medicaid drug copayment policies? *Health Affairs* 18 (2): 201–12.

Thorpe, Kenneth, and Curtis Florence. 1999. Health insurance coverage among children: The role of expanded Medicaid coverage. *Inquiry* 35 (4): 369–79.

Ullman, Frank, Ian Hill, and Ruth Almeida. 1999. CHIP: A look at emerging state programs. Urban Institute Working Paper no. A-35. Washington, D.C.: The Urban Institute, September.

U.S. Congress, Committee on Ways and Means. 2000. *Green book 2000: Background material on programs under the jurisdiction of the Committee on Ways and Means.* Washington, D.C.: U.S. Government Printing Office.

Winkler, A. 1991. The incentive effects of Medicaid on women's labor supply. *Journal of Human Resources* 26:308–37.

Yazici, E. Y., and Robert Kaestner. 1998. Medicaid expansions and the crowding out of private health insurance. NBER Working Paper no. 6527. Cambridge, Mass.: National Bureau of Economic Research.

Yellow Book (YB). *See* Congressional Research Service

Yelowitz, Aaron. 1995. The Medicaid notch, labor supply, and welfare participation: Evidence from eligibility expansions. *Quarterly Journal of Economics* 105:909–40.

———. 1996. Did recent Medicaid reforms cause the caseload explosion in the food stamp program? UCLA Working Paper no. 756. University of California–Los Angeles, July.

———. 1998a. Why did the SSI-disabled program grow so much? Disentangling the effect of Medicaid. *Journal of Health Economics* 17 (3): 321–50.

———. 1998b. Will extending Medicaid to two parent families encourage marriage? *Journal of Human Resources* 33 (4): 833–65.

———. 2000a. Public policy and health care choices of the elderly: Evidence from the Medicare buy-in program. *Journal of Public Economics,* forthcoming.

———. 2000b. Using the Medicare buy-in program to estimate the effect of Medicaid on SSI participation. *Economic Inquiry,* forthcoming.

Zimmerman, David, and Phillip Levine. 1993. The intergenerational correlation in AFDC participation: Welfare trap or poverty trap? Working Paper no. 93–07. Wellesley College, Department of Economics.

Zuckerman, Stephen. 1987. Medicaid hospital spending: Effects of reimbursement and utilization control policies. *Health Care Financing Review* 9 (2): 65–77.

2

The Supplemental Security Income Program

Mary C. Daly and Richard V. Burkhauser

2.1 Introduction

Supplemental Security Income (SSI) is a nationwide federal assistance program for aged, blind, and disabled individuals with low incomes. The SSI program was enacted in 1972 and began paying benefits in 1974, replacing a patchwork of state-run entitlement programs created under the Social Security Act of 1935 and its amendments in 1950. The establishment of SSI was the culmination of a four-year debate over a more overarching welfare reform proposal—the Family Assistance Plan (FAP)—intended to extend the federal social safety net to all low-income Americans. Although Congress eventually rejected the universality of FAP, it passed SSI, a categorical welfare program based on the same negative income tax principles as FAP but targeted on a subset of low-income individuals not expected to work—the aged, blind, and disabled.

SSI began as a relatively small program providing benefits to a largely elderly population. Since that time SSI has grown to become the largest federal means-tested cash assistance program in the United States, with a caseload dominated by children and working-age adults with disabilities. In 2001, an average of 6.7 million people—the vast majority under age

Mary C. Daly is a research advisor at the Federal Reserve Bank of San Francisco. Richard V. Burkhauser is chair and professor of the Department of Policy Analysis and Management at Cornell University.

The authors thank Robert Moffitt, Kathleen McGarry, Kalman Rupp, David Wittenburg, and participants at the NBER Conference on Means-Tested Transfer Programs and two anonymous referees for helpful comments. They thank Andrew Houtenville, Robert Weathers, and David Wittenburg for providing data and Carol D'Souza and Heather Royer for research assistance. They also are grateful to Anita Todd and Rochelle Frank for editorial assistance and to Florence Allen for helping compile the document. The opinions expressed in this paper do not necessarily reflect the views of the Federal Reserve Bank of San Francisco.

sixty-five—received federal and state SSI benefits totaling over $32 billion. Rapid program growth, the changing composition of SSI beneficiaries, and increasing pressure to devolve federal responsibility for social programs to state governments, as well as to integrate traditional "nonworkers" into the labor market, have all raised questions about the role that SSI plays in the broader U.S. social welfare system.

In 1972, those not expected to work included individuals aged sixty-five and older, the blind, and people with disabilities. These categories have always been somewhat arbitrary and difficult to establish and assess, particularly with regard to disability. But dramatic changes in social expectations over who should work and who should be entitled to income transfers have renewed the debate over whom SSI should serve. On the one hand, individuals are living and working longer, and the Americans with Disabilities Act (ADA) has granted people with disabilities a legal right to equal access to employment, suggesting that the aged, blind, and disabled may be better able to work than in the past. On the other hand, the normal retirement age for Social Security benefits is increasing, welfare reforms have placed limits on the number of years single mothers with children may receive benefits in lieu of working, and poverty rates among children remain high. These circumstances suggest that income maintenance programs like SSI will play an increasingly important role in the U.S. social safety net. All these factors will have an impact on the politically determined boundaries of the only remaining federal cash-based means-tested entitlement program without time limits available to both adults and children.

In this chapter we provide the basic information necessary for SSI policymakers to make informed choices about its future. In section 2.2 we review the program's history and describe the structure and evolution of SSI program rules. In section 2.3 we provide expenditure, caseload, and program recipient statistics. In section 2.4 we summarize the primary economic issues related to the SSI program. In section 2.5 we review the empirical evidence regarding these issues. We summarize our findings in section 2.6.

2.2   History and Structure of the SSI Program

The SSI program is a nationwide federal assistance program administered by the Social Security Administration (SSA), which pays cash benefits to low-income individuals who are sixty-five years of age or older or who are blind or disabled. The SSI program was enacted in 1972 and began paying benefits in 1974 replacing the state Old-Age Assistance, Aid to the Permanently and Totally Disabled, and Aid to the Blind Programs created by the Social Security Act of 1935 and its amendments in 1950. In this section we review the history of the SSI program, describe current program structure, eligibility criteria, and benefit levels, and discuss how the program's goals and rules have evolved over time.

2.2.1   Original Rationale and Program Goals

The establishment of a federal income maintenance program for the aged, blind, and disabled, SSI was the culmination of a four-year debate that began with a more overarching welfare reform proposal, FAP, proposed by President Nixon on 8 August 1969.[1] FAP was the first serious attempt to institute a federal negative income tax program equivalent to those proposed by Stigler (1946), Friedman (1962, 1968), and Tobin (1969). FAP departed from existing welfare policy in three important ways: (a) It was universal rather than categorical, with low income and assets as the only eligibility criteria; (b) it was run through the federal tax system rather than being administered by state and local governments; and (c) it had a low benefit reduction rate, in keeping with the notion that low tax rates provide desirable work incentives.[2]

Congress eventually rejected the idea of an income maintenance program for all Americans with low income but on 17 October 1972 created the SSI program, a categorical welfare program targeted on the subset of the poor who were aged, blind, or disabled. The SSI program passed after FAP failed largely because Congress believed that providing income assistance to needy individuals not expected to work was likely to have a much smaller negative impact on employment than a universal negative income tax program. In 1972, those not expected to work included individuals age sixty-five and older, the blind, and people with disabilities, subgroups of the population that already were targets of state-based assistance programs.

In keeping with some of the themes of FAP, the new SSI program federalized benefit administration, set minimum benefit standards, imposed uniform eligibility criteria, and set low benefit reduction rates on labor earnings. Legislative records suggest that SSI was intended to reduce variability in the types of individuals allowed onto the rolls and in the amount of assistance they received, to make economic resources the only determinant of eligibility for those meeting the categorical requirements, and to provide incentives for beneficiaries to work to supplement their income and move toward rehabilitation (U.S. House of Representatives, Committee on Ways and Means 1971).[3,4] Thus, under SSI, Congress federalized benefit administration, set minimum benefit standards, imposed uniform

1. See Burke and Burke (1974) and Smeeding (1994) for a more detailed historical discussion of how SSI became the nation's first negative income tax program.

2. The key features of most negative income tax (NIT) proposals are universality, federal benefit administration, and low benefit reduction rates. For a fuller discussion of the origins of NIT policy see Burkhauser and Finnegan (1989, 1993).

3. Most legislative models of the NIT, including FAP and SSI, impose both an income and an asset test. Throughout this chapter we refer to income and assets as economic resources.

4. Under the former state-run programs the amount of assistance could vary from recipient to recipient according to an individual's assessed needs, age, and living situation.

eligibility criteria, and set relatively low benefit reduction rates on labor earnings. In addition to adopting some of the administrative mechanisms of FAP, the SSI program began to blur the traditional ability-to-work standard for determining who should be entitled to public welfare payments. By extending SSI benefits to the needy families of children with disabilities, Congress expanded the social safety net to include families headed by adults who were "employable."[5,6]

2.2.2   SSI Eligibility Criteria

As noted earlier, SSI is an income support program for low-income individuals who are aged, blind, or disabled. Thus, SSI eligibility is a function of three program-based categorical criteria—age, disability, or blindness—as well as more general requirements associated with income and asset limits, and citizenship and residency rules. The SSA is responsible for screening applicants and making awards for SSI. Table 2.1 summarizes the SSI eligibility requirements described in detail in the remainder of this section.

Means Tests

To be eligible for SSI, individuals must fall below federally mandated income and asset limits. In 2002, the countable income limit was set at $780 per month ($9,360 per year) for individuals and $1,170 per month ($14,040 per year) for couples. The countable income limit is determined by the federal benefit rate (FBR) and increases annually with the average U.S. wage index. In general, the countable income limits fall just short of the U.S. Census Bureau official poverty thresholds.[7] SSI applicants also must meet countable asset limits. In 2002, asset limits were set at $2,000 for individuals and $3,000 for couples. Unlike the countable income limits, the asset limits are not indexed for inflation. Thus, over time, countable asset limits for SSI eligibility have become stricter. Countable asset limits were last changed in 1989, rising from $1,500 for individuals and from $2,250 for couples.

As noted earlier, not all income received by individuals or couples is countable. Exclusions include a $20 monthly income disregard for all forms of income with the exception of means-tested income and an additional $65 monthly disregard for any labor income.[8] After these disregards,

---

5. Poor children with disabilities had previously been included in state AFDC programs.

6. A final category of people allowed onto the SSI rolls, despite their potential to find alternative private support, were noncitizens. By law, legal immigrants had to show income sponsorship before immigrating to the United States. Largely due to the definition of income in the SSI means test, the 1972 legislation allowed sponsored immigrants who were poor to apply for SSI. This primarily affected the SSI aged program.

7. For example, in 2001, the Census Bureau poverty threshold for all single-person households (under and over age sixty-five) was $754 per month ($9,044 per year). The countable income cutoff for SSI was $740 per month ($8,880 per year) in 2001.

8. In certain cases, impairment-related expenses may be deducted from this total. Also, income is disregarded when it is used for Plans for Achieving Self Support (PASS).

Table 2.1   **SSI Eligibility Requirements in 2002**

Requirement	Definition	Exceptions/Exclusions
Limited income[a]	Countable income must be • below $780 a month for single adult or child • below $1,170 a month for couple (In states that pay SSI supplements, countable income can be higher)	Not all income counts. Some exclusions are • $20 per month of most income • $65 per month of wages and one-half of wages over $65 • food stamps • home energy/housing assistance
Limited resources[a] (property and other assets a person owns)	• $2,000 for single adult or child • $3,000 for couple (limit applies even if only one member is eligible)	Not all resources count. Some exclusions are • the home a person lives in • a car, depending on use or value • burial plots for individual and immediate family • burial funds up to $1,500 • life insurance with face value of $1,500 or less
Citizenship/residence[b]	• resides in one of the fifty states, Washington, D.C., or the Northern Mariana Islands; and • U.S. citizen or national; or • certain American Indians; or • lawful permanent resident with forty work credits; or • certain noncitizens with a military service connection; or • certain refugee or asylum-type noncitizens during the first seven years; or • certain noncitizens in the United States or receiving SSI on 22 August 1996	Exception to residence: certain children of U.S. armed forces personnel stationed abroad

(*continued*)

for every $1 in labor earnings a worker loses $0.50 in SSI benefits. Therefore, after all income disregards, an SSI recipient faces a 50 percent implicit tax on labor earnings.[9] Neither the income nor the asset exclusions are indexed for inflation.

In-kind assistance from government programs like food stamps and public housing are not counted as income against the individual's overall SSI benefit. All other benefits from government programs are taxed at 100

---

9. As we will discuss below, for those SSI beneficiaries receiving other means-tested program benefits, the effective marginal tax on work can be much higher.

Table 2.1　　　(continued)

Requirement	Definition	Exceptions/Exclusions
Categorical: sixty-five or older, blind or disabled; blind; disabled	Meet only one of these: • age sixty-five or older • corrected vision of 20/200 or less in better eye • field of vision less than 20 degrees • physical or mental impairment that keeps a person from performing any "substantial" work and is expected to last twelve months or result in death • for a child's impairment, "marked and severe functional limitations" expected to last twelve months or result in death	Person whose visual impairment is not severe enough to be considered blind may qualify under the nonblind disability rules: • A job that pays $780 per month ($1,300 if blind) is generally considered substantial work. • Special work incentives allow some income and resources to be excluded and permit payment of special cash benefits or continuation of Medicaid coverage even when a blind or disabled person is working.

Source: SSA (2002b).

[a]If only one member of a couple is eligible, the income and resources of both are considered in determining eligibility. If a child under age eighteen is living with parents, the parents' income and resources are considered.

[b]If a noncitizen has a sponsor who signed a legally unenforceable affidavit of support (Immigration and Naturalization Services [INS] form I-134), the sponsor's income and resources are considered in determining eligibility and payment amount for three years following the date of lawful admission. (This rule does not apply to noncitizens who become blind or disabled after legal admission for permanent residence or to noncitizens who are not lawful permanent residents.) If the sponsor signed the new legally enforceable affidavit of support (INS form I-864), the sponsor's income and resources are considered until the noncitizen acquires forty work credits or becomes a citizen. (This rule applies to noncitizens who become blind or disabled after admission for permanent residence and to noncitizens who are not lawful permanent residents.)

percent. Countable resources include resources other than the home a person lives in, a car (depending on use or value), and limited amounts of life insurance and burial funds.[10] In cases where an eligible individual resides in a household with ineligible individuals, a portion of the other persons' income is considered when determining the amount of the SSI payment. This process, known as "deeming," applies to married couples with one eligible member, parents of child applicants, and U.S. sponsors of noncitizen applicants. The deeming rules are straightforward: If an individual or couple is living in another person's household and is receiving both food and shelter from the person in the household, the federal benefit rate is reduced by one-third.

Although the federal benefit rate—and, thus, the monthly income test—

10. In 2002, the dollar value on disregards on assets was $4,500 for a car or medical treatment, $1,500 on life insurance, and $2,000 on personal property and household furnishings.

rises with inflation each year, the monthly income disregards, the asset limits, and the value of allowable assets (e.g., car, household effects) are not indexed, and thus have fallen substantially in real terms since SSI began. The real decline in the income disregards and asset limits over time has effectively eroded the value of SSI benefits and narrowed the population of potential recipients relative to 1974 levels. Consider first the 1972 set disregards of $20 on all income and $65 on labor income. Valued in 2002 dollars, these disregards would be $84 and $275 per month, respectively. Adjusting the asset limits for inflation discloses the same pattern. Valued in 2002 dollars, the asset limits set in 1972 would be $6,345 for individuals and $9,517 for couples,[11] compared to the $2,000 and $3,000 limits currently in place. Thus, compared to when it was enacted in 1972, SSI now covers a narrower and less economically advantaged portion of the income distribution.

Citizenship and Residency Criteria

In addition to meeting the economic resource criteria, individuals also must meet residency and citizenship requirements. To be eligible for SSI an individual must be a resident of the United States and a U.S. citizen, a U.S. national, or a "qualified alien" in an SSI-eligible noncitizen category.[12] The current SSI-eligible noncitizen categories generally can be characterized as covering individuals who were lawfully in the United States as of 22 August 1996, individuals who are refugees or in refugee-like situations, and individuals who have contributed to the country either by service in the military or through extended periods of work. These relatively restrictive allowances for noncitizens were implemented under 1996 welfare reform (PRWORA) and were a direct response to concerns that newly arrived noncitizens with immigration sponsors were increasingly applying for, and receiving, SSI benefits. The SSI provisions in the 1996 welfare reform act generally excluded these individuals from receiving SSI by mandating that the income of the noncitizen's immigration sponsor be considered in the means test.

Categorical Eligibility Criteria

Individuals meeting income, asset, and citizenship tests may qualify for SSI benefits based on three categorical criteria: age, blindness, or disability. Applicants need only meet one of the three criteria, although some applicants fit multiple categories. The categorical program requirements for the aged and the blind are straightforward. Individuals are categorically el-

11. Had the asset limits of $2,000 (individuals) and $3,000 (couples) set in 1989 kept up with inflation, they would be $2,856 and $4,284, respectively, in 2002.
12. The term *qualified alien* is defined in section 431 of Public Law (P.L.) 104-193, as amended by P.L. 104-208 and P.L. 105-33. See Parrot, Kennedy, and Scott (1998) for a complete listing of the qualifying criteria.

igible for SSI based on age if they are age sixty-five or older. Individuals may receive SSI benefits for the blind if they have 20/200 vision or less with the use of a correcting lens in their better eye, or if they have tunnel vision of 20 degrees or less. These objective standards make for relatively easy and uniform screening of aged and blind SSI applicants at offices of the SSA across the United States.[13]

In contrast, the disability screening process is more complex. First, there is no simple definition of disability.[14] The most frequently applied model of disability comes from Nagi (1965, 1969a, b, 1991). In the Nagi model, disability is a dynamic process in which an individual's pathology interacts with the socioeconomic environment.[15] The dynamic nature of the disability process is represented by the movement through three stages: pathology, impairment, and disability. The first stage, pathology, is the presence of a physical or mental condition that interrupts the physical or mental process of the human body. An example is deafness. This leads to the second stage, impairment, which Nagi defines as "a physiological, anatomical, or mental loss or abnormality that limits a person's capacity to function." For example, deafness limits the ability to interpret sound. The final stage, disability, is an inability to perform or a limitation in performing roles and tasks that are socially expected. For example, a person with deafness is unable to use the telephone. Under the Nagi model, those with a pathology that causes a physical or mental impairment that subsequently limits one or more life activities—such as work—but who nevertheless work would not be considered to have a work disability.[16] (This is the case whether work was possible through changes in the work environment, ac-

13. Although the measurement of these "objective standards" is relatively straightforward, the justification for using them as standards for inability to work is less so. A literature exists that argues that categorical age is not a useful measure of ability to work. A parallel literature exists that suggests that functional ability rather than medical condition is a superior criterion for determining ability to work (Library of Congress 1998; Wunderlich, Rice, and Amado 2002).

14. Mashaw and Reno (1996) argue that the appropriateness of any definition of disability depends on the purpose for which it is used. They document over twenty definitions of disability used for purposes of entitlement to public or private income transfers, government services, or statistical analysis. In the ADA of 1990, disability is defined as a physical or mental impairment that substantially limits one or more major life activities, a record of such an impairment, or being regarded as having such an impairment. La Plante (1991) provides a useful discussion of alternative definitions that can be used to estimate this population. Burkhauser, Houtenville, and Wittenburg (forthcoming) provide detailed analyses of different definitions of disability in national representative U.S. surveys.

15. The World Health Organization (WHO) has a model of disability very similar to that of Nagi. The key to both of these definitions is the recognition that individuals move from the presence of a health condition to a point where it begins to impinge on activities that are socially expected of them and that this movement is related to the environment in which individuals live. See Jette and Badley (2002) for an excellent comparison of the Nagi and WHO models.

16. This measure closely resembles what Verbrugge (1990) calls social disability, or the intersection of an individual's physical impairment (e.g., deafness) and the environmental challenges of the activities required by a social role, such as work.

cess to rehabilitation, or individual adaptability.)[17] The first component is the presence of a pathology—a physical or mental malfunction, or the interruption of a normal process, or both. This leads to a second component, an impairment, which Nagi defines as a physiological, anatomical, or mental loss or abnormality that limits a person's capacity and level of function. The final component of disability is defined as an inability to perform, or a limitation in performing, socially expected roles and tasks. For men and, increasingly, for women of working age, market work is a socially expected role. Hence, those who are unable to perform or are limited in their ability to work are considered disabled.

The disability determination process for SSI incorporates some of the reasoning put forth in Nagi's disability definition. Applicants for disability benefits move through a multistep process in which their pathology, impairment, and level of functioning are judged. Applicants thought to be unable to engage in any substantial work become eligible for benefits. Below we describe the process of disability determination for both adults and children applying for SSI disability benefits.

Like the aged and blind, persons seeking disability benefits also apply at an office of the SSA. Once the federal officials and the applicant have gathered sufficient information to complete the application, it is submitted to a state agency for determination of disability. State disability examiners, working with vocational and medical consultants, act as the primary gatekeepers of both SSI and Social Security Disability Insurance (SSDI).[18] Disability decisions are made by state agencies acting under contract to the federal government. Therefore, although disability eligibility criteria are uniform across the country, the interpretation of these criteria, and hence the disability determination process itself, can and does systematically vary from state to state and over time. Table 2.2 shows differences in mean allowance rates (initial acceptances to initial applications), by state between 1974 and 1993. As the table indicates, mean allowance rates vary considerably across states, ranging from lows of 28 in Louisiana and New Mexico to highs of 48 in Delaware, New Jersey, and Rhode Island.

Disability Screening for Adults

SSA defines adult disability as the inability to engage in substantial gainful activity by reason of a medically determinable physical or mental impairment that is expected to result in death or last at least twelve months.

---

17. For example, a person with deafness who is accommodated at the workplace with a Telephone Typewriter machine that permits him or her to use the telephone.

18. SSDI is a social insurance program that provides payments to individuals who have paid Social Security taxes for the appropriate number of quarters and who are judged to be disabled under the SSA guidelines. Unlike SSI, it is not means-tested. However, it does have restrictions on labor earnings consistent with its criteria for disability eligibility. See Bound and Burkhauser (1999) for a fuller discussion of this program from an economic perspective.

Table 2.2   **Mean Disability Allowance Rates by State, 1974–93**

Current State of Residence	Mean	Standard Deviation
Alabama	32	4.8
Arizona	41	6.0
Arkansas	32	5.6
California	37	7.5
Colorado	40	5.8
Connecticut	45	8.9
Delaware	48	4.7
District of Columbia	39	8.0
Florida	37	6.4
Georgia	33	7.2
Illinois	37	5.8
Indiana	40	7.3
Iowa	44	8.7
Kansas	41	5.2
Kentucky	33	3.8
Louisiana	28	8.4
Maine	44	6.1
Maryland	37	5.1
Massachusetts	44	7.8
Michigan	37	6.8
Minnesota	45	7.5
Mississippi	31	5.9
Missouri	38	6.8
Montana	37	6.5
Nebraska	43	6.1
Nevada	39	6.9
New Hampshire	42	5.5
New Jersey	48	9.4
New Mexico	28	5.3
New York	41	9.2
North Carolina	40	6.1
North Dakota	42	5.9
Ohio	42	7.8
Oklahoma	33	6.7
Oregon	37	6.7
Pennsylvania	39	7.4
Rhode Island	48	4.7
South Carolina	37	4.7
South Dakota	46	4.5
Tennessee	35	6.4
Texas	34	6.2
Utah	45	5.9
Vermont	46	5.3
Virginia	36	3.4
Washington	40	8.4
West Virginia	30	8.3
Wisconsin	46	6.5
Wyoming	39	5.1
Total	39	8.2

Source: Burkhauser et al. (1999).

Notes: The mean allowance rate for a state is defined as the mean of the state's yearly initial acceptance to initial application ratio for the years 1974–93. Allowance rates are based on SSDI applications and acceptances.

Applicants must be unable to do any work that exists in the national economy for which they are qualified by virtue of age, education, and work experience. The United States does not award federal disability benefits for partial disability.[19]

As a practical matter, SSA asks the state disability determination offices to follow a five-step procedure in their initial disability determination.[20] First, the examiners check to see if applicants are currently working and making more than the "substantial gainful activity" (SGA) amount—$780 a month in 2002. If so, their application is denied. As can be seen in figure 2.1, almost no cases are rejected in this manner, since presumably the SSA field offices have already checked to see if applicants are working before they send applications to the disability determination office.[21] Second, the state disability examiners determine if the applicant has a severe impairment that is expected to last twelve months or result in death. If not, the application is denied. About 20.1 (13 + 7) percent of all applicants were denied at this step in 2000. Third, the state disability examiners look to see if the impairment meets the medical listings. If the impairment is listed, applicants pass the categorical screening for disability. If the impairment is judged to be equivalent to one of the medical listings, then applicants also meet the categorical requirement for benefits. Most recipients who pass the disability screening do so at this stage because their impairment either meets or equals one on the medical listing (22 percent of all applicants were approved at this step in 2000).

Fourth, if a decision cannot be reached on medical factors alone, applicants are evaluated in terms of residual functional capacity. If they are found to be able to meet the demands of "past relevant work" their claim is denied (20 percent of all applicants were denied at this step in 2000). If individuals are deemed unable to do past relevant work, examiners determine if the impairment prevents the applicant from doing any other work. Here vocational factors are considered. If, for example, applicants' maximum sustained work capacity is limited to sedentary work and they are at least age fifty to fifty-four, with less than a high school education and no skilled work experience, then they would be considered disabled and pass the categorical screening. In contrast, if applicants' previous employment experience includes skilled work, then they would not receive benefits. At

19. However, as will be shown later, in some instances the SSI program allows individuals with disabilities to exceed the earnings limit and continue to receive SSI benefits, making it a type of partial disability insurance. Most other western industrialized countries provide partial disability benefits to their working-age populations. For a discussion of disability program rules in other western industrialized nations see Aarts, Burkhauser, and deJong (1996).

20. Our discussion of the adult disability determination process draws heavily on Bound and Burkhauser (1999).

21. The percentages in figure 2.1 are based on outcomes from initial SSDI applications, the data available from published sources. However, there is no reason to believe that the patterns for SSI would be significantly different.

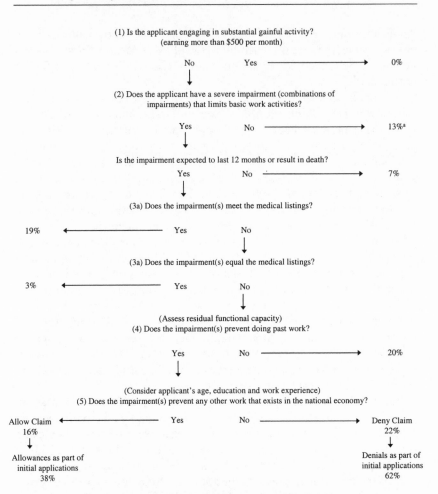

Fig. 2.1   SSA initial disability determinations, sequential decision-making process, and outcomes of decisions on initial SSDI applications, 2000

Source: Authors' calculations using SSA Office of Disability data, SSA-831 Disability Decision file.

[a]This response includes 5 percent of claims that were denied because the applicant failed to cooperate in obtaining evidence needed for the claim. The other 8 percent were denied for "impairment not severe."

this stage, 16 percent of all applicants were determined eligible for benefits and 22 percent were denied benefits in 2000.

Applicants who are denied benefits can ask for a reconsideration. Their file will then be reviewed by a second team of examiners. If they are rejected after reconsideration, individuals may appeal the case to an administrative law judge. It is at this stage that applicants will for the first time come face to face with a gatekeeper. Individuals denied benefits at this stage may appeal the decision to the Social Security Appeals Council and then to the district courts. In 2001, about 33 percent of those initially denied benefits appealed the decision. About 10 percent of those who appealed the decision eventually were awarded benefits (SSA *SSI Annual Statistical Report,* 2002b).[22] For the claimants who are allowed benefits at the initial level or who do not appeal, the application and decision process usually takes a few months. For those who appeal to the administrative law judge, the process can take a year or more.

Disability Screening for Children

Screening children for disability eligibility has proven to be even more complex and contentious than adult disability screening. When the SSI program was originally considered, Congress recognized the potential difficulties of applying the standard SSA disability definition to children. Thus, under the original legislation, Congress wrote that a child should be considered disabled if "he suffers from any medically determinable physical or mental impairment of comparable severity" to a disabling impairment in an adult (SSA 1997). In practice, children originally qualified for SSI if they had "a medically determinable physical or mental impairment which results in marked and severe functional limitations, and which can be expected to result in death, or which has lasted or can be expected to last for a continuous period of not less than 12 months." Between 1974 and 1989 the child disability determination process did not include a functional assessment or take into account the equivalent of adult vocational factors. See figure 2.2 for a comparison of the child and adult initial disability determination process.

This changed in 1990, when the Supreme Court decided the case of *Sullivan v. Zebley.* The court ruled that in order to meet the standard of equal treatment, a functional limitation component parallel to that of adults must be included in the initial disability determination process for children. In response, SSA added two new bases for finding children eligible for benefits: (a) functional equivalence, which was set at the medical listing level of the disability determination process, and (b) an individual functional assessment (IFA), which was designed to be parallel with the functional and vocational assessment provided for adults. By allowing applicants who did not meet the medical listing to be found disabled if their impairments were severe enough to limit their ability to engage in age-appropriate activities, such as attending school, the IFA lowered the level of severity required for children to be eligible for SSI benefits (U.S. GAO 1994, 1995).[23]

22. There is some evidence that the proportion of claimants who appeal and the proportion of decisions that get reversed rise and fall with the percentage of initial denials (Lando, Cutler, and Gamber 1982).

23. Following the Zebley decision a large number of previously denied cases were reassessed and awarded disability benefits. This can be seen in the caseload statistics presented later in this chapter.

Adults	Children: Pre-Zebley	Children: Post-Zebley	Children: Post 1996 Welfare Reform
1. Are you working? Y = Deny	1. Are you working? Y = Deny	1. Are you working? Y = Deny	1. Are you working? Y = Deny
2. Do you have a severe impairment? N = Deny	2. Do you have a severe impairment? N = Deny	2. Do you have a severe impairment?[b] N = Deny	2. Do you have a severe impairment?[d] N = Deny
Compare impairment to medical listings	Compare impairment to medical listings	Compare impairment to medical listings	Compare impairment to medical listings
Mental / **Other**		**Mental**[c] / **Other**	**Mental**[c] / **Other**
3a. Meet both diagnostic (A) and functional (B) criteria? Y = Allow 3a. Meet criteria in medical listings? Y = Allow	3a. Meet criteria in medical listings? Y = Allow	3a. Meet both diagnostic (A) and functional (B) criteria? Y = Allow 3a. Medically meet medical listings? Y = Allow	3a. Meet both diagnostic (A) and functional (B) criteria? Y = Allow 3a. Medically meet medical listings? Y = Allow
3b. Equal? Meet (B) and some of (A)? Y = Allow 3b. Medically equal medical listings? Y = Allow	3b. Medically equal medical listings?[a] Y = Allow; N = Deny	3b. Equal? Meet (B) and some of (A)? Y = Allow 3b. Medically equal medical listings? Y = Allow	3b. Equal? Meet (B) and some of (A)? Y = Allow 3b. Medically equal medical listings? Y = Allow
Assess residual functional capacity (RFC)		3c. Functionally equal medical listings? Y = Allow	3c. Functionally equal medical listings? Y = Allow
4. Can you do past work? Y = Deny		Do individualized functional assessment	
Consider age, education and work experience		4. Given IFA, is impairment(a) of comparable severity to that which would disable an adult? Y = Allow; N = Deny	
5. Can you do any other work? N = Allow; Y = Deny			

Fig. 2.2   Sequential initial disability determination process for children

Source: Created by authors using disability determination guidelines in SSA *Annual Statistical Supplement* (various years).

[a]Before 1990, SSA policy in SS Ruling 83-19 explicitly prohibited using an overall functional assessment to find that a claimant's impairment equaled the medical listings. A claimant with multiple impairments could meet or equal the listings only if at least one impairment, alone, met or medically equaled a specific listing.

[b]A medically determinable physical or mental impairment of comparable severity to one meeting adult definition.

[c]The childhood mental disorders listings were modified in 1990 to include functional criteria similar to those put in the adult listings in 1985.

[d]A medically determinable physical or mental impairment that results in marked and severe functional limitation.

In 1996, as part of welfare reform, Congress modified the definition of disability for children. Legislators replaced the comparable severity (to adults) criterion with a definition of disability that is unique to children. Under the new definition, a child's impairment—or combination of impairments—is considered disabling only if "it (they) results in marked and severe functional limitations, is expected to result in death or has lasted or can be expected to last at least 12 months" (SSA 1996). The new focus on assessing the severity of impairments among children was reflected in changes in the evaluation process. The legislation removed the IFA, replacing it with a criterion based on functional equivalence or evaluations of the extent to which impairments create medical listing–level severity. The revised rules defined medical listing–level severity for functional limitations as (a) marked limitations in two broad areas of functioning, such as social functioning or personal functioning, or (b) extreme limitations in one area of functioning, such as inability to walk (SSA 1997). In practice these changes meant that although functional limitations continued to include behavior-related limitations, they no longer covered the same breadth of functioning included in the IFA. For example, Congress specifically removed maladaptive behavior disorder from the functional listing criteria. Thus, the post-1996 standard represents a broader measure of disability than originally applied to children, but a narrower standard than the one used between 1990 and 1996 (see figure 2.2).

2.2.3   SSI Benefits

Federal Benefit Levels

Each eligible SSI beneficiary in his or her own household with no other countable income received a federal cash payment of $545 per month in 2002 ($817 for jointly eligible couples). The federal SSI benefit is increased each January by the cost-of-living index used to adjust all Social Security Old-Age, Survivors, and Disability Insurance (OASDI) benefits. Although the original objective of the SSI program was to guarantee an income at the poverty level, from the beginning the federal minimum SSI benefit was set below the official Bureau of the Census poverty line. Excluding state supplementation, SSI payments represent about 75 percent of the poverty threshold for an eligible individual, and about 90 percent of the threshold for an eligible couple; these percentages have remained relatively constant over time.[24]

SSI recipients are required by law to apply for every government pro-

---

24. This difference arises in part because the SSI program and the U.S. poverty thresholds assume different economies of scale. The SSI program assumes that a single person needs 67 percent of the couple benefit to be equally well off; the U.S. poverty threshold assumes that a single person needs 80 percent of the couple benefit to maintain an equivalent standard of living.

gram for which they may be eligible. In most states, recipients receive state supplemental payments and become eligible for Medicaid and food stamps without making a separate application.[25,26] Since 1986 SSI benefits and eligibility for Medicaid have been continued for those who earn above the SGA; this is known as 1619(b) status.[27] In general, the special eligibility test for Medicaid applies if the individual has earnings over the level that offsets his or her SSI benefits but is still lower than a threshold amount established in the state in which he or she resides.[28] Adult SSI recipients with disabilities also are eligible for federally funded, state-administered vocational rehabilitation.[29]

State Supplementation

In designing the SSI program Congress recognized that states may want to boost benefit levels beyond the federal program. In addition, Congress wanted to ensure that those states paying above the federal level in 1972 would continue to provide the same level of assistance as they had prior to the federalization of SSI. As a result of these two goals, there are two types of state supplementation for SSI: mandatory and optional.[30] Under mandatory supplementation, states whose Old-Age Assistance and Aid to the Permanently and Totally Disabled benefits were greater than the federal minimum had to make up the difference in mandatory state supplements.[31] Although nearly every state was subject to mandatory supplementation in 1972, increases in federal benefit levels over the years have left only a few SSI beneficiaries receiving mandatory payments today.

In 2000, forty-five states and the District of Columbia provided optional supplemental benefits (columns [1–3], table 2.3). States offering supplements can follow the same rules as the federal SSI program and have the program administered by SSA, or they can administer their own program

25. We discuss states' latitude in determining Medicaid eligibility for SSI recipients later in this section.

26. In most cases, individuals who are eligible for SSI are categorically eligible for food stamps. The exceptions to this general rule are SSI beneficiaries living in households where other members do not receive and are not applying for SSI. These individuals must apply for food stamps at the local food stamp office and meet the household income test to obtain food stamp eligibility.

27. In 1995, only about 46,000 (1.3 percent) of the 3.5 million SSI disability recipients were in 1619(b) status (Mashaw and Reno 1996).

28. In making this determination, the SSA takes the average expenditures on Medicaid and SSI (including state SSI) and compares this amount to an individual's earnings.

29. The Ticket to Work/Work Incentives Improvement Act of 1999 expanded the eligible pool of vocational rehabilitation providers available to disabled SSI recipients by allowing beneficiaries to receive vocational rehabilitation services from not-for-profit and for-profit vendors. The first tickets from this program were issued in 2002.

30. For a detailed description of state supplementation see Ponce (1996).

31. Mandatory state supplements applied to individuals receiving benefits in December 1973.

Table 2.3   SSI State Supplementation and Coordination with Other Programs

United States and District of Columbia	Administration of Optional State Program[a]			Method of Mandatory Passalong		Medical Eligibility Determination			Interim Assistance Reimbursement Agreement with SSA
	State	Federal (SSA)	Federal and State	Payment Levels	Total Expenditures	Federal Criteria	State Criteria	SSA	
Alabama[b]	*			*		*			
Alaska	*			*		*		*	*
Arizona	*			*		*			*
Arkansas[c]		*		*		*		*	*
California	*			*		*		*	*
Colorado	*				*	*		*	*
Connecticut[b]	*			*			*		*
Delaware		*			*	*			*
DC		*		*		*			*
Florida[b]	*			*		*		*	*
Georgia[c]		*		*		*		*	*
Hawaii		*		*		*		*	*
Idaho	*			*			*		*
Illinois	*			*		*			*
Indiana	*			*			*		*
Iowa			*		*	*		*	*
Kansas[c]		*		*		*			*
Kentucky[b]	*			*		*		*	*
Louisiana[d]	*			*		*		*	*
Maine	*			*	*	*		*	*
Maryland[d]		*		*		*			
Massachusetts			*	*		*		*	*
Michigan	*			*		*		*	*[e] *
Minnesota[b]		*		*		*		*	*
Mississippi[c]				*		*		*	
Missouri	*			*	*	*			*
Montana	*			*			*	*	*
Nebraska		*		*		*		*	*
Nevada[b]		*		*			*		*
New Hampshire	*			*		*			*[e] *
New Jersey		*		*		*		*	*

(*continued*)

Table 2.3   (continued)

United States and District of Columbia	Administration of Optional State Program[a]			Method of Mandatory Passalong		Medical Eligibility Determination			Interim Assistance Reimbursement Agreement with SSA
	State	Federal (SSA)	Federal and State	Payment Levels	Total Expenditures	Federal Criteria	State Criteria	SSA	
New Mexico	*			*		*		*	*[e]
New York		*	*	*		*		*	*
North Carolina	*			*		*		*	*
North Dakota[b]	*			*			*		
Ohio[d]	*				*		*		
Oklahoma	*				*	*			
Oregon	*					*	*		*
Pennsylvania		*		*		*		*	*
Rhode Island[b]		*		*		*		*	*[e]
South Carolina[b]	*			*		*		*	
South Dakota[d]	*			*		*		*	
Tennessee[c]	*			*		*		*	*
Texas[f]				*		*		*	
Utah[b]		*		*		*		*	*
Vermont[b]			*			*			*
Virginia	*				*		*		*
Washington			*		*	*		*	*
West Virginia[f]					*	*		*	*
Wisconsin	*			*		*		*	*
Wyoming	*			*		*		*	
Total states	29	11	5	40	10	40	11	33	38

Source: SSI Annual Statistical Report (SSA 2002b).

[a] See body of text for description of the various forms of state supplementation.

[b] State no longer has any recipients receiving mandatory minimum state supplementation.

[c] Mandatory minimum state supplementation program is federally administered. No optional program.

[d] Mandatory minimum state supplementation program is federally administered.

[e] State provides assistance only in initial application cases. No assistance provided during periods that SSI benefits are suspended or terminated.

[f] State does not have a mandatory minimum state supplementation program.

and use state-specific eligibility criteria. Despite the apparent cost advantage to federal administration, states have increasingly opted for state administration of supplemental payments. About three-quarters of states providing optional supplementation administer their own programs or jointly administer them with the federal government. Only eleven states rely solely on federal administration.

Although a majority of states have optional supplementation programs, a number of factors minimize the importance of these programs. First, only twenty-three states provide supplements to the vast majority of SSI recipients living independently in their own households.[32] In the remaining states with optional programs, supplements are paid only to the minority of SSI recipients living in institutions.[33] Second, because state supplements are not annually adjusted for inflation, the real value of the median state supplemental payment to individuals living independently declined by about 60 percent between 1975 and 1997.[34]

That being said, public concern over states' reducing their SSI supplemental payments when federal benefit levels rise led Congress to mandate that states pass along SSI benefit increases resulting from annual cost-of-living adjustments. States may meet this passalong requirement by maintaining payment levels year to year (the payment levels method) or they may spend the same amount of money in the aggregate that they spent the year before the federal benefit rose (the total expenditure method). In 2002, forty states used the payment levels method and ten states used the expenditures method (columns [4–5], table 2.3).

Coordination with Other Programs

In addition to SSI federal and state cash payments, SSI beneficiaries frequently gain automatic eligibility to Medicaid and Food Stamp programs. Generally, SSI recipients are categorically eligible for Medicaid. A state may either use SSI eligibility criteria for determining Medicaid eligibility, or it may use its own criteria as long as the criteria are no more restrictive than the state's January 1972 medical assistance standards.[35] Forty states use SSI criteria and eleven states use eligibility criteria more restrictive than those of the SSI program (see columns [6–7], table 2.3). States may also enter into agreements with SSA to make Medicaid eligibility determinations for them, based on the federal SSI criteria; thirty-three states have such contracts with SSA (column [8], table 2.3).

---

32. Over 90 percent of SSI recipients live in their own households (U.S. House of Representatives, Committee on Ways and Means 1998).

33. One explanation for the ongoing supplementation of SSI recipients living in institutions is that supplementary SSI payments provide states with a mechanism of supporting such facilities.

34. Over time some states have even reduced the nominal value of supplemental payments.

35. This final option is known as the 209(b) option.

With the exception of California, SSI recipients in all states may be eligible for food stamps.[36] The SSA offices notify applicants and recipients of SSI of their potential eligibility for food stamps. Eligibility for the Food Stamp Program is determined by the food stamp office.

Finally, thirty-eight states (column [9], table 2.3) have agreements with SSA to be reimbursed for basic needs assistance provided during the period during which an eligible individual's SSI application for benefits was pending, or an individual's SSI benefits were suspended and subsequently reinstated.

2.2.4   Administration and Financing

As a federal income maintenance program, SSI is funded from general revenues and is administered by the SSA. Although, as discussed earlier, many states supplement federal benefit levels, over time the share of supplemental benefits paid by states has declined. In 1975, state SSI expenditures accounted for approximately 27 percent of total SSI payments. In 2001, state supplemental payments amounted to about 11 percent of annual SSI expenditures (SSA 2002a).[37]

2.2.5   Summary

Although the goals of the SSI disability program have not changed since its inception in 1974, its structure has been subject to numerous legislative, administrative, and court actions. These actions have primarily focused on making the disability criteria more target effective and on enhancing incentives aimed at returning recipients to the workforce. For the child disability component of the program, changes have focused on providing an appropriate vocational criterion for children that does not unduly discourage rehabilitation and school success. Notably, there have been few changes to the means test criteria and no adjustment for inflation in these criteria, meaning that over time, the amount of income that will disqualify one for SSI has fallen in real terms, or, simply put, the means test has become more restrictive. Finally, other legislative efforts have centered on limiting the eligibility of noncitizens. The legislative history of SSI shows that the primary mechanisms used by policymakers to alter the coverage and the generosity of SSI have been changes in the categorical eligibility criteria, rather than changes in the size of SSI benefits.

36. California cashes out food stamps, and SSI recipients in California receive a cash payment in their state supplementary payment in lieu of food stamps.

37. The numbers reported reflect the average for all states. Looking across states, in January 1999, the federal share of the maximum SSI benefit ranged from 58 percent in Alaska and 74 percent in California to 100 percent in the eight jurisdictions without a supplemental program (CRS 1999).

2.3   Program Statistics

2.3.1   Trends in Expenditures, Caseloads, and Benefits

The SSI program has grown substantially in both recipients and expenditures since it first paid benefits in 1974. However, its growth has varied over time (figure 2.3). Between 1974 and 1982, caseloads fell by 4.5 percent and real federal expenditures declined by about 15 percent. This decline caused concern among policymakers that too few potentially eligible recipients were enrolling (Menefee, Edwards, and Schieber 1981). After this slow start, the number of SSI beneficiaries increased steadily until 1996, growing from roughly 3.9 million in 1982 to 6.6 million in 1996, a 70 percent increase. Federal payments for the program rose even faster during this period, with the greatest growth between 1989 and 1992. Valued in 2001 dollars, total annual payments increased from $17.6 billion in 1982 to $32.5 billion in 1996, an increase of about 85 percent. Between 1996 and 2001 (the last year of data available) caseloads and expenditures have risen by less than 2 percent. Despite rapid growth in the SSI program over time, as a percentage of total federal outlays SSI expenditures have remained relatively stable at 1.9 percent since the program began in 1974.

2.3.2   Trends in Characteristics of Recipients

Originally considered a program for the elderly, SSI is now dominated by adults and children with disabilities. Figure 2.4 shows the age composition of SSI beneficiaries between 1974 and 2001. In 1974, the majority of the SSI caseload was over the age of sixty-five. The number of aged beneficiaries peaked at 2.5 million in 1975, gradually dropped to around 2 million in 1982, and remains at about that level. In contrast, the number of blind and disabled adults (aged eighteen to sixty-four) on SSI has more than doubled since 1974, with the most rapid growth occurring after 1982.[38] In December 2001, 3.8 million adults aged eighteen to sixty-four received SSI benefits, about 2.1 million more than in 1982. The number of blind and disabled recipients who are under age eighteen has also grown substantially in recent years.[39] Between 1974 and 1989 the child caseload increased to about 185,000. However, following the Zebley decision in 1990, the number of blind and disabled children rose rapidly, reaching 955,000 by 1996.[40] Since then, child SSI rolls have declined slightly, falling to 881,000 in 2001.

38. This growth is almost entirely due to increases in the number of disabled beneficiaries. The number of working-age SSI recipients eligible due to blindness has remained relatively constant over time (SSA *Annual Statistical Supplement,* various years).

39. Again, the growth is almost entirely explained by increases in the number of disabled children.

40. As noted earlier, this increase was due both to the reassessment of previously denied cases and to the increase in applications due to the more lenient eligibility rules.

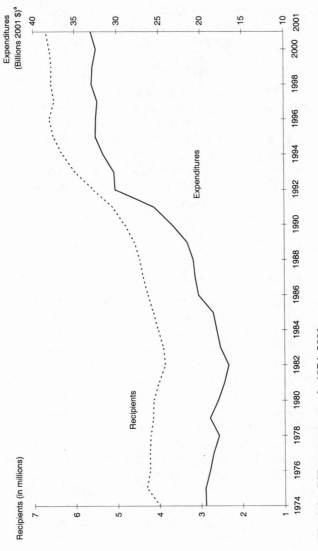

Fig. 2.3 SSI program growth, 1974–2001

Source: SSA (2000, 2002b).

[a]Annual expenditures estimated from monthly amount from December of each year.

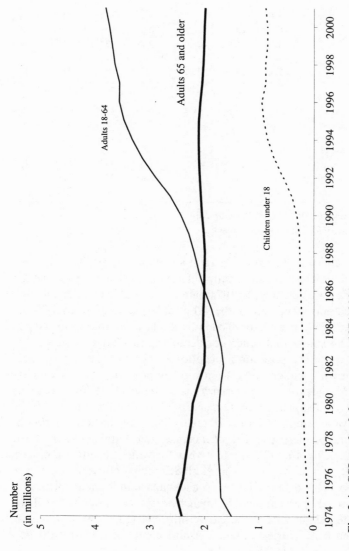

Fig. 2.4 SSI caseloads by age group, 1974–2001
Source: SSA (various years).

Table 2.4   Trends in Key Characteristics of SSI Beneficiaries, 1975–2001

	1975	1984	1987	1990	1992	1994	1996	2001
All SSI Recipients								
Age								
Less than 18	2.5	5.3	5.7	6.4	10.0	13.4	14.4	13.2
18 to 64	39.4	44.2	48.3	50.9	52.3	53.0	54.0	57.0
65 and above	58.1	50.6	46.0	42.7	37.7	33.7	31.6	29.8
Gender								
Male	35.5	34.8	36.1	37.2	39.0	41.1	41.5	41.7
Female	64.2	65.1	63.9	62.8	61.0	58.9	58.5	58.2
Citizenship								
Noncitizens	n.a.	4.5	6.4	9.0	10.8	11.7	11.0	10.4
Disabled SSI Recipients *(under age 65)*								
Qualifying Diagnosis								
Physical	n.a.	n.a.	49.0	47.0	44.7	42.2	41.3	39.0
Mental Retardation	n.a.	n.a.	26.9	26.6	27.1	27.6	27.5	25.0
Psychiatric Disorder	n.a.	n.a.	24.1	26.4	28.2	30.2	31.2	36.0

Source: SSI Annual Statistical Report (SSA 2002b).
Note: n.a. indicates information is not available.

As a result of rapid growth in adult and child disabled beneficiaries, the SSI population looks dramatically different today from the way it did when the program was created. In 1974, blind and disabled adults and children comprised only 40 percent of the SSI population. In 2001, over 70 percent of SSI beneficiaries were disabled individuals under the age of sixty-five.

Table 2.4 shows that other key demographic characteristics have also changed since the program's inception.[41] The first section of the table shows the age, gender, and citizenship composition of all SSI recipients. Since 1975, the proportion of males has increased. In 1976, more than two-thirds of SSI recipients were female. In 2001, about 60 percent of SSI recipients were female. Another notable change in the composition of the SSI population has been the rapid increase in the number of noncitizens receiving benefits. In 1982, the first year for which records on citizenship were kept, a little over 3 percent of all SSI recipients were noncitizens. In 1994, two years before citizenship became a requirement for new applicants, about 12 percent of all SSI beneficiaries were noncitizens. This percentage fell slightly once the citizenship restrictions were imposed, but noncitizen beneficiaries remain a sizable component of the SSI population—10.4 percent in 2001.

41. Notably, race is not included in the table. Information on the racial composition of SSI beneficiaries in the 1998 *Green Book* showed an increase in the number of Latinos enrolled in the program over time. These data also showed that African Americans are disproportionately represented among child and adult disabled beneficiaries. Unfortunately, there are no comparable data on race after 1995.

The second section of table 2.4 shows trends in the three main qualifying diagnostic categories—physical impairments, mental retardation, and psychiatric disorders other than mental retardation—for SSI recipients with disabilities (adults and children). In the early years of the program, less than one-quarter of SSI beneficiaries qualified on the basis of psychiatric disorders other than mental retardation. Following expansions in the eligibility criteria for mental impairments in both adults and children, the number of adults and children qualifying for SSI on the basis of a mental impairment began to grow. As a result, in 2001, 36 percent of all SSI recipients qualified on the basis of mental impairments other than mental retardation.

2.3.3 SSI Participation

An important policy concern with respect to all public assistance programs is the degree of participation among eligible individuals—that is, of the people who meet the categorical, economic resource, and citizenship tests, what proportion is receiving SSI benefits. It is relatively straightforward to make such calculations for those aged sixty-five and older, and a literature exists on this question. Unfortunately, the difficulties of establishing and assessing disability for adults and children not only make it difficult for policymakers and administrators to accurately determine SSI eligibility for those who apply, but also make it difficult for researchers to calculate program participation rates that require some estimate of the eligible disabled population that does not apply for benefits. Existing nationally representative data sources lack sufficient information on either economic characteristics or health characteristics to generate precise estimates of the population eligible for the disability components of SSI. As a result, there is almost no research on SSI participation rates among the eligible population with disabilities.[42]

In table 2.5 we provide a preliminary approximation of take-up rates for SSI that we believe is useful in establishing broad trends. We use the official U.S. Bureau of the Census poverty calculations and show the share of SSI recipients in age-based poverty populations. This method was used in the 1998 *Green Book* for the population aged sixty-five and older. On the one hand, because our estimates do not account for citizenship, assets, and especially disability status, they will understate program participation among those in the poverty population who are eligible. On the other hand, since those eligible for SSI may have household incomes above the official poverty line, our approximations may overstate program participation

---

42. It is possible to estimate the population with some level of disability using national data sources (see Bound and Burkhauser 1999 for examples). It is much more difficult to isolate the subpopulation within this broader category that would meet the medical listing or vocational criteria for SSI eligibility.

Table 2.5   **SSI Participation Rates among Poor, 1974–98, by Age Group**

	Take-Up Rates			Disability Prevalence
	65+	18–64	< 18	18–64
1974	78.5	14.8	0.7	—
1975	75.6	14.8	1.0	—
1976	72.3	15.0	1.2	—
1977	74.1	15.3	1.4	—
1978	71.3	15.4	1.7	—
1979	61.0	14.4	1.7	—
1980	57.4	12.5	1.6	20.3
1981	55.1	11.0	1.6	19.2
1982	53.6	9.7	1.4	17.4
1983	55.3	9.6	1.4	17.5
1984	61.2	10.5	1.6	19.3
1985	58.8	11.3	1.7	19.0
1986	58.0	12.6	1.9	19.2
1987	56.6	13.4	2.0	18.8
1988	57.6	13.9	2.0	18.7
1989	60.3	14.8	2.1	19.6
1990	56.3	14.9	2.3	19.7
1991	55.0	15.0	2.8	18.9
1992	53.5	15.5	3.6	19.3
1993	56.3	15.9	4.6	20.4
1994	57.9	17.5	5.5	21.4
1995	63.7	18.9	6.3	19.9
1996	61.0	19.1	6.6	20.7
1997	60.8	19.7	6.2	21.3
1998	60.0	20.7	6.6	21.3

Source: Authors' calculations using data from the Current Population Survey.

Notes: Dashes indicate data not available. Take-up rates are calculated as the number of SSI recipients divided by the number in poverty in each age group. Data for take-up rates are from the SSA and the Census Bureau. Disability prevalence is calculated as the percentage of the poverty population eighteen to sixty-four years of age answering "yes" to the Current Population Survey question: "(Do you/Does anyone in this household) have a health problem or disability which prevents (you/them) from working or which limits the kind or amount of work (you/they) can do?" This question was not asked of children.

among all eligible households. Nonetheless, the trends in table 2.5 are revealing of how SSI is being used by low-income persons.

As the first column of table 2.5 shows, the participation rate among the poor elderly declined from 78.5 percent in 1974 to 53.6 percent in 1982. Since then, participation rates have fluctuated from year to year but have remained well below the highs recorded in the early years of the program. In general, no more than two-thirds of elderly individuals living in poverty receive SSI benefits. More complete measures of participation suggest that take-up rates among the elderly are lower than the gross measures indicate.

Table 2.6   **Prevalence of Multiple Program Participation by SSI Recipients, 1999, by Gender and Age Group (%)**

Simultaneous Program Participant[a,b]	Male			Female			
	0–17	18–64	65+	0–17	18–64	65+	All
SSI recipients							
OASDI	7.3	31.8	55.9	7.2	29.1	60.4	37.6
Medicaid	79.6	89.9	91.9	78.4	90.8	92.3	89.4
Medicare	c	32.2	77.7	c	27.8	88.0	41.4
General assistance	c	0.5	0.8	c	2.3	0.4	1.0
WIC	c	c	c	c	4.4	c	1.4
School meals	78.6	0.8	c	75.9	0.5	c	10.8
TANF	c	1.9	0.5	1.2	11.8	1.0	4.5
Unemployment insurance	c	c	c	c	c	c	c
SSI households							
Energy assistance	11.7	10.9	9.4	7.3	13.6	10.3	11.4
Housing assistance	9.8	6.6	6.6	11.9	12.4	8.6	9.4
Food stamps	37.0	39.3	31.2	36.2	50.9	42.5	42.6

Source: SSA, *SSI Annual Statistical Report* (2002b).

[a]Based on data from the Survey of Income and Program Participation.

[b]Based on SSA administrative records.

[c]Less than 0.5 percent of SSI recipients in the gender/age group participate in the program.

Researchers consistently find the participation rate among persons eligible for SSI aged benefits at between 45 and 60 percent (Menefee, Edwards, and Schieber 1981; Warlick 1982; Coe 1985; Shields et al. 1990; McGarry 1996).

The remaining columns in table 2.5 show SSI participation rates for poor adults aged eighteen to sixty-four and poor children. Consistent with the caseload growth highlighted in figure 2.4, participation rates among poor working-age adults and children have risen over time. Participation rates among poor adults rose from 14.8 percent in 1974 to 20.7 percent in 1998, with the most rapid increases occurring during the 1990s. Recipiency rates for poor children also increased rapidly during the 1990s, rising from 2.1 percent in 1989 to 6.6 percent in 1998. As column (4) shows, the prevalence of disability has not risen since 1980, which suggests that the increase in SSI take-up rates among the poor is not a function of increased disability.

2.3.4   Multiple Program Participation among SSI Beneficiaries

A large fraction of SSI beneficiaries participate in other government programs. Table 2.6 shows simultaneous program participation for SSI recipients and their households by gender and age in 1999.[43] In 1999, 36.1

---

43. Unless otherwise noted, the percentages reported in table 2.6 are based on estimates from the Survey of Income and Program Participation and taken from the *SSI Annual Statistical Report* (SSA 2002b).

percent of all SSI recipients also received OASDI, either for retirement or disability. Receipt of OASDI was most common among men and women aged sixty-five and older. Medicaid receipt was nearly universal, with 89.4 percent of all SSI recipients on the program. A substantial fraction of SSI recipients also received Medicare benefits—41.4 percent in 1999. Looking at other means-tested programs, 42.6 percent of households with an SSI recipient also received food stamps, and about one in ten received energy or housing assistance.

Separate data from the 1998 *Green Book* produced by the U.S. House of Representatives (not shown) indicate that over time the percentage of SSI recipients receiving OASDI and Medicare has been declining. At the same time the percentage of SSI recipients receiving food stamps, assistance from the special Supplemental Nutrition Program for Women, Infants, and Children (WIC), free or subsidized meals, and public housing has been rising. The fact that a growing share of SSI recipients receive benefits from multiple means-tested programs suggests that the work incentives faced by the typical beneficiary are increasingly complex. SSI beneficiaries face multiple implicit taxes in the form of reduced benefits from SSI and any other transfer programs, plus the regular assortment of federal, state, and local taxes, as well as the loss of medical insurance for those not meeting the 1619(b) provisions. As others have shown, the cumulative marginal tax rates for individuals receiving multiple programs can be quite high (Giannarelli and Steuerle 1995; Keane and Moffitt 1998).

Although the empirical literature on the effects of changes in these various marginal tax rates will be discussed later in this chapter, it is useful to lay out the tax circumstances SSI recipients potentially face. Figure 2.5 (from Burkhauser and Wittenburg 1996) shows how a single male's 1994 net income changes with each additional dollar of his labor if he is eligible to receive the federal SSI benefit of $458 and the average cash value of Medicaid insurance for SSI disability of $540 per month. With no labor earnings, this person would receive $998 per month in SSI benefits and Medicaid insurance.

As the figure shows, the interaction of the Earned Income Tax Credit (EITC) and federal taxes as well as food stamps, which one-half of all SSI beneficiaries receive, significantly alters the marginal tax rates faced by recipients with various amounts of labor earnings. The EITC phase-in subsidy to work offsets Social Security (FICA) taxes, but because the Food Stamp Program subtracts 24 cents in food stamps for every dollar of labor earnings, the net tax on the first dollar of labor earnings is 23.85 percent. This tax rate continues to the SSI disregard level of $85 per month. At this point the 50-cent loss in SSI benefits per dollar of labor earnings interacts with the food stamp program taxes on work, resulting in a net tax of 58.85 percent. When the EITC plateau begins, the net tax on labor earnings rises to 66.5 percent, and when the EITC phaseout tax begins, the net tax on la-

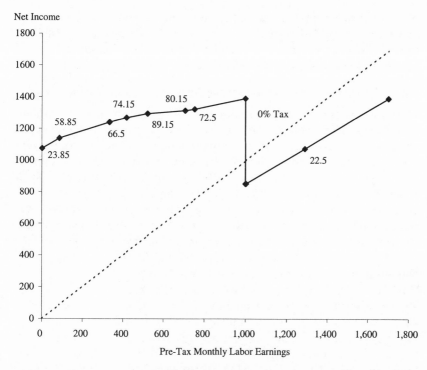

Net Income

Fig. 2.5   Marginal tax rates on labor earnings and net income for a single person receiving Medicaid, SSI, and food stamps in 1994
Source: Burkhauser and Wittenburg (1996).

bor earnings rises to 74.15 percent. When the federal income tax standard deduction level is passed and federal income tax starts, the marginal tax rate rises to 89.15 percent. Marginal tax rates only begin to fall after food stamps and EITC break-even points are reached. The final increase in tax rates occurs just before SSI benefits phase out, when all Medicaid benefits are lost because earned income now equals the Medicaid special eligibility plateau. The reduction of such cumulatively high marginal tax rates via a single universal income support program was one of the arguments made in support of President Nixon's original FAP program.

2.4   Review of Economic Issues

Although economic analysis of social programs frequently takes the goals of the program as given, with SSI the motivation for the program is itself an important determinant of how we view the behavioral reactions to it. In this section we first discuss the economic rationale behind a federal income floor for the subset of the poor who are aged, blind, or disabled.

Next, we review the theory related to individual responses to the existence and structure of SSI including take-up, work, savings, and disability-reporting behavior. Finally, we consider the equity goals of SSI and discuss attempts to evaluate program effectiveness.

2.4.1 Public Income Provision for the Aged, Blind, and Disabled

As noted earlier, SSI was born out of a failed effort to provide a guaranteed income floor under all Americans—FAP. Hence, although the motivation for providing an income floor to the subset of the adult poor who are aged, blind, or disabled is primarily distributional, it also rests on a political compromise that offered this entitlement only to categories of individuals not expected to work. Although this compromise allowed SSI to become law in 1972, social expectations regarding work have changed over time for the three groups targeted by SSI—the aged, blind, and disabled. Individuals are living and working longer; the normal retirement age for Social Security benefits has been raised; and the ADA has granted people with disabilities a legal right to equal access to employment.

Although work expectations have risen for the aged, it is people with disabilities who have experienced the largest shift in public attitudes. In 1990, people with disabilities successfully argued that unequal access to jobs—rather than an impairment—is the primary barrier to employment opportunities. As a result, people with disabilities gained legal rights to accommodation under Title I of the ADA. Some disability advocates even have argued that there is no such thing as a disabled worker; rather, there is only a society that does not provide the appropriate accommodations for such individuals.[44] In a world of full accommodation, the disability-transfer population should be zero. Such attitudinal changes raise basic questions about how society should treat people with disabilities. Most fundamental of these questions is whether people with disabilities should categorically be expected to work or not.

These types of cultural changes potentially shift the boundaries of the population that is not expected to work and hence is eligible for a categorical guaranteed income floor based on age or disability. As the opportunities for employment and the demand for the productivity of people with disabilities and those over age sixty-five increase, the clear categorical lines drawn between them and other groups with similar difficulties finding work, such as low-skilled or less-educated younger persons, or single mothers facing welfare limits, are increasingly blurred.

The original political compromise that made the families of disabled children eligible for SSI was slightly different and represented a departure from the not-expected-to-work criterion applied to the aged and to adults

---

44. See Johnson (1997) for alternative views of the rights and responsibilities of people with disabilities.

with disabilities. Some argued that SSI benefits for disabled children replaced the earnings of parents forced to reduce their work effort in order to care for their newly disabled child. Others argued that SSI-children benefits indirectly offset extra disability-related household expenses. In both cases, SSI-children benefits were intended to offset lost income and partially return the family to its previous level of economic well-being. (See NASI 1995 for a fuller discussion of these issues.)

2.4.2 SSI and Behavioral Change

If the aged and disabled adults are neither able nor expected to work, then many of the disincentives discussed in regard to other means-tested transfer programs are irrelevant. In such a world, cumulative marginal tax rates could approach 100 percent with no change in work behavior, and SSI could provide relatively high income guarantees and still maintain relatively low break-even points (the income level at which a person is no longer eligible for benefits). Moreover, to the degree that age and work disability are clearly defined and immutable categories, differences in the guarantees, time limits, or funding mechanisms for SSI and other programs would have little effect on SSI allowances and caseloads. In such a world SSI program participation is purely a function of the prevalence of health limitations in the low-income population. We will suggest that none of these premises hold with respect to the disability component of SSI. Thus, SSI policymakers must take behavioral changes on the part of potential SSI recipients and state and local governments into account when establishing program eligibility criteria and considering future program rules.

Propensity to Apply for SSI

Disability is neither a static nor a precise concept. Responses to the onset of health conditions depend not only on the severity of the impairment, but also on the social environment that people with health impairments face—including the availability of employment; the availability of accommodation, rehabilitation, and retraining; the presence of legal supports or protections; and the accessibility and generosity of SSI and other government transfer programs. The propensity for individuals to apply for SSI benefits depends on the probability they place on their health impairment and vocational circumstances being sufficient to meet the SSI disability eligibility standards as well as on their employment potential and the generosity of SSI relative to other forms of public assistance. The latter comparison is particularly relevant in light of 1996 welfare reform (PRWORA) that restricts the access to, and generosity of, alternative public assistance programs. If low-income adults have health conditions or have children with health conditions, the generosity of SSI relative to other alternatives may induce individuals to apply for benefits.

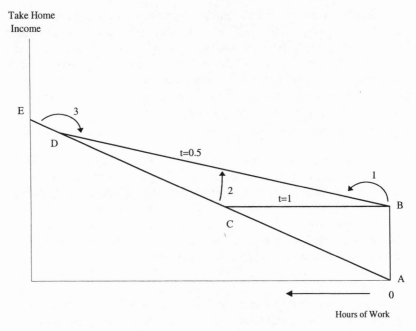

Fig. 2.6   Budget constraints with different marginal tax rates (BC: marginal tax rate = 100 percent; BD: marginal tax rate = 50 percent)
Source: Hoynes and Moffitt (1996).

Program Participation and Work Incentives

The economics of program participation and labor supply for individuals potentially eligible for SSI mirrors the analyses of these issues in programs such as Aid to Families with Dependent Children (AFDC) and Temporary Assistance for Needy Families (TANF). Thus, to understand the work disincentives embodied in the SSI program, we turn to the framework used for other categorical welfare programs. Moffitt (1986) provides a discussion of the basic economic issues. In these models individuals make choices that depend on the income gained from the program and the costs of participating, including the time and money costs associated with applying for and maintaining eligibility for benefits.

To see how this works in the case of SSI, consider the conventional labor-leisure model diagramed in figure 2.6.[45] Figure 2.6 compares the budget constraint of an SSI program with a 50 percent marginal tax rate ($t = 0.5$) to one with a marginal tax rate of 100 percent ($t = 1.0$). Segment

---

45. This discussion draws from the expositions in Moffitt (1986), Hoynes and Moffitt (1996), and Moffitt's review of the AFDC/TANF program (chap. 5) in this volume. This discussion is made primarily in the context of adults with disabilities.

ACDE of the figure represents the budget constraint of those not categorically eligible for SSI. The line has a slope equal to the hourly wage rate, w.
Segment ABCDE applies to the same individuals if they are categorically
eligible and if they face a marginal tax rate of 100 percent. Benefits are
taxed one dollar for each dollar earned and phased out at the break-even
level (point C). That is, even though they are categorically eligible for benefits, their labor earnings offset all SSI benefits at hour levels greater than
point C. Segment ABDE applies to the same people, but now they face a
marginal tax rate of 50 percent. Benefits are taxed at a rate of 50 cents per
dollar earned, and the break-even hours point is D. Under this model, categorical eligibility for SSI benefits unambiguously reduces work effort relative to not being categorically eligible. There is an income effect associated with the guarantee (AB) and a substitution effect associated with the
marginal tax rate (BC or BD). The income and substitution effects work in
the same direction, and hours of work among participants fall. Only those
whose optimal hours worked prior to program eligibility were beyond the
break-even hours point may not be affected, and even then it will depend
on the shape of their indifference curve (i.e., some would be willing to accept less income by substantially reducing work and living on program
benefits).

The next question to ask is what happens if the marginal tax rate is reduced. Here the answer is unclear; the net effect of a reduction in t, from
100 percent (BC) to 50 percent (BD), is ambiguous. The arrows in figure
2.6 show the various responses that could occur following a reduction in
the marginal tax rate (represented by a shift from segment BC to BD). For
individuals initially receiving SSI benefits and not working (i.e., initially at
point B), a reduction in the tax rate may encourage participants to work
more, which is represented by arrow 1. At the same time, a reduction in t
expands the range of individuals eligible for benefits and brings some portion of those categorically eligible but not previously receiving SSI onto the
rolls. As these individuals move onto SSI their work effort is reduced, as
shown by arrow 2. Arrow 3 shows that some categorically eligible individuals who continue to earn too much under the lower tax rate may be motivated to reduce their hours of work enough to become eligible for benefits,
thereby combining work and SSI benefits. Finally, it is also possible that a
reduction in t will increase payments by enough to induce previously eligible persons on earnings grounds but not on categorical grounds (segment
AC) to risk entry onto the rolls.

Taking each of these possibilities into account, the net effect of a lower
marginal tax rate on work effort is ambiguous. The only thing that is clear
is that lower marginal tax rates increase caseloads. A lower tax rate makes
more categorically eligible individuals eligible for the program on income
grounds and, given positive takeup rates, unambiguously boosts the number of individuals on the rolls. Moreover, by lowering the costs associated

with staying on the rolls, lower marginal tax rates reduce exit rates from the program, thereby increasing caseloads. Finally, lower marginal tax rates may induce those on the margin of categorical eligibility on health grounds to apply for benefits, since the gains to program acceptance have increased.

Unlike SSI benefits for the elderly, where categorical age eligibility is easily demonstrated and benefit receipt is automatic if one meets the means test, categorical eligibility for SSI benefits is more difficult to demonstrate. Thus, eligibility for benefits is not certain, and models of SSI application must take this risk of nonacceptance into consideration. In general, those considering applying for SSI will value disability benefits with a probability of less than one. Holding the underlying health condition constant, the probability of acceptance onto the rolls will depend on the disability screening process. Conditional on the same impairment, tighter eligibility criteria are likely to increase the probability of denial and reduce the expected value of applying. In contrast, looser criteria increase the probability of acceptance and increase the expected value of applying.[46] In either case, individuals facing uncertainty surrounding acceptance, informational hurdles, or stigma associated with benefit receipt may be induced to participate by the increase in benefits associated with the lower marginal tax rate.

If those categorically eligible for benefits on health grounds are completely unable to perform any substantial gainful activity under any circumstances, then there is no need to lower the marginal tax rate on SSI, since those on the program are neither expected nor able to work. However, to the extent that work is both possible and expected for people with disabilities who meet the other eligibility criteria, policy discussions with respect to trade-offs between tax rates, guarantees, and break-even points become much closer to those taking place for other income maintenance programs.

The same model also incorporates stigma and other fixed program costs. As in other income maintenance programs, the presence of stigma and other program costs associated with applying for benefits explains why some categorically eligible individuals are observed on segment ACD. As fixed program costs and stigma decline, participation among this group will rise. What the model in figure 2.6 does not show are potential program interaction effects. As discussed in figure 2.5, the actual budget constraint facing those categorically eligible for SSI benefits is more complex, with more nonlinearities due to the cumulation of taxes from multiple programs. In a like manner, multiple program eligibility will cause complications for those interested in the behavioral effects of other transfer programs. Burkhauser and Smeeding (1981) and Powers and Neumark (2001) show that the incentives to accept actuarially reduced Social Security ben-

46. Weathers (1999) develops a multiperiod model of the SSDI application process in which the optimal time of application following the onset of a disability is a function of the opportunity cost of lost wages versus the gain in SSDI, adjusted for the probability of acceptance. A similar model could be used to predict the timing of SSI disability applications.

efits (OASI) at younger retirement ages are increased for those who would be eligible for both SSI and OASI at age sixty-five, since OASI benefits after a small disregard are taxed on a dollar-for-dollar basis by SSI.

Finally, one can also use the model in figure 2.6 to think about the labor-supply behavior of parents of children with disabilities. If a child is judged eligible for SSI benefits, then an able-bodied parent faces the same marginal tax rates, guarantees, and break-even points shown in figure 2.6. Stigma, information costs, and reduced program benefits (adjusted for the probability of acceptance) also apply. One additional issue that affects parents of children with disabilities is how benefit receipt will influence the future well-being of their child.

Saving Behavior

The presence of asset testing in the eligibility criteria for SSI may reduce saving among those meeting other eligibility criteria. This point is made generally about means-tested programs. Hubbard, Skinner, and Zeldes (1995) argue that when eligibility is tied to assets, individuals meeting the income test have incentives to reduce their savings in order to qualify for benefits. Among those applying for SSI benefits, the most likely group to be affected by the asset test is the elderly, who may have accumulated savings over their lifetime.

2.4.3 Balancing Efficiency and Equity Concerns

Our discussion above has focused on the behavioral effects of the SSI program. This focus on the efficiency costs of SSI-induced behavioral change ignores the social benefits of SSI and may lead some to conclude that a socially optimal SSI program would have no behavioral impact on benefit applications, work, or saving. This conclusion is inappropriate for two reasons. First, even if actual disability status were perfectly observable, society would probably still want to target some level of benefits on disadvantaged low-income workers and their families even if it resulted in some efficiency losses. Hence, the more important question is not whether there are program-related behavioral changes but whether they are small relative to the social gains from redistributing income to less advantaged persons. Analyses of the welfare implications of the SSI program should focus on this second and more important question.

Second, in a world where the socially appropriate eligibility standard for SSI is difficult to assess, some individuals will be denied benefits who are less capable of work than is socially acceptable. In such a world, a more lenient eligibility criterion will involve a trade-off between the reduction of type II errors on the one hand and the additional costs of type I errors on the other. The issue is this: In the presence of uncertainty, do the social benefits outweigh the efficiency costs arising from increasing the probability of guaranteeing an income floor to those below some minimum level of work capacity at the cost of also providing these funds to some who are more capable of work? In both cases, it is appropriate to assign some value to SSI as a mechanism for providing social protection against the economic consequences of aging and disability for disadvantaged workers. To do otherwise would be to hold too narrow a view from a social policy perspective. See Bound et al. 2002 for a fuller discussion of these issues.

2.5   Review of the Evidence

In the previous section we reviewed the potential consequences on application, work, and saving behavior of SSI program rules and showed that if the aged or disabled adults are capable of work, the SSI program rules could influence their behavior. We also discussed how SSI program rules could affect the work behavior of the parents of children with disabilities. In this section we review the empirical literature on the effects of the existence and structure of SSI on behavior. Despite the size and importance of the SSI program, the empirical literature on its behavioral effects is relatively small. Moreover, almost without exception, empirical studies focus on only one of the three groups SSI targets. For this reason, the empirical evidence on the behavioral effects of SSI for each target population group will be discussed in turn.

2.5.1   SSI and Adults with Disabilities

Work Effort of Adults with Disabilities[47]

Most of the research on the work effort of those with disabilities focuses on a broader population than those receiving either SSI or SSDI. The most common analyses rely on nationally representative survey data that include questions about whether a health limitation prevents individuals from working or limits their ability to work full time or to do certain jobs.[48] Although such research is not as targeted as one might like, it does provide a backdrop for understanding the types of trends faced by the SSI program.

Based on these data, figure 2.7 shows that over the past two decades employment rates for those with disabilities as well as SSDI and SSI caseloads have varied greatly, fluctuating with the economy, changes in benefit eligibility criteria, and the implementation of other public policies intended to support people with disabilities. The figure shows employment rates of working-age men and women with self-reported disabilities and the number of individuals receiving disability benefits for the period 1980–99. The employment data come from Burkhauser et al. (2002) and reflect the em-

47. This discussion draws from Burkhauser and Daly (2002).
48. Although numerous scholars have questioned the validity of such data, Burkhauser et al. (2002) show that questions of this type can be used to track trends in outcomes, such as employment, for the population with disabilities.

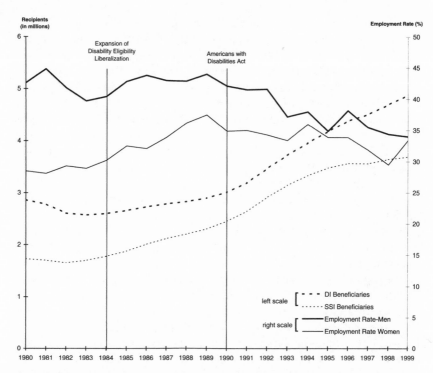

Fig. 2.7   Disability benefit rolls and employment rates among working-age men and women with disabilities

ployment rates of Current Population Survey (CPS) respondents who say they are limited in the amount or type of work they can perform. Data on SSDI and SSI beneficiaries come from the SSA (2002a). Also indicated in the figure are a few key events: the liberalization of disability screening in 1984 and the passage of the ADA in 1990.

The trends in figure 2.7 highlight the major concerns of disability policymakers over the past two decades. First, the number of disability beneficiaries has increased continuously since the eligibility expansion and liberalization in 1984, with especially strong growth during the 1990s (application and acceptance rates in the 1990s rivaled those experienced during the expansion period of the late 1970s). Second, whereas employment rates for those with self-reported work limitations rose through the economic expansion of the late 1980s, they have fallen almost continuously since, even during the strong expansion of the 1990s.

So far, three major hypotheses have been proposed to explain this decline. Kaye (forthcoming) argues that declining employment rates among those with disabilities in the 1990s were caused by dramatic increases in the severity of impairments. Hence, for Kaye, the recent trends are health-based and not a reflection of changes in public policy. Other researchers have taken a more social environment–oriented view. For example, DeLeire (2000) and Acemoglu and Angrist (2001) attribute the downturn in employment among those with disabilities during the 1990s to the passage of the ADA. Bound and Waidmann (2002) argue that changes in disability benefits eligibility and generosity made it easier and more profitable for workers to leave the labor force and take benefits. Autor and Duggan (2001) suggest that a combination of disability benefits that replaced a greater share of labor earnings and declining job opportunities for low-skilled workers induced an increasing share of workers to choose benefits over employment. Which one of the many changing social variables deserves the most credit is a matter for future research, but in all likelihood the true cause is a combination of factors, rather than a single policy action or identifiable event.

While researchers debate the reasons for the declining employment and rising benefit rates of men and women with disabilities during the 1990s, policymakers are debating whether these outcomes are signs of success or failure of U.S. disability policy. For some advocates of those with disabilities, the increasing disability benefit rolls reflect an appropriate increase in support for a group of workers with limited labor market opportunities. For others, the increased rolls reflect the shortcomings of a transfer-focused policy that failed to provide the necessary supports (e.g., universal health insurance, rehabilitation, and job services) to allow individuals to select work over benefits. For others still, the outcomes observed during the 1990s are simply evidence of the law of unintended consequences in policy making, whereby policies to promote economic well-being (in the case of benefits) and work (in the case of the ADA) actually increased the disability benefit rolls and reduced employment.

Whichever explanation accounts for the decline in employment among those with disabilities, research by Bound, Burkhauser, and Nichols (forthcoming) shows that one must be careful in making general statements about the population targeted by SSI based on aggregate data on the population with disabilities or data on the SSDI targeted population. Table 2.7, taken from Bound, Burkhauser, and Nichols, uses longitudinal data from the Survey of Income and Program Participation (SIPP) linked to Social Security administrative files to compare the monthly labor earnings and employment of those who apply for SSI or SSDI three years before application, one to three months before application, and three years after application. As table 2.7 shows, unlike SSDI applicants, the vast majority of SSI applicants are not employed three years before they apply for benefits. Only 25 (28) percent of those awarded (denied) SSI were working three years before their application, and their average monthly labor earnings were only $144 ($260). Moreover, both their employment and their average monthly labor earnings were a small fraction of the employment and labor earnings of SSDI applicants three years prior to application.

Table 2.7   Average Monthly Labor Earnings and Employment Rates and How They Changed before and after Application for SSDI and SSI (in January 1990 dollars)

| | Before Application[a] | | Application[b] | | | After Application[c] | | |
Population	Monthly Labor Earnings[d]	Employment Rate[e]	Monthly Labor Earnings[d]	Employment Rate[e]	% of Before Earnings[f]	Monthly Labor Earnings[d]	Employment Rate[e]	% of Before Earnings[f]
Supplemental Security Income								
Awarded SSI	144	25	17	6	12	63	12	44
Denied SSI	260	28	89	15	34	105	19	40
Social Security Disability Insurance								
Awarded SSDI	1,575	87	248	16	16	87	11	6
Denied SSDI	1,248	81	154	17	12	434	31	35

Source: Bound, Burkhauser, and Nichols (forthcoming): 1990–93 SIPP data merged to SSA disability determination records.

[a]Thirty-six to thirty-eight months prior to application.

[b]One to three months after application.

[c]Thirty-seven to thirty-nine months after application.

[d] Average includes zeros.

[e]Positive labor earnings in at least one month over the period.

[f]Average monthly labor earnings during application period divided by average monthly labor earnings before application.

[g]Average monthly labor earnings after application divided by average monthly labor earnings before application.

The data in table 2.7 suggest that the factors causing the low employment and labor earnings of SSI applicants at the time of application and after they move onto the SSI rolls were in effect well before the time of their application. This is not surprising, since Bound, Burkhauser, and Nichols also show that the typical SSI applicant is less likely than the typical SSDI applicant to be white, a high school graduate, married, wealthy, or living in a high-income household prior to application.

Factors Affecting SSI Participation

Although application for SSI disability benefits is a function of health, it is also influenced by program rules and benefits. These include eligibility criteria and the generosity of benefits relative to work, the comparative generosity and availability of other means-tested welfare and social insurance programs, macroeconomic conditions (national, state, and local), and applicants' education and job skills. During the 1990s, considerable attention was devoted to understanding the link between these nonhealth factors and SSI caseload growth. The following discussion reviews the evidence on determinants of SSI caseload growth, looking first at the relationship between caseload dynamics and screening stringency (benefit supply) and then at factors affecting the demand for SSI benefits, including ease of benefit access, benefit generosity relative to work and other programs, and economic conditions.

The SSA began modifying its disability determination process in the mid-1970s. Concerned that state offices were not consistently and uniformly applying the residual functional capacity (RFC) and vocational standards in adult disability determinations, in 1979 SSA published regulations specifying who was to be classified as disabled, essentially tightening the eligibility criteria. The SSA also tightened its policy towards benefit terminations in continuing disability reviews (CDRs) by state Disability Determination Services (DDS), permitting benefit termination without proof of medical improvement. This policy resulted in a threefold increase in the number of cessation decisions on continuing reviews by state agencies (Lewin-VHI 1999). Consistent with the tighter standards, the yearly allowance rate (initial acceptances divided by initial applications) of adult SSI disability applications began to fall in 1976 (table 2.8).

The Social Security Disability Amendments of 1980 continued the trend of tightening the disability determination and review process. Importantly, the 1980 law changed both the frequency and nature of medical eligibility reviews done on disability beneficiaries.[49] Before 1980, the only beneficiar-

---

49. The 1980 law tightened SSA control over the state disability determination services. In particular, the SSA had previously reserved the right to review initial determinations before they were transmitted to the applicant, but during the 1970s it reviewed only 5 percent. The 1980 amendments required that SSA review two-thirds of successful applications. To enforce administrative control over administrative law judges, the secretary of Health and Human

Table 2.8   **SSI Allowance Rates and Annual Changes in Beneficiaries, Adults 18–64, 1974–2001**

	Allowance Rate (%)	Number of Beneficiaries (thousands)	Yearly % Change in Beneficiaries
1974	47.8	1,503	
1975	52.6	1,699	13.0
1976	47.1	1,714	0.9
1977	42.2	1,737	1.3
1978	36.4	1,747	0.6
1979	31.5	1,727	−1.1
1980	29.5	1,731	0.2
1981	29.5	1,703	−1.6
1982	26.6	1,655	−2.8
1983	32.2	1,700	2.7
1984	38.2	1,780	4.7
1985	32.0	1,879	5.6
1986	36.8	2,010	6.7
1987	36.2	2,119	5.4
1988	37.1	2,203	4.0
1989	39.5	2,302	4.5
1990	40.5	2,450	6.4
1991	39.4	2,642	7.8
1992	44.5	2,910	10.1
1993	41.1	3,148	8.2
1994	39.4	3,335	5.9
1995	42.5	3,482	4.4
1996	41.6	3,569	2.5
1997	40.8	3,562	−0.2
1998	42.9	3,646	2.4
1999	43.0	3,690	1.2
2000	39.4	3,744	1.5
2001	38.0	3,811	1.8

Source: Authors' calculations from SSA data, *SSI Annual Statistical Report 2001* (2002b).
Note: Allowance rates equal initial awards divided by initial applications.

ies targeted for medical eligibility review were those who had conditions that were likely to improve over time. The new law stipulated that all beneficiaries should periodically receive continuing disability reviews and that all but those deemed to have permanent disabilities should be reviewed

---

Services was empowered to appeal administrative law judge rulings that were favorable to the applicant.

Prior to 1980, the law provided that disability determinations be performed by state agencies under an agreement negotiated by the states and the secretary of Health and Human Services. The 1980 amendments required that disability determinations be made by state agencies according to regulations of the secretary. It also required the secretary to issue regulations specifying performance standards to be followed in the disability determinations, and if the secretary found that a state agency was failing to make disability determinations consistent with regulations, then the secretary was required to terminate the state's authority and assume federal responsibility for the determinations.

every three years. The 1980 law made permanent the practice of using the same standards in CDRs that were applied when initially evaluating claimants. In addition to tightening the disability adjudication and review process, the 1980 law established two key work incentives: (a) the 1619(b) provision, and (b) the deduction of impairment-related work expenses (IR-WEs) from earnings when determining the SGA. As noted earlier, the 1619(b) provision authorized a three-year demonstration project, allowing for the payment of special SSI benefits (and the retention of Medicaid coverage) for SSI recipients who exceeded the SGA level. Section 1619 became permanent in 1986.

As could be expected, the 1980 law had a discernible impact on administrative practice. As demonstrated in table 2.8, the yearly allowance rate for adult SSI disability recipients fell from a high of 52.6 percent in 1975 to 26.6 percent in 1982. The number of recipients fell from 1.75 million in 1978 to 1.66 million in 1982. This decrease occurred despite the economic recession of 1980–82. This removal of individuals from the rolls generated a major political response. Most of the people removed from the rolls appealed the decision, requesting a hearing before an administrative law judge and causing a huge backlog of cases. As a result, some state governors instructed their DDS service not to terminate anyone from the disability rolls unless that person's conditions had improved.[50]

In 1984, in response to concerns that federal disability policy had become too restrictive, the SSA agreed to a moratorium on CDRs pending the enactment and implementation of revised guidelines. The 1984 law had profound effects on the standards used to evaluate a person's potential eligibility for SSI. When reviewing existing beneficiaries, the burden of proof was shifted back to the SSA to show that a beneficiary's health had improved sufficiently to allow him or her to return to work. A moratorium was imposed on re-evaluations of the most troublesome cases—those that involved mental impairments or pain—until more appropriate guidelines could be developed. Finally, benefits were continued pending the outcome of an appeal.

The 1984 law substantially increased the weight given to source evidence (i.e., evidence provided by the claimant's own physician) by requiring that it be considered first, prior to the results of an SSA consultative examination. The SSA was also required to consider the combined effect of all impairments, whether or not any one impairment was severe enough to qualify a person for benefits. Perhaps most important, the SSA substantially revised its treatment of mental illness, reducing the weight given to diagnostic or medical factors, and emphasizing the ability of an individual to function in work or worklike settings.

50. For a fuller discussion of disability policy in this period, see Berkowitz and Burkhauser (1996).

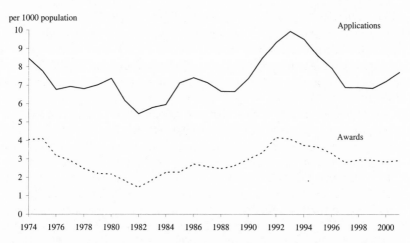

Fig. 2.8   Applications and awards among population 18–64 (per 1,000 in population)

Source: SSA (various years).

Table 2.8 shows that the dip in the SSI adult disability population that occurred between 1978 and 1982 was reversed thereafter and rose about 4 or 5 percent a year during the economic growth years of the later 1980s. When the next economic downturn came in the early 1990s, conditions were ripe for a surge in applications and in the number of people on the SSI disability rolls. The increases in the disability transfer population in the early 1990s exceeded anything seen in SSI since the start of the program. The annual acceptance rate for SSI adult disability benefits was almost 45 percent in 1992, the highest since 1976. Economic recovery and Congressional action with respect to SSI disability eligibility in 1996 have slowed the growth in the working-age adult SSI population, and acceptance rates in 2000 and 2001 were back to the levels of the late 1980s. However, the economic downturn could result in an increase in the rolls.[51]

The legislative history underlying the disability screening process highlights how access to benefits has changed over time. Figure 2.8 shows that the desire for SSI disability benefits has also fluctuated. Fluctuations in applications have been as large as changes in the SSI disability rolls. To some extent these fluctuations have mirrored changes in eligibility standards, contracting when eligibility standards were tightened in the late 1970s and

---

51. As part of more general welfare reforms in 1996, Congress removed drug and alcohol addiction as allowable conditions for SSI eligibility. In 1995, there were about 135,000 SSI recipients whose disability was based solely on drug addiction or alcoholism. The Congressional Budget Office estimated that about 65 percent of these individuals would be eligible for SSI based on other sufficiently disabling conditions. For a full discussion of these reforms and their impact see U.S. House of Representatives, Committee on Ways and Means (1998).

early 1980s, rising after the relaxation of eligibility standards in 1984, and falling again following the tightening of standards in the mid-1990s. However, other factors, including local economic conditions, outreach efforts by both SSA and state governments to search for eligible candidates, and the generosity of SSI relative to other programs, are all likely to have contributed to the variability in applications over time.

A number of scholars have estimated the link between local economic conditions and SSI application rates. The fact that SSI is a national program restricts the extent to which regional variation in benefits can be used to identify the effect of the program on applications. However, Black, Daniel, and Sanders (2002) used regional variation in economic conditions to identify the effect of financial incentives on the decision to apply for SSI (and SSDI) disability benefits. In particular, they examined the impacts of the coal boom during the 1970s and the coal bust during the 1980s on the number of SSI beneficiaries. Using panel data on 186 counties in Kentucky, Ohio, Pennsylvania, and West Virginia, they estimated an elasticity of program payments with respect to local area earnings of between –0.5 and –0.7 for SSI recipients. Although these results lend some support to the notion that labor market conditions in an area affect the decision of individuals to apply for disability benefits, the point estimates are hard to interpret. Black, Daniel, and Sanders interpret the estimated coefficient on the local earnings variable as reflecting the effect of changes in the financial attractiveness of disability benefits. However, given the nature of the specification used, it is possible that the earnings variable is picking up the effect of general economic conditions rather than the relative financial attractiveness of SSI.[52] Furthermore, their estimates reflect the short-run effect of changes in the local economies in Kentucky, Ohio, Pennsylvania, and West Virginia on the number of disability beneficiaries. Given the fact that the typical SSI spell is lengthy in duration, long-run effects likely will be substantially larger than short-run effects.

A considerable amount of government-sponsored research has attempted to explain the dramatic growth in the SSI population in the early 1990s. A useful summary of this work can be found in Rupp and Stapleton (1995). Much of this analysis has used the considerable variation in state-level applications and awards to test the models. Using cross-state data from 1988–92, Stapleton et al. (1998) find convincing evidence that the recession of the early 1990s contributed to the rapid rise in the number of applications for SSI benefits. They estimate that a 1 percentage point rise in the unemployment rate was associated with a 2 percent rise in applications for SSI. The effects on final awards were somewhat lower. Finally, they found that the changes in the unemployment rate had a smaller effect on

52. As will be discussed shortly, the evidence that recessions lead to increases in the number of applications for SSI is strong.

benefit awards than on applications, suggesting that recessions induce those with less severe disabilities to apply for SSDI and SSI benefits.

Stapleton et al. (1998) also provide strong, if indirect, evidence that changes in screening stringency in the 1990s played a central role in explaining program growth. Indeed, the very fact that award rates were rising at the same time that application rates were rising would seem to suggest an important role for changes in screening stringency. They find that changes in the unemployment rate, together with other factors they include in their models, could explain almost all of the growth in applications for impairments related to conditions of internal organs, but could account for much less of the growth in applications for impairments related to musculoskeletal or mental health conditions. These patterns suggest that regulatory changes such as the increased weight given to pain and other symptoms, the increased reliance on source evidence, and the broadening of the standards used for those with mental impairments have contributed importantly to the recent surge in applications for SSI.

Whereas the 1990s recession seems to be part of the explanation for the rapid rise in applications for SSI benefits that occurred during the first part of the 1990s, no such rise occurred during the severe recession of the early 1980s. A reasonable interpretation of these patterns is that the tightening of eligibility standards that occurred during the early 1980s counteracted the effects of the 1980s recession. During the mid-1980s, when eligibility standards were relaxed again, the booming economy slowed any immediate response. However, when the 1990s recession hit, applications grew rapidly.

Researchers studying the increases in SSI caseloads have found evidence that an important factor explaining the growth in SSI over the 1990s has been efforts by states to shift individuals off state-funded programs such as general assistance and onto SSI. States that cut general assistance benefits experienced above-average growth in the application for SSI benefits (Lewin-VHI 1995). Using monthly administrative data from Michigan, Bound, Kossoudji, and Ricart-Moes (1998) find that the increase in the application for SSI benefits exactly coincided with the end of general assistance in Michigan. However, they also find that general assistance benefits are typically less generous than are SSI benefits. This finding is surprising within the context of a simple labor supply model that ignores the relative costs of application for these two types of benefits. The fact that many potentially eligible people did not apply for the more generous SSI benefits suggests that applying for disability benefits may be difficult and onerous. There is also considerable anecdotal evidence that states and third parties often act as intermediaries to facilitate the SSI application process (Livermore, Stapleton, and Zeuschner 1998; Bound, Kossoudji, and Ricart-Moes 1998).

Brown, Hoyt, and Scott (1999) approach a similar question using county-level data on SSI and AFDC participation rates. They find that prior to 1996 welfare reform, variation in AFDC programs across states explains little of the variation in SSI participation. They also find that program and eligibility variables explain more of the county-to-county variation in SSI participation than in AFDC participation, suggesting that SSI is a more tightly targeted program than AFDC. Still, they conclude that given the significant changes in welfare programs embodied in the transition from AFDC to TANF, SSI participation rates likely will be affected.

Increases in the value of Medicaid benefits for individuals on SSI also may have contributed to the recent growth in applications for both programs. Yelowitz (1998) uses cross-state variation in Medicaid benefits to estimate the effect of changes in their value on participation in SSI. In particular, in response to court orders, many states increased Medicaid benefits in 1991. Using these changes, Yelowitz estimates that increases in the value of Medicaid that occurred over the late 1980s and early 1990s can explain about 20 percent of the increase in the working-age population receiving SSI benefits.

However suggestive Yelowitz's results are, they do not seem to be very robust. Stapleton and his colleagues (Lewin-VHI 1995) used Yelowitz's methodology to look at the effect of changes in the value of Medicaid on the application for SSI benefits and found no measurable effects. Given the expectation that increases in the value of Medicaid would initially have a proportionately bigger effect on the number of applications (a flow) than on the beneficiaries (a stock), this nonresult is surprising. Although it is hard to imagine that eligibility for Medicaid benefits does not make SSI more attractive, finding statistical evidence of this effect has proven to be quite challenging.

Effects of Work Incentives and Disincentives

Because the United States has few program alternatives that offer long-term benefits to working-age persons who are not working, the relatively generous benefits and imperfect screening mechanisms in SSI could pose significant work disincentives for persons with disabilities who are considering applying for benefits. Additionally, the high marginal tax rates for those on the program could discourage exit from it and entry into the labor force.

A large empirical literature has tried to estimate the magnitude of moral hazard effects. Some of that literature has examined the net effect of SSI (and SSDI) on labor force participation rates, such as how much higher participation rates would be were it not for these programs. However, this literature has primarily focused on estimating the disincentive effects of SSDI program parameters, benefit generosity, or screening stringency. For a complete review of this literature see Bound and Burkhauser (1999). Although it is tempting to look to the SSDI literature to gain some insights into how the SSI program affects the behavior of low-income adults with disabilities, doing so is problematic. First, whereas both programs use the same criteria of inability to perform substantial gainful activity with respect to establishing categorical eligibility, the benefit structures of the two programs are quite different.[53] Second and perhaps more important, as noted earlier, typical SSDI applicants have much different socioeconomic characteristics and work histories than typical SSI applicants.

As seen in table 2.7, most of the individuals who apply for SSI were not working three years prior to application. More importantly, the causes for their low employment rates at that time likely were more closely associated with the problems faced by low-skilled or poorly educated workers generally than with specific effects of poor health or of the work disincentives of SSI or SSDI. Furthermore, only 19 percent of those who were denied SSI benefits were employed three years after their application (table 2.7). In contrast, 35 percent of denied SSDI applicants were employed three years after application. These patterns suggest that changes in program work incentives and disincentives for those on the SSI rolls are less likely to induce them to leave the rolls and return to employment than would be the case for SSDI beneficiaries. This seems especially likely given that far fewer SSI beneficiaries than SSDI beneficiaries worked three years prior to application when they presumably did not have a work limitation severe enough to qualify for benefits.

Although it is not clear that SSDI research will shed much light on the work behavior of SSI recipients, there is a large literature on the work incentives and disincentives in other welfare programs. This empirical research consistently finds that recipients are unresponsive to changes in marginal tax rates (for reviews of this literature see Moffitt 1986 and Hoynes and Moffitt 1996). This literature provides little evidence that individuals participating in means-tested programs respond to financial incentives by working more. Research on the extent to which individuals with disabilities have the same income and substitution elasticities of participants in other programs would be an important step in determining whether the results discussed are applicable to the SSI population.

Finally, the small amount of research that does exist on the work efforts of SSI recipients suggests that, despite special allowances for SSI recipi-

---

53. For example, SSDI is an insurance-based (non-means-tested) program with its benefits based on past individual earnings history, whereas SSI is a flat-rate means-tested welfare program. SSDI provides recipients Medicare benefits after they are on the program two years and restricts its recipients to labor earnings up to $750 per month for a limited period, after which they face a significant program "notch" and lose all SSDI benefits. The SSI program provides its recipients with immediate access to Medicaid and, once on the program, allows them more generous work options compared to SSDI.

ents who receive earnings (e.g., 1619[a] and [b] status), only a small percentage of disabled adult SSI recipients work.[54] In 1976 only 3.4 percent of all disabled adult beneficiaries worked. Since that time, the percentage of disabled adult SSI recipients with earnings has nearly doubled, but, at 6.3 percent in 2001, it remains quite low.[55] A somewhat more optimistic picture comes from work by Muller, Scott, and Bye (1996), who look at the work history of SSI recipients. They find that among a sample of SSI beneficiaries coming onto the rolls between 1976 and 1988, approximately one-quarter worked at some point during the time they received benefits.

In response to the low number of SSI recipients who work, the SSA has conducted two large-scale return-to-work demonstration projects to study the effectiveness of providing rehabilitation and employment services to SSI beneficiaries. The first, the Transitional Employment Training Demonstration (TETD) project, which operated between 1985 and 1987, focused on SSI beneficiaries whose primary condition was mental retardation. The second, Project NetWork, operated between 1992 and 1995 and included SSDI and SSI beneficiaries with a wide range of diagnoses. The two demonstration projects were run in a similar fashion. Eligible beneficiaries in selected cities were invited to participate in the two projects. Volunteers were then randomly assigned to treatment and control groups. The treatment groups were provided with rehabilitation and employment services, whereas the control group was not. Using both survey and administrative data, the effectiveness of the rehabilitation and employment services could then be studied by comparing outcomes of the experimental and control groups.

Analysis of the impact of the TETD project suggests that the employment and rehabilitation services provided to SSI beneficiaries significantly increased earnings for participants over the six years they were observed (earnings of the treatment group were close to 70 percent higher than the control group, roughly $4,000 in 1996 dollars), but the program only had a small impact on average SSI payments ($870 per participant). This small reduction in SSI payments was not nearly sufficient to cover the average costs of transitional employment services for program participants (Thornton and Decker 1989).[56] However, when the employment and earnings gains for program participants are weighed against the costs of providing the employment services, the program may very well have produced

---

54. Section 1619 (P.L. 96-265) became law in 1986. These provisions dramatically altered the earnings opportunities for SSI disabled adults. Section 1619(a) allows recipients to maintain their SSI (and Medicaid) benefits even when their earnings exceed SGA. Section 1619(b) extends Medicaid coverage to workers whose earnings make them ineligible for SSI cash payments.

55. Data on recipients who work come from SSA (2002b).

56. The net effect of the transitional employment services is harder to evaluate and depends crucially on the extent to which the services provided by the project substitute for other services paid for by the government (Thornton and Decker 1989).

a net social benefit. Similar results were obtained from Project NetWork. Analyses of the program (Kornfeld and Rupp 2000) show that during the first two years of operation Project NetWork produced modest net benefits to persons with disabilities, as earnings gains among participants more than offset reductions in SSI and SSDI benefits. However, the small gain in earnings was not nearly sufficient to offset the costs of administering Project NetWork. Moreover, data for a third-year follow-up on about 70 percent of the sample show that earnings gains declined to about zero, suggesting that the increase in earnings may have been temporary.

Importantly, in both cases the fraction of program eligibles who volunteered for either TETD or Project Network was small—roughly 5 percent in each experiment. This suggests that, however beneficial it might be to those who participate, the provision of transitional employment services to those on SSI who volunteer for services is unlikely to have much of an impact on the overall SSI population. This is hardly surprising. As shown earlier in this chapter, only a small fraction of SSI applicants were working in the years prior to application. In addition, beneficiaries go through a long process to establish that they have medical conditions that prevent them from performing substantial gainful activity. At least at the time they apply for SSI benefits, applicants would appear to have put substantial energy into becoming eligible for program benefits—benefits that must more than compensate applicants both for any loss of income associated with moving onto SSI and for the costs associated with applying for benefits.[57] For the great majority of those awarded benefits, their health is unlikely to improve over time and their labor market opportunities are probably deteriorating. Moreover, those who return to work may be subject to high marginal tax rates.[58] Under such adverse conditions it is not surprising that voluntary returns to work are rare.

2.5.2   SSI and Families of Children with Disabilities

As noted earlier, the primary justification for awarding cash benefits to poor families containing a disabled child is that the families of disabled children face additional economic burdens associated with their child's poor health (see NASI 1996). These economic burdens may include lost earnings from a parent who provides care for the disabled child and medical and nonmedical expenses related to the child's specific disability. How-

---

57. As will be discussed later in this chapter, the cost of applying for SSI disability benefits for the average applicant may be lower today than in previous periods. To the extent that welfare reform has changed the SSI applicant pool, individuals may not be making a choice between work and benefits but rather between other welfare and SSI.

58. The evidence we have on the extent of work activity by those who have been awarded SSI benefits comes mostly from the analysis of Social Security Earnings data. Anecdotal evidence suggests that some fraction of those on SSI are actually working, but are working "off the books." Research targeted on such off-the-books work by SSI beneficiaries along the lines of that done by Edin and Lein (1997) on welfare recipients would be valuable.

ever, SSI child benefits are not based on an earnings replacement or expenditure offset formula but, rather, are means-tested against current income. It is difficult to know a priori whether beneficiary families experience dramatic drops in labor earnings or increases in net-of-disability expenditures in family income. In fact, it is equally possible that recipient families have low incomes prior to the onset of the child's disability, and that the additional burdens placed on families with a disabled child are not the root cause of their current financial situation.

As with the adult SSI program, the child SSI program faces the problems related to moral hazard—incentives for parents to have their children become and remain eligible for SSI. The degree to which this potential moral hazard causes behavioral changes with respect to gaining and maintaining eligibility depends, to some degree, on the pre-disability economic circumstances of the covered families. If the typical family is a middle-income family that experiences a dramatic decline in its economic well-being at the onset of the child's disability, but in all other ways has the market and social characteristics necessary to attain middle-income status, then cash programs that only partially offset these losses are unlikely to lead to major disincentives for labor market participation or the child's recovery. However, if the typical family that comes onto the SSI rolls is already economically vulnerable (e.g., family members have few market skills, it is a one-parent family, etc.) prior to the onset of the child's disability, eligibility for SSI is likely to have much greater economic importance. Poor families that have a child with a disability may be able to completely replace or even increase their family income if their child's disability results in the receipt of SSI benefits. Thus, pre-disability differences in economic well-being alter the replacement rate of SSI among families of children with disabilities and make the moral hazard of behavioral change much greater among pre-disability low-income families than among middle- or high-income families.

Factors Affecting SSI Participation

As is true for the adult disability determination process, the disability determination process for children has undergone substantial revision. As noted earlier, the most important change came in 1990 when the Supreme Court required SSA to significantly broaden the eligibility criteria for childhood disability. The same year as the Zebley decision, SSA also released regulations revising the procedures used to evaluate mental impairments among children. The new rules expanded SSA's medical listings for childhood mental impairments by adding such illnesses as attention deficit hyperactivity disorder (ADHD) and by incorporating functional criteria in the listings. Similar to the changes made in the adult process, SSA modified the types of evidence used to judge the damage of mental illness; less emphasis was placed on the testimony of medical professionals and more weight was given to the information parents, teachers, and counselors provided about the child's condition. As with the IFA, the new mental impairment regulations focused on how disabilities affected a child's performance in school.

Following these changes, the child SSI caseloads grew rapidly. Data from the SSA show that between 1989 and 1996 the number of children under eighteen receiving SSI more than tripled, from 265,000 to 955,000. Applications increased from 132,000 in 1989 to 541,000 per year in 1994, and awards more than quadrupled. The yearly allowance rate on applications rose from 39 percent in 1989 to a peak of 58.1 percent in 1992. In 1992, the number of children on SSI grew by 40 percent (U.S. GAO 1998).

In response to rapid caseload growth and a burgeoning concern that the disability determination process was allowing too many children without serious medical problems onto the disability rolls, Congress narrowed the criteria for childhood disability in 1996. In addition, Congress mandated that SSA redetermine the eligibility of children on the rolls who might not meet the new eligibility criteria because they received benefits on the basis of the former, more lenient, standards.[59] In 1997, the number of SSI recipients under age eighteen fell 7.9 percent and by 2001 was still 7.7 percent below the 1996 high (see figure 2.4).

Economic factors also influence the decision of families to participate in SSI. Evidence suggests that a large fraction of the children coming onto the rolls in the 1990s previously participated in the AFDC program. Daly and Burkhauser (1998), using data from the National Longitudinal Survey of Youth (NLSY), calculate that two-thirds of children found eligible for SSI in the early 1990s were in families already receiving some type of welfare assistance. Other things being equal, families eligible for multiple programs are likely to select those programs that provide the highest net benefit to them. Although additional costs are associated with SSI (e.g., more stringent application rules, greater stigma related to receiving benefits, etc.), as the benefit difference between SSI and other programs increases, more families will be willing to incur these costs to improve their economic situation.

Kubik (1999) tests the empirical significance of this prediction. He finds that AFDC recipient families who successfully qualify a child for SSI benefits can increase family income substantially. Table 2.9 (taken from Kubik 1999) shows how a family's income can change when a child moves from AFDC to SSI. The analysis is for two states, Maryland and Connecticut, and demonstrates two points: (a) Families can significantly improve their economic well-being if someone in the family qualifies for SSI, and (b) the generosity of SSI relative to AFDC has grown over time, implying that the

---

59. The SSA originally identified 288,000 children as potentially affected by changes in the eligibility criteria. In 1998, SSA scaled back its estimates; new estimates suggest that fewer than 100,000 children will become ineligible for SSI (U.S. GAO 1998).

Table 2.9   AFDC and SSI Benefit Levels for Maryland and Connecticut, 1990 and 1994 (in dollars)

State	AFDC Benefit for Family of Three (1)	AFDC Benefit for Family of Two (2)	Difference ([1] − [2]) (3)	Federal SSI Benefit (4)	Net SSI Benefit ([4] − [3]) (5)
Maryland					
1990	4,872	3,804	1,068	4,632	3,564
1994	4,392	3,432	960	5,352	4,392
Connecticut					
1990	6,660	5,424	1,236	4,632	3,396
1994	8,160	6,588	1,572	5,352	3,780

Source: Kubik (1999).

Notes: All benefit levels are state maximums, assuming the family earns no countable income. Both Maryland and Connecticut did not provide SSI state supplements to children during this time period.

incentive to transfer to the SSI program has grown. Table 2.8 shows that a family of three living in Maryland in 1990 could have increased monthly family income by over $3,500 if one child transferred to the SSI rolls. By 1994, this advantage had grown to almost $4,400. Since other in-kind benefits such as Medicaid and food stamps remained constant, the family experienced a net gain in income if the child moved from AFDC to the SSI rolls.

A small number of empirical papers have examined the responses of AFDC participants to changes in the SSI program, including the post-Zebley broadening of the childhood disability criteria, and increases in the relative generosity of SSI benefits during the 1990s (see RAND 1998 for a thorough review of this literature). Garrett and Glied (2000) examine the impact of the Zebley decision on SSI and AFDC caseloads using the Zebley ruling as a "natural experiment," representing an exogenous increase in the supply of SSI benefits (i.e., eligibility criteria are relaxed and more families are allowed onto the SSI program). They exploit the state-level variation in the difference between SSI and AFDC payments to test whether families are responsive to increases in net benefits. Their findings suggest that families are responsive to differences in program generosity. They found that in low-AFDC states, where the difference between AFDC and SSI payments would be largest, about 53 percent of the new post-Zebley child SSI cases switched from the AFDC program; nationally, only about 43 percent of new SSI child cases came from the AFDC program.

Along the same lines, Kubik (1999) examines the incentives for families to identify children as disabled when SSI benefits are more generous than AFDC benefits. Using data from the National Health Interview Survey (NHIS) and changes in the difference in SSI and AFDC benefits, Kubik finds that reported disabilities—particularly mental impairments—were higher in low-AFDC-benefit states than in high-AFDC-benefit states.[60] Using data from the CPS on household SSI receipt, he also finds that relatively generous SSI benefits (relative to AFDC payments) affect SSI participation. Kubik estimates that a 10 percent increase in SSI benefit generosity increases the probability of SSI participation among families with low education by 0.39 percentage points—a 5 percent increase in SSI participation. Overall, Kubik finds a significant and positive relationship between the marginal value of SSI benefits and the prevalence of disability, and receipt of SSI, among children.

Effects of SSI on Work Effort of Families

SSI support for families potentially affects the labor market effort of parents. However, there is not a large empirical literature on this relationship. Indeed, of the literature on childhood SSI, only the Garrett and Glied (2000) and Kubik (1999) papers consider this issue. Garrett and Glied estimate that the Zebley decision had a significant impact on the employment of unmarried women without a high school education. Kubik finds similar results; examining behavior after Zebley, Kubik finds that increases in SSI benefits lowered the probability that low-education household heads work. He estimates that a 10 percent increase in SSI benefits decreases labor force participation of low-education household heads by about 2 percent. The empirical evidence on the effects of SSI benefit levels on parental work effort after Zebley suggest that, in addition to responding to the particular health needs of a child, mothers also respond to the income effect present in the guarantee as well as to the high marginal tax rates placed on their labor earnings.

2.5.3   SSI and the Behavior of the Aged

Factors Affecting Participation

Researchers have offered a number of hypotheses to explain the low enrollment in SSI among the elderly, including lack of knowledge about the program and eligibility criteria, prohibitively expensive application costs (e.g., time cost or cost of learning), and unobserved costs of receiving benefits (e.g., welfare stigma). Early work on this topic focused primarily on the roles of welfare stigma and program knowledge on the decision to apply. Coe (1985) reported that of the SSI nonparticipants classified as eligible (48 percent of all eligible individuals), a significant fraction were not aware of the program or did not think they were eligible. Coe also found that benefit levels were positively and significantly related to participation,

---

60. To account for state-specific factors that may affect the prevalence of disability, Kubik examines this relationship before and after Zebley. Thus, he measures the change in the prevalence of reported disability and compares it to the change in the difference between SSI and AFDC benefits by state.

with each $10 in additional benefits resulting in a 2.4 percentage point increase in the probability of participation. This is consistent with the notion that relatively high benefit levels would outweigh any noninformational barriers to participation, such as access costs. However, Coe notes, noninformational barriers accounted for only 25 percent of the negative effect of low benefits on participation. The primary reason lower benefit levels decreased participation was that eligible individuals facing low benefit levels were more likely to believe that they were not eligible to participate. Warlick (1982) also concluded that program information and the difficulty of the application process were the primary reasons for low participation rates among the eligible elderly.

Recent work by McGarry (1996) draws a slightly different conclusion. McGarry extends previous research by using detailed asset and income information from the 1984 Survey of Income and Program Participation to more accurately classify eligibility by accounting for differences in benefit levels introduced by state supplementation, and by explicitly controlling for measurement error in the estimation process. McGarry concludes that the participation decision is primarily determined by the financial situation of eligible individuals. She finds that although all persons eligible for SSI are poor, the probability of participation declines as the number of alternative resources increases. Similar to Coe, she finds that the elasticity of the expected benefit is about 0.5 and that, after controlling for size of the SSI payment, those with greater resources are less likely to participate.[61]

McGarry departs from previous research in finding little evidence that welfare stigma or informational program costs affect participation. However, as she notes, her results must be interpreted with caution. The estimated model is a reduced-form version, which includes variables likely to affect participation through more than one path. If a variable operates in opposite directions on different factors, its importance may be obscured. Thus, although she argues that the negative coefficient on years of schooling implies that lack of information does not deter participants, this result can just as easily be interpreted as evidence of stigma associated with receiving benefits (i.e., more educated individuals feel more stigma associated with receiving benefits).

In general, the low SSI participation rates among the elderly remain something of a mystery. Although there is reason to believe that some individuals are uninformed about the program or their eligibility for benefits, there is not much evidence that a large fraction of the elderly poor in need of assistance are constrained by transactions costs. What does appear to be the case is that eligible individuals who are close to the margin on the

---

61. Coe's measure of other resources includes only the home ownership variable. McGarry uses a more extensive set of resource measures, including home and other asset ownership, labor earnings over the year, and the ratio of income to needs.

means test are less likely to participate in the program. As Coe (1985) argued, this may be due to individuals' misunderstanding the income disregards and other program rules that determine eligibility. Thus, unless individuals are sufficiently below the means test guidelines, they believe that they will be ineligible and thus do not apply. This interpretation is consistent with McGarry's simulation of responses given a change in benefit levels. McGarry examined how raising the federal income guarantee to the U.S. poverty line affected the participation of those previously and newly eligible for benefits. She finds that raising the benefit level increases the participation rates of those previously eligible by 16.5 percentage points, from 0.534 to 0.699. In contrast, she finds that less than 30 percent of those newly eligible under the increased income limit participate in the program.[62]

Saving Behavior

Although it is well recognized that means-tested programs create incentives for potentially eligible individuals to alter their behavior to ensure qualification, few studies have rigorously reviewed the incentives facing elderly individuals close to the age and resource tests for SSI. Yet it is likely that SSI program features create disincentives for working and saving as individuals approach the age of eligibility. Neumark and Powers (1998) focus on the relation between saving behavior and SSI receipt among the elderly. They argue that SSI's influence on the saving patterns of elderly individuals should vary with the expected level of their benefits and the likelihood of receiving them. In practice, individuals with low lifetime earnings living in high-benefit states should reduce saving more than high lifetime earners living in low-benefit states. Neumark and Powers use state-level variation in the generosity of supplemental SSI payments to identify the effects of SSI on the saving behavior of the elderly. They find that SSI reduces the saving of men and women nearing the age of retirement who are likely participants in the program.

SSI and Labor Force Participation at Older Ages

There only are a handful of papers that discuss SSI and the labor force behavior of older workers. Duggan (1984) finds that SSI has a negative impact on the labor force participation of men and women over fifty-four years of age, with especially strong effects for men. Powers and Neumark (2001) investigate the role that SSI plays in exercising the early retirement option in the Social Security program. Although Powers and Neumark

---

62. McGarry (2000) simulates the effects of changes in eligibility criteria on participation and costs. She finds that extending the income guarantee for all elderly individuals to the poverty line has the largest impact. Modifications to SSI that increase income disregards or eliminate the asset test or base income eligibility are less costly but also have less of an impact on poverty.

find only weak empirical evidence that eligibility for SSI benefits positively influences early retirement decisions, these effects may increase in coming years. The normal retirement age for receiving Social Security benefits is now in the process of increasing from sixty-five to sixty-seven over the next fifteen years, increasing the value to those eligible of the SSI bridge, especially for those in very poor health.

2.6 Summary and Conclusions

The enactment of the SSI program in 1972 was the culmination of a four-year debate over a much more overarching welfare reform—a federally funded minimum income guarantee for all Americans. Unlike Nixon's FAP proposal, SSI was targeted on the subgroup of low-income individuals "not expected to work." Since then, SSI has grown dramatically, with the composition of SSI beneficiaries shifting toward adults and children with disabilities.

How one views the increases in the SSI disability population is largely influenced by one's view of the social purpose of SSI. For those who see SSI as an incomplete substitute for a universal guaranteed income program like the NIT, expansions in the SSI program are seen as appropriate because they bring the United States more into line with most Western European countries that provide such a universal minimum social safety net for all their citizens. However, for those who are worried about the long-term effects of a lifetime on government transfers, the rise in the prevalence of disability transfer recipients—particularly among poor children and younger adults—is of more concern.

Whatever perspective one takes, however, as the population on SSI changes and the group of those not expected to work narrows, the structure of SSI comes into question. As we have shown, the SSI population has dramatically shifted over time. It is now dominated by children and young adults with disabilities. To date, despite some attempts to offset the negative work incentives in SSI (section 1619), exits from SSI to employment, even among this younger population, have been rare. As shown earlier in this chapter, for individuals and families receiving SSI and other transfer program benefits the marginal tax rates can go from 50 to near 100 percent at relatively low earnings levels. Although such high tax rates and relatively generous guarantees make sense for populations not expected to work, in a population where work is possible, they seriously discourage work. Hence, for those with a capacity to work, SSI, together with eligibility for other programs, can become the "poverty trap" that the original supporters of Nixon's single universal FAP program were trying to avoid.

Such concerns are particularly relevant in light of other government policies to protect those with disabilities. Support for civil rights–based legislation like the ADA is based on the idea that people with disabilities should have equal access to employment. Supporters of this type of legislation view unequal access to jobs to be a greater impediment to employment than a health impairment. Furthermore, they ask that social policy focus on altering workplace institutions to more fully accommodate people with disabilities. Hence, in a world of full accommodation, they argue that the disability transfer population should be zero. Fundamentally, the current policy debate over expanding SSI transfer rolls hinges on the role people with disabilities should play in society. Should people with disabilities be expected to work or not? If yes, then policies targeting people with disabilities—particularly the young—would be better focused on education, rehabilitation, job training, and accommodation than on increasing or expanding transfers. Likewise, for children with disabilities, investing more time, energy, and resources in enhancing their education and development, rather than focusing solely on supplementing the income of their households, might be more desirable.

In general, our examination in this chapter suggests that in the absence of a universal guaranteed income program for all Americans, the operational flexibility of the categorical eligibility criteria for SSI has made the program sensitive to both downturns in the business cycle and increases in the pool of vulnerable people. Moreover, when the dividing lines separating the working-age adult and child populations eligible for SSI from those eligible for other income-based benefits are imprecise, as with disability, policy changes in other welfare programs are likely to affect SSI caseloads.

References

Aarts, L., R. V. Burkhauser, and P. R. deJong. 1996. *Curing the Dutch disease: An international perspective on disability policy reform.* Aldershot, U.K.: Averbury.

Acemoglu, D., and J. Angrist. 2001. Consequences of employment protection? The case of the Americans with Disabilities Act. *Journal of Political Economy* 109 (5): 915–57.

Autor, D., and M. Duggan. 2001. The rise in disability and the decline in unemployment. MIT, Department of Economics. Mimeograph.

Berkowitz, E. D., and R. V. Burkhauser. 1996. A United States perspective on disability programs. In *Curing the Dutch disease: An international perspective on disability policy reform,* ed. L. Aarts, R. V. Burkhauser, and P. R. de Jong, 71–92. Adershot, U.K.: Averbury.

Black, D., K. Daniel, and S. Sanders. 2002. The impact of economic conditions on participation in disability programs: Evidence from coal boom and bust. *American Economic Review* 92 (1): 27–50.

Bound, J., and R. V. Burkhauser. 1999. Economic analysis of transfer programs targeted on people with disabilities. In *Handbook of labor economics.* Vol. 3(c), ed. O. Ashenfelter and D. Card, 3417–528. Amsterdam: Elsevier Science.

Bound, J., R. V. Burkhauser, and A. Nichols. Forthcoming. Tracking the household income of SSDI and SSI applicants. *Research on Labor Economics.*

Bound, J., J. B. Cullen, A. Nichols, and L. Schmidt. 2002. The welfare implications of increasing DI benefit generosity. NBER Working Paper no. 9155. Cambridge, Mass.: National Bureau of Economic Research.

Bound, J., S. Kossoudji, and G. Ricart-Moes. 1998. The ending of general assistance and SSI disability growth in Michigan: A case study. In *Growth in disability benefits: Explanations and policy implications,* ed. K. Rupp and D. Stapleton, 223–48. Kalamazoo, Mich.: W. E. Upjohn Institute for Employment Research.

Bound, J., and T. Waidmann. 2002. Accounting for recent declines in employment rates among the working-aged men and women with disabilities. *Journal of Human Resources* 37 (2): 231–50.

Brown, W. H., W. Hoyt, and F. A. Scott. 1999. Substitution between SSI and AFDC: An analysis using county-level data. Working Paper no. E-211-99. University of Kentucky, Department of Economics.

Burke, V. J., and V. Burke. 1974. *Nixon's good deed: Welfare reform.* New York: Columbia University Press.

Burkhauser, R. V., J. S. Butler, Y. Kim, and R. Weathers. 1999. The importance of accommodation on the timing of male disability insurance application: Results from the Survey of Disability and Work and the Health and Retirement Study. *Journal of Human Resources* 34 (3): 589–611.

Burkhauser, R. V., and M. C. Daly. 2002. U.S. disability policy in a changing environment. *Journal of Economic Perspectives* 16 (1): 213–24.

Burkhauser, R. V., M. C. Daly, A. Houtenville, and N. Nargis. 2002. Self-reported work limitation data: What they can and cannot tell us. *Demography* 39 (3): 541–55.

Burkhauser, R. V., and T. A. Finnegan. 1989. The minimum wage and the poor: The end of a relationship. *Journal of Policy Analysis and Management* 8 (1): 53–71.

———. 1993. The economics of minimum wage legislation revisited. *Cato Journal* 13 (1): 123–29.

Burkhauser, R. V., A. Houtenville, and D. Wittenburg. Forthcoming. A user's guide to current statistics on the employment of people with disabilities. In *The decline in employment of people with disabilities: A policy puzzle,* ed. D. Stapleton and R. Burkhauser. Kalamazoo, Mich.: W.E. Upjohn Institute for Employment Research.

Burkhauser, R. V., and T. M. Smeeding. 1981. The net impact of the Social Security system on the poor. *Public Policy* 29 (2): 159–78.

Burkhauser, R. V., and D. C. Wittenburg. 1996. How current disability transfer policies discourage work: Analysis from the 1990 SIPP. *Journal of Vocational Rehabilitation* 7(1/2): 9–27.

Coe, R. 1985. Nonparticipation in the SSI program by the eligible elderly. *Southern Economic Journal* 51 (3): 891–97.

Congressional Research Service (CRS). 1999. Cash and noncash benefits for persons with limited income: Eligibility rules, recipient and expenditure data, FY 1996–FY 1998. Report Code no. RL30401. Washington, D.C.: Library of Congress.

Daly, M. C., and R. V. Burkhauser. 1998. How family economic well-being changes following the onset of a disability: A dynamic analysis. Syracuse University, Department of Economics and Center for Policy Research. Manuscript.

DeLeire, T. 2000. The wage and employment effects of the Americans with Disabilities Act. *Journal of Human Resources* 35 (4): 693–715.

Duggan, J. 1984. The labor-force participation of older workers. *Industrial and Labor Relations Review* 37 (3): 416–30.

Edin, K., and L. Lein. 1997. *Making ends meet: How single mothers survive welfare and low-wage work.* New York: Russell Sage Foundation.

Friedman, M. 1962. *Capitalism and freedom.* Chicago: University of Chicago Press.
———. 1968. The case for the negative income tax. In *Republican papers,* ed. M. Laird, 202–20. Garden City, N.Y.: Anchor.
Garrett, A. B., and S. Glied. 2000. Does state AFDC generosity affect child SSI participation? *Journal of Policy Analysis and Management* 19 (2): 275–95.
Giannarelli, L., and E. Steuerle. 1995. The twice poverty trap: Tax rates faced by AFDC recipients. Urban Institute Research Report. Washington, D.C.: The Urban Institute.
Hoynes, H., and R. Moffitt. 1996. The effectiveness of financial work incentives in Social Security Disability Insurance and Supplemental Security Income: Lessons from other transfer programs. In *Disability, work, and cash benefits,* ed. J. Mashaw, V. Reno, R. V. Burkhauser, and M. Berkowitz, 189–222. Kalamazoo, Mich.: W. E. Upjohn Institute for Employment Research.
Hubbard, R., J. Skinner, and S. Zeldes. 1995. Precautionary saving and social insurance. *Journal of Political Economy* 103 (2): 360–99.
Jette, A., and E. Badley. 2002. Conceptual issues in the measurement of work disability. In *The dynamics of disability: Measuring and monitoring disability for Social Security programs,* ed. G. S. Wunderlich, D. Rice, and N. L. Amado, 183–210. Washington, D.C.: National Academy Press.
Johnson, W. G., ed. 1997. The Americans with Disabilities Act: Social contract or special privelege? *The Annals of the American Academy of Political and Social Sciences* 549 (January): 1–220.
Kaye, S. Forthcoming. Employment and the changing disability environment. In *The decline in employment of people with disabilities: A policy puzzle,* ed. D. Stapleton and R. Burkhauser. Kalamazoo, Mich.: W. E. Upjohn Institute for Employment Research.
Keane, M., and R. Moffitt. 1998. A structural model of multiple welfare program participation and labor supply. *International Economic Review* 39 (3): 553–89.
Kornfeld, R., and K. Rupp. 2000. The net effects of the Project NetWork return-to-work case management experiment on participant earnings, benefit receipt, and other outcomes. *Social Security Bulletin* 63 (1): 12–33.
Kubik, J. 1999. Incentives for the identification and treatment of children with disabilities: The Supplemental Security Income program. *Journal of Public Economics* 73:187–215.
Lando, M. E., R. Cutler, and E. Gamber. 1982. *1978 survey of disability and work: Data book.* Washington, D.C.: Government Printing Office.
La Plante, M. P. 1991. The demographics of disability. *The Americans with Disabilities Act: From policy to practice,* ed. J. West, 55–77. New York: Milbank Memorial Fund.
Lewin-VHI. 1995. Longer-term factors affecting SSDI and SSI disability applications and awards: Final report. Washington, D.C.: Office of the Assistant Secretary for Planning and Evaluation, U.S. Department of Health and Human Services and the Social Security Administration.
———. 1999. Policy evaluation of the overall effects of welfare reform on SSA programs: Final report and appendix. Washington, D.C.: Office of the Assistant Secretary for Planning and Evaluation, U.S. Department of Health and Human Services and the Social Security Administration.
Library of Congress. 1998. Vocational factors in the Social Security disability decision process: A review of the literature. Report prepared under an interagency agreement for the Social Security Administration Office of Disability Research. Washington, D.C.: Federal Research Division, Library of Congress.
Livermore, G., D. C. Stapleton, and A. Zeuschner. 1998. Lessons from case studies of recent program growth in five states. In *Growth in disability benefits: Ex-*

planations and policy implications, ed. K. Rupp and D. C. Stapleton, 249–86. Kalamazoo, Mich.: W. E. Upjohn Institute for Employment Research.

Mashaw, J. L., and V. P. Reno. 1996. *Balancing security and opportunity: The challenge of disability income policy.* Report of the Disability Policy Panel. Washington, D.C.: National Academy of Social Insurance.

McGarry, K. 1996. Factors determining participation of the elderly in SSI. *Journal of Human Resources* 31 (12): 331–58.

———. 2000. Guaranteed income: SSI and the well-being of the elderly. NBER Working Paper no. 7574. Cambridge, Mass.: National Bureau of Economic Research.

———. 2000. Guaranteed income: SSI and the well-being of the elderly. NBER Working Paper no. 7574. Cambridge, Mass.: National Bureau of Economic Research.

Menefee, J., B. Edwards, and S. Schieber. 1981. Analysis of nonparticipation in the SSI program. *Social Security Bulletin* 44 (6): 3–21.

Moffitt, R. 1986. Work incentives in transfer programs (revisited): A study of the AFDC program. *Research in Labor Economics* 8(b): 389–439.

Muller, S., C. Scott, and B. Bye. 1996. Labor-force participation and earnings of SSI disability recipients: A pooled cross-sectional time series approach to the behavior of individuals. *Social Security Bulletin* 59 (1): 22–42.

Nagi, S. 1965. Some conceptual issues in disability and rehabilitation. In *Sociology and rehabilitation,* ed. M. B. Sussman, 100–13. Washington, D.C.: American Sociological Association.

———. 1969a. Congruency in medical and self-assessment of disability. *Industrial Medicine and Surgery* 38:27–36.

———. 1969b. *Disability and rehabilitation: Legal, clinical, and self-concepts of measurement.* Columbus: Ohio State University Press.

———. 1991. Disability concepts revisited: Implications to prevention. In *Disability in America: Toward a national agenda for prevention,* ed. A. M. Pope and A. R. Tarlove, 309–27. Washington, D.C.: National Academy Press.

National Academy of Social Insurance (NASI). 1996. Restructuring the SSI disability program for children and adolescents. *Report from the Committee on Childhood Disability to the Disability Panel of the NASI.* Washington, D.C.: NASI.

Neumark, D., and E. Powers. 1998. The effect of means-tested income support for the elderly on pre-retirement saving: Evidence from the SSI program in the U.S. *Journal of Public Economics* 68 (2): 181–206.

Parrott, T., L. Kennedy, and C. Scott. 1998. Noncitizens and the SSI program. *Social Security Bulletin* 61 (4): 3–31.

Ponce, E. 1996. State optional supplementation of SSI payments, 1974–1995. *Social Security Bulletin* 59 (1): 52–66.

Powers, E., and D. Neumark. 2001. The Supplemental Security Income program and incentives to take up Social Security early retirement: Empirical evidence from matched SIPP and Social Security administrative files. NBER Working Paper no. 8670. Cambridge, Mass.: National Bureau of Economic Research.

RAND. 1998. Background and study design report for policy evaluation of the effect of the 1996 welfare reform legislation on SSI benefits for disabled children. Washington, D.C.: Social Security Administration.

Rupp, K., and D. Stapleton. 1995. Determinants of the growth in Social Security Administration's disability programs: An overview. *Social Security Bulletin* 57 (2): 3–20.

Shields, J. F., B. Barnow, K. Chaurette, and J. Constantine. 1990. Elderly persons eligible for and participating in the Supplemental Security Income program. Final Report prepared for the U.S. Department of Health and Human Services. Washington, D.C.: U.S. Government Printing Office.

Smeeding, T. 1994. Improving Supplemental Security Income. In *Social welfare policy at the crossroads,* ed. R. Friedland, L. Etheridge, and B. Vladeck, 97–108. Washington, D.C.: National Academy of Social Insurance.

Social Security Administration (SSA). 1997. The definition of disability for children. SSA Publication no. 05-11053. Washington, D.C.: U.S. General Printing Office.

———. 2000. *Annual statistical supplement to the Social Security bulletin 2000.* Washington, D.C.: U.S. General Printing Office.

Social Security Administration. 2002a. *Annual report of the Supplemental Security Income Program.* Washington, D.C.: U.S. General Printing Office.

———. 2002b. *SSI annual statistical report 2001.* Washington, D.C.: U.S. General Printing Office.

———. Various years. *Annual statistical supplement to the Social Security bulletin.* Washington, D.C.: U.S. General Printing Office.

Stapleton, D. C., K. A. Coleman, K. A. Dietrich, and G. A. Livermore. 1998. Empirical analyses of DI and SSI application and award growth. In *Growth in disability benefits: Explanations and policy implications,* ed. K. Rupp and D. C. Stapleton, 31–92. Kalamazoo, Mich.: W. E. Upjohn Institute for Employment Research.

Stigler, G. 1946. The economics of minimum wage legislation. *American Economic Review* 36 (June): 358–65.

Thornton, C. V., and P. T. Decker. 1989. The transitional employment training demonstration: Analysis of program impacts. Project report. Princeton, N.J.: Mathematica Policy Research, July.

Tobin, J. 1969. Raising the incomes of the poor. In *Agenda for the nation,* ed. K. Gordon, 77–116. Washington, D.C.: Brookings Institution.

U.S. General Accounting Office. 1994. *Rapid rise in children on SSI disability rolls follows new regulations.* Report no. GAO/HEHS-94-225. Washington, D.C.: U.S. Government Printing Office.

———. 1995. *New functional assessments for children raise eligibility questions.* Report no. GAO/HEHS-95-66. Washington, D.C.: U.S. Government Printing Office.

———. 1998. *SSA needs a uniform standard for assessing childhood disability.* Report no. GAO/HEHS-98-123. Washington, D.C.: U.S. Government Printing Office.

U.S. House of Representatives, Committee on Ways and Means. 1971. Social Security amendments of 1971. House Report no. 92-231. Washington, D.C.: U.S. Government Printing Office.

———. 1998. Background material on data and programs within the jurisdiction of the Committee on Ways and Means. Washington, D.C.: U.S. Government Printing Office.

Verbrugge, L. M. 1990. Disability. *Epidemiology of Rheumatic Disease* 16:741–61.

Warlick, J. L. 1982. Participation of the aged in SSI. *Journal of Human Resources* 17 (2): 236–60.

Weathers, R. 1999. *Essays in applied microeconomics.* Ph.D. diss., Syracuse University.

Wunderlich, G. S., D. Rice, and N. L. Amado, eds. 2002. *The dynamics of disability: Measuring and monitoring disability for Social Security programs.* Washington, D.C.: National Academy Press.

Yelowitz, A. 1998. Why did the SSI-disabled program grow so much? Disentangling the effect of Medicaid. *Journal of Health Economics* 17 (3): 321–49.

The Earned Income Tax Credit

V. Joseph Hotz and John Karl Scholz

3.1 Introduction

The Earned Income Tax Credit (EITC) grew from $3.9 billion in 1975 (in 1999 dollars), the first year it was part of the tax code, to $31.5 billion in 2000. No other federal antipoverty program has grown at a comparable rate. In 2000 EITC spending was within $4 billion of the *combined* federal spending on Temporary Assistance for Needy Families (TANF) and food stamps.[1]

The growth of the EITC has been even more striking given the antipathy most Americans express toward welfare, at least prior to welfare reform in 1996, and the rhetoric of both political parties about recognizing the limitations of government programs.[2] The EITC's popularity relative to means-tested cash transfers like the former Aid to Families with Depen-

V. Joseph Hotz is professor of economics at the University of California—Los Angeles and a research associate of the National Bureau of Economic Research. John Karl Scholz is professor of economics and director of the Institute for Research on Poverty at the University of Wisconsin–Madison and a research associate of the National Bureau of Economic Research.

The authors thank Robert Moffitt for guidance; Janet Holtzblatt for comments and for teaching them a lot about the earned income tax credit over the years; Dan Feenberg and the National Bureau of Economic Research for putting TAXSIM on the Web; and Janet McCubbin, Bruce Meyer, Jeffrey Liebman, John Wolf, and conference participants for helpful suggestions.

1. The fiscal year (FY) 2002 budget showed total food stamp spending in 2000 at $18.3 billion and total TANF spending at $18.4 billion.

2. Views on welfare are illuminated by questions on the General Social Survey, which asks, "Are we spending too much money, too little money, or about the right amount on welfare?" In the 1972–82 surveys, 54.8 percent of the respondents replied "too much." In the 1996 survey, 57.7 percent replied "too much," although the percentage giving this response had fallen to 45.8 percent in 1998 and to 38.9 percent in 2000.

dent Children (AFDC) and new TANF programs stems, at least in part, from the perception that the EITC rewards work.

The credit began as part of a broader effort by Senator Russell Long (Dem.-La.) to derail congressional and presidential interest in a negative income tax (NIT) in the late 1960s and early 1970s. The initial debates highlighted a tension that exists to this day. The attraction of the NIT was that—as a universal *antipoverty* program—it would provide a guaranteed minimal standard of living to all in an administratively efficient way (through the tax system) without having the notches and high cumulative marginal tax rates that characterize a patchwork system of narrower programs. Senator Long's primary objection to the NIT was that it provided its largest benefits to those without any earnings, and hence would dull the labor market attachment of poor families. His alternative, initially called the "work bonus," would phase in and thus increase with earnings up to a point.

Over the years, the EITC has played different tax policy, labor market, and antipoverty roles. In section 3.2, we review the political history of the EITC, its rules, and its goals, and we provide a broad set of program statistics that summarize its growth and coverage. Various goals of the program occasionally come into conflict. For example, when the EITC was increased as part of the 1993 budget bill, it was singled out as an important antipoverty program that has positive (relative to alternatives) labor market incentives. Around the same time, however, studies of EITC noncompliance suggested that the credit was difficult for the Internal Revenue Service (IRS) to administer. One's view of the credit will be influenced significantly by the weight one places on its antipoverty effects, its labor market effects, and the ability of the IRS to administer the credit.

The core of this chapter is a discussion of EITC-related behavioral issues and research. Section 3.3 provides EITC program statistics. As would be expected with a program that has more than tripled in size (in real dollars) in the 1990s, a considerable amount of attention has been paid to the EITC in recent years. In section 3.4, we outline the conceptual underpinnings of much of this recent work and discuss EITC participation and compliance, its effects on labor force participation and hours of work, marriage and fertility, skill formation, and consumption. In this overview, we show that there are theoretical reasons to prefer the EITC to other antipoverty programs if the objective is to encourage work among the poor. At the same time, the predicted effects of the EITC are not all prowork, especially with respect to hours and its labor market incentives for two-earner couples. But a policy focus only on labor markets would be overly narrow, since it is clear that the EITC has the potential to affect a much broader set of economic behaviors.

Section 3.5 reviews the evidence to date on these behavioral issues. Given the design and size of the credit, it is not surprising that it delivers significant resources to working poor families. A large set of studies examine the credit's labor market effects, as would be expected given that a central distinction between the EITC and NIT approach to antipoverty policy is the likely superiority of the EITC in encouraging labor force participation. Recent studies have also focused on the degree to which expansions of the EITC over the last twenty years can account for trends in labor force participation for single women with children in the United States.

As highlighted in Moffitt (1998), many studies over the last ten years have examined the effects of programs like AFDC, Medicaid, and food stamps on family structure and children's well-being. These studies have been motivated by a growing concern that public assistance programs contributed to the rise in out-of-wedlock childbearing and female headship, two behaviors associated with the incidence of poverty, especially among children. Until very recently, however, little attention has been paid to the effects of the EITC expansions on these behaviors. We discuss recent EITC-related studies of this issue. We also discuss recent studies of the EITC's effect on consumption patterns of the poor. Because the credit is administered through the nation's (and, in some cases, state's) income tax systems, EITC payments to low-income households are typically received once a year, as an adjustment to tax liabilities or refunds. This payment pattern contrasts with the monthly payments typically associated with AFDC/TANF and food stamps, and it may provide a way to gain additional insight into the nature of credit markets and consumption behavior for low-income families.

Our goal in section 3.5 is to summarize succinctly what has been done, to evaluate the strengths of this work, and to identify areas where additional work could be useful to either verify existing conjectures or alter what we thought was known.

In the final sections, we briefly discuss EITC-related policy debates and highlight what, if any, critical economic issues underlie these debates. We also briefly identify issues on which future research is needed.

3.2 Program History, Rules, and Goals

It is not surprising that fundamental tensions in the design of the safety net emerge at different points in the program's history, given the EITC's status as the largest cash or near-cash antipoverty program.[3] In the mid-1960s and early 1970s there was a great deal of discussion about the appropriate design of antipoverty policy. At the risk of oversimplifying, one part of the policy debate focused on either direct earnings subsidies (of which the EITC is one) or on subsidies paid to employers to hire disad-

3. Our discussion of the EITC's political history comes directly from Liebman's (1997a) and Ventry's (2000) interesting accounts.

vantaged workers. Remnants of the latter approach are found in the current, modest Work Opportunity and Welfare-to-Work tax credits that are part of the federal income tax.[4] A problem with earnings or employment subsidies is that they do nothing for adults (and the children that live with them) who are unable or unwilling to work. Consequently, they must be matched with programs that help provide food, housing, health care, and other basic needs to those not in the labor market.

The EITC was established amid the political debate over the NIT that occurred in the 1960s and 1970s. The NIT held great promise to the early designers of the war on poverty since it would solve the difficult integration issues that arise with categorical antipoverty programs—the need for bureaucracies to administer and enforce eligibility and benefit rules and the need to mitigate potentially high marginal tax rates that recipients face as earnings increase. Partly for these reasons, in 1966 an NIT was the capstone of the Office of Economic Opportunity's (the federal agency in charge of conducting the war on poverty) plan to eradicate poverty. President Johnson, however, opposed the NIT and a leading alternative proposal at the time, a guaranteed annual income, on the grounds that both proposals undermined work effort. Without the support of the president, an NIT was not adopted. Nevertheless, in the late 1960s and early 1970s, the government launched the first widespread social experiments, the Gary (Indiana), New Jersey, Iowa, and Seattle-Denver Income Maintenance Experiments, to examine the effects of an NIT.

In 1969 President Nixon introduced an NIT called the Family Assistance Plan (FAP) that would have replaced the AFDC program. Although it enjoyed widespread initial support, the FAP was subsequently attacked by liberals as being insufficiently generous and by conservatives as being overly expensive and having insufficiently stringent work requirements.

Russell Long, then chair of the Senate Finance Committee, opposed the FAP and, as an alternative, designed a proposal targeted at those willing to work. His 1972 proposal included a large public service jobs component and a "work bonus" equal to 10 percent of wages subject to Social Security taxation. The FAP was defeated in 1972, but Senator Long aggressively pushed his work bonus scheme over the next three years. His efforts were aided by the confluence of three events. First, from 1960 to 1970 the payroll tax rate increased to 4.8 percent from 3.0 percent (on *both* employers and employees), and it increased further to 5.8 percent in 1973, which focused attention on the rising tax burdens of low-income families. Second, fostered in part by the income maintenance experiments, there continued to be a great deal of intellectual attention paid to the NIT and NIT alternatives in think tanks, universities, and government agencies. Third, a

---

4. For further discussion of employment subsidies and a broader treatment of employment strategies for low-wage labor markets, see Bishop and Haveman (1978) and Haveman (1996).

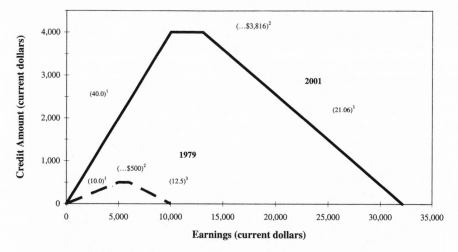

Fig. 3.1   The Earned Income Tax Credit for a family with two or more children in 1979 and 2001

Notes: 1 = subsidy rate; 2 = maximum benefit for two or more children; 3 = benefit reduction (implicit tax) rate.

recession started in 1974. This prompted members of Congress in 1975 to try to stimulate aggregate demand by refunding $8.1 billion in 1974 income taxes and cutting 1975 income taxes by an additional $10 billion. With the passage of a tax bill in 1975, Senator Long was able to enact a variant of his work bonus, called the EITC, on a temporary, eighteen-month basis. The provision added a 10 percent supplement to wages up to $4,000 ($12,387 in 1999 dollars) for taxpayers with children, and it phased out at a 10 percent rate over the $4,000 to $8,000 income range.

Senator Long undoubtedly understood that once a provision is in the tax code, it is likely to remain. Indeed, the EITC remained in the tax code each subsequent year until it was made permanent in 1978. Legislation in 1978 also added a flat range to the EITC's phase-in and phaseout ranges, as shown in figure 3.1.[5] An "advance payment" option was also added to the credit in 1978, so that workers would be able, if they desired, to receive the credit incrementally throughout the year.

Spending on the safety net slowed in the late 1970s and shrank in the 1980s. Between 1978 and the Tax Reform Act of 1986 (TRA86), the fact that the tax credit (and tax code) was not indexed for inflation caused a substantial erosion of the EITC's real value. The TRA86, as part of its provisions to eliminate income taxes on families with incomes below the

5. The phase-in rate for the credit was 10 percent on earnings up to $5,000, for a maximum credit of $500. The maximum credit was available for taxpayers with earnings between $5,000 and $6,000. The phaseout rate for the credit was 12.5 percent on incomes between $6,000 and $10,000.

poverty line, increased the EITC to the point where the maximum credit in 1987 equaled the real value of the credit in 1975. The TRA86 also indexed the credit for inflation. During this period the EITC continued to be supported by liberals and conservatives, both of whom were sympathetic to the idea of reducing tax burdens on low-income families and rewarding work.

Through much of the 1980s and into the 1990s, deficits were a dominant topic in Washington economic policy discussions. By 1990, annual deficit forecasts exceeding $300 billion—"as far as the eye can see"—were common, so that year President Bush agreed to abandon his "no new taxes" pledge and meet with Democratic leaders of Congress to fashion deficit-reduction legislation. The tortuous negotiations led to the 1990 tax bill, which phased out exemptions and itemized deductions on high-income taxpayers and raised the highest marginal tax rate from 28 percent to 31 percent. Whereas distributional issues have always played a role in tax policy, they played an exceptionally important role in 1990, perhaps because of the antipathy of Democratic congressional leaders toward the Republican president and the sense of those leaders that policy in the 1980s disfavored low-income families.[6] The EITC proved to be a straightforward way to alter the distributional characteristics of various deficit-reduction packages, and distributional tables became an important factor behind the 1990 EITC expansion that was phased in over three years. In 1991, the credit for the first time was also made larger for taxpayers with two or more children than for taxpayers with one child.

Another major change to the EITC occurred as part of the 1993 budget bill. In his first State of the Union Address, President Clinton said, "The new direction I propose will make this solemn, simple commitment: By expanding the refundable earned income tax credit, we will make history; we will reward the work of millions of working poor Americans by realizing the principle that if you work forty hours a week and you've got a child in the house, you will no longer be in poverty." This declaration completed the evolution of the EITC from Senator Long's modest "work bonus" to a major antipoverty initiative. President Clinton set a target for the EITC: full-time work at the minimum wage plus the EITC (and any food stamps a family is eligible for) should be enough to raise the family's net-of-payroll-tax income above the poverty line. To achieve this goal, the EITC was again increased, and increased sharply for families with two or more children.[7]

6. Many of the newspaper articles about 1990 budget talks emphasized distributional issues. See, for example, "GOP's Tax Proposal Said to Favor Wealthy; Budget Talks Proceeding at 'Glacial' Pace," *Washington Post,* 14 September 1990, A12, and "Budget Negotiations Recess Amid Confusion on Progress; Officials Disagree on Extent of Disagreement," *Washington Post,* 18 September 1990, A1.
7. The specific goal was achieved only for families with fewer than three children, and only after the minimum wage was increased in 1996 and 1997.

The 1993 budget bill (and EITC expansion) passed by one vote in the Senate and received not a single supporting Republican vote. This too marked a transformation in the EITC's political history. For the first time, the EITC became a policy linked exclusively to Democrats. In subsequent years, there have been highly partisan battles over EITC-related issues.

3.2.1   EITC Rules

To receive the earned income credit, taxpayers file their regular tax return and fill out the six-line Schedule EIC that gathers information about qualifying children. The EITC is refundable, meaning that it is paid out by the Treasury regardless of whether the taxpayer has any federal income tax liability. There are several basic tests for EITC eligibility. The taxpayer must have both earned and adjusted gross income below a threshold that varies by year and by family size. Most EITC payments go to taxpayers with at least one "qualifying child." A qualifying child needs to meet age, relationship, and residence tests. The age test requires the child to be younger than nineteen, younger than twenty-four if a full-time student, or any age if totally disabled. The relationship test requires the claimant to be the parent or the grandparent of the child or for the child to be a foster child.[8] Under the residence test the qualifying child must live with the taxpayer at least six months during the year.[9] Another rule limits the sum of taxable and tax-exempt interest, dividends, net capital gains, rents, royalties, and "passive" income to less than $2,350 (indexed for inflation).

In 2001, taxpayers with two or more children could receive a credit of 40 percent of income up to $10,020, for a maximum credit of $4,008. Taxpayers (with two or more children) with earnings between $10,020 and $13,090 received the maximum credit. Their credit was reduced by 21.06 percent of earnings between $13,090 and $32,121. The EITC schedule in 2001 for families with two or more children is shown in figure 3.1. A small credit available for childless taxpayers between the ages of twenty-four and sixty-five with very low incomes was added in 1994. The credit rate for these taxpayers is 7.65 percent, and the maximum credit in 2001 was $364. Table 3.1 shows the complete evolution of income eligibility thresholds, credit rates, and phaseout (or implicit tax) rates.

Panel A of figure 3.2 shows total tax payments and marginal tax rates for two-parent, two-child families in Illinois (a state with relatively high tax

8. Until late 1999, a foster child was any child for whom the claimant cared for "as if the child is their own." The caring stipulation still holds, but now the child must also be placed in the home by an authorized placement agency. Prior to the 2001 tax legislation, EITC-eligible foster children also needed to live with the taxpayer for twelve, rather than six, months.

9. In 1990 (tax year 1991) the residency and AGI tiebreaker (to be discussed) tests replaced a support test, since in principle it is easier to verify where a child lives than it is to verify who supports a child. Under the support test the taxpayer had to pay for at least half the child's support, where items like transfer payments (e.g., AFDC and housing subsidies) and child support were not considered support provided by the taxpayer.

Table 3.1 **Earned Income Tax Credit Parameters, 1979–2001 (in nominal dollars)**

Year	Phase-in Rate (%)	Phase-in Range ($)	Max Credit ($)	Phaseout Rate (%)	Phaseout Range ($)
1975–78	10.0	0–4,000	400	10.00	4,000–8,000
1979–84	10.0	0–5,000	500	12.50	6,000–10,000
1985–86	11.0	0–5,000	550	12.22	6,500–11,000
1987	14.0	0–6,080	851	10.00	6,920–15,432
1988	14.0	0–6,240	874	10.00	9,850–18,576
1989	14.0	0–6,500	910	10.00	10,240–19,340
1990	14.0	0–6,810	953	10.00	10,730–20,264
1991[a]	16.7[b]	0–7,140	1,192	11.93	11,250–21,250
	17.3[c]		1,235	12.36	11,250–21,250
1992[a]	17.6[b]	0–7,520	1,324	12.57	11,840–22,370
	18.4[c]		1,384	13.14	11,840–22,370
1993[a]	18.5[b]	0–7,750	1,434	13.21	12,200–23,050
	19.5[c]		1,511	13.93	12,200–23,050
1994	23.6[b]	0–7,750	2,038	15.98	11,000–23,755
	30.0[c]	0–8,245	2,528	17.68	11,000–25,296
	7.65[d]	0–4,000	306	7.65	5,000–9,000
1995	34.0[b]	0–6,160	2,094	15.98	11,290–24,396
	36.0[c]	0–8,640	3,110	20.22	11,290–26,673
	7.65[d]	0–4,100	314	7.65	5,130–9,230
1996	34.0[b]	0–6,330	2,152	15.98	11,610–25,078
	40.0[c]	0–8,890	3,556	21.06	11,610–28,495
	7.65[d]	0–4,220	323	7.65	5,280–9,500
1997	34.0[b]	0–6,500	2,210	15.98	11,930–25,750
	40.0[c]	0–9,140	3,656	21.06	11,930–29,290
	7.65[d]	0–4,340	332	7.65	5,430–9,770
1998	34.0[b]	0–6,680	2,271	15.98	12,260–26,473
	40.0[c]	0–9,390	3,756	21.06	12,260–30,095
	7.65[d]	0–4,460	341	7.65	5,570–10,030
1999	34.0[b]	0–6,800	2,312	15.98	12,460–26,928
	40.0[c]	0–9,540	3,816	21.06	12,460–30,580
	7.65[d]	0–4,530	347	7.65	5,670–10,200
2000	34.0[b]	0–6,920	2,353	15.98	12,690–27,413
	40.0[c]	0–9,720	3,888	21.06	12,690–31,152
	7.65[d]	0–4,610	353	7.65	5,770–10,380
2001	34.0[b]	0–7,140	2,428	15.98	13,090–28,281
	40.0[c]	0–10,020	4,008	21.06	13,090–32,131
	7.65[d]	0–4,760	364	7.65	5,950–10,708

Source: U.S. House of Representatives, Committee on Ways and Means (1998, p. 867). 1998 through 2001 parameters come from Internal Revenue Service Publication 596.

[a]Basic credit only. Does not include supplemental young child or health insurance credits.

[b]Taxpayers with one qualifying child.

[c]Taxpayers with more than one qualifying child.

[d]Childless taxpayers.

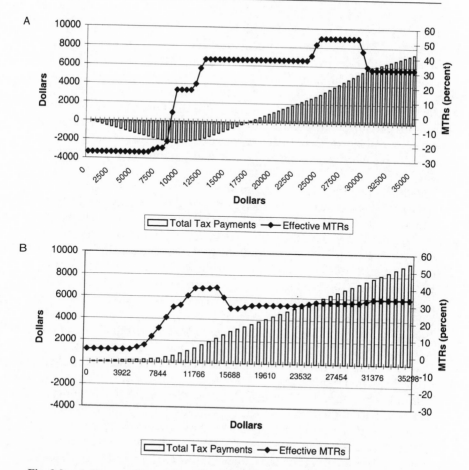

Fig. 3.2   *A,* **Taxes and marginal rates, family of four, Illinois, 1998;** *B,* **Taxes and marginal rates, family of four, Illinois, 1984 (in $ 1998)**

Notes: Calculations only reflect the effects of the state and federal tax system and do not include the effects of transfer programs. See Feenberg and Coutts (1993) for details of the NBER's TAXSIM model used for these calculations.

rates on low-income families) in 1998.[10] We assume workers bear the full burden of payroll taxes, so the employer and employee share of payroll taxes is 14.2 percent.[11] The marginal tax rate line is initially at –25.8 percent, reflecting the sum of the 14.2 percent effective payroll tax rate and

10. Nineteen states impose positive (but typically small) state income taxes on families of four with incomes below the poverty line (Johnson 2001).

11. Employers and employees both contribute 7.65 percent of earnings as payroll taxes, but the standard incidence assumption for payroll taxes implies that after-tax earnings would be 7.65 percent larger in the absence of payroll taxes, so the effective payroll tax rate is (0.153/ 1.0765) or 14.2 percent.

the –40 percent EITC rate. The flat portion of the EITC occurs around $10,000, where the Illinois household would face a 3 percent marginal state tax rate. Effective rates are 38.3 percent over much of the phaseout range, reflecting the sum of the 14.2 percent payroll tax, the 21.1 percent EITC phaseout, and the 3 percent Illinois state income tax. Rates jump to 53.3 percent between $25,000 and $29,000 as this family enters the 15 percent bracket of the federal income tax.[12] The corresponding average tax burdens are shown in the bars. Two-parent, two-child Illinois families would have negative combined income and payroll taxes up to roughly $17,200.[13]

Panel B of figure 3.2 shows the analogous situation for the same type of family in 1984, before the 1986 tax reform, and the 1990 and 1993 EITC expansions, all of which reduced taxes on low-income families. The pattern of marginal and average tax rates is strikingly different from what applied in 1998. The payroll tax (7 percent on employers and employees) was almost as high as it is now, resulting in an effective rate of 13.1 percent. The EITC was only 10 percent on incomes up to $7,844 (in 1998 dollars), so even taxpayers with very low incomes faced positive marginal rates. The EITC was phased out at a 12.5 percent rate beginning at $9,413 (again, in 1998 dollars). In addition, the 11 percent federal marginal tax bracket started at around $9,413 of income. Thus, all but the lowest-income families faced marginal tax rates of at least 28 percent, and some faced significantly higher marginal rates.

In calendar year 2001, fourteen states and the District of Columbia had EITCs as part of their state income tax systems.[14] The parameters of these credits are summarized in table 3.2. Most are structured as percentages of the federal credit and use the same eligibility definitions. In New York, for example, the state EITC was 25 percent of the federal credit in 2001, rising to 30 percent by 2003. Ten of the state EITCs (including D.C.) are refundable, and most make the credit available to workers without qualifying children.

Two unusual features show up in state EITCs. Wisconsin's state EITC has a three-tiered schedule equaling 4 percent of the federal credit for taxpayers with one child, 14 percent of the federal credit for taxpayers with

---

12. The EITC phaseout rate is lower for taxpayers with one child, but because they only receive one child credit and have one less personal exemption, one-child families in 2002 begin to pay the federal 10 percent marginal income tax rate at an income of $22,850. Hence, EITC recipients with one child and incomes between $22,850 and $29,201 have cumulative marginal tax rates around 40 percent (including payroll taxes).

13. Low-income families would generally file returns because their incomes exceed filing thresholds or to get back withheld taxes. With the $600 child credit along with exemptions of $3,000 and the standard deduction of $7,850, a married couple with two children in 2002 will not have a positive income tax liability until their earnings exceed $31,850, even without the EITC.

14. This discussion is from Johnson (2001).

Table 3.2   **State Earned Income Tax Credits, Tax Year 2001**

	Percentage of Federal Credit
Refundable credits	
Colorado (1999)	10
District of Columbia (2000)	25
Kansas (1998)	10
Maryland (1987)[a]	16 (rising to 20 in 2003)
Massachusetts (1997)	15
Minnesota (1991)	Averages 33%, varies by earnings[b]
New Jersey (2000)	15 (20% by 2003), limited to families with incomes below $20,000
New York (1994)	25 (30% by 2003)
Vermont (1988)	32
Wisconsin (1989)	4% one child; 14% 2 children; 43% 3 children
Nonrefundable credits	
Illinois (2000)	5
Iowa (1990)	6.5
Maine (2000)	5
Oregon (1997)	5
Rhode Island (1975)	25.5

Source: Johnson (2001, particularly Table 4). Adoption years are from Dickert-Conlin and Houser (2002), which in turn are from Johnson.

Note: State names are followed by year adopted (in parentheses).

[a]A Maryland taxpayer may claim a refundable credit or a nonrefundable credit (equal to 50 percent of the federal credit), but not both.

[b]Minnesota's credit for families with children, unlike the other credits shown in the table, is not expressly structured as a percentage of the federal credit. Depending on income levels, the credit may range from 22 percent to 46 percent of the federal credit.

two children, and 43 percent of the federal credit for taxpayers with three or more children. This schedule was developed with explicit reference to the higher incomes needed to keep families with three or more children out of poverty. The Minnesota schedule includes a second phase-in range to combat the problem that increases in wages or hours for certain minimum-wage workers made them no better off because of the loss of cash assistance and food stamps and increases in taxes (see Johnson 2001, page 21, for more details).

The state credits in combination with the federal credit can be substantial. A family with three or more children earning $9,600 in Wisconsin, for example, could receive a combined state and federal EITC of $5,457, or a 57 percent supplement to their earned income.

3.2.2   Interaction with Other Social Welfare Programs

The tax system operates independently of transfer programs, so there is relatively little interaction between the EITC and other programs. In 1979 (as part of a technical corrections bill) Congress required both advance and lump-sum EITC payments to be treated as earned income for AFDC, food stamp, and Supplemental Security Income (SSI) recipients. The 1981 tax legislation went even further in requiring welfare agencies to assume that individuals eligible for both the EITC and AFDC received the EITC incrementally through the year, thus likely lowering AFDC and food stamp benefits. In 1984 this position was reversed and states were allowed to reduce AFDC benefits only when they could verify that individuals actually received the EITC. The 1990 tax legislation prohibited the counting of the EITC as income or as a resource in the month received or in the following month when determining eligibility for AFDC, Medicaid, food stamps, SSI, and low-income housing benefits. Finally, the 1993 Mickey Leland Hunger Act prohibited counting the EITC for the first twelve months after receipt for food stamp eligibility and benefits. Beyond these time intervals, the EITC could cause potential recipients to fail program asset tests.

Since the abolition of AFDC, it has not yet become clear how the EITC will interact with state TANF programs. There are two major issues. First, states now have the authority to count the EITC as income when determining eligibility for their welfare programs. Second, many TANF programs contain employer subsidies and other job-related activities, which may or may not trigger tax obligations and potential EITC payments. The 1997 budget bill made clear that the EITC could not be claimed on income resulting from "community service" and "work experience" jobs funded under TANF. Other situations will be judged by their "facts and circumstances" under the general welfare doctrine.[15] The law is not yet well developed in this area.

3.2.3 Quality Control and Noncompliance

Relative to alternative delivery mechanisms, the EITC is inexpensive to administer. Most EITC recipients would be required to file a tax return even in the absence of the credit, so the marginal cost of obtaining the EITC is simply the small cost of filling out Schedule EIC. The cost to the IRS is also quite small. The IRS has a budget of roughly $8 billion to serve some 120 million individual taxpayers and 15 million corporations. The incremental cost of administering the EITC is surely a very small fraction of this total. The costs of administering two other major income-support programs for low-income families are much higher. Administrative costs in fiscal year (FY) 1995 were $3.7 billion for food stamps and $3.5 billion for AFDC, although a significant portion of those costs also paid for client services.

A system based largely on self-assessment (like the U.S. income tax) will

---

15. A loose description of the general welfare doctrine is that if payments are made for the general welfare, meaning that payments are public support for a disadvantaged family, they are not taxable and do not trigger the EITC. If payments are more job-related, they are less likely to be viewed as payments made to support the general welfare and more like compensation for services rendered. In this case they would be taxable and trigger the EITC.

have lower administrative costs than a more bureaucratic approach, but it will also have higher noncompliance. The most recent study of EITC noncompliance examined returns filed in 2000 (for tax year 1999) and found that of the $31.3 billion claimed in EITC, between $8.5 and $9.9 billion, or 27.0 to 31.7 percent of the total, exceeded the amount to which taxpayers were eligible (IRS 2002a).

Of the errors the IRS was able to classify, roughly half involve qualifying-child errors.[16] About half of these arose because the child claimed was not the taxpayer's qualifying child. Of these errors, the most common problem was that EITC-qualifying children failed to live for at least six months (see footnote 8 for the rules applying to foster children) with the taxpayer who was claiming the child. Reasons for mistakes of this type can run the gamut from innocent taxpayers running afoul of complex IRS rules to fraud. Consider, for example, a divorced couple whose divorce agreement gives the dependency exemption to the noncustodial parent, who in turn is regularly paying child support. Since the noncustodial parent receives the dependency exemption, that parent could easily assume that he or she could also claim the child to receive the EITC if he or she is otherwise qualified. But in this case the claim would be inappropriate, since the child does not live with the claimant for more than six months. In the category of clear noncompliance, consider the situation described in the ethnographic study of Romich and Weisner (2000). They write that "one woman relies on her mother to baby-sit her younger daughter every weekend. The grandmother also buys school clothes for the child. In return for this care, the grandmother 'gets hers back at the end of the year' by (illegally) filing the child as her dependent and receiving an EITC" (p. 1256).

Two other sources of qualifying-child errors arise with the adjusted gross income (AGI) tiebreaker and relationship rules. The AGI tiebreaker rule stipulated that if two people could legitimately claim the same EITC-qualifying child (such as a mother and grandmother in the same house), the one with the greater income was supposed to. Something like a tiebreaker rule is necessary to establish legitimacy in cases where more than one taxpayer claims the credit based on the same child. But it led to outcomes where, for example, a parent who lived and cared for a child could not claim the child because the child's grandparent also lived in the house and had a higher income. The AGI tiebreaker rule was simplified beginning in 2002 and now applies only if two taxpayers actually claim the same EITC-qualifying child. This change should significantly reduce errors related to the AGI tiebreaker rules, which accounted for 17.2 percent of all errors in 1999. The relationship test is violated when the person claiming the EITC-qualifying child is not the child's parent (including the parent of an adopted child, stepchild, or foster child) or grandparent.

---

16. Also see McCubbin (2000), Scholz (1997), U.S. General Accounting Office (1998), and Holtzblatt (1991) for discussions of earlier EITC compliance studies.

The IRS found that 21.4 percent of overclaims resulted from income-reporting errors. These problems may arise from both underreporting and overreporting income (including underreporting of investment income, which could make a taxpayer ineligible for the EITC). This category also includes situations where a married couple living together chooses to file two separate tax returns (perhaps two head-of-household returns, or one head-of-household and one single return), strategically splitting their incomes and children to maximize the EITC.

Another source of EITC errors arose in situations where the taxpayer filed as single or head of household but should have used the married-filing-separate status. Like other sources of error, these can range from the innocent to blatant. For example, the custodial parent in a married couple that separates but does not get a divorce should, in some cases, file a joint or married-filing-separate return rather than file as a head of household, where they may be more likely to be eligible for the credit.[17] Only the savviest taxpayers would likely understand these rules.

Several EITC changes since the 1999 compliance study may have beneficial effects on EITC compliance. One that has already been mentioned is the change to the AGI tiebreaker test.[18] Another initiative was put in place as part of the 1997 budget agreement, in which Congress directed the secretaries of the Treasury and Health and Human Services to jointly use the Federal Case Registry (FCR) of Child Support Orders to improve the accuracy of EITC claims. The FCR typically identifies a child, the custodial parent, and a noncustodial parent. Since a large fraction of EITC errors arise in cases where someone other than the person living with the child is claiming the child for EITC purposes, the FCR has the potential to allow the IRS to identify a substantial number of noncompliant cases, where previously they had no useful information to scrutinize residence claims about EITC-qualifying children. It is too early to know whether the FCR's apparent potential can be realized, although the system will be used by the IRS to target prerefund audits in 2002 and Congress has given the IRS authority to treat an EITC claim by a noncustodial parent as a "math error" during return processing beginning in 2004.[19]

The rate of EITC noncompliance appears higher than the overall U.S. tax gap, where it is estimated that 17 percent of total taxes are not paid (Internal Revenue Service 1996).[20] Although compliance appears to be very

17. See Holtzblatt and Rebelein (1999, p. 8) for a discussion of the "abandoned spouses" rules.

18. Income and foster child definitions have also been simplified.

19. Whereas the FCR would appear to be a promising compliance tool, the data in the registry could be low quality; living arrangements could be fluid, making the FCR data insufficiently up-to-date; or it could be infeasible or inefficient (from a cost-benefit standpoint) to use FCR data during processing to stop questionable refund claims before money is paid out. Once inappropriate EITC claims are paid out, it is very difficult to get the money back.

20. There is some question about the reliability of the tax gap estimates since the underlying data are from 1988.

high for wage and salary income, presumably because of third-party information reporting, compliance rates on self-employment income, sales of business property, certain types of capital income, and income earned in the informal sector are comparable to and in some cases far worse than EITC compliance rates.

3.3   Program Statistics

Table 3.3 provides information on the maximum real EITC benefit (in 1999 dollars) over time, real expenditures, and caseloads since the credit was established in 1975. For the first sixteen years of the credit, the real value of the maximum EITC never exceeded its 1975 value by more than $10. Real spending on the credit increased sharply starting with the 1986 EITC ex-

Table 3.3	Maximum Real EITC Credit, Real Spending, and Number of Participants (in 1999 dollars)		
Year	Real Maximum EITC ($)	Real EITC Spending ($ millions)	Number of Claimants (thousands)
1975	1,239	3,871	6,215
1976	1,171	3,792	6,473
1977	1,100	3,098	5,627
1978	1,022	2,678	5,192
1979	1,147	4,709	7,135
1980	1,011	4,015	6,954
1981	916	3,504	6,717
1982	863	3,064	6,395
1983	836	3,002	7,368
1984	802	2,626	6,376
1985	852	3,233	7,432
1986	836	3,054	7,156
1987	1,248	4,973	8,738
1988	1,231	8,303	11,148
1989	1,223	8,861	11,696
1990	1,215	9,614	12,542
1991	1,511	13,584	13,665
1992	1,643	15,470	14,097
1993	1,742	17,913	15,117
1994	2,842	23,725	19,017
1995	3,400	28,374	19,334
1996	3,776	30,607	19,464
1997	3,795	31,800	19,490
1998	3,839	31,959	19,516
1999	3,816	32,270	19,419
2000	3,762	31,471	19,363

Source: U.S. House of Representatives (1998) and general IRS statistics of income data on individuals available at [http://www.irs.ustreas.gov/prod/tax_stats/soi/ind_gss.html].

Note: The data reflect claims (allowed through math error processing) and do not reflect subsequent IRS enforcement actions after math error processing.

pansion. Prior to 1986, the EITC cost between $2.6 and $4.7 billion. The 1986 expansion roughly doubled total spending on the credit by increasing the maximum credit (to make up for the loss in the value of the credit due to inflation), indexing the credit, and extending its phaseout range. The credit rate, maximum credit, and spending increased every year from 1990 through 1996 as a consequence of the three-year phase-ins of the 1990 and 1993 EITC increases. Real EITC spending more than tripled in the 1990s.

The evolution of the number of EITC claimants shown in table 3.3 closely mirrors the changes in EITC statutes and, to a lesser extent, business cycle changes. Between 5.2 and 7.4 million taxpayers claimed the credit between 1975 and 1986. By extending EITC eligibility to taxpayers with incomes up to an indexed level of $18,576 in 1988, the 1986 EITC changes increased the number of EITC recipients by roughly 50 percent. The phased-in 1990 expansions also modestly increased the income thresholds that determine EITC eligibility, so the number of recipients increased by roughly 1 million per year from 1990 to 1993. The number of claimants increased by roughly 4 million as a consequence of the childless-worker credit that became available for the first time in 1994. Possibly due in part to increased compliance efforts, the number of EITC claimants has been constant since 1995, despite the increasing labor force participation rate of single-parent families.

It appears that the EITC reaches a large percentage of its intended beneficiaries. Scholz (1994) used matched data from tax returns and the Survey of Income and Program Participation (SIPP) to calculate that 80 to 86 percent of taxpayers eligible for the EITC appeared to receive it in 1990.[21] Developments since 1990 have an ambiguous effect on EITC participation rates. The maximum credit has increased sharply since then, from $1,215 to around $3,800 in 1999 dollars, and the credit extends further up in the income distribution, where filing propensities are high. The IRS, state agencies, and nonprofit organizations have also expanded outreach efforts. However, there has been a steady increase in labor force participation of single women with children (Meyer and Rosenbaum 2000, 2001), and new workers in this group presumably have lower filing propensities than typical workers in the population. Hill et al. (1999), for example, suggest that EITC participation rates for single mothers who recently had been on AFDC in California were in the range of 42 to 54 percent in 1993 and 1994. In addition, the IRS no longer will intervene (as it did until the early 1990s) and award the credit when taxpayers file and appear eligible but do not take the credit. Instead, the IRS sends a letter to taxpayers encouraging them to consider filing an amended return. EITC compliance efforts may also have discouraged some eligible taxpayers from claiming the credit.

The IRS (2002b) used data from the Current Population Survey (CPS)

21. Blumenthal, Erard, and Ho (1999) present similar participation rates for 1988, making use of detailed audit data from the 1988 Taxpayer Compliance Measurement Program.

matched to tax returns and data from the SIPP for calendar year 1996 to estimate that, of the households that appeared to be eligible for the EITC, between 82.2 and 87.2 percent filed tax returns and hence either claimed the EITC or likely received a notice from the IRS telling them they may have been eligible. These calculations suggest that the EITC changes between 1990 and 1996 had relatively little net effect on EITC participation.

Liebman (2000) uses matched data from the 1990 CPS and tax returns to examine the characteristics of EITC-eligible taxpayers. He writes (p. 1178):

> 50 percent of eligible 1990 EITC taxpayers are married, while 30 percent are formerly married, and 20 percent have never been married. A little more than half are white, a quarter are Black, and 18 percent are Hispanic. Of eligible EITC recipients, 74 percent have a high school education or less; 44 percent live in the South; and 36 percent live in a central city. Fifty-eight percent work 1500 hours or more, though this average is brought down by married couples in which one spouse does not work. Sixteen percent of eligible EITC tax returns are filed by individuals in households that receive welfare income during the year and 26 percent are in households receiving food stamps.

It is difficult to predict how the characteristics of EITC participants have evolved between 1990 and now. The income threshold at which the EITC is fully phased out has increased from $20,000 to over $30,000 (nominal) dollars since 1990. Many taxpayers have incomes in that range, so it is likely that EITC recipients appear somewhat more affluent than what Liebman found. At the same time, labor force participation rates of single women with children have increased over this period, and many of these new workers have low levels of human capital.

3.3.1 Antipoverty Effects, Target Efficiency, Distributional Impact

The EITC was available in 2001 only to taxpayers with earned income and adjusted gross income less than $32,121 if they had more than one qualifying child, $28,281 if they had one qualifying child, and $10,708 if they had no qualifying children. Scholz and Levine (2001) calculate that in April 1997 over 60 percent of EITC payments went to taxpayers with pre-EITC incomes below the poverty line and roughly half of total payments directly reduced the poverty gap.[22] Liebman (1997a) plots density functions for EITC payments following the 1993 expansion that show a right-skewed distribution, centered at roughly $13,000, with most payments going to families with incomes between $7,000 and $26,000.[23]

Figure 3.3 presents data from 1999 tax returns on the distribution of

---

22. The U.S. Department of Health and Human Services poverty guidelines for 2002 are $8,860 for a one-person family, $11,940 for two-person families, $15,020 for three-person families, and $18,100 for four-person families.

23. Burkhauser, Couch, and Glenn (1996) compare the distributional effects of the EITC and minimum wage. They show the EITC is much more "target efficient" than minimum wage increases, if the objective of policy is to increase incomes of low-income workers.

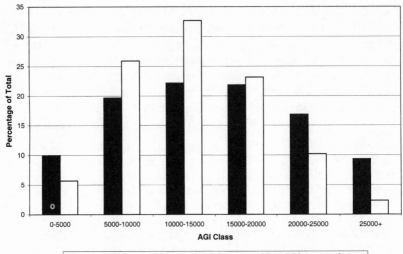

Fig. 3.3   Distribution of total EITC returns and EITC payments of families with children, by AGI, 1999

Source: "Individual Income Tax Returns, 1999," available at [http://www.irs.gov/taxstats/display/0,,i1%3D40%26genericId%3D16882,00.html] (99INDTR.EXE, posted 28 January 2002), and authors' calculations.

EITC returns and payments by adjusted gross income class for EITC claimants with children. Roughly 23 percent of claimants are in the phase-in range of the credit, and they receive 24 percent of total payments. Roughly 19 percent are in the flat range, and they receive 26 percent of total payments. The remaining 58 percent of claimants are in the phaseout range of the credit; they receive roughly half of total payments. Of the 19.3 million total EITC claims in 1999, 3.2 million had no qualifying children and claimed $0.6 billion, 7.8 million had one qualifying child and claimed $12.0 billion, and 8.2 million had two or more and claimed $19.3 billion. Data are not available for the distribution of EITC claims by filing status.

Because the EITC is based on annual family income and not wages, it is possible that people with high hourly wages who, for some reason or another, choose to work relatively few annual hours could receive the credit. In fact, the evidence suggests that in low-wage labor markets, incomes and wages are tightly linked. Scholz (1996) describes tabulations from SIPP showing that roughly two-thirds of EITC payments go to taxpayers with wages in the bottom 25th percentile of all workers with children (below $6.43 per hour) and more than 95 percent of all EITC benefits are paid to workers with wages below the median of $9.42 per hour. Liebman (1997a) reports that in 1990, 75 percent of EITC recipients worked at least 1,000 hours and 60 percent worked more than 1,500 hours per year. Incomes and wages are now even more tightly linked for EITC recipients since EITC-eligible taxpayers cannot have more than $2,350 of capital (and net capital gains) income.

Liebman (1997a) also presents calculations that provide an interesting perspective on the importance of the EITC in low-wage labor markets. Between 1976 and 1996, the share of income received by the lowest fifth of the population fell from 4.4 percent to 3.7 percent. The share received by the top 5 percent increased from 16.0 percent to 21.4 percent over that period. Liebman's calculations show that for households with children, the EITC offsets 29 percent of the decline in incomes in the 1st quintile of the population and 9 percent of the decline in the 2nd quintile.

A more direct measure of the EITC's importance is that in 1997 and 1998 it removed 4.3 million persons from poverty (Council of Economic Advisers 1998, 2000). Recalling President Clinton's antipoverty goal for the EITC, a full-time (2,000 hours) minimum-wage worker heading a single-parent, two-child family would earn $10,300 in wages and be eligible for a $3,656 EITC in 1997. The poverty line for this family was $12,802.[24] The combination of full-time minimum wage work and the EITC for a family of three in 1986 was $7,226, while the poverty line was $8,737. A full-time minimum-wage worker receiving the EITC and heading a family of three in 1975, the first year of the EITC, would have had an income of $107 above the poverty line of $4,293.

3.4 Review of Behavioral Issues

In this section we consider several conceptual issues related to the behavioral effects of the EITC.

3.4.1 Program Participation: Claiming the EITC

Perhaps the most basic behavioral issue associated with the EITC is whether *eligible* taxpayers actually file tax returns to receive it. At first glance the analytic underpinnings of this decision appear straightforward: The benefit of filing for the credit is the dollar value of the EITC. The costs include the transactions costs associated with filing a return (for those who would not otherwise file) and gathering the necessary information to claim the EITC (or resources to pay a professional tax preparer). These cost-benefit considerations lead to straightforward implications. Claiming the credit becomes more likely in cases where the potential credit is larger and where the filer's familiarity with the program and the U.S. tax system is greater.

---

24. A married family with two children would have had an EITC and earnings of $13,956, and the poverty line was $16,400. We look at 1997 since this is the most recent minimum wage increase. Given the absence of minimum-wage indexing, full-time minimum-wage work supplemented by the EITC after 1997 will be a smaller percentage of the poverty line than in 1997.

From the work of Holtzblatt (1991), McCubbin (2000), and others, however, we know that a significant fraction of taxpayers receive the EITC when they are not technically eligible. Thus, a focus on participation among eligibles may, in some circumstances, be too narrow. For policymakers and scholars interested in overall EITC participation, participation and compliance issues are intertwined. Even when thinking about participation of eligibles, participation and compliance are linked, since legitimate current-year claims, for example, may lead to scrutiny of past tax returns or the possibility that funds may be garnished to cover defaulted student loans, past taxes, or child support.

Compliance issues can usefully be thought of in the classic tax evasion framework of Allingham and Sandmo (1972). Taxpayers will adopt an optimal reporting strategy, weighing the trade-off between the return to misreporting a dollar of income and the corresponding increased risks of detection and penalty. Interestingly for the case of the EITC, some taxpayers may gain by *overreporting* income, a situation the IRS has little experience with.[25] Also, unlike the classic tax evasion model that focuses on income reporting, a central issue with EITC noncompliance has to do with the residence of the qualifying child. The IRS (until recently, perhaps) has had little information with which to examine these claims.

3.4.2   The Decision to Work and Hours of Work

As noted in both the introduction and the political history of the EITC, one of the arguments frequently given for the EITC is that it provides stronger work incentives than the NIT or entitlement programs like AFDC, food stamps, and Medicaid. This assessment, although true in a comparative sense, obscures a complicated set of work and labor supply incentives created by the EITC for different household structures and individuals at different parts of the income distribution. As a result of these complicated incentives, the overall effect of the EITC on hours of work is ambiguous.

The simplest framework in which to consider the work incentive effects of the EITC is the static labor-leisure model displayed in figure 3.4. In this stylized setting, the EITC creates, for eligible households, an expanded budget constraint, shifting out the constraint from ade to $abcde$. The phase-in region is represented by the segment ab, the flat region by bc, and the phaseout region by cd. Consider the implications for individuals who do not work, whose well-being is indexed by utility level, U_0^I, in the absence of the EITC. As illustrated in figure 3.4, the introduction of the EITC induces such individuals to enter the labor force and work, and their utility increases to U_1^I from U_0^I. The EITC creates an incentive for these nonworkers to enter the labor force since it increases the marginal value of

---

25. Steuerle (1991) has referred to this phenomenon as the "superterranean economy."

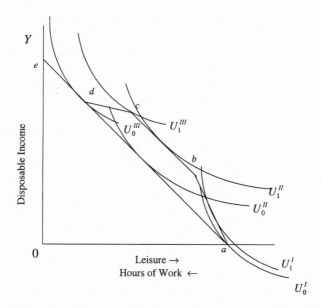

Fig. 3.4   Effects of the EITC on labor force participation and hours of work

working by raising the effective wage. More formally, the rise in the effective wage rate due to the EITC for individuals initially out of the labor force results in only a positive substitution effect and no income effect.

Figure 3.4 also displays preferences for two additional types of individuals, indexed by II and III, who, in the absence of the EITC (or other social programs), would participate in the labor force. As can be seen, the introduction of an EITC program does not alter their decision to work. Thus, the incentive effects of the EITC with respect to labor force participation are unambiguously positive: The EITC will encourage some workers to enter the labor force and should not induce individuals, low-skilled or otherwise, to leave it. This result stands in contrast to the labor force participation predictions that arise with programs related to the NIT (like AFDC), where a guaranteed benefit at zero hours of work creates incentives for some people to leave the labor force.

At the same time, the predicted effect of an EITC from the simple static labor-leisure model on the *extent* of work (i.e., number of hours of work) is ambiguous. As figure 3.4 illustrates, this is because of the differential effects that the credit has in its flat and phaseout regions. The EITC structure implies different marginal returns to work (i.e., effective marginal wage rates) for different parts of the preprogram income distribution. For type II individuals, who would participate in the labor force in the absence of the EITC, the introduction of the EITC does not change the value of their time in the labor market and only alters the income they can receive through the tax credit. Thus, there is only an income effect associated with the introduction of the EITC for type II individuals. Whether this income effect is negative (leisure is a normal good) or positive is not clear a priori. The empirical evidence on income effects associated with labor supply decisions suggests that leisure is a normal good, so, as illustrated in figure 3.4, the EITC may result in a reduction of hours of work for this type of individual.

The phaseout region of the EITC is relevant for the type III individuals in figure 3.4. These individuals, as drawn, have an incentive to reduce their hours of work enough so that they actually receive a credit. This final case illustrates the potentially negative effect on hours that is generated in the phaseout region of the EITC. There the EITC implies a *lower* effective wage rate relative to the absence of the EITC, which, by itself, results in a negative substitution effect. In addition, there is an income effect that, if negative, will lead to a further reduction in hours of work.

The above considerations suggest that the consequences of the EITC expansions for affecting the work behavior of low-income workers are more complicated than the commonly held view that the EITC is prowork. In particular, the labor market effects of the credit depend on the distribution of taxpayers within the credit's ranges and the degree to which people in and out of the labor market respond to incentives. On the former issue, as noted earlier, around 77 percent of EITC recipients will have incomes that fall in the flat or phaseout range of the credit, which raises the concern that the EITC may lead to a net reduction in the labor supplied by low-income workers. The latter issue concerning the responsiveness to the "effective" wage and income changes associated with the EITC expansions also cannot be resolved a priori. It is an empirical matter. Below, we discuss the empirical evidence to date on the magnitudes of these effects.

The simple model illustrated in figure 3.4 focuses on the behavioral effects for individuals and ignores an important feature of the U.S. tax code applicable to the EITC. *Married* couples generally file joint tax returns and, thus, the AGI subject to taxes depends on their combined income and not the separate incomes of each spouse. The fact that families, rather than individuals, are the unit of analysis for the tax system has consequences for the effective wage rates of secondary earners, which is an issue made even more important by the EITC. To see this, consider the following example discussed in Eissa and Hoynes (1998).

Suppose that the husband earns $11,650 (in 1997) and that the couple makes its time allocation decisions sequentially, with the wife taking actions under the assumption that her husband's income is given. In this case, the family will receive the maximum credit of $3,656 (assuming the couple has two children) if the wife does not participate in the labor force. If she does participate, the family's credit, at the margin, will be reduced by $0.21 and that dollar will be subject to the Social Security payroll tax of $0.142

percent and any state taxes. Consequently, her marginal tax rate is at least 35 percent; that is, her effective wage rate will be only 65 percent of her gross wage rate.

This lowering of the wife's effective wage provides an incentive for the wife *not* to participate in the labor force, even though the presence of an EITC might induce her husband to enter the labor force. Furthermore, if she works, she has an incentive to reduce her hours of work in the presence of the EITC (compared to no EITC) due to lowering of her effective wage (inducing a substitution effect) and to the higher income the family receives from the EITC (inducing an income effect). Note that the ambiguous effect of the EITC on the labor force participation choice of one of the spouses does not hinge on the sequential decision-making assumption noted above. Under a more general model of joint decision-making, the greater the disparity in the gross wage rates and/or tastes for nonwork time across spouses, the greater the incentive for an expansion of the EITC to induce one of the spouses to *not* participate in the labor force. Again, the importance of this potential work disincentive effect of the EITC depends on the magnitudes of the labor supply and labor force participation wage elasticities of husbands and wives, on the degree to which people correctly perceive tax incentives, and on the distributions of their wage rates relative to the phase-in, flat, and phaseout regions of the EITC. We examine empirical evidence on the labor force participation and labor supply effects of the EITC for married couples below.

3.4.3 Marriage and Fertility

The previous discussion of the potential for differential effects of the EITC by marital status raises an important issue about the potential effects of the EITC on family structure. As noted above, the tax treatment of married couples is different from that of single parents or individuals, which leads to situations where a married couple may face larger total tax liabilities than they would pay if they separated. Similarly, two unmarried people may pay lower taxes than they would if they got married. This is the well-known "marriage penalty" that has been the focus of attention in the public finance literature and policy circles.[26] In practice, marriage penalties tend to accrue to two-earner couples if both partners have similar earnings, and marriage bonuses tend to accrue to couples if the partners have disparate earnings or only one earner. Two recent studies have suggested that the EITC and its expansions over the last ten years are an important contributing source of the marriage penalty (see Dickert-Conlin and Houser 1998 and Holtzblatt and Rebelein 1999). For example, Holtzblatt and

26. See Feenberg and Rosen (1995), Alm and Whittington (1995), U.S. Congressional Budget Office (1997), and Bull et al. (1999). The general statement of the problem is that the tax system cannot simultaneously be progressive, treat the family as the unit of taxation, and be neutral with respect to marriage.

Rebelein (1999) estimated that the EITC increased the net marriage penalties in the individual income tax by between $3.6 and $9.9 billion in 2000, depending on the specific assumptions, and that these EITC-related net penalties accounted for 10.0 to 31.7 percent of the total net projected marriage penalties.

A natural question to ask is whether changes in the EITC are likely to affect rates of marriage and divorce among the poor. That is, the EITC may decrease the incentive for single parents to marry by providing resources to families with children. The credit also provides fairly substantial incentives for some people to marry and others to separate or not marry. This potential for the EITC to influence marital status is reminiscent of the concerns about the effects of other public assistance programs, most notably the AFDC program, on marriage and the incidence of female headship.[27] To date, much less attention has been paid in the literature to the impacts of the EITC on marital status than to those of other assistance programs.

A related question arises as to whether the structure of the EITC also may affect the fertility decisions of households. As noted in section 3.2, the EITC was only available to families with children prior to 1994, and, even now, the maximum credit available to families with children is much larger than that available to childless taxpayers. In addition, households with two or more children were able to claim a higher EITC than households with only one child, starting in 1991. Both of these EITC features constitute a modest pronatalist incentive for taxpayers. There is a substantial literature that examines the effects of AFDC on fertility, especially on out-of-wedlock births.[28] Furthermore, studies have found nonnegligible effects of provisions of the tax code, namely the presence and generosity of the dependent exemptions, on fertility and the timing of birth (see Whittington, Alm, and Peters 1990 and Dickert-Conlin and Chandra 1999).

There is no direct empirical evidence on whether EITC fertility incentives have actually influenced behavior. The question, however, is important for two reasons. First, the effects of policy on fertility are of general interest as part of an effort to assess the potential for unintended consequences of tax policy. Second, many of the methods used by researchers to isolate the effects of the EITC on other behaviors, especially labor supply, hinge crucially on the assumption that the EITC expansions have had no effects on the fertility of couples. We return to this issue below.

3.4.4   Consumption Behavior and Income Smoothing

The fundamental tenet of the life-cycle consumption model is that utility-maximizing households will vary their consumption and saving so as to

---

27. See Moffitt (1998) for a discussion of this issue and a summary of the empirical evidence on it.
28. Again, see Moffitt (1998) for a summary of that literature and its findings.

equate the marginal utility of consumption across periods. To do this, families typically save in periods when income is unusually high and borrow when income is unusually low. Families eligible for the EITC generally have lower incomes and are younger than other taxpayers. Thus, one would expect EITC-eligible households to include many who would like to borrow.

There is evidence, however, that some of these families that would like to borrow are unable to do so.[29] For these liquidity-constrained families, the EITC could enhance utility more than it would for an otherwise equivalent consumer who was not liquidity-constrained. The EITC advance payment option might seem like a particularly important feature for credit-constrained taxpayers. By delivering a portion of the EITC incrementally with every paycheck, it presumably offers families an enhanced ability to smooth the marginal utility of consumption.[30] As we discuss below, however, only 1.1 percent of EITC recipients took advantage of the advance payment option in 1998, although "refund anticipation loans" (with very high implied interest rates) are popular.

Further evidence of credit constraints among the EITC-eligible population might be inferred from unusual patterns of seasonality in consumption. In particular, most EITC payments are received in February and March of each year (Barrow and McGranahan 2000). Since these payments can be a large fraction of a family's quarterly income, one might expect to see a corresponding increase in consumption for credit-constrained families. Souleles (1999), for example, presents evidence based on consumption Euler equations for the entire population that is consistent with tax refunds' influencing the seasonality of consumption, which in turn is consistent with the existence of liquidity-constrained consumers.

Consumption-related issues also arise if one steps away from the canonical life-cycle model of consumption. Thaler (1994) and others have argued that self-control problems are pervasive in the economy. If rules of thumb, habit, innumeracy, or other psychological factors have a dominant influence on economic behavior, the forward-looking model of utility-maximizing consumers may not do a particularly good job of characterizing economic behavior. In this case, it is possible that self-control problems or other factors prevent families from accumulating resources that might

29. Jappelli (1990) looks at direct measures from the 1983 Survey of Consumer Finances and finds that roughly 20 percent of the population appears to be constrained. Also see Jappelli, Pischke, and Souleles (1998).

30. Taxpayers can receive a portion of their EITC incrementally throughout the year via the advance payment option. They do this by filing Form W-5 with their employers, who then include the advance payment in their regular paycheck (the employers are held harmless because they reduce payroll tax remittances to the government). To reduce the possibility that advanced EITC payments will lead to an end-of-year tax liability, advance payments are limited to 60 percent of the maximum credit available to families with one child. Taxpayers receiving the advance payment are obligated to file at the end of the year to reconcile their tax liabilities.

allow them to enhance their long-run economic well-being. The lump-sum EITC may therefore provide a substantial one-time payment that can be used to purchase a car, enhance human capital, or move out of an undesirable neighborhood (and in doing so break a cycle of economic deprivation). It is difficult to develop and test rigorous formulations of nonoptimizing consumption behavior.

3.5   Review of Evidence on the Behavioral Effects of the EITC

In this section, we summarize the empirical evidence concerning the effects of changes in the EITC on a range of behavioral outcomes. We begin by discussing empirical studies of EITC take-up (or participation) decisions and what is known about the extent of noncompliance in actual claims of the credit. We then summarize the literature on the effects of the EITC expansions on labor force behavior, including labor force participation and labor supply decisions. Most of the empirical investigations of the EITC have focused on the latter set of behaviors. We discuss the econometric approaches taken in these studies and consider their potential shortcomings. We then provide a summary of the less extensive literature on the effects of the EITC on other behaviors, including marriage and living arrangements, human capital investment decisions, and consumption decisions, commenting on the importance of expanding on these studies in future work.

3.5.1   Evidence on EITC Participation and Noncompliance

It would be helpful to policymakers to know what fraction of EITC nonparticipation (among eligible taxpayers) is due to information barriers and what fraction is due to purposeful nonparticipation. The decision of individuals or households to participate in the EITC entails at least two choices: Households must work and have income below the EITC breakeven thresholds, and households must file a tax return to claim the credit.

As mentioned in section 3.4, there are three studies of EITC participation among eligibles: Scholz (1994) for 1990; Blumenthal, Erard, and Ho (1999) for tax year 1988; and IRS (2002b) for tax year 1996. None of the studies model the EITC participation decision based a formal optimizing model. Scholz (1994) presents reduced-form regressions of factors correlated with nonparticipation. He finds some evidence, based on his analysis of linked data from the 1990 SIPP and tax returns, that factors like working in the household service sector or being eligible for a small EITC were positively correlated with not claiming the credit when eligible. The question is still open, however, about the degree to which EITC participation can be increased by additional outreach and information.

Formally modeling the decision to claim the EITC will require one to confront several information and noncompliance issues. There is mixed anecdotal evidence on the degree to which taxpayers are aware of the EITC.[31] The only systematic evidence comes from Phillips (2001), who presents tabulations from the 1999 National Survey of America's Families showing that roughly two-thirds of Americans have heard about the EITC. Past welfare recipients and parents with incomes near the poverty line were among the most knowledgeable.

The degree of awareness of the credit is critical for some issues and less important for others. The credit could, for example, significantly increase labor force participation even if people know little about it as long as workers have some understanding that the tax system rewards work at low levels of earnings. The link between the marginal incentives of the credit shown in figure 3.2 and the labor supply decisions discussed in figure 3.4 depends on people understanding the specific incentives inherent in the credit's structure. Given the lag between labor market decisions and receipt of the credit, which can be as much as sixteen months, informational considerations suggest that the credit's effect on participation may be larger than its effect on hours, compared to a world where taxpayers have perfect knowledge of the credit.

Informational issues are probably less fundamental when thinking about EITC participation among taxpayers eligible for the credit. Scholz (1997) reports that roughly 95 percent of EITC claimants are either legally required to file tax returns or would file to recover overwithheld taxes, so most eligible taxpayers would get into the system even in the absence of the EITC. In 1996, 56.5 percent of claimants used paid tax preparers, who surely are aware of the credit. The IRS also has a policy of notifying all taxpayers who do not claim the credit but appear to be eligible for it based on their filing information that they may be eligible and can file an amended return to claim the credit.

Behavioral work on overall EITC participation and noncompliance must take into consideration three central facts. First, there appears to be little scope for overstating EITC claims by systematic, ongoing misreporting of wage and salary income. The IRS, using information returns filed by employers, can in principle corroborate wage and salary reports.[32]

Second, there appear to be ample opportunities to misreport self-

---

31. Liebman (1997a) suggests that awareness of the credit might be quite low. Smeeding, Ross-Philips, and O'Connor (2000) and Romich and Weisner (2000) find greater awareness, although the former study is based on a sample seeking help with tax preparation and the latter is based on a small sample from Project New Hope, a work-based welfare reform project in Milwaukee.

32. The IRS (1996) reports that, in aggregate, net underreporting on wage and salary income was 0.9 percent, lower than any items other than state tax refunds (at 0.8 percent). Wage and salary errors related to EITC can still occur because claimants may not realize that employers provide independent information to the IRS, may unintentionally omit a Form W-2 for a second job, may wish to use the IRS as a "loan shark" for the period between submitting a claim and being audited (Andreoni 1992), or may wish to take the chance that the IRS will be unable to recover money once it is paid out (and spent).

employment income to strategically manipulate the size of the available EITC, since most forms of self-employment do not include information reporting. McCubbin (2000), however, reports that only a small fraction of EITC noncompliance in 1994 involved self-employment income. In addition, only 17.6 percent of all EITC filers claim any self-employment income, and 54.3 percent of those reporting self-employment income have incomes in the phaseout range of the credit (IRS 1999), so it appears that strategic misreporting of self-employment income is not currently a dominant feature of EITC noncompliance. Perhaps this is because EITC incentives can be complicated for those wishing to strategically manipulate self-employment income. To be effective, would-be tax cheats need to be sophisticated enough to *overstate* self-employment income in the phase-in range of the credit or *understate* self-employment income in the phase-out range.

Third, as pointed out by Liebman (1997a, 2000) and McCubbin (2000), among others, the major area of EITC noncompliance—particularly participation by ineligibles—has to do with qualifying-child errors. This is a particularly difficult area for the IRS to enforce, since information on children (beyond ages and Social Security numbers) is not collected in the tax system.[33] Liebman (1997b) develops the following intuitive idea: If noncompliance is inadvertent, it should not respond to the size of the available credit. He examines this by looking at whether the probability of erroneously claiming a dependent child depends on the tax gain to such a claim (McCubbin 2000 pursues a similar strategy). He estimates that roughly one-third of ineligible claimants in 1988 did so in response to the EITC incentive.

Good compliance studies will be difficult to conduct outside of the Treasury, IRS, or Census Bureau because of data-access limitations. An interesting question for public servants and affiliated scholars at these agencies is whether data gathered for one purpose—for example, administering child support laws—could be useful in reducing erroneous EITC claims. To be useful for tax administration, ways to identify erroneous payments before money goes out must be developed, since once payments are made they are rarely recovered. In addition, the IRS has limited resources, so research is also needed on the cost-effectiveness of alternative ways of improving compliance, focusing on both the EITC and the broader tax system. Although EITC compliance has received considerable scrutiny in recent years, comparable work on other areas of the tax code is badly dated or nonexistent.

---

33. Despite some evidence that error rates are high for certain subgroups—for example, Liebman (2000) reports that roughly one-third of male heads of households did not appear to have children in matched CPS data—audits are expensive, so "hit rates" need to be much higher than one in three for compliance initiatives to pass any sensible cost-benefit test. The U.S. General Accounting Office (2000), for example, reports that 86 percent of EITC claims selected for audit in fiscal year 1999 were, in fact, noncompliant.

New studies documenting changes in EITC participation rates of eligible taxpayers in the late 1990s are needed, given the sharp changes in the credit over the decade and changes in low-wage labor markets. Greater detail on the characteristics of nonparticipants would also be useful, both for outreach and for understanding linkages between programs. These studies would be straightforward, although in order to do them, data rich enough to determine eligibility need to be linked with data indicating whether or not a potentially eligible taxpayer files a return and receives the credit.

3.5.2   Effects of EITC on Labor Force Participation and Labor Supply

Most of the existing empirical investigations have focused on the consequences of the expansion of the EITC for labor force participation rates and hours of work. Most of these studies have sought to estimate the overall, or "reduced-form," effects of the historical expansions of this program on these labor market outcomes. Another strand of these studies focuses on estimating the effects of the EITC with now-standard labor supply models by exploiting the fact that the EITC expansions have varied the effective wages and incomes confronting individuals and households over the last twenty-five years. We also provide a brief discussion of the evidence derived from more structural optimizing models of time allocation and program participation decisions in which household preferences and budget and time constraints are explicitly parameterized.

Reduced-Form Effects of EITC

Reduced-form studies typically exploit statutory EITC changes to assess their effects on behavior. This approach is a time-honored strategy in policy analysis and applied economics, and it is often referred to as "natural experiments" or "difference-in-differences."[34]

Consider the following framework to help clarify the underlying identification issues. Suppose we are interested in estimating the effect of a policy (or bundle of policies) on some outcome, y. In most of the reduced-form studies of the EITC, the identifying variation used comes from the periodic legislative expansions and other changes in the credit. For example, Eissa and Liebman (1996) study the effects of the changes in the EITC contained in the TRA86. Furthermore, as noted above, these changes were not always applicable to everyone in the population. Prior to 1994, childless adults were not eligible to claim the EITC and adults with qualifying children were eligible for the same schedule of credits, whereas, starting in 1994, childless adults were eligible and adults with two or more children were eligible for a more generous credit than adults with only one

---

34. The following discussion draws heavily on Moffitt and Wilhelm (2000). Also see Blundell and MaCurdy (1999), Meyer (1995), and Angrist and Krueger (1999) for other discussions of approaches to estimating the effects of policy interventions.

child. To characterize these sources of policy variation, let $d_t(Q_{it})$ denote the EITC regime prevailing as of period t, where the particular features of the EITC code applicable to the ith individual or household depend on their characteristics, Q_{it} (e.g., presence and number of children). That is:

(1) $d_t(Q_{it}) = \begin{cases} 1 \text{ if individual } i \text{ is eligible for a policy reform that} \\ \text{prevails in period } t, 0 \text{ otherwise} \end{cases}$

Finally, consider the following linear specification of the determinants of behavioral outcomes, y_{it}, such as labor force participation or hours of work,

(2) $y_{it} = \beta d_t(Q_{it}) + \lambda_t X_{it} + \alpha_t + u_{it},$

where X_{it} is a vector of individual and household characteristics that may include Q_{it}, u_{it} is an error term, and β, λ_t, and α_t are parameters to be estimated.

To understand what is required to identify β, the overall effect of the policy change, consider what would be learned if one could assign the values of $d_t(Q_{it})$ by a controlled experiment, where some individuals (experimentals) would face a new policy regime $[d_t(Q_{it}) = 1]$ and others (controls) would not have access to this new regime $[d_t(Q_{it}) = 0]$. It would follow, by design, that $d_t(Q_{it})$ would be uncorrelated with (orthogonal to) u_{it} and, for that matter, to X_{it}. In this case, the standard conditions for consistently estimating the parameters in equation (2) would apply. In fact, in this case, the mean difference in outcomes for experimentals and controls would consistently estimate β.

In the absence of random assignment of individuals to policy regimes, we must rely on temporal changes (or, possibly, locational differences) in policies *and/or* variation in $d_t(Q_{it})$ due to individual differences in Q_{it}. However, these sources of variation, in general, are not sufficient for identifying β. For example, reliance only on the changes in the EITC over time to identify the credit's effect is confounded with other temporal changes in the economy (or environment) that may have influenced the labor supply of the low-income population. Thus, additional assumptions, in conjunction with the availability of certain types of data, are required in order to identify the effects of the EITC. Existing studies of the EITC, and studies of related tax and public assistance policy changes, make use of alternative data sources and assumptions.

Suppose d_t is defined as in equation (1) and assume we have data, either repeated cross-section or panel data, on households for periods t'' and t', where t' denotes a period before an EITC expansion and t'' is a period after the expansion. Furthermore, recall that prior to 1994 the EITC required claimants to have children present to be eligible for the credit. This implies that households without children both *before* and *after* EITC expansions (such as occurred in 1986) were not eligible for the EITC, whereas households with children faced a change in the credit with the expansion. In this case Q_{it} can be represented as an indicator variable, where $Q_{it} = 1$ if children are present in household i and in period t and 0 if not, and $d_t(0) = 0$ for t' and t''. The difference-in-differences estimator of β results from differencing equation (2) for periods t' and t'' for each individual/household:

$$(3) \quad y_{it''} - y_{it'} = \beta[d_{t''}(Q_{it''}) - d_{t'}(Q_{it'})] + \lambda_{t''}X_{it''} - \lambda_{t'}X_{it'} + (u_{it''} - u_{it'}).$$

The validity of the difference-in-differences estimator for β relies on several additional assumptions about Q_{it} and its effects on y in equation (2). The first concerns the nature of independent effects of Q_{it} on y. Recall that we allowed for the possibility that X_{it} includes Q_{it}. In the current context, this amounts to assuming that the presence of children affects the labor supply decisions of parents, an assumption consistent with various behavioral models of optimal time allocation.[35] The standard difference-in-differences estimator maintains either the assumption that Q_{it} is excluded from X_{it} or the less restrictive, but not innocuous, assumption that $\lambda_t = \lambda$, that is, the effect of children on y does not vary with time. Second, the standard difference-in-differences estimator typically assumes that Q_{it} is uncorrelated with u_{it} in equation (2). Note that strict exogeneity of Q_{it} in equation (2) is not required. The consistency of the difference-in-differences estimator holds under weaker assumptions, especially if one is willing to maintain that Q_{it} is a time-invariant variable. (See Moffitt and Wilhelm 2000 for details.) Under these two sets of assumptions, the difference-in-differences estimator of β will be consistent.

As noted earlier, the difference-in-differences studies rely on explicit comparisons between groups that are and are not affected by changes in the EITC. Figure 3.5 plots trends in the labor force participation between 1984 and 1996 (from the March CPS, taken from Meyer and Rosenbaum 2000) for six groups in the population—including households with and without children—that are commonly used to examine the effects of the EITC. It is these trends that the difference-in-differences studies of labor force participation seek to explain.

It is clear from figure 3.5 that labor force participation of three groups commonly used as controls has no discernible trends. Single women with no children and black men, the top two lines in the figure, have high and unchanging rates of labor force participation. Single women who dropped out of high school but have no children also have steady (or even declining) rates of labor force participation. The three groups of women eligible for the EITC all had rising rates of labor force participation, particularly after 1992. These are all single women with children, single women who dropped out of high school and have children, and single women with children under six.

---

35. See Browning (1992) for a discussion of such models and the effects of children.

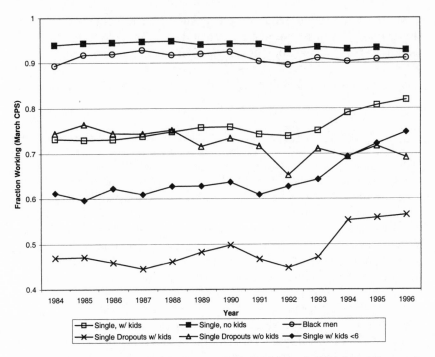

Fig. 3.5   Labor force participation rates, 1984–1996, March CPS, from Meyer and Rosenbaum (2000)

Selected EITC studies of the estimated impacts of the EITC on labor force participation and hours of work are summarized in table 3.4. We first discuss papers adopting the difference-in-differences approach.

Eissa and Liebman (1996) estimate the effects of the 1986 EITC expansion on labor force participation of single women and, conditional on working, their hours of work. To isolate those affected by the policy from those who are not, they treat single women with children as being in the experimental group and single women without children as being in the control group. They find that the 1986 tax reform (including the EITC changes) increased labor force participation among all single women with children by as much as 2.8 percentage points (from a base of 74.2 percent). The effects are much larger (on the order of 6 percentage points) for women with children and less than a high school education.

Eissa and Hoynes (1998) use a similar difference-in-differences estimator to examine the EITC's labor market effects on couples, in addition to an alternative quasi-structural approach discussed below. Recall that the EITC would be expected to have *negative* labor market effects for secondary workers. They find modest negative effects of the EITC on married women's labor force participation, estimating that the EITC expansions

Table 3.4   **Summary of Empirical Evidence on the Effects of the EITC on Labor Force Participation and Hours of Work**

Study	Data Source and Population Covered	Years Covered	Estimation Method Used and Source of Identification	Impact Estimates
Labor force participation (LFP)				
Dickert, Houser, and Scholz (1995; DHS)	SIPP data. Cross-sectional, using state-level variation. Focus on participation effects of single parents and couples. Drop cases with high assets.	1990 calendar year file.	Variation in budget sets is measured by the effects that cross-state variation in tax and transfer rules have on the returns to moving from zero to twenty (forty) hours in the labor market. The responsiveness of LFP to the cross-state variation in budget sets is used to make inferences about EITC expansions.	The 1993 OBRA expansions would increase LFP by 3.3 percentage points for single women from a base of 56.4 percent. This implies the elasticity of LFP with respect to net income is roughly 0.85.[a]
Eissa and Liebman (1996)	Repeated cross sections of the CPS. Focus on single women with children.	1985–87 March CPS for the "pre" period, 1989–91 March CPS for the "post" period	Difference-in-difference. "The difference between the change in labor force participation of single women with children and single women without children is our estimate of the effect of TRA86 on participation."	TRA86 resulted in a 2.8 percentage point increase in labor force participation from a base of 74.2 percent. This implies the elasticity of LFP with respect to net income is roughly 1.16.[b]
Keane and Moffitt (1998) and Keane (1995)	SIPP data. Cross-sectional. The sample is single women with children. Drop cases with high assets.	Fourth wave of the 1994 SIPP	Estimate a structural model taking detailed account of the tax and transfer system on budget sets. Families make hours decisions moving from zero to twenty to forty, and participation decisions for food stamps, AFDC, and housing programs.	Changes in the EITC between 1984 and 1996 would increase labor force participation rates by 10.7 percentage points, from a base of 65.4 percent. This implies the elasticity of LFP with respect to net income is roughly 0.96.[c]

(continued)

Table 3.4 (continued)

Study	Data Source and Population Covered	Years Covered	Estimation Method Used and Source of Identification	Impact Estimates
Meyer and Rosenbaum (2001)	Repeated cross sections of the CPS. Focus on single women with children.	1985–97 March CPS and Merged Outgoing Rotation Group data from 1984–96.	Cross-state variation in budget sets as measured by the effects that cross-state variation in tax and transfer rules have on after-tax wages, where wages are randomly drawn from empirical distributions *and* over-time variation in these rules.	$1,000 reduction in income taxes if a woman works, increases employment by 2.3 to 2.9 percentage points. These imply elasticities of LFP with respect to net income of 0.69 and 0.70. See footnote 35 of Meyer and Rosenbaum (1999).
Eissa and Hoynes (1998)	Repeated cross sections of the CPS. Focus on married couples with fewer than twelve years of schooling.	1985–97 March CPS.	Two approaches: difference-in-difference, and intertemporal variation in tax rates caused by tax reforms. The latter is captured by using predicted net of tax wages for everyone in the sample assuming a full-time, full-year job.	The EITC expansions between 1984 and 1996 increased the LFP of married men by 0.2 percentage points and reduced the LFP of married women by 1.2 percentage points. The elasticity of LFP with respect to net wages is 0.03 for husbands and 0.29 for wives (page 22).
Hotz, Mullin, and Scholz (2002a)	Longitudinal administrative data from the California welfare, unemployment, and federal income tax systems.	1987–98	Rely on the phased-in EITC expansions beginning in 1990 that, beginning in 1994, disproportionately benefited families with two or more children relative to one child.	LFP increased by 6 percentage points and EITC claimed by $439 for families with two or more children relative to those with one child. The elasticity of LFP with respect to labor market earnings is between 0.97 and 1.69, depending on what year is used to estimate average LFP and earnings.

Hours of Work

Study	Data	Period	Method	Findings
Hoffman and Seidman (1990), U.S. General Accounting Office (1993), and DHS	PSID for Hoffman and Seidman, CPS for GAO; and SIPP for DHS.	1990 calendar year file for DHS	Each study *simulates* hours responses using parameters from the NIT experiments, and, in the DHS study, parameters from the kinked budget set literature.	DHS simulate labor supply responses to the 1993 EITC expansion (1993–96) of −0.09 to −4.04 percent. These range from 0 to −3.17 percent for husbands, −1.47 to −11.36 percent for wives, and −0.53 to −4.02 percent for single women heads.[d]
Eissa and Liebman (1996)	Repeated cross sections of the CPS. Focus on single women with children.	1985–87 March CPS for the "pre" period, 1989–91 March CPS for the "post" period.	Difference-in-difference. Regression of annual hours on characteristics and dummy variables for kids, post-86 and their interaction.	Statistically insignificant effect on hours (the 1986 expansions were associated with an increase of 25.2 hours, with a standard error of 15.2).
Keane and Moffitt (1998) and Keane (1995)	SIPP data. Cross-sectional. The sample is single women with children. Drop cases with high assets.	Fourth wave of the 1994 SIPP.	Estimate a structural model taking detailed account of the tax and transfer system on budget sets. Families make hours decisions moving from zero to twenty to forty, and participation decisions for food stamps, AFDC, and housing programs.	The estimates show a modest increase in aggregate hours worked from the EITC expansions between 1984 and 1996. Mean weekly hours increase to 26.5 from 24.1 These changes are not broken into the contribution of new labor market participants and potential reductions of hours of those already in the labor market.

(continued)

Table 3.4 (continued)

Study	Data Source and Population Covered	Years Covered	Estimation Method Used and Source of Identification	Impact Estimates
Eissa and Hoynes (1998)	Repeated cross sections of the CPS. Focus on married couples with fewer than twelve years of schooling.	1985–97 March CPS.	Instrumental variables with two sets of instruments. One has EITC parameters and interactions with birth cohort and education. The second uses imputed marginal tax rates for incomes in $5k increments from $0 to $100k.	The EITC expansions between 1984 and 1996 reduced hours of married men by 45 (or 2 percent) and reduced hours of married women between 13 and 93 (or 0.8 to 6 percent). Uncompensated wage elasticities are 0.06 to 0.07 for men and 0.08 to 0.52 for women. Income elasticities for men were −0.03 and for women, −0.04 to −0.41.

[a]The paper reports that the EITC increases the probability of working by 3.3 percentage points. Table 3 of the paper shows that the mean labor force participation rate of single parents was 56.4 percent. Meyer and Rosenbaum (1999, appendix table 1) shows that taxes fell by $732 for single women with children in their sample between 1992 and 1996. Mean wages in DHS (1995) are $6.55. Data from table 1 of Eissa and Liebman (1996) imply that single women with children worked 1,620 hours (conditional on working). This implies the elasticity of labor force participation with respect to the net-of-tax wage is $(3.3/56.4)/[732/(6.55 \times 1,620)] = 0.85$, as shown in the table. The sample used in DHS differs somewhat from the samples used in Eissa and Liebman and in Meyer and Rosenbaum primarily in that they drop families that would not be eligible for transfer program benefits even if they did not work (because they fail asset tests).

[b]TRA86 altered many aspects of the tax system in addition to expanding the EITC. From 1984–86, the pre-period, the maximum EITC was between $500 and $550. From 1988 to 1990, the maximum EITC ranged between $874 and $953. The TRA86 also increased the standard deduction for head of household to $4,400 in 1988 from $2,480 in 1986, increased the dependent exemption to $1,950 in 1988 from $1,086 in 1986, and extended the 15 percent bracket for head of household filers. Meyer and Rosenbaum (1999, appendix table 1) show that taxes fell by $492 for single women with children in the sample between 1984 and 1988. Eissa and Liebman report that earnings, conditional on working, in their sample were $15,188. This implies the elasticity of labor force participation with respect to the net-of-tax wage is $(2.8/74.2)/(492/15,188) = 1.16$, as shown in the table.

[c]Table 5 of Keane (1995), which is based on Keane and Moffitt (1998), shows that increasing the EITC to 40 percent increased labor force participation rates by 10.7 percentage points from a base of 65.4 percent. In the text, this experiment is characterized as increasing the EITC to its 1996 level from its 1984 level. Meyer and Rosenbaum (1999, appendix table 1) show that taxes fell by $1,443 for single women with children in their sample between 1984 and 1996. Mean wages in Keane and Moffitt (1998) are $5.20. Data from table 1 of Eissa and Liebman (1996) imply that single women with children worked 1,620 hours (conditional on working). This implies the elasticity of labor force participation with respect to the net-of-tax wage is $(10.7/65.4)/[1,443/(5.20 \times 1620)] = 0.96$, as shown in the table. Like DHS the sample drops families that would not be eligible for transfer program benefits even if they did not work (because they fail asset tests). This elasticity calculation may be biased downward if the Keane and Moffitt model did not take into account other features of TRA86 (see note b). That would make the implied average change in after-tax income smaller than $1,443, which would increase the elasticity estimate.

[d]The high end of the range of these estimates comes from the study of Hausman (1981), who reported much larger elasticities than have been reported elsewhere. If instead, we focus on the mean parameters from the NIT studies and the preferred parameters from the study by Triest (1990), which adopts the Hausman methodology. DHS (1995) report labor supply responses to the 1993 EITC expansion (1993–96) of −0.54 to −1.17 percent. These ranges from −0.34 to −1.32 percent for husbands, −2.64 to −3.03 percent for wives, and −1.08 to −1.11 percent for single women heads. See table 2 of DHS (1995). Triest (1990) finds uncompensated wage elasticities of around 0.05 for men and 0.25 for women, and his estimates of virtual income elasticities are 0.0 for men and −0.15 for women.

between 1984 and 1996 reduced the likelihood of labor market participation by around 1.2 percentage points (or 2 percent).

Ellwood (2000) exploits the difference-in-differences approach in which he classifies parents according to their position in the distribution of predicted wages, comparing women in the lowest (predicted) wage quartile with those in higher quartiles to distinguish groups that are likely to be affected by the EITC (the lowest quartile) from those that are not (the higher quartiles). He concludes that it is "perilous to impossible" to decompose the relative impacts of welfare reform, the strong economy, and EITC changes in the 1990s on the labor force participation patterns of low-skilled workers, but notes that the combination has led to a "truly unprecedented increase in labor market activity by low-income single parents" (p. 1100).[36]

To the extent that changes in policies other than the EITC or other "environmental" factors are coincident with the EITC expansions, there is the potential for bias in difference-in-differences estimates. Many states, for example, implemented changes in their welfare programs during the latter part of the 1980s, including reducing the growth in guarantees and the imposition and tightening of work rules for recipients (see Moffitt, chap. 5 in this volume). Given the AFDC eligibility criteria, these changes are likely to have differentially affected single women with children relative to those without children. Furthermore, there is potential for the composition of the treatment and control groups in these studies to have changed over time.[37]

These concerns are addressed by Hotz, Mullin, and Scholz (2002a), who assess the employment effects of the EITC changes in the 1990s using data on a sample of families who received welfare benefits in California during the early part of the 1990s. Their study has four distinctive differences from previous work. First, their sample is composed of former (or current) welfare recipients, a more disadvantaged population than that examined in other papers. Second, they used administrative data from the welfare, unemployment insurance, and federal tax systems and focused on four counties in California that were part of a welfare demonstration (see Hotz,

36. Neumark and Wascher (2001) examine correlations between income and income-to-needs ratios and state and federal EITC parameters. They find small effects of the federal EITC on earnings but large effects of state EITCs. They emphasize the state-level results, but variation in state EITC policy is somewhat limited in the years spanned by their data, so the discrepancy is puzzling.

37. Ellwood (2000) raises similar concerns (with different language), pointing out that with comparisons of single women with and without children, one cannot disentangle the separate effect of policy changes and everything else going on in the economy. One can only hope to test the overall impact of the combination of policies in a strong economy. He also notes that the temporal pattern of labor force participation of the two groups is often different before the enactment of the EITC, so drawing inferences from differential trends afterwards is troubling. Moreover, a large fraction of childless single women were already workers even before EITC expansions, so their employment cannot grow much.

Mullin, and Scholz 2002b for a more complete description). The data allow the authors to account more directly than other studies for potentially confounding changes in local labor markets and welfare reform. Third, the authors identify the employment effects of the EITC by comparing families with two or more children to families with one child, since after 1994 the EITC increased substantially for the former group relative to the latter. They argue that this approach focuses on groups that are likely to be more similar than studies that compare, for example, families with and without children.

They find that the EITC has large, positive effects on employment of adults from welfare families in California. Employment rates of families with two or more children increased 6 to 8 percentage points more than the employment rates of one-child families. The implied-elasticity of labor force participation with respect to net income ranges from 0.97 to 1.69 depending on assumptions used in the underlying elasticity calculations. Most of this range exceeds the next highest estimate reported in table 3.4. Larger elasticity estimates are consistent, however, with the previously mentioned result for Eissa and Leibman (1996) for women with children and less than a high school education. The fourth distinctive feature of the Hotz, Mullin, and Scholz study is that through a special arrangement with the California Franchise Tax Board, the authors were able to request grouped tabulations from the federal tax returns filed by the sample members. If the EITC accounts for the relative employment increase of families with two or more children, they should be filing tax returns and claiming the EITC at a significantly greater rate than their one-child counterparts. In fact, they do.

Estimates from the natural experiment (or difference-in-differences) studies described above are limited in their ability to assess the effects of alternative EITC designs. As can be seen in table 3.1, all major expansions in the EITC entailed simultaneous changes in EITC phase-in rates, phaseout rates, and the maximum credit. In section 3.3, we noted that a simple labor-leisure model predicts that households in the phaseout region of the credit would reduce their labor supply in response to an increase in the phaseout rate, all else being equal, while the effect of increases in the phase-in rate on hours of work depends on the relative strength of the substitution and income effects associated with this change. Determining the direction and magnitude of the behavioral responses to changes in each of these parameters is useful for assessing the validity of this model and for assessing the likely impacts of alternative designs of the EITC beyond those actually implemented.

Effects of the EITC Based with Standard Labor Supply Models

As noted above, several studies have analyzed the effects of the EITC on labor force participation and hours of work with standard labor supply models, using the fact that the EITC alters the effective wage or effective tax rates that certain types of individuals and households face.[38] The studies by Dickert, Houser, and Scholz (1995); Eissa and Hoynes (1998); and Meyer and Rosenbaum (2001) are based on this approach.[39]

Dickert, Houser, and Scholz (1995) measure labor force participation elasticities using data from the 1990 SIPP. They construct a detailed tax and transfer simulation model that reflects precise estimates of state and federal income taxes, payroll taxes, AFDC, food stamps, and Supplemental Security Income. The simulation model allows them to characterize the enormous variation in budget sets that families face in different states. They use an instrumental variables approach (described presently), calculating the after-tax change in incomes that would result from taking a half-time (and in some specifications, full-time) job at the predicted wage relative to being out of the labor market. The intuition underlying the study is that in high-benefit states (like New York at the time), the after-tax return to work is fairly low since substantial benefits are clawed back, while in low-benefit states (like Texas at the time), the after-tax return to work is high since there are few benefits to lose. Thus, if labor market participation decisions are sensitive to the after-tax returns to work, participation rates should be higher in low-benefit states than in high-benefit states, all else being equal.

Dickert, Houser, and Scholz find that a 10 percent increase in the after-tax wage results in a 2 percentage point (or 3.5 percent) increase in labor market participation among single parents (they also jointly estimate a reduced-form equation for the welfare participation decision), which suggests that EITC-induced changes in the returns to work increase labor market participation. Their estimates also show that participation of secondary wage earners will fall as a consequence of the EITC. Their new empirical work on participation, coupled with simulation work on the effect of the EITC on hours for those already in the labor market, suggests that the aggregate positive participation effects of the 1993 EITC expansions likely outweighed the negative hours effects, resulting in a net increase in aggregate hours of work.

A potential problem with the Dickert, Houser, and Scholz (1995) study is that EITC effects are inferred from correlations of employment with other aspects of the tax and transfer system.[40] Moreover, idiosyncratic state-level factors correlated with family budget sets and labor market de-

38. The approach builds on the neoclassical labor supply and labor force participation models. See Pencavel (1986), Killingsworth and Heckman (1986), and Blundell and MaCurdy (1999) for surveys of this work.

39. Also see the simulation studies of Hoffman and Seidman (1990); U.S. General Accounting Office (1993); Holtzblatt, McCubbin, and Gillette (1994); and Browning (1995).

40. The data are a cross section and the EITC is a uniform federal program, so EITC effects are inferred from the cross-state variation in net wages generated by state-level differences in tax and transfer rules.

cisions could bias estimates. Hoynes (1997), for example, shows that including state fixed effects can significantly alter estimates of the effects of AFDC on female headship.

Meyer and Rosenbaum (2001) significantly advance the literature in their analysis of the effects of the EITC and other policy changes on the labor force participation of single women. They develop an econometric model of labor force participation, calculating the probability that the utility of working exceeds the utility associated with not working. That is, the probability of working is given by

(4) $\Pr(U(Y_w, L_w, P_w, X, \varepsilon_w) > U(Y_{nw}, L_{nw}, P_{nw}, X, \varepsilon_{nw}))$

where $U(Y_k, L_k, P_k, X)$ are the indirect utility functions associated with the work (w) and nonwork (nw) states, Y_k is the income the woman receives in the kth state, L_k is her leisure time in alternative states, P_k denotes her participation in welfare programs (to capture potential transaction costs and stigma associated with participation in such programs), X denotes observable characteristics, and ε_k represents unobserved, stochastic components of tastes. The influence that the EITC and other programs have on wages and income enters through the specifications of the incomes associated with the work and nonwork states.

Meyer and Rosenbaum specify Y_w and Y_{nw} as functions of parameterizations of the EITC, federal and state tax rules, and the characteristics of other welfare programs facing women at different times and in different states, utilizing an exhaustive set of data on the tax structure and welfare programs. Linearizing $U(\cdot)$ with respect to its arguments and using a nonparametric strategy to calculate *expected* values of income associated with the work state for women in their data, they use a probit specification to estimate their labor force participation model.

They find that EITC changes account for roughly 60 percent of the increase in the employment rate of single mothers from 1984 to 1996 and roughly 31 percent of the increase from 1992 to 1996. Given the changes in employment rates and the size of the EITC changes over this period, their results are broadly consistent with the earlier papers, although, as we show in table 3.4, their estimated elasticities of labor force participation with respect to net income are the smallest of the range of existing studies (although all estimates are quite close, with the exception of the larger estimate of Hotz, Mullin, and Scholz 2002a).

There are at least two notable features of Meyer and Rosenbaum's work. First, they account for EITC changes that occurred between 1984 and 1996, making use of time series variation in the credit to identify employment effects. Second, they construct an elaborate simulation model of the tax and transfer system that allows them to net out the influence of changes in other policies, both over time and across place of residence. Dealing with the influence of other policy changes is potentially important, especially to the extent that such changes had differential impacts on households with and without children.

Structural Choice Models of Time Allocation and Program Participation

The nonlinear or kinked nature of the budget set induced by the EITC program can result in nonmarginal changes in behavior that complicate efforts to rely on wage and income elasticities drawn from other econometric studies. This can be seen in figure 3.4 for the type *III* individuals. The optimal pre-EITC labor supply choice for a type *III* individual would generate labor earnings that exceed the upper threshold for EITC eligibility. Because of the nonconvexity introduced with the EITC phaseout range, one could observe individuals reducing their labor supply and earnings so as to be eligible for a credit. Such nonconvexities in the phaseout region require one to know more than just the income and substitution effects in order to assess the response to EITC changes. It requires knowledge of the underlying preferences for work versus leisure to determine whether such behaviors are likely to occur.

The structural approach explicitly parameterizes the preferences and constraints facing individuals and then exploits the theory of optimal decision-making to characterize the likelihood function used to reconcile observed labor supply and program participation behaviors. This approach is exemplified in the work of Hausman (1985) on the effects of income tax structure on the labor supply and Moffitt (1990) and Keane and Moffitt (1998) in the study of the labor supply impacts of welfare and other social programs.

Keane and Moffitt (1998) and Keane (1995; based on the Keane and Moffitt model) use their model estimates to examine a wide range of policy reforms, including changes to AFDC and food stamp tax rates, a variety of wage and work subsidies, and changes to the EITC. Their EITC simulations find that the expansions between 1984 and 1996 increased labor force participation by 10.7 percentage points, from a base of 65.4 percent. They also find that the aggregate effect of the EITC expansions was to increase hours of work. This paper is notable as the only EITC study to recover underlying household preference parameters.

A study by Blundell et al. (2000) sought to estimate the likely impact of alternative implementations of an EITC-like tax credit scheme in the United Kingdom (called the Family Working Tax Credit) before it was actually implemented. This type of application is one of the most valuable uses for structural estimates. In general, greater knowledge of the "structure" of individual and household preferences and their choice processes is required to predict the behavioral responses to complicated, hypothetical policy changes than is needed to assess the net impacts of straightforward, observed changes in the credit. At the same time, identification of these structural features of decision making is inherently more difficult than estimating net effects of observed expansions.

3.5.3 Estimates of the EITC and Hours of Work

Studies estimating the effects of the EITC on hours of work for those households that are working find small, negative effects. These studies are summarized in the second panel of table 3.4. Liebman (1997a) finds no bunching of taxpayers at the beginning and end of the phaseout range, as might be expected if the EITC significantly affects hours and taxpayers are cognizant of the discontinuities in implied marginal tax rates generated by the credit. As Liebman notes, it is not surprising that negative effects on hours for people already in the labor market are small because the precise relationship between the EITC and hours worked is likely to be poorly understood by most taxpayers. The majority of EITC recipients pay a third party to prepare their tax returns, and it is difficult to infer the implicit tax rates embodied in the credit from the look-up table that accompanies the EITC instructions. This confusion is less likely to mitigate positive participation effects, since for these to be operative, taxpayers only need to understand that there is some tax-related bonus to work. Abundant anecdotal evidence indicates that taxpayers have this understanding (see, e.g., Jason DeParle, "Once a Forlorn Avenue, Tax Preparers Now Flourish," *New York Times,* 21 March 1999).

The standard approach to estimating the effects of policies on hours of work is based on the labor supply equation that takes the following generic form:

$$(5) \qquad h = \alpha_0 + \alpha_1 w^* + \alpha_2 Y^* + \beta X + u,$$

given $h > 0$, where h is the number of hours worked, w^* is the effective wage rate, Y^* is the individual's effective nonlabor income, the Xs are again used to capture observable differences, and u is an error term. The parameters α_1 and α_2 in equation (5) represent the uncompensated wage effect and income effect, respectively, and $\alpha_1 - \alpha_2 h_0$ represents the compensated wage, or substitution, effect, evaluated at some level of hours of work, h_0. In the context of estimating the effects of taxes and other social programs on hours of work, one crucial issue is how to deal with the potential endogeneity of w^* and Y^* when estimating α_1 and α_2. The endogeneity of effective wages and incomes facing individuals arises because of the nonlinearities in the budget sets in the presence of taxes and transfer programs that individuals face. Even if before-tax and transfer wages and before-tax sources of unearned income are assumed to be exogenous (and these are controversial assumptions), effective wages and income levels are presumed to be endogenous. This is due to the fact that individuals' choice of the segment of the budget constraint may depend upon their tastes and preferences, which are, in part, reflected in their value of u, giving rise to endogeneity bias in the estimation of α_1 and α_2. Such bias is likely to be more problematic when individuals face nonconvex budget sets created, for example, by the phaseout region of the EITC.

Several econometric strategies have been employed in an attempt to mitigate these biases. They differ in the sources of variation they use to identify the effects of tax and transfer programs, the degree to which the estimates can be used to estimate more general sets of counterfactual regime changes, and the extent to which they rely on maintained assumptions about unobserved components of preferences and their distributions. The most common strategy in papers examining the EITC and hours is to use instrumental variables (IV) methods. Eissa and Hoynes (1998) use the IV strategy to estimate variants of α_1 and α_2, which they then use to simulate the effects of changes in the EITC on hours of work. The IV approach also has the benefit of its relative simplicity and holds the promise of obtaining wage elasticities that can be used to analyze more general policy changes. At the same time, these methods are vulnerable to the concerns raised above about reliance on wage and income elasticities to make inferences about the effects of program changes characterized by nonlinear, and especially nonconvex, budget sets. Furthermore, the usefulness of these estimates depends on the validity and power of the instrumental variables themselves— that is, that the variation in the instrument reflects variation that is exogenous to the (endogenous) net wages and incomes of individuals.

Summary of Studies of Effects of the EITC on Labor Market Outcomes

We draw four broad conclusions from the empirical work on the EITC and labor force participation and hours. First, based on the evidence from many studies, the EITC positively affects the labor force participation of single-parent households. Second, in aggregate, the positive participation effects appear to be fairly substantial. Meyer and Rosenbaum (2001), for example, suggest that as much as 62 percent of the increase in single mothers' labor force participation between 1984 and 1996 could be attributed to the EITC, while as much as 35 percent of the increase from 1992 to 1996 could be attributed to the credit. Labor force participation elasticities with respect to net-of-tax income reported in table 3.4 range from 0.69 to 1.16, and could be as large as 1.7 for former and current welfare recipients. Third, as would be expected given the tax treatment of secondary workers in two-earner couples, the EITC has a modest, negative effect on labor force participation for secondary workers in two-parent families. Fourth, the EITC appears to have a small negative effect on hours worked by those in the labor force, but some studies (Dickert, Houser, and Scholz 1995; Keane and Moffitt 1998; and Meyer and Rosenbaum 2001) suggest that the aggregate hours effect of the EITC, once participation effects are accounted for, is positive.

Labor market issues have receive more attention than other EITC-related issues, but more could usefully be done. First, Hotz, Mullin, and Scholz (2002a) find that employment elasticities with respect to EITC changes are significantly higher for welfare recipients than they are for others. Further work on the EITC and employment, particularly for subpopulations, may be useful. Second, additional attention could be paid to augmenting the labor market proxies employed in the studies. Some evidence suggests that state unemployment rates, the variable typically used, are too blunt, which makes it hard to disentangle business cycle effects from policy changes. Third, the behavioral responses to the EITC *may change* over time. This possibility is suggested by Moffitt (1999), who finds that welfare participation appears to be more sensitive to changes in labor market conditions during the 1990s than was the case in earlier decades. Ellwood (2000) also emphasizes the fact that the "combination of welfare sticks, EITC carrots, and a remarkably strong economy had a multiplicative effect that is far greater than any one or two of these policies would have had on their own" (p. 1084). Work would be valuable that helps policymakers better anticipate the effects of policy changes, adopted individually and in packages, in different economic environments.

3.5.4   Estimates of the Effects of the EITC on Other Behavioral Outcomes

Marriage and Family Formation

As noted earlier, the EITC can lead to large marriage penalties and bonuses depending on the relative incomes between potential partners. Once these incentives have been clearly documented, as is done by Dickert-Conlin and Houser (1998) and Holtzblatt and Rebelein (1999), it is natural to ask whether they affect behavior.

Three recent papers examine whether the EITC encourages the existence of female-headed families.[41] Dickert-Conlin and Houser (2002) look at correlations between EITC changes and female headship. They account for the fact that couples affect their EITC through their marital and labor supply choices, and they find little effect of the EITC on marriage decisions. Eissa and Hoynes (1999) also find modest or nonexistent effects on family formation.

Ellwood (2000) takes a different strategy. Rather than isolating the specific effect of marriage on tax and transfer payments, he looks at data from the Panel Study of Income Dynamics (PSID) and focuses on 1,671 marriages that women in the sample entered between 1983 and 1991. He measures penalties and bonuses by income in the last year prior to marriage

41. Also see Dickert-Conlin (1999) for a more general look at taxes, transfers, and separations.

and in the first year after marriage to look at whether families would be net winners or losers had the 1996 EITC provisions been in place when they married. Clearly other factors (like postmarital childbearing or other changes in income) can affect these comparisons. Ellwood then looks at patterns of marriage incentives over time across wage and skill groups and at the corresponding marriage patterns. He finds no evidence that EITC marriage penalties or bonuses affected marriage.

The evidence on the EITC's effects on marriage and fertility mirrors the broader evidence from the literature on transfer programs. Moffitt (1998) surveys studies of the effects of welfare on marriage and fertility and concludes that "a neutral weighing of the evidence still leads to the conclusion that welfare has incentive effects on marriage and fertility," but the effects tend to be small and cannot explain time series increases in nonmarital fertility and declines in marriage rates. Moffitt also notes that results tend to vary significantly based on the methodology used and other specification differences.

Human Capital Formation[42]

Until now, we have ignored the potential impacts of the EITC on an important issue related to the ability of the EITC to alleviate poverty—namely, its effect on human capital or skill development among workers. The argument is sometimes made that prowork programs provide a double bonus, because they induce people to work, and, by going to work, low-skilled individuals can acquire productive skills that can enhance their future earnings. Drawing from the literature on human capital investment, the issue is what effect the EITC has on skill formation and wage growth among low-skilled populations.

Formal models of human capital investment emphasize that the decision of workers to invest in skill formation depends on the comparison of the opportunity cost associated with time spent acquiring skills with the future returns to wages that result from the acquired human capital. As noted by Heckman, Lochner, and Cossa (2002), programs that affect the value of market work, such as the EITC, may affect these costs and returns. The effect of the EITC is further complicated by the differential impacts it has on effective wage rates. As noted above, the EITC raises the effective wage rate in the phase-in region, leaves it unchanged in the flat region, and lowers it in the phaseout region. Thus, whether the opportunity costs of human capital investments and the returns from such investments are raised or lowered by the EITC depends critically on which part of the EITC applies and over what time intervals.

Moreover, exactly how programs like the EITC affect skill acquisition and life-cycle wage growth depends on what model characterizes the hu-

---

42. This section draws heavily on Heckman, Lochner, and Cossa (2002).

man capital accumulation, or production, process. In particular, if one assumes that work-related skills are largely acquired as a by-product of work—that is, via "learning by doing" (LBD)—then programs that encourage greater labor force participation and hours of work will tend to encourage skill acquisition.[43] In contrast, if learning, either via formal schooling or while on the job, is rivalrous with working, as is the case with an "on-the-job training" (OJT) model, policies that encourage work may discourage skill acquisition.[44]

Using data from the 1980 CPS, Heckman, Lochner, and Cossa (2002) estimate the structural parameters for hours of work and wage equations profiles for OJT and LBD models of life-cycle human capital investment and time allocation. Based on these models, the authors simulate the effects of the presence of an EITC on life-cycle labor supply decisions, human capital investments, and wage growth. Their simulations imply very different patterns of EITC effects on these decisions across the OJT and LBD models of human capital formation, even though the models do not appreciably differ in their fit of the data. For example, their simulations show that although the two models yield similar predictions of the effects of the EITC on human capital formation via its effect on labor market entry by females, they yield different effects on the intensive labor supply margins. In particular, the EITC has large effects on training in an OJT model but weak effects on labor supply. It has little effect on skills and larger labor supply effects within the LBD model they examine.

These provocative findings by Heckman, Lochner, and Cossa suggest the need to devote attention to the life-cycle implications of EITC changes in order to understand the potential for the credit to improve the skills, and thus the well-being, of disadvantaged populations in the United States.

Consumption

A central issue when thinking about the EITC and consumption is the degree to which the credit allows people to smooth the marginal utility of consumption. One would think that the advance payment option might help people do this. However, in 1998 only 185,027 (1.1 percent) of 16,118,328 of EITC claimants with qualifying children took advantage of this option.

Barrow and McGranahan (2000) examine whether consumption appears to increase for EITC-eligible families in months, particularly February, when they are likely to receive the EITC. The topic is an interesting one, since the models economists typically use to think about consumption would predict that families would not immediately spend their EITC upon

43. See, for example, Weiss (1972) for an exposition of the formal model of LBD applied to the human capital investment context.
44. This is true in the human capital models of Becker (1964) and Ben-Porath (1967).

receipt, but rather would spread EITC-financed consumption over the year (or lifetime). Hence, standard models would predict no discernible effect. Yet there is some evidence that significant portions of the population are liquidity constrained and hence have consumption patterns that track income receipt very closely.

The authors use monthly data from the Consumer Expenditure Survey of nondurables and durables from 1982 through 1996. Using regression models of monthly consumption with month dummies, month dummies interacted with (simulated) EITC eligibility, and family economic and demographic characteristics, they find that EITC-eligible households spend approximately 9 percent more on durable goods in February, the modal month of EITC refund, than do households not eligible for the credit. They show that these results are not driven by income differences or differences in family size between EITC-eligible and EITC-ineligible families. They also show that the seasonal effects are larger after the 1990 EITC expansions, as would be expected. The estimated magnitudes suggest that EITC recipients spend roughly one-fifth of the full amount of their refund in the month of receipt.

Smeeding, Ross-Phillips, and O'Connor (2000) fielded a survey of low-income taxpayers who used tax preparation services at a neighborhood legal clinic in Chicago and solicited detailed information about the anticipated and actual uses of the EITC. The study provides information on how the EITC is used by families, such as for purchasing a car, paying tuition, changing residences, paying bills, or purchasing food. A next step in this research program would be to examine what families would do at the margin with, say, an additional $100 a month through regular earnings (or welfare) and compare that to the uses to which the lump-sum EITC is put. The authors suggest that the lumpiness of the EITC might allow people to make investments that enhance social mobility. Further work examining this conjecture would be valuable.

3.6   Assessing Proposed and Potential Modifications to the EITC

Given the central role played by the EITC in the nation's antipoverty programs, it is not surprising that a broad range of possible credit modifications has been raised. Like the historical forces shaping the credit, these ideas tend to push the credit toward improving behavioral incentives or toward enhancing its antipoverty effectiveness. In this section we discuss some of these issues.

3.6.1   Marriage Penalties

Proposals regularly address EITC-related marriage penalties. Several things should be kept in mind when thinking about these. First, the tax system cannot simultaneously be progressive (have increasing average effective tax rates), treat the family (as opposed to individuals) as the unit of taxation, and be neutral with respect to marriage. Hence, either penalties for singles or marriage penalties are inevitable, unless the structure of individual income taxation is dramatically altered. Second, as noted by Holtzblatt and Rebelein (1999), 62 percent of EITC-related marriage penalties are borne by couples with incomes above the amount necessary to be eligible for the EITC. We suspect that policymakers are considerably less concerned about the marriage penalty that arises for a worker with earnings of $40,000 and his spouse with earnings of $10,000 (if they split and the spouse took the children, she could get a large EITC) than they are about the family-formation incentives that apply to unemployed or sporadically employed workers with or without children. Third, an extensive literature has examined the effects of antipoverty programs on marriage and fertility generally and has found relatively small effects.

3.6.2 Administering the EITC through the Tax System and Other Issues of Credit Design

During debates over restructuring the IRS,[45] the EITC was sometimes referred to as a "non-tax function of the IRS." The rationale for this sentiment is that tax rules are sufficiently complex that it is already beyond the IRS's ability to effectively administer the laws required to accurately collect taxes. Asking the IRS to administer the EITC diverts resources that could help the IRS better collect taxes.

There is, of course, a clear relationship between all tax expenditures and spending programs so that any deviation from a comprehensive income tax could be viewed as a situation where the IRS is being asked to carry out some function other than tax collection to achieve some social purpose.[46] The practical question to pose in optimally configuring the tax system and spending programs is what the marginal cost is of providing specific incentives through the tax system relative to the best alternative delivery mechanism. In the case of the EITC, there are strong arguments in support of running the EITC through the tax code. Because filing thresholds are fairly low and because of overwithholding, most low-income families with earnings already file tax returns. Consequently, they are already in the system, so the incremental cost of claiming the EITC is low. The IRS collects income information from both employers and employees, so it is straightforward in most circumstances to verify income eligibility. The IRS has little ability to document living arrangements, however, so a significant number of errors arise in determining who is able to claim an EITC-qualifying child. New developments with the Federal Case Registry of Child Support

---

45. See, for example, "The New IRS Law," Albert Crenshaw, *Washington Post,* 23 July 1998, A6.
46. See Surrey (1973) for an early discussion of the concept of tax expenditures.

Orders may improve the IRS's ability to handle this aspect of EITC eligibility.

Just because a case can be made that an EITC-like subsidy may appropriately be delivered through the tax code does not mean that the EITC is optimally designed. Liebman (1999) examines the optimal phaseout rate of the EITC. A more rapid phaseout will reduce the utility of some EITC recipients and may cause some taxpayers to leave the labor market. At the same time, it will reduce the cost of the program, which, if the marginal excess burden of tax collections is high enough, may lead to an increase in overall welfare given specific social welfare weights on different income groups. Liebman uses simulation analyses to highlight the magnitudes of the various behavioral issues in question. Results are naturally sensitive to the compensated labor supply, the marginal excess burden of taxes, and the characteristics of the assumed social welfare function. His simulations tend to result in optimal phaseout rates that bracket the current rates for families with one child and two or more children.

3.6.3 Adjusting Further for Family Size and Tighter Integration with the Tax System

In 1998 the child poverty rate for families with three or more children was 28.5 percent, twice the 11.9 percent rate for children in smaller families. A way to address the higher poverty rates of families with three or more children is to add a third tier to the federal EITC schedule for these families, which would result in an EITC schedule similar to the structure of the Wisconsin state EITC. One specific proposal implemented this idea by increasing the phase-in rate to 45 percent from 40 percent, adding nearly $500 to the maximum EITC available to a taxpayer with three or more children. The potential drawbacks of the idea are that it costs money and it further increases incentives for people to have children and, in some circumstances, to become single parents.

The Minnesota state EITC also may have worthwhile lessons for the federal credit. Recall that Minnesota adjusts its phase-ins and phaseouts of the state credit to smooth notches that are generated by features of the federal and state tax and transfer programs. As is clear when plotting the budget sets facing families with one child and two children, there are unusual notches and kinks, particularly when the effects of transfer programs are taken into account. It would be straightforward to alter the phaseout rates to smooth marginal tax rates at the income levels around which families begin to pay positive levels of federal income taxes (in the absence of the EITC). This would increase headaches for people trying to describe the structure of the credit, but it would have little practical consequence for people taking the credit since the credit amount is invariably found from look-up tables in the EITC instructions or by requesting the IRS to calculate the credit. At the same time, although smoothing the phaseout rates would have clear esthetic value, it might have very little practical consequence, since it is unlikely that any but the most sophisticated workers would recognize the link to incremental labor market decisions and the size of their lump-sum EITC after filing tax returns.

Cherry and Sawicky (2000) and Ellwood and Liebman (2000) go well beyond the Minnesota model and develop more systemic policy proposals that would, under some options, integrate the EITC, dependent exemption, and child credit. The Cherry-Sawicky "unified universal child credit," for example, would rise for an initial range of earnings, flatten out over an additional range, and then phase down to a minimum benefit of $1,270 per child, an amount that equaled the value of the dependent exemption and child credit for a taxpayer in the 28 percent bracket when their proposal was designed. The unified universal child credit would cost more than $30 billion per year, but the modification would reduce some of the labor market disincentives and marriage penalties that arise in the current EITC, significantly increase benefits available to low- and moderate-income families with many children, and provide considerable additional tax benefits to families with children and incomes between roughly $25,000 and $50,000.[47] Although a complete analysis of this idea is well beyond the scope of this chapter, both papers offer far-reaching ways to improve the tax system.

3.6.4   EITC and TANF Interactions

As state TANF programs evolve, clear rules need to be made about what kinds of state-subsidized activities will trigger EITC eligibility and what activities will not. The polar cases are easy to identify: TANF payments that are like payments made under AFDC would not qualify as income for the purposes of the EITC. Wages earned while a single mother works and receives a TANF grant for child care will be considered income for the EITC. Congress has explicitly indicated that "work-experience" and "community-service" jobs will not trigger the EITC. But there is a vast gray area of other TANF-supported activities that need to be clarified. The trade-offs in clarifying the rules are apparent: making as many people engaged in worklike activities eligible for the EITC as possible will be more costly than having more restrictive rules, but it will also provide an additional source of support to poor families, and the EITC may help reinforce the work-expectation message that is at the core of many state TANF programs. Attention might also be paid to the link between the EITC and TANF-based asset tests.

47. Somewhat thorny technical issues would need to be worked out, such as who would receive the unified universal child credit in situations where a noncustodial parent is currently paying child support and receiving the dependent exemption and the custodial parent is receiving the EITC. Integrating the dependent exemption and EITC could result in pressure to rewrite many divorce settlements.

3.6.5   The Advance Payment Option

Only 1.1 percent of EITC recipients with children used the advance payment option in 1998. Low use of the advance payment option has generated considerable discussion in policy circles, although we think this attention is somewhat misplaced. Simple calculations suggest that eschewing the advanced payment option, as currently designed, costs the taxpayer at most $52.77 (assuming the taxpayer could receive the maximum available advance payment each month, earns 8 percent interest, and does not receive his or her refund until May). Given that low-wage workers may change jobs frequently, the transactions costs associated with setting up advanced payments can be fairly high. This, coupled with the possibility that someone will receive too much in advance payments and have to pay it back at tax time,[48] suggests that the utility cost of failing to take advantage of the advance payment option is probably small.

It is sometimes suggested that greater use of the advance payment option would reinforce the prowork message of the EITC. Partly for this reason, officials in the United Kingdom designed their EITC-like program, the Working Families Tax Credit (WFTC), to include incremental receipt of payments throughout the year. There are significant differences between the U.S. and U.K. experiences, however.[49] The WFTC is paid through the employer and is retrospectively based on earnings, hours worked, and family income during the six-week period prior to the beginning of the payment period (the previous six months). Thus, someone could have a job, become eligible for the WFTC, and then leave the job and still receive the WFTC for the duration of the six months. Rules are in place to curb efforts to manipulate income to maximize the WFTC, but there is not yet any evidence of their effectiveness. Other aspects of the British tax system suggest that less emphasis is placed on compliance (and perhaps that greater emphasis is placed on minimizing the intrusiveness of tax authorities and associated forms) than occurs in the United States, which may result in a greater willingness to tolerate overpayments or underpayments that might arise with the WFTC. The WFTC replaced the Family Credit, which was also delivered incrementally through the year.

3.7   Summary and Conclusions

Over the last twenty-five years, the EITC has become, by a considerable margin, the country's largest cash or near-cash program directed at low-

---

48. Holtzblatt and Liebman (1998) note that taxpayers are less likely to receive too much in EITC advance payments if income is only from wages. Only about one in four EITC claimants has income from only one source during the year, however. Advance payments also lengthen the time between when money is paid out and when the IRS is able to verify eligibility.

49. See Holtzblatt and Liebman (1998) for a more detailed discussion.

income families. Its popularity is fairly easy to account for. Unlike safety net programs such as AFDC, TANF, and food stamps, the EITC gives no benefits to those without labor earnings. Thus, it subsidizes the incomes of people who in some sense are "doing the right thing." The appeal of this reaches across party lines. In addition, unlike the safety net programs, the EITC has unambiguously positive labor market participation incentives. By virtue of the fact that it provides no benefits for the most destitute, the EITC is not a *substitute* for the safety net. But its desirable labor market effects (relative to other safety net programs) and its targeting of the working poor undoubtedly account, at least in part, for its rapid growth.

Research on the EITC has been a growth industry in the last decade. In our review we have been struck by the variety of different topics and approaches taken by researchers. We can think of no major EITC-related topic that has not received at least some attention from serious scholars, possibly with the exception of the economic incidence of the credit. But that is not to say that we know everything necessary about the credit. We lack information about the participation rate of the credit since the mid-1990s. Research on the labor market effects of the credit have pushed quasi-experimental and IV repeated cross-sectional analyses using the CPS to their logical limits, but there have not been utility-based structural analyses of the EITC. Nor have there been any longitudinal analyses of the EITC, which hold considerable promise for controlling for unobservables in ways that are impossible with the CPS. Research on the EITC and family structure and fertility is in its infancy. Work initiated by Heckman, Lochner, and Cossa (2002) also has considerable potential for enhancing understanding of the effects of the EITC and other policies directed at low-wage labor markets.

Stepping back further from current thrusts of the literature, two potentially promising new ways for research to develop are apparent. First, Smeeding, Ross-Phillips, and O'Connor (2000) raise an important issue. To what extent and through what channels can the EITC enhance economic well-being? Are there nonlinearities associated with the EITC, possibly through its lumpiness, that allow the credit to enhance well-being in a way that differs significantly from equivalent-sized (in total) payments received throughout the year?

Second, it is easy for researchers to focus on narrow, well-defined questions that lend themselves to standard (or possibly innovative) methodological tools. Perhaps as a consequence, however, less attention has been paid to the design of the constellation of public policies that are or could be directed at low-wage labor markets. Questions along these lines would include the following: What are the relative merits of the EITC and employer-based wage subsidies, of the EITC, and of the minimum wage? Do the answers differ given existing tax and transfer provisions? Can the broader tax and transfer system be altered or more tightly integrated in

welfare-enhancing ways? The specific research questions that have dominated the EITC agenda are critical stepping stones for satisfactory answers
to these more global issues, but it would be inappropriate as research
evolves to study only the narrower issues at the expense of the broader.

References

Allingham, M., and Agar Sandmo. 1972. Income tax evasion: A theoretical analysis. *Journal of Public Economics* 1 (3/4): 323–38.
Alm, James, and Leslie A. Whittington. 1995. Does the income tax affect marital
decision? *National Tax Journal* 48 (4): 565–72.
Andreoni, James. 1992. IRS as loan shark: Tax compliance with borrowing con-
straints. *Journal of Public Economics* 49 (3): 35–46.
Angrist, Joshua, and Alan Krueger. 1999. Empirical strategies in labor economics.
In *Handbook of labor economics.* Vol. 3A, ed. O. Ashenfelter and D. Card, 1277–
366. Amsterdam: North-Holland.
Barrow, Lisa, and Leslie McGranahan. 2000. The effects of the Earned Income Tax
Credit on the seasonality of household expenditures. *National Tax Journal* 53 (4,
part 2): 1211–43.
Becker, Gary. 1964. *Human capital.* New York: Columbia University Press.
Ben-Porath, Yoram. 1967. The production of human capital and life-cycle earn-
ings. *Journal of Political Economy* 75 (4): 352–65.
Bishop, John, and Robert Haveman. 1978. Targeted employment subsidies: Issue
of structure and design. Institute for Research on Poverty Special Report no. 24.
Madison, Wis.: Institute for Research on Poverty.
Blumenthal, Marsha, Brian Erard, and Chih-Chin Ho. 1999. Participation and
compliance with the Earned Income Tax Credit. University of St. Thomas, B.
Erard and Associates, and Internal Revenue Service. Mimeograph.
Blundell, Richard, Alan Duncan, Julian McCrae, and Costas Meghir. 2000. The la-
bor market impact of the working families tax credit in the U.K. *Fiscal Studies*
21:65–74.
Blundell, Richard, and Thomas MaCurdy. 1999. Labor supply: A review of alter-
native approaches. In *Handbook of labor economics.* Vol. 3A, ed. O. Ashenfelter
and D. Card, 1560–695. Amsterdam: North-Holland.
Browning, Edgar. 1995. Effects of the Earned Income Tax Credit on income and
welfare. *National Tax Journal* 48:23–43.
Browning, Martin. 1992. Children and economic household behavior. *Journal of
Economic Literature* 30 (3): 1434–75.
Bull, Nicholas, Janet Holtzblatt, James R. Nunns, and Robert Rebelein. 1999.
Defining and measuring marriage penalties and bonuses. OTA Paper no. 82-R.
Washington, D.C.: U.S. Treasury Department, Office of Tax Analysis.
Burkhauser, Richard V., Kenneth A. Couch, and Andrew Glenn. 1996. Public poli-
cies for the working poor: The Earned Income Tax Credit versus minimum wage
legislation. In *Research in labor economics,* ed. S. Polachek, 65–109. New York:
JAI Press.
Cherry, Robert, and Max B. Sawicky. 2000. Giving tax credit where credit is due.
Economic Policy Institute briefing paper. Washington, D.C.: Economic Policy
Institute.

Council of Economic Advisers. 1998. Good news for low income families: Expansions in the Earned Income Tax Credit and the minimum wage. Washington, D.C.: Council of Economic Advisers, December.

———. 2000. *Economic report of the president.* Washington, D.C.: Council of Economic Advisers, February.

Dickert, Stacy, Scott Houser, and John Karl Scholz. 1995. The Earned Income Tax Credit and transfer programs: A study of labor market and program participation. In *Tax policy and the economy,* 9th ed., ed. James M. Poterba, 1–50. Cambridge, Mass.: National Bureau of Economic Research and the MIT Press.

Dickert-Conlin, Stacy. 1999. Taxes and transfers: Their effects on the decision to end a marriage. *Journal of Public Economics* 73:217–40.

Dickert-Conlin, Stacy, and Amitabh Chandra. 1999. Taxes and the timing of births. *Journal of Political Economy* 107 (1): 161–77.

Dickert-Conlin, Stacy, and Scott Houser. 1998. Taxes and transfers: A new look at the marriage penalty. *National Tax Journal* 51 (2): 175–217.

———. 2002. EITC and marriage. *National Tax Journal* 60 (1): 25–39.

Eissa, Nada, and Hilary Williamson Hoynes. 1998. The Earned Income Tax Credit and the labor supply of married couples. NBER Working Paper no. 6856. Cambridge, Mass.: National Bureau of Economic Research.

———. 1999. Good news for low income families? Tax-transfer schemes and marriage. University of California–Berkeley, Mimeograph.

Eissa, Nada, and Jeffrey B. Liebman. 1996. Labor supply response to the Earned Income Tax Credit. *Quarterly Journal of Economics* 111 (2): 605–37.

Ellwood, David T. 2000. The impact of the Earned Income Tax Credit and social policy reforms on work, marriage, and living arrangements. *National Tax Journal* 43 (4, part 2): 1063–105.

Ellwood, David T., and Jeffrey B. Liebman. 2000. The middle class parent penalty: Child benefits in the U.S. tax code. Harvard University, John F. Kennedy School of Government. Mimeograph, May.

Feenberg, Daniel R., and Elizabeth Coutts. 1993. An introduction to the TAXSIM model. *Journal of Policy Analysis and Management* 12 (1): 189–94. Available at [http://www.nber.org/taxsim].

Feenberg, Daniel R., and Harvey Rosen. 1995. Recent developments in the marriage tax. *National Tax Journal* 48 (1): 91–101.

Hausman, Jerry. 1985. Taxes and labor supply. In *Handbook of public economics.* Vol. 1, ed. A. Auerbach and M. Feldstein, 213–61. Amsterdam: North-Holland.

Haveman, Robert. 1996. Reducing poverty while increasing employment: A primer on alternative strategies, and a blueprint. *OECD Economic Studies* 26:7–42.

Heckman, James J., Lance Lochner, and Ricardo Cossa. 2002. Learning-by-doing vs. on-the-job training: Using variation induced by the EITC to distinguish between models of skill formation. NBER Working Paper no. 9083. Cambridge, Mass.: National Bureau of Economic Research, July.

Hill, Carolyn J., V. Joseph Hotz, Charles H. Mullin, and John Karl Scholz. 1999. EITC eligibility, participation, and compliance rates for AFDC households: Evidence from the California caseload. Final report for the State of California. University of California–Los Angeles, April.

Hoffman, Saul D., and Laurence S. Seidman. 1990. *The Earned Income Tax Credit: Antipoverty effectiveness and labor market effects.* Kalamazoo, Mich.: W. E. Upjohn Institute for Employment Research.

Holtzblatt, Janet. 1991. Administering refundable tax credits: Lessons from the EITC experience. In *Proceedings of the eighty-fourth annual conference on taxation,* 180–86. Washington, D.C.: National Tax Association.

Holtzblatt, Janet, and Jeffrey B. Liebman. 1998. The EITC abroad: Implications of the British Working Families Tax Credit for pay-as-you-earn administration of the EITC. In *Proceedings of the ninety-first annual conference on taxation,* 198–207. Washington, D.C.: National Tax Association.

Holtzblatt, Janet, Janet McCubbin, and Robert Gillette. 1994. Promoting work through the EITC. *National Tax Journal* 47 (3): 591–607.

Holtzblatt, Janet, and Robert Rebelein. 1999. Measuring the effect of the EITC on marriage penalties and bonuses. Washington, D.C.: U.S. Treasury Department. Mimeograph, November.

Hotz, V. Joseph, Charles H. Mullin, and John Karl Scholz. 2002a. The Earned Income Tax Credit and labor market participation of families on welfare. University of California–Los Angeles Vanderbilt, and University of Wisconsin–Madison. Mimeograph, March.

———. 2002b. Welfare, employment, and income: Evidence on the effects of benefit reductions from California. *American Economic Review Papers and Proceedings* (May): 380–84.

Hoynes, Hilary. 1997. Does welfare play a role in female headship decision? *Journal of Public Economics* 65 (2): 89–117.

Internal Revenue Service (IRS). 1996. Federal tax compliance research: Individual income tax gap estimates for 1985, 1988, and 1992. Publication no. 1415 (rev. 4-96). Washington, D.C.: IRS.

———. 1999. Individual income tax returns, 1997. Available at [http://www.irs. ustreas.gov/prod/tax_stats/soi/ind_gss.html] (97INDTR.EXE, 97in04ag.xls). Posted 28 December.

———. 2002a. Compliance estimates for Earned Income Tax Credit claimed on 1999 returns. Washington, D.C.: IRS, February.

———. 2002b. Participation in the Earned Income Tax Credit program for tax year 1996. Washington, D.C.: IRS, January.

Jappelli, Tullio. 1990. Who is credit constrained in the U.S. economy? *Quarterly Journal of Economics* 105 (1): 219–34.

Jappelli, Tullio, Jorn-Steffen Pischke, and Nicholas S. Souleles. 1998. Testing for liquidity constraints in Euler equations with complementary data sources. *Review of Economics and Statistics* 80 (2): 251–62.

Johnson, Nicholas. 2001. A hand up: How state Earned Income Tax Credits help working poor families escape poverty in 2001. Washington, D.C.: Center on Budget and Policy Priorities. Mimeograph.

Keane, Michael P. 1995. A new idea for welfare reform. *Federal Reserve Bank of Minneapolis Quarterly Review* 19 (2): 2–28.

Keane, Michael, and Robert Moffitt. 1998. A structural model of multiple welfare program participation and labor supply. *International Economic Review* 39 (3): 553–89.

Killingsworth, Mark, and J. Heckman. 1986. Labor supply of women. In *Handbook of labor economics.* Vol. 1, ed. O. Ashenfelter and R. Layard, 103–204. Amsterdam: North-Holland.

Liebman, Jeffrey. 1997a. The impact of the Earned Income Tax Credit on incentives and income distribution. *Tax Policy and the Economy,* ed. James Poterba, 83–119. Cambridge: MIT Press.

———. 1997b. Noncompliance and the Earned Income Tax Credit: Taxpayer error or taxpayer fraud? Harvard University, John F. Kennedy School of Government. Mimeograph, August.

———. 1999. The optimal design of the Earned Income Tax Credit. Harvard University, John F. Kennedy School of Government. Mimeograph.

———. 2000. Who are the ineligible EITC recipients? *National Tax Journal* 53 (4, part 2): 1165–85.

McCubbin, Janet. 2000. EITC noncompliance: The determinants of the misreporting of children. *National Tax Journal* 53 (4, part 2): 1135–64.

Meyer, Bruce D. 1995. Natural and quasi-experiments in economics. *Journal of Business and Economic Statistics* 13 (2): 151–61.

Meyer, Bruce D., and Dan T. Rosenbaum. 1999. Welfare, the Earned Income Tax Credit, and the labor supply of single mothers. NBER Working Paper no. 7363. Cambridge, Mass.: National Bureau of Economic Research, September.

———. 2000. Making single mothers work: Recent tax and welfare policy and its effects. *National Tax Journal* 53 (4, part 2): 1027–61.

———. 2001. Welfare, the Earned Income Tax Credit, and the labor supply of single mothers. *Quarterly Journal of Economics* 116 (3): 1063–1114.

Moffitt, Robert. 1990. The econometrics of kinked budget constraints. *Journal of Economic Perspectives* 4 (2): 119–39.

———. 1998. The effect of welfare on marriage and fertility. In *Welfare, the family, and reproductive behavior,* ed. R. Moffitt, 50–97. Washington, D.C.: National Academy Press.

———. 1999. The effect of pre-PRWORA waivers on AFDC caseloads and female earnings, income, and labor force behavior. Johns Hopkins University, Department of Economics. Manuscript, May.

Moffitt, Robert, and Mark Wilhelm. 2000. Taxation and the labor supply decisions of the affluent. In *Does Atlas shrug? The economic consequences of taxing the rich,* ed. Joel Slemrod, 193–234. Cambridge: Harvard University Press.

Neumark, David, and William Wascher. 2001. Using the EITC to help poor families: New evidence and a comparison with the minimum wage. *National Tax Journal* 54 (2): 281–317.

Pencavel, John. 1986. Labor supply of men: A survey. In *The handbook of labor economics,* Vol. 1, 3–102. Amsterdam: North Holland.

Phillips, Katherin Ross. 2001. Who knows about the Earned Income Tax Credit? New federalism: National survey of American families. Series no. B-27. Washington, D.C.: The Urban Institute.

Romich, Jennifer, and Thomas Weisner. 2000. How families view and use the EITC: Advance payment versus lump sum delivery. *National Tax Journal* 53 (4, part 2): 1245–64.

Scholz, John Karl. 1994. The Earned Income Tax Credit: Participation, compliance, and anti-poverty effectiveness. *National Tax Journal* 47 (March): 59–81.

———. 1996. In-work benefits in the United States: The Earned Income Tax Credit. *Economic Journal* 106 (January): 156–69.

———. 1997. Testimony for the House Ways and Means Committee. 8 May, Washington, D.C.

Scholz, John Karl, and Kara Levine. 2001. The evolution of income support policy in recent decades. In *Understanding poverty,* ed. S. Danziger and R. Haveman, 193–228. Cambridge and New York: Harvard University Press and Russell Sage Foundation.

Smeeding, Timothy M., Katherine Ross-Phillips, and Michael O'Connor. 2000. The EITC: Expectation, knowledge, use, and economic and social mobility. *National Tax Journal* 53 (4, part 2): 1187–209.

Souleles, Nicholas S. 1999. The response of household consumption to income tax refunds. *American Economic Review* 89 (September): 947–58.

Steuerle, C. Eugene. 1991. The "superterranean" economy. *Tax Notes,* 6 May, 647.

Surrey, Stanley. 1973. *Pathways to tax reform: The concept of tax expenditures.* Cambridge: Harvard University Press.

Thaler, Richard H. 1994. Psychology and savings policies. *American Economic Review Papers and Proceedings* 84 (2): 186–92.

Triest, Robert K. 1990. The effect of income taxation on labor supply in the United States. *Journal of Human Resources* 25 (3): 491–516.

U.S. Congressional Budget Office. 1997. For better or worse: Marriage and the federal income tax. Washington, D.C.: U.S. Congressional Budget Office, June.

U.S. General Accounting Office (GAO). 1993. Earned Income Tax Credit: Design and administration could be improved. Report no. GAO/GGD-93-145. Washington, D.C.: U.S. GAO.

———. 1998. Earned Income Tax Credit: IRS' tax year 1994 compliance study and recent efforts to reduce noncompliance. Report no. GAO/GGD-98-150. Washington, D.C.: U.S. GAO.

———. 2000. Financial audit: IRS' fiscal year 1999 financial statements. Report no. GAO/AIMD-00-76. Washington, D.C.: U.S. GAO.

U.S. House of Representatives, Committee on Ways and Means. 1998. *1998 Green Book.* Washington, D.C.: U.S. Government Printing Office.

Ventry, Dennis. 2000. The collusion of tax and welfare politics: The political history of the Earned Income Tax Credit 1969–1999. *National Tax Journal* 53 (4, part 2): 983–1026.

Weiss, Yoram. 1972. On the optimal lifetime pattern of labour supply. *Economic Journal* 82 (328): 1293–315.

Whittington, Leslie A., James Alm, and H. Elizabeth Peters. 1990. Fertility and the personal exemption: Implicit pronatalist policy in the United States. *American Economic Review* 80 (3): 545–56.

U.S. Food and Nutrition Programs

Janet Currie

4.1 Introduction

The U.S. government operates a wide variety of food and nutrition programs (FANPs), which reach an estimated one out of every five Americans every day.[1] Most FANPs were developed with the primary goal of assuring adequate nutrient intakes in populations deemed to be at risk of undernutrition. However, the nature of nutritional risk has changed over time from a situation in which significant numbers of Americans suffered food shortages to one in which obesity is prevalent even among the homeless. For example, Luder et al. (1990) examined a sample of homeless shelter users in New York City and found that 39 percent were obese. This observation raises the question of whether supplying food is the most effective way to address the nutritional needs of the majority of FANP recipients.

A secondary goal of many FANPs is to improve the nutritional choices of recipients through nutrition education. This goal has received increasing attention in recent years, in response to the finding that many FANP recipients consumed diets sufficient in calories but of poor quality. But the research reviewed in this chapter suggests that we still know little about

Janet Currie is professor of economics at the University of California, Los Angeles, and a research associate of the National Bureau of Economic Research.

The author thanks Hillary Hoynes, Aaron Yelowitz, Robert Moffitt, and participants in the NBER conference on Means-Tested Social Programs for providing helpful comments. Jwahong Min provided excellent research assistance. This research was supported by the National Science Foundation (NSF) and by the National Institute of Child Health and Human Development (NICHID), but these institutions do not necessarily endorse any of its findings.

1. See "Food and Nutrition Service Program Data" at fns1.usda.gov/fns/menu/about/programs/progdata.htm.

the best ways to improve the quality rather than the quantity of food consumed.

In a country in which much of the social safety net is implemented at a state or even at a local level, an important third goal of federal FANPs is to provide a uniform, minimum, nationwide threshold below which assistance cannot fall. The safety-net role of FANPs is likely to become increasingly important in this era of welfare reform as states cut back on cash assistance and FANP benefits form an increasing proportion of the total aid provided to low-income families.

The vast majority of the research on FANPs focuses on the three largest programs: The Food Stamp Program (FSP), The Special Supplemental Nutrition Program for Women, Infants, and Children (WIC), and the National School Lunch Program (NSLP). Accordingly, this review will focus primarily on these three programs. The rest of this chapter is laid out as follows: Section 4.2 provides a brief overview of the history, rules, and program statistics of these three programs. The rest of the paper offers an evaluation of the evidence from these three programs regarding the overall effectiveness of FANPs (section 4.3); factors affecting take-up (section 4.4); the efficacy of in-kind versus cash programs (section 4.5); work disincentives created by the programs (section 4.6); and the role of nutrition education as compared to simple changes in budget constraints (section 4.7). Section 4.8 concludes with a discussion of current policy issues and suggestions for future research.

4.2   Program History, Rules, and Statistics

Table 4.1 offers a brief overview of the history, costs, participation, eligibility requirements, and benefits associated with the twelve most important FANPs. The table indicates that in addition to being the most studied, the FSP, WIC, and NSLP are by far the largest and most widely available FANPs. However, as table 4.1 makes clear, there are many other programs serving smaller subsets of the population. For example, the School Breakfast Program (SBP) serves 7.4 million children per day, compared to the NSLP's 27 million. One reason for the lower participation rate is that 25 percent of schools that offer NSLP do not participate in the SBP. Although income cutoffs for the two programs are the same, the SBP also serves a poorer population on average, which is reflected in the fact that more of the children qualify for a free meal in SBP (77 percent of participating children receive free breakfasts, compared to 48 percent who receive free lunches). The Child and Adult Care Food Program serves 2.5 million children in day care, and 57,000 adults daily. Together these two programs cost $2.8 billion per year, which is about half the cost of the NSLP. The other seven smaller programs together cost only $623 million annually, which is suggestive of their much smaller scale and scope.

Table 4.1 Overview of U.S. Food and Nutrition Programs

Program and Date of Introduction	Federal Cost (1998$)	Population Served	Eligibility Requirements	Benefits
FSP 1961 pilot	19 billion	Low-income households	Household gross income < 130% poverty	Thrifty Food Plan amount less 30% of countable income
1975 nationwide		20.8 million persons/ month	Meet countable income limit, which nets out allowable expenses; asset limit $2000 or $3000 elderly; TANF, SSI, GA recipients eligible; household members may be required to meet state welfare work and training requirements; strikers, noncitizens, postsecondary students, institutionalized not eligible	Difference issued as monthly coupons or as Electronic Benefit Transfers; maximum monthly benefit in 1999 = $125 for 1 person household, $329 for 3 person household, $597 for 6 person household; average benefit per person in 1998 = $71
WIC 1972 pilot	4 billion	Low-income children < 5, pregnant or women	Income cutoffs and verification requirements vary by state but must be ≥ 100% and ≤ 185% poverty	Two nutrition education contact per certification period
1974 permanent program		7.4 million people/ month; 77% = children	Certified as "at nutritional risk"; adjunctive eligibility through TANF, Medicaid, food stamps, may raise effective income cutoffs	Supplemental foods rich in protein, iron, calcium, vitamins A and C; delivered in kind or as vouchers; average worth = $31 monthly; referrals to health and social services
NSLP 1946	5.8 billion	Low income children 27 million lunches/day	Free lunch if ≤ 130% poverty; reduced-price lunch if ≤ 185% poverty	Nutrients = ⅓ daily requirements; as of 1996/97 school year, meals to conform to *Dietary Guidelines for Americans*; average subsidy to school of $2.10 per meal in schools where most meals subsidized

(continued)

Table 4.1 (continued)

Program and Date of Introduction	Federal Cost (1998$)	Population Served	Eligibility Requirements	Benefits
SBP				
1966 pilot	1,267 million	Low-income children	Same as NSLP	See NSLP; subsidy of $1.05 for free meals (1997/98) and $.75 for reduced-price meals
1975 permanent		7.4 million breakfasts/day		
CACFP				
1968 daycare	1.5 billion for children	Children in day care	Day care centers in poor areas (½ kids ≤ 185% poverty)	Reimbursements for meals and snacks which conform to meal patterns (e.g., child care centers get $1.09 per free breakfast, $1.98 per free lunch, $.54 per free snack [1998]; corresponding tier 1 rates = $.92, $1.69, $.50
1976 family care	32 million for adults	Adults in care	Family child care homes sponsored by nonprofit agencies; those in poor areas get Tier 1 rates; others, Tier 2	
1987 adult care		2.5 million children/day; 57,400 adults/day		
SFSP				
1968 pilot	256 million	Children at approved sites	Open sites located in poor areas (see above); enrolled sites, where 50% ≤ 185% poverty	Meals and snacks that follow specified meal food patterns
1975 permanent program		2.3 million children/day		Residential summer camps

Program				
TEFAP 1933 (Federal Surplus Relief)	241 million	3.8 million households served	Soup kitchens, homeless shelters, and similar organizations	USDA purchases, packages, and distributes commodities to eligible agencies.
NPE 1972	141 million	Needy persons aged 60+; 20 million meals/month	No income requirement; targets those with greatest nutritional and social needs	Funds agencies that provide "Congregate Feeding Programs" as well as organizations like "Meals on Wheels"
CSFP 1969	93 million	377,642 people/month; 63% elderly; 30% children	Elderly (60+) ≤ 130% poverty; pregnant or breast-feeding women; new mothers, infants, children < 6; income cutoffs for women, children, set by states	Food packages tailored to individual needs; participating local agencies include health clinics and visiting nurses
SMP 1940 some areas / 1971 permanent program	17 million	134 million ½ pints milk	Children eligible for free lunch who do not have access to other school nutrition programs	½ pints milk
The WIC Farmer's Market Nutrition Program 1989 pilot / 1992 permanent program (*continued*)	12 million	819,972 people received coupons in 1994	WIC participants	Coupons for fresh fruits and vegetables from participating farmer's markets

Table 4.1 (continued)

Program and Date of Introduction	Federal Cost (1998$)	Population Served	Eligibility Requirements	Benefits
NET 1977	3.75 million	All school children	Benefits not targeted by income	USDA grants NET funds to states; NET may be used to develop curricula and materials, nutrition education for children, and training for food service staff and teachers

Notes: FSP = Food Stamp Program; WIC = Special Supplemental Nutrition Program for Women, Infants, and Children; NSLP = National School Lunch Program; SBP = School Breakfast Program; CACFP = Child and Adult Care Food Program; SFSP = Summer Service Program; TEFAP = The Emergency Food Assistance Program; NPE = Nutrition Program for the Elderly; CSFP = Commodity Supplemental Food Program; SMP = Special Milk Program; NET = Nutrition Education and Training Program. The Nutrition Assistance Program for Puerto Rico, American Samoa, and the Northern Marianas has been excluded from the table. This block grant program replaced the FSP in these areas in 1981. The Food Distribution on Indian Reservations Program has also been excluded.

The FSP, WIC, and NSLP have adopted very different approaches to meeting the goals discussed in the introduction. As shown in table 4.1, the NSLP (and the smaller SBP) provide free or reduced-price meals conforming to certain nutritional guidelines directly to their target population. The FSP provides coupons (or, more recently, electronic debit cards) that can be redeemed for food with few restrictions on the types of foods that can be purchased. The WIC program offers coupons that may be redeemed only for specific types of food, to women, infants, and children certified to be at nutritional risk. It also involves a nutrition education component, something that is absent from the other two programs. The remainder of this section offers further details about these programs.

4.2.1   History and Evolution of Program Rules: The FSP[2]

The FSP began as a small pilot program in 1961 and gradually expanded over the next thirteen years: In 1971, national eligibility standards were established, and all states were required to inform eligible households about the program. In 1974, states were required to extend the program statewide if any areas of the state participated. Food Stamp Program benefits have traditionally been provided in the form of coupons that can be exchanged for food at participating stores. These coupons may be used to purchase a wide range of foods, the most significant exception being hot foods that are for immediate consumption.

In contrast to the rules for cash welfare receipt under the old Aid to Families with Dependent Children (AFDC) program and the new Temporary Aid for Needy Families (TANF) programs, most rules for the FSP are set at the federal level. This is because the FSP is designed to offset state variation in welfare programs to some extent, as shown in table 4.2. For example, food stamp benefits amount to less than a third of the combined AFDC/TANF and food stamp benefits in states such as California or Wisconsin that have high cash welfare benefit levels, whereas in low-welfare-benefit-level states such as Texas, FSP income constitutes over half of the household's combined benefits (U.S. Committee on Ways and Means 2000). As table 4.2 shows, there is much more uniformity in the combined benefit levels than in AFDC/TANF benefits alone. Moreover, unlike AFDC/TANF, the FSP is available regardless of family structure, which makes it a particularly important part of the social safety net for low-income households. Congress deliberately retained the centralized nature of the FSP when it further decentralized the welfare system via the Personal Responsibility and Work Opportunity Reconciliation Act (PRWORA) in 1996, which underlines the importance many policymakers attach to providing a minimum federal safety net.

2. Much of the information in this section comes from U.S. Committee on Ways and Means (1999) or from Castner and Anderson (1999).

Table 4.2   Maximum TANF and FSP Benefits for a Family of Four (January 2000, selected states)

State	Maximum TANF	Maximum Combine	TANF vs. WI	Combined vs. WI
California	626	813	.93	.96
New York City	577	779	.86	.92
Illinois	377	639	.56	.76
Texas	201	515	.30	.61
Wisconsin	673	846	1.0	1.0
Ohio	373	636	.55	.75
Massachusetts	579	780	.86	.92
Mississippi	170	494	.25	.58

Source: U.S. Committee on Ways and Means (2000). Note that in states that have more than one benefit level, the one reported is the highest (with the exception of New York City, which has lower benefits than other parts of New York State).

Although most program rules are set at a federal level, the FSP is usually operated through the same state welfare agencies and staff that run the TANF and Medicaid programs. States do have a say about some administrative features such as the length of eligibility certification periods, the design of outreach programs (which may receive 50 percent federal cost sharing), and any "workfare" requirements for participation in the program.

In the early years of the program, households had to pay cash for their food coupons, with the amount depending on the household's income. This purchase requirement was eliminated in 1977 (Kuhn et al. 1996). In the early 1980s, Congress enacted revisions to the FSP that were designed to hold down costs and tighten eligibility. In 1985, rules were liberalized— AFDC and Supplemental Security Income (SSI) recipients became automatically eligible; sales taxes on FSP purchases were prohibited; benefits were increased for the disabled and those with earnings; and deductions for child care and shelter were increased. Legislation passed in 1988, 1989, and 1993 has also liberalized eligibility rules for some specific groups.

Eligibility

Currently, the FSP operates as follows: The FSP household is defined as either a person living alone or a group of people who live together and customarily purchase food and prepare meals together. Generally, people who live together will receive higher benefits if they can be counted as separate food stamp households; however, married couples, and parents with children under twenty-one, are excluded from doing this, although elderly people living with others because of disability may qualify as separate households. The rationale for this last rule is that elderly people who are constrained to live with others by disability should not be penalized by the loss of their food stamp benefits.

Households made up entirely of TANF, SSI, or general assistance recipients are automatically eligible for food stamps. For other households, monthly cash income is the main determinant of eligibility. The FSP uses both the household's gross monthly income and its counted (or "net") monthly income, except for elderly or disabled households, for whom only the net monthly income is counted. This procedure has the effect of creating a more lenient eligibility test for these households. Gross income includes all of the household's cash income, including income from welfare programs, but excluding several smaller sources of income including (a) any payments made to third parties rather than directly to members of the household; (b) unanticipated, irregular, or infrequent income, up to $30 per quarter; (c) loans; (d) income received for the care of someone outside the household; (e) nonrecurring lump-sum payments such as income tax refunds; (f) federal energy assistance; (g) expense reimbursements; (h) income earned by school children aged seventeen or younger; (i) the cost of producing self-employment income; (j) federal postsecondary student aid (such as Pell grants and loans); (k) advance payments of federal Earned Income Tax Credits; (l) on-the-job training earnings of children under nineteen who are in Job Training and Partnership Act programs; (m) income set aside by disabled SSI recipients as part of an approved plan to achieve self-sufficiency; and (n) some other federal payments such as payments under laws relating to Native Americans.

To derive net income in households without an elderly or disabled member, the following amounts are subtracted from gross income: (a) a standard deduction of $134 per month (standard deductions in Alaska, Hawaii, Guam, and the Virgin Islands are $229, $189, $269, and $118, respectively); (b) any amounts paid as legally obligated child support; (c) 20 percent of any earned income; (d) dependent care expenses related to work or training up to $175 a month per dependent and $200 a month for children under age two; and (e) shelter expenses that exceed 50 percent of counted income after all other deductions have been applied, up to a periodically adjusted ceiling of $250 per month (different ceilings apply in Alaska, Hawaii, Guam, and the Virgin Islands).

For households with an elderly or disabled member, net monthly income is equal to gross monthly income less the same standard child support, earned income, and dependent care deductions; any shelter expenses that exceed 50 percent of counted income after all other deductions, without any limit; and out-of-pocket medical expenses (other than those for special diets) that are incurred by the elderly or disabled household members to the extent that they exceed a threshold of $35 per month.

All households must have net monthly income that does not exceed the

Table 4.3   Net and Gross Income Limits for Food Stamps, and Maximum
                   Monthly Allotments

	Net Income	Gross Income	Maximum Benefit
1 person	658	855	122
2 persons	885	1,150	224
3 persons	1,111	1,445	321
4 persons	1,338	1,445	408
5 persons	1,565	2,034	485
6 persons	1,791	2,329	582
7 persons	2,018	2,623	643
8 persons	2,245	2,918	735
Each additional person	+227	+295	+92

Source: U.S. Committee on Ways and Means (1999).

Note: Alaska and Hawaii have higher income limits and maximum benefit levels.

federal poverty line. Households without an elderly or disabled member must also have gross income that does not exceed 130 percent of the federal guidelines. Finally, household assets must be less than $2,000 in households without elderly members, and less than $3,000 in households with elderly members. The family home and one car are excluded from the asset limits, as long as the car's value does not exceed $4,500. These asset limits apply regardless of the household's size. The net and gross monthly income eligibility limits and maximum benefit levels for families of different sizes are summarized in table 4.3.

FSP Program Benefits and Marginal Tax Rates

Benefit levels are based on the cost of the U.S. Department of Agriculture's Thrifty Food Plan (TFP) for a family of four, adjusted for household size. It is interesting to note that nutritional needs could actually be satisfied at a far lower cost than that given by the TFP. However, the foods included in the TFP are chosen to approximate the food consumption patterns of low-income Americans (Ohls and Beebout 1993).

Table 4.4 offers an example of the benefit calculation for a single mother with two children, and her own mother (the grandmother). This table illustrates a situation in which this family would get substantially more in food stamp benefits if the grandmother lived apart from her daughter than they would receive if they lived together. Thus, the program appears to be designed (in part) to support the independence of elderly people.

The discussion so far highlights some of the ways in which the FSP program rules tend to favor households containing elderly members. We can compare the four-person household in table 4.4 with one in which there is a father earning $1,500, a stay-at-home mother, and two children, with rental payments of $650. This household would receive a monthly benefit

Table 4.4   **Example Calculations of Food Stamp Benefits**

1. Single mother, 2 children, earnings of $1,000 per month, rent $400 per month
   Standard deduction = $134
   20% of earned income = $200
   Dependent care deduction = $350
   Rent deduction = $242
   Net income = 1,000 – 134 – 200 – 350 – 242 = 74
   .3 × 74 = 22.2
Maximum food stamp benefit for family of 3 = 321. 321 – 22.2 = **$298.80 food stamp benefit**

2. Elderly grandmother, income from pension = $500, rent $250 per month
   Standard deduction = $134
   Medical expenses = $200
   Rent deduction = $167
   Net income = 500 – 134 – 200 – 167 = 0
Maximum food stamp benefit for family of 1 = 122. **$122 food stamp benefit**

3. Same single mother, 2 children, and grandmother, household income = $1,500, rent =
     $650 per month
   Standard deduction = $134
   20% of earned income = $200
   Dependent care deduction = $350
   Medical expenses = $200
   Rent deduction = 342
   Net income = 1,500 – 134 – 200 – 350 – 200 –342 = 274
   .3 × 274 = 82.8
Maximum food stamp benefit for family of 4 = 408. 408 – 82.2 = **$325.80 food stamp benefit**

of $268.20, compared to the benefit of $325.80 for the household with the elderly member, even though this household has the same income and rental payments.

Note that households participating in the FSP are taxed at a rate of 30 percent for each additional dollar of earnings. Under certain circumstances, households may face even larger tax rates. For example, in 1998, the gross income limit for a family of three was $1,445, and the maximum food stamp allotment was $321 per month. If the household earned $1,446 they would be ineligible for food stamps because of the gross income limit. If they earned $1,444, then they would be eligible. If they took the deduction for one child and had excess shelter expenses of $200, then they would qualify for a benefit of $127 per month. Thus, by earning $2 more per month, the household would lose $127, for a net loss of $125!

The FSP's 30 percent tax rate on other income can also be regarded as a tax on state efforts to transfer income to poor families. For every dollar that a state transfers in the form of TANF benefits, the federal government reduces FSP transfers by $.30. This tax may serve as a disincentive for states to increase the generosity of their own cash transfer programs. Conversely, the fact that in-kind benefits are not counted as income for the purposes of eligibility determination in most federal means-tested programs may give states an incentive to provide aid in kind rather than in cash.

Electronic Benefit Transfer

Food stamp benefits are usually issued monthly by welfare agencies. In the past this was generally done either by mailing recipients an authorization-to-participate card that could be redeemed for coupons at specified places (such as a post office) or by directly mailing food stamp coupons to recipients. The introduction of Electronic Benefit Transfer (EBT) represents the first major shift in the way the program has been administered since 1977. Maryland pioneered EBT in 1993, and twenty other states had adopted EBT by 2000. The 1996 PRWORA legislation mandated that all states switch to EBT by October 2002.

Most EBT systems work much like bank debit cards. Recipients are given EBT cards with a magnetic stripe. At the checkout, the recipient enters a personal identification number in a terminal to authorize EBT payment of the food stamp purchase. The terminal connects to the EBT system's central computer, which maintains an account for the recipient. If the PIN is verified and the recipient has enough funds to cover the transaction, then the purchase is authorized, and the amount is deducted from the recipient's balance. The retailer is reimbursed at the end of the day via an electronic transfer of funds from an EBT account maintained by the U.S. Treasury to the store's financial institution.

Welfare Reform and the FSP

In addition to the requirement that states switch to EBT, PRWORA required able-bodied adults without dependents (ABAWDs) to meet stiff work requirements and limited their participation in the program to only three to six months in any thirty-six-month period, unless the person is enrolled in a work or training activity. However, most states have waived these requirements for at least some fraction of their ABAWD caseloads (Gabor and Botsko 1998).

PRWORA also disqualified legal immigrants and allowed states to alter FSP eligibility rules in order to make the program more compatible with other state welfare programs. In principle, states can use this latter provision to sanction FSP recipients who do not comply with the work requirements of other welfare programs, who fail to cooperate with child support enforcement, or who fail to ensure that minors attend school. However, enforcement of these types of sanctions has been relatively lax—in 1996, 40 percent of the 5.5 million people technically subject to work and training requirements were exempted (U.S. Committee on Ways and Means 1998). Finally, the PRWORA beefed up the nutrition education component of the FSP considerably. Between fiscal year 1997 and 1999, nutrition education spending increased from \$32.7 million to a projected \$75 million in fiscal year 1999.

FSP Participation

Trends in program participation and expenditures from 1975 to the present are shown in table 4.5. Participation in the FSP hovered around 20 million persons per year during the 1980s but rose sharply in the early 1990s to a peak of approximately 27 million persons in 1994. Participation then began to fall again, declining back to 20.8 million participants by 1998. The passage of PRWORA coincided with the decline in FSP enrollment, which has provoked a debate about the extent to which changes in FSP participation can be attributed to PRWORA.

Table 4.5   **Trends in Caseloads and Expenditures for the Three Largest FANPs**

	1975	1980	1985	1995	1995	1998
Expenditures (billions $1998)						
FSP	12.7	18.9	20.4	22.1	29.3	19.0
WIC	.7	.9	2.3	2.6	3.7	4.0
NSLP	5.6	6.0	4.6	4.6	5.6	5.8
Average Monthly Caseload (millions participants)						
FSP	16.3	19.2	19.9	20.0	26.6	20.8
WIC						
Women	.2	.4	.7	1.0	1.6	1.7
Children	.7	1.5	2.5	3.5	5.3	5.7
NSLP						
Any meals	26.3	26.6	23.6	24.1	25.6	27.0
Free meals	10.5	10.0	9.9	9.9	12.4	13.5
Caseload (as % Relevant Low-Income Population)						
FSP (as % < 130% poverty)		46.3	39.0	40.9	48.6	38.9
WIC (as % < 185% poverty;						
children < 5)		20.3	27.6	39.2	53.9	61.8
NSLP						
% any meals; children aged 5–17		53.4	49.7	50.0	48.2	48.7
% free meals; children aged 5–17						
< 130% poverty		86.1	73.3	78.9	81.4	87.2

Source: U.S. Committee on Ways and Means (various years), plus author's calculations of size of the relevant poor population from Current Population Surveys, various years. Note that the 1975 CPS had a noncomparable format, so estimates for 1975 are not included for "Caseloads as % Relevant Low-Income Population." For WIC, we have no estimate of the extent of nutritional risk, so the figures show participation as a percent of the infants and children in the relevant income range. We cannot identify pregnant or postpartum women in the CPS. "Any meals" refers to free meals, plus reduced-price meals, plus full-price meals served under the NSLP. We use all children ≥ 5 and ≤ 17 as the base for the NSLP, recognizing that some five-, 16-, and 17-year-olds will not be in school, but that some eighteen- and nineteen-year-olds will be.

Note: See table 4.1 for explanation of abbreviations.

An alternative hypothesis is that the decline in FSP participation is due to the booming economy of the 1990s. However, if one examines the FSP caseload as a percentage of the population that is in poverty, one also sees an increase followed by a decline. For example, as table 4.5 shows, 40.9, 48.6, and 38.9 percent of the population with incomes less than 130 percent of poverty participated in the FSP in 1990, 1995, and 1998, respectively (U.S. Committee on Ways and Means 1998). This suggests that the increase in the caseload was not driven by business-cycle effects alone since downturns would be expected to increase the fraction of poor, but not necessarily to increase the fraction of the poor who participated in the program. Estimates of the extent of the decline in FSP that can be attributed to good economic conditions range from 28 to 44 percent, suggesting that some of the remainder may be due to welfare reform, as is discussed further below (Dion and Pavetti 2000; Wilde et al. 2000).

Composition of the FSP Caseload

Table 4.6 shows that the recent changes in the FSP caseload were also accompanied by changes in its composition. After remaining remarkably stable during the 1980s and early 1990s, the fraction of the food stamp caseload with any earnings rose from 21 percent in 1995 to 26.3 percent in 1998. Over the same time interval, the fraction with AFDC (TANF) income fell from 38 percent to 31.4 percent, while the fraction with SSI income rose from 23 percent to 28.1 percent. It is possible that some of this change in the FSP caseload reflects households who took up SSI when they become ineligible for TANF, although the beginning of the increase in the fraction of households receiving SSI appears to predate the onset of welfare reform. The fraction of households with children and single heads also fell dramatically from 50 percent to 39.6 percent between 1995 and 1998. However, the fraction of FSP households with children fell only slightly, to 58.3 percent from 60 percent (U.S. Committee on Ways and Means 1998).

Table 4.6   Percent of Food Stamp Households with Selected Characteristics

	1980	1985	1990	1995	1998
Gross monthly income below poverty	87	94	92	92	92
With earnings	19	20	19	21	26
With AFDC income	n.a.	39	43	38	31
With SSI income	18	19	19	23	28
With children	60	59	61	60	58
With children and female heads	n.a.	46	51	50	40
With elderly members	23	21	18	16	18

Sources: U.S. Committee on Ways and Means (1999).
Note: n.a. indicates not available.

Finally, McConnell and Ohls (2000) show that decline in the caseload has been much more dramatic in urban than in rural areas, where about one-quarter of the FSP caseload is located. In fact, the decline that did occur in rural areas can be entirely accounted for by a reduction in the number of eligible households. McConnell and Ohls also show that rural households are somewhat less likely to know that they are eligible for the FSP or to know where and how to sign up. Nonetheless, rural households have higher take-up conditional on eligibility than urban households, and their level of satisfaction with the program is higher. For example, they are more likely to feel that they are treated respectfully by their caseworkers. Because of this difference in perceptions about treatment, McConnell and Ohls speculate that the sharper decline in FSP take-up in cities may be attributable to unhelpful caseworkers who, for example, do not inform people who lose TANF benefits that they remain eligible for the FSP.

4.2.2   History and Evolution of Program Rules: WIC[3]

As table 1 has shown, WIC differs from FSP along a number of key dimensions. First, it is not an entitlement program, which means that when the funds Congress allocates to the program run out, eligible participants can no longer be served.[4] Second, WIC is targeted only to pregnant, postpartum, or lactating women, infants, and children less than five. Third, WIC provides only nutritious foods, in contrast to food stamps, which can be used to purchase virtually anything edible other than alcohol, tobacco, hot foods intended for immediate consumption, and (paradoxically) vitamins. The WIC program also has more specific nutritional goals than the FSP: It seeks to improve fetal development and reduce the incidence of low birth weight, short gestation, and anemia. Recently, WIC has recognized that the reduction of overweight is also a goal of the program.

The 1969 White House Conference on Food, Nutrition, and Health documented nutritional deficiencies among low-income pregnant women, infants, and children, and was one of the major factors leading to the establishment of WIC in 1972 (by amendment to the Child Nutrition Act of 1966). In 1975, the age limit was changed to allow children to participate up until their fifth birthdays, and amendments in 1978 established income eligibility standards, defined "nutritional risk," required that one-sixth of administrative funds be allocated to nutrition education, and directed the secretary of agriculture to regulate the types of foods provided to WIC par-

---

3. Most of the following information about the WIC program comes from these sources: Bitler, Currie, and Scholz (2002); U.S. Congress (1996); Randall, Boast, and Holst (1995); U.S. Committee on Ways and Means (1999); and Hamilton, Fox, et al. (2000). Other sources are noted where appropriate.

4. Technically, FSP is not an entitlement program either, but Congress has always appropriated sufficient monies to fully fund the program.

ticipants. Legislation in 1989 required states to seek rebates on purchases from infant formula manufacturers.

WIC is administered by the Food and Consumer Service (FCS) of the U.S. Department of Agriculture (USDA) and by state WIC agencies (in 1994 there were eighty-four "state" agencies covering the fifty states, District of Columbia, Guam, Puerto Rico, the Virgin Islands, and thirty Indian Tribal Organizations). In turn, these state organizations operated 2,129 local WIC agencies, which operated at about 10,000 sites. Most local agencies are state, county, or municipal health departments, but other organizations such as hospitals or maternal and child health programs can also serve as WIC agencies.

WIC Benefits

The program provides a combination of food supplements, nutrition education, and access to health services. The food packages are tailored to provide the specific nutrients that are most likely to be lacking in the diets of the target populations. The included foods are good sources of protein, iron, calcium, and vitamins A and C. Food packages are usually provided in the form of vouchers or checks that are redeemable only for certain types of food at participating grocers, although in a few areas participants receive deliveries of food items, or pick them up from a central location. The monthly value of the food package provided in 1994 varied from $40.49 in the Southeast to $52.68 in the West. With rebates for infant formula, the costs to state agencies for these packages were $29.08 and $43.34, respectively. Food retailers enter into annual contracts with state or local WIC agencies, in which they agree to accept WIC coupons, to charge less than or equal to the going price, to accept training, and to submit to reviews by WIC agencies.

WIC agencies are required to offer participants at least two nutrition education sessions during each certification period. These may include one-on-one counseling, group classes, or films and videos, for example. Participants are usually required to pick up WIC vouchers during scheduled nutrition education sessions (although the sessions themselves are not compulsory), although at times when such sessions are not scheduled vouchers may be mailed. WIC agencies are also required to assist WIC participants in obtaining preventive health care services, either through the provision of services on-site or through referrals to other agencies. In fact, state WIC agencies are required to give priority for funding to local agencies that provide "ongoing, routine pediatric and obstetric care" (U.S. Congress 1996).

WIC Eligibility

A person must be categorically eligible in order to receive WIC benefits. That is, the individual must be a pregnant, breastfeeding, or postpartum woman; an infant up to the age of one year; or a child aged one through four years. In addition to falling into one of these categories, the individual must be income eligible. Income cutoffs are set by the states, but must be between 100 percent and 185 percent of the federal poverty line. In fact, all states have adopted 185 percent of poverty as the income cutoff. When determining income eligibility, cash income from Social Security, welfare, or other public assistance is counted, whereas in-kind transfers in the form of NSLP and FSP benefits are excluded. Some small sources of income such as income from Home Energy Assistance, youth employment demonstration programs, and payments made to volunteers are also excluded.

In addition, individuals may qualify because they are "adjunctively eligible." That is, people who participate in AFDC/TANF, food stamps, or Medicaid are eligible for WIC even if their incomes exceed the 185 percent cutoff. Some states also have adjunctive eligibility for other programs, such as Head Start and SSI. Recent expansions of the Medicaid income cutoffs for pregnant women, infants, and children mean that many people with incomes above 185 percent of poverty are now eligible for WIC. In some states, children with incomes up to 300 percent of poverty may be eligible. Some commentators feel that these largely unintended expansions of the WIC program to people of higher income are inappropriate and should be reversed (see Besharov and Germanis 2001).

Participants must also be "at nutritional risk." Among women, inadequate or inappropriate nutrient intakes, general obstetrical risks, hemoglobin or hematocrit measures below specified state cutoffs, and high weight for height are commonly reported risks. Among children, common risks include inappropriate or inadequate nutrient intake and low hemoglobin or hematocrit levels. Over two-thirds of WIC infants are classified as being at risk, either because their mothers are currently at risk or because the mothers were at risk during pregnancy. In practice, it seems that virtually all income-eligible individuals are certified as "at risk," usually on the basis of inappropriate nutrient intakes if they do not meet any other risk criteria (Institute of Medicine 2002). This fact becomes less surprising when one considers that current nutritional guidelines state that everyone should have five servings of fruits and vegetables per day.

Participants are certified "WIC eligible" for fixed periods. For example, pregnant women are certified for the duration of their pregnancies and up to six weeks postpartum. Postpartum women are certified for up to six months. Breastfeeding women and infants may be recertified at intervals of six months, up to the infant's first birthday, and children are certified every six months up to the month in which the child reaches the fifth birthday. States may also establish shorter certification periods for applicants deemed to present a risk of fraud or abuse.

Areas of State Discretion: WIC

As discussed earlier, the number of participants served is limited by each year's congressional appropriation. In each state, a maximum caseload is

Table 4.7   Priority System for WIC

Priority	Description
1	Pregnant and breast-feeding women and infants demonstrated to be at nutritional risk via anthropometric or hematological assessment or by other documented nutritionally related medical condition.
2	Infants up to six months of mothers who participated in WIC during pregnancy or who would have been eligible to participate during pregnancy under priority 1. Breast-feeding mothers of priority 2 infants may also be assigned priority 2.
3	Children demonstrated to be at nutritional risk via anthropometric or hematological assessment or by other documented nutritionally related medical condition. States have the option of including high-risk postpartum women at this priority level.
4	Pregnant and breast-feeding women and infants, at nutritional risk because of inadequate dietary pattern. States have the option of including high-risk postpartum women at this priority level.
5	Children at nutritional risk due to inadequate dietary pattern. States may also include high-risk postpartum women in this priority level.
6	Postpartum women, not breast-feeding, at nutritional risk on either medical or dietary criteria.
7	Previously certified participants who are likely to regress in nutritional status without continuation of supplemental foods.

set for each local agency. When the agency reaches this ceiling, a priority system is used to allocate scarce places, and other eligible applicants go on a waiting list. These priorities are intended to give preference to medically based nutritional risks, rather than to those that are based only on inadequate diets. The priority system is illustrated in table 4.7, which shows that states have some latitude in assigning priority rankings. In practice, no states have had waiting lists for the program in recent years.

Table 4.8 describes other dimensions of state discretion, including the tailoring of food packages, the frequency with which food instruments are issued, whether or not participants in other programs are automatically eligible, income documentation and verification policy, policies for obtaining dietary information, documentation of nutritional risk, and standards for determining nutritional risk. For example, whereas most states specify brands that can be purchased using WIC coupons, some large and important states such as Texas do not. Also, although most states issue WIC coupons monthly, there is a sizable number that issue them bimonthly, quarterly, or at intervals determined at the discretion of the local office. In ten states, family members of NSLP participants are automatically eligible for WIC. A surprising number of states (twenty-six) did not require documentation of income until the federal government ordered states to begin requiring such documentation in April 1999. Standards for nutritional risk have also varied considerably from state to state. For example, in New

Table 4.8   **WIC Regulations That Have Varied at the State Level**

I. Food Package Adjustment Practices
   A. Designation or disallowance of food brands.
   B. Specification of size of food container.
   C. Elimination or reduction of specified food types.
   D. Specified form of food within food types.
   E. Specified type of milk, cheese, or formula.
II. Frequency of WIC Food Instrument Issuance
   A. May be every month, every two months, every three months, or other. Some states
      have different standard frequencies for different types of recipients, and others do
      not have a standard frequency of issuance.
III. Interactions with Other Programs
   A. In all states except Georgia and Illinois, AFDC participants are automatically eli-
      gible. In all states but Georgia and Hawaii, FSP participants are automatically eli-
      gible.
   B. Participants in Medicaid, the NSLP, SSI and other programs may also be auto-
      matically eligible for WIC.
IV. Income Documentation and Verification Policy
   A. Many states did not require income documentation, allow applicant self-
      declarations, or demanded documentation at local agency discretion. As of April,
      1999, all states were required to demand such documentation.
V. Policies for obtaining dietary information
   A. Dietary information may be obtained from all participants, or only those who are
      at risk because of dietary patterns (rather than for example, because of anemia).
   B. Data may be collected using 24 hour dietary recalls, food frequency checklists,
      food diaries, or other methods.
VI. Documentation of nutritional risk factors
   A. In some states, only the most important risk factor is reported, while in others, all
      risk factors, or a set number of risk factors are reported.
VII. Standards for determining nutritional risk.
   A. Standards are set separately for each category of recipient (infants, children, preg-
      nant, breast-feeding, and postpartum women).
   B. Anthropometric standards may be set for weight-for-age, height-for-age, and
      weight-for-height.
   C. Standards are also set for hemoglobin and hematocrit values. These may vary with
      the trimester of pregnancy. The federal government has been standardizing these
      cutoffs across states.
VIII. Priority System (see table 4.7).

Source: Randall, Boast, and Holst (1995).

Hampshire, infants below the 25th percentile of height-for-age are considered to be at risk, whereas in neighboring Massachusetts, infants must be
below the 11th percentile to be deemed at risk.

WIC Participation

In the quarter century since it was authorized as a permanent program,
WIC has shown virtually continuous growth from fewer than 1 million participants in 1977 to approximately 7.4 million participants per month in
1998, as was shown in table 4.5. The caseload in 1999 was composed of 23

percent women and 20 percent infants, while the rest were children (U.S. Committee on Ways and Means 2000). However, Burstein et al. (2000) show that child WIC participation tends to fall off greatly after the child's first birthday, presumably because the value of the WIC food package is much reduced once the child stops using infant formula.

Table 4.5 shows our estimate of the WIC population as a fraction of infants and children meeting the categorical and income eligibility standards (but not including the adjunctively eligible). We ignore the nutritional risk criteria, since most people who are income-eligible seem to satisfy them in practice. The figures show that by 1998, approximately 60 percent of the low-income population of infants and children less than five participated in WIC.[5] A 1996 study indicated that 60 percent of those participating in WIC were poor, 25 percent were on AFDC, 36 percent received food stamps, and 55 percent were on Medicaid.

Bitler, Currie, and Scholz (2002) present a more detailed analysis of participation using data from the Survey of Income and Program Participation, which allows them both to identify monthly income and to identify pregnant and postpartum women more accurately than the Current Population Survey (CPS) data allow. They include those that were adjunctively eligible through participation in other programs and calculate that 58 percent of all infants in any given month in 1998 were eligible for WIC! Roughly 45 percent received WIC benefits, so that the take-up rate among eligible infants was 73.2 percent. Among children one to four, 57 percent were eligible for WIC and 38 percent of eligible children received benefits. The difference between this estimate and that in table 4.5 reflects the low take-up among relatively high-income children who are adjunctively eligible. Estimates for pregnant and postpartum women are less accurate, since it is not possible to observe infant feeding practices, but they estimate that 54 percent of all pregnant and postpartum women are eligible for WIC and that 66.5 percent of these women received benefits.

4.2.3   History and Evolution of Program Rules: NSLP

The NSLP is in some respects an intermediate program between the FSP and WIC. Like the FSP, it is an entitlement program, and most schools with eligible children participate. Like WIC, it is targeted to children. Unlike FSP, benefits include only meals that follow USDA-approved meal plans. However, until recently, these meal plans did not have to follow the *Dietary Guidelines for Americans* (U.S. Department of Health and Human Services [DHHS] and USDA 1995), and school meals were often criticized

5. Concern has recently been expressed about participation among infants that exceeds USDA estimates of the number of eligibles. However, there are several problems with the way that the USDA calculates the number of eligibles. For example, they do not include those who are adjunctively eligible (National Research Council 2001).

for being high in fat and sodium and low in carbohydrates, fruits, and vegetables (see Gordon, Devaney, and Burghardt 1995).

The NSLP was established in 1946 in response to nutrition deficiency–related health problems identified among young men being drafted during World War II. Perhaps this is why the legislation governing the program states that "It is declared to be the policy of Congress, as a measure of national security, to safeguard the health and well-being of the Nation's children and to encourage the domestic consumption of nutritious agricultural commodities and other food . . . [through] school lunch programs" (U.S. Congress 2000). As this language suggests, a primary goal of the program is to provide meals that include minimum daily requirements of key nutrients. A secondary purpose is the disposal of agricultural surplus.

Changes to the program over the past twenty years include attempts to alter meal guidelines in order to provide healthier meals and reduce waste, as well as a decreasing emphasis on the use of surplus commodities. These changes include the development of the "offer versus serve" option, which allowed schools to be reimbursed for lunches in which students were offered all five components of the school lunch meal pattern, as long as students chose at least three components.[6]

The Food and Nutrition Service of the USDA oversees administration of the program through local state agencies (usually departments of education). In turn, the state agencies provide technical assistance to local school food authorities, who provide assistance to individual schools.

NSLP Benefits

The program provides a flat per-meal subsidy to participating schools, as long as the meals served conform to program guidelines. The subsidy depends on the income of the students served, as shown in table 4.9. Note that the NSLP subsidizes school lunches served to children at all income levels, so that in principle, even schools without poor students can participate. The subsidies can be compared to the average full prices charged to children with incomes above 185 percent of poverty, which are also shown in the table. Additionally, schools receive commodities for use in school lunches. These commodity subsidies are available regardless of the incomes of the students served. Schools can ask for cash instead of actual food products, and they can ask for additional bonus commodity aid, if it can be used without waste.

In 1994, Congress passed the Healthy Meals for Healthy Americans Act, which required the USDA to develop a new menu planning system that

---

6. The five elements were the following: one serving of a meat or meat alternate; two servings of vegetables, fruit, and/or juice; one serving of bread or bread alternate; and one serving of milk.

Table 4.9   Percent of Households Receiving AFDC/TANF or SSI and Also Receiving
                   Assistance from FANPs

	1984	1987	1990	1992	1993	1994	1995	1997–98
AFDC								
Food stamps	81.4	81.7	82.7	86.2	88.9	88.3	87.2	81
WIC	15.3	18.6	18.7	21.5	18.5	21.4	24.7	30.6
Free or reduced-								
price meals	49.2	55.6	52.7	55.5	56.9	57.5	63.1	60.3
SSI								
Food stamps	46.5	39.7	41.3	46.2	48.0	50.1	50.0	43.7
WIC	2.5	2.5	3.0	4.3	3.7	5.4	5.6	5.5
Free or reduced-								
price meals	12.7	11.9	15.3	18.2	21.3	23.8	25.2	18.4

Source: U.S. Committee on Ways and Means (2000, 864).

Table 4.10   Current Dietary Standards for School Lunches

I. Provision of one-third of the recommended dietary allowances of protein, calcium, iron, vitamin A, and vitamin C for the applicable age or grade group.

II. Provision of the lunchtime energy allowances for children based on the appropriate age or grade group.

III. The applicable recommendations of the *1990 Dietary Guidelines for Americans,* which are
   A. Eat a variety of foods.
   B. Limit total fat to 30 percent of calories.
   C. Limit saturated fat to less than 10 percent of calories.
   D. Choose a diet low in cholesterol.
   E. Choose a diet with plenty of vegetables, fruits, and grains.
   F. Use salt and sodium in moderation.

IV. The following measures of compliance with the applicable recommendations of the *1990 Dietary Guidelines for Americans:*
   A. A limit on the percent of calories from total fat to 30 percent based on the actual number of calories offered.
   B. A limit on the percent of calories from saturated fat to less than 10 percent based on the actual number of calories offered.
   C. A reduction of the levels of sodium and cholesterol.
   D. An increase in the level of dietary fiber.

Source: U.S. Congress (2000, p. 22).

schools can use to meet the specific nutrient standards set out in the *Dietary Guidelines for Americans.* Now, rather than choosing a specific number of items from a list, schools can use whatever portions and combinations of food they wish in order to meet these guidelines. Table 4.10 shows the guidelines that school lunches are currently required to meet. In response to the act, the USDA has also implemented the School Meals Initiative for Healthy Children to provide nutrition education to both children and food service staff (Hamilton and Fox 2000).

The USDA is also working to improve the nutritional quality of commodities distributed to NSLP schools by, for example, reducing the sodium in canned vegetables and offering low-fat beef patties. It is worth noting that a historical goal of the NSLP has been to provide an outlet for surplus agricultural commodities. In the past, there was less conflict between this goal and that of guaranteeing minimum daily intakes of important nutrients. However, in a world where obesity is an increasing problem, the disposal of large amounts of foods such as full-fat milk, cheese, and peanut butter can pose problems for program staff who are attempting to provide a healthy diet to program recipients.

NSLP Eligibility

Determination of income eligibility for the program is left to the schools. For example, in the Los Angeles Unified School District, parents are asked to fill in a form at the beginning of the year, and children who are certified eligible on the basis of these self-reports receive coupons that can be redeemed for meals.[7] The standard form parents fill out requires them to give the names and Social Security numbers of all adult household members, as well as the household's current income (i.e., income last month) and its sources. Some subsample of parents is chosen for verification of income eligibility. In principle, parents are required to report changes in income that would make their children ineligible for the program. In practice, it appears that this provision is not enforced and so certifications are generally for the duration of the school year.

NSLP Participation

Ninety-nine percent of public schools and 83 percent of all (public and private) schools participate. Nationally, 92 percent of students have the program available at their schools (Burghardt, Gordon, and Devaney 1995). In 1996, 57 percent of the 45.3 million children enrolled in participating institutions (i.e., almost all schools) participated in the NSLP. Eighty-six percent of these participants received free lunches, indicating that they came from households with incomes less than 1.3 times the federal poverty line (U.S. Committee on Ways and Means 1998).

As table 4.5 shows, participation in the NSLP fell in the mid-1980s but has recovered steadily since 1985, and it is now at historically high levels. In 1998, 27 million children received meals under the program. An increasingly large fraction of the total meals served are free: That is, they are served to children from households with incomes less than 130 percent of poverty. This increase in the numbers of poor children participating in the NSLP is particularly remarkable given the economic expansion of the

---

7. This description came from a graduate student whose children participate in the program.

1990s and the fact that much of the recent decline in the FSP caseload has been attributed to buoyant economic conditions. The bottom panel of table 4.5 shows that although NSLP participation as a fraction of the five- to seventeen-year-old child population has remained roughly constant over the past fifteen years, participation in the free meals part of the program as a fraction of the five- to seventeen-year-old population with incomes less than 130 percent of poverty has increased steadily.

4.2.4   Interactions of FANPs with Other Programs

Many participants in FANPs also qualify for other types of social assistance. As has been discussed, those on AFDC and SSI qualify automatically for the FSP, children in TANF and FSP are qualified to receive free school meals, and in most states, income criteria for WIC are automatically deemed to have been met by participants in Medicaid, FSP, and TANF. In-kind benefits such as those provided by FANPs are not included as income for the purposes of calculating eligibility for other FANPs. Participation in one social program may also increase knowledge about other programs. For example, staff in WIC agencies often provide information to those eligible for other programs, which may contribute to multiple program use among WIC participants (Randall, Boast, and Holst 1995).

Table 4.6 indicates that in 1998, 31 percent of food stamp households received AFDC, whereas 28 percent received SSI. Food stamp households also received assistance from General Assistance (6 percent), Social Security (23 percent), and Unemployment Insurance (1.6 percent); U.S. Committee on Ways and Means 1998). In all, 79 percent of FSP households received some other form of cash assistance. Table 4.11 shows the fraction of AFDC and SSI households who also received assistance from FANPs over the period 1984 to 1998.

Households participating in WIC and in NSLP face "notches" in their budget constraints that are similar to those previously described for the

Table 4.11   **Subsidies and Prices for NSLP, 1997–98**

	Per Meal Federal Subsidy	Average Price Charged
Family income		
≤ 130% of poverty	1.89	0
130–185% of poverty	1.49	0.38
> 185% of poverty	0.18	1.14
Commodity assistance (all meals)	0.15	—

Source: Rossi (1998).
Note: Dash indicates not applicable.

FSP. If households participate in more than one program, then the notches can be even bigger. For example, both the FSP and NSLP have income cutoffs of 130 percent of poverty. Thus, in the example above, if the household had participated in both programs, then it would lose $125 in FSP benefits and would also have to start paying for school lunches (at the "reduced price" rate). If we assume that a student attends school twenty-two days a month, then the move from free to reduced-price status would cost the household a further $8.36 per month.

Currie and Grogger (2001) show that among single heads, a quarter of the reduction in food stamp participation rates may be attributable to increases in the generosity of the Earned Income Tax Credit program, which moved many of these households above the income threshold for the program. Thus, this study suggests that it is important to consider other programmatic changes that may have had effects on food stamp participation.

Finally, an interesting feature of the FSP is that it subsidizes rents and so to some extent is actually a housing program.[8] For example, suppose that the four-person household depicted in table 4.4 moved from a $650 apartment to an $800 per month apartment. The deduction that they could claim for rent would rise from $342 to $492 per month, and the value of their food stamp benefit would increase from $325.80 per month to $370.80 per month. Thus, the increase of $150 in rental payments would be offset by an increase in $45 in food stamp benefits. On the other hand, if this household did not contain an elderly member, rental deductions would be capped at $250 and there would be no offset. Similarly, for the elderly, the FSP subsidizes out-of-pocket medical expenditures and thus can be viewed as a medical insurance policy that "wraps around" coverages provided by the Medicare and Medicaid programs.

4.2.5   Financing and Quality Control Issues

The FSP

Funding for the FSP is overwhelmingly federal. In addition to funding the benefits, the federal government pays its own administrative costs, and at least 50 percent of the state's administrative costs. The USDA Food and Consumer Service retains responsibility for approving and overseeing participation by retail food stores and other outlets that may accept food stamps. The FNS is responsible for monitoring stores that participate in the FSP, whereas states are responsible for monitoring individuals.

It is difficult to come up with any reliable estimate of the extent of fraud in the FSP. Various types of abuse are possible. For example, recipients may sell coupons at a discount to other individuals or to stores. Or stores

---

8. I am grateful to Edward Olson for pointing out this feature of the FSP.

may allow recipients to keep most of the change from a small food purchase or to purchase nonfood items. Or ineligible individuals may attempt to qualify for benefits.

The federal quality control system is directed at reducing erroneous determinations about individuals' eligibility for benefits. Under this system, state welfare agencies continuously sample their active food stamp caseloads as well as decisions to end or deny benefits. Over 90,000 cases are reviewed each year. These reviews yield a picture of the extent to which states erroneously award or deny benefits, as well as estimates of the dollar amounts of benefits involved. In 1996, the national weighted average overpayment rate was estimated at 6.9 percent, and the underpayment rate was estimated at 2.3 percent. The rate of improper denial of benefits was 3.8 percent (U.S. Committee on Ways and Means 1998).

States are subject to sanctions if their combined over- and underpayment dollar rates exceed the national average error rate for the year in question. In most cases these sanction amounts can be used by states to improve the administration of FSP benefits. The Food and Nutrition Service (FNS) of the USDA is also active in matching FSP databases to other databases in order to track down households that are receiving benefits for deceased individuals and prisoners. Four states have developed systems for using fingerprints to verify FSP recipients' identities.

However, a series of U.S. General Accounting Office (GAO) reports documents the fact that these efforts to monitor individual eligibility are not always successful. The GAO has found that millions of dollars in overpayments were accounted for by payments to households including inmates, deceased individuals, households that were receiving benefits in more than one state, and individuals who had already been disqualified for program violations. For example, a four-state audit study found that $500,000 had been collected by 3,000 previously disqualified individuals. However, although this is a substantial dollar amount, it is very small relative to the $5.6 billion in food stamps that was paid to 6.4 million individuals over the period of the study in these four states (U.S. GAO 1999b).

A second type of abuse involves individuals who illegally sell their food stamp benefits. The extent of this type of trafficking is unknown, but one interesting study of the issue found that it was not uncommon for the same individual to both buy and sell food stamp benefits within the month, usually to other individuals (Ciemnecki et al. 1998). For example, a recipient might receive his or her cash TANF benefit at the beginning of the month and use this cash to buy needed food. The recipient's monthly FSP benefit might be received some days later and be exchanged (at a 30 to 50 percent discount) for cash. Then, if cash is received at some later point in the month, it might be used to purchase FSP benefits (again at a discount), which would then be exchanged for food.

In this scenario, severe liquidity constraints drive the trafficking. The value of the FSP benefit may be less than the household's monthly food budget, but the household is forced to budget on a day-to-day basis, and the monthly FSP allotment is likely to exceed the amount the household plans to spend on food in the next few days. The study authors note that EBT technology per se is not likely to be a particularly effective deterrent to this type of trafficking, since the buyer and the seller can simply go to the store together. However, the study results suggest that crediting the FSP benefits to the recipient's card at smaller time intervals might prevent this type of trafficking.

A second form of trafficking occurs when individuals sell their benefits at a discount to stores, which then redeem them at full value. This form may be viewed as more pernicious, in that it reduces the total amount of food that is purchased using the FSP benefits. The USDA estimates that about 2 percent of FSP benefits are lost due to this type of fraudulent claim, and that a further 3.7 percent are illegally trafficked in this way (U.S. Committee on Ways and Means 1998).

These estimates appear to be based on extrapolations of verified instances of fraud to the population of food stamp retailers. For example, Macaluso (1995) found that although 9.4 percent of stores investigated by FNS were trafficking, only a small percentage of the large, publicly owned grocery stores that were investigated engaged in trafficking. Since these stores account for most of the redemptions of food stamp coupons, he infers that the total amount of trafficking is small. On the other hand, he finds that more than one in every seven dollars of benefits is trafficked in those small, privately owned stores not stocking a full line of food that were investigated by FNS. Similarly, in neighborhoods where the poverty rate exceeds 30 percent, one in five stores investigated by FNS was trafficking.

The problem with extrapolations from estimates based on FNS investigations to the national level is that, first, FNS is more likely to investigate stores where abuses are suspected than those in which abuses are not suspected. Second, FNS is unlikely to catch all of the offending stores. The first factor means that extrapolations tend to produce overestimates of trafficking, while the second factor means that extrapolations tend to produce underestimates.

Although trafficking in food stamps is illegal, penalties do not appear to be particularly harsh. Individuals are typically disqualified from the program for one year for a first offense, two years for a second offense, and permanently for a third offense or for trafficking an amount that exceeds $500 (U.S. GAO 2000). Stores are generally assessed a fine, but these fines are apparently seldom collected. The GAO reports that between 1993 and 1999, the FNS levied $78 million in fines but collected only $11.5 million (U.S. GAO 1999c). The GAO suggests that the FNS would have more success if it referred the delinquent debt to the Department of the Treasury, which could deduct the debt from any future federal payments made to the store owners.

The WIC Program

The seven regional offices of the FNS issue regulations and provide cash grants to state WIC agencies. In turn, the state agencies provide funds to local agencies, monitor local compliance with regulations, and provide technical assistance to local staff. State WIC agencies are required to report to the FCS a "minimum data set" of eighteen items from their client and management information systems. These items may be reported either for all clients or for a representative sample. They include state agency identification; local agency identification; service site identification; case identification; date of birth; race/ethnicity; certification category (i.e., pregnant woman, breastfeeding woman, postpartum woman, infant, child); expected date of delivery or weeks gestation; date of certification; sex; priority level; participation in TANF, Medicaid, or food stamps; migrant farmworker status; number in family; family income; nutritional risks present at certification; hemoglobin, hematocrit, or "EP value"; weight; height; and date of height and weight measure. However, despite these requirements, in 1994 data on income were submitted for only 86 percent of the caseload, and data on other program participation were submitted for only 92 percent of the caseload (Randall, Boast, and Holst 1995). In addition to this minimum data set, some states also report information on birth weight, birth length, source of prenatal care, duration of breastfeeding, and food package codes.

State agencies are also required to conduct on-site reviews of at least 10 percent of their vendors each year and to submit the results of this monitoring to FCS annually. Methods of on-site monitoring may include reviews of checkout procedures, inventory records, and prices charged to WIC recipients. In the two-year period between 1 October 1996 and 30 September 1998, about 9 percent of WIC vendors were identified as having committed fraud or abuse (U.S. GAO 1999a). This estimate is remarkably close to Macaluso's (1995) findings for the FSP. Presumably the fraud takes much the same form (e.g., vendors purchasing WIC coupons at a discount). However, no estimate of the dollar losses associated with WIC coupon trafficking is available. It is also unclear whether these vendors are sanctioned any more effectively than those defrauding the FSP.

In contrast to the FSP, where an extensive effort is made to monitor individual compliance with eligibility standards through the federally mandated quality control system, there does not appear to be any federally coordinated attempt to eliminate fraud at the individual level. Bitler, Currie, and Scholz (2002) estimate using data from the Survey of Income and Program Participation (SIPP) that of the infants receiving WIC in any given month in 1998, 5.9 percent were ineligible for the benefits. Similarly, of the

3.7 million children receiving benefits, 5.4 percent did not meet the income or adjunctive eligibility criteria (and had not done so for the past six months). These error rates are consistent with those reported in the National Survey of WIC Participants (2001). The GAO recently recommended FCS to direct state agencies to require participants to provide evidence that they reside in the states in which they receive WIC benefits and to provide identification when their eligibility is certified and when they receive food or food vouchers (U.S. GAO 2000).

One type of fraud that may occur with WIC is the trafficking of infant formula obtained free under the program. Given the high cost of formula, it might be tempting for a low-income mother to sell the formula she receives from WIC and give her older infant either solid food or cow's milk as a replacement. It is not known whether many mothers engage in this practice, but there is anecdotal evidence of a substantial market in WIC formula.

NSLP

Table 4.9 indicates that the federal subsidies for lunches served to those below 185 percent of the federal poverty line exceed the "full price" of lunch charged to wealthier students. Glantz et al. (1994) conducted a more detailed analysis of the costs of the lunch program and found that federal subsidies for the free or reduced-price meals often produce a surplus. Because the program is required to be nonprofit, these subsidies are generally used to subsidize either the cost of full-price meals and "a la carte" food items consumed by wealthier students, or kitchen equipment (Rossi 1998). In addition to the federal funds represented by these subsidies, states are required to match 30 percent of the federal expenditures on the program, less the percentage by which the state per capita income is below the per capita income of the United States.

Quality control procedures in the NSLP are aimed primarily at insuring that participating schools comply with program regulations (U.S. Congress 2000). The first set of requirements covers the "lunch counting and claiming system." Schools submit monthly claims to the responsible state agency (usually the Department of Education) for reimbursement. School food authorities are required to conduct annual, on-site reviews of each school's procedures for establishing the "counts" of free, reduced-price, and full-price lunches that are claimed and to compare these counts to data regarding the number of eligible children in each school and attendance records.

Schools are further required to maintain files of approved and denied applications for free and reduced-price lunches that include the child's name and documentation certifying that the child is in an eligible household. In households that are selected for income verification, parents are asked to send either papers that show that they get food stamps or TANF, or papers that show the household's current income. The latter may include pay stubs for each job, Social Security retirement benefit letters, unemployment or disability compensation check stubs, benefit letters from welfare agencies for those receiving General Assistance, child support checks, or a brief note explaining how food, clothing, and housing are obtained by those who report "no income." Parents who do not reply to this request for income verification have their benefits cut off. All records pertaining to income eligibility must be maintained for a period of three years.

School food authorities are required to provide a list of all schools in which 50 percent or more of the children are certified eligible for free or reduced-price lunches to state authorities, and states are required to check that these schools are indeed in high-poverty areas. Finally, schools are required to keep production and menu records sufficient to demonstrate that the nutritional content of lunches served meets federal requirements when the lunches are averaged over the course of a week.

4.3   Evidence About the Overall Efficacy of FANPs

The apparent decline in the extent of hunger in America (as measured by the prevalence of nutritional deficiencies such as anemia or vitamin deficiencies rather than by food insecurity) begs the question of the extent to which FANPs can be credited with bringing about the decline. For example, an alternative hypothesis is that the reduction in hunger reflects steady decreases in the real price of food as well as increases in its availability over time. The fraction of income that a typical American family spends on food has declined from one-third to less than one-sixth since the mid-1960s (Citro and Michael 1995), and as we will see, even among FSP households the typical family spends less than fifteen cents out of every dollar of cash income received on food. On the other hand, Bhattacharya et al. (2001) find evidence of a "heat or eat" effect in which the food consumption of poor families suffers when cold weather strains the family budget. This suggests that FANPs do not provide complete insurance against this type of shock.

This section discusses evidence regarding the overall effectiveness of FANPs. Tables 4.12, 4.13, and 4.14 provide an overview of the large number of studies that have been devoted to identifying effects of the FSP, WIC, and NSLP on a long list of outcomes. Before proceeding with a discussion of selected studies, I offer some comments regarding what types of effects one might expect, the different types of outcomes that can be measured, the identification of program effects, and other methodological issues.

4.3.1   Theory

Economic theory suggests that if the value of the FANP benefit is less than the amount the family would have expended on food in any case, then it will have no more effect on consumption of food than an equivalent cash transfer. Hence, if the family spent only fifteen cents of every dollar of income on food, a dollar's worth of FANP benefits would also be expected to increase spending on food by only fifteen cents. The rest of the dollar would presumably be spent on other goods. FANPs like WIC and NSLP that provide specific food items may also affect the type of goods that are consumed, to the extent that they supply goods that would not otherwise have been chosen by the family. For example, a child may drink more milk and fewer soft drinks if milk is supplied in the school lunch or subsidized through WIC.

On the other hand, the impact of programs that target benefits to a specific individual in the household may be mitigated by compensatory actions taken in the household. For example, if a child is participating in school breakfast and lunch, a parent may feed that child less at dinner and might feed another nonparticipating child more. Thus, it is not obvious that increasing the consumption of certain nutrients at some meals will increase overall consumption of those nutrients. The first thing evaluators of FANPs typically examine is whether participation in the FANP increases food expenditures and/or changes nutrient intakes.

If the FANP does change nutrient intakes, then it may or may not have a measurable impact on other aspects of child well-being. For example, if a FANP encourages a child to consume more of a nutrient that is already consumed in adequate amounts, then this is unlikely to have any beneficial effect, and could in fact be harmful if it encouraged overeating. Only FANPs that help children to overcome nutritional deficiencies, improve their diets, or stabilize their consumption patterns (in the case of households that are food insecure but consuming an adequate number of calories) are likely to have a positive impact.

4.3.2 Measurement Issues

Whether or not FANPs are judged to be effective depends in part on what outcome measure is chosen. There are three broad classes of nutritional outcome measures that have been examined. The first group measures food insecurity. For example, people may be asked how often they missed a meal because there was no food in the house, or whether they worried about running out of money to buy food. A recent USDA report (Nord, Jemison, and Bickel 1999) found that one in ten U.S. children suffered from food insecurity.[9] Food insecurity has been linked to higher levels of hyperactivity, absenteeism, aggression, and tardiness as well as impaired academic functioning among children (Murphy et al. 1998).

---

9. The definition used in this study included those who answered yes to items ranging from "We worried whether our food would run out before we got money to buy more" to "In the last twelve months did any of the children ever not eat for a whole day because there wasn't enough money for food?"

A second set of measures indicates whether or not a person suffers from an identifiable nutritional deficiency. For example, even mild iron anemia has been linked to cognitive shortfalls and inability to pay attention in children. These deficiency measures may be assessed using actual blood or urine tests, but due to the cost of collecting these measures, most studies rely on self-reported food diaries that keep track of either household nutrient availability or individual nutrient intakes over a specified period of time. One problem with all of these deficiency measures is that many contemporary threats to health are linked to overconsumption rather than underconsumption of nutrients.

The third set of nutritional measures consists of anthropometric indexes such as birth weight, body mass index, height-for-age, or weight-for-height. These measures have the advantage of being objective and accurate (when taken by trained technicians). Birth weight is the single most important indicator of a newborn's health. Infants weighing less than 2500 grams at birth are considered to be low birth weight, whereas those who weigh less than 1500 grams are very low birth weight. Low or very low birth weights are linked to higher-than-average risks of infant mortality, chronic conditions, and delayed development.

Body mass index (BMI) is defined as weight in grams divided by the square of height in meters. Adults with a BMI over thirty are considered to be obese and are at higher risk of mortality from a range of illnesses. Height-for-age is considered to be a long-term measure of nutritional status. However, in developed countries, few individuals are stunted (i.e., far below normal height-for-age). Weight-for-height can be viewed as a shorter-run measure of nutritional status, although again, in developed countries individuals are more likely to suffer from excessive weight that from wasting (i.e., low weight-for-height).

The link between food insecurity and other measures of nutritional outcomes is quite weak. In the USDA study, only 3.5 percent of households had food insecurity severe enough that one or more household members ever went hungry. Bhattacharya, Currie, and Haider (2001) show that among children, standard poverty measures are more highly correlated with nutritional deficiencies than food insecurity, and that among teens, neither measure correlates well with objectively measured nutritional deficiencies. It is possible that in many cases food insecurity reflects social problems such as dysfunctional families, homelessness, alcohol and drug abuse, or (especially in the elderly) inability to shop for and prepare food more than it reflects actual food shortages.

Finally, many studies of FANPs examine the effects of the programs on food expenditures. The implicit assumption seems to be that families with higher food expenditures will be better nourished, although, as previously discussed, this assumption is suspect in a world in which many people both consume excessive calories and have nutrient deficiencies.

4.3.3   Identification of Program Effects and Other Econometric Issues

As table 4.12 illustrates, the modal study of the FSP, for example, compares eligible participants to eligible nonparticipants using a multiple regression model. The main problem with drawing inferences about the efficacy of the FSP from this exercise is that participants are likely to differ from eligible nonparticipants in ways that are not observed by the researcher. Thus, for example, Basiotis, Kramer-LeBlanc, and Kennedy (1998) and Butler and Raymond (1996) both find that participation in the FSP *reduces* consumption of some important nutrients. Since it is hard to imagine how giving people food coupons could do this, one suspects that these results are driven by negative selection into the FSP program. That is, those who participate may be less likely to eat a healthy diet for reasons that have not been controlled for in the regression models estimated by these researchers. Since participation of eligibles is not complete in any of these programs, the selection problem is ubiquitous in this literature and applies to all studies that attempt to examine impacts of the programs.

The standard approach to this problem is to find an instrument—that is, a variable that affects program determination but has no independent effect on outcomes. For example, if there was a lot of variation in the rules determining eligibility, and the variation in these rules was not related to variation in the outcomes of interest, then program rules could be used as instruments for predicting participation, and the outcome of interest would then be linked to predicted participation. However, if states were less likely to require income verification for WIC applicants in states with a high incidence of low birth weight, then variation in this program rule might not be a valid instrument for WIC participation.

Unfortunately, at least from the point of view of researchers, most FSP and NSLP rules are set at the federal level and have shown little change over time, which means that these rules are not good candidate instrumental variables. However, some rules, such as those setting recertification periods for the FSP, are set at the state level, although this potential source of identification has not been exploited in any extant study of child outcomes. In contrast to FSP and NSLP, there is a great deal of variation in WIC program rules across states, and also some variation over time. Thus, WIC program rules offer an apparently more promising source of instrumental variables, although to date only one study (Brien and Swann 1999) has taken advantage of this source of identification to examine effects on child outcomes. Bitler, Currie, and Scholz (2002) show that these differences in state program rules are correlated with WIC participation in the ways that one might expect.

One promising identification strategy is to exploit interactions between programs. For example, as discussed above, households receiving cash welfare are generally categorically eligible for FANPs. Thus, it could be argued

Table 4.12   Studies of the Food Stamp Program

Study	Data[a]	Design	Results
Studies of Multiple Outcomes			
Allen and Gadson (1983)	1977–78 NFCS-LI Aided recall for food use from household supply (7 days); FSP-eligible households ($n = 3,850$)	Multivariate regression including benefit amount	MPS$_F$ from food stamps: 0.30; increases the availability of food energy; protein; carbohydrate; vitamin A, vitamin B-6, vitamin B-12, vitamin C; thiamin; riboflavin; niacin; calcium; iron; magnesium; phosphorus; also increases fat availability
Basiotis et al. (1983)	1977–78 NFCS-LI Aided recall for food use from household supply (7 days); FSP-eligible households ($n = 3,562$)	Multivariate regression including participation dummy	Impact on at-home food cost per household per week: $3.7 (20.4%); increases the availability of food energy, vitamin C, thiamin
Basiotis et al. (1987)	1977–78 NFCS-LI Aided recall for food use from household supply (7 days); 24-hour recall followed by two days of food records; FSP-eligible households ($n \sim 3,000$)	Simultaneous equations for food cost/nutrient availability/nutrient intake relationship, including participation dummy and benefit amount	MPS$_F$ from food stamps: 0.17; no significant impact on calcium availability
Hama and Chern (1988)	1977–78 NFCS-Elderly Supplement Aided recall for food use from household supply (7 days); FSP-eligible households with elderly members ($n = 1,454$)	Simultaneous food expenditure/nutrient availability equation including participation dummy	Impact on per capita at-home food expenditure per week: $0.64 (3.7%); increases the availability of vitamin B-6, calcium, iron, magnesium
Johnson, Burt, and Morgan (1981)	1977–78 NFCS-LI Aided recall for food use from household supply (7 days); low-income households ($n = 4,535$)	Multivariate regression including participation dummy and benefit amount, weights used to deal with missing data	MPS$_F$ from food stamps: 0.17; increases the availability of food energy, and Modified Diet Source[b]

Kisker and Devaney (1988)	1979–80 NFCS-LI Record of household food use (7 days); FSP-eligible households ($n \sim 2,900$)	Bivariate t-tests of participation dummy	Impact on money value of food used at-home per equivalent nutrition unit per week: $2.49 (10.8%); increases the proportion of households with household nutrient availability above 100% or 80% of RDA for energy and 10 nutrients; FSP participants more likely to experience food insecurity
Kramer-LeBlanc, Basiotis, and Kennedy (1997)	1989–91 CSFII 24-hour recall followed by two days of food records; FSP-eligible individuals ($n = 793$)	Multivariate regression including benefit amount	MSP_F from food stamps: 0.35; Increases HEI[c]

Studies of Impact on Food Expenditures

Brown, Johnson, and Rizek (1982)	1977–78 NFCS-LI FSP participant households ($n = 911$)	Multivariate regression including benefit amount	MPS_F from food stamps: 0.45
Chavas and Yeung (1982)	1972–73 BLS-CES FSP-eligible households, Southern region ($n = 659$)	Seemingly unrelated regression model, interactions between benefit amount and demographic variables	MPS_F from food stamps: 0.37
Chen (1983)	1977–78 NFCS-LI FSP participant households ($n = 1,809$)	Multivariate regression including participation dummy and benefit amount	MPS_F from food stamps: 0.20 (Pre-EPR); 0.23 (Post-EPR)
Devaney and Fraker (1989)	1977–78 NFCS-LI FSP-eligible households ($n = 4,473$)	Multivariate regression including participation dummy and benefit amount	MPS_F from food stamps: 0.42 (weighted); 0.21 (unweighted)
Levedahl (1991)	1979–80 NFCS-LI FSP participants who used all their food stamps ($n = 1,210$)	Multivariate regression including benefit amount	MPS_F from food stamps: 0.69

(continued)

Table 4.12   (continued)

Study	Data[a]	Design	Results
Price (1983)	1973–74 BLS-CES All households ($n = 10,359$)	Multivariate regression including participation dummy and benefit amount	Impact on at-home food expenditure per week per adult male equivalent (AME): $2.01 (18.2%); MPS_F from food stamps: 0.42
Ranney and Kushman (1987)	1979–89 counties and county groups in CA, IN, OH, VA FSP-eligible households ($n = 896$)	Multivariate regression including participation dummy and benefit amount	MPS_F from food stamps: 0.4
Salathe (1980)	1973–74 BLS-CES FSP-eligible households ($n = 2,254$)	Multivariate regression including participation dummy and benefit amount	Impact on per capita food purchase per week: at-home $1.45 (18.8%), total $0.88 (9.4%); MPS_F from food stamps: 0.36
Senauer and Young (1986)	1978 PSID FSP participant households ($n = 573$)	Multivariate regression including benefit amount	MPS_F from food stamps: 0.3 (Pre-EPR); 0.26 (Post-EPR)
Smallwood and Blaylock (1985)	1977–78 NFCS-LI FSP-eligible households ($n = 3,582$)	Two-equation selection bias model including participation dummy and expected weekly benefit amount	MPS_F from food stamps: 0.23
West (1984)	1973–74 BLS-CES FSP-eligible households ($n = 2,407$)	Multivariate regression including participation dummy and benefit amount	MPS_F from food stamps: 0.17 (participants); 0.47 (eligibles)
Studies of Impact of Cashout			
Beebout et al. (1985)	1977 Puerto Rico Supplement to the NFCS and 1984 Puerto Rico Household Food Consumption Survey 7-day food use from records and recall; participant and FSP eligible nonparticipant households using 1977 eligibility criteria ($n = 3,995$)	Precashout compared to cashout (1977 vs. 1984); two-equation selection bias models including group membership dummy, participation dummy, and benefit amount	Impact of cashout (NAP) on at-home food expenditure per AME per month: −$2.95 (−2.4%); impact of cashout (NAP) on MPS_F from food stamps: −0.06

Cohen and Young (1994)	1990 Washington State Cashout Demonstration 7-day food use from records and recall; households participating in AFDC and who applied after FIP implementation (*n* = 780)	Comparison of treatment and matched comparison counties; multivariate regression including group membership dummy and benefit amount	Impact of cashout (FIP) on at-home food expenditure per household per month: −$28.08 (−12.1%); on total food expenditure per AME per month: −$22.12 (−17.2%); increases the availability of food energy, protein, vitamin C, calcium, iron, zinc
Davis and Werner (1993)	1990 Alabama ASSETS Demonstration ASSETS and FSP Participants (*n* = 1,371)	Comparison of treatment and matched comparison counties; multivariate regression including group membership dummy and benefit amount	Impact of cashout (ASSETS) on at-home food expenditure per household per month: −$56.44 (−21.9%); on total food expenditure per AME per month: −$25.43 (−21.9%)
Fraker et al. (1992)	1990 Alabama Cashout Demonstration 7-day food use from records and recall; FSP participants (*n* = 2,386)	Random assignment of participants to check or coupon; multivariate regression including group membership dummy and benefit amount	Impact of cashout on at-home food expenditure per household per month: $2.66 (+1.1%); on total food expenditure per AME per month: −$0.34 (−0.3%); impact of cashout on MPS_F from food stamps: +0.01
Levedahl (1995)	1990 San Diego Cashout Demonstration FSP participant households receiving coupons (*n* = 494)	Multivariate regression including benefit amount	MPS_F from food stamps: 0.26
McCracken (1995)	1990 Washington State Cashout Demonstration FIP targeted pregnant and parenting teens (*n* = 1,172)	Comparison of treatment and matched comparison counties; two step endogenous switching model for self-selection bias including group membership dummy and benefit amount	Impact of cashout (FIP) on at-home food expenditure per household per month: −$36.00

(continued)

Table 4.12 (continued)

Study	Data[a]	Design	Results
Ohls et al. (1992)	1990 San Diego Cashout Demonstration 7-day food use from records and recall; FSP participants ($n = 1,143$)	Random assignment of participants to check or coupon; multivariate regression including group membership dummy and benefit amount	Impact of cashout on at-home food expenditure per household per month: $-$22.25 (-7.5\%)$; on total food expenditure per AME per month: $-$9.39 (-6.9\%)$; impact of cashout on MPS_F from food stamps: -0.17; increases the availability of food energy, protein
Whitmore (2002)	1990 San Diego and Alabama Cashout (see above)	Divide households into those who spent more than the value of food stamps on food and those that did not; supplementary phone survey of food stamp recipients	Only households where value of food stamps exceeded desired food purchases reduced spending; reductions in spending had no nutritional consequence; food stamps trafficked at $0.65 on the dollar
Studies of Impact on Nutrient Availability and Nutrient Intake			
Basiotis, Kramer-LeBlanc, and Kennedy (1998)	1989–90 CSFII 24-hour recall followed by two days of food records; low-income households ($n = 1,379$)	Multivariate regression (survey weights) including participation dummy and benefit amount	Reduces HEI
Bishop, Formby, and Zeager (1992)	1977–78 NFCS-LI 24-hour recall followed by two days of food records; FSP-eligible individuals ($n = 2,590$)	Stochastic dominance methods using participation dummy	Increases the intake of calcium
Butler, Chls, and Posner (1985)	1980–81 FNS SSI/ECD 24-hour recall via telephone; low-income elderly individuals	Multivariate regression including participation dummy, with selection bias adjustment	Increases the intake of calcium

Study	Data	Methodology	Findings
Butler and Raymond (1996)	1980–81 FNS SSI/ECD and 1969–73 Rural Income Maintenance Experiment 24-hour recall via telephone and in person; low-income elderly individuals ($n = 1,542$); low-income individuals in rural areas ($n = 1,093$)	Multivariate endogenous switching model including participation dummy and benefit amount, with selection bias adjustment	Increases the intake of food energy (for those living in rural areas), calcium; reduces the intake of food energy (for the elderly), protein, riboflavin, niacin, iron
Cook, Sherman, and Brown	1986 CSFII-LI 24-hour recall followed by two days of food records; children aged 1–5 in households under 125% of poverty	Bivariate chi-squared tests using participation dummy	Increases the intake of vitamin B-12, folate, calcium, magnesium, zinc
Devaney and Moffitt (1991)	1979–80 NFCS-LI Record of household food use (7 days); FSP-eligible households ($n = 2,925$)	Multivariate OLS and selection bias models including benefit amount	Increases the availability of food energy, protein, vitamins A, vitamin B-6, vitamin C, thiamin, riboflavin, calcium, iron, magnesium, phosphorus
Fraker, Long, and Post (1990)	1985 CSFII 4 nonconsecutive 24-hour recalls; women aged 19–50 ($n = 381$) and their children aged 1–5 ($n = 818$)	Participation dummy; multivariate regression including participation dummy, with selection bias adjustment	Increases the intake of food energy, protein, and zinc; reduces the intake of vitamins A and E
Gregorio and Marshall (1984)	1971–74 HANES-I 24-hour recall; preschool children ($n = 2,774$), school-aged children ($n = 3,509$)	Bivariate and multivariate regression using participation dummy and participation interacted with poverty index ratio	No significant impact estimated
Lopez (1984)	1971–73 HANES-I and 1976–80 NHANES-II 24-hour recall; low-income elderly ($n = 1,684$ and $n = 1,388$)	Multivariate ANOVA using participation dummy	Reduces the intake of iron
Posner et al. (1987)	1980–81 FNS SSI/ECD 24-hour recall via telephone; elderly ($n = 1,900$)	Multivariate regression including participation dummy	Increases the intake of calcium

(continued)

Table 4.12 (continued)

Study	Data[a]	Design	Results
Rose, Smallwood, and Blaylock (1995)	1989–91 CSFII 24-hour recall followed by two days of food records; children aged 1–5 ($n = 800$)	Multivariate regression (weight not used) including participation dummy	Increases the intake of iron
Rose, Habicht, and Devaney (1998)	1989–90 CSFII 24-hour recall followed by two days of food records; non-breastfeeding pre-schoolers ($n = 499$)	Multivariate regression (unweighted) including benefit amount	Increases the intake of vitamin A, thiamin, niacin, iron, zinc
Weimer (1998)	1989–91 CSFII 24-hour recall followed by two days of food records; elderly individuals ($n = 1,566$)	Multivariate regression including participation dummy	No significant impact estimated
Whitfield (1982)	1978 Tulsa Oklahoma 24-hour call; FSP-eligible individuals ($n = 195$)	Multivariate regression including participation dummy and benefit amount	Increases the intake of iron; reduces the intake of vitamins A and C
Studies of Impact on Other Nutrition and Health Outcomes			
Alaimo et al. (1998)	1988–94 NHANES-III Low-income ($n = 5,285$)	Logistic regression (survey weights) using participation dummy	FSP participants more likely to experience food insecurity
Bhattacharya and Currie (2000)	1988–94 NHANES-III Youths aged 12 to 16 ($n = 1,358$)	Multivariate regression including participation dummy	FSP participants less likely to experience food insecurity
Currie and Cole (1993)	1979–87 NLSY Young, poor women ($n = 4,900$)	Multivariate two-state least squares using participation dummy (participation endogenous) and fixed effects model	No significant effect of mother's food stamp receipt on the likelihood of low-weight birth

Study	Data source, population (sample size)[a]	Method	Findings
Hamilton, Cook, and Thomsen (1997)	1995 CPS Low-income households (n = 21,810)	Comparison of means using participation dummy	Only 4.4% of food stamp households were food secure, compared with 68.1% of all households under 130% of poverty
Lopez and Habicht (1987)	1971–73 HANES-I and 1976–80 NHANES-II Low-income elderly (n = 1,684 and n = 1,388)	Multivariate ANOVA using participation dummy	No systemic effect of FSP participation on participants' iron status
Rose, Gunderson, and Oliveira (1998)	1989–91 CSFII and 1992 SIPP All households (n = 6,620 and n = 30,303)	Logistic regression using annual dollar amount of food stamps	Food insufficiency was inversely related to the size of food stamp benefit, and this relationship was stronger with food stamp than with other income

Source: The tables are based largely on research reviewed in Hamilton and Fox et al. (2000).

Note: BLS-CES = Bureau of Labor Statistics Consumer Expenditure Survey; CPS = Current Population Survey; CSFII = Continuing Survey of Food Intake by Individuals; FNS SSI/ECD = Food and Nutrition Service Supplementary Security Income/Elderly Cashout Demonstration; HANES = Health and Nutrition Examination Survey; NHANES = National Health and Nutrition Examination Survey; NFCS-LI = Nationwide Food Consumption Survey (Low Income Supplement); NLSY = National Longitudinal Survey of Youth; PSID = Panel Study of Income Dynamics; MPS_F = Marginal Propensity to Spend on Food; EPR = Elimination of the Purchase Requirement; NAP = Nutrition Assistance Program in Puerto Rico; FIP = Family Independence Program; ASSETS = Avenue to Self-Sufficiency through Employment and Training Services.

[a]Data source, data collection method, and population (sample size).

[b]Modified Diet Score is defined as the sum of ratios of actual nutrient values to RDA standards for seven nutrients (protein, vitamins A, C, thiamin, riboflavin, calcium and iron)

[c]Healthy Eating Index (HEI) measures the extent to which individual intake, in terms of 10 food groups and these nutrients—sodium, fat, and saturated fat—conform to the Dietary Guidelines for Americans and the USDA Food Guide Pyramid.

that factors that encourage participation in welfare programs also affect participation in FANPs by reducing the transactions costs associated with enrolling in the program. If these factors have no direct impact on outcomes, then they will be valid instruments. For example, recent expansions of eligibility for the Medicaid program may have had the effect of bringing people into welfare offices, where they also signed up for the FSP. If Medicaid has no direct effect on food expenditures, then changes in Medicaid rules may be valid instruments for FSP participation in models of food expenditures. Welfare reform may be having the opposite effect, driving people out of welfare offices and increasing the transactions costs associated with claiming and maintaining FSP eligibility. Thus welfare reform offers a potential source of identifying variation in program rules, although one would have to be cautious about assuming that, for example, termination of cash benefits had no independent effect on the outcomes of interest.

In the absence of strong instruments, many studies either have simply punted on the issue of identification or have used a weaker design. For example, many studies reviewed in tables 4.12, 4.13, and 4.14 use what might be termed a "dose-response" methodology in which it is argued that other things being equal, the greater the size of the benefits, the greater the effect of a program ought to be. There is some variation in the benefit levels received, for instance, by FSP households of similar size, because these households may have differing levels of earned and unearned income (e.g., different TANF payments), pay different amounts of rent, and have different demographic structures. However, since all of these sources of variation (with the possible exception of state differences in TANF payments) reflect choices made by households, it is not clear that they are a legitimate source of identification of program effects. These identification problems should be kept in mind in the following discussion of estimated program effects.

Other econometric issues that are sometimes noted in studies of FANPs include discussions about functional form, controls for household size and composition, controls for the number of meals consumed away from home, and weighting issues. All of these issues raise thorny questions for which there are no obvious answers. In terms of functional form, there is little evidence to suggest that any particular form is correct. However, a general rule of thumb might be to estimate as flexible a functional form as the data will permit.

Controlling for household size and composition is also tricky. The reason one would want to control for these factors is that children are presumed to need less food than adults, and women to need less food than men, on average. Researchers often use "equivalence scales" that seek to convert all household members into the equivalent number of adult males. However, given that the equivalence is unlikely to be exact, this practice

Table 4.13   **Studies of the WIC Program**

Study	Data[a]	Design	Results
Studies of Impact on Birth Outcomes			
Ahluwalia et al. (1992)	Linked WIC and birth record files for 1992 WIC and non-WIC Medicaid recipients with full-term births ($n = 53,782$)	Multivariate regression including length of prenatal WIC "exposure"	Reduces the likelihood of low birth weight
Bailey et al. (1983)	Primary data collection at one WIC site and one non-WIC site in Florida (dates not reported) WIC and income-eligible nonparticipants who were 30 weeks pregnant at time of recruitment and receiving identical prenatal care ($n = 101$)	Multivariate regression and analysis of variance using participation dummy	Increases mean birth weight; participating pregnant women consume more of vitamin B-6 and iron
Brien and Swann (1999)	NMIHS-live births file (1988) (a) WIC and income-eligible non-Hispanic women who are at nutritional risk ($n = 7,778$) (b) WIC and income-eligible non-Hispanic women with at least one live birth prior to 1988 ($n = 6,254$ pairs of births)	(a) Multivariate regression using participation dummies (one for every participated and one for participated during first trimester), with several selection bias adjustment models (b) Fixed effects model using participation status for each pregnancy, separate for blacks and whites	Increases mean birth weight (for blacks)
Brown, Watkins, and Hiett (1996)	Medical records, birth and death certificates for births in one Indiana hospital between January 1988 and June 1989 Non-Hispanic women who delivered at the area's primary hospital for the "underserved" ($n = 4,707$)	Multivariate regression including participation dummy	No significant impact estimated on birth weight, the likelihood of low/very low birthweight, and infant mortality rate

(continued)

Table 4.13 (continued)

Study	Data[a]	Design	Results
Buescher et al. (1993)	Linked WIC, Medicaid, and birth record files for 1988 births in North Carolina WIC and non-WIC Medicaid recipients who were enrolled in prenatal care ($n = 21,900$)	Multivariate regression including participation dummy and months on WIC and percent of pregnancy on WIC	Reduces the likelihood of low/very low birth weight
Covington (1995)	NMIHS-live births file (1988) WIC and non-WIC African American women who received some prenatal care ($n = 3,905$)	Multivariate regression including participation dummy; separate models for LBW vs. normal weight and VLBW vs. normal weight for each of four subgroups based on combinations of income and receipt of Medicaid and/or AFDC	Reduces the likelihood of low/very low birth weight (except the subgroup with annual income > 12000 and no public aid, which showed negative impact)
Devaney and Schim (1993)	FNS WIC/Medicaid (1987–88) WIC and non-WIC Medicaid recipients ($n = 111,958$)	Probit analysis using participation dummy: enrolled by 30 weeks gestation	Reduces neonatal and infant mortality rate
Devaney (1992)	FNS WIC/Medicaid (1987–88) WIC and non-WIC Medicaid recipients ($n = 111,958$)	Probit analysis using participation dummy: (a) participated; (b) participated during first trimester	Increases mean birth weight and reduces the likelihood of very low birth weight
Devaney, Bilheimer, and Shore (1990, 1991)	FNS WIC/Medicaid (1987–88) WIC and non-WIC Medicaid recipients ($n = 111,958$)	Multivariate regression and probit analysis using participation dummy: (a) participated; (b) participated during first trimester; attempted but rejected selection bias adjustment	Increases mean birth weight and mean gestational age/length of gestation, and reduces the likelihood of low birth weight and premature birth, Medicaid/health care costs
Frisbie et al. (1997)	NMIHS-live births file (1988) WIC and non-WIC women ($n = 8,424$)	Multivariate regression including participation dummy	Reduces the likelihood of small for-gestational-age birth/intrauterine growth retardation

Study	Data	Methods	Findings
Gordon and Nelson (1995)	NMIHS-live births file (1988) WIC and income-eligible women ($n = 6,170$)	Multivariate regression and logit analysis using participation dummy; birth weight analysis included separate models for blacks and whites, as well as several alternative models to control for simultaneity; attempted, but rejected, selection bias adjustment (using per capita state-level WIC food expenditures, an indicator of whether the family had income from wages and an indicator of WIC participation during previous pregnancies as identifying variables)	Increases mean birth weight and mean gestational age/length of gestation, and reduces the likelihood of low/very low birth weight and premature birth
Heimendinger et al. (1984)	WIC and medical records in 3 WIC clinics and 4 non-WIC clinics in the same Boston neighborhoods (1979–81) WIC and Medicaid-eligible infants and toddlers up to 20 months of age with at least 2 height and weight measurements ($n = 1,907$)	Multivariate regression of value added measures by age group (3-month intervals), using participation dummy based on mother's participation in WIC during pregnancy	Increases mean birth weight
Joyce, Corman, and Grossman (1988)	Census data for large counties in the United States in 1997 Data for 677 counties with 50,000+ residents for white analysis and 357 counties with 5,000+ blacks for black analysis	Cost-effectiveness study using aggregate data; multivariate regression using state-specific number of pregnant women enrolled in WIC per 1,000 state-specific eligible women, with selection bias adjustment. Separate models for blacks and whites.	Reduces neonatal mortality rate (for blacks)
Kennedy and Kotelchuck (1984)	WIC and medical records in WIC sites and non-WIC health facilities in 4 geographic areas of Massachusetts (1973–78) (reanalysis of data from Kennedy et al. 1982) Matched WIC and non-WIC pairs of pregnant women ($n = 418$ pairs)	t-tests and chi-square tests using participation dummy and number of months vouchers received	Increases mean birth weight and mean gestational age/length of gestation, and reduces neonatal mortality rate

(continued)

Table 4.13 (continued)

Study	Data[a]	Design	Results
Kennedy et al. (1982)	WIC and medical records in WIC sites and non-WIC health facilities in 4 geographic areas of Massachusetts (1973–78) WIC and WIC-eligible women ($n = 1,297$)	Multivariate regression including participation dummy and number of vouchers received, months on WIC	Increases mean birth weight and reduces the likelihood of low birth weight
Kotelchuck et al. (1984)	Linked WIC, birth and death records for 1978 births in Massachusetts Matched WIC and non-WIC pairs of pregnant women with singleton births ($n = 4,126$ pairs)	t-test and chi-square tests using participation dummy and months on WIC and percent of pregnancy on WIC	Increases mean gestational age/length of gestation and reduces the likelihood of low birth weight, neonatal mortality rate
Kowaleski-Jones and Duncan (2002)	NLSY Mother-Child data; 2,000 children, 1990–96; 104 sibling pairs, 71 pairs in which one child participated and one didn't	Sibling fixed effects	Increase of 7 ounces in mean birth weight; positive effect on temperament score; no effect on social or motor skills test scores
Mays-Scott (1991)	WIC records in one county health department in Texas (1987–89) Prenatal WIC participants who were ≤17 years and had at least one previous pregnancy ($n = 217$)	Analysis of variance using number of months enrolled, nutrition education contacts, and voucher pickups	Increases mean birth weight
Metcoff et al. (1985)	Primary data collection at a prenatal clinic in one hospital in Oklahoma (1983–84) Income-eligible pregnant women selected at midpregnancy based on predicted birth weight; roughly equivalent numbers were predicted to have average-size babies vs. small or large babies ($n = 410$)	Randomized experiment; multivariate regression using participation dummy	Increases mean birth weight (in the case of smoking mothers); also estimated the impact on the nutritional biochemistries of pregnant women, but no significant result obtained

Study	Data	Method	Findings
Moss and Carver (1998)	NMIHS-live birth and infant death files (1988) WIC and income-eligible non-Hispanic women ($n = 7,796$)	Logit analysis using participation dummy with and without Medicaid	Reduces neonatal mortality rate
New York State Department of Health (1990)	Linked WIC, birth record and hospital discharge files for births in last 6 months of 1998 Singleton births to WIC and non-WIC women ($n = 132,994$)	Multivariate regression including participation dummy defined on the basis of insurance coverage (Medicaid, private, none)	Increases mean birth weight and mean gestational age/length of gestation, and reduces the likelihood of low/very low birth weight and premature birth, Medicaid/health care costs
Rush, Alvir, et al. (1988a)	Vital statistics records for 1,392 counties in 19 states and D.C. (1972–80)	Multivariate regression for trend analysis relating WIC program penetration over time to birth outcomes	Increases mean birth weight and mean gestational age/length of gestation, and reduces the likelihood of premature birth
Schramm (1986)	Linked WIC, Medicaid, birth record, hospital care, and death record files for 1982 births in Missouri WIC and non-WIC Medicaid recipients ($n = 8,546$)	Multivariate regression including participation dummy and WIC food costs adjusted for length of pregnancy	Increases mean birth weight and reduces the likelihood of low birth weight, Medicaid/health care costs
Schramm (1985)	Linked WIC, Medicaid, birth and hospital care records for 1980 births in Missouri WIC and non-WIC Medicaid recipients ($n = 7,628$)	Analysis of covariance using participation dummy and WIC food costs adjusted for length of pregnancy	Reduces the likelihood of low birth weight, Medicaid/health care costs
Silverman (1982)	Medical records for random sample of women enrolled in MIC in Allegheny Co., Pennsylvania before (1971–74) and after (1974–1977) initiation of WIC WIC and income-eligible nonparticipants ($n = 2,514$)	Multivariate regression using participation dummy	No significant impact estimated on birth weight and the likelihood of low birth weight

(continued)

Table 4.13 (continued)

Study	Data[a]	Design	Results
Simpson (1988)	Aggregate county-level data for North Carolina, including vital statistics, demographic and service infrastructure characteristics, and program penetration and expenditures (1980–85) Data for 75 (out of 100) counties, all of which provided WIC and other prenatal care services for all county residents (rather than sharing responsibility with another county)	Trend analysis relating WIC penetration over time to birth outcomes; multivariate regression using program "intensity" variable based on county-level WIC expenditure	No significant impact estimated on the likelihood of low birth weight
Stockbauer (1987)	Linked WIC, birth, and death record files for 1982 births in Missouri Matched WIC and non-WIC women with singleton births ($n = 9{,}411$ pairs)	Analysis of covariance using participation dummy and dollar value of redeemed vouchers	Increases mean birth weight (for blacks) and mean gestational age/length of gestation, and reduces the likelihood of low/very low birth weight (for blacks) and premature birth; increases the likelihood of small-for-gestational-age birth/intrauterine growth retardation (for whites)
Stockbauer (1986)	Linked WIC, birth, and death record files for 1980 births in Missouri WIC and non-WIC Missouri residents with singleton births ($n = 6{,}732$ for WIC, sample for non-WIC not given)	Analysis of covariance for WIC participant vs. three different comparison groups: (a) all non-WIC births; (b) random sample of non-WIC births; (c) matched group of non-WIC births, using participation dummy, duration of participation, and dollar value of redeemed WIC coupons; separate analyses for white, nonwhite, and total group	Increases mean birth weight (for nonwhite) and mean gestational age/length of gestation, and reduces the likelihood of low birth weight (for nonwhite) and small-for-gestational-age birth/intrauterine growth retardation, neonatal mortality rate (for nonwhite); increases neonatal mortality rate (for whites)

Impact on Breastfeeding and Infant Feeding Practices

Balcazar, Trier, and Cobas (1995)	NMIHS-live births file (1988) Mexican-American and non-Hispanic white women who were not undecided about infant feeding plans prior to the infant's birth ($n = 4,089$)	Multivariate regression including participation dummy	Increases the intention to breast-feed (with advice); reduces the intention to breast-feed (overall)
Chatterji et al. (2002)	NLSY Mother-Child file. 1,282 children born 1991–95. 970 siblings born 1989–95.	IV with WIC state program characteristics as instruments; sibling fixed effects	OLS and IV indicate WIC reduces breast-feeding initiation, but no effect on duration; fixed effect suggests reductions in length breast-feeding
U.S. GAO (1993)	RLMS (1989–92) Nationally representative sample of mothers of 6-month-olds (analysis included all respondents with complete data for questions of interest [$n = 79,428$])	Multivariate regression including participation dummy based on prenatal or postpartum participation	Reduces the incidence of breast-feeding initiation
Ryan et al. (1991)	RLMS (1984 and 1989) Respondents in 1984 and 1989 ($n = 120,334$)	Multivariate regression including participation dummy	Reduces the incidence of breast-feeding initiation and the duration of breast-feeding
Schwartz et al. (1992)	NMIHS-live births file (1988) WIC participants and income-eligible nonparticipants ($n = 6,170$)	Three-stage regression with selection bias adjustment, using participation dummy and advice (to breastfeed) dummy	Increases the incidence of breast-feeding initiation (if given advice); reduces the incidence of breast-feeding initiation (otherwise)
Tuttle and Dewey (1994)	Primary data collection in WIC clinics and neighborhoods in one northern California community Hmong and Vietnamese WIC participants whose youngest child was less than 1 year ($n = 122$)	Multivariate regression including the number of times previously participated in WIC	Increases the incidence of breast-feeding initiation

(continued)

Table 4.13 (continued)

Study	Data[a]	Design	Results
Impact on Nutrition and Health Outcomes of Pregnant Women			
Endres, Sawicki, and Casper (1981)	Dietary recalls for sample of pregnant WIC participants in 22 counties in Illinois (1978–79) Newly enrolling pregnant WIC participants and participants who were on the program for 6 months or more (n = 766)	t-tests for participant before vs. after, separate groups	Participants consume more of food energy, protein, vitamins A, B-6, B-12, C, and D, folate, thiamin, niacin, riboflavin, calcium, iron magnesium, zinc
Kennedy and Gershoff (1982)	WIC and medical records in WIC sites and non-WIC health facilities in 4 geographic areas of Massachusetts (1973–78) WIC and WIC-eligible women (n = 232)	Multivariate regression including the number of WIC vouchers received	Increases final hemoglobin levels (measured at 34 weeks gestation or later)
Rush, Sloan, et al. (1988)	Primary data collection, laboratory measurements, and record abstractions (data on nutritional and health status of mothers were collected at the time of enrollment in WIC or prenatal care and again at about 8th month of gestation) Nationally representative sample of pregnant WIC participants and income-eligible nonparticipants receiving prenatal care in surrounding public health clinics or hospitals (n = 3,935)	Multivariate regression including participation dummy	Participants consume more of food energy, protein, fat, carbohydrate, vitamins B-6, B-12, and C, thiamin, niacin, riboflavin, calcium, iron magnesium, phosphorus; also estimated the impact on breast-feeding practices, but no significant result obtained

Impact on Nutrition and Health Outcomes of Infants and Children

Study	Data source/sample	Method	Findings
Burstein, Fox, and Puma (1991)	Primary data collection (24-hour recall; body measurements; blood samples) in Florida and North Carolina (1990–91) Random sample of WIC and income-eligible non-WIC infants (6 months old) stratified by birth weight (n = 807)	Multivariate regression including participation dummy; both single-equation and instrumental variable models are used to control for selection bias. But findings from single-equation models are stressed because selection bias–adjusted models yielded some implausible findings	Participants consume more iron; reduces head circumference; also estimated the impact on mother's breast-feeding practices and found that WIC improves infant feeding practices among non-breast-feeding mothers
Burstein et al. (2000)	NHANES-III (1988–91) SIPP 1993 panel (1993–95) Comprehensive Child Development Program (nonrepresentative sample of 2-year-olds from 10 sites, 1994–97)	Charts and cross-tabulations	Sharp falloff in WIC participation after child's 1st birthday, and with exit from AFDC, even with no change in household income; WIC children worse off in many dimensions than eligible non-participants, but have higher consumption of calcium and folate
Centers for Disease Control (1996)	NHANES-III (1988–91) WIC and income-eligible infants and children of 2–59 months (n = 3,488)	Multivariate regression including participation dummy	No significant impact estimated on the incidence of overweight
Fraker, Long, and Post (1990)	CSFII (1985) WIC and WIC-eligible children 1–4 years (n = 445)	Multivariate regression with selection bias adjustment, using proportion of 4 recall days on which child was enrolled in WIC; also tested for combined WIC and FSP participation	Participants consume more vitamin B-6
Hicks and Langham (1985)	Blind interviewer-administered tests and record retrieval for school grades Siblings WIC pairs, one who "participated" in WIC prenatally and one who enrolled after one year of age (n = 19 sibling pairs)	Multivariate regression including participation dummy	Increases IQ, attention span, visual-motor synthesis, and school GPA

(continued)

Table 4.13 (continued)

Study	Data[a]	Design	Results
Hicks, Langham, and Takenaka (1982)	Blind interviewer-administered tests and record abstractions for sample members of 3 rural counties in Louisiana Siblings WIC pairs, one who "participated" in WIC prenatally and one who enrolled after one year of age ($n = 21$ sibling pairs)	Multivariate regression including participation dummy	Reduces height/length
James (1998)	Medical records for one health center in Mt. Vernon, NY Randomly selected sample (matched on age and gender) of children who were up to date on immunizations at 12 months of age; equal size groups ($n = 150$; total)	Chi-square tests of the difference in percentage up-to-date at 24 months, using participation dummy	No significant impact estimated on the immunization status
Oliveira and Gunderson (2000)	CSFII (1994–96) WIC and income-eligible children (1–4 years) in households where at least one other person also participates in WIC ($n = 180$)	Multivariate regression including participation dummy; authors also ran regression for full sample of WIC and income-eligible children. That model resulted in more significant effects.	Participants consume more of vitamin B-6, folate, iron
Rose and Habicht (1998)	CSFII (1989–91) Non-breast-feeding preschool children (1–4 years) in FSP-eligible households ($n = 499$)	Multivariate regression including value of monthly household per capita WIC benefit. Investigated selection bias but reportedly "found no evidence of it"	Participants consume more of protein, vitamins B-6 and E, folate, thiamin, niacin, riboflavin, iron, magnesium, zinc
Rose, Smallwood, and Blaylock (1995)	CSFII (1989–91) Non-breast-feeding preschool children 1–5 years ($n = 800$)	Multivariate regression including participation dummy	Participants consume more iron

Study	Sample/Data	Methods	Findings
Rush, Leighton, et al. (1988)	Primary data collection, 24-hour recall, physical and laboratory measurements (1983–84) Random sample of infants and children of women included in the longitudinal study of women ($n = 2,370$)	Multivariate regression including participation dummy, defined on the basis of age of "inception" into WIC, including prenatally	Participants consume more of vitamins B-6 and C, iron, but less of protein, calcium, magnesium, phosphorus; reduces height/length; improves receptive vocabulary scores and digit memory at age; improves the immunization status; also estimated the impact on mother's breastfeeding practices, but no significant result obtained
Sherry, Bister, and Yip (1997)	PedNSS data for Vermont (1981–94) 12,000 to 19,500 records per year	Prevalence estimates for each year for overall sample and for 6–23 months and 24–59 months; trend analysis and chi-square tests	Reduces the prevalence of anemia
Smith et al. (1986)	Medical records for children in one health center in Los Angeles; initial and 6-month follow-up measures Subset of random sample of WIC and non-WIC children under the age of 5 who were diagnosed with anemia; matched on age, gender, and ethnicity ($n = 25$ each group)	Analysis of variance using participation dummy	Increases mean hematocrit, hemoglobin
Vasquez-Seoane, Windom, and Pearson (1985)	Medical records for children in an inner-city health center in New Haven, CT before and after initiation of WIC (1971 vs. 1984) Infants and children between 9 and 36 months of age ($n = 583$)	t-tests for pre-WIC vs. post-WIC group level comparison over time	Increases mean hematocrit and hemoglobin and reduces the prevalence of anemia

(continued)

Table 4.13 (continued)

Study	Data[a]	Design	Results
Yip et al. (1987)	(a) PedNSS data for Arizona, Kentucky, Louisiana, and Tennessee (1975–85; most data provided by WIC programs) (b) Linked PedNSS and birth records for WIC participants in Tennessee PedNSS database (1975–84) Infants and children between 6 and 60 months of age (a) $n = 499,759$; (b) $n = 72,983$	Multivariate regression and angular chi-square tests for overall and age-specific prevalence estimates for each year: initial measures vs. follow-up measures	Reduces the prevalence of anemia

Source: The tables are based largely on research reviewed in Hamilton and Fox et al. (2000).

Note: CSFII = Continuing Survey of Food Intake by Individuals; FNS WIC/Medicaid = FNS; WIC/Medicaid database; NHANES-III = Third National Health and Nutrition Examination Survey; NMIHS = National Maternal and Infant Health Survey; PedNSS = Pediatric Nutrition Surveillance System; RLMS = Ross Laboratories Mother's Survey; MIC = Maternity and Infant Care Project.

[a]Data source and population (sample size).

Table 4.14   **Studies of the National School Lunch Program**

Study	Data[a]	Design	Results
Studies of Impact on Food Energy and Nutrient Intake (at Lunch or Daily)			
Akin et al. (1983)	NFCS (1977–78) 24-hour recall; food record for 2 days; children/adolescents aged 6–18 (n = 1,554)	Multivariate regression (GLS) including the ratio of the number of days when the respondent ate school lunch to total number of days of dietary data	Increases daily intake of food energy, protein, vitamins A, B-6, B-12, and C, thiamin, niacin, calcium, iron, phosphorus, magnesium
Akin, Guilkey, and Popkin (1983)	NFCS (1977–78) 24-hour recall; food record for 2 days; children/adolescents aged 6–18 (n = 1,554)	Switching regression and Chow tests, including the ratio of the number of days when the respondent ate school lunch to the number of days when he/she ate any lunch	Increases daily intake of food energy, vitamins A, B-6, C, iron
Devaney, Gordon, and Burghardt (1993)	Nationally representative sample of students from 329 public and private schools 24-hour recall and questionnaire (parent); children/adolescents of grades 1–12, families (n = 3,350)	Multivariate regression (OLS) with selection bias adjustment, including participation dummy of whether the respondent ate NSLP lunch on recall day	Increases at-lunch intake of protein, vitamins A, B-12, riboflavin, calcium, phosphorus, magnesium, zinc, and in case of some subgroup(s) of the sample, fat, saturated fat, cholesterol; reduces at-lunch intake of carbohydrate and vitamin C; also increases daily intake of vitamins A, C, carbohydrate, fat, saturated fat; increases the consumption of milk (products), meat and fish, grain products, fruits (juices), vegetables; reduces the consumption of dry beans and peas, sugar, and sweets

(continued)

Table 4.14 (continued)

Study	Data[a]	Design	Results
Hoagland (1980)	HANES-I (1978–79) 24-hour recall and biochemical tests; children/adolescents, aged 6–21 ($n = 3,155$)	Comparison of means; linear regression, where participants are defined as those who ate school lunch on recall day	Increases daily intake of vitamin C
Howe and Vaden (1980)	Sample of randomly selected students in selected grades from one public city high school in KS 24-hour recall; adolescents of grades 10–11 ($n = 104$)	2-way ANOVA, where participants are defined as those who ate school lunch on recall day	Increases at-lunch intake of protein, vitamins A, C, thiamin, riboflavin, calcium, iron
Perry et al. (1984)	All 5th grade classes from two schools and 4/30 6th grade classes in a third school; one SFA in AL Food record for 3 days; observation (plate waste); questionnaire (student); children of grades 5–6 ($n = 233$)	Unmatched t-test, where participants are defined as those who ate NSLP lunch on data collection days	Increases at-lunch intake of vitamins A, C, riboflavin, calcium, phosphorus
Wellisch et al. (1983)	Nationally representative sample of student and families from 276 public schools; included students in no-NSLP schools 24-hour recall; food expenditure recall for 1 week; anthropometrics; in-person interview (parents and children); children/adolescents of grades 1–12, families ($n = 6,556$)	Multivariate (OLS) and logistic regression, including participation variables on whether the student ate NSLP lunch on recall day or on past/current weekly participation	Increases at-lunch intake of food energy, protein, vitamins A, B-6, thiamin, riboflavin, niacin, calcium, phosphorus, magnesium; reduces at-lunch intake of vitamin C; same results with respect to daily intake, for all of the above nutrients except thiamin and vitamin C; NSLP lunches are more dense in protein, vitamins A, B-6, riboflavin, niacin, calcium, phosphorus, magnesium, and iron (elementary school); NSLP lunches are less dense in vitamin C and iron (secondary school); increases weight, percent body fat,[b] the probability of overweight/overfatness[c] of the older subgroup of the participants; increases household's food expenditure

Studies of Impact on Children's Nutrition and Health Status, Food Consumption, and Household Food Expenditure[d]

Bhattacharya and Currie (2000)	NHANES-III (1988–94) Youths aged 12 to 16 (n = 1,358)	Multivariate regression including dummies for income eligibility and school being in session and an interaction term of the two, measuring "exposure" to school meals, to address the endogeneity of program participation	Exposure to school meals improves the overall quality of the diet (measured by HEI) and reduces blood cholesterol and sweets consumption
Gretzen and Vermeersch (1980)	All students from two intervention programs and two comparison programs in one semi-rural SFA in CA Review of school records; children of grades 1–8 (n = 332)	Comparison of means, t-test, and ANOVA for participant vs. matched control groups (two low-income and one mid-income group), where participants are defined as those who received school lunch regularly from grade 1 to 8	Male participants in NSLP are shorter in height compared to those in Head Start
Long (1991)	NESNP (1980–81) Food expenditure recall for 1 week; questionnaire (parent); families of children/adolescents of grades 1–12 (n = 5,997)	Multivariate regression with selection bias adjustment, where participants are defined as the households of which any member participated in NSLP at least once during a week	Increases household food expenditure
Melnick, Rhoades, Wales et al. (1998)	All children randomly selected classrooms from 25/50 NYC public and private schools 24-hour recall (nonquantitative) and questionnaire (parent); children of grades 2 and 5 (n = 1,397)	Gender-adjusted ANCOVA, where participants are defined as those who ate school lunch on recall day	Increases food and vegetables/5-A-Day Index Score, Food Guide Pyramid[e] Index Score

(*continued*)

Table 4.14 (continued)

Study	Data[a]	Design	Results
Wolfe, Campbell, Frongillo et al. (1994)	All children in selected grades from 51/110 schools in 7 regions in NY state Anthropometric and questionnaire (parent); children of grades 2 and 5 ($n = 1,797$)	Multivariate (OLS) and logistic regression, where participants are defined as those whose parent report that the child eats school lunch	Increases the body mass index[f] and percent of body fat of the participants; reduces the probability of underweight[g]

Source: The tables are based largely on research reviewed in Hamilton and Fox et al. (2000).

Note: NESNP = National Evaluation of School Lunch Programs; NFCS = Nationwide Food Consumption Survey; NHANES = National Health and Nutrition Examination Survey; HEI = Healthy Eating Index; ANCOVA = analysis of covariance; ANOVA = analysis of variance.

[a]Data source, data collection method and population (sample size).

[b]Based on measurements of triceps skinfold (Wellisch et al. 1983) or arm fat area (Wolfe et al. 1994).

[c]Based on weight for age and triceps fatfold > 75th NCHS percentile.

[d]Devaney, Gordon, and Burghardt (1993) and Wellisch et al. (1983) also did some relevant works. Their results are included in the section for "Studies of Impact on Food Energy and Nutrient Intake (at Lunch or Daily)."

[e]Based on the following number of daily recommended servings for children: Bread group 9 or more servings, Milk 2 or more servings, Meat group 2 or more servings, Vegetables 4 or more servings, and Fruit 3 or more servings.

[f]Based on weight/(height)^2 above 90th percentile in NHANES I and II.

[g]Based on arm fat area < 10th percentile.

undoubtably introduces measurement error. For example, female-headed households might be more likely to meet their recommended daily allowances (RDAs) of nutrients just because the targets levels are set lower for these households. A cleaner solution to the problem of heterogeneity in household composition may be to include a full set of controls for household composition in the model.

There is no usual practice regarding the treatment of the number of meals consumed away from home. Many studies ignore the issue entirely, whereas others use an ad hoc adjustment. These adjustments may also introduce biases. If, for example, the nutritional content of food consumed away from home is assumed to be too low, then households that eat out less will be more likely to meet their RDAs. Clearly, what can be done is limited by the data available in any particular survey.

Finally, many studies are based on surveys with complex sampling designs, and the use of sampling weights may have a considerable impact on the estimates. However, it is often unclear which weights should be used, particularly in studies in which subsets of participants are examined.

4.3.4   The Efficacy of the FSP

The National FSP Survey of 1996 found that 50 percent of FSP participants experience some level of food insecurity. Although on average the levels of nutrients available to respondents exceeded RDAs, substantial numbers of FSP recipients failed to meet the RDAs for some nutrients. For example, 31 percent of FSP households did not meet the RDA for iron, and 21 percent did not meet the RDA for folate (Cohen et al. 1999). Simple comparisons of FSP participants with nonparticipants also typically find that the former are more likely than the latter to report food insecurity, are more likely to suffer vitamin deficiencies, and, at the same time, have higher BMI (Bhattacharya and Currie 2000). Clearly participation in the FSP does not eliminate nutrition-related problems. Still, it is possible that the FSP makes households significantly better off nutritionally than they otherwise would have been. There has been a great deal of research devoted to investigating this question, although much of it is now dated. As table 4.12 indicates, most researchers have focused on three measures: household food expenditures, household nutrient availability, and individual nutrient intakes.

The studies reviewed in table 4.12 suggest that participation in the FSP has generally positive effects on household food expenditures. However, even the most recent of these studies are based on data from over twenty years ago. Fraker (1990) provides a synthesis of virtually all of the pre-1989 studies reviewed in table 4.12 that examine the marginal propensity to spend on food (MPS_f) out of FSP income. He concludes that the most reasonable estimates range between \$0.17 and \$0.47. That is, a \$1 increase in FSP benefits would lead to an additional \$0.17 to \$0.47 being spent on food. More recent estimates, such as those of Kramer-LeBlanc, Basiotis, and Kennedy (1997), also appear to fall in this range.

Note that this finding implies that although the FSP does increase food expenditures, there is a lot of leakage in this bucket of aid, since most of the money is spent on other goods. Most of these studies are based on comparisons of FSP households with eligible nonparticipants. If FSP households have higher MPS_f than nonparticipant households even in the absence of the program, then selection effects may cause the effects of the FSP to be overstated.

A second question is whether higher expenditures on food are translated into increased nutrient availability at the household level. In order to determine household nutrient availability, researchers keep track of the food purchased for consumption in the household and compare the nutrient content of this food with household RDAs. Judging by table 4.12, the evidence on this question is mixed. However, one of the better studies of this issue is Devaney and Moffitt (1991), which uses data from the 1979–80 National Survey of Food Consumption. This survey collected a seven-day record of household food use. Devaney and Moffitt compare FSP participants with eligible nonparticipants and attempt to control for selection into the FSP. They find a significant positive impact of the FSP on the consumption of food energy, protein, vitamin A, vitamin B-6, vitamin C, thiamin, riboflavin, calcium, iron, magnesium, and phosphorus.

All of these studies start from a presumption of scarcity. That is, if people are short of nutrients, then moving them toward the U.S. RDA is an achievement. However, if most people are meeting or exceeding the U.S. RDA, as they certainly are for calories, protein, and some vitamins, then encouraging them to consume even more is wasteful, if not actually harmful. What we would like to know is whether the FSP increases the consumption of households who are not meeting their RDAs for specific nutrients, and how it affects the composition of the diet (e.g., the percentage of total calories derived from fat) in all the participating households. However, little evidence is available on these questions.

Increases in household nutrient availabilities may or may not lead to increases in individual nutrient intakes. Nutrients may be lost during food preparation or wasted. Some individuals may not consume some items, and individuals may consume food outside the home (e.g., school lunches). Studies of individual nutrient intakes typically find much weaker effects than studies of the effects of the FSP on household nutrient availabilities, as table 4.12 shows.

However, Fraker, Long, and Post (1990) found a significant difference in the consumption of calories between preschool children in FSP and non-FSP households. Rose, Smallwood, and Blaylock (1995) and Cook, Sherman, and Brown (1995) also find positive effects on intakes of some nutrients among preschool children. There is little evidence of significant positive effects on intakes for other groups, although Basiotis, Kramer-LeBlanc, and Kennedy (1998) find that FSP participants have healthier diets than nonparticipants. It is likely, as Fraker (1990) suggests, that individual nutrient intakes are measured with more error than household nutrient availabilities, so that it is more difficult to find statistically significant effects for nutrient intakes.

A few studies have examined the effects of FSP participation on anthropometric outcomes. For example, Currie and Cole (1993) use data from the National Longitudinal Survey of Youth to examine the effect of participation in both AFDC and the FSP during pregnancy. They find that although there is a negative correlation in ordinary least squares (OLS) models, this correlation disappears in instrumental variables models, or when fixed effects for the mother are employed. Korenman and Miller (1992) use the same data and find a statistically significant effect of FSP participation during pregnancy on the birth weight of first-born children in OLS models. However, they find no effect on children of higher birth order, or when they attempt to control for selection into the FSP using models with mother fixed effects.

Finally, a few recent studies have also examined the effect of the FSP on food insecurity. Bhattacharya and Currie (2000) show that controlling for standard demographic factors such as age, education, race, and household structure, the standard positive correlation between food insecurity and FSP participation is reversed. Conditional on these factors, their sample of adolescents was 6 percent less likely to report food insecurity if the household participated in the FSP. Similarly, Rose, Gunderson, and Oliveira (1998) found that among FSP participants in the SIPP, the incidence of food insecurity decreased with the size of the FSP benefit.

4.3.5 The Efficacy of WIC

WIC is the most studied FANP, but significant gaps remain in our knowledge. As table 4.13 illustrates, most of the existing studies focus on the effects of participation by pregnant women on the health of newborns, even though infants and children make up 75 percent of the caseload. In addition, there are few studies of postpartum women.

Possible selection biases also pose a significant problem for the interpretation of most studies of WIC. These selection biases could take several forms. For example, since many women are referred to WIC when they seek prenatal care, it may be only women who are highly motivated to bear a healthy child who enroll. Conversely, given limited funds, program administrators may pick the most at-risk individuals to participate. In the first case, one might expect overestimates of the true program effects, whereas in the second, one would expect underestimates.

A 1992 GAO study (U.S. GAO 1992) reviewed seventeen studies of the effects of prenatal WIC participation on newborns that it judged to be adequate in terms of sample size and design. The seventeen studies found that WIC participation reduced the incidence of low birth weight by between 10 and 43 percent, and that it reduced the incidence of very low birth weight between 21 and 53 percent. The GAO conducted a meta-analysis of these studies and concluded that providing WIC services to mothers of babies born in 1990 will ultimately prove to have saved federal tax payers more than $337 million. Their estimates suggest that $1 invested in WIC saves at least $3.50 in other costs. However, it should be kept in mind that these studies covered only prenatal WIC recipients, and that most WIC recipients are infants, postpartum women, and children.

Moreover, these conclusions are subject to several caveats. First, the GAO study placed a lot of weight on a series of studies that were conducted by matching information about WIC recipients to Medicaid records (such as Buesher et al. 1993 and Schramm 1985, 1986). Since the income cutoff for Medicaid was well below the income cutoff for WIC over the period covered by the study, the estimates may apply to the poorest WIC recipients rather than to the average WIC recipient. Moreover, none of the studies included by the GAO was able to adequately deal with the problem of potential selection bias.

Additional studies of the effects of WIC on pregnant women have been completed since the GAO study, most of which come to similar positive conclusions. These include Ahluwalia et al. (1992); Brown, Watkins, and Hiett (1996); Covington (1995); Gordon and Nelson (1995); Devaney (1992); and Kowaleski-Jones and Duncan (2000). Some of these studies attempt to deal with the selection problem using statistical methods, but as Gordon and Nelson point out, in most data sets it is difficult to find variables that affect WIC participation that will not also affect birth outcomes.

Brien and Swann (1999) address this problem by merging data about the characteristics of state WIC programs to their individual-level data from the National Maternal and Infant Health Survey. They find that characteristics of state WIC programs affect the probability of enrollments among blacks, although they have little impact on whites. In particular, whether or not the state required that applicants provide documentation of their income affected black enrollments. Using these instruments in two-stage least squares regression models, they find that WIC participation lowers the probability of low birth weight by 8 percent among blacks.

Brien and Swann also estimate models with mother fixed effects (for mothers with two or more births) as an alternative way of controlling for the possible unobserved differences between WIC participants and nonparticipants. The findings of these models are consistent with the instrumental variables results for blacks. Among whites, they find no effect of WIC. However, it is important to keep in mind that fixed effects models are likely to understate the true effect of WIC if WIC participation is measured with error or if there are positive spillovers of WIC participation from one child to another, as one might expect as a result of educational interventions. Kowaleski-Jones and Duncan (2000) also use sibling fixed effects methods, and they find that participation in WIC increases birth weight by seven ounces.

Table 4.13 lists three studies that have found positive results of WIC participation on the nutritional status of pregnant women, something that one would expect to lead to higher birth weights. Moreover, the pattern of increases in nutrient intakes is consistent with the tailoring of food packages by WIC, suggesting that it is related to the consumption of WIC foods. However, the most recent study of this issue (Rush, Sloan, et al. 1988) uses data collected in 1983–84.

A few studies have examined the effects of WIC participation on breast-feeding and infant feeding practices. Although breast milk is universally acknowledged to be the best food for infants, WIC gives free formula to mothers who choose not to breast-feed. In fact, it is estimated that 40 percent of the infant formula sold in the U.S. is sold (at a negotiated discount) to WIC agencies (Randall, Boast, and Holst 1995). Since formula is expensive, this feature of the program removes a powerful incentive to breast-feed. Even in the absence of this incentive, however, one would expect WIC mothers to be less likely to breast-feed than other mothers because women who are poor, young, minority, or less educated are less likely to breast-feed. One countervailing influence may be the nutrition education that WIC is mandated to provide. WIC centers are required to teach pregnant women that "breast is best."

Table 4.13 provides an overview of studies of the effects of WIC on breast-feeding. These studies suggest that WIC does discourage breast-feeding unless strong attempts are made to counterbalance this effect through education and that, even with education, the net effect of WIC on breast-feeding is negative. It is likely, however, that WIC has a positive impact on infant feeding practices among women who choose not to breast-feed. The provision of free formula appears to encourage women to delay the introduction of cow's milk (which is not recommended before one year) and of solid foods (which are not recommended before four months; Burstein, Fox, and Puma 1991). The use of iron-fortified formula rather than cow's milk would also be expected to reduce the risk of anemia among infants.

Table 4.13 indicates that the estimated effects of WIC on infants and children tend to be much more variable than the estimated effects on birth outcomes. Some studies actually report reductions in anthropometric measures such as head circumference, which presumably reflects selection bias. A consistent finding is that WIC does raise consumption of target nutrients. For example, a recent study by Rose, Habicht, and Devaney (1998) uses 1989–91 data from the Continuing Survey of Food Intakes to examine the effects of WIC on non-breast-feeding preschool children in FSP eligible households. They found that WIC had positive effects on the consumption of protein, vitamin B6, vitamin E, folate, thiamin, riboflavin, niacin, iron, magnesium, and zinc. However, the mean intakes of most of these nutrients exceeded 100 percent of the RDA for both the participants and nonparticipants. Rose, Habicht, and Devaney find no significant effect of WIC on the fraction of calories from fat, and a recent Centers for Disease Control study finds no effect of WIC on the incidence of overweight. Thus, one might conclude that too little attention is being paid to reducing intakes of the wrong types of foods among children at risk of obesity. Burstein et al. (2000) report similar findings using the National Health and Nutrition Examination Survey.

Although these studies do not control for selection into WIC, the Burstein et al. (2000) study provides some insight into the question of how children who participate in WIC differ from eligible nonparticipants. The study finds that the WIC children are more likely to have been born to women who smoked or drank during pregnancy, and are more likely to be low birth weight. They have a poorer home environment along a number of dimensions, and their mothers score more poorly on tests of "locus of control," financial skills, and coping skills. These comparisons suggest that fears that WIC studies are biased by the selection of the most capable mothers into the program are misplaced. More research into the question of exactly how mothers are selected into WIC (and other FANPs) offers one possible resolution to the problem of nonrandom selection.

WIC has also been found to lower the incidence of anemia. Yip et al. (1987) look at the prevalence of anemia from 1975 to 1985, a period when WIC was growing rapidly. They find that over this period the incidence of anemia fell from 7.8 percent to 2.9 percent. It is highly plausible that this decrease is due to WIC, given that (a) WIC mandates that iron-fortified formulas and cereals be included in its food packages, (b) half of all infants born in the United States during the 1980s participated in WIC, and (c) three-quarters of these children were formula-fed since birth (Schwartz et al. 1992).

Improvements in the consumption of micronutrients such as iron may be responsible for differences in cognitive performance that have been observed in two studies. Rush, Alvir, et al. (1988b) found that infants and children whose mothers participated in WIC prenatally had significantly higher scores on the Peabody Picture Vocabulary Test than other infants. Hicks, Langham, and Takenaka (1982) studied twenty-one sibling pairs in Louisiana. Because of the way that WIC was introduced in Louisiana, one sibling had received WIC benefits starting prenatally, while the other had received benefits only after one year of age. The sibling with greater WIC exposure fared better on virtually all of the measures assessed including IQ and school grade point averages. This study has been criticized, however, because the measured effects are greater than those reported in many studies of food supplementation in severely malnourished populations (Pollitt and Lorimor 1983). Also, the siblings with the greater WIC exposure were more likely to be first born, which might conceivably account for the fact that they were also found to be shorter than their siblings. Kowaleski-Jones and Duncan (2000) use data from the National Longitudinal Survey of Youth to examine the effect of maternal participation in WIC on motor and social skills and temperament in addition to birth weight. They used sibling fixed effects models to control for unobservables and found some evidence of a positive effect of WIC on temperament, although not on motor or social skills.

4.3.6   The Efficacy of NSLP

Two large national studies of the impact of school lunch have been conducted: the National Evaluation of School Nutrition Programs (NESNP) conducted in 1980 to 1981 and the School Nutrition Dietary Assessment Study (SNDA) conducted in 1991 to 1992 (Devaney, Gordon, and Burghardt 1993; Gordon, Devaney, and Burghardt 1995). The SNDA was also the first study to attempt to account for selection into the program and to evaluate the effects of NSLP on the quality of the diet as well as the probability that RDAs were met. The SNDA found that controlling for selection overturned some of the findings of the NESNP; hence, I focus on the SNDA here.

Both studies predate the latest changes to the NSLP, so it is not possible to assess the effects of these changes. By allowing students to drink nonfat rather than whole milk, for example, the recent changes may reduce the amount of fat provided by meals without affecting their nutrient densities. The fourth National Health and Nutrition Examination Survey, which is currently in the field, may shed some light on these issues.

As table 4.14 shows, most studies of the NSLP have focused on individual nutrient intakes. Studies conducted as part of the SNDA found that the number of calories consumed at lunch was similar for NSLP participants and nonparticipants but that the NSLP lunches were higher in fat and sodium. On the other hand, the NSLP had a positive impact on the consumption of some important nutrients such as vitamin A and calcium, which are found in the mandatory milk component of the lunch meal pattern. Younger NSLP participants also had higher lunchtime intakes of vitamin B-12, phosphorus, magnesium, and zinc. NSLP lunches generally met or exceeded the goal of providing one-third of the RDA for all vitamins and minerals. Nonparticipants were more likely to be short of vitamin A, vitamin B-6, calcium, iron, and zinc (Devaney, Gordon, and Burghardt 1993). Together with the results for total calories, these results suggest that the NSLP influences consumption of these nutrients by providing foods rich in specific nutrients, rather than by increasing total food intake. In particular, NSLP participants consume more milk, meat or meat substitutes, and vegetables at lunch than nonparticipants.

Changes in nutrient intakes at lunch may be offset by other changes in eating patterns over the course of the day. The SNDA asked about nutrient intakes over a twenty-four-hour period and concluded that the positive effects of the NSLP on lunchtime nutrient intakes were somewhat offset. This finding is analogous to the conclusion from the FSP literature that much of the value of the benefit is spent on goods other than food. On the other hand, the NSLP did not have any statistically significant impact on twenty-four-hour intakes of cholesterol or sodium, indicating that the negative effects of the NSLP on diet also tend to be offset over a twenty-four-hour period. Thus, findings that NSLP participants are more likely to be overweight than nonparticipants (see Wolfe et al. 1994; Bhattacharya and Currie 2000) may reflect selection into the program.

There has been virtually no research on the question of whether the NSLP has positive effects on the schooling attainments of participating students. This omission is curious given the fact that one of the rationales for school nutrition programs is that hungry children are likely to have difficulty learning.

Similarly, there has been little research on the question of whether participation in the NSLP improves food security. One would think that the availability of at least one nutritious meal per day might have a major impact on the food security of children in some households. Bhattacharya and Currie (2000) address this issue using data from the National Health and Nutrition Examination Surveys. They estimate a difference-in-difference model where adolescents are either eligible or ineligible for the NSLP, and schools are either in session or out of session. They do not find any statistically significant effect of NSLP participation on the degree of food insecurity reported by households of adolescents, although they do find that the NSLP is linked to reductions in the fraction of adolescents with high blood cholesterol and improvements in the quality of the diet as measured by the Healthy Eating Index.

Although the SBP is not a focus of this review, it is useful to discuss some of the evaluations of SBP alongside those of the NSLP because the SBP evaluations address a somewhat different set of questions. One of the major goals of the SBP is to promote breakfast consumption among children who would not otherwise eat breakfast. Devaney and Stuart's (1998) recent reexamination of the SNDA data indicates that the SBP does encourage poor children to eat more than a nominal breakfast. Some smaller-scale studies (see Myers et al. 1989) have found positive effects of SBP on school attendance and test scores. This study followed children before and after the SBP was introduced into their school.[10]

This research suggests that school nutrition programs can have positive effects on nutrient intakes and perhaps on scholastic achievement, al-

10. Unfortunately, this study suffered from many missing observations, which undermines its credibility somewhat. However, one would not want to draw sweeping conclusions about the effects of school meal programs on the basis of one study, in any case.

though more research is needed on this question. It will be interesting to see whether the recent sweeping changes to the programs will enhance these effects.

4.4 Evidence about Take-up

In order for programs to be effective, eligible families must take up their benefits. Nonparticipation by eligibles is a significant problem. For example, only 69 percent of households eligible for the FSP participated in 1994. The 40 percent increase in enrollments between 1988 and 1993 was due mainly to a higher participation rate among eligibles rather than to an increase in the number of eligibles (U.S. Committee on Ways and Means 1998), suggesting that changes in take-up have important impacts on participation rates. Possible reasons for nonparticipation include lack of knowledge about eligibility, transactions costs associated with enrolling in the program, and stigma associated with participation (see Moffitt 1983). Welfare reform has the potential to affect participation via all three channels as is discussed further below.

4.4.1 Take-up of the FSP

Takeup of FSP benefits is high among some subgroups of eligibles, but low among others. For example, in 1994, 86 percent of eligible children participated, but only one-third of eligible elderly persons. Virtually all eligible single-parent households were enrolled compared to only 78 percent of eligible households with children and two or more adults (U.S. Committee on Ways and Means 1998).

Participation rates for FSP also varied by ethnicity, with 92 percent of eligible African Americans participating compared to 61 percent of eligible Hispanics and 59 percent of eligible white non-Hispanics. Participation rates were higher in some states than others, ranging from 38 percent in Alaska to virtually 100 percent in Vermont and Maine. Participation rates also tended to fall as income rose (U.S. Committee on Ways and Means 1998; Schirm 1998).

The available evidence suggests that all three of the explanations for nonparticipation that have been suggested (lack of information, transactions costs, and stigma) may be important in explaining these patterns. A recent USDA study of FSP eligibles found that three-quarters of nonparticipating households said that they were not aware that they were eligible. Only 7 percent of households gave stigma as their main reason for nonparticipation, but half answered affirmatively to at least one of the survey questions about stigma. Haider, Schoeni, and Jacknowitz (2002) investigate low participation rates among the elderly using information from the Health and Retirement Survey and conclude that many elderly people who are eligible for food stamps say that they do not need benefits, which may indicate that there is stigma associated with using the program unless one is very needy.

Turning to transactions costs, the average FSP application took nearly five hours of time to complete, including at least two trips to an FSP office. Recertification for benefits took 2.5 hours and at least one trip. Out-of-pocket application costs averaged about $10.31 or 6 percent of the average monthly benefit (Ponza et al. 1999). Blank and Ruggles (1996) found that participation in the FSP increased with the size of the benefit, suggesting that households trade off the costs and benefits when deciding whether or not to participate.

Daponte, Sanders, and Taylor (1999) investigate these issues further using a sample of 405 households in Allegheny County, Pennsylvania. They found that many households that satisfy the gross income requirement for the FSP (i.e., they have incomes less than 130 percent of poverty) are ineligible for other reasons. Many of them have liquid assets in excess of the asset limits. This means that it is treacherous to try to impute eligibility for social programs using the limited asset information usually available in general surveys. The authors also conducted a randomized experiment. The treatment group was informed about their eligibility status and about the size of any benefits they were eligible for. The control group was not. Information had a significant effect in that people informed about their eligibility status were much more likely to subsequently apply for the FSP. In keeping with Blank and Ruggles, those entitled to the largest benefits were most likely to apply when given this information: The take-up rate was over 90 percent for those eligible for over $202 in benefits, compared to only 40 percent among those eligible for less than $41. This finding demonstrates that transactions costs are a significant barrier to take-up.

Yelowitz (2000) also provides evidence that suggests that lack of information and transactions costs associated with enrollment in the FSP have important effects. He studies increases in income cutoffs for Medicaid over the late 1980s and early 1990s. Newly eligible families who applied for Medicaid may have learned of their eligibility for the FSP at the same time. Alternatively, families who did not find it worthwhile to incur the transactions costs associated with applying for food stamps may have found it worthwhile to apply for both Medicaid and food stamps. In any case, Yelowitz finds that for every ten newly eligible families who took up Medicaid benefits, four also took up food stamps. The fact that only 40 percent took up suggests either that those who applied for Medicaid were not all informed about eligibility for food stamps, or that transactions costs are important in addition to lack of information. These changes in Medicaid eligibility may have accounted for as much as half of the run-up in the FSP caseload in the early 1990s.

4.4.2   Take-up in WIC and the NSLP

Estimating take-up of the WIC program is complicated by the fact that one must be at nutritional risk in order to qualify. Hence, estimates of take-up are sensitive to assumptions about the fraction of the population that is at risk. The USDA estimated that 9.2 million persons were eligible for WIC in 1995 and that 75 percent participated in the program. Among some subgroups of the eligible population, such as infants, take-up has been closer to 100 percent (Rossi 1998), and in recent years concern has been expressed about take-up rates greater than 100 percent of those infants the USDA deems to be eligible for the program (National Research Council 2001).

Perhaps the best potential sources of evidence about the factors that affect participation in WIC are studies that have tried to control for selection into the program. Unfortunately, these studies seldom report the first-stage estimates from their selection correction models. As discussed above, Brien and Swann do report these estimates and show that several characteristics of state programs influence WIC participation. Their results suggest that administrative barriers (such as procedures to verify income) may discourage people from applying for WIC. Chatterji et al. (2002) show that in addition, restrictions on the types of foods that can be purchased (such as restrictions that mothers buy low-fat milk) discourage participation. Bitler, Currie, and Scholz (2002) find that requiring more frequent visits to WIC offices also has negative effects on participation. Some of their models use administrative state-level data, so that they are not contaminated by underreporting of WIC participation, which is a significant problem in survey data. Poor and minority women are also more likely to be enrolled, as were high school dropouts and single mothers.

Similarly, participation in the NSLP is higher among children from the poorest families. This may be due in part to the fact that these children are eligible for free meals, whereas other children have to pay at least part of the cost of the meals. In his analysis of the SNDA data, Gleason (1995) finds that girls are less likely to eat school meals than boys, and that older girls are less likely than younger ones to eat these meals.

Gleason also shows that the characteristics of the meals are important determinants of participation. The most common reason given for not eating school lunch was that students didn't like the food. His results suggest that implementation of the *Dietary Guidelines'* recommendation that fat make up no more than 30 percent of the calories in a meal would lead to a substantial drop in participation. However, this drop-off could be counterbalanced by reducing the price of meals, restricting the ability of students to go off campus, eliminating vending machines, or reducing the number of a la carte menu items offered in addition to the school lunch.

Approximately a quarter of children eligible for free or reduced price meals do not become certified. In a study of the parents of eligible non-participants, Burghardt et al. (1993) found that over half believed that they were ineligible, 10 percent thought the certification process was onerous, and 20 percent cited stigma. In contrast, Glantz et al. (1994) find that children's preferences are the largest single factor affecting the parents' decision to apply for certification. If children indicate that they will not eat the meals, then parents do not apply.

Gordon, Devaney, and Burghardt (1995) compare OLS and selection-corrected models of participation in school meals programs. They find that the OLS estimates indicate that NSLP increases the number of calories consumed, while the selection-corrected models do not. In other words, the students who choose to participate in NSLP are those who would eat bigger lunches in any case. This is especially true for adolescent girls, indicating that those girls who do choose to participate are those who are big eaters. These findings suggest that implementation of the *Dietary Guidelines* may reduce the number of participants in school meal programs, particularly among adolescent girls, unless special care is taken to serve meals that appeal to these students.

4.4.3   Welfare Reform and Take-up

There is a good deal of debate about the mechanism through which PRWORA may have affected take-up of FSP caseloads. Welfare reform can affect FSP participation in many ways. First, households that leave the welfare rolls because they either find work or run into time limits may not know that they remain eligible for FSP. In some instances, their caseworkers may not even know that they remain eligible, since under the prior regime, welfare recipients were automatically eligible for food stamps.

Second, state "diversion programs" intended to discourage people from applying for welfare benefits by, for example, requiring them to engage in job search before applying for benefits may also discourage them from applying for food stamps. In these two scenarios, people who are eligible for FSP benefits are not receiving them because of administrative barriers created by welfare reform.

A third possibility is that welfare reform has been successful in terms of encouraging people to leave the welfare rolls for jobs that pay more than the income limit for the FSP. However, the available evidence is that most of those who transition from welfare to work continue to have incomes low enough to qualify for the FSP, so this is not a likely explanation for the decline in FSP caseloads (Dion and Pavetti 2000). For example, Zedlewski and Brauner (1999) examine data on households with children who had participated in the FSP between January 1995 and the survey date. When surveyed between February and October 1997, one-third of these families had left the program. Zedlewski and Brauner find that families who had been on welfare were more likely than other families to have exited, and that the difference was greatest at the lowest levels of income. If families were choosing not to participate because of improvements in their financial positions, then one might expect differences in participation to be greatest at the highest levels of income.

Fourth, the publicity surrounding welfare reform may have increased the stigma surrounding all means-tested programs. For example, there is some evidence that the degree of underreporting of means-tested program participation in the CPS has increased in recent years.

Fifth, some categories of persons, such as resident aliens and adults without dependents who do not meet work requirements, have become ineligible as a result of PWRORA. However, since these groups did not make up much of the FSP caseload before PWRORA, it is unlikely that their exclusion is responsible for much of the decline in caseloads. Temporary sanctions of TANF recipients who fail to comply with work requirements may also lead to a loss of food stamp benefits.

Sixth, even if eligible households are aware of their entitlements, losing automatic eligibility for food stamps increases transactions costs greatly, as families are typically required to be recertified for FSP benefits four times a year. Many states have shorter recertification intervals for working families than for families entirely on cash assistance, because working families have more variable incomes and hence may be more likely to receive food stamps in error. Currie and Grogger (2001) and Kabbani and Wilde (2002) both show that reductions in recertification intervals reduce participation. Thus, by reducing the fraction of the low-income population that relies solely on welfare, welfare reform has resulted in an increase in the transactions costs associated with staying on the FSP for many families and decreases in participation.

Loprest (1999) found that two years after leaving AFDC/TANF, less than a third of former welfare recipients were receiving food stamps. This study was based on a national survey of former recipients, but similar findings have been reported using state-level administrative data (Dion and Pavetti 2000). It is evidently important to distinguish between the possible reasons for nonparticipation, but most of the available evidence regarding effects of welfare reform on participation in the FSP is anecdotal. Still, enough evidence of negative effects of welfare reform is available that the GAO recently recommended that the FNS require states to inform welfare applicants of their eligibility for food stamps during the first meeting; to publicize eligibility requirements for the FSP and distinguish them from the eligibility requirements for TANF; and to aggressively evaluate access to food stamp benefits when reviewing states' FSP operations (U.S. GAO 1999b).

Little information is available about the effects of welfare reform on participation in other FANPs. However, in a study using SIPP data from 1993 to 1995, Burstein et al. (2000) find that 22 percent of child exits from the WIC program were associated with parents leaving AFDC (holding income constant). This suggests that declines in welfare participation due to welfare reform may also lead to the loss of WIC benefits.

4.5 Evidence Regarding the Efficacy of Cash versus In-Kind Transfers

What do evaluations of food and nutrition programs have to say about whether the provision of services in-kind makes economic sense? Economic theory suggests that if the goal of nutrition programs is to improve the utility of the household decision maker, then this could be done more efficiently by replacing in-kind benefits with cash. Moreover, having a large number of in-kind programs is more expensive administratively than simply mailing a check, and in-kind programs are more subject to some types of fraud (e.g., recipients attempting to trade food stamps for cash). Viewed from this perspective, the growth in the proportion of assistance to low-income households that is delivered in-kind over the past thirty years (see Currie 1991) is hard to explain.

On the other hand, in-kind programs have several features that are attractive to at least some constituencies. First, the benefits may be more targeted to the truly needy. On the other hand, provision of benefits in kind is stigmatizing, and those who suffer most from stigma are not necessarily those least in need of aid. Second, the fact that the benefits are in kind may deter some types of fraud. For example, people may be less likely to falsely claim eligibility for food stamps than they are to falsely claim eligibility for cash assistance. Of course, to the extent that food stamps can be converted easily to cash, this argument for the provision of in-kind benefits will be undermined.

A third, and perhaps more compelling argument, is that advocacy groups, the agricultural industry, and the general public all support the idea of giving food aid in kind. It is this political support that allowed the FSP to survive the latest round of welfare reform unscathed. Public support for the in-kind nature of food aid may indicate that the general public is not particularly interested in increasing the utility of aid recipients. Rather, the goal of nutrition programs is to alter the behavior and consumption bundles of recipient households in specific ways.

4.5.1   Administrative Costs

Supplying benefits in kind increases the transactions costs associated with running safety-net programs. For example, one study found that in the case of a FSP program operated using paper coupons, these costs amounted to $13.39 per case month for the program, $24.73 per $1,000 redeemed for participating retailers, and $3.50 per $1,000 redeemed for financial institutions (who eventually receive deposits of FSP coupons).

These costs may be substantially reduced by EBT. One demonstration found that the corresponding costs in an EBT system were $2.52 per case month, $15.21 per $1,000 for retailers, and $.23 per $1,000 for financial institutions (USDA 1994).[11] Notwithstanding these cost savings, EBT may result in lower participation by vendors, who may need to install special equipment in order to participate.

11. In a single month in 1997, retailers deposited 1.7 million dollars' worth of food stamp coupons in more than 26,000 banks. Banks in turn made 27,000 deposits to Federal Reserve District Banks. At each step, coupons had to be counted (see fns1.usda.gov/fsp/menu/admin/ebt/ebt.htm).

Total administrative costs associated with the FSP vary considerably from state to state. For example, in 1988, the annual administrative cost per case varied from $238 in the highest quintile of states (excluding Alaska, which had very high costs of $522 per case) to $108 in the lowest quintile of states (Ohls and Beebout 1993). A comparison of the difference in these figures to the direct costs of operating a coupon program (given earlier) suggests that the administrative cost savings that would be obtained by cashing out the FSP are dwarfed by regional differences in administrative costs that are driven by other factors.

4.5.2 Fraud and Stigma

It is possible that the provision of benefits in kind reduces the number of households that fraudulently claim eligibility for FANPs, relative to the number that would claim equivalent cash benefits. However, little evidence is available on this question. What is clear from the discussion above is that the provision of in-kind benefits opens the door to another type of abuse, which is the illegal trafficking of benefits for cash. It is also clear that some fraction of the potential FANP caseload is deterred from using these programs by stigma, although, again, there is little evidence available regarding whether these households would find a cash program less stigmatizing.

A major goal of the EBT program is to reduce fraud in the FSP. In studies of this issue, FNS has found that FSP recipients reported by a three-to-one margin that it was harder to sell benefits with EBT cards. Sixty-nine percent of retailers surveyed also perceived FSP fraud to be decreased under EBT (USDA 1994). However, although in principle EBT data could be used to identify fraudulent use of FSP benefits by both individuals and stores, a recent GAO report found that most state agencies were not yet equipped to effectively analyze these data (U.S. GAO 2000). EBT could also increase the participation of eligibles by reducing stigma: The use of an electronic card may be less likely to draw attention than the use of coupons.

4.5.3 Are In-Kind Benefits Treated Differently from Cash?[12]

The FSP typically provides benefits that are less than a household's monthly food budget. Thus, in principle, the benefits should be equivalent to a cash transfer, since households can use the FSP benefits to buy food that they would have purchased in any case and use the money released to buy other goods. On the other hand, the fact that some people sell their food stamps suggests that at least these people are receiving more in the form of stamps than they wish to consume in the form of food purchases.

---

12. A related question is whether we can learn anything from the FSP about running welfare programs using a voucher system. However, Moffitt (1999) argues that there are several features about the market for food that may make it difficult to draw inferences from the FSP about the general question of whether it is advantageous to provide benefits in the form of vouchers.

Studies of this issue have found that approximately 11 percent of the caseload receive food stamp benefits larger than their food budgets (Ohls and Beebout 1993).

In contrast to the FSP, WIC and the NSLP provide food "packages" that are likely to differ from those that would be chosen by households in the absence of the programs. Other things being equal, then, one might expect these programs to have larger effects on the composition of the diet than the FSP.

As table 4.12 shows, many studies have attempted to estimate the MPS_f out of FSP benefits and to compare it to the MPS_f out of cash income. Surprisingly, these studies have typically found that the former is greater than the latter. For example, in his review of the literature Fraker finds that estimates of the MPS_f out of FSP benefits center around \$0.25, whereas the MPS_f out of cash income is estimated to be less than \$0.15. As discussed above, given the fungibility of FSP benefits, one might expect the two quantities to be the same for most households. It is possible that the small fraction of households that receive food stamp benefits greater than or equal to their preferred food budgets have a very high MPS_f out of FSP benefits, and that this high value is largely offset by the many other households who are not "constrained" by the FSP.

More recent evidence on this question is provided by several food stamp "cashout" demonstrations, which are also summarized in table 4.12. In these cashouts, households were issued checks instead of the usual FSP coupons. The study with perhaps the cleanest design was carried out in San Diego. This demonstration randomly assigned households receiving welfare payments and FSP benefits to a treatment group that received a check combining the two benefits and to a control group that continued to receive FSP coupons separately. The treatment group spent an average of \$22 per month less on food.

However, Whitmore (2002) has reexamined these data and finds that only households that were constrained in the sense that the initial value of their food stamps was greater than or equal to their food budgets spent less on food after the cashout. She further finds that households reduced spending on relatively nonnutritious items such as soda and juice, and that the reductions in expenditure did not have any negative effect on nutritional status. Whitmore also provides some direct evidence regarding trafficking of food stamps from a survey of food stamp recipients. She finds that food stamps sell for about 65 percent of their face value.

The results from several other cashout demonstrations show little evidence of effects on expenditures. For example, studies of the cashout of the Puerto Rican FSP system[13] did not show any change in the MPS_f out of

13. In 1982 the FSP program in Puerto Rico was changed to a cash program called the Nutrition Assistance Program.

program benefits (Beebout et al. 1985; Devaney and Fraker 1986; Moffitt 1989). However, in Puerto Rico, FSP coupons were widely circulated as currency even before the cashout. A demonstration in Alabama also failed to find a significant effect of cashout, but in this demonstration the FSP benefit was issued as a separate rather than a combined check, and the demonstration was introduced with little publicity as an explicitly short-term demonstration (Fraker et al. 1992). Lastly, a cashout demonstration that dealt with elderly households found little impact on food expenditures (Butler, Ohls, and Posner 1985).

Whitmore's findings cast doubt on the hypothesis that, on average, households with children treat FSP benefits differently from cash. However, it is possible that some subset of these households does benefit from receiving benefits in kind. It is thought that female heads of household may have more control over the use of FSP coupons than they have over the cash income they receive from other sources, and that they have higher marginal propensities to spend on food. Welch (1999) documents the fact that many prime age men live in households where other members are receiving some form of public assistance. And Moffitt, Reville, and Winkler (1998) point out that many unmarried welfare mothers are in fact cohabiting with a partner. In these households, the fact that FSP benefits are issued in the woman's name and earmarked for food purchases may increase her ability to spend the income on food. The fact that elderly recipients are more likely to live alone might then explain the finding that their MPS_fs out of FSP benefits and cash are equal. It would be very interesting to test this hypothesis using detailed information about the composition of FSP households.

Further evidence about the efficacy of in-kind transfers comes from WIC and the NSLP. As discussed above, these programs appear to increase the consumption of targeted nutrients, not by increasing the total amount of food consumed (as any kind of transfer would be expected to do), but by changing the composition of foods consumed.

4.6 Evidence Regarding Work Disincentives

As discussed earlier, social programs with fixed income cutoffs create a notch in the budget constraint facing households. Households located near these notch points may face very high marginal tax rates on additional earnings, which are likely to discourage them from increasing their hours of work. Moreover, some households that were initially located above the notch may find it in their interests to cut back work hours to the notch point. On the other hand, removing the notch (for example, by eliminating a program like WIC) would not necessarily increase work effort.

The bulk of the research on the effects of cash welfare programs such as AFDC has been directed at measuring the work disincentives created by these programs. These studies often consider the combined effect of AFDC and FSP benefits on the behavior of female-headed households, since, as discussed above, most households that receive AFDC (now TANF) also receive FSP benefits. The combined data offer some purchase on the problem because FSP benefits are reduced thirty cents for every dollar of AFDC benefits. Hence, the variation in AFDC benefits across states creates some variation in FSP benefits. Moffitt and Fraker (1988) use data on female heads participating in AFDC and FSP in 1979 to estimate that the FSP reduces labor supply by 9 percent. However, they also found that small changes in guarantee levels and benefit reduction rates would have little impact on hours of work. Moffitt and Keane (1998) estimate a structural model of participation in multiple welfare programs and again conclude that high welfare tax rates have relatively little effect on work effort.

Hagstrom (1996) examines the effects of FSP participation on the labor supply of married couples and finds that the labor supply effects are even smaller than those found in studies focusing on single persons. These findings are consistent with the literature on cash welfare programs, which also finds small labor supply effects (see Moffitt 1992, 1998). Hagstrom identifies his model using variation in FSP benefits stemming from differences in nonlabor income and deductions (such as shelter deductions) across households with identical labor incomes.

Although they are now very dated, it is worth mentioning the results of several randomized experiments involving work programs for FSP recipients that were conducted in the early 1980s. Ohls and Beebout (1993) discuss several different models including (a) an applicant job search model, which required participants to contact a specified number of employers; (b) a job club model, which required participation in a two- to four-week training session designed to improve job search skills; (c) a group job search assistance model, which required participation in a two-day employability skills training workshop followed by eight weeks of job search with biweekly group meetings; and (d) a job club/workfare model, which required participation in a three-week job club followed by assignment to workfare jobs for those who were unsuccessful in finding employment on their own. All of these treatments increased earnings among treatment groups relative to controls, although the effects were not always statistically significant. Treatment effects tended to be larger for women than men. The treatments were also successful in reducing food stamp benefit amounts to the extent that the experimental programs produced modest cost savings.

Another notable finding, however, was that approximately two-thirds of the FSP recipients in the experimental sites were exempt from FSP work requirements due to age, the presence of young children in the household, disability, participation in other programs, or other factors. In principle, those who participate in programs such as AFDC/TANF are responsible for meeting the work requirements of those programs and so are exempted from compliance with FSP work requirements. Thus, it seems fair to conclude that although FSP recipients have technically been subject to work requirements for a long time, efforts to actually force most recipients to work have not been vigorously pursued.

4.7 Evidence about the Importance of Production Functions versus Budget Constraints

Is the typical FANP's emphasis on changing household budget constraints the best way to improve the nutritional status of the population, or should more attention be paid to altering household "production functions"? For the average American, obesity, a poor quality diet, and lack of exercise are much greater threats to health than food scarcity. An extensive body of evidence links diets high in fat and low in fiber to coronary artery disease, stroke, diabetes, and some forms of cancer (U.S. DHHS 1991). Moreover, individuals in poor households are both more likely to be obese and more likely to purchase foods with little nutritional value (e.g., soft drinks) compared to those in higher-income households, and the concentration of obesity among households of lower income has become more pronounced over time (Bhattacharya and Currie 2000).

FANPs differ in their implicit answers to this question of budget constraints versus production functions. The FSP allows households to use their benefits to purchase a very wide range of foods. The underlying assumption, then, is that households need larger food budgets but that they do not need direction in terms of what foods to purchase. On the other hand, the NSLP offers meals that conform to specific nutritional guidelines. WIC not only tailors its food packages to meet specific nutritional needs but also offers nutrition education. Thus, the FSP program is directed primarily at loosening household budget constraints, whereas the NSLP and WIC also attempt to alter household "health production functions" by changing the composition of the foods that are eaten. Evaluations of these programs reflect these differences in goals, since most evaluations of the FSP focus on whether household food expenditures are increased, whereas evaluations of the NSLP and WIC generally focus on individual nutrient intakes and (at least in the case of WIC) health outcomes.

It is possible then that a comparison of the effects of these programs can shed light on the issue of whether FANPs should be directed primarily at loosening budget constraints or at altering household production functions (or both). But it is difficult to compare the effectiveness of FANPs given that evaluations tend to focus on different sets of outcomes. Still, a perusal of the results in tables 4.12, 4.13, and 4.14 suggests that the NSLP and, especially, the WIC programs have greater positive effects on the composition of the diet than the FSP. This comparison suggests, then, that efforts to change household production functions may be productive. However, the fact that programs like WIC improve diets may reflect the effects of nutrition education, but it may also simply reflect the constraints of the program—that is, the fact that only nutritious foods are provided. There is little evidence about whether the nutrition education component of WIC is effective (although, as discussed above, there is some evidence of positive effects on infant feeding practices). Thus, for evidence of the effects of nutrition education, we must look elsewhere.

Evaluations of government-sponsored educational interventions show that intervention can be successful in improving young children's eating patterns. For example, Harrell et al. (1998) find that both classroom and individual nutritional education had positive effects on third- and fourth-grade children in terms of reducing blood cholesterol levels. Glenny et al. (1997) report similar results for family therapy and other interventions aimed at lifestyle modification.

Evaluations of the federal Nutrition Education and Training (NET) Program, which provides grants to states that implement nutrition education programs in their schools, have found that it is much easier to improve nutrition knowledge than it is to affect behavior. However, some evaluations of school-based programs have shown that children's willingness to try new foods offered in school lunch and the quality of snacks chosen away from home improved, and that children were more likely to consume fruits, vegetables, protein foods, and foods with vitamin A. Poor children have been shown to be more likely to consume dairy products and foods with vitamin C in response to NET programming. Not surprisingly, longer programs (e.g., fifty classroom hours or more) have been found to have larger effects on behavior (Contento, Manning, and Shannon 1992).

An important point with respect to nutrition education programs is that since many of them are still at the demonstration stage, the opportunity exists to conduct sensible, randomized evaluations of the efficacy of different types of programs. If it is not possible to randomize within schools, it may be possible to randomize across schools, as was done in the CATCH study (Luepker et al. 1996). In this study, ninety-six elementary schools located in four states were randomly chosen to be intervention or control sites. Five thousand third- to fifth-grade children took part over a three-year period from 1991 to 1993. The intervention involved training for food service staff and teachers, a nutrition curriculum for students, and outreach to parents. By 1993, the number of calories provided in school meals, and the number of calories provided in the form of fat and saturated fat, had fallen significantly in intervention schools relative to controls.

Kenkel (2000) summarizes a number of studies by Pauline Ippolito and Alan Mathios (1990, 1995, 1996) that have examined the effects of attempts by both government and the private sector to inform the public about the health benefits of diets low in fat and high in fiber. Government efforts to get this message out during the 1970s were relatively unsuccessful. But in the mid-1980s, the Federal Trade Commission and the Food and Drug Administration relaxed rules that had prevented food manufacturers from making health claims for their products. Ippolito and Mathios show that after declining very slowly between 1977 and 1985, the consumption of fats and cholesterol fell dramatically between 1985 and 1990, and the consumption of cereals rich in fiber increased. The Nutrition Labeling and Education Act of 1990 is apparently also influencing consumer choices (Ippolito and Mathios 1993).

In summary, the available evidence indicates that many households have imperfect information about diet and nutrition, and that both government and private programs can be effective in providing nutrition education, particularly to young children. Further research into these questions would be very useful.

4.8   Current Policy and Research Questions

In conclusion, I would like to offer five broad areas that merit future research. First, it would be useful to know more about the links between FANPs and changes to cash welfare programs such as TANF and the EITC. The policy debate leading up to the passage of the PRWORA included a good deal of discussion about overhauling the FSP. Congress considered cashing out the program and greatly reducing federal oversight by distributing the funds as block grants to the states. Yet the program survived the most recent round of welfare reform intact. Still, because of the links between FANPs and participation in other welfare programs, welfare reform is likely to have an important impact on the effectiveness of these programs. Households that were once automatically eligible for participation in FANPs because of their status as welfare recipients may not be aware that they remain eligible for FANPs even after their cash assistance has been cut off. Or they may find it difficult to go through the process of applying and reapplying for these benefits. The stigma associated with participation in any welfare program may also be increasing over time. Assessing the extent to which welfare reform affects participation in FANPs, and the channels through which participation is affected, is an important area for future research. We need a better understanding of the determinants of participation in the program if we are to effectively combat decreases in participation that may be linked to welfare reform.

A second important question for FANP research is the extent to which these programs should focus on improving the quality of diets rather than the quantity of foods consumed. As has been discussed, some FANPs such as WIC already place some emphasis on diet quality, whereas programs like FSP are designed to promote overall food consumption. In addition, the NSLP and SBP have recently been overhauled in order to place a greater emphasis on diet quality. In principle, the adoption of EBT could make it easy to place restrictions on the foods that could be purchased using FSP benefits (Kirlin and Adam 1998) if this proved to be an effective way to improve nutritional choices and health outcomes.

A third area for research concerns the extent to which any new monies allocated to FANPs should be allocated to nutrition education rather than to the provision of food to low-income Americans. As discussed above, some of the NSLP funds have been earmarked for nutrition education under the Healthy Meals for Healthy Americans Act. Funding for NET has also increased in recent years. The available evidence suggests that educational initiatives of this kind can have a positive effect on the diets of young children. Still, funding for this type of program is a drop in the bucket compared to overall spending on traditional food subsidies. As policymakers consider whether this funding should be increased further, it would be useful to have more information about the effects of nutrition education (as conducted by the WIC program, for example) on the behavior of adults as well as children.

Fourth, it would be useful for researchers and policymakers to think about FANPs in a more integrated manner. At present, it is difficult to compare the effectiveness of these programs, since each is evaluated in terms of a separate and largely non-overlapping set of outcomes. It would be useful, for example, to have more studies of the effects of the FSP and WIC on outcomes such as the cognitive attainments of young children and the food security of their households, and it would be useful to know more about the effects of the NSLP on household food expenditures. It would be of great interest to have a better sense of the way in which FANPs as a group contribute to the food security, nutritional outcomes, and general well-being of American households.

Finally, it is encouraging that more attention is being paid in recent studies to the ubiquitous issue of sample selection. It is particularly difficult to evaluate the impact of programs like FANPs that are implemented on a national basis and often show little change over time. Some researchers have shown considerable ingenuity identifying and exploiting the limited amount of variation in programs that exists across jurisdictions, and in using designs such as sibling comparisons to control for the background characteristics of families who choose to participate in these programs. Yet many questions remain about the effects of these programs. For programs and populations for whom coverage is not yet complete (such as WIC participation among children), and in cases where changes to programs are contemplated, well-designed social experiments could provide great insight into program effects.

References

Ahluwalia, I. B., V. K. Hogan, L. Grummerstrawn, W. R. Colville, and A. Peterson. 1992. The effect of WIC participation on small-for-gestational-age births. *American Journal of Public Health* 88 (9): 1374–77.

Akin, J. S., D. K. Guilkey, P. S. Hanes, and B. M. Popkin. 1983. Impact of the School Lunch Program on nutrient intakes of school children. *School Food Service Research Review* 7 (1): 13–18.

Akin, J. S., D. K. Guilkey, and B. M. Popkin. 1983. The School Lunch Program and nutrient intake: A switching regression analysis. *American Journal of Agricultural Economics* 65 (3): 477–85.

Alaimo, K., R. R. Briefel, E. A. Frongillo, Jr., and C. M. Olson. 1998. Food insufficiency exists in the United States: Results from the Third National Health and Nutrition Examination Survey (NHANES-III). *American Journal of Public Health* 88 (3): 419–26.

Allen, J. E., and K. E. Gadson. 1983. *Nutrient consumption patterns of low-income households.* Washington, D.C.: Economic Research Service, U.S. Department of Agriculture.

Bailey, L. B., M. S. O'Farrell-Ray, C. S. Mahan, and D. Dimperio. 1983. Vitamin B6, iron, and folacin status of pregnant women. *Nutrition Research* 3:783–93.

Balcazar, H., C. M. Trier, and J. A. Cobas. 1995. What predicts breastfeeding intention in Mexican-American and non-Hispanic white women? Evidence from a national survey. *Birth* 22:74–80.

Basiotis, D., S. Johnson, K. Morgan, and J. S. A. Chen. 1987. Food stamps, food costs, nutrient availability, and nutrient intake. *Journal of Policy Modeling* 9:383–404.

Basiotis, P., P. M. Brown, S. R. Johnson, and K. J. Morgan. 1983. Nutrient availability, food costs, and food stamps. *American Journal of Agricultural Economics* 65:685–93.

Basiotis, P., C. S. Kramer-LeBlanc, and E. T. Kennedy. 1998. Maintaining nutrition security and diet quality: The role of the Food Stamp Program and WIC. *Family Economics and Nutrition Review* 11 (1–2): 4–16.

Beebout, H., et al. 1985. *Evaluation of the Nutrition Assistance Program in Puerto Rico.* Vol. II, *Effects on food expenditures and diet quality.* Washington, D.C.: Mathematica Policy Research.

Besharov, D. J., and P. Germanis. 2001. *Rethinking WIC: An evaluation of the Women, Infants, and Children Program.* Washington, D.C.: AEI Press.

Bhattacharya, J., and J. Currie. 2000. Youths at nutritional risk: Malnourished or misnourished? In *Youths at risk,* ed. J. Gruber, 483–522. Chicago: University of Chicago Press.

Bhattacharya, J., J. Currie, and S. Haider. 2001. Food insecurity or poverty? Measuring need related dietary adequacy. University of California–Los Angeles, Department of Economics. Mimeograph, August.

Bhattacharya, J., T. DeLeire, S. Haider, and J. Currie. 2001. Heat or eat? Income shocks and the allocation of nutrition in American families. University of California–Los Angeles, Department of Economics. Mimeograph, July.

Bishop, J. A., J. P. Formby, and L. A. Zeager. 1992. Nutrition and nonparticipation in the United States Food Stamp Program. *Applied Economics* 24 (9): 945–49.

Bitler, M., J. Currie, and J. K. Scholz. 2002. WIC participation and eligibility. University of California–Los Angeles, Department of Economics. Mimeograph, May.

Blank, R., and P. Ruggles. 1996. When do women use AFDC and food stamps? The dynamics of eligibility vs. participation. *Journal of Human Resources* 31 (1): 57–89.

Brien, M. J., and C. A. Swann. 1999. Prenatal WIC participation and infant health: Selection and maternal fixed effects. University of Virginia, Department of Economics. Unpublished Manuscript.

Brown, H. L., K. Watkins, and H. K. Hiett. 1996. The impact of the Women, Infants, and Children Food Supplemental Program on birth outcome. *American Journal of Obstetrics and Gynecology* 174:1279–83.

Brown, M., S. R. Johnson, and R. L. Rizek. 1982. *Food stamps and expenditure patterns: A statistical analysis.* Report submitted to the Food and Nutrition Service, U.S. Department of Agriculture. University of Missouri–Columbia.

Buescher, P. A., L. C. Larson, M. D. Nelson, and A. J. Lenihan. 1993. Prenatal WIC participation can reduce low birth weight and newborn medical costs: A cost-benefit analysis of WIC participation in North Carolina. *Journal of American Dietetic Association* 93 (2): 163–66.

Burghardt, J., A. Gordon, N. Chapman, P. Gleason, and T. Fraker. 1993. *The School Nutrition Dietary Assessment Study: School food service, meals offered, and dietary intake.* Alexandria, Va.: U.S. Dept. of Agriculture, Food and Nutrition Service.

Burghardt, J., A. Gordon, and B. Devaney. 1995. Background of the School Nutrition Dietary Assessment Study. *American Journal of Clinical Nutrition* 61 (1 Supp.): 178S–81S.

Burstein, N., M. K. Fox, J. B. Hiller, R. Kornfeld, K. Lam, C. Price, and D. T. Rodda. 2000. *WIC general analysis project, profile of WIC children.* Cambridge, Mass.: Abt Associates.

Burstein, N., M. K. Fox, and M. J. Puma. 1991. *Study of the impact of WIC on the growth and development of children: Field test.* Vol. 2, *Preliminary impact estimates.* Cambridge, Mass.: Abt Associates.

Butler, J. S., J. C. Ohls, and B. Posner. 1985. The effect of the Food Stamp Program on the nutrient intake of the eligible elderly. *The Journal of Human Resources* 20 (3): 405–20.

Butler, J. S., and J. E. Raymond. 1996. The effect of the Food Stamp Program on nutrient intake. *Economic Inquiry* 34:781–98.

Castner, L., and J. Anderson. 1999. *Characteristics of food stamp households: Fiscal year 1998.* Advance Report. Washington, D.C.: USDA Food and Nutrition Service, July.

Centers for Disease Control. 1996. Nutritional status of children participating in the special: Supplemental Nutrition Program for Women, Infants, and Children: United States, 1988–1991. *Morbidity and Mortality Weekly* 45 (3): 65–69.

Chatterji, P., K. Bonuck, S. Dhawan, and N. Deb. 2002. WIC participation and the initiation and duration of breast-feeding. Working Paper no. 1246–02. Madison, Wis.: Institute for Research on Poverty, February.

Chavas, J.-P., and M. L. Yeung. 1982. Effects of the Food Stamp Program on food consumption in the southern United States. *South Journal of Agricultural Economics* 14 (1): 131–39.

Chen, J.-S. 1983. *Simultaneous equations models with qualitative dependent variables: A Food Stamp Program participation and food cost analysis.* Ph.D. diss., University of Missouri.

Ciemnecki, A., L. Hulsey, J. Ohls, I. Piliavin, M. Sullivan, and J. Rossol. 1998. *Final report for the Food Stamp Participant Trafficking Study.* Report no. 8171–091. Washington, D.C.: Mathematica Policy Research, March.

Citro, C., and R. Michael. 1995. *Measuring poverty: A new approach.* Washington, D.C.: National Research Council.

Cohen, B., J. Ohls, M. Andrews, M. Ponza, L. Moreno, A. Zambrowski, and R. Cohen. 1999. *Food stamp participants' food security and nutrient availability, final report.* Contract no. 53-3198-4-025. Washington, D.C.: Food and Nutrition Service, U.S. Dept. of Agriculture, July.

Cohen, B. E., and N. Young. 1994. Impacts of the Washington State Food Stamp Cashout Demonstration on household expenditures and food use. In *New directions in food stamp policy research,* ed. N. Fasciano, D. Hall, and H. Beebout. Washington, D.C.: U.S. Department of Agriculture.

Contento, I. R., A. D. Manning, and B. Shannon. 1992. Research perspectives on school-based nutrition education. *Journal of Nutrition Education* 24 (5): 247–60.

Cook, J. T., L. P. Sherman, and J. L. Brown. 1995. *Impact of food stamps on the dietary adequacy of poor children.* Medford, Mass.: Center on Hunger Poverty and Nutrition Policy, Tufts School of Nutrition.

Covington, M. T. 1995. Protective factors in the content of prenatal care services that promote normal birth weight deliveries among African-American women. Ph.D. diss., University of North Carolina–Chapel Hill.

Currie, J. 1991. *Welfare and the well-being of children.* Chur, Switzerland: Harwood Academic Publishers.

Currie, J., and N. Cole. 1993. Welfare and child health: The link between AFDC participation and birth weight. *American Economic Review* 8 (4): 971–85.

Currie, J., and J. Grogger. 2001. Explaining recent declines in Food Stamp Program participation. In *Brookings Wharton Papers on Urban Affairs,* ed. W. Gale and J. Rothenberg-Pack, 313–35. Washington, D.C.: Brookings Institution.

Daponte, B. O., S. Sanders, and L. Taylor. 1999. Why do low-income households not use food stamps? Evidence from an experiment. *Journal of Human Resources* 34 (3): 612–28.

Davis, E. E., and A. Werner. 1993. *Effects of food stamp cash-out on participants and food retailers in the Alabama ASSETS demonstration.* Cambridge, Mass.: Abt Associates.

Devaney, B. 1992. *Very low birthweight among Medicaid newborns in five states: The effects of prenatal WIC participation.* Alexandria, Va.: Food and Nutrition Service, U.S. Department of Agriculture.

Devaney, B., L. Bilheimer, and J. Schore. 1990. *The savings in Medicaid costs for newborns and their mothers from prenatal WIC participation in the WIC program.* Executive summary and vol. 1. Alexandria, Va.: Food and Nutrition Service, U.S. Department of Agriculture.

———. 1991. *The savings in Medicaid costs for newborns and their mothers from prenatal WIC participation in the WIC program.* Vol. 2. Alexandria, Va.: Food and Nutrition Service, U.S. Department of Agriculture.

Devaney, B., and T. Fraker. 1986. Cashing out food stamps: Impacts on food expenditures and diet quality. *Journal of Policy Analysis and Management* 5:725–41.

———. 1989. The effect of food stamps on food expenditures: An assessment of findings from the Nationwide Food Consumption Survey. *American Journal of Agricultural Economics* 71 (1): 99–104.

Devaney, B., A. R. Gordon, and J. A. Burghardt. 1993. *The School Nutrition Dietary Assessment Study: Dietary intakes of program participants and nonparticipants.* Alexandria, Va.: Food and Nutrition Service, U.S. Dept. of Agriculture.

Devaney, B., and R. Moffitt. 1991. Dietary effects of the Food Stamp Program. *American Journal of Agricultural Economics* 73 (1): 202–11.

Devaney, B., and A. Schirm. 1993. *Infant mortality among Medicaid newborns in five states: The effects of prenatal WIC participation.* Alexandria, Va.: Food and Nutrition Service, U.S. Department of Agriculture.

Devaney, B., and E. Stuart. 1998. Eating breakfast: Effects of the School Breakfast Program. *Family Economics and Nutrition Review* 60–62.

Dion, M. R., and L. Pavetti. 2000. *Access and participation in Medicaid and the Food Stamp Program: A review of the recent literature.* Washington, D.C.: Mathematica Policy Research.

Endres, J., M. Sawicki, and J. A. Casper. 1981. Dietary assessment of pregnant women in a supplemental food program. *Journal of American Dietetic Association* 79:121–26.

Fraker, T. M. 1990. *Effects of food stamps on food consumption: A review of the literature.* Washington, D.C.: Mathematica Policy Research.

Fraker, T. M., S. K. Long, and C. E. Post. *Analyses of the 1985 Continuing Survey of Food Intakes by Individuals.* Vol. 1, *Estimating usual dietary intake, assessing dietary adequacy, and estimating program effects: Applications of three advanced methodologies using FNS's four-day analysis file.* Washington, D.C.: Mathematica Policy Research.

Fraker, T. M., A. P. Martini, J. C. Ohls, M. Ponza, and E. Quinn. 1992. *Evaluation of the Alabama Food Stamp Cash-out Demonstration.* Vol. 1, *Recipient impacts.* Washington, D.C.: Mathematica Policy Research.

Frisbie, W. P., M. Biegler, P. deTurk, D. Forbes, and S. Pullum. 1997. Racial and ethnic differences in determinants of intrauterine growth retardation and other compromised birth outcomes. *American Journal of Public Health* 87 (12): 1977–83.

Gabor, V., and C. Botsko. 1998. *State food stamp policy choices under welfare reform: Findings of the 1997 50 state survey.* Contract no. 53-3198-6-020. Washington, D.C.: Food and Nutrition Service, U.S. Dept. of Agriculture, May.

Glantz, F. B., R. Berg, D. Porcari, et al. 1994. *School lunch eligible nonparticipants.* Cambridge, Mass.: Abt Associates.

Gleason, P. M. 1995. Participation in the National School Lunch Program and the School Breakfast Program. *American Journal of Clinical Nutrition* 61 (1S): 213S–20S.

Glenny, A. M., S. O'Meara, A. Melville, T. A. Sheldon, and C. Wilson. 1997. The treatment and prevention of obesity: A systematic review of the literature. *International Journal of Obesity and Related Metabolic Disorders* 21 (9): 715–37.

Gordon, A. R., B. L. Devaney, and J. A. Burghardt. 1995. Dietary effects of the National School Lunch Program and the School Breakfast Program. *American Journal of Clinical Nutrition* 61 (1S): 221S–31S.

Gordon, A., and L. Nelson. 1995. *Characteristics and outcomes of WIC participants and nonparticipants: Analysis of the 1988 National Maternal and Infant Health Survey.* Alexandria, Va.: Food and Nutrition Service, U.S. Dept. of Agriculture.

Gregorio, D. I., and J. R. Marshall. 1984. Fine tuning well-being: Food stamp use and the adequacy of children's diets. *Social Science Quarterly* 65:1137–46.

Gretzen, D., and J. A. Vermeersch. 1980. Health status and school achievement of children from Head Start and free school lunch programs. *Public Health Reports* 95 (4): 362–68.

Hagstrom, Paul. 1996. The food stamp participation and labor supply of married couples: An empirical analysis of joint decisions. *Journal of Human Resources* 31 (2): 383–403.

Haider, S., R. Schoeni, and A. Jacknowitz. 2002. Food stamps and the elderly: Why is participation so low? Santa Monica, Calif.: RAND. Mimeograph, April.

Hama, M. Y., and W. S. Chern. 1988. Food expenditure and nutrient availability in elderly households. *Journal of Consumer Affairs* 22 (1): 3–19.

Hamilton, W. L., J. T. Cook, and W. W. Thomsen. 1997. *Household food security in the United States in 1995: Summary report of the food security measurement project.* Cambridge, Mass.: Abt Associates.

Hamilton, W. L., M. K. Fox, et al. 2000. *Nutrition and Health Outcomes Study: Review of the literature.* 2d draft. Cambridge, Mass.: Abt Associates.

Harrell, J. S., S. A. Gansky, R. G. McMurray, S. I. Bangdiwala, A. C. Frauman, and C. B. Bradley. 1998. School-based interventions improve heart health in children with multiple cardiovascular disease risk factors. *Pediatrics* 102 (2): 371–80.

Heimendinger, J., N. Laird, J. Austin, P. Timmer, and S. Gershoff. 1984. The effects of the WIC program on the growth of infants. *American Journal of Clinical Nutrition* 40:1250–57.

Hicks, L. E., and R. A. Langham. 1985. Cognitive measure stability in siblings following early nutritional supplementation. *Public Health Reports* 100 (6): 656–62.

Hicks, L. E., R. A. Langham, and J. Takenaka. 1982. Cognitive and health measures following early nutritional supplementation: A sibling study. *American Journal of Public Health* 72 (10): 1110–18.

Hoagland, G. W. 1980. *Feeding children: Federal child nutrition policies in the 1980s.* Washington, D.C.: U.S. Government Printing Office.

Howe, S. M., and A. G. Vaden. 1980. Factors differentiating participants and nonparticipants of the National School Lunch Program. Part 1: Nutrient intake of high school students. *Journal of American Dietetic Association* 76 (5): 451–58.

Institute of Medicine. 2002. Framework for dietary risk assessment in the WIC program. Washington, D.C.: National Academy Press.

Ippolito, P., and A. Mathios. 1990. Information, advertising, and health: A study of the cereal market. *RAND Journal of Economics* 21 (3): 459–80.

———. 1993. New food labeling regulations and the flow of nutrition information to consumers. *Journal of Public Policy and Marketing* 12:188–205.

———. 1995. Information and advertising: The case of fat consumption in the United States. *American Economic Review* 85 (2): 91–95.

———. 1996. Information and advertising policy: A study of fat and cholesterol consumption in the United States, 1977–1990. Bureau of Economics Staff Report. Washington, D.C.: Federal Trade Commission.

James, J. M. 1998. *Immunization and its implication on WIC and non-WIC participants.* Master's thesis, New York Medical College.

Johnson, S. R., J. A. Burt, and K. J. Morgan. 1981. The Food Stamp Program: Participation, food cost, and diet of low-income households. *Food Technology* 35 (10): 58.

Joyce, T., H. Corman, and M. Grossman. 1988. A cost-effectiveness analysis of strategies to reduce infant mortality. *Medical Care* 26 (4): 348–60.

Kabbani, N., and P. Wilde. 2002. Short recertification periods in the U.S. Food Stamp Program: Causes and consequences. Washington, D.C.: USDA Economic Research Service.

Kenkel, D. 2000. Prevention. In *The handbook of health economics,* ed. A. Culyer and J. Newhouse, 1675–714. Amsterdam: North Holland.

Kennedy, E. T., and S. Gershoff. 1982. Effect of WIC supplemental feeding on hemoglobin and hematocrit of prenatal patients. *Journal of American Dietetic Association* 80:227–30.

Kennedy, E. T., S. Gershoff, R. Reed, and J. E. Austin. 1982. Evaluation of the effect of WIC supplemental feeding on birth weight. *Journal of American Dietetic Association* 80 (3): 220–27.

Kennedy, E. T., and M. Kotelchuck. 1984. The effect of WIC supplemental feeding on birth weight: A case-control analysis. *American Journal of Clinical Nutrition* 40:579–85.

Kirlin, J., and W. Adam. 1998. *Food stamp EBT systems and program-eligible vs. non-eligible food items.* Contract no. 53-3198-6-029. Washington, D.C.: Food and Nutrition Service, U.S. Department of Agriculture, August.

Kisker, E. E., and B. Devaney. 1988. *Food choices of low-income households: Final report.* Washington, D.C.: Mathematica Policy Research.

Korenman, S., and J. Miller. 1992. *Food Stamp Program participation and maternal and child health.* Washington, D.C.: Food and Nutrition Service, U.S. Department of Agriculture, May.

Kotelchuck, M., J. B. Schwartz, M. T. Anderka, and K. Finison. 1984. WIC participation and pregnancy outcomes: Massachusetts Statewide Evaluation Project. *American Journal of Public Health* 74 (10): 1086–92.

Kowaleski-Jones, L., and G. Duncan. 2000. Effects of participation in the WIC food assistance program on children's health and development. Working Paper no. 1207-00. Madison, Wis.: Institute for Research on Poverty.

Kramer-Leblanc, C., P. Basiotis, and E. Kennedy. 1997. Maintaining food and nutrition security in the United States with welfare reform. *American Journal of Agricultural Economics* 79 (5): 1600–07.

Kuhn, B., P. Dunn, D. Smallwood, K. Hanson, J. Blaylock, and S. Vogel. 1996. Policy watch: The Food Stamp Program and welfare reform. *Journal of Economic Perspectives* 10 (2): 189–98.

Levedahl, J. W. 1991. *Effect of food stamps and income on household food expenditures.* Technical bulletin. Washington, D.C.: Economic Research Service, U.S. Department of Agriculture.

———. 1995. A theoretical and empirical evaluation of the functional forms used to estimate the food expenditure equation of food stamp recipients. *American Journal of Agricultural Economics* 77:960–68.

Long, S. K. 1991. Do the school nutrition programs supplement household food expenditures? *Journal of Human Resources* 26 (4): 654–78.

Lopez, L. M. 1984. *Food stamps and the nutritional status of the U.S. elderly poor.* Ph.D. diss., Cornell University.

Lopez, L. M., and J. P. Habicht. 1987. Food stamps and the iron status of the U.S. elderly poor. *Journal of American Dietetic Association* 87 (5): 598–603.

Loprest, P. 1999. *Families who left welfare: Who are they and how are they doing?* Washington, D.C.: Urban Institute Press.

Luder, E., E. Ceysens-Okada, A. Korenroth, and C. Martinezweber. 1990. Health and nutrition surveys in a group of urban homeless adults. *Journal of the American Dietetic Association* 90:1387–92.

Luepker, R. V., C. L. Perry, S. M. McKinlay, P. R. Nader, G. S. Parcel, E. J. Stone, L. S. Webber, J. P. Elder, H. A. Feldman, C. C. Johnson, S. H. Kelder, and M. Wu. 1996. Outcomes of a field trial to improve children's dietary patterns and physical activity: The Child and Adolescent Trial for Cardiovascular Health (CATCH). *Journal of the American Medical Association* 275 (10): 768–76.

Macaluso, T. 1995. *The extent of trafficking in the Food Stamp Program.* Washington, D.C.: USDA Food and Consumer Service.

Mays-Scott, C. L. 1991. *Adolescent pregnancy and infant outcome: The influence of physiological and socioeconomic determinants on pregnancy outcome.* Ph.D. diss., Texas Women's University.

McConnell, S., and J. Ohls. 2000. Food stamps in rural America: Special issues and common themes. Washington, D.C.: Mathematica Policy Research, May.

McCracken, C. A. 1995. *The effects of a Food Stamp Program cashout on household food allocation and nutrient consumption: The case of Washington.* Ph.D. diss., Washington State University.

Melnik, T. A., S. J. Rhoades, K. R. Wales, C. Cowell, et al. 1998. Food consumption patterns of elementary school children in New York City. *Journal of American Dietetic Association* 98 (2): 159–64.

Metcoff, J., P. Costiloe, W. M. Crosby, L. Bentle, S. Dutta, F. Weaver, G. Burna, H. H. Sandstead, and C. E. Bodwell. 1985. Effect of food supplementation (WIC) during pregnancy on birth weight. *American Journal of Clinical Nutrition* 41:933–47.

Moffitt, R. A. 1983. An economic model of welfare stigma. *American Economic Review* 73 (5): 1023–35.

———. 1989. Estimating the value of an in-kind transfer: The case of food stamps. *Econometrica* 57 (2): 385–410.

———. 1992. Incentive effects of the U.S. welfare system: A review. *Journal of Economic Literature* 30 (1): 1–61.

———. 1998. *Welfare, the family, and reproductive behavior: Research perspectives.* Washington, D.C.: National Academy Press.

———. 1999. Voucher programs for transfer payments: Lessons from the food stamp program. Johns Hopkins University, Department of Economics. Manuscript, April.

Moffitt, R. A., and T. Fraker. 1988. The effect of food stamps on labor supply: A bivariate selection model. *Journal of Public Economics* 35 (1): 25–56.

Moffitt, R. A., and M. Keane. 1998. A structural model of multiple welfare program participation and labor supply. *International Economic Review* 39 (3): 553–89.

Moffitt, R. A., R. Reville, and A. Winkler. 1998. Beyond single mothers: Cohabitation and marriage in the AFDC program. *Demography* 35 (3): 259–78.

Moss, N. E., and K. Carver. 1998. The effect of WIC and Medicaid on infant mortality in the United States. *American Journal of Public Health* 88 (9): 1354–61.

Murphy, J. M., C. Wehler, M. Pagano, M. Little, et al. 1998. Relationship between hunger and psychosocial functioning in low-income American children. *Journal of the American Academy of Child and Adolescent Psychiatry* 37 (2): 163–70.

Myers, A., A. E. Sampson, M. Weitzman, B. L. Rogers, and H. Kayne. 1989. School Breakfast Program and school performance. *American Journal of Diseases of Children* 143:1234–39.

National Research Council. 2001. Estimating eligibility and participation for the WIC program. Washington, D.C.: National Academy Press.

New York State Department of Health. 1990. *The New York State WIC evaluation: The association between prenatal WIC participation and birth outcomes.* Albany, N.Y.: New York State Department of Health, Bureau of Nutrition.

Nord, M., K. Jemison, and G. Bickel. 1999. *Prevalence of food insecurity and hunger by state, 1996–1998.* Washington, D.C.: Food and Rural Economics Division, U.S. Department of Agriculture.

Ohls, J. C., and H. Beebout. 1993. The food stamp problem: Design tradeoffs, policy, and impacts. Washington, D.C.: Urban Institute Press.

Ohls, J. C., T. M. Fraker, A. P. Martini, et al. 1992. *Effects of cash-out on food use by Food Stamp Program participants in San Diego.* Princeton, N.J.: Mathematica Policy Research.

Oliveira, V., and C. Gunderson. 2000. *WIC and the nutrient intake of children.* Washington, D.C.: U.S. Department of Agriculture, Economic Research Service.

Perry, L. H., E. C. Shannon, K. Stitt, et al. 1984. Student lunch practices: A comparison of cost and dietary adequacy of school lunch and brown bag lunches. *School Food Service Research Review* 8 (2): 114–18.

Pollitt, E., and R. Lorimor. 1983. Effects of WIC on cognitive development. *American Journal of Public Health* 73 (6): 698–700.

Ponza, M., J. Ohls, L. Moreno, A. Zambrowski, and R. Cohen. 1999. *Customer service in the Food Stamp Program.* Contract no. 53-3198-40-025. Washington, D.C.: Food and Nutrition Service, U.S. Department of Agriculture, July.

Posner, B. M., J. C. Ohls, and J. C. Morgan. 1987. Impact of food stamps and other variables on nutrient intake in the elderly. *Journal of Nutrition for the Elderly* 6 (3): 3–16.

Price, D. W. 1983. *Effects of socioeconomic variables and food stamp participation on the consumption of selected food groups.* Research Bulletin no. XB 0932. Agricultural Research Center, Washington State University.

Randall, B., L. Boast, and L. Holst. 1995. *Study of WIC participant and program characteristics, 1994.* Food and Nutrition Service Report no. 53-3198-9-002. Washington, D.C.: Office of Analyses and Evaluation, Food and Consumer Service, December.

Ranney, C. K., and J. E. Kushman. 1987. Cash equivalence, welfare stigma, and food stamps. *South Economic Journal* 53 (4): 1011–27.

Rose, D. C., C. Gunderson, and V. Oliveira. 1998. *Determinants of food insecurity in the United States: Evidence from the SIPP and CSFII datasets.* Technical Bulletin no. 1869. U.S. Department of Agriculture.

Rose, D. C., J. P. Habicht, and B. Devaney. 1998. Household participation in the Food Stamp and WIC programs increases the nutrient intakes of preschool children. *Journal of Nutrition* 128:548–55.

Rose, D. C., D. Smallwood, and J. Blaylock. 1995. Socio-economic factors associated with the iron intake of preschoolers in the United States. *Nutrition Research* 15 (9): 1297–309.

Rossi, P. 1998. *Feeding the poor: Assessing federal food aid.* Washington, D.C.: AEI Press.

Rush, D., J. M. Alvir, D. A. Kenny, S. S. Johnson, and D. G. Horvitz. 1988a. The National WIC Evaluation: Evaluation of the Special Supplemental Food Program for Women, Infants, and Children, III: Historical study of pregnancy outcomes. *American Journal of Clinical Nutrition* 48:412–28.

———. 1988b. The National WIC Evaluation: Evaluation of the Special Supplemental Food Program for Women, Infants, and Children, IV: Study of infants and children. *American Journal of Clinical Nutrition* 48:429–38.

Rush, D., J. Leighton, N. L. Sloan, J. M. Alvir, D. G. Horvitz, W. B. Seaver, G. C. Garbowski, S. S. Johnson, and R. A. Kulka. 1988. The National WIC Evaluation: Evaluation of the Special Supplemental Food Program for Women, Infants, and Children, VI: Study of infants and children. *American Journal of Clinical Nutrition* 48:484–511.

Rush, D., N. L. Sloan, J. Leighton, J. M. Alvir, D. G. Horvitz, W. B. Seaver, G. C. Garbowski, S. S. Johnson, and R. A. Kulka. 1988. The National WIC Evaluation: Evaluation of the Special Supplemental Food Program for Women, Infants, and Children, V: Longitudinal study of pregnant women. *American Journal of Clinical Nutrition* 48:439–83.

Ryan, A. S., D. R. Rush, F. W. Krieger, and G. E. Lewandowski. 1991. Recent declines in breast-feeding in the United States: 1984 through 1989. *Pediatrics* 88 (4): 719–27.

Salathe, L. E. 1980. The Food Stamp Program and low-income households' food purchases. *Agricultural Economic Research* 32 (4): 33–41.

Schirm, A. 1998. *Reaching those in need: How effective is the food stamp Program?* Washington, D.C.: Food and Nutrition Service, U.S. Department of Agriculture, August.

Schramm, W. F. 1985. WIC prenatal participation and its relationship to newborn Medicaid costs in Missouri: A cost/benefit analysis. *American Journal of Public Health* 75 (8): 851–57.

———. 1986. Prenatal participation in WIC related to Medicaid costs for Missouri newborns: 1982 update. *Public Health Reports* 101 (6): 607–15.

Schwartz, J. B., D. K. Guilkey, J. S. Akin, and B. M. Popkin. 1992. *WIC breast-feeding report: The relationship of WIC program participation to the initiation and duration of breastfeeding.* Alexandria, Va.: Food and Nutrition Service, U.S. Department of Agriculture.

Senauer, B., and N. Young. 1986. The impact of food stamps on food expenditures: Rejection of the traditional model. *American Journal of Agricultural Economics* 68 (1): 37–43.

Sherry, B., D. Bister, and R. Yip. 1997. Continuation of decline in prevalence of anemia in low-income children: The Vermont experience. *Archives of Pediatrics and Adolescent Medicine* 151:928–30.

Silverman, P. R. 1982. *The effect of a local prenatal nutrition supplementation program (WIC) on the birth weight of high risk infants.* Ph.D. diss., University of Pittsburgh.

Simpson, K. N. 1988. *Analyzing the influences of selected public prevention programs on low birthweight in North Carolina counties.* Ph.D. diss., University of North Carolina–Chapel Hill.

Smallwood, D. M., and J. R. Blaylock. 1985. Analysis of Food Stamp Program participation and food expenditures. *West Journal of Agricultural Economics* 10 (1): 41–54.

Smith, A. L., G. Branch, S. E. Henry, et al. 1986. Effectiveness of a nutrition program for mothers and their anemic children under 5 years of age. *Journal of American Dietetic Association* 86 (8): 1039–42.

Stockbauer, J. W. 1986. Evaluation of the Missouri WIC program: Prenatal components. *Journal of American Dietetic Association* 86 (1): 61–67.

———. 1987. WIC prenatal participation and its relation to pregnancy outcomes in Missouri: A second look. *American Journal of Public Health* 77 (7): 813–18.

Tuttle, C. R., and K. G. Dewey. 1994. Determinants of infant feeding choices among Southeast Asian immigrants in Northern California. *Journal of American Dietetic Association* 94 (3): 282–86.

U.S. Committee on Ways and Means. 1998. *Green book 1998.* Washington, D.C.: U.S. Government Printing Office.

———. 1999. *Green book 1999.* Washington, D.C.: U.S. Government Printing Office.

———. 2000. *Green book 2000.* Washington, D.C.: U.S. Government Printing Office.

———. Various years. *Green book.* Washington, D.C.: U.S. Government Printing Office.

U.S. Congress. 1996. *Consolidated federal regulations.* 1 January 1996 ed. Washington, D.C.: U.S. Government Printing Office.

———. 2000. *Consolidated federal regulations.* 1 January 2000 ed. Washington, D.C.: U.S. Government Printing Office.

U.S. Department of Agriculture (USDA). 1994. The impacts of the off-line electronic benefits transfer demonstration. Washington, D.C.: Food and Nutrition Service, U.S. Department of Agriculture, April.

U.S. Department of Health and Human Services (DHHS). 1991. *Healthy people 2000: National health promotion and disease prevention objectives.* Report no. 91-50213. Washington, D.C.: DHHS.

U.S. Department of Health and Human Services (DHHS) and U.S. Department of Agriculture (USDA). 1995. *Dietary guidelines for Americans.* 4th ed. Washington, D.C.: U.S. Government Printing Office.

U.S. General Accounting Office (GAO). 1992. *Federal investments like WIC can produce savings.* Report no. GAO/HRD9218. Washington, D.C.: U.S. Government Printing Office.

———. 1993. Breastfeeding: WIC's efforts to promote breastfeeding have increased. Report no. 94-13. Washington, D.C.: U.S. Government Printing Office.

U.S. General Accounting Office. 1997. *Food Assistance: A Variety of Practices May Lower the Costs of WIC* (Washington D.C.: U.S. Government Printing Office) GAO/RCED-97-225, Sept. 17, 1197.

———. 1999a. *Food assistance: Efforts to control fraud and abuse in the WIC program can be strengthened.* Report no. GAO/RCED-99-224. Washington, D.C.: U.S. Government Printing Office, August.

———. 1999b. *Food Stamp Program: Households Collect Benefits for Persons Disqualified for Intentional Program Violations.* Report no. GAO/RCED-99-180. Washington, D.C.: U.S. Government Printing Office, July.

———. 1999c. *Food Stamp Program: Storeowners seldom pay financial penalties owed for program violations.* Report no. GAO/RCED-99-91. Washington, D.C.: U.S. Government Printing Office, May.

———. 1999d. *Food Stamp Program: Various factors have led to declining participation.* Report no. GAO/RECD-99-185. Washington, D.C.: U.S. Government Printing Office, July.

———. 2000. *Food Stamp Program: Better use of electronic data could result in disqualifying more recipients who traffic benefits.* Report no. GAO/RCED-00-61. Washington, D.C.: U.S. Government Printing Office, March.

Vasquez-Seoane, P., R. Windom, and H. A. Pearson. 1985. Disappearance of iron-deficiency anemia in a high-risk infant population given supplemental iron. *New England Journal of Medicine* 313 (19): 1239–40.

Weimer, J. P. 1998. *Factors affecting nutrient intake of the elderly.* Agricultural Economic Report no. 769. Washington, D.C.: U.S. Department of Agriculture, Food and Rural Economics Division, Economic Research Service.

Welch, F. 1999. In defense of inequality. *American Economic Review* 89:1–17.

Wellisch, J. B., S. D. Hanes, L. A. Jordan, K. M. Mauer, and J. A. Vermeech. 1983. *The National Evaluation of School Nutrition Programs.* Vols. 1 and 2. Santa Monica, Calif.: Systems Development Corp.

West, D. A. 1984. *Effects of the Food Stamp Program on food expenditures.* Research Bulletin no. XB 0922. Washington State University, Agricultural Research Center.

Whitfield, R. A. 1982. A nutritional analysis of the Food Stamp Program. *American Journal of Public Health* 72 (8): 793.

Whitmore, D. 2002. What are food stamps worth? Princeton University Industrial Relations Section. Mimeograph, January.

Wilde, P., C. Gunderson, M. Nord, and L. Tiehen. 2000. The decline in food stamp participation in the 1990s. Washington, D.C.: USDA Food and Nutrition Research Program, June.

Wolfe, W. S., C. C. Campbell, E. A. Frongillo, J. D. Haas, and T. A. Melnik. 1994. Overweight school children in New York State: Prevalence and characteristics. *American Journal of Public Health* 84 (5): 807–13.

Yelowitz, A. 2000. Did recent Medicaid reforms cause the caseload explosion in the Food Stamps Program? University of California–Los Angeles, Department of Economics. Unpublished manuscript.

Yip, R., N. Binkin, L. Fleshood, and F. L. Trowbridge. 1987. Declining prevalence of anemia among low-income children in the United States. *Pediatrics* 258 (12): 1619–23.

Zedlewski, S., and S. Brauner. 1999. Declines in food stamp and welfare participation: Is there a connection? Washington, D.C.: The Urban Institute.

5

The Temporary Assistance for Needy Families Program

Robert A. Moffitt

The Temporary Assistance for Needy Families (TANF) program was created by legislation passed by the U.S. Congress and signed by the president in 1996. The Personal Responsibility and Work Reconciliation Act (PRWORA) created the TANF program out of the preexisting Aid to Families with Dependent Children (AFDC) program, which itself was created by Congress in 1935 as part of the Social Security Act. The PRWORA legislation represented the most fundamental restructuring of the AFDC program since its inception. The most important restructured elements are (a) the devolution of major program design elements, and financing through block grants, to the individual states; (b) the imposition of strict work requirements in order to qualify for federal aid; and (c) lifetime limits on the number of years of benefit receipt which could be paid out of federal funds.

This paper reviews the rules and structure of the TANF program and compares them with the historical AFDC program. In addition, it reviews the caseloads, costs, and participation rates of the TANF and AFDC programs. Finally, it reviews the research that has been conducted on both programs. Given the relative youth of the former, relatively little scholarly research has been conducted on it to date. Consequently, the bulk of the research will be reviewed for the AFDC program. Some discussion will also be provided of the extent to which the results of the AFDC research can be expected to apply to the TANF program.

Robert A. Moffitt is professor of economics at Johns Hopkins University and a research associate of the National Bureau of Economic Research.

The author would like to thank Daniel Gubits for research assistance.

Table 5.1   Major Legislation in the AFDC and TANF Programs

Date	Title of Legislation	Main Provision
1935	Social Security Act	Created the AFDC program for low-income children without a parent present in household
1961	Amendments to the Social Security Act	Created AFDC-UP program for children in two-parent families where primary earner is unemployed
1967	Amendments to the Social Security Act	Lowered the benefit reduction rate to two-thirds; created the WIN program
1981	Omnibus Budget Reconciliation Act of 1981	Increased the benefit reduction rate to 1; imposed a gross income limit; counted income of stepparents; expanded waiver authority
1988	Family Support Act of 1988	Created the JOBS program for education, skills training, job search assistance, and other work activities; created transitional child care and Medicaid programs; mandated AFDC-UP in all states
1996	Personal Responsibility and Work Reconciliation Act	Abolished the AFDC program and created the TANF program

The first section reviews the rules and history of the programs. The second section reviews the trends in caseloads and expenditures and other program characteristics, followed by a section on the research results. Section 5.4 reviews research on the TANF program. A final section discusses reforms of the financial incentives in the program.

5.1   History, Rules, and Goals

5.1.1   History and Rules of the AFDC Program

Table 5.1 shows the major pieces of legislation creating and altering the AFDC program over its history, 1935–96.[1] The program was created by the Social Security Act of 1935 along with the Old-Age Social Security and Unemployment Insurance programs. The AFDC program provided cash financial support to families with "dependent" children, who are defined as those who were deprived of the support or care of one natural (i.e., biological) parent by reason of death, disability, or absence from the home, and were under the care of the other parent or another relative. Although the language of the legislation was gender-neutral, in practice the vast majority of families of this type consisted of a mother and her children, or what are today called single-mother families. Although the presence of the father was possible if he was the single parent or if he was disabled, the

1. A short, but more detailed, history of the major developments in the AFDC program can be found in Garfinkel and McLanahan (1986, chap. 4). That discussion also includes an account of the history of income support programs prior to AFDC.

overwhelming majority of participating families were initially, and have continued to be, those in which the father is not present. In 1935 the primary reason for the absence of the father was death, but this was to change in later years as that absence was more a result of divorce or out-of-wedlock childbearing. Eligibility also required that families have income and assets below specified levels.

The AFDC program was created as a shared federal and state responsibility. The states had a large role in the program, for they were responsible for not only creating and administering their own AFDC programs but also setting the level of basic benefits. States subsequently picked very different benefit levels, with benefits ranging sixfold from the most generous to the least generous. The federal role was both financial and regulatory. Financially, the federal government was responsible for providing open-ended matching grants to the states, with declining match rates at higher state benefit levels. On the regulatory side, the federal government put many restrictions on the definition of eligibility and allowable resources but also on the benefit formula. In terms of eligibility, for example, the federal government defined what family structures were eligible and put restrictions on who could and could not be counted as part of the assistance unit, and also on what income and assets could be counted for eligibility determination. Regarding the benefit formula, the federal government put restrictions on allowable deductions for earned income and also for child care and work-related expenses, effectively constraining the state's ability to set the benefit reduction rate in the program. Thus the states ended up being primarily responsible for the level of benefits, or what economists call the "guarantee," while the federal government effectively set the benefit reduction rate, which economists sometimes call simply the "tax rate." The nominal benefit reduction rate in the program in 1935 was 100 percent, for benefits were determined by a straightforward subtraction of income from "needs" (i.e., the guarantee), and there were few deductions for income allowed.[2]

The definition of a dependent child as resulting from the absence or disability of a parent implicitly allowed families to be eligible where the mother (or father) had remarried or was cohabiting with a partner who

---

2. Additional complexities were present because the states actually had the right to manipulate the benefit formula in ways that altered even the tax rate. For example, states could impose maximums on the benefit paid to a family, which creates a range of a zero tax rate; they could reduce the difference between the guarantee and net income (defined as income less deductions) by a defined fraction (called the "ratable reduction"), which effectively reduces the tax rate by that fraction; and they could impose gross income ceilings for eligibility, which create a notch in the budget constraint. They also had discretion in setting allowable deductions, which alters the effective tax rate as well. See U.S. Congress, Committee on Ways and Means (1996), Keane and Moffitt (1998, appendix), and Meyer and Rosenbaum (2001, appendix 1) for more details on the formula in different states. States are allowed even more discretion over the benefit formula under the new TANF program (see subsequent discussion).

was not a parent of the child. Further, stepparents and cohabitors were excluded from the definition of the assistance unit for purposes of eligibility and benefit determination, so their income was not automatically counted against benefits. In principle the income they provided to the eligible children should be counted as income to the assistance unit, but rigorously measuring intrahousehold income flows is difficult, so the enforcement of this principle was minimal. However, in 1935 the rate of remarriage was fairly low and the rate of cohabitation was even lower, so these issues did not attract discussion; they did so only later when these types of families grew in the general population and in the AFDC recipient population.

A significant expansion of the program took place in 1961 when Congress created the AFDC-UP (for "unemployed parent") program to include families in which both natural parents were present but where the primary earner was unemployed, with unemployment defined as the inability to find work in excess of 100 hours per month. The income and asset eligibility conditions and benefit formulas were identical to those in the basic AFDC program. The AFDC-UP program was made optional to the states, with financing at the same rate as in basic AFDC, and twenty-five states had created and operated such programs by the end of the decade.

The next major change in the program occurred in 1967 when Congress, concerned with work incentives in the program, lowered the nominal tax rate on earnings from 100 percent to 67 percent (by two-thirds, to be exact). States were required to deduct $30 and one-third of remaining monthly earnings from total monthly income before calculating the benefit (hence the "thirty-and-one-third" rule). The Social Security Amendments in 1967 also created a program called the Work Incentive (WIN) Program, which required women whose youngest child was older than six and who did not fall into a number of exempt categories (disabled, in school, etc.) to register for some type of work or education activity, usually some type of job placement program. The WIN program was never effective, for, while the majority of nonexempt recipients were registered, states did not provide the funds or exert the effort to set up the necessary activities to engage more than a small number of registrants. Although there were almost no evaluation studies of WIN conducted (see below), there was nevertheless a widespread perception that the job placement operations in place were also quite ineffective.[3]

A number of Supreme Court decisions in the late 1960s and early 1970s were also important in modifying key features of the program. One outlawed what were called state "man-in-the-house" rules, rules which made ineligible for benefits mothers who were living, even on a temporary basis, with men who were not the natural fathers of the children. The court

---

3. See Lalonde (chap. 8 in this volume) for a more detailed discussion of the WIN program and its evolution.

judged these laws to violate the original Social Security Act provision stipulating that eligibility was based solely on the absence of the natural father. A second, related decision prohibited states from counting the income of any such cohabiting men against the AFDC benefit without specific evidence that the men were providing income support to the woman and children; some states had been automatically including the male's income when calculating benefits. A third decision outlawed so-called residency requirements that some states had adopted, which required families who had moved into a state to live there for a few years before eligibility could be established. The court judged these laws to violate the equal protection clause of the Constitution and to impose an unlawful restriction on freedom of residential location.

The growth of the Food Stamp and Medicaid programs in the late 1960s and early 1970s also affected the AFDC program. Eligibility for the Food Stamp Program, although open to all individuals regardless of family type, was made automatic for AFDC recipients. Thus a close tie between the programs was established, and participation in the AFDC program constituted a guaranteed entry to the Food Stamp Program. Families in the AFDC program were also made categorically eligible for the Medicaid program, significantly raising the generosity of program benefits. Unlike the case of food stamps, however, non-AFDC recipients faced more difficult eligibility hurdles for Medicaid and were often ineligible until the 1980s (see the chapter on Medicaid in this volume). A third program of some importance that grew more in the 1980s is the Earned Income Tax Credit, whose amounts were required by Congress to be excluded from AFDC recipient income for the purpose of benefit calculation in order to encourage work.[4]

Throughout the 1970s a number of welfare reform proposals were considered by the federal executive branch but were either never proposed to Congress or were proposed and not passed. The Nixon administration proposed, with its Family Assistance Program, replacing AFDC with a program more resembling a negative income tax—with a low marginal tax rate—and which would have federalized the program and hence removed it from the control of the states, a reform much discussed in the 1970s in an attempt to eliminate the large cross-state variation in benefits. The legislation did not pass Congress. The Ford administration considered a welfare reform proposal with a number of features but, most notably, a considerable strengthening in the work requirements of the program. The program was never submitted to Congress. The Carter administration submitted to Congress a major welfare reform proposal which, like the Family Assis-

4. Food stamp benefits were also excluded from the AFDC benefit calculation, as were housing subsidies in most states. Supplemental Security Income benefits were excluded, but SSI recipients were not allowed to be covered by AFDC anyway (i.e., they were excluded from the AFDC assistance unit).

tance Program, would have federalized the program but which introduced, for the first time, significant added work requirements. The legislation was not passed by Congress.

The next major piece of legislation passed by Congress was the Omnibus Budget Reconciliation Act of 1981, which had several important features. The tax rate on earnings in the program was increased to 100 percent, up from the 67 percent provided for in the 1967 amendments, on the argument that this would concentrate benefits on the lowest income families and hence those most in need.[5] In addition, for the first time Congress required states to count a portion of stepparent income against the grant regardless of the amount of financial support that the stepparent might be determined, by some calculation, to have provided to the mother and her children. Congress also put an upper limit on the gross income that a family could have to be eligible, thus eliminating the possibility that high levels of deductions could allow such families onto the rolls. A fourth important feature of the legislation, little noticed at the time but which became important later, was a provision encouraging states to experiment with new AFDC work provisions that were at variance with federal law and federal regulations, and to seek waivers to test alternative provisions that they might be interested in. The "WIN demonstrations" of the 1980s, as they were called because they were modifications of WIN, allowed states to experiment with community work programs, work supplementation programs, heightened job search, and other programs to strengthen the emphasis on work and improve upon their WIN programs.

Subsequent to 1981 and throughout the early and mid-1980s, states began taking advantage of the waiver provisions in the 1981 Act and, eventually, virtually all states conducted WIN demonstrations. These demonstrations typically tested low-cost programs that required some type of job search activity, although some also required recipients to simply work— usually in some community service job like cleaning up a public park—in exchange for their benefits ("workfare"). A few states were more ambitious and tested more expansive employment programs that attempted to provide more basic skills training or substantive work experience. Many of the demonstrations also narrowed the list of conditions allowing a recipient to be exempt from participating in these programs. The 1980s thus witnessed the beginning of significant AFDC reform activity initiated at the state and local levels, a new trend in light of the history of reform activity, which had theretofore occurred primarily at the federal level.

The state activity on increased work requirements led to increased congressional interest in work and culminated in the passage of the 1988 Fam-

---

5. The recipient was allowed to work for four months with the thirty-and-one-third reduction rule, but further earnings were taxed at the 100 percent rate. Later, the flat $30 exemption amount was allowed for twelve months.

ily Support Act, whose most important feature was the creation of the Job Opportunities (JOBS) program. The JOBS program replaced WIN and was to require much larger numbers of welfare recipients to engage in work-related activities, both by reducing the number of exempt recipients and by mandating that states engage a minimum fraction of eligible recipients in some type of acceptable activity (called "participation" requirements). In addition, and equally important, the legislation strongly encouraged, and partly required, states to conduct not only low-cost job search programs that had been dominant in the WIN demonstrations but also some human capital, education, and training programs that would increase job skills of AFDC recipients, a major change in orientation.[6]

However, over the years subsequent to 1988, states failed to implement JOBS programs to any significant degree. They failed to draw down all the federal matching funds made available to them to subsidize the programs, and they did not put in place the necessary programs to enroll eligibles on a wide scale. As a result, many states never achieved the participation requirements in the act. The most common explanation for this failure was the onset of a recession in the late 1980s, which put pressure on state budgets and made it difficult to allocate funds to JOBS, but the administrative difficulty in creating JOBS programs was gradually realized to have been underestimated, and this also played a role. It was also gradually realized that full implementation of the JOBS program would require a significant increase of expenditures and hence was unlikely in the short run to generate cost savings.[7]

In an attempt to provide more financial work incentives, the Family Support Act also required states to offer transitional child care and Medicaid benefits, benefits provided to families who had left the welfare rolls because of employment or increased earnings, for up to twelve months following exit. States were allowed to require copayments for child care and were required to charge premiums for the second six months of Medicaid benefits. In practice, these provisions were little used by exiting welfare mothers, for reasons that have never been fully studied. Some experts speculated that the paperwork burden of continuing to establish eligibility combined with the relatively short time frame of extended benefits (twelve months), together with the copayment and premium provisions, discouraged take-up.

Finally, the Family Support Act expanded AFDC-UP, mandating that all states offer the program. However, the law only required states to offer benefits to unemployed families for six months out of the year, and many states initially without UP programs elected to meet only this minimum requirement when creating their program subsequent to the act.

6. See U.S. Congress, Committee on Ways and Means (1994) for a discussion of the JOBS program rules and see Gueron and Pauly (1991) for a discussion of the shift in employment philosophy that JOBS represented.

7. See the chapter by LaLonde in this volume for a more detailed discussion of JOBS.

Although the Family Support Act of 1988 was considered at the time to be landmark legislation that would lead to fundamental changes in the program, its failure to do so has left it as a fairly minor and transitional piece of legislation in the history of the AFDC program. Interest in further reforms of the system did not die down after the act but instead increased in intensity. For example, the goals of reform started shifting almost immediately from the human capital, education, and training emphasis embodied in the act to an emphasis on work per se, regardless of training content. Another notable shift subsequent to the act was a shift toward caseload reduction per se as a goal, which had not been a major focus of the act. In part this change may have been a result of the rising caseloads and expenditures in AFDC over the late 1980s and early 1990s (see below). Finally, an increased interest in family structure issues and nonmarital childbearing occurred in the period subsequent to the act.

This increased welfare reform activity took place, as it had in the 1980s, mainly at the state level. With encouragement from the Bush and Clinton administrations, states over the early 1990s increased their initiation of AFDC waiver programs testing alternative features of reform. An increased emphasis on work requirements, in particular to the exclusion of human capital and education programs as just noted, was present in almost all state efforts. Most states also began imposing sanctions (i.e., temporary or permanent withdrawal of benefits) on recipients for failure to comply with work and other requirements. Although such sanctions had been present in some form previously, they had never been as aggressively enforced. The increased emphasis on work requirements was often accompanied in the waiver programs as well by a reduction of marginal tax rates on earnings to provide financial incentives to work, for the federal rules still required 100 percent rates. Many other features also began to be introduced, including (a) the provision of time limits on benefits, stipulating that recipients could not receive benefits for more than a certain number of years (two to five, for example), at least within a given calendar period; (b) the imposition of family caps, which specified that AFDC recipients would not receive higher benefits if they had additional children while on AFDC; and (c) an attempt to reintroduce residency requirements by formulating two-tier programs under which immigrants were not denied benefits but rather were given lower benefits than initial residents for some specified period.

Another new feature of the state waiver programs in this period was an increased tendency to test programs that contained multiple reform features simultaneously, for example, simultaneously strengthening work requirements, enforcing sanctions, imposing time limits and family caps, and the like. Prior to this period, the waiver programs formulated by states had tested only one or two reform features at one time. These reform packages were intended to test new programs that differed in their entirety from the

AFDC program and were intended to have a cumulative impact greater than the sum of the impact of each reform individually. More generally, they represented a political desire for a major, wholesale change in the AFDC program rather than incremental change.[8]

A final new feature of the waiver programs over this period was an increased tendency to test the new programs on the entire state AFDC caseload, whereas prior to this period the waiver programs had been tested on the caseload in only one or two counties, cities, or local offices. These statewide waivers had the effect of essentially replacing the existing AFDC program with the reform program for the entire state, at least for the lifetime of the waiver, which was usually several years. As waivers of this type grew in number—forty states had requested and been granted waivers by 1995—the waivers gradually ceased to be small-scale experiments and began to envelope a major portion of the national caseload and hence to gradually eliminate the AFDC program de facto.[9]

5.1.2 TANF

Congress subsequently took action in 1996 by enacting PRWORA, which simultaneously reduced federal authority over the program but also mandated many (but not all) of the popular state-level waiver features with federal law. Table 5.2 summarizes the differences between AFDC and TANF. The PRWORA legislation converted the previous matching grant to a block grant and removed much of the federal regulatory authority over the design of the program. Thus states are free to set their benefit levels, as before, but also the tax rate, income limits, asset requirements, and even the form of assistance (cash or in-kind services). The last provision is important because it allows states to use TANF dollars to support child care, job search support, social services, and other types of expenditure; there are no requirements on how much or little must be spent on cash aid directly. In addition, no federal definition of who is to be included in the assistance unit is imposed; the AFDC-UP program is abolished, and states cover two-parent families at their own discretion. States are free to impose family caps. In addition, and importantly, the entitlement nature of the program is abolished and states are not required to serve all eligibles.

At the same time, however, the law imposed new federal authority in a

---

8. See U.S. Department of Health and Human Services (DHHS; 1997) and Harvey, Camasso, and Jagannathan (2000) for a summary of the provisions of the state waiver programs in this period.

9. The federal government generally required states to conduct random-assignment evaluations of their reforms. When states moved to implementing reform programs on the full state caseload, they usually complied with this requirement by holding out a small group of control families to be administered the old AFDC program. A major problem with these experiments was that it was difficult to prevent the control families from perceiving, and being affected by, the overall programmatic change in the state that occurred around them. See subsequent discussion.

Table 5.2   **Comparison of the AFDC and TANF Programs**

Item	AFDC	TANF
Financing	Matching grant	Block grant
Eligibility	Children deprived of support of one parent or children in low-income two-parent families (AFDC-UP)	Children in low-income families as designated by state; AFDC-UP abolished; minor mothers must live with parents; minor mothers must also attend school
Immigrants	Illegal aliens ineligible	Aliens ineligible for five years after entry and longer at state option
Form of aid	Almost exclusively cash payment	States free to use funds for services and non-cash benefits
Benefit levels	At state option	Same
Entitlement status	Federal government required to pay matched share of all recipients	No individual entitlement
Income limits	Family income cannot exceed gross income limits	No provision
Asset limits	Federal limits	No provision
Treatment of earnings disregards	After four months of work, only a lump sum $90 deduction plus child care expenses, and nothing after twelve months	No provision
Time limits	None	Federal funds cannot be used for payments to adults for more than sixty months lifetime (20 percent of caseload exempt)
JOBS program	States must offer a program that meets federal law	JOBS program abolished
Work requirements	Parents without a child under three required to participate in JOBS	Exemptions from work requirements are narrowed and types of qualified activities are narrowed and prespecified (generally excludes education and classroom training) and must be twenty hours per week rising to thirty hours per week for single mothers
Work requirement participation requirements	JOBS participation requirements	Participation for work requirements rise to 50 percent by fiscal year 2002
Child care	Guaranteed for all JOBS participants	No guarantee, but states are given increased child care funds
Sanctions	General provisions	Specific provisions mandating sanctions for failure to comply with work requirements, child support enforcement, schooling attendance, and other activities
Child support	States required to allow first $50 of child support received by mother to not reduce benefit	No provision

Source: Burke (1996).

few specified areas. Federal funds are not to be used to pay adults for more than sixty months of TANF benefits over their lifetimes, although states are allowed an exemption from this requirement for 20 percent of their caseloads. Minors who have dependent children are required to stay in school and live with their parents in order to receive federal TANF dollars. Aliens are ineligible for five years after their entry into the United States and longer at state option. In addition, while the JOBS program is abolished, new work requirements are imposed that require that much greater fractions of the caseload be involved in them, and which exempt many fewer families (as many as 50 percent of single mother recipients and 90 percent of two-parent families must comply). Recipients involved in general education and training cannot be counted toward these participation requirements. The hours of work per week required are also greatly increased (up to thirty hours per week for single mothers and more for two-parent families).[10]

The most dramatic departures from the AFDC program are the time limit and work requirement provisions. Lifetime time limits are a new concept in U.S. transfer programs and are based on a quite different philosophy of the aims of public assistance than has been the case heretofore. States are allowed certain types of exemptions from the time limits and are also allowed to grant temporary extensions to individual families, so long as the total number does not exceed 20 percent of the caseload. The work requirements in the new legislation are much stronger than in previous law and change the orientation from education and training to work per se. The law also allows states to impose sanctions on recipients for failure to comply with the work requirements, sanctions that are much stronger than in past law and which have been enforced rigorously. The work emphasis of the law is further reinforced by an increase in the funds made available for child care.[11] At the same time, any system of work requirements must specify some exemptions from them, and states are allowed to exempt families with specified types of difficulties.

Several other PRWORA provisions are worth noting for their importance. States are required to maintain expenditures from their own funds at a level at least 75 percent of that prior to PRWORA (the so-called

10. The law imposed specific penalties on the states for not complying with these mandated provisions. These penalties took the form of percentage reductions in the block grant allocation for each type of violation. The work participation requirements have been considerably ameliorated thus far by another provision of the law that reduces those requirements in proportion to the amount of caseload reduction a state experiences. Because caseloads have fallen dramatically, these participation requirements have been greatly reduced as well. However, this provision of the law also gives states an incentive to reduce the caseload because it lowers the level of mandated work requirements.

11. However, the guarantee of child care that existed under AFDC is abolished. That guarantee was widely seen by states as a constraint on their ability to increase employment among recipients.

"maintenance of effort" provisions). This maintains a semblance of a matching grant system in the short to medium run. A major point of discussion between the federal government and the states has been over whether these funds can only be spent on recipients eligible for TANF dollars or can be more generally spent and, if the latter, whether there are any categories of expenditure that funds cannot be spent on. Regulations issued in the spring of 1999 by the U.S. Department of Health and Human Services (DHHS) interpret the law fairly broadly and allow the funds to be spent on a wide variety of sources, giving states considerable flexibility as a result. Another important financing provision was the creation of a contingency fund for the states to draw on in times of high unemployment. The strong performance of the U.S. economy since 1996 has made this contingency fund of little relevance thus far, but it could be important in the future if the economy turns down. Another provision in PRWORA provides for bonuses to the five states who most reduce their out-of-wedlock childbearing rates and their abortion rates.

Since the 1996 act, states have moved forward vigorously to design TANF programs that are very different from their AFDC programs prior to 1990, not only to comply with the provisions of the law but also to alter program features that go beyond the minimum required. A good example is the important case of time limits. Table 5.3 shows the limits adopted by the states in the first year after TANF. Only a slight majority of the states—twenty-seven—have adopted the simple PRWORA standard of a sixty-month lifetime time limit. The rest of the states have adopted some other type of plan and, in fact, most of these states have adopted time limits that

Table 5.3   State Time Limits, August 1998

States	Time Limits
27 states	60 months
8 states	Intermittent (e.g., 24 out of 60 months); lifetime of 60 months
8 states	Less than 60 months lifetime
Arizona, Indiana	24 out of 60 months, lifetime of 60 for adults only; 60 months lifetime
California	For applicants: 18 months but can be extended to 24 months if extension will lead to employment or 60 months if no job available and adults participate in community service. For recipients: 24 months but can be extended to 60 months if no job available and adults participate in community service
Illinois	No limit if family has earned income and works 20 hours per week; 24 months for families with no child under age 13 and no earnings; 60 months for all other families
Iowa	Individualized; lifetime of 60 months
Massachusetts	24 out of 60 months; no lifetime limit
Michigan	No time limit; will use state funds after 60 months
Texas	12, 24 and 36 months lifetime for adults only; time period depends on employability of head of household

Source: U.S. DHHS (1998).

are stricter than those required by PRWORA, sometimes dramatically so.[12] For example, eight states impose not only a lifetime limit but also a shorter limit over fixed calendar intervals (e.g., no more than twenty-four months of receipt in every sixty months of calendar time). Eight other states simply impose a shorter lifetime limit than sixty months; the shortest of these is Connecticut, at twenty-one months, a very stringent limit. However, Arizona illustrates a variation that many states have considered—a lifetime limit only for adults, so that children can continue to receive benefits beyond sixty months (paid for out of state funds). Six other states besides Arizona have adopted these "reduction" rather than "termination" policies, which constitute a relaxing of the time limits implicit in PRWORA (Gallagher et al. 1998, table 6).[13] The other six states in the table have more complex provisions that introduce new criteria into the time limit imposed and hence open the door to individual-specific considerations related to need and job availability.

The states have also embraced work requirements and sanctions vigorously. The most notable movement has been toward a "work first" approach in which recipients and new applicants for benefits are moved as quickly as possible into work of any kind, with a deemphasis on education and training. States have imposed strong sanctions for failure to comply with these requirements, usually beginning with an initial partial sanction at first noncompliance and then graduating to a more severe, full sanction at subsequent noncompliance. Seven states have imposed a lifetime ban on eligibility if an adult receives a certain number of sanctions; in Georgia, for example, two sanctions will trigger this prohibition. Many states have also lowered the age of the youngest child that furnishes exemption from the requirement to one year or six months and have otherwise tightened up on exemptions from the regulations (Gallagher et al. 1998). The work requirements have also been strengthened by frequent requirements for job search and work registration at the point of application for TANF benefits that must be complied with before benefit receipt can begin.

With the aim of reinforcing these work requirements, states have generally lowered their tax rates. Table 5.4 shows state-by-state changes as of October 1997. Although ten states have kept the AFDC disregards (i.e., no disregards beyond $90 after twelve months of benefit receipt), the rest of the states have lowered their tax rates considerably. Many states have a tax rate of 50 percent, while there is a distribution above and below this value as well. A few states have 100 percent disregards, implying a tax rate of

12. However, the large states in the United States—who have a disproportionate share of the caseload—do not have time limits below sixty months (and Michigan has none at all).

13. It is worth noting at this point that the PRWORA legislation imposes the limit only on a family in which there is an adult caretaker who has been on welfare for sixty months, regardless of how long the children have been supported. In principle, children could be put under the care of a different relative and be eligible for another sixty months of benefits.

Table 5.4   Monthly Earnings Disregards in TANF as of October 1997

State	Flat Disregard	% of Remainder
Alabama	0	20
Alaska	$150	0
Arizona	$90	33
Arkansas	20 percent	50
California	$225	50
Colorado	AFDC	AFDC
Connecticut	0	100[a]
Delaware	AFDC	AFDC
District of Columbia	AFDC	AFDC
Florida	$200	50
Georgia	AFDC	AFDC
Hawaii	$200	36
Idaho	0	40
Illinois	0	67
Indiana	AFDC	AFDC
Iowa	20 percent	50
Kansas	$90	40
Kentucky	AFDC	AFDC
Louisiana	$120–1,020	0
Maine	differs by county	differs by county
Maryland	0	26
Massachusetts	$120	50
Michigan	$200	20
Minnesota	0	36
Mississippi	$90	0
Missouri	AFDC	AFDC
Montana	$200	25
Nebraska	0	20
Nevada	0	$90 or 20[b]
New Hampshire	0	50
New Mexico	$150	50
New Jersey	0	50
New York	90	42
North Carolina	AFDC	AFDC
North Dakota	0	27[c]
Ohio	$250	50
Oklahoma	$120	50
Oregon	0	50
Pennsylvania	0	50
Rhode Island	$170	50
South Carolina	AFDC	AFDC
South Dakota	$90	20
Tennessee	$150	0
Texas	AFDC	AFDC
Utah	$100	50
Vermont	$150	25
Virginia	0	100[d]
Washington	0	50

Table 5.4   (continued)

West Virginia	0	40 on average (varies)
Wisconsin	0	0
Wyoming	$200–400	0

Source: Gallagher et al. (1998, table 14)

Notes: In cases where the disregards change with the length of the spell, those for the longest spell are shown. AFDC = $90 flat disregard and zero percent of remainder after twelve months.

[a]Disregard is 100 percent as long as earnings are below poverty line; benefit goes to zero above.

[b]Disregard is $90 or 20 percent, whichever is greater.

[c]There is an additional disregard that varies with earnings and family size.

[d]Disregard is 100 percent as long as net income is below poverty line; disregard is 0 if net income is above poverty line but earnings are below poverty line; and benefits go to zero if earnings are above poverty line.

zero; these states limit benefits by imposing income limits of one form or another on eligibility (at which point the tax rate is effectively greater than 100 percent).

States have altered some of the other financial aspects of eligibility and the benefit formula but not all.[14] Asset limits have generally been raised, as have gross income limits, but benefit levels themselves have for the most part been left the same as they were prior to PRWORA (Gallagher et al. 1998). The 100-hour rule limiting work in two-parent families has been dropped in the majority of states, although work requirements are now imposed on both parents in such families. Family caps have been adopted in twenty-two states, and one state (Wisconsin) has adopted a flat benefit that does not vary at all with family size. There has been significant reduction in the use of the child support pass-through (the requirement that the welfare recipient receive the first $50 of child support payment from the father). Finally, the majority of states have adopted some type of "diversion" program which seeks to divert families who have applied for TANF from coming onto the rolls. One type provides a family with a lump-sum cash payment together with a stipulation that they cannot reapply for a fixed number of months. Another provides families with child care, medical, or transportation services to assist them in cases where they are judged to be only temporarily needy. A third, common, program requires recipients to engage in a specified period of job search, sometimes merely by registering with a work agency but often requiring that the applicant show evidence of having applied for jobs or having contacted employers. The individual cannot be considered for assistance until the requirement is met.

14. Details on state-specific benefit formulas can be found in the Welfare Rules Database of the Urban Institute (http://anfdata.urban.org/wrd).

5.1.3   Goals of AFDC and TANF

The AFDC and TANF rules implicitly reveal many of the goals of the programs as they have changed over time. Originally the AFDC program was intended only to provide cash support for widows and their children, at a time when married women were commonly expected not to work and to stay at home to raise their children. Over time, as the general labor force participation rate of women with children rose, and as the composition of the caseload shifted toward divorced and unmarried mothers, the goals of the program gradually shifted as well, toward encouraging and requiring work to accompany the cash benefit. This shift took a major additional step with the state-level welfare reform efforts in the early 1990s and with the 1996 passage of PRWORA, whereby the goals of the program were moved toward the employment goal much more strongly than had been the case in the past.

Another significant shift in goals in the 1990s has been the shift from an education-training strategy toward a pure work strategy. There has been a tension between these two strategies ever since the employment goal began to enter into programmatic discussions in the late 1960s. The education-training strategy, or what was sometimes called the human capital strategy, aimed to improve recipient skills and potential wage rates in the labor market, whereas the pure work strategy emphasized instead work per se, even if the education or training content was not high. The education-training strategy is more expensive and has an uncertain rate of return but holds the promise of long-run improvement, whereas the pure work strategy is relatively inexpensive and promotes employment directly but may do less for long-run earnings capacity. The education-training, or human capital, strategy was most forcefully embodied in the Family Support Act of 1988, but the 1996 PRWORA strongly reoriented the strategy toward a pure work goal.

But the PRWORA legislation represented more than simply a redirection of the employment goal and an increased emphasis on work. A new goal appeared, which was to reduce "dependency," a term much used in public discussions, which is more or less defined as long-term receipt of welfare benefits. Such dependency is presumed by the PRWORA legislation to have deleterious effects on adults and children, a hypothesis upon which research has a bearing. The time limits embodied in PRWORA are intended to reduce dependency directly by simply disallowing long-term receipt, thereby providing only temporary assistance to families. There is also an implicit hypothesis in the notion of a time limit by which welfare recipients are capable of becoming "self-sufficient" off the rolls, where "self-sufficiency" is meant as the attainment of a reasonable and sustainable level of income that is enough to allow a family not to have to apply for public support. The time limit provisions implicitly presume that it is possible to become self-sufficient after five years or less of welfare receipt, another hypothesis that is in principle possible to test.

Another new goal of welfare programs in the 1990s has been to reduce the rate of nonmarital childbearing and to encourage marriage. This goal is explicitly stated in the preamble to the PRWORA legislation, but the law itself has very few provisions directly relating to it.[15] In part this is because it is presumed that reductions in dependency will lead to reductions in such childbearing and an increase in marriage, another hypothesis that can be subjected to test. The lack of direct provisions in PRWORA on childbearing and marriage is also partly the result of a lack of confidence by Congress in the efficacy of any specific set of programs directly aimed at those outcomes.

5.2   Caseloads, Expenditures, Participation, and Recipient Characteristics

5.2.1   Expenditure, Caseload, and Benefit Trends

The AFDC program experienced uneven growth of expenditures and caseloads over its lifetime. Whereas program growth was essentially comparable to population growth from 1935 through the late 1950s, expenditures and caseloads began to pick up in the 1960s. Figure 5.1 shows the growth of real per capita expenditures in the AFDC program from 1970 to 1995.[16] A notable increase in AFDC expenditures occurred in the early 1970s (a continuation of an upward trend that began in the late 1960s) and ran through about 1977, a period known as the "welfare explosion." Expenditures subsequently declined in real terms, until the early 1990s, when they underwent another period of growth, albeit much smaller in magnitude than that in the 1970s. This period of growth was not sufficient to offset the long-period decline, however, and by 1995 per capita expenditures on the AFDC program were at about the same level they were in 1972.

The second line in figure 5.1 shows per capita expenditure trends in the TANF program and for a reconstructed set of expenditures for the AFDC program to restore some measure of comparability. The TANF program's expenditures cover many types of activities (e.g., jobs programs and emergency assistance) that were not included in official AFDC expenditures. As the line shows, expenditures including these additional programs were slightly higher than official AFDC expenditures but have fallen rapidly in the TANF program. This decline is largely a result of the decline in the caseload, as discussed next.

15. Of the four principal goals of the PRWORA legislation given in its preamble, only one relates solely to assisting the poor; the other three relate to increasing marriage and employment and to reducing nonmarital childbearing.

16. This figure and all subsequent ones use the Personal Consumption Expenditure deflator (base 1996) for conversion to real amounts.

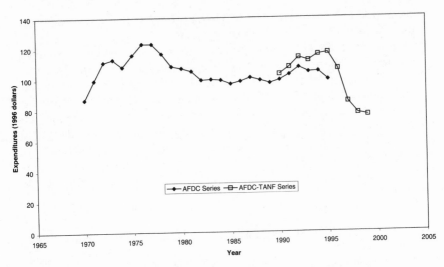

Fig. 5.1   **AFDC and TANF real expenditures per capita, 1970–99**
Sources: U.S. DHHS (2001, table TANF 3); U.S. Congress, Committee on Ways and Means (2000, table 7-15); U.S. Department of Commerce (2000, table 2, Population).

The upper line in figure 5.2 shows the per capita caseload in the AFDC and TANF programs. The AFDC caseload grew dramatically in the early 1970s (again, a continuation of a trend that began in the 1960s) and then gradually declined until 1982 and leveled off for the rest of the decade. A new surge of growth occurred in the early 1990s, followed by a decline that began before 1996 but accelerated after it and led to a caseload level by 1999 that had fallen below its level in 1970. Overall, the pattern of caseload growth generally follows the pattern of expenditures in figure 5.1. Indeed, a decomposition of the per capita expenditure growth into caseload per capita and expenditures per recipient through 1995 shows that the former explains essentially all of the expenditure patterns (Moffitt 2001). The same correlation appears after 1995. Expenditures per recipient changed very little over the entire period.

The lower lines in figure 5.2 show trends in the fraction of single-mother families who received AFDC or TANF benefits, and trends in the fraction of earnings-poor single-mother families who did so.[17] Participation rates grew rapidly in the 1970s and then declined somewhat through the early 1990s. Moffitt (2001) has shown that the fraction of the population that is in single-mother families grew steadily over the period and accelerated during the 1980s and early 1990s; this growth kept the caseload from

17. Earnings-poor families are those below their poverty threshold on the basis of family earnings alone. Only single-mother families are shown because married families have always been a minor fraction of the caseload.

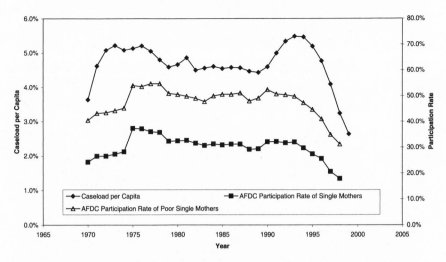

Fig. 5.2   AFDC and TANF caseload per capita and participation rates per capita, 1970–99

Sources: U.S. DHHS (2001, table TANF 1); U.S. Department of Commerce (2000, table 2, Population); author tabulations from the Current Population Survey.

falling even more than it did from the decline in participation rates of single mothers alone. Indeed, the spike in the caseload in the early 1990s is not reflected in participation rates and is instead a result of the continued growth of single-mother families. Starting around 1994, participation rates declined drastically along with the caseload. The caseload decline was entirely the result of the drop in participation, for, at least through 1999, there was no dropoff in the number of single mother families (U.S. DHHS 2001, pp. III–50).[18]

Figure 5.3 shows trends in real welfare benefits for a family of four over the 1970–98 period.[19] The lower line in the figure shows trends for AFDC-TANF, while the upper two lines show figures for the combined sum of AFDC-TANF, food stamps, and Medicaid. The higher of the two latter lines shows the straight sum of the three, and the lower of the two discounts the Medicaid benefit by an estimate of its cash-equivalent value and also takes into account the taxation of AFDC-TANF income by the Food Stamp Program.

The figure shows that AFDC-TANF benefits by themselves have declined secularly since 1970, and hence cannot provide an explanation for

18. The decline in participation was not a result of increases in income that made more single mothers ineligible. The decline in the participation rate of poor single mothers in figure 5.2 suggests this, but when income eligibility is more precisely determined, the data show a decline in the participation rate of income-eligible families as well (U.S. DHHS 2001, pp. II–21).

19. The figures show the maximum amount paid for a family with no other income, or what economists commonly call the guarantee.

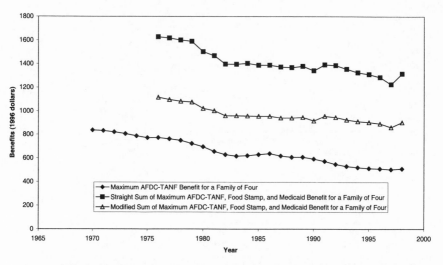

Fig. 5.3   Real monthly AFDC-TANF, food stamp, and Medicaid benefits, 1970–98
Source: Welfare benefits data file, [http://www.econ.jhu.edu/People/Moffitt/DataSets.html].

any of the positive or negative fluctuations in the caseload or in participation rates conditional on single motherhood shown in figure 5.2. Mechanically, the decline in benefits results from a failure of states to raise nominal benefit levels to keep up with inflation. There has been very little change in this trend during the TANF program, although the benefit decline has slightly leveled off.

Nevertheless, it is important to note that food stamps and Medicaid were not received by many families in the late 1960s and came into their own only in the early 1970s, when they rapidly expanded around the country. Recipients of AFDC were automatically eligible for benefits from both programs (as TANF recipients continue to be). Consequently, a proper comparison of the change in benefits received by AFDC recipients is more closely approximated by comparing the AFDC benefit alone in 1970 to the combined benefit in 1975 and after. By that comparison, there was a strong growth of benefits in the early 1970s, thus providing a possible explanation for the growth in the caseload and in participation rates over that period. Moreover, the decline in the combined benefit subsequently has been entirely the result of the decline in AFDC benefits, for food stamp benefits have remained relatively constant in real terms and real Medicaid benefits have grown slightly. On net, by 1998, the combined benefit was still higher than the AFDC benefit alone in 1970.

The AFDC-TANF benefit decline after 1996 is also somewhat misleading because of the increase in the fraction of TANF expenditures spent on noncash services. Figure 5.4 shows the distribution of 1999 TANF expenditures by spending category and shows that only 59 percent of monies

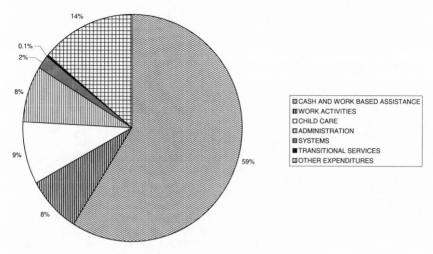

Fig. 5.4   TANF expenditures by spending category, FY 1999
Source: U.S. DHHS (2000, chart 2.4).

were expended on cash aid. The rest was spent on work activities, child care, administration, and a number of other categories (including social services). Indeed, when the post-TANF expenditures in figure 5.1 are divided by the number of cash recipients shown in figure 5.2, it can easily be seen that expenditures per recipient have actually increased after 1996, rather than fallen. In large part this is simply because the caseload has declined so drastically that states have used their block grant monies for other, noncash categories.[20]

5.2.2   Recipient Characteristics

Table 5.5 shows the trends in a few characteristics of the AFDC and TANF caseload 1969 to 1999. The percent of the caseload with earnings was only 13 percent in 1979 but dropped further in the 1980s, largely because of 1981 federal legislation that increased the tax rate on earnings to 100 percent (see table 5.1), effectively making many working families formerly on AFDC ineligible for benefits. The percent with earnings is a much higher 25 percent by 1999, a reflection of the emphasis of current welfare reform on work.

The age of recipients appears to be slightly increasing and family size is declining, although most of this decline occurred in the 1970s. The fraction

---

20. There are unfortunately no concrete data on how many of the recipients of the noncash expenditures are AFDC-TANF recipients and how many are either former recipients—namely, those who have left the welfare rolls—or even poor families who have never been on AFDC-TANF. This makes the expenditure per recipient calculation potentially misleading, for the monies are now spread over a large population. Along with the decline in expenditures has probably been a redistribution within the poor population.

Table 5.5   **Selected Characteristics of AFDC and TANF Families, 1969–99**

	1969	1979	1988	1999
% with earnings	—	12.8	8.4	25.2
age (median)	—	—	29.0	31.2
% with less than high school education	76.7	57.8	47.2	48.9
Family size	4.0	3.0	3.0	2.8
% whose youngest child is less than two	—	—	43.1	32.3
% child-only families	10.1	14.6	9.6	29.1

Sources: First, fourth, and sixth rows: U.S. DHHS (2001, table TANF 7). Second and fifth rows: Oellerich (2001, table 3). Third row: for 1969, 1979, and 1988, U.S. Congress, Committee on Ways and Means (1998, table 7-19); for 1999, U.S. DHHS (1999, table 17); figures shown here represent the originals inflated by the fraction nonmissing.

Note: Dashes indicate data not available.

whose youngest child is less than two has also decline in the 1990s, either because of a general decline in the population of families with children in this age range or because mothers with very young children have left the welfare rolls. Another important trend has been an enormous increase in the 1990s in the fraction of the caseload composed of child-only cases. These are cases in which benefits are received by children but the parent, or other adult caretaker, is herself ineligible for benefits. Such ineligibility can occur if the parent is a noncitizen immigrant but the children are citizens; if the children are cared for by a nonparent with income above the TANF eligibility level; or if the parent has been sanctioned for violating one of many TANF rules (including those for work requirements) or has reached a TANF time limit and has gone off the rolls. The last category occurs only in those states with partial sanctions—that is, in the case of a violation only the portion of the benefit designated for the adult is terminated—and in those states where the time limit is applied only to the adult, not to the children. In child-only families, none of the work requirements or time limits affect benefits or eligibility because they are assessed only on adults.

The last row of the table shows trends in the fraction of the caseload without a high school education. This fraction declined secularly, as it did for the population as a whole from rising levels of education. However, it has increased slightly since 1996, possibly a sign that more educated recipients have left the rolls in the massive caseload decline illustrated earlier. This would leave the caseload more disadvantaged than it had been before.[21]

The types of single mothers on AFDC also shifted over time, as shown in figure 5.5. Initially most single mothers were widows, but in the 1960s

---

21. The evidence on whether this type of selectivity has occurred is weaker than one would predict. See Moffitt and Stevens (2001), Moffitt et al. (2001), and Smith (2001), and the references therein.

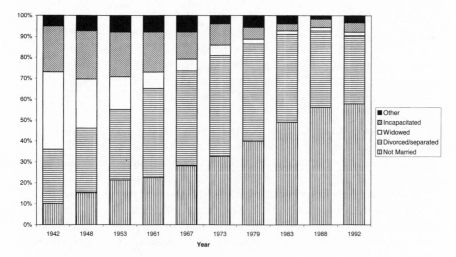

Fig. 5.5   Basis of AFDC eligibility, 1942–94
Source: U.S. DHHS (1995, 63).

and 1970s the majority were divorced and separated women. In the 1980s and 1990s, the majority were unmarried single mothers. These trends have contributed importantly to the perception of welfare recipients by the general public and have probably increased its unpopularity.[22]

5.3   Research on the AFDC Program

This section reviews the research literature on the AFDC program. The AFDC program has received more research attention from economists than any other welfare program. It was the best-known cash means-tested program in the mind of the general public and policymakers. Its benefit structure was also fairly simple and came closest, among all means-tested programs, to the simple textbook model of such a program with a single guarantee and a single tax rate on income. This made it particularly well suited to the study of work incentives, which has always been the main interest of economists, beginning with the discussions of a negative income in the 1960s.

Research on the TANF program is considered later in a separate section.[23] There is much less research on TANF, and, further, the character of that research is generally quite different from that on the AFDC pro-

22. For a study of how the general public perceives welfare recipients, and how that perception is affected by the marital status of recipients, see Moffitt (1999b).

23. That section includes research on the AFDC waivers of the 1990s because those waivers, while conducted within the AFDC program, are best understood as precursors to TANF.

gram, as will be seen from the review. Nevertheless, research on AFDC is still quite relevant to the TANF program because academic AFDC research deals, by and large, with fundamental response issues—the effects of benefits and tax rates on behavior—and not with the effects of specific subfeatures of AFDC, which are not so generalizable. Consequently, AFDC research is still relevant in the TANF era, albeit in a generalized sense.

Although the issue of work incentives is by far the major area in which AFDC research has been conducted, some studies have also been conducted on many other issues as well. The review below will include the main areas of such research: dynamics and turnover in the program; employment and training programs; effects of the program on demographic and family outcomes; and research on the state determination of benefits. The sections below on each of these topics will first consider the economic models used to analyze them, followed by a review of the empirical evidence.

5.3.1   Work Incentives

Models

Economists' research on AFDC, as on most welfare programs, generally has taken the redistributive goals of the program as given and has tended to focus on the behavioral incentives and disincentives provided by the program structure and benefit formula. For work incentives, there is a well-developed model for analyzing these incentives—the static labor supply model—which has been the workhorse of this literature. The model has endured because it can capture the simple labor supply effects of a wide range of elementary program alternatives.

The model is illustrated with the familiar income-leisure diagram in figure 5.6, where the nontransfer constraint is shown as ADE with slope $-W$ (the hourly wage rate) and it is assumed that there is no nonprogram non-labor income (N). The benefit formula (allowing positive N) is $B = G - t(WH + N)$, where H is hours of work, generating the transfer constraint shown as ACD, with slope $-W(1 - t)$. Here t is the marginal tax rate on benefits and the intercept G is the guarantee level. The introduction of the program where there was none before uncontrovertibly reduces (or at least does not increase) labor supply because income and substitution effects go in the same direction. Those initially on constraint AD will move to CD, reducing labor supply, and a few of those initially above point D will reduce labor supply to go onto the program (indifference curves not shown).

An increase in G, which shifts segment CD up in parallel fashion, reduces hours of work in this model if leisure is a normal good, but the more

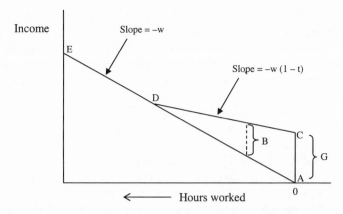

Fig. 5.6 Budget constraint with a means-tested transfer program

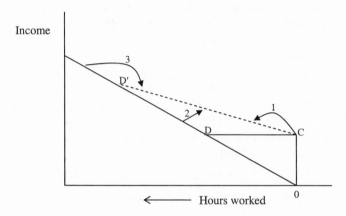

Fig. 5.7 Effect of change on *t* on labor supply

important comparative static is that induced by a reduction in *t*. The negative income tax, a program originally proposed by Friedman (1962) and promoted by Lampman (1968), Tobin (1966), Tobin, Pechman, and Mieszkowski (1967), and many others thereafter, was intended to provide work incentives by such a reform. Figure 5.7 shows the effect of a reduction in *t* from 1.0 to some lesser value by the shift from CD to CD′. It is now a well-known result that the effect of such a reduction on average hours of work is ambiguous in sign. While some of those who are initially on welfare and not working increase their hours of work (arrow 1), those in the newly created eligible region will reduce their labor supply (arrow 2), as will some of those at higher income levels who are initially ineligible (arrow 3). Whether labor supply on net increases or decreases depends on the relative numbers of individuals at different points and on the magnitudes of their responses.[24] The ranges of G and t in the AFDC program typically resulted in a program breakeven point (D or D') somewhere in the part-time hours range, so the effect of a reduction in t was thought to increase part-time work both by pulling nonworkers up to that range and inducing some full-time workers to reduce work to part time (to obtain benefit supplementation).

This result is a special case of a larger principle that has bedeviled welfare reform, namely, that any reform that provides a benefit to those on welfare that is not available off welfare tends to draw families onto the program, thereby increasing the caseload and decreasing labor supply. Providing benefit supplementation to those who work while on welfare—but not to those who are off welfare—is one example, but so is providing medical benefits, child care subsidies, and education and training programs, if those are provided only to those on welfare and not those off. There is no way within this general class of budget-constraint manipulations of the welfare formula to avoid these effects entirely, although they may be avoided by making such benefits universal and hence available to those off welfare as well as on.

With a minor modification, the model also provides a simple theory of welfare participation, which is also a useful tool in analyzing the AFDC program. Denoting $V(W', N')$ as the indirect utility obtained by an individual on a linear budget segment with slope W' and rightmost intercept N', we can write the determinants of welfare participation—P, equal to 1 if the individual participates and 0 if not—as

$$(1) \qquad P^* = V[W(1 - t), N(1 - t) + G] - V[W, N] - C$$

$$(2) \qquad P = 1 \text{ iff } P^* > 0; \quad P = 0 \text{ otherwise}$$

where C is some implicit cost attached to being a welfare recipient. That cost may be a stigma cost—the individual suffers a utility loss from being on welfare per se—or a time and money cost arising from the process of applying for the program and complying with its ongoing reporting and other requirements. The first two terms in equation (1) imply that participation propensities are increasing in G and decreasing in t, and there is a presumption (although not strictly required by theory) that they are decreasing in W. The basic trade-off in the model faced in the participation choice is between the potential benefit, on the one hand, and potential earnings off welfare, on the other. Welfare costs (C) are needed to explain why participation rates of eligibles are less than 100 percent—as all data

---

24. The decrease in t has ambiguous effects on work effort but unambiguously increases the caseload and the participation rate in the program. The early literature on reductions in t (e.g., Aaron 1973) emphasized that there is a trade-off between work incentives and program costs for this reason. But, in fact, the trade-off is more unfavorable than this implies because a reduction in t may not only increase costs, it may also not increase labor supply.

calculations show them to be—for this implies that some families will be observed to be on segment AD in figure 5.1 and do not take advantage of a potential increase in income by going onto welfare. Note that equations (1)–(2) also cover the participation choice between locating above the break-even point D in figure 5.1 and below it, as well as the choice between segment AD and CD.

Evidence

There have been three major reviews of the literature on the effect of AFDC on labor supply (Danziger, Haveman, and Plotnick 1981; Moffitt 1992b; Hoynes 1997), which cover most of the work on that topic. The studies as a whole confirm that AFDC reduces labor supply, and the estimates of its effect range from 10 to 50 percent of non-AFDC levels. Mean labor supply in the absence of AFDC is generally only about twenty hours per week, however (including nonworkers), so the absolute magnitude of the reduction is not as large as might be expected.[25] Probably the major methodological problem with these estimates is the obvious one that they are not based on any data in which AFDC was literally absent, but rather are extrapolations from estimated effects of the existing, positive level of AFDC benefits down to a benefit level of zero. Benefit-level estimates (really, effects of G) are obtained from cross-state variation in benefits, which, although large, does not include zero benefits. These estimates must therefore be treated with some caution.

This literature also generally estimates income and substitution effects on labor supply, usually based, at least in part, on variation in G and t across states. This itself is also problematic because, while there was considerable variation in G in the AFDC program, as just noted, the nominal level of the tax rate was set by the federal government and hence was constant across states. Sometimes this problem was circumvented by constraining the effect of t to enter the labor supply function through $W(1 - t)$, thereby allowing wage variation to identify the coefficient, but often variation in effective tax rates arising from a variety of sources was used.[26] Either approach has problems. In any case, however, the elasticities estimated in the papers generally fell into acceptable ranges as those are defined

25. The estimates suffer from a data problem, namely, that they use household surveys that only contain information on hours of work over an entire year (divided by 52), which includes both welfare and nonwelfare weeks. Thus the estimates are themselves some average over weeks in which the individual was on welfare and weeks in which she was not.

26. See note 2 for ways in which states could manipulate the tax rate. These variations only changed the tax rate over some ranges of the data and hence still require some parametric restrictions to obtain general estimates of substitution effects. Some studies, rather than using the official manipulations of the tax rate, simply used estimated effective tax rates obtained by regressing benefits on income on a state-by-state basis (see Fraker, Moffitt, and Wolf 1985, and McKinnish, Sanders, and Smith 1999 for such estimates). However, these incorrectly linearized the benefit formula and also incorporated taxes and work-related expenses that should not be included.

by the general labor supply literature for women and single mothers, with moderately large and negative income effects and moderately sized and positive uncompensated substitution effects.

However, as noted in the Models section above, the net effect of changes in t on labor supply depends on the relative magnitudes of offsetting positive and negative effects, regardless of whether uncompensated substitution effects are positive. On this issue, the evidence suggested that the net effect was reasonably close to zero; that is, that the positive and negative incentive effects of changes in t essentially cancel each other out. The nonexperimental evidence, such as that provided by simulations from nonexperimental labor supply elasticities, demonstrates this, as does evidence from the NIT experiments. In the latter, comparisons of labor supply across alternative treatment groups that had the same G but different t showed no consistent evidence of differences in hours of work (SRI International 1983, table 3.9). As noted by Moffitt (1992b), the finding of a small or nonexistent effect of changes in t on labor supply is consistent with the relative invariance of hours of work among female heads in time series before and after the 1967 and 1981 changes in the tax rate in the AFDC program.

There have been relatively few new studies of AFDC and labor supply since the past reviews. Three are noted in table 5.6. Hoynes (1996) studied the AFDC-UP program and found it to have significant negative effects on the labor supply of husbands and wives, but that marginal reductions in t had little effect, consistent with prior work. Keane and Moffitt (1998) focused on the labor supply effects of participating in multiple programs, including not only AFDC but also food stamps, subsidized housing, and the Medicaid program. They showed that cumulative marginal tax rates were generally greater than 100 percent in this case. Nevertheless, although their estimated substitution and income elasticities were sizable, the net effect on labor supply of reducing the marginal tax rates to a level below 100 percent was negligible, again for the same reasons already noted. Meyer and Rosenbaum (2001) focused on an attempt to explain the increase in employment rates among single mothers from 1984 to 1986. They found that AFDC benefits and tax rates (the latter affecting potential benefits if working) had expected effects on employment probabilities, but that the time series increase in single-mother employment was less affected by changes in those parameters and other welfare variables than by a change in the generosity of the Earned Income Tax Credit (EITC) over the period (see the EITC chapter in this volume).[27]

Simple static models of participation in AFDC also form a part of this

---

27. Because Meyer and Rosenbaum examined employment rather than hours of work, the "perverse" effect of a change in t could not occur. They briefly examined effects on hours of work as a sensitivity test, but they noted that the model independent variables were not set up for that dependent variable.

Table 5.6 **Recent Studies of the Effect of AFDC on Labor Supply**

Study	Data	Population	Dependent Variable	Welfare Variables	Results
Hoynes (1996)	Survey of Income and Program Participation, 1983–86	Low-asset married couples	Labor supply and participation in the AFDC-UP program	AFDC guarantee and tax rate evaluated at specific labor supply points	AFDC-UP has sizable negative effect on labor supply; marginal changes in G and t have little effect
Keane and Moffitt (1998)	Survey of Income and Program Participation, 1984	Low-asset single mothers	Labor supply and participation in AFDC, food stamps, and subsidized housing	Guarantees and tax rates in AFDC, food stamps, and subsidized housing evaluated at specific labor supply points	Substitution elasticity is 1.82 and total income elasticity is −.21; marginal changes in t have no effect on labor supply
Meyer and Rosenbaum (2001)	Current Population Survey, 1984–96	Single mothers	Probability of working	AFDC and food stamp guarantee and expected benefits if work	Guarantees reduce employment probability and benefits if work increase it

literature, generally estimating some version of equations (1)–(2). Again, most of this literature is summarized by prior reviews. The studies overwhelmingly confirm that participation propensities are positively affected by G and negatively affected by t, and generally confirm that those propensities are negatively affected by W and N. Two of the recent studies (Hoynes 1996 and Keane and Moffitt 1998) estimated participation equations jointly with labor supply equations and obtained results consistent with these findings.

Researchers have also sought to use this model to explain the time-series pattern of caseload and participation rates in different periods shown in Figure 2. Most explanations for the welfare caseload increase in the late 1960s and early 1970s rely on the gradual expansions of the Food Stamp and Medicaid programs to more counties in the United States, which, given the ties of these programs to AFDC receipt, made the program more attractive. Such an explanation is consistent with the economic model. However, most observers attribute part of the increase as well to court decisions relaxing eligibility restrictions and to declines in welfare stigma, although the latter may be endogenous. The relatively stable caseload trend in the late 1970s and 1980s is generally attributed to two offsetting and contradictory forces, one an increase in the fraction of single mother families in the population and the other a decline in the participation rate conditional on single motherhood. The latter is most often attributed to the decline in the real benefit level, while the causes of the former are still in considerable dispute. The economic model is better at explaining changes in participation conditional on single motherhood than changes in single motherhood, in general. Finally, the increase in caseloads in the early 1990s, which resulted from a rise in the participation rate conditional on single motherhood more than a rise in single motherhood, is more difficult to explain with the economic model, for neither declining wage rates nor increasing benefits can be reasonably tied to most of the growth. Blank (2001) shows that the majority of the caseload increase over this period arose from increases in child-only cases and the AFDC-UP caseload, neither of which is easily explainable by the economic model, whereas the remaining growth of the traditional single-mother AFDC caseload is reasonably well explained by an expanded model that includes not only benefits but also demographics, political factors, and other policy variables.[28]

28. Blank also argues, however, that the growth of the single-mother AFDC caseload over this period was more a result of an increase in the number of single mothers with income below the eligibility level than of an increase in take-up conditional on this eligibility. Moffitt (2001) showed that the caseload increase over this period was half a result of increases in the numbers of single mothers and half a result of increases in take-up conditional on single motherhood (but not conditional on income). Moffitt also argued that, over the period 1971–95, participation rates so defined fluctuated around a constant mean and hence had no effect on the long-run growth of the caseload, which is instead essentially entirely explained by the growth in single motherhood.

A small literature has also developed on the concept of welfare stigma, which, as mentioned above, is conceived of as a disutility of welfare participation which lowers participation rates in the program. Moffitt (1983) introduced the concept to the literature but considered it to be an exogenous heterogeneous parameter of the individual utility function that could be used to rationalize the need to estimate a participation equation and not just a labor supply equation.[29] However, other studies have developed the idea of welfare stigma as a disutility that declines with the number of other families who are on welfare, setting up a social interactions, or contagion, model that can have multiplier effects once participation rates exceed a threshold. Besley and Coate (1992a), for example, assumed that the utility of being on welfare is reduced by some function of the fraction of the population that is not truly needy and is instead reducing labor supply to go onto welfare. Lindbeck, Nyberg, and Weibull (1999) simply assumed that the utility of being on welfare is reduced by the number of others who are on welfare, but they went on to analyze the voting equilibria that would set benefit levels that would generate different welfare caseloads as an equilibrium outcome. In a somewhat different vein, Nechyba (2001) assumed that the stigma of having nonmarital births (which is a condition for welfare eligibility) is reduced by the magnitude of the aggregate nonmarital birth rate, and he then showed that a change in welfare benefits can initiate a nontrivial change in that birth rate through multiplier effects.

5.3.2   Participation Dynamics

A continuing area of research on the AFDC program focuses on participation dynamics, that is, the study of entry rates, exit rates, and spell distributions of time on AFDC. Interest in this issue arises from several sources. One is the recognition that, contrary to the impression given by the static labor supply model where participation seems to be a one-time, permanent decision, turnover rates in the AFDC program are quite high. Another is that attitudes toward the program, and policy measures to assist recipients, may differ depending upon whether recipients have only short spells of AFDC receipt or long spells. Short-spell recipients are likely to be those with stronger labor market skills who use the program for temporary support, whereas long-term recipients are likely to be those with the weakest skills. Further, long-term receipt may reduce skill levels further, as time out of the labor force results in deterioration of skills.

Models

The two building blocks of dynamic participation analysis are an entry rate and an exit rate. The standard static labor supply–participation model

---

29. If participation rates of eligibles are 100 percent, then all individuals are on the boundary of their constraints, and their observed values of labor supply uniquely determine their welfare participation status; hence there is no need to estimate a welfare participation equation.

is easily adapted to entry and exit in order to generate a conventional economic model of turnover. Supposing that the relevant population of eligibles is composed of myopic individuals who make decisions only on the basis of current period values, the decision for women who are off welfare at time $\tau - 1$ to enter or not enter the program (designate EN_τ as an entry dummy variable) and the decision for women who are on welfare at time $\tau - 1$ to exit or not exit the program (designate EX_τ as an exit dummy) can be formulated as

(3) $EN_\tau^* = V[W_\tau(1 - t), N_\tau(1 - t) + G] - V[W_\tau, N_\tau] - C - F1$

(4) $EN_\tau = 1$ iff $EN_\tau^* > 0$; $EN_\tau = 0$ otherwise

(5) $EX_\tau^* = V[W_\tau, N_\tau] - V[W_\tau(1 - t), N_\tau(1 - t) +] + C - F2$

(6) $EX_\tau = 1$ iff $EX_\tau^* > 0$; $EX_\tau = 0$ otherwise,

where F1 are fixed costs associated with moving onto welfare and F2 are fixed costs associated with moving off welfare (and possibly into the workforce). Starting with initial positions on or off welfare, and with G, t, and C fixed, transitions on and off welfare are driven by fluctuations in private market income opportunities W_τ and N_τ, which are assumed to follow some stochastic process. Individuals leave welfare when good job or other income opportunities arise and enter welfare when those job or income circumstances deteriorate; benefit levels and tax rates affect the relative attractiveness of welfare in the decision.

Given that the utility structure of the entry and exit decisions in equations (3)–(6) is the same as that in equation (1), the same comparative statics apply: Entry rates are increasing in G and decreasing in t and W, while exit rates are decreasing in G and increasing in t and W. Since labor supply on welfare is always less than labor supply off welfare, we can also say that these entry and exit decisions operate to make labor supply decreasing in G and increasing in t and W. That work incentives are implied to increase in t reflects the adverse work incentive effects noted above and can be seen in a dynamic context to operate through entry and exit: Decreases in marginal tax rates tend to decrease exit from the rolls and increase entry onto the rolls. Although the fixed costs reduce transition rates, an individual's participation will tend to gradually move over time toward welfare if equation (3) is more positive than equation (5) conditional on W_τ and N_τ and toward nonwelfare if the opposite occurs.

If μ is the entry probability, λ is the exit probability, and p_τ is the probability of being on welfare at time τ, then we have the flow identity

(7) $$p_\tau = \mu(1 - p_{\tau-1}) + (1 - \lambda)p_{\tau-1}$$
$$= \mu + (1 - \mu - \lambda)p_{\tau-1}$$

which approaches the equilibrium value

(8)
$$p_\tau = \frac{\mu}{\mu + \lambda}$$

Thus participation on welfare will be more likely if μ is greater than λ, and nonwelfare participation will be more likely if λ is greater than μ. Unless the fixed costs are large relative to the utility differences, these participation tendencies will be driven by the relative values of G, t, W, and N, as before.

In this simple setup, short-term recipients can be thought of as those with higher values of mean W_τ and N_τ, which will generate lower entry rates, higher exit rates, and shorter spell lengths, and long-term recipients can be thought of as those with lower mean values of those variables, resulting in higher entry rates, lower exit rates, and longer spell lengths. A logical alternative in this model is that short-termers and long-termers have the same means for wages and nonlabor income, but short-termers have a higher variance, which will lead them to have higher turnover rates as well. If the variation in wage and nonlabor income from period to period, which generates turnover in this model, is not exogenous but rather depends on effort, then it is also possible that short-termers are those who put more effort into job search. Heterogeneity in the distaste for welfare can also generate differences in turnover rates, as those with greater distaste have a lower reservation wage for going off or failing to enter welfare.

These models can be made more realistic by allowing foresight, particularly if wage growth is made endogenous and allowed to be affected by whether the individual is on or off welfare. Current entry and exit decisions will then be affected by expectations of the future consequences for wages and labor market opportunities. Liquidity constraints are important because those going onto welfare may be those who are more greatly constrained and who cannot sustain themselves off welfare after a negative wage shock, and those on welfare may be discouraged from saving by the asset tests in the program (see Hubbard, Skinner, and Zeldes 1995).

Evidence

The empirical literature on participation dynamics has two strands, one consisting of simple descriptive work on the distribution of AFDC spells in the population and of what types of individual characteristics are associated with that distribution, and another consisting of estimates of entry and exit rate equations. The most influential descriptive work in the literature is that of Bane and Ellwood (1983, 1994) and Ellwood (1986), who used panel data to estimate distributions of AFDC spell lengths and also distributions of "total time on" AFDC in a fixed calendar interval. These authors realized upon examination of the data not only that turnover rates were high but that many of those who exited the AFDC rolls returned in fairly short order, a finding that has been repeatedly found in subsequent work. This implies that many women do not have many long spells but nevertheless accumulate a considerable amount of time on welfare because of their high return rates. Consequently, they may have a high total time on welfare even though they do not have long spells. The data used by Bane and Ellwood indicated that up to one-quarter of all (new) recipients would be on AFDC for more than ten years in the subsequent twenty-five-year period, as compared to only 10 percent who would have a spell that lasted that long.[30]

In their later work (Bane and Ellwood 1994), the authors took the existence of high reentry rates to extend the categorization of welfare recipients to a threefold classification, consisting of long-termers, short-termers, and "cyclers." Long-termers have long spells, short-termers have only brief periods of AFDC receipt, and cyclers have relatively short spells but return to the rolls frequently. The authors argued that policy toward the three groups should be different. In a recent paper, Moffitt (2002) has provided evidence, however, that cyclers do not appear to have greater labor market skills than long-termers, which is an implication of the conventional economic model, where high turnover is generated by higher labor market skill. Moffitt found that the education and wage rates of cyclers were equal to those of long-termers, if not lower, and that they are a very disadvantaged group of recipients. This suggests that their cycling on and off for the rolls must be arising from some other kind of behavior, such as an inability to comply with program rules.

The literature on estimating entry and exit equations is fairly large and is well summarized, for the most part, by the previous reviews of research on AFDC referred to earlier. Table 5.7 lists some of the more recent studies that have been conducted, which explore a variety of issues. On the issue of whether AFDC benefits affect the probability of entry and exit, the literature confirms prior work that the guarantee generally decreases exit and increases reentry. None of the studies estimated the effects of the tax rate. Blank and Ruggles (1994) emphasized the high rates of reentry in the program, and Blank and Ruggles (1996) emphasized that spells of eligibility are not the same as spells of welfare receipt, and some women enter the rolls after being eligible for some time and others leave the rolls and remain eligible, usually for unknown reasons. Fitzgerald (1995) and Hoynes (2000) examined the effects of local labor market conditions on exit rates, while Harris (1993, 1996) examined the "routes" to exit from the rolls and reen-

30. The U.S. Department of Health and Human Services now routinely publishes these total time on figures. A recent report (U.S. DHHS 2001, table IND 10) shows that, in a period later than Bane and Ellwood considered and for the total recipient population (not just those with a new spell), one-quarter of recipients were on AFDC more than five years in a ten-year period, a much higher rate of dependence. Gottschalk and Moffitt (1994) examined how total-time-on had been trending, however, and found no trend from the 1970s to the 1980s. They also proposed an alternative measure, which was the percentage of income received from AFDC over a fixed calendar period.

Table 5.7   **Recent Studies of Participation Dynamics in the AFDC Program**

Study	Data	Population	Dependent Variable	Welfare Variables	Results
Blank and Ruggles (1994)	Survey of Income and Program Participation, 1986 and 1987 panels	Single mothers who have been on AFDC and have left	Probability of returning to AFDC	AFDC guarantee	Guarantee positively affects reentry rate
Blank and Ruggles (1996)	Survey of Income and Program Participation, 1986 and 1987 panels	Single mothers	Probability of exiting AFDC and probability of becoming ineligible for AFDC	AFDC guarantee	Guarantee has a negative effect on exit; many women are still eligible after the exit
Fitzgerald (1995)	Survey of Income and Program Participation, 1984 and 1985 panels	Single mothers on AFDC	Probability of exiting AFDC	AFDC guarantee	Guarantee negatively affects exit rate
Harris (1993)	Michigan PSID, 1984–86	Single mothers who are on AFDC	Probability of exiting AFDC	AFDC guarantee	Guarantee is insignificant; two-thirds of exits are for employment
Harris (1996)	Michigan PSID, 1983–88	Single mothers who have exited AFDC	Probability of returning to AFDC	AFDC guarantee	Guarantee is insignificant; other variables do matter
Hoynes (2000)	California administrative data on AFDC recipients, 1987–92	California welfare recipients	Probability of exiting AFDC and probability of reentry	None	Local labor market variables affect transition rates
Hoynes and MaCurdy (1994)	Michigan PSID, 1968–89	Single mothers who received AFDC	Probability of exiting AFDC	AFDC guarantee	Guarantee explains changes in length of welfare spells in some periods but not others

try to it. The literature on "routes" was initiated to a large extent by Bane and Ellwood (1983), who found that most exits from AFDC were to marriage. Harris (1993, 1996) and others found that this was a result of using annual data and that when monthly data are used, exits are usually to work. The literature on these routes on and off welfare and reasons for exit are frought with conceptual problems, for the immediate reasons for entry and exit may not be the long-run reasons. In addition, reasons that particular individuals enter and exit are endogenous to their unobserved characteristics, and it is difficult, as a result, to draw any implications about whether government policy should be to encourage certain routes off welfare.[31]

5.3.3 Employment Programs

In addition to simply providing cash with a specified benefit formula, the AFDC program long conducted various types of employment programs for recipients. One type was an education or training program that attempted to provide labor market skills and hence to improve the wage rate of the recipient. In policy discussions, these programs are often termed "human capital" programs. A second type provided assistance in job search, or assisted recipients in locating transportation and child care for employment, or even instructed recipients on the kinds of behavior and dress needed at regular jobs. In policy discussions, these are generally not termed human capital programs, but economists' conception of human capital should include them because there is some type of investment, or instruction, involved, which has a future return, however small and short-lived that return might be. A third type was a pure workfare program that simply required a recipient to work some minimum number of hours per week, without the assistance or other guidance from the welfare department (except, in the case of public service employment, to actually provide the job). Such a program should not be expected to affect the wage rate and is not a human capital program under any definition. Most programs had at least some elements of two or more of these ideal types, and it is not always easy to find any of the types in pure form. Nevertheless, prior to TANF and the pre-PRWORA waiver programs, AFDC employment programs typically drew mostly on elements from the first two of these program types, even though variations on the third were present to some degree.

Models

These programs, when viewed as human capital programs that require an investment of time (in education, training, job search, etc.) and yield some rate of return in the form of a higher future wage, can be simply ana-

---

31. In a review of the earlier literature in this subarea (Moffitt 1992b, 26), I noted that the studies needed more theoretical structure and content. This observation would seem still to hold.

lyzed with the standard investment framework familiar from human capital theory.[32] The value to an individual of participating in the program is the present value of future wage and earnings gains minus the present value of the time costs and, if any, money costs. Here it is important to know whether the program is voluntary or mandatory. If it is voluntary, no recipient will participate in the program unless its net present value is positive, but if it is mandatory, then it is conceivable that the net present value will be negative for some recipients. If so, this will reduce the value of being on welfare and should be subtracted from the welfare benefit itself (or the present value of such benefits) to obtain the value of being on welfare.

There are a number of minor alterations in this familiar model that change things slightly but not in the main. Future gains in earnings must be multiplied by the probability of employment if the latter is less than one, and programs that change only that probability and not wages also have a potentially positive net present value. Second, the rate of return will depend on whether earnings are raised sufficiently to induce the individual to go off welfare altogether; if so, incremental earnings gains go untaxed (by the welfare department), but if not, earnings gains will be taxed at the welfare tax rate t and hence will be reduced. The rhetoric of most education and training programs is that they are intended to move recipients off welfare altogether, but the reality is otherwise (see empirical review). The phrase "welfare trap" is sometimes used to describe a situation in which a very large rate of return is needed to make the recipient financially better off off welfare—this is particularly likely to occur if there is a notch at the point of going off welfare where tax rates are over 100 percent. Third, if there are opportunity costs in the form of forgone earnings—as in the classic education case of human capital—these forgone earnings will only be $W(1 - t)$, not W, and hence will be lower than they would be for such investment off welfare.[33] If the recipient is not working, there is forgone leisure rather than forgone earnings but the former is not taxed.

Assuming that the opportunity cost is in earnings rather than leisure, the net present value of the program in a two-period model can be written as

$$(9) \qquad NPV = -W_1(1 - t)I + \frac{1}{1 + r} \{P_2[(W_2 - W_1)(1 - t)H_2]$$

$$+ (1 - P_2)[(W_2 - W_1)H_2 - (G - tW_1H_2)]\}$$

---

32. Although traditional human capital theory presumes the effect of investment to affect the wage rate, a generalized interpretation would allow it to affect employment as well. For example, an investment in teaching a recipient improved job search techniques may lead to a better ability of the recipient to find a job at all, which would affect hours of work and not the wage rate. Although the theoretical discussion here assumes it is the wage rate that is affected, the same model can be extended to include effects on hours of work.

33. This point was made long ago by Kesselman (1976). The theoretical literature on the effect of transfer programs on human capital investment is virtually nonexistent. See Kesselman and Miller and Sanders (1997).

where W_1 is the wage if the recipient does not undergo the program, W_2 is the (higher) wage in period two if she does, I is the amount of time required in period one, H_2 is hours worked in period 2, and P_2 is a welfare participation dummy in period two if the recipient undergoes the program.[34] A second equation for the determination of P_2 is required but that is omitted for brevity. The welfare trap is illustrated by the last term, which shows that the gain to the program if the recipient goes off welfare subtracts off the lost benefit relative to the earnings gain.

The key empirical questions raised by this model are (a) what effect past programs have had on the wage rate or earnings and (b) to what degree they have moved recipients off welfare in subsequent periods.

Moffitt (1996) has noted that there is a third empirical question, which is (c) whether these programs affect the desirability of being on welfare in the first place, which is commonly termed an effect on entry into the program.[35] If the program is voluntary, no recipient can be made worse off by its presence and the welfare program can only be enhanced in value, which will increase the caseload by making welfare more attractive. If the program is mandatory, it may reduce the caseload to the extent that recipients or potential recipients see it as making them worse off.

Evidence

The main employment programs in the history of the AFDC program—at least prior to the waiver programs of the 1990s—were the WIN program, the WIN demonstrations of the 1980s, and the JOBS program, all referred to in section 5.2 in the discussion of the history of the AFDC program. As noted there, the WIN program was a work-registration program that provided simple job placement and job search assistance to eligible recipients; the WIN demonstrations tested new employment programs involving community work experience (close to workfare), work supplementation, and heightened job search; and the JOBS program required states to offer some mix of education, job skills training, job search, on-the-job training, work supplementation, and community work experience.[36]

---

34. The change in H_2 resulting from the increase in the wage is ignored for simplicity.

35. This is a slight misnomer given the high turnover in the program. Recipients who are already on welfare but who know that they may be engaged in a program subsequently may also change their exit decisions given the presence of the program (e.g., whether to accept a job offer off the rolls or not).

36. "Community work experience" meant workfare because it was usually work at a publicly created job in the community such as cleaning up public parks. "Work supplementation" allowed welfare departments to use welfare benefits to subsidize private sector jobs. See U.S. Congress, Committee on Ways and Means (1994, table 10.4) for the programs chosen by the states under the JOBS programs; these usually were job search, on-the-job training, and community work experience, with sometimes some type of education. Although education was required to be one of the programs offered, states rarely supplied the necessary funds to establish significant programs of that type.

Neither the WIN demonstrations nor the JOBS program was ever evaluated in a nationally representative sense, that is, by a random sample of all programs around the country or by a universal sample of all programs. Instead, there were a series of evaluations of the programs in selected state and local areas. In both cases, probably enough areas were selected that a reasonably good sense of the effects of different types of programs were obtained. For the WIN program, however, there was one major evaluation, which was national in scope (Ketron 1980). It used a methodology that is now regarded as undesirable (the use of individuals on waiting lists as a comparison group) and found very modest impacts of the program on recipient earnings, between $200 and $300 per year on average but larger for public service employment.

The results of the WIN demonstration and JOBS evaluations have been reviewed and summarized in several other places (Burtless 1995a, b; Devere, Falk, and Burke 2000; Gueron and Pauly 1991; Moffitt 1992b; O'Neill and O'Neill 1997; Plimpton and Nightingale 2000; U.S. General Accounting Office 1999; see also LaLonde, chap. 8 in this volume). Both the WIN demonstration and JOBS evaluations concentrated on answering the first empirical question noted above, namely, whether there is a positive return to the programs in terms of wage rates or earnings, and devoted some attention as well to the second question—whether caseloads were reduced. Virtually no attention was paid to the third question (whether there was induced entry) primarily for methodological reasons, for most of the estimates of program effects were obtained from random assignment trials, and those trials are inherently incapable of estimating entry effects (Moffitt 1992a).

The results of the evaluations of the WIN demonstration programs show generally positive impacts on employment and earnings, with impacts on the latter usually in the range of $300 to $600 per year. However, some programs had a much smaller impact, close to zero, and others had larger impacts, occasionally around $900 per year. These impacts are not large enough to make a major dent in the poverty rate, but are large enough to make the programs worth considering, especially in light of the view in the 1980s that most employment programs for welfare recipients had no impact at all. Furthermore, the expenditure on the WIN demonstration programs was quite small, around $500 per recipient in some cases, because only a modest amount of services were provided; these were very small-scale programs. The earnings impacts are perhaps larger than one might expect from such a minor investment.[37]

---

37. The evaluations also showed that most employment impacts arose from increases in the amount of time employed rather than on the hourly wage rate. This is not too surprising given that the programs made little investment in human capital. However, it also implies that the impacts are likely to fade over time, and, indeed, Friedlander and Burtless (1995) showed that they were gone in most sites after five years.

On the other hand, another finding from the WIN demonstrations was that the reduction in AFDC participation, caseloads, and expenditures on AFDC benefits was quite modest. The employment and earnings impacts were either not enough to move recipients over the break-even point, or not enough to prevent recipients from coming back onto the AFDC rolls in sufficient frequency to result in significant declines in welfare expenditures.

The evaluations of the JOBS program have also generally yielded positive impacts on employment and earnings. Evaluations of the California Greater Avenues to Independence (GAIN) program, the best-known of the early JOBS evaluations, showed positive earnings gains of $636 (about 25 percent) in the third year after the evaluation began (Riccio, Friedlander, and Freedman 1994). The GAIN evaluation involved six different counties in California, and the results from an evaluation of one of the counties—Riverside—showed especially large earnings gains (almost 50 percent) for reasons that have never been completely resolved, partly because the random assignment methodology used does not enable any rigorous investigation of mechanisms by which the treatment has an effect. Speculation has been that the Riverside program was so successful because it offered a particularly strong "work first" program that emphasized immediate job placement through job search (although others believe it had a good mix of rapid-employment job search and human capital education and training); because the labor market in Riverside was relatively weak and hence control families did not do well; and even because of a charismatic and energetic director. Whatever the reason, the Riverside evaluation has come to be one of the genuine success stories of employment programs in the 1990s.

One of the problems with evaluations that this illustrates is that conducting experimental tests of a program in only a handful of areas, and allowing each area to offer a different variation on the general program, essentially prevents learning whether differential effects that occur across areas are the result of site-specific factors (the economy, charismatic directors, etc.) or of the particular program that was tested in the area. Hotz, Imbens, and Klerman (2000) compared different sites in the GAIN evaluation to determine if the different impacts across sites could be ascribed instead to differences in the types of recipients enrolled in each site; they found that such differences did not explain the cross-site differences. Greenberg et al. (2001) ran regressions of the estimated program effects in each of several JOBS sites on characteristics of the area, the sample, and the program, and found it impossible to explain the cross-site differences. This makes it difficult to use the results for policy because extrapolation to the nation as a whole or to any other particular area around the country is very problematic.

A JOBS evaluation involving eleven different sites has also yielded results but is still in progress at this writing.[38] A unique aspect of this evaluation was that it tested different program strategies within the same sites, thus eliminating some of the site effects just described. For the most part, the variation of interest was whether the program tested a rapid-employment, low-cost job search program or a human capital, high-cost education and training program. The distinction is important because the TANF program that replaced AFDC emphasized the former over the latter, as part of the work first philosophy (this was also an issue in the Riverside GAIN program, as just noted). The results to date indicate that, four years after the evaluation began, positive employment and earnings gains resulted, falling generally in the range of $300 to $500 per year (Freedman 2000). Both rapid-employment and human capital programs were found in this range, although some of the human capital programs yielded results that were lower. The trend in impacts after three years suggests that the rapid-employment programs have large initial impacts that fade over time, whereas the human capital programs have impacts that do not decline as fast or may even grow over time, and that the earnings and employment gains end up by the third year not far different (Bloom and Michalopoulos 2001).[39] This has led some observers to conclude that the two strategies yield about the same impacts.[40] If the two have the same impacts, then, because the human capital strategy is more expensive than the job-search strategy (up to double the cost by some estimates), the former must necessarily have a lower rate of return than the latter.

Another important finding from this JOBS evaluation was that, although earnings impacts of the programs were positive, household income changed very little as a result of the program. This occurred because the increases in earnings were mostly cancelled out by declines in welfare benefits. This implies that recipients would have very little incentive themselves

38. The evaluation began in the early 1990s, and results from a five-year follow-up measuring impacts have not yet been completed.

39. In a study of the earlier GAIN program that followed recipients nine years after enrollment, Hotz, Imbens, and Klerman (2000) found the same pattern when comparing treatment effects in different counties—those with rapid-employment programs had impacts that faded over time compared to those emphasizing education, and after nine years they were statistically no different from each other.

40. A later analysis (Bloom and Michalopoulos 2001) concluded that "mixed" strategies were best, rather than a pure rapid-employment or pure human capital strategy. This conclusion was based largely on a comparison of pure strategies in this JOBS evaluation with several of the earlier GAIN evaluations, which were characterized as "mixed" as well—with a dominant emphasis on one strategy but with elements of the other. The only JOBS evaluation with such a mixed strategy was tested in one site (Portland), which stood out from the rest and had above-average impacts. Portland was initially known as a rapid-employment program city, but in fact it offered some education and training to certain recipients. Perhaps more important, it offered individualized treatments to different types of individuals after assessing their needs. There were other differences in the program operated in Portland as well, together with differences in its local economic environment from those in the other cities. Unfortunately, as with the Riverside GAIN program, it is almost impossible to determine what the true reason for the difference in impacts in Portland was.

to engage in these programs, unless they expected greater gains in the future than were measured by the evaluation. This suggests that the programs would have to be mandatory in order for the welfare departments to induce recipients to enroll in them.

Although the overall sense of the JOBS evaluations is that there are indeed employment and earnings gains from these programs, both inherent problems and practical problems with the random-assignment methodology limit what has been learned. Aside from the difficulty of incorporating entry effects and separating site effects from treatment effects, as already noted, many of the programs allowed control group members to start receiving the program after three years or so. Thus, impact estimates beyond that period are not true estimates of the program by itself. In addition, in many of the areas the local program environment continued to change after the evaluation was initiated, further affecting the outcomes of experimentals and controls.

5.3.4   Family Structure

Models

The suggestion that the AFDC program encourages women to have children out of wedlock has been a staple of popular views of welfare for decades. This popular view is consistent with the fact that AFDC benefits are primarily provided only to single-parent families and those are virtually all families with a female single parent. This view has been addressed by a large volume of research by economists in the last fifteen years or so and by a smaller volume of work by demographers in prior years. It has been accompanied by a more expansive examination of the effects of AFDC on family structure in general, including not only its effects on whether a woman is a single mother, but also on cohabitation, childbearing, and whether a woman lives with her parents or other relatives.

Virtually any economic model of marriage, including Beckerian utility-differences, or gains-to-marriage, models, predicts that the offer of a benefit to an individual contingent entirely on whether he or she is unmarried and has children will induce behavior that leads to a higher incidence of such events. One theoretical framework that would predict the opposite is one in which marriage is entered into voluntarily but where marital dissolution is an exogenous event. In this case, single motherhood is in part an unlucky random outcome of marriage that should in principle be insured against, and AFDC is a form of public insurance that plays that role. The presence of such insurance should, therefore, encourage individuals to take the risky action, namely, to enter into marriage, to a greater degree than they would in the absence of insurance. However, the moral hazard problem is severe, for individuals can clearly exert much control over becoming a single mother and, further, much single motherhood takes place prior to marriage. This makes insurance forces unlikely to change the net direction of effect of AFDC.

The precise rules of the AFDC program, and its two-parent counterpart, the AFDC-UP program, complicate the incentives in several respects (Moffitt, Reville, and Winkler 1994). Because eligibility for AFDC is based on the deprivation of the support of a biological parent, a woman who marries a man who is not the father of her children, or who cohabits with a man who is similarly not the biological parent, is eligible for AFDC. Thus AFDC does not discourage marriage or cohabitation universally but only if it is with the male who is the children's actual father. If a woman does marry or cohabit with a nonbiological male, and that male provides financial support to the children, the income will be counted in full or in part against the grant, and it is possible that the woman in question may end up financially ineligible for the program. However, at least for cohabitation, enforcing this provision is difficult. On the other hand, the AFDC-UP program does provide some outlet, for it provides benefits not only to families where both biological parents are married, but also where they cohabit; eligibility is only based on the presence of both parents, not on the presence of a legal union. However, the eligibility provisions in AFDC-UP have been sufficiently strict historically that it is more difficult to qualify for benefits under it than under AFDC, so the incentives for a woman against joining up with the father of her children are still quite strong.

The literature on the effects of AFDC on marriage has a parallel in models of the effect of the income tax, and of the Earned Income Tax Credit (EITC), in creating marriage disincentives (for the latter, see Hotz and Scholtz, chap. 3 in this volume). That literature is instructive because it implies that even if AFDC benefits were provided to married couples (or unmarried biological parents), there would still be a potential for incentives for or against marriage. If the unit of taxation is the family, then married couples are more likely to be above the income eligibility point—assuming that both male and female have income—than if they are separate, to take just one example. As the taxation literature demonstrates, the only neutral program that does not distort family structure private incentives is one in which benefits are paid entirely on an individual basis. But then such a program would violate vertical equity considerations and would also be complicated by the presence of children. As Hotz and Scholz note, a tax or benefit system cannot simultaneously be progressive, treat the family as the unit of taxation, and be neutral with respect to marriage (see also Alm, Dickert-Conlin, and Whittington 1999).

Another theoretical observation worth noting in this context is that a universal benefit system that provides nonzero benefits to all household structures—in particular, to single individuals—could alter predictions of the effect of AFDC on marriage. If the AFDC system were altered so as to allow benefits to be paid to both married couples and single individuals, then some marriages would dissolve so that the single individual—most often the male—could collect the benefits for which he is newly eligible. In addition, some currently single mothers and absent fathers would choose not to marry despite the new benefits they could obtain from that action because the absent father would now also receive increased income. These effects would have to be counted against the marriage-increasing results of the program change, with unknown, and therefore ambiguous, net effect.

The AFDC program alters incentives for childbearing and living arrangements as well. With regard to childbearing, the effect is through the route of single motherhood, for childbearing outside of marriage makes a mother eligible for benefits whereas childbearing inside marriage generally does not. An additional incentive for childbearing appears in the benefit structure in states in which benefits are calibrated to family size and higher benefits are paid to larger families. In this case there is an income gain to having additional children that is not present in the absence of a government welfare program and hence distorts choices in that direction. Living arrangements refer generally to whether a single mother lives with others, either her parents or a cohabiting male. The rules governing cohabitation have already been discussed, and it is only necessary to note that living with parents is governed by the same rules. That is, living with parents does not alter the basic eligibility condition based on the absence of a biological parent, and it will affect the grant only if the parents provide financial support to the mother or child. However, because that type of support is more verifiable than support from a cohabiting male, states are more likely to reduce the benefit in this case. The less-than-full taxation of parental support provides an incentive for a woman to live with her parents, as noted by Hutchens, Jakubson, and Schwartz (1989). The fact that support is partly taxed provides a disincentive for a woman to live with her parents relative to a family-structure-neutral system in which the AFDC benefit is not affected by this type of family structure. This provides another example of the trade-offs noted above that always come up in balancing equity with neutrality in tax and transfer systems.

Evidence

There has been built up in recent years a fairly large literature on the effect of AFDC benefits on family structure, mostly concerned with the effects of benefits on the probability of being a single mother. The literature has been reviewed many times, but the most recent review is by Moffitt (1998) and reviewed sixty-eight separate estimates of the effect of AFDC on various aspects of marriage, fertility, and single motherhood. This review covered studies conducted through approximately 1996. The results of this survey are shown in table 5.8, which reports counts of estimates showing insignificant, significant, or a mixture of insignificant and significant effects of welfare. The results are broken down by race, when pos-

Table 5.8   **Counts of Estimates of Effect of Welfare on Marriage and Fertility**

Type	All Races			White			Nonwhite or Black		
	Insignificant	Significant	Mixed	Insignificant	Significant	Mixed	Insignificant	Significant	Mixed
All	8	5	1	8	13	5	10	12	6
Cross-state levels	6	3	1	2	9	4	7	6	3
Cross-state changes	1	2	—	4	4	—	1	5	2
Within-state	1	—	—	1	—	—	1	1	—
Time series	—	—	—	1	—	1	1	1	1

Source: Moffitt (1998, table 1).

Note: Dashes indicate absence of data.

sible, and by the source of variation in benefits used to identify welfare effects—either cross-state variation in benefit levels, cross-state changes in benefits (i.e., state fixed effects models), within-state variation assuming the existence of some determinant of benefits that does not simultaneously directly affect family structure, or pure time series studies. Overall, although there is a very slight excess of significant estimates over insignificant ones across all races, it is quite small. However, the patterns differ by race and source of benefit variation, with stronger effects appearing for white women, and for white women using cross-state levels and for black women using cross-state changes in benefits. The difference in how benefit variation affects family structure between the two races is a result of a different sorting of single mothers by state for the two races, with white single mothers tending to be concentrated in high-benefit states but black single mothers tending to be concentrated in low benefit states.

Nevertheless, the most important implication of the review is that none of the significant estimates were in the "wrong" direction—all were in the expected direction (positive on single motherhood, negative on marriage, etc.). A simple unweighted average of the estimates, therefore, reveals a central tendency suggesting the presence of an effect of welfare benefits on family structure. Moreover, when distinctions are made between the studies by the likely credibility of the estimates—those controlling for the most other variables, which concentrate on the most appropriate part of the distribution of women, and use the most careful econometric methods— effects are sometimes stronger, sometimes substantially so (Moffitt 1998). Therefore, although there is still considerable uncertainty in the literature and there remain a large number of studies reporting insignificant estimates, this reading of the literature leads to the conclusion that welfare is likely to have some effect on family structure.[41]

There have been a few newer studies not included in the review just described. One of particular note is that of Hoffman and Foster (2000), who were able to replicate a study of Rosenzweig (1999) using Michigan Panel Study of Income Dynamics data, finding significant effects of welfare on nonmarital fertility, albeit only in certain age ranges. Foster and Hoffman (2001) conducted another study with the National Longitudinal Survey of Youth and found, as have many prior studies, that welfare impacts are greatly reduced when state fixed effects are added to the model. Blau, Kahn, and Waldfogel (2000) use microdata from the 1970, 1980, and 1990 censuses to estimate metropolitan-area fixed effects models of the effect of

41. This is a slight change from the author's earlier reading of the literature (Moffitt 1992b). As discussed in Moffitt (1998), the magnitude of the effect is more uncertain than the existence of an effect. Estimates range from quite small effects to rather large ones. The difference is not easily explainable by the preferred study characteristics just mentioned, and is consequently not currently resolved.

AFDC benefits on marriage rates and find them to have no statistically significant effect in their preferred models.

An issue in the literature has been that real AFDC benefits have declined over time while single motherhood rates have increased, suggesting that benefits could not have caused the rise in headship. Nechyba (2001) constructs a theoretical model in which social interactions between low-income families cause lags in the response to a change in benefits, consistent with the hypothesis that rising welfare benefits in the late 1960s and early 1970s could have had lagged effects over the next two decades (a hypothesis also suggested by Murray 1984). Moffitt (2000) takes a more direct approach and conducts a time series analysis of the relative importance of trends in female wages, male wages, and welfare benefits, and finds that a decline in the wages of less-educated males was the main contributor to the rise in female headship, and that the decline in welfare benefits slowed that rise, thus providing one possible reconciliation between the cross-sectional and time series evidence.

The living arrangements literature has examined the effects of welfare on the propensity of a single mother to live with her parents, and on her propensity to cohabit. Ellwood and Bane (1985) found that higher AFDC benefits were associated with greater propensities for single mothers to live independently of parents, whereas Hutchens, Jakubson, and Schwartz (1989) argued that the proper variable is the relative benefit between living with and without parents—equal to the benefit penalty imposed for living with parents—and found it to have a statistically significant effect on the propensity to live independently. Hu (2001) found that the probability that a teenager in a welfare family leaves the household is inversely related to the size of the benefit reduction suffered by the parent if the teen were to leave. Moffitt, Reville, and Winkler (1998) found cohabitation rates to be very high among AFDC recipients, but their econometric model did not turn up any strong effects of benefits, or state rules governing cohabitation, on the likelihood of cohabiting. Evenhouse and Reilly (1999), examining the issue with the Survey of Income and Program Participation, find stronger effects of benefits, however, on the likelihood of cohabiting with a male who is not the natural parent of the children.

5.3.5   State Benefit Determination

Models

A final area of considerable economic research has been on the determinants of state benefit level and on the effects of federal matching grants on the level of state benefits. The models used in this literature for state benefit determination are generally drawn straight from the literature on median voter models of public choice, considering aid to the poor as a positive argument in that voter's utility function but with the taxes needed to pay for those benefits to be a negative argument. Income effects are generally assumed to be positive, with higher median voter income leading to greater benefit levels. In the typical model, assuming a head tax on all voters to finance benefits, the price of benefits is equal to the per capita caseload times one minus the federal matching rate. Thus higher caseloads imply that the cost of a dollar increase in the benefit level is greater, and a lower matching rate implies the same. Lower matching rates, assuming they are partially spent on tax relief or other public goods, have some "leakage" because a dollar of grant does not translate into an extra dollar of welfare expenditure. For many years the matching rate structure of the federal subsidy formula for AFDC was progressive, with higher matching rates at low benefit levels than at high benefit levels, thus indirectly encouraging a reduction in the dispersion of benefit levels across different states. However, this structure was gradually replaced over the 1970s by a simple constant proportional matching rate, regardless of the level of the state benefit, in an open-ended match at that rate.

Evidence

One focus of the empirical literature has been to estimate price and income elasticities for benefits, usually from a regression of benefit levels on state median income and on a price variable, usually constructed as the caseload times one minus the matching rate, as just discussed.[42] There are several econometric issues that arise in such estimation that will not be discussed in detail here. The first model of this type was conducted by Orr (1976), who found that the federal matching rate, state per capita income, and other variables measuring the characteristics of the taxpaying population and the recipient population all had effects on a state's chosen benefit. Orr concluded that the results were generally supportive of a public choice view of state benefit determination. A number of additional studies were conducted thereafter and a range of price and income elasticities obtained. Ribar and Wilhelm (1999) have surveyed the estimates, and they conclude that price elasticities are of the correct sign but weak in significance and relatively small in magnitude—in the range (–0.14, 0.02)—in contrast to income effects, which are generally significantly positive and somewhat larger in size—in the range (0.11, 0.82). Chernick (1998) also reviews the evidence and argues that the price elasticities of changing the matching rate are somewhat greater than this. Baicker (2001) uses a different estimation strategy and obtains yet higher price elasticities.

A puzzle that has garnered additional attention is the reason for the

---

42. There are a number of issues in using aggregate state median income to proxy the income of the median voter, and also whether median income itself identifies the median preference voter. See Moffitt, Ribar, and Wilhelm (1998) for a discussion.

long-term decline in real AFDC benefits over the 1970s and 1980s. Neither changes in matching rates nor in income can explain the decline; in fact, real income growth should have led to an increase in benefits. Several hypotheses have been suggested, including that AFDC benefits were replaced by food stamp and, possibly, Medicaid benefits in the voter's utility function, or simply that voters' preferences shifted. Shifts in the nature of the caseload, from divorced women to unmarried mothers, has also been posited to be partly responsible for the trend. Others have suggested that the decline in real wages for low-skilled workers led to an increase in the price of redistribution as well as an increase in "distance" from the median voter, both leading to a decline in the desire for redistribution. No consensus has emerged in the literature on the reasons for the change.[43]

5.4   Research on the TANF Program

Research on the TANF program is much smaller in volume than that on AFDC, not only because TANF has been in existence for a shorter period but also because economists and other researchers have encountered many difficulties in studying the program that were not present, at least to the same degree, for the AFDC program. Estimating the overall impact—that is, the combined effect of all individual component changes—of the transition from AFDC to TANF, for example, is hampered by the fact that it was introduced in all states at approximately the same time. This is a traditional problem in studying the effects of national legislation that introduces a program simultaneously in all states and areas.[44] A second problem is that cross-state variation under TANF is much more complex than it was under AFDC, for in the AFDC environment most state programs were of the same general type—because they were required to be so by federal regulation—and hence differences could be characterized by differing levels of only a few simple parameters (the guarantee, tax rate, etc.). Under TANF, each state has freedom under the block grant to develop programs that differ from those in other states in dozens of ways. States have taken advantage of this freedom to tailor their programs individually, with the result that there are more than fifty-one dimensions by which state programs differ, leaving no degrees of freedom to estimate their effects. A related problem is that each dimension is itself quite complex and difficult to measure; for example, the way a simple concept such as time limits is imple-

---

43. See Orr (1979) and Gramlich (1982) for two early contributions, and Moffitt, Ribar, and Wilhelm (1998) for a recent one. See Chernick (1998) for some discussions of the issues and a review of the literature and Moffitt (1999b) for a discussion of the implications of this literature for explaining the 1996 welfare legislation.

44. As will be noted below, some of the pre-TANF AFDC waiver programs discussed in section 5.2 have, however, been used in an attempt to estimate TANF effects. Also, not all states implemented their TANF programs at exactly the same time.

mented can vary tremendously by the number and types of exemptions and extensions granted, whether the state allows the "clock" to stop temporarily for families, and so on. Documentation of these differences across states has also been spotty, at times, and this has also limited research.

In what follows, the discussion will first consider models of behavior under TANF and will then consider evidence on those behaviors as well as any other TANF issues that have been discussed in the literature.

5.4.1 Models

Many of the features of TANF can be understood as variations in parameters that were present in the simple AFDC models discussed earlier, with equivalent predictions. Among these are reductions in welfare tax rates, which, as noted previously, should increase the employment rate of women initially on welfare but which has ambiguous effects on overall labor supply including initial ineligibles.[45] Another is the imposition of family caps, which reduce or eliminate the increase in benefits ordinarily provided by the presence of additional births; this represents a simple change in the relationship of the guarantee level to family size, with expected effects on both welfare participation and the birth rate. A third is the provisions which make minor mothers ineligible for benefits if they live apart from their parents, which, as the living arrangements literature in AFDC makes clear, should be expected to reduce the incidence of such living apart.

There are three new features of TANF whose effects are not directly apparent in the simple AFDC models discussed previously. These are work requirements, time limits, and, to some extent, the increase in general costs of welfare participation through provisions for diversion, numerous requirements for continued participation, and informal pressure on women to leave the welfare rolls. Each of these three will be discussed in turn.

Work requirements can, at one level, be easily incorporated in the standard static labor supply model, for they can be modeled simply as a requirement that a recipient work some minimum number of hours. As illustrated in figure 5.8, where H_{min} is the minimum required work hours, the portion of the welfare constraint CJ is eliminated by the requirement. An individual initially at C (work requirements are aimed at nonworkers) will move either to J (arrow 3) or to segment AK (arrow 2)—increasing labor supply in either case—or to point A (arrow 1), remaining as a nonworker.[46] The caseload and participation rate in welfare both fall, as do expenditures

---

45. Giannarelli and Wiseman (2000) have suggested that the popularity of earnings disregards in the post-TANF period may partly arise from the need to satisfy federal requirements under the TANF program that minimum fractions of the caseload be employed or engaged in a work-like activity. Ironically, the more successful a state is in moving employable recipients off welfare and into jobs, the more likely it is to run afoul of these federal requirements. These create a perverse incentive for states.

46. The latter is more realistic if N is positive.

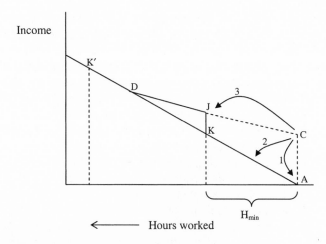

Fig. 5.8   Effect of work requirements on labor supply

on benefits, and average hours of work rise. If H_{min} falls to the left of the hours corresponding to point D, the work requirement is equivalent to eliminating welfare completely. Holding H_{min} fixed, this is more likely in low-guarantee states and has been shown to hold for some recipients in those states with sufficiently high hourly wage rates and using the official hours of work requirements in PRWORA.

Although work requirements achieve the goals of increased labor supply and reduced caseloads, they do so by redefining the underlying goals of the program. Work requirements achieve work incentives by giving up on the original negative income tax goal of achieving work incentives at the same time as providing support to those who "cannot" work in a single, integrated system that provides a guarantee to all families with no questions asked. Welfare programs with work requirements at their center must instead predefine those who can work and those who cannot work; the former are provided with the benefit formula illustrated in figure 5.8, and the latter are simply given G, or possibly G plus a low tax rate as an encouragement to work even a small number of hours. Because making the separation of the population—or categorization—into those who can and cannot work is fraught with practical as well as conceptual problems, the desirability of work requirements depends upon the magnitude of the costs incurred by whatever system of categorization is implemented.

There have been two strands of research on these issues. One dates from the late 1960s and early 1970s, during debates over the negative income tax. Categorical systems were heavily criticized by economists at that time for a variety of reasons. One was that the administrative difficulty in assigning recipients to categories is too great, and, more generally, because economists tend to believe that everyone can work, at least some amount, at some wage and with some kind of work support; that is, the variation in individual ability is continuous rather than discrete. Another was that, because true ability to work is partly unobserved by the policy maker, work requirement systems provide individuals with incentives to switch categories by altering, to the extent possible, the observable characteristics that the government uses to assign recipients to different categories. Yet another was that, because work requirements necessarily involve individual-specific judgments on ability to work, they would result in excessive caseworker discretion and consequent inequitable treatment across individuals.[47]

The second strand of literature examines the possible optimality of work requirements in various models of optimal taxation. An early set of papers demonstrated that, if heterogeneity in preferences and abilities is unobserved by the government, then tying in-kind transfers to cash transfers could be used to induce individuals to self-select into welfare according to need (Blackorby and Donaldson 1988; Dye and Antle 1986; Nichols and Zeckhauser 1982). Work requirements are an inverse case in which the imposition of negative tied transfer—work—along with cash can be used to induce those with higher ability to opt out of the welfare program. Beaudry and Blackorby (1998) and Cuff (2000) make this connection explicit and introduce additional heterogeneities into the model, in both cases demonstrating the optimality of workfare as a screening device when unobservables are present. Besley and Coate (1992b, 1995) showed that, under a different optimization criterion, workfare can be also used as a screening device to ensure that higher-wage individuals do not take advantage of the program. In this rather different justification for work requirements, all recipients must undergo the cost of complying with work requirements, but benefits can be higher because high-wage individuals no longer have an incentive to apply. Another strand of the literature was that begun by Akerlof (1978), who showed that if individuals can be tagged as truly needy, they can be given a greater G and lower t than they could under a noncategorical negative income tax. He likewise directly dealt with the incentive problem to change categories by requiring that an incentive compatibility constraint be set that would discourage such behavior. Although not directly related to work requirements, it is easily extended in that direction. Unlike the prior papers, Akerlof assumes that there are at least some observables that can be used to discriminate between different types of individuals. This literature is continuing with further refinements and special cases.[48]

The 1996 legislation has made these issues of renewed importance. The

47. See Barth and Greenberg (1971), Browning (1975), Lurie (1975) for examples of these early critiques of work-requirement systems as compared to a negative income tax. Barth and Greenberg note that the drawbacks to a system that requires separating the employable and nonemployable was a principle criticism of the AFDC program as it existed in the 1960s.

48. For example, Chone and Laroque (2001) and Immonen et al. (1998). See also Parsons (1996) for an analysis, albeit in the context of social insurance programs, of the consequences for these models of assuming "two-sided" error—that is, that some tagged individuals can indeed work as well as that some untagged individuals cannot work.

PRWORA requires states to more rigorously enforce work requirements by regularly assessing benefit penalties (called "sanctions") on those who do not comply with the requirements (i.e., those who work less than H_{min}). Indeed, to some extent the most important work-related feature in the legislation was the requirement that states, for the first time, actually enforce the benefit reductions that figure 5.8 portrays. Within the federal guidelines, states now have much more freedom to assess sanctions than they did under the AFDC program, and many have adopted very stringent sanction policies.[49] The federal government has also tightened up the definition of H_{min}, setting specific values for it such as twenty hours per week for single mothers with children under six, for example. States are allowed to exempt families from the work requirement (e.g., women who are ill or incapacitated, elderly, pregnant, or have a child under one year old), which can be interpreted as the assignment of families to the "cannot work" status. However, the federal legislation also sets numerical minimums on the fraction of a state's recipients that must be engaged in a work activity and most of these exempt families are not excluded from the denominator of the ratio.

Time limits are a relatively new programmatic feature and have yet to be subjected to much economic analysis. In one sense time limits require no new models because they simply eliminate welfare after some point and this necessarily moves the individual to the nonwelfare constraint in figure 5.5, thereby increasing labor supply and decreasing the welfare caseload. However, the dynamics of this response could be fairly complex if welfare recipients anticipate the onset of time limits and alter their behavior before hitting the limit. For example, similar to behavior that has been found for the response to unemployment benefits with a fixed exhaustion point, welfare recipients may begin to leave welfare prior to the time limit date, and their leaving rates may accelerate as the time limit approaches. In the unemployment insurance (UI) case, this behavior is generally explained by the randomness of wage offers and the desire to accept an attractive offer when it arrives even if it does so somewhat in advance of the benefit exhaustion date. The same may apply for welfare recipients approaching a time limit. A more complex response can occur if recipients "bank" their benefits by going off the rolls during good (labor market) times and saving their benefits for bad times (a downturn in the labor market, unexpected negative income shock, etc.).[50] Whatever the model, time limits will tend to increase labor supply and reduce welfare participation and the caseload.

The implementation of time limits in the states has been far from this

49. For example, as noted previously, in Georgia, two violations result in a lifetime ban on welfare receipt. Lurie (2001, 4), in a study of implementation of sanctions in local welfare offices, notes as well that discretion in using sanctions is widespread and inevitable: "While states decide the amount of the sanctions, the decision to impose or lift a sanction is inevitably at the discretion of the frontline worker."

50. A few states have programs that allow recipients to receive benefits for a maximum of x years out of every y years, $y > x$. This would set up cyclical welfare participation response as well as banking within the y interval.

textbook portrayal. Many states have made liberal use of exemptions and extensions from time limits, resulting in many fewer families' hitting the limits than anticipated. In many cases these exemptions and extensions are granted at the discretion of individual caseworkers and local welfare offices, who make subjective judgments on whether recipients have made a good faith effort to find work. Other states have put in place programs funded out of state revenues that will support families after they exhaust their benefits, although sometimes at a reduced level and sometimes only for the children. Still other states stop the clock from ticking if the recipient works more than a specified number of hours of work, if the recipient has not been offered a job training slot, or under other conditions. At this writing, many fewer families have exhausted their benefits than anticipated for all these reasons as well as because so many families have left the rolls; the latter could be either because of the favorable economy or from banking behavior. However, despite these factors, in the long run the time limit will bind on more families if it is kept in place.

Finally, the numerous additional costs and penalties that have been imposed on welfare participation have resulted in many more involuntary terminations under TANF than were present under AFDC. Indeed, it is no longer clear that a simple voluntary model of welfare participation—even one with work requirements and time limits added to the model—adequately describes reality. Diversion programs and related devices to discourage women who apply for the rules can still be retained in a voluntary model but one in which the cost of application is much higher than before, discouraging application. The cost of being on welfare even after applying and being accepted is also raised by the many rules that TANF recipients must obey, ranging from mandatory attendance at meetings with caseworkers to compliance with child support enforcement, requirements for school attendance (minor TANF mothers without a high degree only), and requirements that children of the TANF mother have regular school attendance, receive immunization shots, or have health exams. Failure to comply with any of these rules carries a penalty that may either reduce benefits or even terminate the families from the rolls. Finally, much anecdotal evidence suggests that welfare departments have exercised discretion to push women off welfare by using administrative devices to end eligibility. These administrative terminations were thought to be present in the AFDC program but are now much more common. This should probably be modeled as a random involuntary termination rate from the program.

5.4.2   Evidence on TANF and Pre-TANF Waiver Reforms

As noted previously, the volume of research on TANF is necessarily much less than that for the AFDC program. In addition, the largest volume of data analysis conducted on TANF is descriptive in nature and does not seek to estimate the effect of the 1996 legislation in a causal sense—that is, the effect of the legislation on outcomes relative to what would have happened if the law had not been passed. The descriptive literature, for example, has demonstrated that poverty rates have mostly fallen since 1996, the TANF caseload has dropped by over 50 percent since 1994, women who have left the TANF rolls have employment rates of approximately 60 percent, and there is a lower tail of the single-mother income distribution whose income has fallen since 1996. Separating the PRWORA contribution to these outcomes from the effects of general trends, the improving economy, and other programmatic developments (e.g., EITC and Medicaid expansions) is not attempted in this literature. The review to follow will instead discuss only studies that attempt to make causal inferences.[51]

Table 5.9 lists the studies that have estimated the overall impact of 1990s welfare reform (i.e., the effect of all the individual components combined) on income, employment, and welfare participation outcomes.[52] Studies of the effects of pre-1996 waiver reforms are shown in the first panel of the table. Most of these studies made use of the differential timing at which states introduced their reforms in the pre-1996 period. With a few exceptions, the studies show waivers to have had positive effects on most measures of labor supply and negative effects on measures of AFDC participation, as expected. All of these studies include variables for the state unemployment rate or related cyclical variables in their models, and hence the estimated effects of welfare reform are all intended to be net of the strong economy.

Two exceptions to the results are Bartik and Eberts (1999) and Ziliak et al. (2000) who find very little effect of welfare reform, net of the economy, on the size of the AFDC caseload. The main difference between these two studies and the others is that these two enter the lagged AFDC caseload into the regression model. The reduction in the estimated size of the effect of welfare reform is an indirect sign that states that implemented reforms had above-average caseloads and that caseloads regressed to the mean thereafter, causing a spuriously estimated decline in the caseload in the studies that omit this lag. A debate has ensued over the econometric properties of including lagged dependent variables in the models in question, which has not yet been resolved.[53]

Randomized trials are represented in two of the entries in table 5.9.

---

51. See Moffitt and Ver Ploeg (2001) for a list of all types of studies that have been conducted on TANF as of approximately spring 2001, including descriptive studies, as well as a comprehensive discussion of the alternative evaluation methodologies that have been used to estimate causal effects of welfare reform.

52. A number of studies are excluded from the table, including those conducted on a single state but which were not random assignment, and a number of random assignment evaluations that were discontinued or that have not produced results (Harvey, Camasso, and Jagannathan 2000 has a comprehensive list).

53. Klerman and Haider (2001) demonstrate that building up an aggregate caseload model from a more fundamental set of entry and exit equations will necessarily result in the need for lags in the aggregate model. However, they argue that the caseload model that results from this aggregation is easily misspecified because of duration dependence and other properties of the underlying dynamic model.

Table 5.9 Studies of the Overall Effect of Welfare Reform on Labor Supply, Earnings, Income, and AFDC-TANF Participation

Study	Program(s) Studied	Dependent Variable	Source of Program Variation	Estimated Effect of Welfare Reform
Pre-1996 Waiver Programs				
Bartik and Eberts (1999)	All state waiver programs	AFDC caseload	Cross-state variation in timing of waiver introduction	Essentially zero
Blank (2001)	All state waiver programs	AFDC caseload	Cross-state variation in timing of waiver introduction	Negative
Bloom and Michalopoulos (2001)	Waiver programs in Connecticut, Florida, and Vermont	Employment, earnings, income, AFDC participation	Randomized assignment on population of AFDC recipients	Positive effect on employment and earnings, no effect on income, small or zero effects on AFDC participation
Council of Economic Advisors (1997)	All state waiver programs	AFDC caseload	Cross-state variation in timing of waiver introduction	Negative
Fein et al. (2001)	Waiver program in Delaware	Employment, earnings, AFDC participation	Randomized assignment on population of AFDC recipients and applicants	After two years, no effect on employment and earnings but negative effect on AFDC participation
Figlio and Ziliak (1999), Ziliak et al. (2000)	All state waiver programs	AFDC caseload	Cross-state variation in timing of waiver introduction	Essentially zero
Moffitt (1999a)	All state waiver programs	AFDC participation rate, labor supply, and earnings of less educated women	Cross-state variation in timing of waiver introduction	No effect on employment or earnings; positive effect on weeks and hours worked; negative effect on AFDC participation rate
Mueser et al. (2000)	Waiver programs in five urban areas	AFDC entry and exit rates, employment rate of welfare leavers	Cross-state variation in timing of waiver introduction	Negative effect on entry rate, positive effect on exit rate, positive but small effect on employment rate of leavers

Study	Program	Outcome	Identification	Result
O'Neill and Hill (2001)	All state waiver programs	Employment, AFDC participation	Cross-state variation in timing of waiver introduction	Positive on employment, negative on AFDC participation
Schoeni and Blank (2000)	All state waiver programs	Labor supply, earnings, income, AFDC participation	Cross-state variation in timing of waiver introduction combined with difference-in-difference using high-educated control group	Positive effects on labor supply, earnings, income; negative effects on AFDC participation
Wallace and Blank (1999)	All state waiver programs	AFDC caseload	Cross-state variation in timing of waiver introduction	Negative
Ziliak et al. (2000)	All state waiver programs	AFDC caseload	Cross-state variation in timing of waiver introduction	Zero (or positive)
TANF				
Council of Economic Advisors (1999)	—	AFDC-TANF caseload	Cross-state variation in timing of TANF implementation	Negative
Ellwood (2000)	—	Employment, earnings	Difference-in-difference with high-wage control group	Cannot separate effect of EITC and welfare reform
McKernan et al. (2000)	—	Employment	Difference-in-difference with childless women control group	Positive
O'Neill and Hill (2001)	—	Employment, AFDC-TANF participation	Cross-state variation in timing of TANF implementation	Positive on employment, negative on AFDC-TANF participation
Schoeni and Blank (2000)	—	Labor supply, earnings, income, AFDC-TANF participation	Difference-in-difference with high-educated control group	No effect on labor supply or individual earnings, positive effect on family earnings and income, negative effect on AFDC-TANF participation
Wallace and Blank (1999)	—	AFDC caseload	1996+ year dummy	Negative

Note: Dashes indicate that program studied is TANF.

These studies made use of traditional random-assignment methods rather than cross-state variation to estimate the effects of reform. These studies generally also find positive effects on employment and earnings and negative effects on welfare participation, like the nonexperimental studies.[54] However, the estimated effects on both income and welfare participation are considerably smaller than those estimated from the nonexperimental literature. This may be because random-assignment methods are not well suited for major structural reforms like the pre-1996 welfare waivers—or for TANF itself—because such structural reforms tend to cause changes in local labor markets and local communities that feed back onto the control group. The policy-induced changes in the economic and programmatic environment, and in the expectations of the eligible population for what level of work is to be required of welfare recipients, are unlikely not to have affected the control group. This is likely to have made control and experimental group behavior more similar and therefore to have biased estimated effects downward. Another important difference between experimental and nonexperimental estimates is that the former cannot capture entry effects, whereas the latter can. Much of the effect of welfare reform on the caseload, and therefore also on labor supply and earnings, has occurred through decreased entry onto welfare. This will also lead to bias in the experimental estimates.

The more important policy issue is the effect of TANF, for the welfare waivers fell far short of the major restructuring that occurred after 1996 and hence cannot be taken as predictive of the effects of TANF. Unfortunately, estimating TANF effects is more difficult than estimating the effects of waivers because the vast majority of the states more or less implemented TANF at the same time, leaving no cross-state variation in the timing of introduction to use for estimation. Two studies made use of the fact that four or five states actually implemented reforms somewhat later than the rest of the states, but this source of variation is unlikely to be reliable because there may have been unique differences between those states and the others which were correlated with their late implementation, and because there are likely to be significant lags in the effects of the reforms. Most studies have, instead, used difference-in-difference methods which compare trends in outcomes for low-wage or less-educated single mothers to trends in outcomes of various other groups (high-wage or highly educated single mothers, or women who are not single mothers) to assess the effect of welfare reform. As Ellwood (2000) and Schoeni and Blank (2000) note, use of these methods is particularly problematic when other reforms, such as the EITC, were occurring roughly simultaneously, and when business-cycle and

---

54. There have been many more random-assignment studies in this period, but those listed in table 5.9 are those that had the main features of PRWORA, namely, time limits, work requirements, sanctions, and enhanced earnings disregards, and that made these reforms within the AFDC system rather than outside of it.

economywide trends were occurring that could affect different groups differently. Ellwood concludes that these difficulties are sufficiently severe that the separate contributions of welfare reform, the EITC, and the economy cannot be identified. The only remaining studies in the table (excluding Wallace and Blank 1999, which uses pure time series variation) are McKernan et al. (2000) and Schoeni and Blank (2000), one of which finds TANF to have increased employment, whereas the other finds it not to have done so but to have affected family earnings, income, and AFDC participation. The two studies used different control groups, so this may be the source of the difference. What evidence there is, therefore, indicates some TANF effects in the expected direction, but the small number of studies and problems in statistical inference make the conclusions rather uncertain.

There have also been a number of studies that have attempted to estimate the separate effects of different components of pre-1996 waiver reforms or of TANF, such as time limits, work requirements, sanctions, earnings disregards, and other features. Unfortunately, the results from these studies have been inconsistent with each other (often providing opposite-signed effects) have generated many insignificant effects, and have generally yielded an uninterpretable set of findings.[55] There are many likely reasons for this pattern, including the enormous proliferation of different policies across the states and the difficulty in accurately characterizing those differences with a few simple variables; inherent difficulty in separating the effects of one component from another when they no doubt strongly interact; differences in the official characterization of policies from those implemented in practice; and lack of statistical power in the data to detect reasonable-sized effects. For whatever reason, despite the initial view that the devolution that would follow PRWORA would generate useful cross-state variation in policies for research, very little progress has been made in that direction to date.[56]

There has been some research as well on the impact of pre-1996 waivers and TANF on demographic outcomes such as marriage, fertility, and living arrangements. The direction of impact of reform on marriage and fertility is ambiguous at the simplest level, for although a reduction in the caseload and generosity of a program that mainly supports one-parent families should have positive effects on marriage and negative effects on childbearing, an increase in women's employment should have the opposite effects, as demonstrated by a large empirical literature on the effect of

55. See Bell (2001) for a discussion of the results with caseloads as a dependent variable.

56. In addition, with a few exceptions, there have been no random-assignment evaluations that have varied each feature of reform individually while holding all the other features fixed, even though this is possible in principle in an experiment. It should also be noted that Grogger (2000, 2001) has attempted to estimate the independent effects of time limits by using age variation in children combined with assumptions that that variation does not interact identically with other welfare reform features. The validity of the assumptions needed for these methods to be valid is unknown.

female wages and labor supply on marriage and fertility. In addition to these broad factors, TANF allows states to impose family caps (restrictions on additional benefits from extra births while on welfare) and denies benefits to minor mothers who wish to live apart from their families, both of which should be expected to have direct effects on family structure.

The evidence to date on the presence of an effect of welfare reform as a whole on these outcomes is suggestive of a weak effect, at best. Analyses of pre-1996 waivers are inconsistent, with some showing a negative effect on nonmarital fertility (Horvath and Peters 1999) and others showing no effect (Fitzgerald and Ribar 2001). Analyses of TANF using difference-in-difference methods, comparing either more-educated and less-educated women or high-wage and low-wage women, show no effect of TANF on marriage but possibly a negative effect on living independently (Ellwood 2000; Schoeni and Blank 2000). Bitler, Gelbach, and Hoynes (2002) found a positive effect of TANF on the likelihood that a child lives with neither parent and a negative effect on the probability of living with an unmarried parent, but the effects were estimated only on cross-state variation in TANF implementation dates within a fourteen-month window. Random-assignment evaluations are particularly problematic for the study of family structure because of the entry-effect problem and the problems of contamination noted earlier. Of those noted in table 5.9, only one (the Delaware study) showed a significant effect on marriage. The reason that particular experiment showed an effect and others did not is not clear.

The evidence on the specific effects of family caps and living arrangements restrictions in the law is quite weak, for the same reason that separating the impacts of the individual components of welfare reform from each other has not been successful in the study of employment and earnings impacts. Some waiver evaluations, particularly one conducted in New Jersey (Camasso et al. 1998a, b), have been used to assess the effects of family caps, but these evaluations are problematic because the family cap was bundled in with changes in work requirements, earnings disregards, and other features common in welfare waiver programs. Thus there is no direct evidence from random-assignment evaluations of family cap effects because none has varied the presence of the family cap, holding other reform features fixed.

Finally, there has been considerable analysis of the effect of the block grant structure of TANF on spending on the poor. As noted previously, the shift from a matching to a block grant should be expected to reduce spending. Predictions of the magnitude of the spending decline depend directly on the size of the price elasticity of benefits, which, as noted before, is not agreed upon in the empirical literature. Ribar and Wilhelm (1999) predict very small reductions, whereas Chernick (1998) predicts benefit declines in the range of 15 to 30 percent (see also Chernick and McGuire 1999); Inman and Rubinfeld (1997) predict spending declines of 40 to 66 percent in low-income states and 0 to 18 percent in high-income states. In addition, there has been considerable speculation that there will be a "race to the bottom," as states facing a higher price of benefits become more sensitive to the influence of cross-state migration in search of higher benefits, leading to a cascading series of real benefit cuts across the states. Theoretical work supports this intuitive prediction, and simulations suggest that benefits could be seriously underproduced in such a system relative to the social optimum (Brueckner 2000; Wheaton 2000).

To date, none of these predictions have been capable of testing because the block grant levels in the 1996 legislation were set at 1994 AFDC levels. Because the AFDC-TANF caseload has fallen so drastically since 1994, states have generally not been able to spend all of their block grant funds. Thus the block grant constraint has not become binding, and hence one should not expect either the (extra) spending declines or the race to the bottom predicted in the literature to have occurred. Further work on this issue must await a rise in spending up to the block grant level.[57]

5.5 Reforms: Financial Incentives

Most reform discussions at the current point in the evolution of the AFDC-TANF program concern whether the provisions of the 1996 welfare law should be modified in some way, such as changing or removing the time limits, work requirements, rules governing sanctions, block grant and funding formulas, and the like. There has been no research on the effects of altering these provisions beyond what has already been discussed in the review of research on AFDC and TANF; as noted, the research base for forecasting the effects of altering most of these provisions is exceedingly slim.

One area of discussion where economists have a strong research base is in the area of additional financial incentives to encourage TANF recipients to work, which is the traditional area of interest in the economics literature. Three different types of reforms have been discussed: (a) reductions in the tax rate on earnings in the TANF program (or what are called "enhanced earnings disregards" in policy discussions); (b) earnings or wage subsidies made available only to those on TANF; and (c) earnings or wage subsidies made available universally to the low-income population. Each will be discussed in turn.

Reductions in the tax rate on earnings have been enacted by many states

---

57. In fact, TANF spending by the states stopped declining in 1998 and has risen since then, even though the economy was still strong, because states began spending their funds on ancillary services like child care. If this trend continues, it is likely that a relatively modest recession could force spending up to the block grant level. Other issues debated in the literature are the adequacy of countercyclical funds to alleviate the potential spending volatility under a block grant system, and how to reduce inequities in the block grants to high- and low-income states.

in their post-reform benefit schedules, as noted earlier in this review, as a means to encourage work among recipients in addition to work requirements. Economic models predict that the effect of reducing welfare tax rates on labor supply is ambiguous in sign because new recipients are drawn onto the welfare rolls, whose labor supply is thereby reduced. The majority of the evidence, both from nonexperimental and negative income tax (NIT) experimental studies, indicates that the net effect of such reductions on labor supply is approximately zero. This should, therefore, be the prediction one should make for the recent tax rate reductions enacted by the states.

A few recent experiments have addressed the labor supply effects of reduced welfare tax rates and have shown, instead, that they generally increase earnings and employment (Berlin 2000; Blank, Card, and Robins 2000). However, the majority of these experiments only test the effects of reduced tax rates on those who are initially on welfare, and, for that group, positive effects on labor supply should occur. Consequently, although the experimental results are of value because they confirm, in broad outlines, the predictions of the static labor supply model for how initial recipients would respond, they do not contradict the literature from prior econometric studies and the NIT experiments because they do not account for the offsetting labor supply effects of new entry.[58]

A new element in recent discussions, however, is an emphasis on coupling work requirements and minimum hours restrictions with tax rate reductions. The argument is that the work requirement limits the negative labor supply effects that serve as an offset to the work incentives of tax rate reductions and is thus superior to welfare programs with tax rate reductions but no work requirements, and that tax rate reductions accompanied by such restrictions are more likely to increase labor supply.[59] However, this

58. See Blank, Card, and Robins (2000) for a discussion of entry and how it might be reduced by imposing barriers such as a waiting period before the financial incentives are allowed (see also Card, Robins, and Lin 1998). Berlin (2000, 35) also draws a contrast between the findings of these recent experiments and those of the NIT experiments, noting that the NIT reduced labor supply whereas the tax rate reductions in the new experiments increased labor supply. However, this is not a proper comparison because the negative labor supply effects in the NIT experiments pertained to the effect of an NIT versus nothing at all (i.e., the treatment–control group comparison), which is expected to be negative from simple theory. In fact, as noted previously, the alternative treatment groups in the NIT experiments that tested alternative welfare tax rates holding the guarantee fixed found generally a zero net effect on labor supply, consistent with the findings of complete offset in nonexperimental econometric models. The NIT experiments included not just recipients but rather a sample of the entire low-income population, so that the offsetting, negative effects of lowering the tax rate were captured by the comparison of outcomes across alternative treatment groups. This is entirely consistent with a positive effect on labor supply of those initially on welfare, and therefore the results of the NIT experiments and recent recipient-only experiments are not inconsistent.

59. Again, see Berlin (2000) and Blank, Card, and Robins (2000) for a discussion of these programs, such as New Hope and the SSP program. Some of the programs tested in these demonstrations allowed recipients to take their "earnings supplements" (i.e., benefits) off welfare. However, in the type of pure transfer program illustrated in figure 5.8, it is immaterial whether individuals receiving benefits in the region above point K are called welfare recipients or not; they are incontrovertibly welfare recipients in the behavioral sense.

is an incorrect comparison because, as discussed previously, work requirements achieve their positive effects on labor supply by eliminating government support for those who do not work, which is the rationale for an income support program in the first place. Consequently, they must be accompanied by a categorization of the population into those who can and cannot work. The relative merits of the two approaches depend on whether the stronger labor supply effects provided by the work requirement system are countered by the inefficiencies, disincentives, and possible inequities created by a feasible categorization system.

Some programs with such minimum full-time work conditions have been voluntary instead of mandatory (e.g., New Hope, Self-Sufficiency Program [SSP], and some treatments in the Minnesota Family Investment Program [MFIP]). That is, the greater benefits made possible by the reduction in the tax rate, and which are available only if hours worked are close to full time, are simply offered to the recipient as an option. Such a program is not a work requirement program at all but is instead just an NIT with part of the budget constraint deleted (namely, the portion in the part-time range). Relative to an NIT with no hours restrictions, a voluntary program of this type would affect labor supply in an ambiguous direction, as some who would have worked part time chose to work full time but some chose not to work at all. Relative to a program with a tax rate of 100 percent, however, such a restricted tax reduction is indeed more likely to increase labor supply than an unrestricted NIT. But that does not mean that it is preferable, because then the issue is why part-time work is not desirable and why the benefits of work supplements should be denied to those who can only work part-time, some of whom will instead choose not to work at all.[60]

The second type of program, offering wage or earnings subsidies to welfare recipients instead of reducing welfare tax rates, has essentially the same effect if those subsidies are permitted only for those who remain on welfare. It is immaterial whether an increase in $W(1 - t)$ comes from an increase in W or a reduction in t.[61] The major alternative proposal is instead that welfare recipients be allowed to carry those subsidies off the welfare rolls and to keep them after exiting. The effect of this reform on the budget

60. This illustrates the more general principle that increases in labor supply should not be the sole criterion for judging a reform because it must always take into account how the relative benefits of program expenditure are spread across individuals at different points on the budget constraint and therefore different points in the income distribution. For example, it should always be possible in principle to increase labor supply simply by offering the population a large increase in income to anyone willing and able to work high enough hours; that is incontrovertible. But that costs money, and the proper comparison for such a program is instead with an equal-expenditure program which would therefore have to reduce funds going to low-hours workers. The issue of distributional weights, and the relevant optimal tax problem, cannot be avoided.

61. The two may have different effects around the break-even level, however depending on how the phaseout and cutoff of the earnings or subsidy are handled. A simple graphical analysis easily demonstrates this (not shown for brevity).

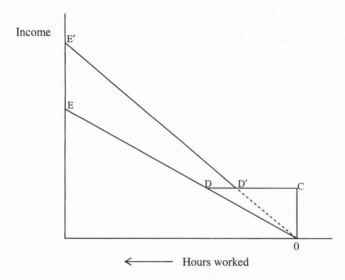

Fig. 5.9   Effect of earnings subsidy on budget constraint

constraint is shown in figure 5.9, where CDE is the initial constraint and CD'E' is the constraint after the subsidy is implemented.[62] Assuming that substitution effects dominate income effects and therefore that labor supply curves for this population group are forward-bending, this change has an unambiguously positive effect on labor supply relative to the initial welfare program for those initially on the welfare portion of the constraint. The drawbacks to such subsidies are the same as those for a universal wage or earnings subsidy, to be considered next.

It is worth noting that this type of program would approach that of a universal subsidy program if (a) those who carry the subsidy off the program are allowed to keep it indefinitely and (b) all eligibles in the population have a finite probability of entering the program within their lifetimes. If both of these conditions hold, all eligibles, including those initially on segment DE, will eventually cycle through the program and hence will have the subsidy available to them off welfare.

The third reform is indeed the offer of a universal earnings or wage subsidy to all low-income families. Graphically, this is identical to figure 5.9 except that those initially off welfare, on segment DE, are also eligible. The relative merits of wage rate and earnings subsidies, on the one hand, and

62. Assuming the subsidy is s percent of earnings, the on-welfare portion of the constraint, segment CD', has slope $W(1 + s)(1 - t)$, while the off-welfare portion of the constraint, segment D'E', has slope $W(1 + s)$. This assumes that the subsidy is included in countable income by the welfare agency along with presubsidy earnings; if it does not, the on-welfare portion of the constraint has slope $W(1 - t + s)$. The figure assumes $t = 1.0$, but all statements in the text apply as well for $t < 1$.

an NIT or similar income support program with a G and t, on the other, were debated extensively in the late 1960s and early 1970s (e.g., Barth and Greenberg 1971; Garfinkel 1973; Kesselman 1969, 1973; Zeckhauser 1971). That literature showed that there will almost certainly be positive effects on labor supply if an income support program is completely replaced by a wage or earnings subsidy. This should not be surprising since benefits are no longer paid to nonworkers under a wage or earnings subsidy, and since, from a equity and distributional point of view, a progressive tax system is replaced by a regressive one. As this early literature recognized (Kesselman 1969; Barth and Greenberg 1971), and has been noted in this review, replacing an income support program with such a subsidy would require a categorization of the eligible population that has its own difficulties which would have to be factored into the comparison.

The literature also addressed the relative merits of wage rate versus earnings subsidies. In general, the former were shown to be superior but were acknowledged to have implementation problems created by the need for employers and workers to document hours of work, and the strong incentives for fraudulent reporting of those hours and for collusion between workers and employers to overreport hours worked. To date, these difficulties have prevented a wage rate subsidy from being enacted in the United States. Earnings subsidies, on the other hand, have the disadvantage that they must be phased out at some earnings level; at and above that point, labor supply disincentives are created.[63] The corresponding issue for welfare reform is how eligibility for a universal earnings or wage subsidy program aimed at the welfare-eligible population would be determined. If family income is used as the eligibility criterion, then a notch will be created at that income level where the subsidy is lost, creating disincentives to go beyond that point as well as incentives for those with higher income to reduce labor supply to become eligible. Alternatively, if the subsidy is phased out gradually, as it is in earnings subsidies such as the EITC, then work disincentives will be created in that region, which will have to be counted against the positive labor supply incentives created at lower earnings levels. Thus the offsetting effects of earnings subsidies on labor supply cannot be avoided.[64]

---

63. See the chapter on the EITC (Hotz and Scholz, chap. 3 in this volume) for a discussion.

64. Once again, an alternative program offers universal earnings subsidies to low-income families but with a minimum hours constraint. As before, the increased labor supply effects of this program would have to be balanced by the increased need for categorization of the population, at least if it were made mandatory. If it is made voluntary, then, as noted previously, the only issue is whether part-time work should not also be subsidized. It should also be noted that, with a mandatory minimum hours constraint, there is little difference between a wage or earnings subsidy program and an NIT-like income support program with a reduced tax rate, for the two only differ in the nature of the budget constraint above the hours constraint point. If the major labor supply decision is the margin between working at the constraint point or locating below it off welfare, the two programs would have the same effects.

5.6 Summary

Although the 1996 legislation is now six years past, the TANF program must still be regarded as being in a state of transition and not as having fully coalesced into a final form. The implementation of the program, as well as myriad of its provisions, such as the imposition of stricter work requirements with more rigorously enforced sanctions for noncompliance and the imposition of time limits, continues to evolve. States are continuing to modify their programs and attempt to change them over time, as they search for new ways to deal with the difficulties of the population that they aim to serve. The uncertainties created by a possible recession, the increasing impact of time limits as more recipients hit those limits over the next few years, and the possibility of further congressional action, all have the potential to lead to further modifications in the program.

While research on the AFDC program is still useful in many ways, and while the models developed for that program are still applicable to TANF, there are many new features of TANF whose effects cannot be easily extrapolated from AFDC research results. At the same time, direct evaluation of the effects of the TANF program, particularly the evaluation of the independent contributions of its separate individual components, poses many empirical challenges. Although the evidence to date is reasonably strong that the TANF program has increased employment and earnings and decreased the caseload, relative to what would have occurred if AFDC had remained in place, the separate effects of work requirements, time limits, sanctions, family caps, and other individual features are essentially unknown. These continuing research challenges, as well as those posed by additional modifications in the TANF program as they occur, will provide a rich agenda for further research.

References

Aaron, H. 1973. *Why is welfare so hard to reform?* Washington, D.C.: Brookings Institution.

Akerlof, G. 1978. The economics of "tagging" as applied to the optimal income tax, welfare programs, and manpower planning. *American Economic Review* 68 (March): 8–19.

Alm, J., S. Dickert-Conlin, and L. Whittington. 1999. Policy watch: The marriage penalty. *Journal of Economic Perspectives* 13 (Summer): 193–204.

Baicker, K. 2001. Extensive or intensive generosity? The price and income effects of federal grants. NBER Working Paper no. 8384. Cambridge, Mass.: National Bureau of Economic Research, July.

Bane, M. J., and D. Ellwood. 1983. The dynamics of dependence: The routes to self-sufficiency. Cambridge, Mass.: Urban Systems Research and Engineering, Inc.

————. 1994. Understanding welfare dynamics. In *Welfare realities: From rhetoric to reform,* ed. M. J. Bane and D. Ellwood, 119–57. Cambridge: Harvard University Press.

Barth, M., and D. Greenberg. 1971. Incentive effects of some pure and mixed transfer systems. *Journal of Human Resources* 6 (Spring): 149–70.

Bartik, T., and R. Eberts. 1999. Examining the effect of industry trends and structure on welfare caseloads. In *Economic conditions and welfare reform,* ed. S. Danziger, 119–57. Kalamazoo, Mich.: Upjohn Institute.

Beaudry, P., and C. Blackorby. 1998. Taxes and employment subsidies in optimal redistribution programs. NBER Working Paper no. 6355. Cambridge, Mass.: National Bureau of Economic Research.

Bell, S. 2001. Why are caseloads falling? Discussion Paper no. 01-02. Washington, D.C.: The Urban Institute.

Berlin, G. 2000. Encouraging work, reducing poverty: The impact of work incentive programs. New York: Manpower Demonstration Research Program.

Besley, T., and S. Coate. 1992a. Understanding welfare stigma: Taxpayer resentment and statistical discrimination. *Journal of Public Economics* 48 (July): 165–63.

————. 1992b. Workfare versus welfare: Incentive arguments for work requirements in poverty-alleviation programs. *American Economic Review* 82 (March): 249–61.

————. 1995. The design of income maintenance programmes. *Review of Economic Studies* 62 (April): 187–221.

Bitler, M., J. Gelbach, and H. Hoynes. 2002. The impact of welfare reform on living arrangements. NBER Working Paper no. 8784. Cambridge, Mass.: National Bureau of Economic Research.

Blackorby, C., and D. Donaldson. 1988. Cash versus kind, self-selection, and efficient transfers. *American Economic Review* 78 (September): 691–700.

Blank, R. 2001. What causes public assistance caseloads to grow? *Journal of Human Resources* 36 (Winter): 85–118.

Blank, R., D. Card, and P. Robins. 2000. Financial incentives for increasing work and income among low-income families. In *Finding jobs: Work and welfare reform,* ed. D. Card and R. Blank, 373–419. New York: Russell Sage Foundation.

Blank, R., and P. Ruggles. 1994. Short-term recidivism among public assistance recipients. *American Economic Review* 84 (May): 49–53.

————. 1996. When do women use Aid to Families with Dependent Children and food stamps? *Journal of Human Resources* 31 (Winter): 57–89.

Blau, F., L. Kahn, and J. Waldfogel. 2000. Understanding young women's marriage decisions: The role of labor and marriage market conditions. *Industrial and Labor Relations Review* 53 (July): 624–47.

Bloom, D., and C. Michalopoulos. 2001. How welfare and work policies affect employment and income: A synthesis of research. New York: Manpower Demonstration Research Corporation.

Browning, E. 1975. *Redistribution and the welfare system.* Washington, D.C.: American Enterprise Institute.

Brueckner, J. 2000. Welfare reform and the race to the bottom: Theory and evidence. *Southern Economic Journal* 66 (January): 505–25.

Burke, V. 1996. New welfare law: Comparison of the New Block Grant Program with Aid to Families with Dependent Children. Report no. 96-720EPW. Washington, D.C.: Congressional Research Service.

Burtless, G. 1995a. Employment prospects for welfare recipients. In *The work alternative: Welfare reform and the realities of the job market,* ed. D. S. Nightingale and R. Haveman, 71–106. Washington, D.C.: Urban Institute.

————. 1995b. What is the proper balance among various types of welfare-to-work programs? In *Looking before we leap: Social science and welfare reform,* ed. R. Weaver and W. Dickens, 52–57. Washington, D.C.: Brookings Institution.

Camasso, M., C. Harvey, R. Jagannathan, and M. Killingsworth. 1998a. A final report on the impact of New Jersey's Family Development Program: Experimental-control analysis. New Brunswick: Rutgers University School of Social Work.

————. 1998b. A final report on the impact of New Jersey's Family Development Program: Results from a pre-post analysis of AFDC case heads from 1990–1996. New Brunswick: Rutgers University School of Social Work.

Card, D., P. Robins, and W. Lin. 1998. Would financial incentives for leaving welfare lead some people to stay on welfare longer? An experimental evaluation of "entry effects" in the self-sufficiency project. NBER Working Paper no. 6449. Cambridge, Mass.: National Bureau of Economic Research.

Chernick, H. 1998. Fiscal effects of block grants to the needy: An interpretation of the evidence. *International Tax and Public Finance* 5:205–33.

Chernick, H., and T. McGuire. 1999. The states, welfare reform, and the business cycle. In *Economic conditions and welfare reform,* ed. S. Danziger, 275–303. Kalamazoo, Mich.: Upjohn Institute.

Chone, P., and G. Laroque. 2001. Optimal incentives for labor force participation. INSÉÉ Working Paper no. 2001-25. Paris: Institut National de la Statistique et des Études Économiques.

Council of Economic Advisors. 1997. Explaining the decline in welfare receipt, 1993–1996. Washington, D.C.: Council of Economic Advisors.

————. 1999. The effects of welfare policy and the economic expansion on welfare caseloads: An update. Washington, D.C.: Council of Economic Advisors.

Cuff, K. 2000. Optimality of workfare with heterogeneous preferences. *Canadian Journal of Economics* 33 (February): 149–74.

Danziger, S., R. Haveman, and R. Plotnick. 1981. How income transfers affect work, savings, and the income distribution. *Journal of Economic Literature* 19 (September): 975–1028.

Devere, C., G. Falk, and V. Burke. 2000. Welfare reform research: What have we learned since the Family Support Act of 1988? Washington, D.C.: Congressional Research Service.

Dye, R., and R. Antle. 1976. Cost-minimizing welfare programs. *Journal of Public Economics* 30 (July): 259–65.

Ellwood, D. 1986. Targeting the would-be long-term recipient: Who should be served. Princeton, N.J.: Mathematica Policy Research.

————. 2000. The impact of the Earned Income Tax Credit and social policy reforms on work, marriage, and living arrangements. *National Tax Journal* 53, pt. 2 (December): 1063–105.

Ellwood, D., and M. J. Bane. 1985. The impact of AFDC on family structure and living arrangements. In *Research in labor economics,* vol. 7, ed. R. Ehrenberg, Greenwich: JAI Press.

Evenhouse, E., and S. Reilly. 1999. Pop-swapping? Welfare and children's living arrangements. Vanderbilt University, Department of Economics. Mimeograph.

Fein, D., D. Long, J. Behrens, and W. Lee. 2001. The ABC evaluation: Turning the corner: Delaware's a better chance welfare reform program at four years. Cambridge: Abt Associates.

Figlio, D., and J. Ziliak. 1999. Welfare reform, the business cycle, and the decline in AFDC caseloads. In *Economic conditions and welfare reform,* ed. S. Danziger, 17–48. Kalamazoo, Mich.: Upjohn Institute.

Fitzgerald, J. 1995. Local labor markets and local area effects on welfare duration. *Journal of Policy Analysis and Management* 14 (Winter): 43–67.

Fitzgerald, J., and D. Ribar. 2001. The impact of welfare waivers on female headship decisions. George Washington University, Department of Economics. Mimeograph.

Foster, E. M., and S. Hoffman. 2001. The young and the not quite so young: Age variation in the impact of AFDC benefits on nonmarital childbearing. In *Out of wedlock: Causes and consequences of nonmarital childbearing,* ed. L. Wu and B. Wolfe, 173–201. New York: Russell Sage Foundation.

Fraker, T., R. Moffitt, and D. Wolf. 1985. Effective tax rates and guarantees in the AFDC program, 1967–1982. *Journal of Human Resources* 20 (Spring): 251–63.

Freedman, S. 2000. Four-year impacts of ten programs on employment stability and earnings growth. New York: Manpower Demonstration Research Corporation.

Friedlander, D., and G. Burtless. 1995. *Five years after: The long-term effects of welfare-to-work programs.* New York: Russell Sage Foundation.

Friedman, M. 1962. *Capitalism and freedom.* Chicago: University of Chicago Press.

Gallagher, L. J., M. Gallagher, K. Perese, S. Schreiber, and K. Watson. 1998. *One year after federal welfare reform: A description of state Temporary Assistance for Needy Families (TANF) decisions as of October 1997.* Washington, D.C.: Urban Institute.

Garfinkel, I. 1973. A skeptical note on "the optimality" of wage subsidy programs. *American Economic Review* 63 (June): 447–53.

Garfinkel, I., and S. McLanahan. 1986. *Single mothers and their children.* Washington, D.C.: Urban Institute Press.

Giannarelli, L., and M. Wiseman. 2000. The working poor and the benefit door. Washington, D.C.: Urban Institute.

Gottschalk, P., and R. Moffitt. 1994. Welfare dependence: Concepts, measures, and trends. *American Economic Review* 84 (May): 38–42.

Gramlich, E. 1982. An econometric examination of the new federalism. *Brookings Papers on Economic Activity,* Issue no. 2:327–70. Washington, D.C.: Brookings Institution.

Greenberg, D., R. Meyer, C. Michalopoulos, and M. Wiseman. 2001. Explaining variation in the effects of welfare-to-work programs. Discussion Paper no. 1225-01. Madison, Wis.: Institute for Research on Poverty.

Grogger, J. 2000. Time limits and welfare use. NBER Working Paper no. 7709. Cambridge, Mass.: National Bureau of Economic Research.

———. 2001. The effects of time limits and other policy changes on welfare use, work, and income among female-headed families. NBER Working Paper no. 8153. Cambridge, Mass.: National Bureau of Economic Research.

Gueron, J., and M. Pauly. 1991. *From welfare to work.* New York: Russell Sage.

Harris, K. 1993. Work and welfare among single mothers in poverty. *American Journal of Sociology* 99 (September): 317–52.

———. 1996. Life after welfare: Women, work, and repeat dependency. *American Sociological Review* 61 (June): 407–26.

Harvey, C., M. Camasso, and R. Jagannathan. 2000. Welfare reform evaluation under section 1115. *Journal of Economic Perspectives* 14 (fall): 165–88.

Hoffman, S., and E. M. Foster. 2000. AFDC benefits and nonmarital births to young women. *Journal of Human Resources* 35 (spring): 376–91.

Horvath, A., and H. Peters. 1999. Welfare waivers and non-marital childbearing. Cornell University, Department of Policy Analysis and Management. Mimeograph.

Hotz, V. J., G. Imbens, and J. Klerman. 2000. The long-term gains from GAIN: A re-analysis of the impacts of the California GAIN Program. NBER Working Paper no. 8007. Cambridge, Mass.: National Bureau of Economic Research.

Hoynes, H. 1996. Welfare transfers in two-parent families: Labor supply and welfare participation under AFDC-UP. *Econometrica* 64 (March): 295–332.

———. 1997. Work, welfare, and family structure: What have we learned? In *Fiscal policy: Lessons from economic research,* ed. A. Auerbach, 101–46. Cambridge: MIT Press.

———. 2000. Local labor markets and welfare spells: Do demand conditions matter? *Review of Economics and Statistics* 82 (August): 351–68.

Hoynes, H., and T. MaCurdy. 1994. Has the decline in benefits shortened welfare spells? *American Economic Review* 84 (May): 43–48.

Hu, W. 2001. Welfare and family stability. *Journal of Human Resources* 36 (spring): 274–303.

Hubbard, G., J. Skinner, and S. Zeldes. 1995. Precautionary saving and social insurance. *Journal of Political Economy* 103 (April): 360–99.

Hutchens, R., G. Jakubson, and S. Schwartz. 1989. AFDC and the formation of subfamilies. *Journal of Human Resources* 24 (fall): 599–628.

Immonen, R., R. Kanbur, M. Keen, and M. Tuomala. 1998. Tagging and taxing: The optimal use of categorical and income information in designing tax/transfer schemes. *Economica* 65 (May): 179–92.

Inman, R., and D. Rubinfeld. 1997. Rethinking federalism. *Journal of Economic Perspectives* 11 (fall): 43–64.

Keane, M., and R. Moffitt. 1998. A structural model of multiple welfare program participation and labor supply. *International Economic Review* 39 (August): 553–89.

Kesselman, J. R. 1969. Labor-supply effects of income, income-work, and wage subsidies. *Journal of Human Resources* 4 (summer): 275–92.

———. 1973. Incentive effects of transfer systems once again. *Journal of Human Resources* 8 (winter): 119–29.

———. 1976. Tax effects on job search, training, and work effort. *Journal of Public Economics* 6 (October): 255–72.

Ketron, Inc. 1980. The long-term impact of WIN II: A longitudinal evaluation of the employment experiences of participants in the Work Incentive Program. Report to the Employment and Training Administration, U.S. Department of Labor. Wayne, Penn: Ketron, Inc.

Klerman, J., and S. Haider. 2001. A stock-flow analysis of the welfare caseload. Santa Monica, Calif.: RAND Corporation.

Lampman, R. 1968. Expanding the American system of transfers to do more for the poor. U.S. Congress, Joint Economic Committee. Washington, D.C.: Government Printing Office.

Lindbeck, A., S. Nyberg, and J. Weibull. 1999. Social norms, the welfare state, and voting. *Quarterly Journal of Economics* 114 (February): 1–35.

Lurie, I., ed. 1975. *Integrating income maintenance programs.* New York: Academic Press.

———. 2001. Changing welfare offices. Policy Brief no. 9. Washington, D.C.: Brookings Institution.

McKernan, S. M., R. Lerman, N. Pindus, and J. Valente. 2000. The relationship between metropolitan and non-metropolitan locations, changing welfare policies, and the employment of single mothers. Washington, D.C.: Urban Institute. Mimeograph.

McKinnish, T., S. Sanders, and J. Smith. 1999. Estimates of effective guarantees and tax rates in the AFDC Program for the post-OBRA period. *Journal of Human Resources* 34 (spring): 312–45.

Meyer, B., and D. Rosenbaum. 2001. Welfare, the Earned Income Tax Credit, and the labor supply of single mothers. *Quarterly Journal of Economics* 116 (August): 1063–114.

Miller, R., and S. Sanders. 1997. Human capital development and welfare participation. *Carnegie-Rochester Conference Series on Public Policy* 46 (June): 1–43.

Moffitt, R. 1983. An economic model of welfare stigma. *American Economic Review* 73 (December): 1023–35.

———. 1992a. Evaluation methods for program entry effects. In *Evaluating welfare and training programs,* ed. C. Manski and I. Garfinkel, 231–52. Cambridge: Harvard University Press.

———. 1992b. Incentive effects of the U.S. welfare system: A review. *Journal of Economic Literature* 30 (March): 1–61.

———. 1996. The effect of employment and training programs on entry and exit from the welfare caseload. *Journal of Policy Analysis and Management* 15 (winter): 32–50.

———. 1998. The effect of welfare on marriage and fertility. In *Welfare, the family, and reproductive behavior,* ed. R. Moffitt, 50–97. Washington, D.C.: National Academy Press.

———. 1999a. The effect of pre-PRWORA waivers on AFDC caseloads and female earnings, income, and labor force behavior. In *Economic conditions and welfare reform,* ed. S. Danziger, 91–118. Kalamazoo: Upjohn Institute.

———. 1999b. Explaining welfare reform: Public choice and the labor market. *International Tax and Public Finance* 6:289–316.

———. 2000. Welfare benefits and female headship in U.S. time series. *American Economic Review* 90 (May): 373–77.

———. 2001. Demographic change and public assistance expenditures. In *Demographic change and fiscal policy,* ed. A. Auerbach and R. Lee, 391–425. Cambridge: Cambridge University Press.

———. 2002. Experienced-based measures of heterogeneity in the welfare caseload. In *Data collection and research issues for studies of welfare populations,* ed. C. Citro, R. Moffitt, and S. Ver Ploeg, 473–99. Washington, D.C.: National Academy Press.

Moffitt, R., A. Cherlin, L. Burton, and L. Chase-Lansdale. 2001. Disadvantage among families remaining on welfare. Paper prepared for the Chicago-Northwestern Joint Center for Poverty Research.

Moffitt, R., R. Reville, and A. Winkler. 1994. State AFDC rules regarding the treatment of cohabitors: 1993. *Social Security Bulletin* 57 (Winter): 26–33.

———. 1998. Beyond single mothers: Cohabitation and marriage in the AFDC program. *Demography* 35 (August): 259–78.

Moffitt, R., D. Ribar, and M. Wilhelm. 1998. The decline of welfare benefits in the U.S.: The role of wage inequality. *Journal of Public Economics* 68 (June): 421–52.

Moffitt, R., and D. Stevens. 2001. Changing caseloads: Macro influences and micro composition. *New York Federal Reserve Bank Economic Policy Review* 7 (September): 37–49.

Moffitt, R., and S. Ver Ploeg, eds. 2001. *Evaluating welfare reform in an era of transition.* Washington, D.C.: National Academy Press.

Mueser, P., J. Hotchkiss, C. King, P. Rokicki, and D. Stevens. 2000. The welfare caseload, economic growth and welfare-to-work policies: An analysis of five urban areas. University of Missouri, Department of Economics. Mimeograph.

Murray, C. 1984. *Losing ground.* New York: Basic Books.

Nechyba, T. 2001. Social approval, values, and AFDC: A re-examination of the illegitimacy debate. *Journal of Political Economy* 109 (June): 637–72.

Nichols, A., and R. Zeckhauser. 1982. Targeting transfers through restrictions on recipients. *American Economic Review* 72 (May): 372–77.

Oellerich, D. 2001. Welfare reform: Program entrants and recipients. Washington, D.C.: Office of the Assistant Secretary for Planning and Evaluation, Department of Health and Human Services. Mimeograph.

O'Neill, J., and M. A. Hill. 2001. Gaining ground? Measuring the impact of welfare reform on welfare and work. New York: Manhattan Institute.

O'Neill, D., and J. O'Neill. 1997. *Lessons for welfare reform: An analysis of the AFDC caseload and past welfare-to-work programs.* Kalamazoo, Mich.: Upjohn Institute.

Orr, L. 1976. Income transfers as a public good. *American Economic Review* 66 (June): 990–94.

———. 1979. Food stamps for AFDC families: Income supplementation or fiscal relief. Washington, D.C.: Department of Health and Human Services. Mimeograph.

Parsons, D. 1996. Imperfect "tagging" in social insurance programs. *Journal of Public Economics* 62 (October): 183–207.

Plimpton, L., and D. Nightingale. 2000. Welfare employment programs: Impacts and cost-effectiveness of employment and training activities. In *Improving the odds: Increasing the effectiveness of publicly funded training,* ed. B. Barnow and C. King, 49–100. Washington, D.C.: Urban Institute.

Ribar, D., and M. Wilhelm. 1999. The demand for welfare generosity. *Review of Economics and Statistics* 81 (February): 96–108.

Riccio, J., D. Friedlander, and S. Freedman. 1994. GAIN: Benefits, costs, and three-year impacts of a welfare-to-work program. New York: Manpower Demonstration Research Corporation.

Rosenzweig, Mark. 1999. Welfare, marital prospects, and nonmarital childbearing. *Journal of Political Economy* 107, part 2 (December): S3–S32.

Schoeni, R., and R. Blank. 2000. What has welfare reform accomplished? Impacts on welfare participation, employment, income, poverty, and family structure. NBER Working Paper no. 7627. Cambridge, Mass.: National Bureau of Economic Research.

Smith, S. 2001. Background on the composition of the TANF caseload since welfare reform. Washington, D.C.: Brookings Institution.

SRI International. 1983. *Final report of the Seattle/Denver income maintenance experiment.* Vol. 1, *Design and results.* Menlo Park, Calif.: SRI International.

Tobin, J. 1965. On improving the economic status of the Negro. *Daedalus* 94 (fall): 878–97.

Tobin, J., J. Pechman, and P. Mieszkowski. 1967. Is a negative income tax practical? *Yale Law Journal* 77 (November): 1–27.

U.S. Congress Committee on Ways and Means. 1994. *Background material and data on programs within the jurisdiction of the Committee on Ways and Means.* Washington, D.C.: U.S. Government Printing Office.

———. 1996. *Background material and data on programs within the jurisdiction of the Committee on Ways and Means.* Washington, D.C.: U.S. Government Printing Office.

———. 1998. *Background material and data on programs within the jurisdiction of the Committee on Ways and Means.* Washington, D.C.: U.S. Government Printing Office.

———. 2000. *Background material and data on programs within the jurisdiction of the Committee on Ways and Means.* Washington, D.C.: U.S. Government Printing Office.

U.S. Department of Commerce, Bureau of the Census. 2000. *Statistical abstract of the U.S.: 1996.* Washington, D.C.: U.S. Government Printing Office.

U.S. Department of Health and Human Services (DHHS). 1995. *Report to Congress on out-of-wedlock childbearing.* Washington, D.C.: U.S. Government Printing Office.

————. 1997. *Setting the baseline: A report on state welfare waivers.* Washington, D.C.: Office of the Assistant Secretary for Planning and Evaluation.

————. 1998. *Temporary Assistance for Needy Families Program: First annual report to Congress.* Washington, D.C.: Administration for Children and Families.

————. 1999. *Characteristics and financial circumstances of TANF recipients: Fiscal year 1998.* Washington, D.C.: Administration for Children and Families, Office of Planning, Research, and Evaluation.

————. 2000. *Temporary Assistance for Needy Families Program: Third annual report to Congress.* Washington, D.C.: Administration for Children and Families.

————. 2001. *Indicators of welfare dependence: Annual report to Congress 2001.* Washington, D.C.: Office of the Assistance Secretary for Planning and Evaluation.

U.S. General Accounting Office (GAO). 1999. Welfare reform: Assessing the effectiveness of various welfare-to-work approaches. Washington, D.C.: U.S. Government Printing Office.

Wallace, G., and R. Blank. 1999. What goes up must come down? In *Economic conditions and welfare reform,* ed. S. Danziger, 49–89. Kalamazoo, Mich.: Upjohn Institute.

Wheaton, W. 2000. Decentralized welfare: Will there be underprovision? *Journal of Urban Economics* 48 (November): 536–55.

Zeckhauser, R. 1971. Optimal mechanisms for income transfer. *American Economic Review* 61 (June): 324–34.

Ziliak, J., D. Figlio, E. Davis, and L. Connelly. 2000. Accounting for the decline in AFDC caseloads: Welfare reform or economic growth? *Journal of Human Resources* 35 (Summer): 570–86.

Housing Programs for Low-Income Households

Edgar O. Olsen

"Those who do not remember the past are condemned to repeat it"
—George Santayana

6.1 Introduction

Unlike other major means-tested transfers, no low-income housing program is an entitlement for any type of household. Despite the failure to serve all eligible households who want to participate, federal, state, and local governments in the United States spend substantially more on housing subsidies to the poor than on other better-known parts of the welfare system such as food stamps and Temporary Assistance for Needy Families (TANF). The most widely cited figures for government expenditures on housing subsidies refer to the direct expenditures of the U.S. Department of Housing and Urban Development (HUD). They ignore the U.S. Department of Agriculture (USDA) programs that account for about 20 percent of all subsidized units, the tax expenditures on the Low-Income Housing Tax Credit ($3.5 billion per year in 2000 and growing rapidly), the expenditures of state and local governments often funded by block grants from the federal government, and the many indirect subsidies such as local property tax exemptions and abatements received by all public housing projects and many privately owned projects, the federal income tax exemption of interest on the bonds issued by state and local governments to finance housing projects, and the underpriced mortgage insurance received by many privately owned projects.

Given the enormous amount of money that has been spent on means-

Edgar O. Olsen is professor of economics at the University of Virginia.

The author is grateful to Neil Seftor for superb research assistance, Robert Olsen and Michael Schill for detailed comments, and Fred Eggers, Dennis Fricke, Bob Gray, Steve Malpezzi, Jim Mikesell, Kathy Nelson, Carla Pedone, Joe Riley, John Quigley, Mark Shroder, Jim Wallace, and John Weicher for helpful conversations.

tested housing assistance over the years, the amount of research on the most important effects of these programs is shockingly small. There is no evidence on the effects of some major programs and little evidence on the effects of other large programs. For example, there are only two studies of the most important effects of Section 236, a program that still serves almost a million people. There are almost no studies of the important effects of the Low-Income Housing Tax Credit (LIHTC), a program that has been the fastest-growing housing program over the last decade accounting for the majority of additional recipients of housing subsidies. The evidence on the most heavily studied programs is old. For example, the studies of the effects of the public housing program on housing consumption are based on data from 1965 through 1977. At the midpoint of this period, the median age of public housing units was ten years. Today, the median age is about thirty years. It stands to reason that the effect of public housing on the housing consumption of tenants is very different today from what it was at the time of these studies. Since direct HUD expenditure on public housing in the form of operating and modernization subsidies is about $6 billion annually and the real resource cost of continuing to use these units to house low-income households is much larger due to their opportunity cost and the substantial local property tax abatement that they receive, this is a sad state of affairs.

If a housing program consists of a set of eligible households and suppliers operating under one set of rules, the United States has had an enormous number of programs intended to improve the housing of low-income households since the federal government became seriously involved in this activity in 1937. There have been many programs as this term is commonly used, each of these programs has typically had a number of variants, and each change in the regulations produces a new program. For example, the public housing program has at least twenty-nine variants. Each has its own rules, and these rules have changed from time to time, although they have many rules in common.

To keep the length of this paper within reasonable limits, it will focus on four broad programs that account for the bulk of all subsidized *rental* units. These programs are public housing, project-based assistance under the Section 236 and Section 8 New Construction/Substantial Rehabilitation Programs, and tenant-based assistance under the Section 8 Existing Housing Program. They illustrate the three basic approaches that have been used to provide housing assistance: government ownership and operation of housing newly built for occupancy by low-income households; government contracts with private parties to build (or substantially rehabilitate) and operate housing for these households; and subsidies to eligible households who select housing in the private market meeting certain minimum quality standards and, under some variants, other restrictions. These programs account for about 70 percent of all subsidized *rental* units and about

50 percent of *all* units for low-income households that have received federal housing subsidies.

Even though there have been almost no studies of their major effects, a more comprehensive paper would have devoted considerable attention to the LIHTC program (that serves more than a million households and has been growing rapidly since 1988), Section 515 (a rental housing program operated by the USDA in rural areas and small towns that produces few new units each year but still serves more than half a million households), and the HOME housing block grant program from the federal government to state and local housing agencies on which we currently spend about $1.85 billion annually, primarily for project-based assistance. In light of the continuing interest in increasing the homeownership rate of the near poor, it would also be desirable to devote considerable attention to several fairly large homeownership programs—HUD's Section 235 program, which provided subsidies to about a half a million households since 1969, and USDA's Section 502 program, which has subsidized almost two million households since 1949 and currently provides subsidies to about half a million households.

The primary purposes of this paper are to (a) consider the arguments that have been offered for housing subsidies to low-income households and the implications of valid arguments for the evaluation and design of housing programs, (b) describe the most important features of the largest rental housing programs for low-income households in the United States, (c) summarize the empirical evidence on the major effects of these programs, and (d) analyze the most important options for reform of the system of housing subsidies to low-income households. The effects of these programs that will be considered include effects on the housing occupied by recipients of the subsidy and their consumption of other goods, effects on labor supply of recipients, the participation rates of different types of households, the distribution of benefits among recipients and all eligible households, effects on the types of neighborhoods in which subsidized households live and the effect of subsidized housing and households on their neighbors, effects on the rents of unsubsidized units, and the cost-effectiveness of alternative methods for delivering housing assistance. Since we continue to seriously consider or embark upon new programs that have the same basic features of older programs and the major effects of the newer programs have not been estimated, an understanding of the older programs is highly relevant for current discussions of housing policy.

Section 6.2 discusses the justifications for housing subsidies for low-income households and goals consistent with these justifications, gives a brief overview of the development of the current system of housing subsidies, and describes in more detail the development and most important rules of the major rental housing programs. Section 6.3 provides information about the number of households served by major programs, direct federal expenditures on these programs, and the characteristics of the households assisted. Section 6.4 discusses what can be said on theoretical grounds about the effects of the programs and reviews the evidence on these effects. Section 6.5 analyzes options for reform of the system of housing subsidies to low-income households. Section 6.6 summarizes the major results.

6.2   Program Justifications, Goals, History, and Rules

6.2.1   Justifications and Goals

Without a clear understanding of the justifications for government activity in a particular area, it is difficult (but not impossible) to conduct an incisive evaluation of current programs or design better programs. For example, a person who has not thought seriously about the justifications for housing subsidies to low-income households might imagine that a housing program for these households is successful if it induces them to occupy better housing. However, a program of cash grants with no strings attached would have this effect for all recipients whose income elasticity of demand for housing is positive—that is, almost everyone. Indeed, it would be possible to devise a subsidy that led to a smaller improvement in housing for all recipients than would result from an equally costly lump-sum grant. A subsidy equal to a fraction of expenditure on all goods except housing would have this effect for recipients whose price elasticity of demand for these other goods is less than one. Should this be considered a successful housing program?

In general, a justification for a government program is an explanation of why we should have a program of that type. Obviously, this involves value judgments. The value judgment underlying this paper is that we should have a program of a particular type if and only if an appropriately designed program of that type will lead to an efficient allocation of resources that is preferred by everyone to the allocation in the absence of government action. Although this simple view leaves much to be desired because it ignores the impact of the multiplicity of external effects, market imperfections, and informational problems that justify other programs and hence the design of a set of programs to deal simultaneously with all of these problems, it is at least a step in the direction of clear thinking about policy evaluation and design.

The major justification for housing subsidies to low-income households is that some taxpayers care about these households but feel that at least some low-income households undervalue housing. If some taxpayers feel this way while others are either completely selfish or nonpaternalistic altruists, it is possible for the government to achieve an efficient allocation and to make everyone better off as they judge their own well-being by providing these low-income households with housing subsidies (Olsen 1981). Politicians and lobbyists for housing subsidies rarely use this argument because it is insulting to potential supporters. However, conversations with ordinary citizens about why they prefer to provide housing assistance rather than cash grants usually leads to this argument.

It is clear that paternalistic altruists do not think that all low-income households undervalue housing. In recent years, proponents of housing subsidies have frequently argued that the primary housing problem of low-income households is an excessive rent-income ratio rather that inadequate housing. That is, the majority of low-income households occupy adequate housing by spending too much of their income on it and hence too little on other goods. People who make this argument must be saying that these low-income households undervalue other goods. If we want to attain an efficient allocation of resources that is preferred by everyone to the allocation in the absence of government action, we must provide nonhousing, rather than housing, subsidies to this group. The implications of these feelings for housing policy are not clear. If housing programs are designed to deal with both poor housing and excessive rent burden, what is the role of food stamps, Medicaid, and other programs designed to subsidize various nonhousing goods?

It is often claimed that housing subsidies to low-income households are justified by more tangible externalities. For example, it has been argued that better housing for low-income families leads to better health for its occupants and, since some diseases are contagious, to better health for the middle- and upper-income families with whom they come in contact. Improvements in the exterior appearance of housing confer benefits on others. Available evidence suggests that some such externalities exist but that their magnitudes are small (Weicher 1979, 489–92). If the goal of housing subsidies is to make both recipients and taxpayers better off, it is doubtful that substantial expenditure can be justified on the basis of these externalities.

Some argue for particular housing programs based on their effects on the members of subsidized households without specifying the nature of the external effect or market imperfection involved and without considering whether the housing program involved is a part of an efficient strategy for dealing with these market failures. For example, many consider a positive effect of a housing program on the educational attainment of children in the subsidized household to be a justification for the program. This argument alone does not justify government action.

No attempt has been made to derive implications for the evaluation and design of government housing programs of a coherent set of justifications for programs of this type. However, the following properties seem broadly consistent with the preceding justifications. First, the program must induce the worst-housed families at each income level to occupy better housing than they would choose if they were given equally costly cash grants with no strings attached. This goal is consistent with the stated purposes of the two major housing acts, namely "to remedy the acute shortage of decent, safe, and sanitary dwellings" (Housing Act of 1937) and "the elimination of substandard and other inadequate housing" (Housing Act of 1949).[1] Second, families that are the same with respect to characteristics of interest to taxpayers should be offered the same assistance. Third, the greatest assistance should go to the neediest families. Finally, the housing provided to participants should have the lowest possible total cost to tenants and governments given its overall desirability.

Other goals for housing programs have been suggested, for example, increasing homeownership, reducing racial segregation in housing, or stabilizing new construction. The rationales for achieving these goals are different from those underlying housing subsidies to low-income families, and they are arguably best achieved by other means.

6.2.2   History

Table 6.1 contains some milestones in the development of the system of housing subsidies for low-income households in the United States.[2] This subsection provides a brief overview of the development of each part of the system, namely public housing, privately owned projects, tenant-based certificates and vouchers, homeownership programs, and housing block grants. The next subsection provides details about the rules governing the four largest rental programs.

Public Housing

Substantial government involvement in subsidizing the housing of low-income households began with the Public Housing Program enacted in the U.S. Housing Act of 1937. Public housing projects are owned and operated by local public housing authorities established by local governments. Almost all are newly built for the program. Until 1969, with minor exceptions, federal taxpayers paid the initial development cost of public housing and tenants and local taxpayers paid the operating cost. Between 1968 and 1972, the federal government greatly increased its previously modest subsidies for operating public housing projects in conjunction with restrictions on the rents that local housing authorities could charge their tenants. In 1969, the federal government began to provide subsidies to local housing authorities for the modernization of their projects. These additional subsidies and restrictions on rent were intended to insure that public hous-

1. In discussions of housing policy, the word "shortage" is not used as economists use it. Instead it means that the market outcome does not provide all households with the type of housing that the speaker thinks they should occupy. All major HUD programs were enacted in these laws or as amendments to them.
2. The dates listed in the table are the dates that programs were enacted. Programs do not become operational until regulations have been written, and this sometimes requires considerable time.

Table 6.1   **Development of System of Housing Programs**

New Programs and Major Modifications of Existing Programs

1937	Public housing, HUD, rental, publicly owned
1949	Section 502, USDA, homeownership
1954	Section 221(d)(3) MIR, HUD, rental, privately owned
1959	Section 202, HUD, rental, privately owned, elderly and handicapped
1961	Section 221(d)(3) BMIR, HUD, rental, privately owned
1962	Section 515, USDA, rental, privately owned
1965	Rent supplements, HUD, rental, extra subsidy to private projects
1965	Section 23, HUD, rental, leasing existing units for public housing tenants
1968	Section 235, HUD, homeownership
1968	Section 236, HUD, rental, privately owned
1969	Modernization subsidies for public housing
1969	Rents in public housing limited to 25 percent of income
1970	Substantial operating subsidies for public housing
1974	Section 8 Existing, HUD, rental, tenant-based
1974	Section 8 New Construction/Substantial Rehabilitation, HUD, rental, privately owned
1975	Operating subsidies for public housing (Performance Funding System)
1976	Operating subsidies for privately-owned projects (LMSA and PD)
1979	Modernization subsidies for privately owned projects (Flexible Subsidy)
1983	Housing Voucher Demonstration, HUD, rental, tenant-based
1986	LIHTC, IRS, rental, privately owned
1990	HOME, HUD, rental and homeownership, block grants to states and localities
1998	Housing Choice Voucher Program, HUD, rental, tenant-based

ing would provide satisfactory housing to its tenants without charging rents that were regarded as excessive.

Privately Owned Projects

In 1954, the federal government began to contract with private parties to provide housing for low-income households. Under most programs, these parties agreed to provide housing meeting certain standards to households with particular characteristics for a specified number of years. The overwhelming majority of the projects were newly built. Almost all of the rest were substantially rehabilitated as a condition for participation in the program. The federal government insures the mortgages on the vast majority of these projects, and default loss in excess of mortgage insurance payments is a major indirect cost of many of the programs. It is important to realize that none of these programs provide subsidies to all suppliers who would like to participate. Since subsidies are provided to selected private suppliers, the market mechanism does not insure that subsidies are passed along to occupants of the subsidized units. In all cases, civil servants are involved in ranking proposals. In most programs, political appointees make the final decisions.

The earlier programs such as HUD's Section 221(d)(3) Market Interest Rate Program and Section 202 limited the private parties who operate the projects to nonprofits and cooperatives.[3] They were succeeded by programs that allowed the participation of for-profit firms, while attempting to limit their profits by restricting their net revenues during the period of the use agreement. For-profit firms have accounted for the majority of the units in the most recent programs such as Section 8 New Construction/ Substantial Rehabilitation and the LIHTC. Despite this trend, nonprofits still account for a substantial minority of units under some recent programs such as the LIHTC.[4]

The earlier programs (Section 221[d][3] MIR and Section 202) did not have income limits. Instead they attempted to insure occupancy by households of low and moderate income by limiting the per-unit cost of the project, thereby providing relatively modest housing. The subsidy under the earlier programs was a below-market interest rate on the loan used to finance the project, and the subsidy received by an occupant of the project did not depend on the household's income. The modest magnitude of the subsidy and the high cost of newly built housing meeting the program's standards resulted in few units occupied by the poorest households.

The initial response to this situation (HUD's Section 221[d][3] BMIR Program) was to provide a larger interest subsidy, thereby reducing the rent to tenants at all income levels by the same amount. Another response (for example, the Rent Supplement Program) was to provide an additional subsidy to many of the poorest households in projects that received an interest subsidy in order to reduce their rents to 25 percent of their adjusted incomes. (The poorest of the poor paid a flat rent equal to 30 percent of the rent that would otherwise be charged for the apartment.) Rent supplements were used almost exclusively with the Section 221(d)(3) MIR and the Section 236 programs.

The basic HUD Section 236 program and the USDA's 515 program are similar to the Section 221(d)(3) BMIR program in providing a substantial interest subsidy that reduces the rent of all of the poorest households occupying identical apartments in a project by the same amount. The more affluent among the eligibles initially paid 25 percent of their adjusted incomes. Over time, an increasing fraction of the poorest occupants of these projects have received additional subsidies under a succession of programs that initially reduced their rents to 25 percent of adjusted income and later to 30 percent.[5] Some of these programs were intended to insure that proj-

3. The original Section 221(d)(3) program is usually called the Market Interest Rate Program (MIR). This is misleading because the program does provide financing at below-market interest rates, albeit not as far below market as the later Section 221(d)(3) Below-Market Interest Rate (BMIR) Program.

4. The extent of the involvement of the two types of sponsor is not well documented because they often work in partnership and only one is listed as the sponsor in official records.

5. The programs involved were the Rent Supplement Program, the Rental Assistance Payments Program, Section 8 Conversion Assistance, and the Section 8 Loan Management Set-Aside (LMSA) and Property Disposition (PD) Programs.

ects built under construction programs continued to house low-income households and to avoid defaults on loans insured by the federal government. However, about a fourth of the occupants of apartments in privately owned HUD-subsidized projects have rents that do not vary with their income (HUD 1997, 3).

In 1978, Congress enacted the Flexible Subsidy Program to provide modernization subsidies to older privately owned subsidized projects, especially under Section 236, 221(d)(3), and 202, just as it had done earlier for public housing. The money is awarded on a competitive basis rather than by formula.

The largest program of subsidized privately owned projects for low-income households is HUD's Section 8 New Construction/Substantial Rehabilitation Program, enacted in 1974. Section 8 New Construction/Substantial Rehabilitation provides not only subsidies for the construction or rehabilitation of projects but also rental assistance payments that initially reduced the rents paid by all tenants to 25 percent of their adjusted incomes.[6]

With minor exceptions, Congress had terminated all of HUD's construction programs by 1983. Section 236 replaced Section 221(d)(3) BMIR, Section 8 New Construction/Substantial Rehabilitation replaced Section 236, and Section 8 New Construction/Substantial Rehabilitation was terminated in 1983 in the sense that no additional applications for projects under this program were accepted after this time.[7] This was in response to the large per-unit cost under all new construction programs compared with tenant-based Section 8 Certificates and studies indicating that these costs were also large relative to the market rents of the units provided. Only public housing and the small Section 202 program for the elderly and handicapped, which had been revised to operate like the Section 8 New Construction/Substantial Rehabilitation Program, were allowed to approve a modest number of additional applications.

The LIHTC was enacted hastily as a part of the Tax Reform Act of 1986 to replace other tax subsidies for low-income housing that were eliminated.[8] Within a few years, it will become the second largest program of

6. Beginning on 1 August 1982, it increased periodically until it reached 30 on 1 October 1985.

7. It is a testimony to the long lags between the appropriation of money under construction programs and their completion that the number of occupied units under this program continued to grow for thirteen years after its termination. For systematic evidence on these lags, see Schnare et al. (1982, table 4-8).

8. Virtually nothing is known about the effects of the LIHTC. There is no repository of information on the characteristics of the households served by this program or the characteristics of the housing provided. Some rudimentary statistical information can be found at http://www.huduser.org/datasets/lihtc.html. What is known about the program is the result of a few studies. Wallace (1995, 794–801) provides an accurate description of the program's rules and a summary of basic descriptive statistics that had been produced by earlier studies. Cummings and DiPasquale (1999) add an unusually thorough analysis of all of the subsidies pro-

housing subsidies to low-income households, surpassing public housing. For projects not financed by tax-exempt bonds, the tax credit pays 70 percent of the cost of developing the project. The tax credit is not available to all developers who want to build housing under the terms specified in the law. Instead each state housing finance agency is allocated an amount of money that is proportional to the state's population to distribute to selected private suppliers. In recent years, developers have proposed projects that would use three times the amount of money appropriated for the program, and many do not apply because the probability of success is too small to justify the effort.

The overwhelming majority of tax credit projects receive subsidies from other sources, primarily development grants or loans at below-market interest rates from state and local governments and rental assistance payments that depend upon the income of the tenants. These additional development subsidies account for about a third of the total capital subsidy (Cummings and DiPasquale 1999, table 7), and owners of tax credit properties receive rental assistance payments on behalf of about 39 percent of their tenants (GAO 1997, 40). The typical project receives subsidized financing from many sources, thereby complicating the task of insuring that the subsidy is passed along to the tenant. The median was five in Stegman's nonrandom sample of twenty-four projects (Stegman 1991, 362).

Under the LIHTC, the tenant's maximum rent is 30 percent of the upper income limit for eligibility.[9] Tenant rent within a project does not vary with income except for households who receive assistance from other programs that require it. As a result, the poorest households occupy relatively few LIHTC units. According to Wallace (1995, 790), only 28 percent of households in LIHTC projects are very low-income as HUD defines this term (50 percent of local median for a family of four). The percentages are 90 for Section 8 New Construction, 81 for public housing, and 77 for Section 236 and 221(d)(3) BMIR.

Tenant-Based Assistance

Until 1965, all housing assistance to the poor was project based and the overwhelming majority of units were newly constructed under a govern-

---

vided for the development of LIHTC projects. This analysis does not, however, include the substantial tenant-based and project-based Section 8 subsidies received by about 39 percent of the units (GAO 1997, 40). GAO (1997) and Buron et al. (2000) provide additional descriptive material. Despite the absence of evidence on the effects of the LIHTC, Congress in 2000–01 increased tax expenditure for this program by more than 40 percent to about $5 billion per year and indexed appropriations to inflation. Shortly thereafter, GAO (2002) produced the first independent analysis of the cost-effectiveness of the program.

9. The upper income limit for a family of four is effectively 60 percent of the local median. Increasing or decreasing these income limits by nationally uniform percentages used for the largest HUD programs yields the income limits for households of other sizes.

ment program. In 1965 Congress created Section 23, a program under which public housing authorities could lease apartments in existing private unsubsidized housing for the use of households eligible for public housing.[10] One variant of this program allowed tenants to locate their own apartments meeting the program's minimum standards. This was the first program of tenant-based assistance in the United States. In 1974, the Section 8 Existing Housing Program replaced Section 23. Since then, tenant-based Section 8 has become the country's largest program of housing assistance. This program was called the Certificate Program. Another program of tenant-based housing assistance, called the Section 8 Voucher Program, that had somewhat different constraints than the Certificate Program was introduced in 1983. This program operated simultaneously with the Certificate Program until 1998, when the two programs were consolidated into another tenant-based program that combined features of the two earlier programs.

Despite the rapid growth of the tenant-based Section 8 Certificate and Voucher programs, the majority of additional recipients of rental housing assistance since 1975 have received project-based assistance. Between 1975 and 1990, the major sources of this assistance were Section 8 New Construction/Substantial Rehabilitation and Section 515. Since 1990, the overwhelming majority of HUD's incremental assistance has been tenant based, but project-based assistance has continued to account for the majority of additions to number of subsidized households in the United States due to the rapid growth of the Internal Revenue Service's LIHTC. Furthermore, HUD spends a substantial fraction of its budget providing additional assistance to units in subsidized housing projects beyond the subsidies initially promised.

Homeownership Programs

The United States has had two major homeownership programs that provide housing assistance to low-income households. The Housing Act of 1949 established the USDA's Section 502 Single Family Direct Loan Program.[11] Until 1968, the magnitude of the subsidy was modest and did not depend on the household's income. The subsidy consisted of lending at the federal borrowing rate to farmers and others living in rural areas. (Farmers now account for a small share of all borrowers.) The Housing Act of 1968 authorized the USDA to pay a portion of the loan repayments for low-income households. For the poorest households, the USDA paid the

10. For a comprehensive analysis of this program and a detailed survey of the literature on it, see Reid (1989).
11. See Carliner (1998, 314–15) for a brief history of the development of the program and Mikesell et al. (1999) for descriptive statistics and the first analysis of this program based on a nationally representative survey.

difference between principal and interest payments at the government's borrowing rate and at an interest rate of 1 percent. For eligible households with higher incomes, the USDA paid the difference between property taxes, homeowners insurance, operating expenses, and principal and interest payments at the government's borrowing rate and 20 percent of the household's adjusted income. During its fifty-year history, the Section 502 Single Family Direct Loan Program has provided over $51 billion in homeownership loans to about 1.9 million households. The program currently provides subsidies to over 500,000 low-income households.

The Housing Act of 1968 established Section 235, a HUD program similar in many respects to USDA's Section 502. Unlike Section 502, this program suffered from scandals and high default rates (Carliner 1998, 313–14). Section 235 was suspended in 1973, reactivated in 1975, severely limited in geographical scope in 1983, and terminated in 1987. Over this period, it provided subsidies to more 500,000 low-income households. Little is known about the reasons for the difference in outcomes of the two programs. The poor performance of Section 235 is usually attributed to consumer naivete and Federal Housing Administration (FHA) mismanagement. More plausible explanations would rely on differences in the structures of the programs such as the magnitude of the down payment required and whether the subsidy is allocated to the seller or the buyer of the house.

Housing Block Grants

The HOME Investment Partnerships Program enacted in 1990 is a block grant for housing assistance. It allocates federal funds by formula to state and local governments to spend on any type of housing assistance subject to certain limits on the incomes of the households served, the cost to acquire and develop units, and the rents that may be charged for rental units. This program is based on the untested assumptions that the best mix of housing programs differs from locality to locality and local officials are better able to determine and implement the best mix.[12]

6.2.3   Rules

This section presents information concerning many of the important rules governing HUD's four largest programs of rental housing assistance for low-income households and the evolution of these rules over the history of the programs. The rules considered determine who is eligible to receive assistance, how the limited assistance is allocated among households that would like to participate, upper and lower limits on the desirability of the

---

12. These assumptions could be tested by comparing the outcomes of different federal programs across localities to see whether one program performs better than all others on all measures and then comparing the overall effect of the mix of programs chosen by local officials with the federal mix in a random sample of localities.

housing that can be occupied, and upper limits on spending on goods other than housing. These rules affect which households are served and a program's effects on consumption patterns.

Other rules that determine the incentives facing potential and actual suppliers will not be discussed. For construction and rehabilitation programs, these rules affect the types of housing that will be proposed and selected. For all programs, they affect how well the units will be maintained and the total cost of the housing provided. Although these rules determine the cost-effectiveness of a program and the level of housing services provided, they have not been seriously analyzed by housing policy analysts. This represents a major gap in our knowledge of housing programs.

It is not possible within reasonable time and space constraints to describe accurately the rules of the four programs that are the focus of this paper over their histories. The rule describing what is and is not included in a household's annual income in determining its eligibility for assistance illustrates the problem. The current rule is more than three pages single spaced. This rule is now the same for all major low-income housing programs. In earlier years, it was different for different programs, and it has been changed on a number of occasions over the history of each program.

Researchers who want to conduct empirical studies of the effects of housing programs, or indeed any program, should consult the Code of Federal Regulations (CFR) for the time period to which their data refer to determine the rules that were in effect at that time.[13] The regulations for HUD are in Title 24 of the CFR. That is, references to them all begin with 24CFR. For example, since 1996 the reference for HUD's physical condition standards for virtually all subsidized housing has been 24CFR5.703. In earlier years, the standards for each program were located in the CFR under the regulations for that program.

The CFR is an annual publication that contains the updated regulations of the federal government as of April 1. A searchable electronic version containing the CFR and the Federal Register since 1981 is available at http://web.lexis-nexis.com/congcomp/. Virtually all rules of interest must be published in the Federal Register along with the date on which they became effective, and each regulation in the CFR cites the relevant passage

---

13. In the case of housing programs, secondary sources, even government publications or agency websites, are always incomplete and sometimes erroneous. For example, it is often said in official HUD documents that the upper income limit for admission to public housing is 80 percent of the local median. This might lead the unsuspecting to conclude that the income limit is the same for families of all sizes, or perhaps that for families of each size it is 80 percent of the local median for families of that size. Neither is correct. Reading the legislation is not a substitute for reading the regulations. Legislation typically specifies some, but not all, of a program's rules. It provides general guidelines concerning other matters, but leaves the design of specific regulations to the administering agency. Furthermore, the operation of a program does not change with the passage of legislation. This does not occur until after new regulations have been announced in the Federal Register.

in the Federal Register. For example, the citation for the proposed regulation that ultimately led to a unified set of physical condition standards applying to all low-income housing programs is 63FR35650. As usual, this source contained a history of previous regulations. The citation for the final rule is 63FR46566, which contains the date on which the regulation became effective.

These sources are useful not only for researchers who have a data set that identifies which households participate in housing programs and are attempting to determine the parameters of the budget spaces of these households but also to others who are trying to learn when major changes in program parameters occurred with an eye to selecting which data to use to maximize exogenous variation in budget constraint parameters. Using these sources, it is easy to determine when important changes in the regulations have occurred.

Prior to the regulations implementing the Housing and Community Development Act of 1974, there was considerable diversity in the rules of different housing programs. This legislation introduced many similarities in the rules across programs, and this trend has continued over the past twenty-five years, culminating in the 1990s with the placement of many common rules in Part 5 of Title 24 of the CFR. These include rules for preferences for admission into subsidized housing (24CFR5.4XY since 1996), income limits, the definitions of annual income and adjusted income, tenant rents, and certifying eligibility (24CFR5.6XY since 1997), and minimum physical housing standards (24CFR5.7XY since 1999).

To help aspiring housing policy analysts navigate through the regulations and to provide others with an overview of the rules that have governed low-income housing programs, this section describes the key rules that prevailed on 1 April 1999 and some of the major changes that have occurred in these rules over the years.

Before proceeding, it is useful to mention several general features of the rules. In recent years, the majority of privately owned projects under HUD's programs receive project-based Section 8 housing assistance payments and are therefore subject to the key rules of the Section 8 program. Since the enactment of the Section 8 program in 1974, Section 8 and public housing have had very similar rules in many respects. This means that the overwhelming majority of HUD's subsidized households are subject to many of the same rules.

Eligibility

With a few minor exceptions such as Section 221(d)(3) MIR and Section 202 in its early years, all housing programs have had upper income limits for eligibility. Indeed, the earlier programs such as public housing had two limits for households of each size—one for initial receipt of a subsidy and a larger limit for retaining the subsidy.[14] The income limits that are discussed here and elsewhere are limits for initial receipt of a subsidy unless otherwise stated.

Prior to the 1974 Housing Act, local public housing authorities chose their own upper income limits based on a vaguely worded provision of the law. The upper income limits for other programs were related to the limits for public housing and always greater than these limits. For example, the income limits for Section 236 in its early years were 35 percent above the limits for public housing in the same locality.

Since the 1974 Housing Act, public housing, Section 236, and all variants of Section 8 have had a common set of income limits. These programs account for the overwhelming majority of HUD-subsidized households. Each year, the Economic and Market Analysis Division (EMAD) in HUD's Office of Policy Development and Research estimates these limits in accordance with the regulations.

The basic income limit for a family of four is 80 percent of the median income of all families in a locality.[15] Income limits for families of other sizes are obtained from the four-person income limit by applying the following percentages.[16]

Family Size and Percentage Adjustments

1	2	3	4	5	6	7	8
70%	80%	90%	100%	108%	116%	124%	132%

In the terminology of housing regulations and policy discussions, these families are described as low-income families.[17] In the absence of excep-

14. The earliest housing programs involved construction and so households had to move in order to receive the subsidy. Even after these programs stopped producing additional units, households entering the program had to move into a project in order to receive a subsidy. The higher limit for continued occupancy was introduced to avoid forcing a household to move if its income rose too much. This problem only arises if the market rent of the unit occupied exceeds the tenant's rent at the upper income limit for admission, that is, if there is a notch at this upper income limit. This is almost surely the case for every construction program in its early years when the housing is new. Based on a vague provision in the law, many local housing authorities set their upper income limits for continued occupancy 25 percent above their limits for admission. Public housing has not had a separate upper income limit for continued occupancy for many years. If a public housing tenant's income rises above the income limit for admission, the housing authority could force the tenant to leave the project, but this rarely happens. Under Section 8 certificates and vouchers, the effective upper income limit for continued receipt of a subsidy is the income at which the subsidy is zero.

15. Income limits were related to local median incomes in an attempt to account for geographical price differences, but differences in median incomes obviously also reflect other factors such as differences in skill levels.

16. There is no good rationale for these percentages. For example, they are not based on differences in poverty lines for households of different sizes.

17. To put these limits in perspective, the poverty line is about 30 percent of median income.

tions, only low-income families are eligible for the housing programs that account for almost all means-tested housing subsidies.

However, there are important exceptions to these simple rules. In 2000, these affected the limits for 37 percent of the metropolitan areas and 86 percent of the non-metropolitan areas. The most important exception in terms of the number of areas affected is the requirement that the income limits in a nonmetropolitan area may not be less than limits based on the state nonmetropolitan median family income.

In a series of amendments to housing laws since 1975, Congress has specified that an increasing percentage of recipients of housing subsidies have incomes below 50 percent of the local median for four-person families and the aforementioned adjustments for family size.[18] These households are called very low-income households, and these laws are codified in 24CFR1275 (1975), 24CFR882 (1976), 24CFR813 (1985), and 24CFR982 (1999).

Finally, the Quality Housing and Work Responsibility Act of 1998 created a new category called extremely low-income families, whose incomes were 30 percent of the local median for families of four and required a high percentage of new recipients of housing subsidies to be in this category (24CFR982.201 [2000]). Consistent with a trend over several decades to avoid concentrations of the poorest households in public housing, the required percentage was much lower for public housing than tenant-based vouchers and certificates. Specifically, the act required that at least 75 percent of new recipients of tenant-based vouchers and only 40 percent of new recipients of HUD's project-based assistance have extremely low incomes.

The details concerning the rules and methods for calculating income limits are contained in fiscal year (FY) 2000 Income Limits Briefing Material available at http://www.huduser.org/datasets/il.html. Fortunately, understanding these complexities is not important for most purposes because the income limits themselves are available in electronic form for all areas from 1990 to the present at the aforementioned website. They can be obtained for earlier years through HUD's Economic Market Analysis Division (EMAD).

Unlike many other means-tested welfare programs, there are no asset tests for eligibility for housing assistance. Actual or imputed income from specified assets is included in income in determining eligibility and rent.

---

18. The income limits calculated based on 80 percent of the local median and income limits for virtually all other housing programs, including non-HUD programs, that use different percentages are calculated by first calculating the limits based on 50 percent, then applying the exceptions, and finally multiplying by the relevant percentage. For example, almost all LIHTC projects involve a program option that restricts the rents of tenants to income limits based on 60 percent of the local median. To calculate these limits, the limits based on 50 percent are multiplied by 1.2.

Preferences

Since housing programs are not entitlements, some system is required to allocate the available money to the many families that would like to participate.[19] The most salient feature of the system is that there has never been a uniform national system to rank families on a waiting list. Instead Congress has specified that some preference must be given to certain types of families but left it to local housing authorities and owners of subsidized private projects to devise preference schemes. For example, in 1971 Section 10(g)(2) of the United States Housing Act of 1937 read as follows:

> The public housing agency shall adopt and promulgate regulations establishing admissions policies which shall give full consideration to its responsibility for the rehousing of displaced families, to the applicant's status as a serviceman or veteran or relationship to a serviceman or veteran . . . , and to the applicant's age or disability, housing conditions, urgency of housing need, and source of income: Provided, That in establishing such admission policies the public housing agency shall accord to families of low income such priority over single persons as it determines to be necessary to avoid undue hardship.

HUD has never been authorized to establish a nationally uniform preference system. Its role has been to review preference systems for consistency with congressional intent.

Obviously, there are infinitely many schemes for ranking families on a waiting list that give some preference to the types of households mentioned in this passage. There are now about 3,400 local public housing authorities and more than 22,000 privately owned HUD-subsidized projects. Although some undoubtedly copy the schemes of others, it seems likely that there have always been an enormous number of different schemes in existence. A common scheme has been to assign points to different family attributes mentioned in the law. However, there are infinitely many different weights that could be assigned to the favored household types consistent with the wording of the law.[20]

Although the language of the law with respect to priorities for receipt of housing subsidies has changed from time to time and other types of families have been singled out for preferential treatment, some of the family types mentioned in the preceding passage have been accorded preferential

19. The next section discusses the extent of the excess demand for assistance to the extent possible with existing data.

20. This creates a problem for research where information on the preference scheme is important. These preference systems could be collected because each public housing agency and manager of a privately owned project is required by law to have a written preference scheme that is available to the public. However, it would be quite expensive to do it for all subsidized housing because they are not available in HUD's central office.

treatment for receipt of housing assistance under many programs over much of their histories. The elderly and handicapped have been given a preference for subsidized housing for at least forty years. There are two programs (Section 202 and 811) limited to such households, many projects built under other programs are built exclusively for them, and they have typically been given priority for admission into projects not built exclusively for them. Families living in substandard housing or displaced by government action have always been given a preference for housing subsidies.[21] Single persons who are not elderly, disabled, or displaced by government action have always been given a low priority for assistance.

Congress suspended federal preferences on 26 January 1996 and repealed them in the Quality Housing and Work Responsibility Act of 1998 (64FR23460, 65FR16692). The final regulations implementing these changes became effective 30 April 2000. Since these legislative changes did not require housing authorities to alter their current preference system, it is likely that they had little immediate effect. Immediately prior to the suspension of federal preferences, federal law required that for the overwhelming majority of new recipients of housing assistance, local housing authorities must give preference to families who were occupying substandard housing, involuntarily displaced, or paying more than 50 percent of income for rent. They were allowed to use local preferences for a small minority of new recipients (53FR1122).

Restrictions on Housing Consumption

Under all forms of project-based housing assistance, households that reach the top of the waiting list are offered a particular unit. To a first approximation, they have no choice concerning the quantity of housing services that they consume if they want to receive housing assistance. It is only to the extent that they can reject particular units without dropping to the bottom of the waiting list and the possibility of being simultaneously on the waiting lists for public housing and individual private projects that eligible families have a range of housing choices.[22] Even if we ignore the complexities resulting from these possibilities, it is not the case that all households offered assistance under a project-based program are offered the same housing. Under mature construction and substantial rehabilitation programs, the variance in the desirability of the program's units of a particular size is enormous. Therefore, the housing offered by these programs at a point in time cannot be characterized by a single number such as its

21. Many involved in discussions of housing policy view living in substandard housing as something that happens to a person rather than something that is chosen.

22. Some housing authorities allow tenants to reject a few units before being dropped from the waiting list. Nothing prevents eligible households from being on the public housing waiting list and simultaneously applying for an apartment in any privately owned subsidized project.

market rent divided by a housing price index or a single vector of characteristics. As explained later and depicted in figure 6.4, families eligible for tenant-based housing vouchers or certificates have a wide range of housing choices, but the program adds the same consumption bundles to the budget spaces of all eligible families with the same characteristics living in one locality provided that they are offered assistance.

Since a primary goal of housing programs is to improve the housing occupied by participants, it should not be surprising that almost all housing programs have minimum housing standards. For some programs such as the older programs involving privately owned projects, these standards have been so vague as to be unenforceable. They require that the housing be decent, safe, and sanitary. For others such as tenant-based vouchers and certificates, much more specific standards have existed.[23] It was not until 1999 that the same detailed standards applied to virtually all subsidized housing (63FR46566).

With the exception of the housing voucher program that began as a demonstration in 1983 and is currently being phased out, all housing programs place upper limits on the quantity of housing available to participants. In the case of production programs, these result from upper limits on construction costs and limits on the amount of money that the housing authority or owner of a private project can receive from the tenant and the government each month. Although this limits how good any program unit can be, it is not a parameter of the budget space of most households offered units under the program. Due to depreciation, units under mature production programs differ widely in their condition. A household's budget space depends on which unit it is offered. With the exception of the aforementioned voucher program, the other programs of tenant-based assistance impose upper limits on the rents that landlords can receive. This upper limit is a parameter of the budget space of each household offered assistance under a particular program in a specific locality.

Under all housing programs, the size of the apartment offered to a household depends on the size and composition of the household. For example, two children of the same sex will be expected to share a bedroom. Beyond a certain age, two children of different sexes will have their own bedrooms.

Tenant Rent

For more than thirty years, the tenant's contribution to rent under all construction programs has been specified in the program's regulations. For all units in the largest programs (public housing and Section 8 New Construction/Substantial Rehabilitation) and many units in other programs, it has depended on household characteristics, but not on the desirability of the housing occupied. Similar remarks apply to the Section 8 Certificate

---

23. See 63FR35650 for a history of the occupancy standards.

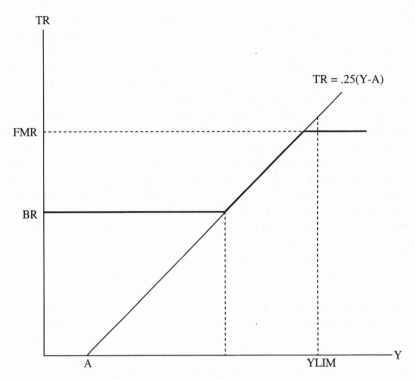

TR

TR = .25(Y-A)

FMR

BR

A   YLIM   Y

Fig. 6.1   Tenant rent under section 236 without rent supplements

Program since 1980. For the other programs of tenant-based assistance, the tenant's contribution to rent depends on the market rent of the apartment selected.

In public housing prior to 1969, each local housing authority had its own system for determining the rent paid by public housing tenants subject to very general guidelines. Some housing authorities charged a fixed fraction of adjusted income (usually 20 percent), others charged the same rents for all apartments of the same size, and still others charged a certain minimum rent to the poorest households and a fraction of adjusted income to households for which this was larger. In 1969, legislation imposed a uniform upper limit on rents at 25 percent of adjusted income, and almost all local authorities charged the maximum rents permitted. Between 1982 and 1985, a transition to a higher percentage—30 percent—occurred, and the authorities were required to charge this rent. The Section 8 New Construction/Substantial Rehabilitation Program and the Section 8 Certificate Program after 1980 used the 25 percent rule initially and made the aforementioned transition to 30 percent in the early 1980s.

The history of the rules for tenant rent in the Section 236 program is similar to the history in several other construction programs. The thick lines in figure 6.1 depict how the tenant's rent TR under Section 236 without rent

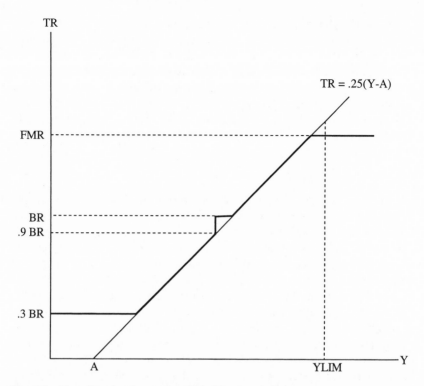

Fig. 6.2   Tenant rent under section 236 with rent supplements

supplements or other additional subsidies varies with the tenant's income
Y. In the diagrams, FMR is the sum of the allowed monthly costs of providing an apartment, including repayment of the mortgage loan at the interest rate charged by the lender.[24] HUD directly pays enough of the mortgage payment to reduce the effective interest rate to one percent. This
determines the basic rent BR paid by the poorest participants. Richer participants paid 25 percent of their adjusted incomes, and owners rebated to
HUD the excess of this amount over BR. If the upper income limit for eligibility YLIM is sufficiently high that 25 percent of the adjusted incomes
of some tenants exceeds FMR (as in figure 6.1), their rent is FMR.

The thick lines in figure 6.2 depict how the tenant's rent varies with income for Section 236 with rent supplements. The Rent Supplement Program was an attempt to make it more attractive for the poorest households
to occupy units in these projects and for the owners of the projects to accept these tenants by guaranteeing a part of the rent payment.[25] To achieve

24. This interest rate is below the market rate due to indirect interest subsidies. For this and
other reasons, FMR should not be interpreted as the market rent of the unit.
25. The Rent Supplement Program enacted in 1965 was always used in conjunction with
subsidized construction programs involving private ownership of housing projects, especially
Section 236 and Section 221(d)(3) MIR. Piggybacks with other construction programs were

this goal, the program paid a portion of the rent that the poorest house-holds would otherwise have to pay to live in these projects. Specifically, these extra payments reduced tenant rents to 25 percent of adjusted income except when this was less than 0.3·BR. In that event, the tenant paid 0.3·BR. The minimum rent supplement payment was 0.1·BR. A succession of later programs replaced the Rent Supplement Program in providing additional subsidies to the poorest households in privately owned subsidized projects.

6.3 Program Statistics

Table 6.2 contains the standard information on the number of households assisted by each broad type of housing program. In some respects, these numbers are misleading.

First, the numbers concerning assisted homeowners are not comparable to the numbers for rental assistance. When the loan on a unit subsidized under a means-tested homeownership program is repaid that household is no longer counted as being assisted even though it continues to live in the house. That is one reason why the number of homeowners assisted has declined. This contrasts sharply with rental assistance where households living in housing built under new construction programs are counted independent of whether the mortgage has been repaid as long as these households continue to receive a subsidy. In fact, the purchase of more than 2.5 million houses has been subsidized under Section 235, Section 502, and other smaller programs.

Second, the numbers in table 6.2 reflect only households assisted by HUD and USDA. They take no account of the large number of households assisted by the LIHTC. About 700,000 households lived in such units in 1998 (table 6.5). Further, these numbers do not account for households that receive subsidies from only state and local programs.

With these caveats in mind, we see that in percentage terms the fastest-growing part of the system of rental housing subsidies over this period has been household-based assistance to live in existing units. Recall, however, that there were no programs in this category prior to 1965 when the small precursor to the Section 8 Existing Housing Program was established. In total, more additional households have been served over the past twenty years by new construction programs than by household-based certificates and vouchers even when the LIHTC is ignored.

Table 6.3 contains the standard numbers on HUD outlays. It shows that, contrary to newspaper accounts, real expenditure on housing assistance

---

rare. Except for providing supplements for projects in the pipeline at the time, no new commitments under this program have been made since 5 January 1973. At its peak, the program provided subsidies to about 180,000 households.

Table 6.2   **Total Households Receiving Assistance by Type of Subsidy, 1977–97 (in thousands)**

Fiscal Year	Assisted Renters				Total Assisted Renters	Total Assisted Homeowners[a]	Total Assisted Homeowners and Renters[a]
	Existing Housing		Subtotal	New Construction			
	Household-Based	Project-Based					
1977	162	105	268	1,825	2,092	1,071	3,164
1978	297	126	423	1,977	2,400	1,082	3,482
1979	427	175	602	2,052	2,654	1,095	3,749
1980	521	185	707	2,189	2,895	1,112	4,007
1981	599	221	820	2,379	3,012	1,127	4,139
1982	651	194	844	2,559	3,210	1,201	4,411
1983	691	265	955	2,702	3,443	1,226	4,668
1984	728	357	1,086	2,836	3,700	1,219	4,920
1985	749	431	1,180	2,931	3,887	1,193	5,080
1986	797	456	1,253	2,986	3,998	1,176	5,174
1987	893	473	1,366	3,047	4,175	1,126	5,301
1988	956	490	1,446	3,085	4,296	918	5,213
1989	1,025	509	1,534	3,117	4,402	892	5,295
1990	1,090	527	1,616	3,141	4,515	875	5,390
1991	1,137	540	1,678	3,180	4,613	853	5,465
1992	1,166	554	1,721	3,204	4,680	826	5,506
1993	1,326	574	1,900	3,196	4,851	774	5,625
1994	1,392	593	1,985	3,213	4,962	751	5,714
1995	1,487	595	2,081	3,242	5,087	705	5,792
1996	1,413	608	2,021	3,293	5,079	670	5,748
1997	1,465	586	2,051	3,305	5,120	631	5,751

Source: U.S. House of Representatives, Committee on Ways and Means (1998, table 15-26).

Notes: Figures for total assisted renters have been adjusted since 1980 to avoid double-counting households receiving more than one subsidy. Data are for beginning of fiscal year.

[a]Starting in 1988, figures reflect a one-time decrease of 141,000 in the number of assisted homeowners because of asset sales by the FmHA to private investors.

Table 6.3   Outlays for Housing Aid Administered by HUD, 1977–97

| | Outlays | |
Fiscal Year	Current Dollars (millions)	1997 Dollars (millions)
1977	2,928	7,515
1978	3,592	8,660
1979	4,189	9,275
1980	5,364	10,687
1981	6,733	12,189
1982	7,846	13,273
1983	9,419	15,257
1984	11,000	17,096
1985	25,064	37,569
1986	12,179	17,813
1987	12,509	17,784
1988	13,684	18,684
1989	14,466	18,860
1990	15,690	19,484
1991	16,898	19,973
1992	18,243	20,936
1993	20,490	22,817
1994	22,191	24,079
1995	24,059[a]	25,394
1996	25,349[a]	26,032
1997 (estimate)	26,110[a]	26,110

Source: U.S. House of Representatives, Committee on Ways and Means (1998, table 15-28).

Notes: The bulge in outlays in 1985 is caused by a change in the method of financing housing, which generated close to $14 billion in one-time expenditures. This amount paid off, all at once, the capital cost of public housing construction and modernization activities undertaken between 1974 and 1985, which otherwise would have been paid off over periods of up to forty years. Because of this one-time expenditure, however, outlays for public housing since that time have been lower than they would have been otherwise.

[a]Figures have been adjusted to account for $1.2 billion of advance spending that occurred in 1995 but that should have occurred in 1996.

has more than tripled over the past twenty years, and table 6.4 shows that real expenditure per household has increased more than 80 percent over this period. With minor exceptions, both have increased continuously for the last twenty years.

Although there is no good reason to believe that these numbers give an erroneous view of the trends over time, it is important to realize that the outlay for a particular year is not the total cost of providing HUD-subsidized housing in that year, for several reasons. First, it does not include the many indirect subsidies involved, such as local property tax exemptions and abatements received by all public housing projects and some privately owned projects; the federal income tax exemption of interest on the bonds issued by state and local governments to finance housing projects; and the underpriced mortgage insurance received by many privately

Table 6.4   **Per-Unit Outlays for Housing Aid Administered by HUD, 1977–97**

Fiscal Year	Per-Unit Outlays	
	Current Dollars	1997 Dollars
1977	1,160	2,980
1978	1,310	3,160
1979	1,430	3,160
1980	1,750	3,480
1981	2,100	3,810
1982	2,310	3,900
1983	2,600	4,220
1984	2,900	4,500
1985	6,420	9,620
1986	3,040	4,440
1987	3,040	4,320
1988	3,270	4,460
1989	3,390	4,420
1990	3,610	4,480
1991	3,830	4,530
1992	4,060	4,670
1993	4,450	4,960
1994	4,720	5,120
1995	5,080	5,360
1996	5,350	5,490
1997 (estimate)	5,490	5,490

Source: U.S. House of Representatives, Committee on Ways and Means (1998, table 15-29).

Notes: The peak in outlays per unit in 1985 of $6,420 is attributable to the bulge in 1985 expenditures associated with the change in the method for financing public housing. Without this change, outlays per unit would have amounted to around $2,860.

owned projects.[26] Second, it includes outlays that are mainly used to provide housing in future years and excludes costs that are the result of past outlays. For example, if HUD pays the cost of building a public housing project this year, that outlay will appear this year. This enormously exceeds the real cost of providing the public housing units for whatever part of the current year they are available. It also greatly understates the cost of providing these units in all future years. That the development costs have been paid does not mean that the cost of using the land and structure to house low-income households is zero. These units have an opportunity cost. To the extent that few units have been built recently or the units built have been financed with upfront capital grants rather than annual payments, the real resource cost of HUD's programs is understated. HUD has built few

26. Mortgage insurance is underpriced when the present value of the losses exceeds the present value of insurance premiums. Some programs are designed to provide a subsidy in this form.

units recently and has moved toward development grants and away from partially or fully subsidizing mortgage payments. However, without knowledge of the trend in the importance of indirect subsidies in the total cost of providing housing assistance, it is impossible to say whether the trends reported in tables 6.3 and 6.4 are understated or overstated.

Table 6.5 shows the number of units under the larger individual rental programs. The decline in the number of public housing units in recent years is due in part to the demolition of some projects, although most of the large decline between October 1997 and October 1998 is due to the exclusion of about 73,000 Indian public housing units from the total. It is a testimony to the difficulty in producing information on the number of units receiving various combinations of subsidies that this table indicates that only 38 percent of Section 236 units received rent supplements or Section 8 project-based assistance in 1997, whereas HUD's Picture of Subsidized Households indicates that 67 percent receive Section 8 project-based assistance. The decline in the number of units under the Section 236 and Section 8 programs reflects in part the decisions of owners of some projects not to continue to participate at the termination of their contract with the government.

Table 6.6 presents information about the characteristics of the households served by HUD's four largest programs. Although household income is about the same across the four programs, the substantial differences in household sizes leads to substantial differences in per capita income. Mean household sizes are 2.8 for tenant-based vouchers and certificates, 2.4 for public housing, 2.1 for Section 236, and 1.6 for Section 8 New Construction/Substantial Rehabilitation. The latter program serves the elderly and disabled to a much greater extent than the other programs. Three-fourths of the households served by this program are in this category, as opposed to about 45 percent in public housing and Section 236 and only 34 percent with vouchers and certificates. Section 8 New Construction/Substantial Rehabilitation serves minorities to a much lesser extent than the other programs. More than half of the households served by the three other programs are members of a minority group, but only 37 percent of households served by this program are minorities. Finally, public housing projects are much more often located in neighborhoods with a high poverty rate and a high fraction of households that are minorities.

One of the most salient features of the system of housing subsidies is the extent to which it fails to offer assistance to all eligible households.[27] Consider the largest group that has been given priority for assistance by the biggest housing programs. For many years, Congress has required that public housing and Section 8 reserve a substantial majority of newly allocated units for households whose incomes are less than limits based on 50

---

27. See HUD (2000) for the numbers reported in this and the next paragraph.

Table 6.5   Number of Units Eligible for Assisted Housing Payments by Program Type, End of Fiscal Year

Year	Public Housing	Section 515 Total	Section 515 With Section 8	Rent Supplement	Section 236 Total	Section 236 With Rent Supplements or Section 8	Section 8 Tenant-Based	Section 8 New/Substantial Rehabilitation[a]	Section 8 Other Project-Based[b]	LIHTC[c]
1957	365,896	0	0	0	0	0	0	0	0	0
1958	374,172	0	0	0	0	0	0	0	0	0
1959	401,467	0	0	0	0	0	0	0	0	0
1960	425,481	0	0	0	0	0	0	0	0	0
1961	465,481	n.a.	0	0	0	0	0	0	0	0
1962	482,714	n.a.	0	0	0	0	0	0	0	0
1963	511,047	n.a.	0	0	0	0	0	0	0	0
1964	539,841	n.a.	0	0	0	0	0	0	0	0
1965	577,347	n.a.	0	0	0	0	0	0	0	0
1966	608,554	n.a.	0	0	0	0	0	0	0	0
1967	639,631	n.a.	0	930	0	n.a.	0	0	0	0
1968	687,336	n.a.	0	2,731	0	n.a.	0	0	0	0
1969	767,723	n.a.	0	12,299	0	n.a.	0	0	0	0
1970	830,454	n.a.	0	30,804	5,437	n.a.	0	0	0	0
1971	892,651	n.a.	0	57,786	32,322	n.a.	0	0	0	0
1972	989,419	n.a.	0	92,070	98,699	n.a.	0	0	0	0
1973	1,047,000	n.a.	0	118,184	191,261	n.a.	0	0	0	0
1974	1,109,000	n.a.	0	147,847	293,831	n.a.	0	0	0	0
1975	1,151,000	n.a.	0	165,326	400,360	n.a.	0	0	0	0
1976	1,172,000	25,702	0	174,339	447,126	n.a.	162,085	5,701	105,480	0
1977	1,174,000	50,261	647	179,908	543,360	n.a.	297,256	30,281	125,598	0
1978	1,173,000	80,842	7,064	171,598	544,515	n.a.	427,331	88,738	174,845	0
1979	1,178,000	114,429	15,800	178,891	541,460	n.a.	521,329	191,815	185,297	0
1980	1,192,000	150,714	24,422	164,992	538,285	163,000	599,122	333,153	221,036	0
1981	1,204,000	185,253	32,274	157,779	537,206	161,000	650,817	474,465	193,645	0
1982	1,224,000	216,974	40,412	153,355	536,531	174,600	690,643	571,298	264,742	0
1983	1,313,816	247,164	44,129	76,919	533,469	176,736	728,406	664,395	357,103	0
1984	1,340,575	273,928	45,465	55,606	530,735	178,115	748,543	730,148	431,121	0

(continued)

Table 6.5   (continued)

		Section 515			Section 236			Section 8		
Year	Public Housing	Total	With Section 8	Rent Supplement	Total	With Rent Supplements or Section 8	Tenant-Based	New/Substantial Rehabilitation[a]	Other Project-Based[b]	LIHTC[c]
1985	1,355,152	300,602	45,510	45,611	527,978	196,280	797,383	757,091	455,832	0
1986	1,379,679	326,212	45,510	34,376	529,121	192,000	892,863	777,656	472,820	0
1987	1,390,098	349,178	45,510	23,487	528,174	189,389	956,181	793,812	489,510	17,086
1988	1,397,907	368,456	45,510	23,476	528,174	202,575	1,024,689	798,551	509,222	52,896
1989	1,403,816	385,677	45,510	20,000	528,000	197,329	1,089,598	803,618	526,650	95,653
1990	1,404,870	401,941	45,510	20,000	530,625	199,617	1,137,244	822,962	540,256	139,094
1991	1,410,137	417,998	45,510	20,000	528,115	199,000	1,166,257	827,474	554,264	180,656
1992	1,409,191	433,616	45,510	20,000	510,442	199,000	1,326,250	822,383	573,844	230,587
1993	1,407,923	448,767	45,510	19,270	510,105	190,140	1,391,794	826,791	593,423	290,529
1994	1,409,455	463,742	45,510	18,808	504,966	190,140	1,486,533	844,663	594,763	348,819
1995	1,397,205	476,213	45,510	20,860	508,353	190,140	1,413,311	890,241	608,140	427,759
1996	1,388,746	482,980	45,510	20,860	505,305	190,140	1,464,588	907,215	586,359	509,119
1997[d]	1,372,260	482,980	45,510	20,860	494,121	190,140	1,499,329	880,369	563,937	593,650
1998[d]	1,295,437	482,980	45,510	20,860	476,451	190,140	1,605,898	853,523	541,514	680,229

Sources: Wayne Baker, Housing Budget Office, U.S. Department of Housing and Urban Development (HUD), Washington, D.C., December 1979, for 1941–75; Carla Pedone, Congressional Budget Office (CBO), U.S. Congress, Washington, D.C., April 2000, for 1976–98 except for LIHTC. CBO tabulations based on Congressional Justifications for the Department of Housing and Urban Development (HUD) and unpublished data from HUD and the Rural Housing Administration. Nolden et al. (2002) provide numbers for the LIHTC.

Notes: N.a. indicates not available. Because reliable data are not available at this point, this table excludes rental assistance for units funded through the various block grant programs to state and local governments, including the McKinney Homeless programs, Housing Opportunities for Persons with AIDS (HOPWA), HOME, and, starting in FY 1998, all units assisted through the Indian Housing Block Grants program. CBO has made some adjustments to published data in certain years to smooth out extremely weird patterns in those years. In particular, figures were reduced for the end of FY 1992 because renewals of expiring contracts in the LMSA program were being double-counted as additional units. Some other strange patterns remain in the data, however.

[a]Excludes units funded with capital grants and project rental assistance through the Section 202/811 program.

[b]Includes units receiving assistance through the Section 8 LMSA, PD, Conversion (from Rent Supplement and Section 236 RAP), and Moderate Rehabilitation programs.

[c]An additional 57,426 units have been completed but cannot be allocated to a particular year. Due to the lag between authorization and completion, the number of units completed by a particular time is much less than the number authorized. For example, more than a million units had been authorized by 1998.

[d]Numbers for these years are estimates.

Table 6.6   **Characteristics of HUD-Subsidized Households 1997**

	Section 8 Vouchers and Certificates	Public Housing	Section 8 New and Substantial Rehabilitation	Section 236
Number of projects	—	13,755	15,177	4,224
Subsidized people (thousands)	3,973	2,859	1,403	902
Subsidized units (thousands)	1,433	1,322	895	448
Average rent per month, inc. utilities	204	192	190	255
Average household income per year	9,100	8,900	8,900	10,000
Average people per household	2.8	2.4	1.6	2.1
Per capita income	3,250	3,708	5,563	4,762
Neighborhood poverty rate	20	37	20	21
% age 62+, head or spouse	16	32	60	34
% age 62+ or disability	34	48	74	43
% with children under 18	66	45	23	45
% single parent	57	39	20	37
% minority total	58	68	37	53
% black	39	48	23	35
% Hispanic	15	17	11	13
Minority as % of neighborhood	39	59	34	40

Source: 1997 Picture of Subsidized Households Quick Facts (http://www.huduser.org/datasets/assthsg/picqwik.html).

Notes: Dash indicates not applicable. Most Section 236 units (67 percent) use Section 8 Loan Management as well as Section 236 subsidy.

percent of the local median income for four-person households, with nationally uniform percentage adjustments for households of other sizes as previously described. These households account for 27 percent of all households in the country. Only 28 percent of the renters in this income group receive housing assistance. Local housing agencies have been allowed to admit households into these programs with incomes up to 60 percent higher than the limits based on 50 percent of the local median for almost twenty years. Forty-two percent of all households meet these higher income limits, and 23 percent of the renters in this larger group receive housing assistance.

Because participants whose income rises above the upper limits applicable for admission into the program are rarely terminated, because exceptions to the limits are allowed in some cases, and because some programs have higher upper income limits, many households with higher incomes receive housing subsidies under means-tested housing programs. Specifically, 10 percent of all renters with incomes between limits based on 50 and 80 percent of the local median for four-person households and the standard HUD adjustments for households of other sizes receive means-tested housing assistance. Seven percent with incomes between limits based on 80 and 120 percent of the local median and 7 percent with incomes in excess of limits based on 120 percent of the local median also receive means-tested housing assistance.

Obviously, the overwhelming majority of eligible households do not receive housing assistance. This is not because they do not want it on the terms offered. There are long waiting lists to get into subsidized housing in all localities, and the length of the waiting list understates excess demand in many localities because housing authorities often close their waiting lists when they get sufficiently long.[28]

Two numbers clearly reveal the extent to which HUD's housing assistance is focused on the poorest households. Forty-three percent of the households served by HUD's programs are above the poverty line (HUD 1992, table 1-1), while 70 percent of renters below the poverty line are not served (U.S. Department of Commerce 1991, table 4-12; HUD 1992, table 1-1).

6.4 Program Effects

This section discusses what program effects should be expected based on each program's rules and the general assumptions of economic theory, and it describes the evidence on important effects of public housing, Section 236, Section 8 New Construction/Substantial Rehabilitation, and tenant-based Section 8 certificates and vouchers. To the best of my knowledge, no research on Section 515 or the LIHTC deals with the effects considered in this paper except their cost-effectiveness.

One theme of this section is that little can be said about many effects of government housing programs based on the usual assumptions of economic theory even combined with plausible additional assumptions such as the normality of housing and leisure. For example, housing programs change budget spaces in ways that do not imply that recipients will occupy better housing or work less.

6.4.1 Cost-Effectiveness

Since large sums of money are spent on housing subsidies and many different methods are used to deliver them, it is important to consider the cost-effectiveness of alternative approaches. When needlessly expensive methods of delivering housing assistance are used, many low-income households who could have been provided with adequate housing at an affordable rent within the current budget continue to live in deplorable housing.

All cost-effectiveness analyses of housing programs involve a comparison of the total cost of providing the housing with its market rent, an index of the overall desirability of the dwelling. For tenant-based vouchers and

---

28. HUD does not regularly collect data on the size of the waiting lists under any of its programs. However, a telephone survey in 1999 by HUD staff revealed that the Los Angeles Housing Authority alone had 342,000 households on its waiting list for Section 8 vouchers.

certificates, the approach is straightforward because all of the costs associated with providing the housing during a period occur in that period and they are all in the records of the administering agency. Estimating a statistical relationship between the rent and characteristics of unsubsidized apartments and then substituting the characteristics of the subsidized units into it yields estimates of the market rents of the units occupied by subsidized households.

Dealing with construction or rehabilitation programs is more difficult because the time path of cost bears no particular relationship to the time path of the market rent of a unit, and all of these programs involve indirect costs that are not in the records of the administering agency. The most widely accepted measure of cost-effectiveness for programs of this type is the ratio of (a) the present value of the rents paid by tenants and all direct and indirect costs incurred by federal, state, and local governments to (b) the present value of the market rents of the units over the period that the units are used to house subsidized families. If a government owns the project at the time that it stops being used to house subsidized families, the present value of the project's market value at that time should be subtracted from the present value of the costs. A severe practical problem in implementing this approach is that data on the condition of the apartments in subsidized housing projects over their lives are not available, and some of the costs are difficult to obtain for each year. As a result, only one study (HUD 1974, 123–28) has fully implemented this approach. Other studies take various shortcuts or rely on strong assumptions about missing data.

This measure of cost-effectiveness focuses on effectiveness in providing housing to the recipient. It does not capture benefits or costs of a housing program to others. For example, it is possible that some housing projects make the neighborhoods in which they are located more attractive places to live. Other projects may have the opposite effect. The standard measure of cost-effectiveness captures neither positive nor negative effects of this sort.

Broadly speaking, there are three potential sources of cost-ineffectiveness of housing programs—distortions in input usage in the production of housing services, insufficient incentives for efficiency on the part of civil servants, and excessive profits to developers of private projects. This section discusses each source.

Almost all of the subsidies for housing projects are subsidies for the initial development of the project or subsidies that are independent of the mix of inputs used to provide a particular quantity of housing service. For example, some programs provide direct loans for development at below-market interest rates, others pay a fixed proportion of the mortgage payment on private loans, still others provide tax credits that are proportional to development cost, and some pay directly the entire development cost. Among subsidies that do not depend on input usage are rental assistance payments under the Section 8 New Construction/Substantial Rehabilitation Program and public housing operating subsidies since 1975. (Recall that the latter do not depend on the housing authority's actions.)

The preceding facts about the nature of the subsidy have led some to conclude that housing services in these projects will be produced with too much initial capital and too little of other inputs from the viewpoint of efficient production. However, since all of these programs contain limits on per-unit development cost, the net effect on input usage is ambiguous on theoretical grounds. Nevertheless, the combination of capital subsidies and development cost limits surely results in some productive inefficiency. This argument applies most directly to for-profit firms that own and operate housing for low-income households. However, to the extent that the decision makers in local housing authorities and the nonprofits who sponsor subsidized projects are interested in the well-being of their tenants rather than other taxpayers, they apply with some force to them as well.

Another incentive for inefficient production of housing services in privately owned projects is that the supplier's revenue is independent of the condition of the apartment, provided that it meets the program's minimum occupancy standards. Given the below-market rents that subsidized households are charged, there is a tremendous excess demand for these units for many years after they are built. Therefore, owners will have no trouble renting them even if they are allowed to deteriorate substantially. Just as in the case of simple rent control, this should lead to too little maintenance from the viewpoint of efficient production of housing services.

The absence of important incentives facing administrators of public housing is another source of inefficiency. Under the public housing program, government employees make all of the decisions that are made by managers of profit-maximizing firms in the private market. These include the exact specifications of the project to be built and exactly what maintenance and renovations to undertake. These decisionmakers also must monitor the performance of the employees of the housing authorities. The government managers involved do not have the same financial incentives to operate efficiently as owners of private rental housing. If they make good decisions, they are not rewarded. If they make bad decisions, they suffer no consequences over a wide range of bad decisions. Indeed, they cannot easily learn whether they have made good or bad decisions. Due to the subsidy, they will not lose their tenants unless they make extraordinarily bad decisions.

The other construction and rehabilitation programs such as Section 8 New Construction/Substantial Rehabilitation and the LIHTC provide subsidies to selected private suppliers, albeit with restrictions concerning who may live in the units, how much rent may be charged, and the like. The subsidies and restrictions are designed (or redesigned based on initial experience) to insure that the money budgeted is spent. In all cases, the result has been that many more suppliers want to participate than can be accom-

Table 6.7   **Ratio of Present Value of Cost to Present Value of Market Rent**

Source	Location	Year	Ratio
Housing vouchers			
Mayo et al. (1980b)	Phoenix	1975	1.09
Mayo et al. (1980b)	Pittsburgh	1975	1.15
Wallace et al. (1981)	National	1979	0.91
Public housing			
Olsen and Barton (1983)	New York City	1965	1.14[a]
Olsen and Barton (1983)	New York City	1968	1.10[a]
HUD (1974)	Baltimore, Boston, Los Angeles, St. Louis		
	San Francisco, Washington	1971	1.17[a]
Mayo et al. (1980b)	Phoenix	1975	1.79
Mayo et al. (1980b)	Pittsburgh	1975	2.20
Section 236			
Mayo et al. (1980b)	Phoenix	1975	1.47
Mayo et al. (1980b)	Pittsburgh	1975	2.01
Section 8 New Construction			
Wallace et al. (1981)	National	1979	1.24[b]

[a]Excludes cost of program administration of about 14 percent.
[b]Excludes all indirect costs estimated to add 20 percent to 30 percent.

modated with available funds. For example, developers have requested three times as much money as state housing agencies have to allocate under the LIHTC in recent years. The reason for the excess demand for program funds by suppliers of housing is that those who are allowed to participate make excessive profits, provided that they do not have to pay anything for the privilege. This explains the bribery and influence peddling under these programs that periodically comes to light.

Four major studies attempt to compare the costs incurred to provide units under various housing programs with the market rents of these units.[29] Table 6.7 reports the results of these studies. In assessing the results in this table, it is important to realize that the Olsen-Barton and HUD studies of public housing did not include the extra cost of administering a means-tested program (such as checking eligibility) as opposed to the cost of managing the housing. The other studies did include all administrative cost. Including all administrative costs would add about 14 percent to the total cost of public housing in the Olsen-Barton and HUD studies. Furthermore, the study of the Section 8 New Construction Program did not include any indirect costs such as the tax exemption of the interest on state

29. See Olsen (2000) for a description and appraisal of the data and methods used in these studies. This paper also discusses a study by Schnare et al. (1982) that focuses on differences in development costs across programs and contains problematic results on overall cost-effectiveness. Weinberg (1982) summarizes the research in Wallace et al. (1981) and Mayo (1986) summarizes his studies of the cost-effectiveness of U.S. and German housing programs.

bonds issued to finance state housing agency projects and the interest subsidy involved in the Tandem Plan financing of FHA-insured projects. Previous research on the magnitudes of these subsidies led Wallace and his coauthors to conclude that these indirect subsidies add 20 to 30 percent to the total cost of the projects.

With the aforementioned adjustments to insure comparability, these studies are unanimous in finding that it costs significantly more than a dollar to provide a dollar's worth of housing under construction programs such as public housing, Section 236, and Section 8 New Construction. The studies of housing certificates and vouchers show that the total costs of these programs exceed the market rents of the units by approximately the cost of administering the program. Excluding administrative cost, the two earliest studies find excess costs of public housing in the range of 10 to 17 percent. The more recent studies find excess costs for this program in the range of 65 to 106 percent. The range of the estimated excess cost of Section 236 is 33 to 87 percent, and the estimated excess cost of Section 8 New Construction/Substantial Rehabilitation is 30 to 40 percent.

These estimates almost surely understate the extent of the inefficiency of construction programs compared with tenant-based certificates and vouchers for two reasons. First, the studies using data before 1975 based their estimates of market rent on an estimated hedonic equation containing a short list of easily observed housing characteristics. Older public housing projects did not have many of the unobserved amenities that were common in the private sector. So there is good reason to expect the estimated hedonic equation to overstate the market rents of public housing units. The more recent studies are based on much more detailed data on housing characteristics and hence are likely to provide more accurate estimates of the market rents of public housing units. Second, unlike tenant-based assistance, the construction programs involve indirect subsidies that do not appear in the program's records. All studies attempt to estimate the magnitude of the major indirect subsidies. However, no study attempts to estimate the magnitude of all of the indirect subsidies. For example, some public housing units were built on land donated by federal, state, and local governments. No study has attempted to add the market value of this land to the cost of public housing. Nonprofit developers of Section 8 New Construction projects sometimes receive property tax exemptions or abatements. No study has attempted to account for this indirect subsidy.

The U.S. GAO (2001, 2002) provides similar results for the major active construction programs—LIHTC, HOPE VI, Section 202, Section 515, and Section 811. Using the conceptually preferable life cycle approach, the excess total cost estimates range from at least 12 percent for Section 811 to at least 27 percent for HOPE VI (GAO 2001, 3).

The GAO study will not be the last word on the cost-effectiveness of the programs studied. Like the previous studies, this study ignores some important costs of production programs. For example, all HOPE VI projects receive substantial local property tax abatements. The GAO analysis ignores this cost to local taxpayers. It also ignores the cost of demolishing old structures on the sites of HOPE VI projects and assumes that the opportunity cost of the land is zero. Obviously, the excess cost of HOPE VI is substantially understated on these accounts. The other major shortcomings of the study are that it is based on assumptions about costs beyond the first year that are not rooted in actual program experience and it fails to account for differences in the desirability of the housing over the period of time considered.[30] Instead it simply compares the average cost of units with the same number of bedrooms in the same type of location (metropolitan or nonmetropolitan). Clearly, the GAO study is improvable in many respects. However, it provides the only independent cost-effectiveness analysis of these programs.

An influential view in discussions of housing policy is that subsidized new construction is needed in localities with the lowest vacancy rates. This suggests that construction programs will be more cost-effective than vouchers in these areas. Obviously, the small number of studies of cost-effectiveness and the different methodologies used in these studies preclude making any definitive judgment about this matter. Whether there are any market conditions under which construction programs are more cost-effective than vouchers is surely one of the most important unanswered questions in housing policy analysis.

The GAO study contains suggestive evidence. In addition to the national estimates, the GAO collected data for seven metropolitan areas. The data for the GAO study refer to projects built in 1999. In that year, the rental vacancy rates in the seven metropolitan areas ranged from 3.1 percent in Boston to 7.2 percent in Baltimore and Dallas, with a median of 5.6 percent. The overall rental vacancy rate in U.S. metropolitan areas was 7.8 percent. So all of the specific markets studied were tighter than average. Only five of the largest seventy-five metropolitan areas had vacancy rates lower than Boston's. In each market, tenant-based vouchers were more cost-effective than each production program studied (GAO 2002, tables 7 and 8).

6.4.2 Consumption Patterns

Since housing programs are intended to produce particular changes in consumption of housing services compared with consumption of other

---

30. Lobbyists for construction programs always argue that these programs produce better housing than that occupied by voucher recipients. Although this is typically true when the units are new, it is not true over the entire time that the units are used for subsidized housing. David Vandenbroucke's unpublished research indicates that in eight of the eleven metropolitan areas studied the median market rent of voucher units exceeded the median market rents of units in both public and subsidized private projects.

goods, knowledge of these changes is important for evaluating the programs. This section explains why the design of housing programs does not insure that the programs change consumption patterns in a way that is consistent with their justifications. It also describes the empirical evidence on the effects of the programs on overall consumption of housing services and other goods.

Ideally, a theoretical analysis of the possible effects of housing programs on consumption patterns would consider all of the other welfare programs for which a household is eligible in describing its budget space in the absence of the housing program and define preferences over at least three composites—housing, other produced goods, and leisure. This has never been done in a theoretical analysis.[31] In this section, we will follow the more traditional approach in the literature, namely to assume that income is not subject to choice and that households would face a linear budget frontier defined by this income and market prices for all goods in the absence of housing subsidies. These assumptions underlie almost all empirical studies of the effects of housing programs on consumption patterns. Even with these simplifying assumptions, little can be said on theoretical grounds about the effect of any housing program on consumption of housing and other goods. For example, the public housing program could induce households to consume more housing services and consume less of other goods, more of all goods, or less housing service and more of other goods.

To see why the usual assumptions of economic theory have no important implications for consumption of housing services and other produced goods under any form of project-based assistance, consider figure 6.3. In this figure, consumption of housing services is measured on the horizontal axis and consumption of other produced goods on the vertical axis.[32] The line segment is the budget line in the absence of the housing subsidy. Since housing assistance is not an entitlement, each subsidized privately owned project and each local housing authority has a waiting list. When a unit becomes available, it is offered to a household on the waiting list of an appropriate size for that apartment. This apartment provides a certain quantity of housing service Q_H^G and the rent that the eligible household must pay enables it to consume a certain quantity of other goods Q_X^G. Normally, if the household declines the offer, it is removed from the waiting list. In some

31. Schone (1994) accounts for several major welfare programs and taxes in her empirical study of the effects of housing and other programs on consumption patterns, which will be discussed when we consider work disincentive effects.

32. The quantity of housing service is an index of all of the attributes of housing valued by consumers, including its neighborhood characteristics. In much of the empirical literature, it is measured by the market rent of the dwelling divided by a housing price index. A housing price index across areas or over time is the market rent of dwellings with the same characteristics. The more comprehensive the list of housing characteristics, the better the housing price index. A few studies based on the housing occupied immediately before and after receipt of housing assistance provide information on the program's effect on a few particular housing characteristics.

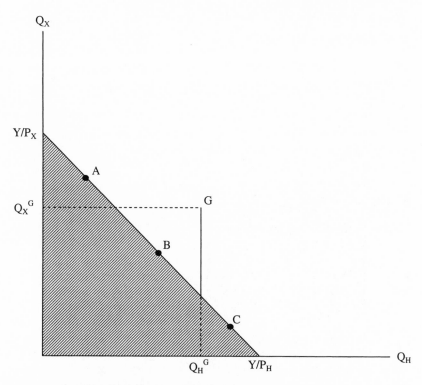

Fig. 6.3   Budget space for project-based program

cases, the household is allowed to decline several offers before removal. This does not change the argument in any fundamental way. In essence, the household is offered an all-or-nothing choice of a particular bundle. The household accepting this offer might choose bundle A, B, or C in the absence of the program. Therefore, the program can have any effect on the consumption bundle of a participant other than reducing its consumption of both goods.

The same conclusion is reached for any type of tenant-based assistance that has been used except for the form of housing voucher that was used between 1983 and 1999. Figure 6.4 depicts the budget spaces of eligible households who were offered assistance under the major certificate and voucher programs. In this diagram, Y is the household's income and P_H and P_X are unsubsidized prices of housing services and other goods. Since participation in these programs is voluntary, a household that is offered assistance can consume any bundle on or below the usual budget line defined by these parameters. All of these programs of tenant-based assistance require recipients to live in apartments meeting minimum housing standards in order to receive assistance. To describe the budget space accurately, it would be necessary to decompose the housing bundle into its components be-

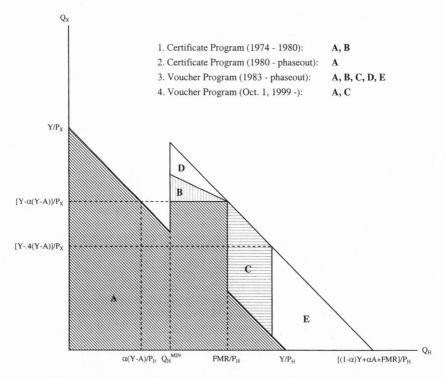

Fig. 6.4   Budget spaces under Section 8 certificate and voucher programs

cause the standards apply to some, but not all, characteristics of housing. When a scalar index of the quantity of housing services is used, this constraint places a lower limit on housing consumption Q_H^{MIN} as a condition for receipt of a subsidy.[33]

Under the original certificate program, participants had to occupy units renting for less than the local fair market rent (FMR) for units of the size occupied. The FMR in an area for units with a certain number of bedrooms has always been the rent at a specified percentile of the distribution of rents of a subset of units of this size. Currently, it is the 40th percentile of the rents of standard quality units occupied within the past fifteen months and not built within the last two years.[34] Since there is an upper

33. In research on these programs, this minimum quantity has been measured as the market rent of units that just meet the program's standards but are minimal in other respects divided by a housing price index (Olsen and Reeder 1983; Cutts and Olsen 2002).

34. Fair market rents apply to entire metropolitan areas and their surrounding counties and groups of nonmetropolitan counties. They are published in the Federal Register each year (for example, 64FR53450) and are available on the HUD website. For the purpose of establishing FMRs, a standard quality unit is a dwelling that is adequate according to the definition used in the American Housing Survey. This characterization is based on the detailed housing characteristics collected in the survey.

limit on the number of bedrooms that may be occupied by each household depending upon its size and composition and a ceiling rent for apartments of each size, the FMR places an upper limit FMR/P_H on each participant's consumption of housing services.[35] A participant that occupied a unit renting for the applicable FMR paid a fraction α of its adjusted income $Y - A$ in rent. (The fraction is currently .3.) In this case, the subsidy was FMR $- \alpha \cdot (Y - A)$ and the participant's consumption of other goods would be $[Y - \alpha \cdot (Y - A)]/P_x$. If the participant occupied a unit renting for less than the applicable FMR, she paid a fraction $\alpha \cdot (Y - A)/FMR$ of the rent. Therefore, the budget space under the original certificate program was the areas A and B in figure 6.4.

The feature of the original certificate program that reduced the rent of a tenant occupying a unit renting for less than the FMR was intended to create an incentive for participants to be economical. However, surveys revealed that few participants understood the rent reduction credit, and it was eliminated in 1980. The budget space under the revised certificate program was the area A.

The voucher program that was introduced as a demonstration in 1983 and operated simultaneously with the certificate program had a simpler structure. It paid a fixed amount toward the participant's rent provided that the participant occupied a unit meeting the program's standards. The fixed amount was PS $- \alpha \cdot (Y - A)$, where PS refers to the payment standard. The payment standard for households of each size and composition could not exceed the applicable FMR, but housing authorities could set payment standards at lower levels.[36] For simplicity, figure 6.4 assumes that PS is equal to FMR. In this case, the budget space under the original voucher program is areas A, B, C, D, and E.

The preceding certificate and voucher programs are being phased out in favor of a voucher program that has some features of each of its predecessors. Starting from the budget space under the most recent certificate program (the area A), the new voucher program enables participants to occupy apartments renting for more than FMR, but neither increases nor decreases their subsidy if they do it. The program places an upper limit on housing consumption by limiting the tenant's contribution to rent to 40 percent of adjusted income. The tenant's contribution is simply the excess of the rent received by the landlord over the government's subsidy, FMR $-$

35. Given the methodology used to calculate them, differences in FMRs between areas do not reflect only geographical differences in housing prices, that is, the difference in the mean rent of identical units in different areas. Therefore, the ceiling on housing consumption has been different for identical households in different localities.

36. Since each authority was allocated a fixed amount of money, setting the payment standard below the FMR enabled it to serve more households. Under the Certificate Program, the authority was allocated a certain number of certificates. This created an incentive for each authority to lobby for higher FMRs in its area to increase the subsidies received by local residents.

$\alpha \cdot (Y - A)$. Since α is currently .3, the upper limit on housing consumption is currently FMR $+ .1 \cdot (Y - A)$.

If housing is a normal good, the type of voucher program in operation between 1983 and 1999 will induce households to occupy better housing than in the absence of the program, although not necessarily better than they would choose if given a cash grant equal to the amount of the housing subsidy. This type of voucher could have the same effect as the cash grant for some, all, or none of its recipients. It is easy to show that each of the other certificate or voucher programs can have any effect on consumption patterns of recipients except less of both goods.

In short, the design of housing programs does not insure that these programs change consumption patterns in a way that is consistent with their justifications. It is an empirical matter whether they have the desired effects.

The available evidence reported in table 6.8 strongly suggests that all housing programs result in substantially better housing for participants. The percentage increase tends to be greatest for new construction programs in their early years, when most of the units are new. As the average age of the units under a construction program increases, the percentage increase in housing consumption of participants declines. The results reported in table 6.9 illustrate this feature of construction programs. In 1970, the median age of public housing units was twenty-two years and the mean market rent of these units differed little from the mean rent of all unsubsidized rental units. At the same time, all Section 236 units were only a few years old. The mean market rent of these units was almost twice as great as the mean rent of all unsubsidized rental units.

Almost all housing programs at almost all times have also increased the consumption of other goods by participants. That is, participants spend less on housing than they would have spent in the absence of the program. Because the overwhelming majority of participants in each housing program pay the same percentage of their adjusted income for rent, there is little difference in expenditure on other goods among households with the same income. Expenditure on other goods under the program differs on account of different adjustments to income and possibly because the household must pay more than 30 percent of adjusted income in order to live in a privately owned subsidized project (about 25 percent of the households in privately owned HUD projects are in this category).

The numbers reported in table 6.8 indicate that the percentage increase in consumption of other goods is less than the percentage increase in housing consumption in public housing, that the opposite is true for tenant-based certificates, and that Section 236 had little effect on consumption of other goods in its early years when the rent schedule required the poorest participants to pay a flat rent exceeding 25 percent of their income. Currently, about two-thirds of the occupants of Section 236 units pay 30 per-

Table 6.8   **Percentage Increase in Consumption of Housing and Other Goods**

Source	Location	Year	Housing (%)	Other (%)
Public housing				
Olsen and Barton (1983)	New York City	1965	58	17
Olsen and Barton (1983)	New York City	1968	66	17
HUD (1974)	Austin, Boston, Honolulu, Indianapolis, Minneapolis, Pittsburgh, Washington	1971	82	19
HUD (1974)	Baltimore, Boston, Los Angeles, St. Louis, San Francisco, Washington	1971	71	16
HUD (1974)	Boston, Pittsburgh, St. Louis, San Francisco, Washington	1971	59	5
Kraft and Olsen (1977)	National	1971	33	14
Mayo et al. (1980a)	Phoenix	1975	35	n.a.
Mayo et al. (1980a)	Pittsburgh	1975	22	n.a.
Hammond (1987)	National	1977	41	[a]
Section 236				
HUD (1974)	n.a.	1972	51	0
Mayo et al. (1980a)	Phoenix	1975	31	n.a.
Mayo et al. (1980a)	Pittsburgh	1975	26	n.a.
Section 8 New Construction				
Wallace et al. (1981)	National	1979	58	n.a.
Section 8 Existing (tenant-based)				
Reeder (1985)	National	1976	16	50
Wallace et al. (1981)	National	1979	31	n.a.
Leger and Kennedy (1990b)	Large urban public housing authorities	1986		
Certificates			59	n.a.
Vouchers			63	n.a.
All programs				
Hammond (1987)	National	1977	40	[a]

Notes: N.a. indicates not available. The percentage increase in consumption is the percentage increase in the real market value (that is, market value divided by an index of the prices of the goods in a category).

[a]Not comparable with other results due to intertemporal approach used.

cent of their adjusted income in rent because they receive project-based Section 8 subsidies, and so this program's effect on consumption of other goods is almost surely positive now.

Unfortunately, the contract reports done for HUD have consistently failed to calculate the percentage increase in consumption of other goods resulting from the programs studied or to provide the relevant mean incomes that would allow others to do it. However, these studies do indicate the dollar magnitude of the decrease in expenditure on housing. Ignoring work disincentive effects, this is the dollar magnitude of the increase in ex-

Table 6.9   **Mean Gross Market Rents of Subsidized and Unsubsidized Units, 1970**

Metropolitan Area	Unsubsidized All Renters	Public Housing	Section 236	
			New	Rehabilitated
Baltimore	116	113	—	—
Boston	135	125	245	206
Los Angeles	128	117	—	—
Pittsburgh	110	92	226	214
St. Louis	97	103	224	—
San Francisco	144	133	224	—
Washington, D.C.	134	136	215	197

Source: HUD (1974, tables 18 and 31).

Notes: Dashes indicate data not available. The mean rents for all renters include the rents paid by subsidized households. Since the mean rent paid by subsidized households was below the mean rent of unsubsidized households, these mean rents understate the mean rent of unsubsidized households. However, since less than 5 percent of renters received housing assistance, the bias is surely small. Section 236 market rents are from 1972–73 data, adjusted to 1970 dollars using a national consumer price index.

penditure on other goods. These studies consistently report that housing programs lead to decreases in housing expenditure.

A careful consideration of the justifications for housing subsidies to the poor suggests that a housing program is not successful unless it induces the worst-housed households with each income to occupy better housing and consume less of other goods than they would choose if they were given cash grants involving the same subsidy.[37] These are the households who undervalue housing in the eyes of paternalistic altruists. Since other programs such as food stamps and Medicaid are intended to induce households who overvalue housing in the eyes of paternalistic altruists (that is, households with excessive rent burdens) to consume more nonhousing goods than they would choose if they were given cash grants involving the same subsidy, it is not clear how housing programs should change the consumption patterns of these households.

Since substantial empirical evidence supports the view that the mean income elasticity of demand for housing is no greater than one, the results in table 6.8 strongly suggest that in aggregate occupants of public housing projects consume more housing services than they would consume if given cash grants equal to their housing subsidies. If the relevant numbers had been included in the reports of HUD's contractors, it might have been possible to make similar statements about other programs.

Although many studies compare housing consumption with and without the program, only four make the more relevant comparison between

37. The subsidy is the excess of the market value of goods consumed under the program over the market value of goods consumed in the absence of the program.

Table 6.10   **Percentage Increase in Housing Consumption Beyond Cash Grants**

Source	Location	Year	% Increase
Public housing			
Olsen and Barton (1983)	New York City	1965	48
Olsen and Barton (1983)	New York City	1968	53
Hammond (1987)	National	1977	40
Schone (1994)	National	1984	49
Section 8 Existing (tenant-based)			
Reeder (1985)	National	1976	10
All programs			
Hammond (1987)	National	1977	39

Note: Cash grant involved in these calculations is equal to the subsidy (that is, market rent minus tenant rent) rather than the cost to taxpayers.

housing consumption under the program and housing consumption with cash grants equal to the housing subsidies. Table 6.10 reports the results of these studies. They show that public housing, tenant-based Section 8 certificates, and the entire system of housing subsidies increase housing consumption more in aggregate than unrestricted cash grants in the aforementioned amounts.

The existing studies do not tell us whether the households whose consumption is "distorted" toward housing by these programs would have been among the worst-housed households with the same budget constraint in the absence of housing assistance. Recall that the rationale for housing subsidies implies that these are the households who should be encouraged to consume more housing than they would with a cash grant.

In deciding how many households should be subsidized to consume housing beyond the levels resulting from cash grants, it is important to realize that the overwhelming majority of households eligible for housing assistance would not live in housing with severe or moderate physical problems or more than one person per room in the absence of the assistance. (See HUD 2000, A28–A29 for HUD's definition of these terms.) In 1997, only 23 percent of unassisted eligible households lived in such housing (HUD 2000, table A5). Since the preprogram housing of recipients of housing assistance differs little from the housing of all eligible households (Wallace et al. 1981, 171), about three-fourths of all eligible households would not have these housing problems in the absence of housing programs.

6.4.3   Neighborhoods of Assisted Households

The landmark 1949 Housing Act established as a goal of low-income housing policy the achievement of a suitable neighborhood for all Americans, and a few studies have estimated the extent to which housing programs achieve this goal. In the absence of housing subsidies, each assisted

Table 6.11   Distribution of Units by Poverty Rate (%)

	Assisted Housing			Welfare Households	All Rental Units
	Public Housing	Private Developments	Certificates and Vouchers		
Less than 10%	7.5	27.4	27.5	25.3	42.1
10–29%	38.9	50.7	57.8	51.0	45.4
20–39%	17.1	11.5	9.5	12.1	6.8
40% or more	36.5	10.4	5.3	11.6	5.7

Source: Newman and Schnare (1997, table 3).

household would live in a neighborhood with certain characteristics. With housing assistance, many of these households live in neighborhoods with different characteristics. This section summarizes the evidence on the difference in neighborhood characteristics for program participants.

Before considering program effects, it is useful to provide some information on the neighborhoods occupied by households under the three broad types of rental housing assistance. Until quite recently, good national information on the neighborhoods in which subsidized households live did not exist. Sandra Newman and her collaborators have remedied this deficiency. (See Newman and Schnare 1997 for a description of the database that they have assembled and some initial results based on it.) Table 6.11 reports one of the results of their efforts. It shows that the neighborhoods occupied by public-housing tenants have many more households with incomes below the poverty line than the neighborhoods occupied by recipients of other types of project-based assistance, certificates and vouchers, and welfare recipients. Recipients of certificates and vouchers live in noticeably better neighborhoods in this regard than households in the other categories.

If households under each broad type of housing assistance would live in neighborhoods with the same characteristics as welfare-recipient neighborhoods in the absence of housing subsidies, table 6.11 would indicate the effect of housing subsidies on the neighborhoods of assisted households. However, since there are some marked differences in the characteristics of the households served by the three types of program (see table 6.6), it is not reasonable to expect that average characteristics of the neighborhoods of the households in these three groups would be the same in the absence of a housing subsidy. So we must look elsewhere for estimates of the effect of housing subsidies on the neighborhoods of assisted households.

A number of studies attempt to estimate this program effect directly by comparing the characteristics of the neighborhoods of households immediately before and after receipt of a housing subsidy. Tables 6.12 through 6.15 report some results of studies of the project-based Section 8 New Con-

Table 6.12 Minority Percentage of All Households by Location Before and After Enrollment: Section 8 New Construction and Substantial Rehabilitation Program

	Destination (%)		
Origin	Central City	Suburb	All Locations
Central city	57	11	68
Suburb	2	30	32
All locations	59	41	100

Source: Wallace et al. (1981, table 3-8).
Note: The sample size is 1,385 observations.

Table 6.13 Mean Change in Minority Concentration from Origin Tract to Destination Tract for Major Demographic Groups: Section 8 New Construction and Substantial Rehabilitation

Household Type	N	Mean % Minority in Tract of Origin	Mean % Minority in Destination Tract	Mean Change in % Minority (%)
Black	1,001	54	35	−19
Hispanic	184	34	32	−2.3
Minority	1,314	47	32	−15
Nonminority white	5,918	7.2	7.0	0.2

Source: Wallace et al. (1981, table 3-9).

Table 6.14 Income and Housing Market Characteristics of Census Tracts Occupied by Recipients Before and After Participation: Section 8 Existing

	Housing Voucher Program	Certificate Program
Median Family Income (1,000s)		
Stayers	13.3	13.3
Movers' origin tract	12.6	12.5
Movers' destination tract	13.7	13.5
% of families receiving welfare		
Stayers	16.2	16.9
Movers' origin tract	19.3	19.9
Movers' destination tract	17.2	16.1
Median monthly rent		
Stayers	233	240
Movers' origin tract	217	215
Movers' destination tract	235	234
% of units without adequate plumbing		
Stayers	2.6	2.6
Movers' origin tract	2.6	2.2
Movers' destination tract	1.7	1.9

Source: Leger and Kennedy (1990b, tables 4.20 and 4.22).

Table 6.15   **Change in Racial/Ethnic Concentration of Tracts Occupied by Black (Non-Hispanic) Recipients Who Moved from their Preenrollment Unit: Section 8 Existing**

	Housing Voucher Program	Certificate Program
% minority		
Origin census tract	75.8	77.1
Destination census tract	73.8	73.7
% Hispanic		
Origin census tract	7.9	8.8
Destination census tract	8.4	94
% black		
Origin census tract	63.9	64.0
Destination census tract	61.9	61.2

Source: Leger and Kennedy (1990b, table 4.25B).

struction/Substantial Rehabilitation Program and the tenant-based Section 8 Existing Housing Program. The data underlying these studies are for a random sample of units in a random sample of projects (in the case of project-based assistance) within a random sample of urban areas.

Table 6.12 reveals that 57 percent of the minority households who moved into Section 8 New Construction/Substantial Rehabilitation projects lived in the central city before and after their move and that 32 percent lived in the suburbs before and after their move. Only 11 percent of these households moved from the central city to the suburbs. So this program does not induce mass migration of minorities from central cities to suburbs.

Table 6.13 indicates that participation in this program typically induced black households to move to a neighborhood with a substantially lower minority percentage.

Tables 6.14 and 6.15 show the effects of the tenant-based Section 8 Existing Housing Program on the types of neighborhoods in which assisted households live. Many participants in this program receive subsidies without moving because their initial units already meet the program's standards or (less often) are repaired to meet the standards and they choose not to move, at least initially. The program has no immediate effect on their neighborhoods. Table 6.14 indicates that those households who move on receipt of the subsidy have fewer poor neighbors and live in neighborhoods where the housing is better. However, these effects are modest. Table 6.15 indicates that tenant-based certificates and vouchers also have a modest effect in reducing racial segregation in housing.

Finally, studies done as a part of the Experimental Housing Allowance Program indicated that public housing induces its participants to live in neighborhoods with a much higher fraction of low-income households and its black participants to live in neighborhoods with a significantly higher fraction of minority households (Kennedy 1980, tables 3-9 and 3-14).

All of the preceding studies estimate the immediate effect of housing programs on the types of neighborhoods in which assisted households live. No studies attempt to estimate the long-run effect of the programs on the location of households. That is, none attempt to estimate the movement of other households and the changes in the housing stock in response to the initial changes in the location of assisted households.

6.4.4   Work Disincentives

Since low-income housing programs are means tested, it is plausible to believe that they will have work disincentive effects. This section describes how the magnitude of housing assistance varies with labor earnings, considers what can be said based on general economic theory about work disincentive effects of housing programs, and discusses empirical research on this topic.

Low-income housing programs are means-tested in two senses. With minor exceptions, all programs mentioned in this paper have always been means-tested in the sense that there have been upper income limits for eligibility for households of each size.[38] Even the programs that have not been means-tested in this sense for all participants over their entire histories have had income limits for many participants for at least twenty years primarily because some occupants of older projects now receive extra subsidies under other programs that have income limits.

The largest programs (Section 8 certificates and vouchers, and public housing) and three-fourths of the units in privately owned HUD projects are also means-tested in the sense that the magnitude of the subsidy received by a household occupying a particular dwelling depends upon its earned income (HUD 1997, 3). All units in the Section 8 New Construction Program, the largest HUD program involving privately owned projects, are means-tested in this sense. For more than fifteen years, the tenant has paid 30 percent of adjusted income in rent under these programs.[39]

Under some project-based programs such as the LIHTC, Section 221(d)(3), and Section 202 (older projects), the subsidy does not depend on income unless the unit or household receives a subsidy from some other source. In each of these cases, the basic program reduces the rent for each unit below the market rent, and the occupant pays this rent independent of its income. However, as far back as 1965, some households in the projects funded under these programs have received additional subsidies that reduced their rents to a fixed fraction of their incomes, and a significant mi-

38. The primary exceptions have been the Section 202 and Section 221(d)(3) MIR.
39. This ignores several alternative rent schemes that applied to a small minority of recipients.

nority of the current participants in these programs receives these extra subsidies. For example, about 40 percent of LIHTC units receive Section 8 assistance (GAO 1997, 40).

The basic Section 236 program was between the two extremes of proportional adjustment of rent to changes in adjusted income for all participants and no adjustment of rent for all participants. Under the basic program, all households who occupied identical units in a Section 236 project and had incomes below a certain level paid the same rent.[40] If income exceeded the cutoff, the rent was 25 percent of adjusted income. Therefore, the benefit reduction rate was zero at low levels of income and .25 at higher levels. Substantial numbers of households were in each category.

Between 1965 and 1974, some, but not all, of the poorest households living in Section 236 projects received rent supplements that reduced their rents to 25 percent of their adjusted incomes over a larger range of adjusted income. After 1974, many more of the poorest households in Section 236 projects received subsidies under the Section 8 Loan Management Set-Aside Program that initially reduced their rents to 25 percent of their adjusted incomes and later to 30 percent.[41]

In studying the work disincentive effects of housing programs, it is important to realize that the subsidy is not the same function of earnings for all households with the same characteristics, even within a given program and the same locality. The subsidy is the excess of the market rent of the unit occupied over the rent paid by the tenant. The preceding paragraphs pointed out the differences in the rents paid by households with the same characteristics under some programs. Even more important are the enormous differences in the market rents of the units occupied by similar households under all mature construction programs. The newest units under these programs are typically very good and hence have a high market rent. The worst are deplorable in part because the program's minimum occupancy standards are not always enforced. The maximum subsidy within a locality under each certificate or voucher program is the same for households with the same characteristics. However, the maximum real subsidy under this program to a household with the same real income will vary across localities because the program's guarantee (the FMR) is not the same everywhere in real terms.

For the overwhelming majority of recipients of housing assistance, the magnitude of the housing subsidy received by a household is a decreasing function of its earned income for small changes in earned income. For others, it is independent of earned income. Therefore, it seems plausible that the standard assumptions of economic theory together with the assump-

---

40. Within a project, the income cutoff was different for households occupying apartments of different sizes.

41. See footnote 6.

tion that leisure is a normal good would imply that each recipient would work less as a result of the program.

Schone (1992) has shown that this intuition is incorrect for a program such as public housing that offers a household a specified apartment for a rent that is proportional to its earned income. She does this by producing a counterexample that involves no peculiar assumptions about preferences or the budget space of the household offered a public housing unit. As usual, this theoretical ambiguity is a result of the nonlinearities of the budget frontier. Since the axioms of the theory of consumer choice do not have an implication concerning the qualitative effect of low-income housing programs on labor earnings, we must rely on empirical studies of this effect.

In the seminal study of the labor supply effects of means-tested housing programs, Murray (1980) estimated that public housing induces tenants to reduce their labor earnings by about 4 percent. Since his study predated data on the hours worked by participants in housing programs and information about multiple program participation, many highly restrictive assumptions were required to make this estimate. First, Murray assumed that leisure is separable from produced goods in household preferences. Many utility functions used in empirical research have this property. Second, he relied on a utility function defined over leisure and a composite of produced goods that was estimated ignoring all nonlinearities in budget frontiers and all differences in market prices facing households living in different localities. It also ignored differences in tastes for leisure versus produced goods across different households, thereby ignoring selection bias. Participants in housing programs may have a different taste for leisure from others. Third, in estimating the subutility function defined over housing and other produced goods, he ignored the other in-kind subsidies for which public housing participants were eligible. However, he did allow for differences in taste based on certain observed characteristics of households, and he did account for the possibility that public housing tenants have stronger than average tastes for housing by using data on these households immediately prior to entering the program to estimate the subutility function.

Since the Survey of Income and Program Participation (SIPP), it has been possible (although extremely difficult) to estimate household preferences accounting for many of the nonlinearities in budget frontiers that result from government programs and to predict the effects of changes in the parameters of these programs in a way that avoids selection bias. In the most important published attempt to estimate the work disincentive effects of housing assistance, Keane and Moffitt (1998) estimate a model of labor supply and program participation for female heads of household who are eligible for AFDC, food stamps, and housing assistance. They model Medicaid as a benefit automatically received by all participants in AFDC and account for federal income and Social Security taxes. The estimated model is then used to predict the effects of a wide variety of changes in the welfare system.

The treatment of housing assistance is the most problematic part of their analysis. Since estimation is extremely challenging without disaggregation of produced goods into housing and other produced goods, they did not do it. However, they recognized that housing subsidies, unlike food stamps, are worth much less to many recipients than cash grants in the amount of the subsidy. They also recognized that housing subsidies are not entitlements and that many households that want to participate are not offered assistance. Keane and Moffitt attempted to capture these aspects of reality by assuming that each household could choose to participate in a program that would provide them with a cash grant equal to an unknown fraction of the difference between the local fair market rent under the Section 8 Certificate/Voucher Program for a household with its characteristics and 30 percent of its adjusted income. That is, housing assistance was treated as an entitlement negative income tax whose known parameters are parameters of the Section 8 Certificate/Voucher Program. However, they judged the results based on this specification to be so implausible that they abandoned this approach and reestimated the model treating the housing subsidy as an exogenous component of nonlabor income for participants without attempting to explain housing program participation.

Estimation of the work disincentive effects of housing programs requires data on consumption of leisure, housing, and other produced goods for a random sample of households and the parameters of their budget spaces. Ignoring the possibility that the household alters its behavior to affect the probability that it will be offered housing assistance, the information missing from the SIPP that precludes estimation of preferences in a straightforward manner is whether a household that is not receiving housing assistance was offered it during the period under consideration and what housing assistance was offered. For example, was the household offered a Section 8 voucher? Was it offered a particular public housing unit, and what were the characteristics of that unit? (Even without this detailed information on what the household was offered, it would be possible to proceed based on a knowledge of which households rejected offers and approximations of the offer.) Accounting for the possibility that the household alters its behavior to affect the probability that it will be selected to participate in a housing program would require a model of decision making under uncertainty and a model of administrative selection.[42]

The best study of the work disincentive effect of a housing program is

42. Crews (1995) has developed a model of administrative selection to study the effects of housing programs on the consumption of produced goods, treating labor earnings as exogenous.

Table 6.16   Simulation of Cashing Out Public Housing (for current public housing recipients)

Original Program Participation Combination	N	Predicted Labor Supply per Week		Predicted Housing Consumption per Month	
		Baseline	Public Housing Cashed Out	Baseline	Public Housing Cashed Out
Public housing only	23	26.28	27.95	399.88	283.51
Public housing, AFDC	2	0.98	0	492.46	230.53
Public housing, food stamps	10	8.57	6.42	356.95	242.15
All programs	39	0	0	394.44	259.14
All public housing recipients	74	9.35	9.56	393.71	263.65

Source: Schone (1994, table 8).

also one of the most sophisticated econometric studies of the labor supply effects of any government program. In this study, Schone (1994) uses data from the SIPP to estimate the distribution of preferences defined over leisure, housing, and other produced goods for a population of female-headed households. These estimates account for many of the nonlinearities in the budget frontier resulting from eligibility for AFDC, food stamps, public housing, federal and state income taxes, and Social Security taxes. (She deleted households who are assisted by other housing programs from the sample because the specific program was not identified and hence she could not describe the household's budget frontier.) She then uses these estimates to predict the effects of several changes in policy. She estimates that the combined effect of AFDC, food stamps, and public housing is to reduce the labor supply of female-headed households by 42 percent and to increase their consumption of housing by 18 percent (Schone 1994, table 7). Table 6.16 reproduces her table 8. It shows that cashing out housing programs—that is, eliminating housing programs and adding the housing subsidy to the AFDC guarantee of the participants in these programs—will increase the labor supply of these households only 2 percent but will reduce their consumption of housing 33 percent.

One assumption underlying these estimates is that households who did not receive housing assistance during the last quarter of 1984 were not offered housing assistance during that period. Since it is certainly not the case that all households who are offered housing assistance accept it, this assumption is violated. For example, Kennedy and Finkel (1994) found that 13 percent of the households offered Section 8 vouchers and certificates in the early 1990s did not use them. The figure was 27 percent in the mid-1980s (Leger and Kennedy 1990). (Similar figures for public housing and subsidized privately owned projects are not available.) However, since turnover in housing programs is low and the number of assisted households was not increasing rapidly at this time, it is safe to say that only a minute fraction of Schone's sample declined an offer of housing assistance during the last quarter of 1984.

Of course, some households surely declined to apply for housing assistance based on the cost of participation broadly conceived and their perceptions of the likelihood of being chosen to participate in each program and, in the case of project-based assistance, the likelihood of being offered particular units. Modeling the decision to apply may enable us to estimate the distribution of taste parameters in the population with less bias and more precision. Two problems in implementing this approach are that few databases contain information on whether a household is on a waiting list for housing assistance and waiting lists are frequently closed to additional applicants. Therefore, it is incorrect to conclude that households that are not on the waiting list do not want to participate. Furthermore, many households on the waiting list decline the offer to participate in the program.

6.4.5   Mean Benefit and Subsidy

Since many economists are interested in the extent to which housing subsidies differ from lump-sum grants, many studies compare the recipient benefit and the subsidy. The most common measure of recipient benefit used in studies of housing programs is the equivalent variation, that is, the lump-sum grant that is just as satisfactory to the recipient as the housing program. The subsidy is the excess of the market rent of the unit occupied over the rent paid by the tenant.[43] Since most housing programs change budget spaces in ways very different from lump-sum grants, we certainly expect any satisfactory measure of benefit to be less than the subsidy for almost all participants. In other words, we expect almost every household to consume a different bundle of goods than it would choose if it were given a cash grant equal to its subsidy. Therefore, the mean benefit should be less than the mean subsidy.

Table 6.17 contains the results of seven studies that estimate both the mean benefit and mean subsidy for one of the four programs or for the entire system of housing subsidies. Estimated benefits are based on estimated indifference maps or equivalently estimated Marshallian demand functions.

Clearly, there are few estimates for programs other than public housing, and there are no recent estimates for any program or for the system as a whole. The median of the estimated ratios of mean benefit to mean subsidy for public housing is .76, and 70 percent of the estimated ratios are between .71 and .81. Based on one study apiece, the ratio is between .63 and .77 for

---

43. The subsidy is less than the taxpayer cost due to administrative costs and the excess of nonadministrative cost over market rent under most programs discussed in section 6.4.1. From the viewpoint of measuring the extent of the consumption distortion, benefit is best compared with the subsidy rather than taxpayer cost.

Table 6.17   **Ratio of Mean Benefit to Mean Subsidy**

	Location	Year	Measure	Sample	Ratio
Public housing					
Olsen and Barton (1983)	New York City	1965	EV	1366	0.77
Olsen and Barton (1983)	New York City	1968	EV	1515	0.73
Murray (1975)	7 cities	1968	EV	1388	
Cobb-Douglas					0.81
CES					0.84
Kraft and Olsen (1977)	Boston, Pittsburgh, St. Louis, San Francisco, Washington, D.C.	1972	EV	333	0.73
Clemmer (1984)	33 SMSAs	1977	EV	>20,000	
Cobb-Douglas					0.92
Stone-Geary					0.80
Linear demand					0.71
Nonlinear demand					0.76
Hammond (1987)	National	1977	EV	804	0.64
Section 8 New Construction					
Schwab (1985)	13 metro areas	1979	CV	167	
Log-linear H expenditure function					0.63
Linear H expenditure function					0.77
Section 8 Existing (tenant-based)					
Reeder (1985)	National	1976	EV	1,099	0.83
All programs					
Hammond (1987)	National	1977	EV	1,088	0.61

Notes: EV = equivalent variation; CES = constant elasticity of substitution; CV = compensating variation; SMSA = standard metropolitan statistical area.

Section 8 New Construction/Substantial Rehabilitation, .83 for tenant-based Section 8 Existing, and .61 for the system as a whole. In assessing the significance of these results for public policy, it is important to realize that mean recipient benefit will be less than the mean subsidy for any successful housing program.

6.4.6   Distribution of Benefits

Many taxpayers care about how benefits are distributed across recipients of housing assistance. They are interested in how mean benefit varies with household characteristics and the variance in benefit among households with the same characteristics. This section explains why little can be said about these matters based on economic theory, and it describes the results of empirical research.

Little can be said on the basis of the program's rules and the general assumptions of economic theory about how mean benefit will vary with household characteristics under any of the programs even within a single locality. Since larger households are entitled to larger apartments under the programs considered, the subsidy will be greater for larger households on this account. However, since larger units under new construction programs may typically be in worse condition or in worse neighborhoods than smaller units, they are not necessarily better overall. Therefore, the mean subsidy is not necessarily greater for larger households. The certificate and voucher programs provide a larger maximum subsidy to larger households within a locality. However, if larger households experience a larger consumption distortion than smaller households, they could receive a smaller benefit even though they receive a larger subsidy.

Similarly, the design of housing programs does not insure that mean benefit will vary with household income within a locality in a particular manner. For all units under many project-based housing programs and many units under the rest, the rent that the tenant pays varies directly with income among households of the same size. Therefore, if all households of a particular size served by a program lived in apartments with the same market rent, the subsidy would be larger for the poorest households of that size. Under all variants of tenant-based Section 8, the maximum subsidy varies inversely with income among households of the same size. However, it is far from the truth that all households served by a mature construction program (that is, a construction program that has been in existence for many years) occupy housing with the same real market rent. Furthermore, a larger subsidy does not imply a larger benefit. If poorer households experience a larger consumption distortion than richer households, they could receive a smaller benefit even though they receive a larger subsidy.

Table 6.18 summarizes the results of regressions of estimated benefit on household characteristics in which a linear relationship between mean benefit and income, family size, age, race, and other characteristics are assumed.[44] Some results are consistent across the studies. In public housing, tenant-based Section 8, and the system as a whole, the mean benefit is larger for poorer households that are the same with respect to other characteristics. Similarly, mean benefit is larger for larger households. These results continue to hold when the authors allow for the possibility of a nonmonotonic relationship by including income and family size squared. The results are less consistent for race and age of the head of the household. The coefficients have different signs in different studies, they are often statistically insignificant, and the magnitudes of the coefficients indicate small differences in mean benefit among otherwise similar households who differ in these respects.

44. Except for Kraft and Olsen, all of the studies used real benefit and income in their analyses. That is, they divided money benefit and income by a cross-sectional price index. Since Kraft and Olsen's study is based on data for five of the country's largest metropolitan areas, it is not clear that taking account of overall differences in prices would have had much effect on their results.

Table 6.18   **Distribution of Benefits Among Program Recipients**

	Income	Family Size	Black	Age	SE/Benefit	Sample
Public housing						
Olsen and Barton (1983), 1965	–**	+**	—	—	0.38	1,366
Olsen and Barton (1983), 1968	–**	+**	—	—	0.43	1,515
Murray (1975)	–	+	+**	+**		1,388
Kraft and Olsen (1977)	–**	+**	–**	–**	0.93	333
Hammond (1987)	–**	+**	—	+**	0.89	804
Section 8 Existing (tenant-based)						
Reeder (1985)	–**	+**	—	+	0.42	1,099
All programs						
Hammond (1987)	–**	+**	+	+**	1.23	1,088

Notes: This table summarizes the results from multiple regression analyses in several articles. In each case, the benefit is regressed on the variables presented in the first four columns and other variables. Olsen-Barton and Kraft-Olsen included sex of the head of the household; Hammond included sex and education of the head and dummy variables for region of the country and size of the locality; and Reeder included dummy variables for sex of the head, other minority, and nonmetropolitan residence as well as an overall price index and the squares of income and family size. In Murray, age is a dummy variable that indicates whether the head is 62 years or older. Murray also includes dummy variables for different household compositions rather than a single variable for family size. The signs presented in the table indicate whether mean benefit varies directly (+) or inversely (–) with the household characteristic. The fifth column presents the standard deviation of the error term divided by the mean benefit, as a measure of the amount of variation present. Finally, the last column gives the number of observations used in the regression.

*The coefficient was statistically significant at the 5 percent level.

Two other noteworthy results emerged from these analyses. First, when Murray (1975) included dummy variables for the different cities represented in his data in the regression equation, he found substantial differences in the real mean benefit of public housing for households with the same characteristics living in different urban areas. In her study of public housing and the entire system of housing subsidies, Hammond (1987) also found substantial differences in real mean benefit for otherwise similar households living in different regions and in places with different degrees of urbanization. Reeder (1985) found large differences in the real mean benefit of the Section 8 Existing Housing Program between otherwise similar households living in expensive and inexpensive locations. Second, when Reeder included in the regression equation a measure of the household's taste for housing based on its preprogram housing consumption, he found that households with the strongest taste received the largest benefit from the Section 8 Existing Program.

6.4.7   Participation Rates

Since taxpayers with any interest in helping low-income households are more interested in helping some types of households than others, information on participation rates of different types of households is useful for discussions of housing policy. This section summarizes the evidence on this matter.

Reeder (1985, table 6) presents the percentage of households in each income and family size class who participate in any HUD program in 1977. The highest participation rate in any of the seventy-seven classes was less than 25 percent. The regularities are that, for any family size, the participation rate first rises and then falls as income increases. For unknown reasons, the poorest households of each size have very low participation rates. Within each income class, participation rates are highest for one-person households, reflecting the strong preference received by the elderly in housing programs.

Wallace et al. (1981, figure S-3 and table 2-8) compare the fraction of eligible households and participants in the Section 8 Existing and New Construction programs with particular characteristics. These comparisons do not hold other characteristics constant. For Section 8 Existing they find that in 1979 the percentage of participants who were elderly was about the same as the percentage of eligibles in this category, that minorities were a slightly larger fraction of participants than eligibles, and very low-income households were a noticeably larger fraction of participants than eligibles.[45] For Section 8 New Construction, the elderly, whites, females, and small families were greatly overrepresented in the sense that they were a higher fraction of participants than eligibles.

Olsen and Barton (1983, 325) use a linear probability model to estimate how the participation rate in public housing in New York City in 1965 and 1968 varied with the household's income and size and with the age, race, and sex of the head of the household. (At that time, public housing accounted for almost all subsidized housing for the poor in the city.) The most striking finding is that blacks had a much higher participation rate (about 20 percentage points) than whites with the same other characteristics. No attempt has been made to determine the explanation for this finding. Participation also increased noticeably with family size (about 4 percentage points per person).

In her attempt to account for both self- and administrative selection in estimating the preferences of recipients of housing subsidies and the benefits that they receive from housing programs, Crews (1995) used data from the eleven metropolitan areas in the 1987 American Housing Survey to estimate a probit model explaining whether a household receives housing assistance. Her explanatory variables reflect participation costs broadly conceived and the factors involved in the preference systems of housing authorities. She found that the poorest households, nonwhites, food stamp

45. Recall that in HUD's terminology very low-income households are not necessarily poor. A family of four is considered to have a very low income if its income is less than 50 percent of the local median.

and welfare participants, and the unemployed had higher participation rates that were statistically significant at the 1 percent level. The elderly have a much higher participation rate that is statistically significant at the 5 percent level.

6.4.8   Market Prices

It is often argued that housing programs will have effects on the rents of unsubsidized units with specified characteristics throughout the housing market. For example, it has been argued that housing vouchers will lead to a higher demand and hence higher rents for units that just meet the standards of the housing program and lower demand and hence lower rents for the worst units because these units will be abandoned by households who receive vouchers. This argument is certainly well founded on economic theory, at least in the short run. Others argue that new construction programs will lead to lower prices for existing apartments. If the new construction comes as a complete surprise to private suppliers, this is also a clear implication of standard economic theory. However, if the new construction under the program is completely anticipated by private suppliers, the opposite effect is to be expected. To the extent that subsidized construction programs lead to greater production of housing, they drive up the prices of inputs that are most important in the production of housing and thereby increase the cost of producing housing with any specified characteristics.

With the exception of Susin (2002), there are no studies of the effects of any of the programs under consideration on market rents of units with a given set of characteristics.[46] NBER and Urban Institute simulation models have been used to study the effects of hypothetical programs bearing some resemblance to the programs under consideration (De Leeuw and Struyk 1975; Kain 1981). The Housing Allowance Supply Experiment did study the effect on market prices of an entitlement housing voucher program similar to the Section 8 voucher program in operation between 1983 and 1999. This study found little effect on the market rents of units of any type (Barnett and Lowry 1979; Mills and Sullivan 1981; Rydell, Neels, and Barnett 1982). For units that were significantly below standards prior to the experiment, rents fell. For modest units meeting the standards or falling slightly below them, rents rose. If an entitlement housing allowance program for which 20 percent of households were eligible had no discernible effect on housing prices, it is perhaps reasonable to conclude that existing tenant-based programs have little effect.

Susin (2002) reports results inconsistent with this conclusion and with the implications of standard economic theory. Since vouchers induce re-

---

46. Studies of the effects of housing programs on the rents of units in the immediate neighborhoods of subsidized housing deal with a different issue. These studies measure the magnitude of nonpecuniary external effects rather than market effects due to changes in the pattern of demand and supply.

cipients to vacate the worst housing and occupy housing in the middle of the quality distribution, this program should decrease rents of the worst apartments and increase rents of units of average quality. Susin finds that *unsubsidized* poor households in metropolitan areas with more vouchers per poor household pay higher rents for units that are the same with respect to many observed housing characteristics.

To obtain this result, he first uses data from the 1993 National American Housing Survey to estimate a hedonic regression explaining the rent of unsubsidized apartments as a function of housing characteristics and dummy variables for combinations of metropolitan area and income group, for example, the poorest households in Oakland.[47] He interprets differences in the coefficients of the dummy variables for a particular type of household across metropolitan areas as reflecting differences in the price of identical housing.[48] For each of the three income classes separately, he regresses these estimated coefficients on the number of vouchers per poor household and a few other potential determinants of the price of identical units.

The reason for the discrepancy between Susin's findings and the implications of the usual theoretical argument about the effects of vouchers on rents is not clear. His results concerning the differences across income groups in the rents of units with the same observed characteristics in the same metropolitan area suggest the importance of unobserved characteristics. He finds that households with higher incomes consistently pay higher rents. The only plausible explanation for this result is that richer households living in apartments that are the same with respect to observed characteristics occupy units that are better with respect to unobserved characteristics. So one possible explanation for Susin's puzzling result is that unobserved housing characteristics are correlated with the number of vouchers per poor household. Since assertions about the effects of different types of housing programs on market prices are influential in discussions of housing policy, additional studies of this question are important.

6.4.9   Tangible External Benefits

Many of the alleged tangible external benefits and costs of particular types of housing program would accrue to neighbors of subsidized households. To the extent that they existed, these external benefits and costs

47. The division of the population into thirds is not based entirely on income, but it is based on household rather than housing characteristics. This is important because the theory explaining the market effects of housing vouchers divides the housing market based on housing characteristics. Most importantly, it distinguishes between units that do and do not meet the program's housing standards. It is important to realize that many households in the lowest third of the income distribution live in units in the middle third of the housing desirability distribution. Many households in the middle third of the income distribution live in units in the lowest third of the housing desirability distribution.

48. Susin (2002, 126) recognizes the importance of unobserved housing characteristics, but this does not affect his procedures or interpretation of results.

would be reflected in neighboring property values. Although the oldest study of this matter was conducted more than forty years ago, there have been relatively few studies over the years.[49] Until recently, these studies have usually been limited to a small number of projects in one city or based on crude methods and data. Recent advances in software for analyzing geographical data have led to several detailed analyses based on data on sales of all unsubsidized single-family units and the location of all subsidized households or projects in several large metropolitan areas.

Lee, Culhane, and Wachter (1999) studied the effects of all major urban rental-housing programs.[50] They find small positive effects on neighboring property values on average for some programs and small negative effects for others. Galster, Tatian, and Smith (1999) find statistically significant effects of the occupancy of units by recipients of Section 8 certificates and vouchers on neighborhood property values. The direction of the effect depends on the nature of the neighborhood and the concentration of program participants in the neighborhood, and the magnitudes are relatively small.

6.4.10   Other Issues

One of the most active areas of research on housing policy over the past few years has been the effect of offering vouchers to occupants of public or private subsidized projects located in central city neighborhoods with high concentrations of poverty on the condition that they move to low-poverty neighborhoods. This research is based on data from HUD's Moving to Opportunity (MTO) Demonstration Program that has been in operation since 1994 in Baltimore, Boston, Chicago, Los Angeles, and New York. Eligible participants were randomly assigned to one of three groups: those who received a Section 8 voucher on the condition that they occupy a unit in a census tract with a poverty rate of less than 10 percent as well as adhering to the other program requirements, those who received regular Section 8 vouchers, and those who continued to receive their current project-based assistance. Households in the first group receive counseling and assistance in finding a private unit, and the experiment was not designed to estimate the effect of this intervention separately from other aspects of the offer.

Although the MTO Demonstration affects few households (about 1,300), its carefully controlled experimental design should permit definitive answers to the main questions posed. The research to date indicates

---

49. See Galster, Tatian, and Smith (1999) for a review of the literature.

50. They incorrectly assume that the FHA-assisted units in their data are owner-occupied units. In fact, these are units in privately owned subsidized rental projects under programs such as Section 221(d)(3) and 236 whose mortgages are insured by the FHA. Therefore, their conclusions about the effect of homeownership programs on neighboring property values is not supported by their results.

that offering households Section 8 vouchers on the condition that they move to low-poverty neighborhoods (combined with assistance in finding a unit) reduces welfare dependency by adults and violent crimes by teenagers in recipient households and increases the educational attainment of younger children in these households. They are also less likely to be the victims of crimes or suffer injuries or asthma attacks (Katz, Kling, and Liebman 2001; Ludwig, Ladd, and Duncan 2001). Kling's web page (http://www.wws.Princeton.EDU/~kling/mto/) contains a comprehensive account of the experiment and research based on it.

Other important issues dealt with in the literature on housing policy are the extent to which subsidized new construction reduces unsubsidized construction (Murray 1983, 1999), the effect of subsidized housing on homelessness (Early 1998), the effect of living in public housing on the educational attainment of children and their earnings as adults (Currie and Yelowitz 2000; Newman and Harkness 2002), and the effect of public housing waiting lists on intra-urban mobility (Painter 1997). The former is particularly important because erroneous views about this matter contribute importantly to bad policy.

6.4.11   Experimental Housing Allowance Program

No discussion of housing policy research would be complete without some mention of the Experimental Housing Allowance Program (EHAP). The major goals of EHAP were to determine the market effects of an entitlement program of tenant-based housing assistance and the effects of various types of such assistance on household choices. Congress authorized this program in 1970, planning for the experiment occurred in the early 1970s, data were collected during the mid-1970s, and the final reports were completed in the late 1970s and early 1980s. The experiment cost almost $200 million (that is, more than $500 million in 2000 prices); research and data collection accounted for almost half of this amount.[51] The research firms that ran the experiments issued more than 300 reports, technical notes, and professional papers. As a result of these expenditures, we know more about the effects of the experimental programs studied than any established housing program.

The experiment had four components: the Supply Experiment, the Demand Experiment, the Administrative Agency Experiment, and the Integrated Analysis. The first two were the largest and most important.

The primary purposes of the Supply Experiment were to determine the market effects of an entitlement program of household-based assistance, such as its effects on the rents of units with specified characteristics and how suppliers alter their units in response to the program. The Supply Experiment research still accounts for the bulk of what is known about these

51. Sadly, HUD lost all of the data that had been so carefully collected and documented.

matters. The RAND Corporation conducted the Supply Experiment. The experiment involved operating entitlement housing allowance programs in the Green Bay and South Bend metropolitan areas. At the time of the experiment, Green Bay had few minorities and a very low vacancy rate. South Bend had a large minority population and a high vacancy rate. About 20 percent of the households in each area were eligible for housing assistance. Unlike established housing programs, both renters and homeowners could participate. These households were offered a cash grant on the condition that they occupy housing meeting certain standards. These payments could continue for up to ten years provided that the household remained eligible.

The Demand Experiment, conducted by Abt Associates in the Pittsburgh and Phoenix metropolitan areas, was primarily intended to see how recipients would respond to different types of household-based housing assistance and, for a given type, to different program parameters. To this end, eligible households were assigned at random to the different programs or to a control group that was paid a small amount of money to provide needed information. One type of housing assistance offered eligible households a cash grant under the condition that they occupy housing meeting certain standards, another offered a cash grant under the condition that they spend at least a certain amount on housing (two different amounts were tested), and another offered the same cash grant with no strings attached. Two other plans offered to pay different fractions of the household's housing expenditure with no other strings attached. Since the Demand Experiment provided subsidies for only three years and large changes in housing consumption have a large fixed-cost component, the Demand Experiment results undoubtedly understate the responsiveness to a permanent program (Bradbury and Downs 1981, 367–68).

The most influential Demand Experiment research went beyond a comparison of different types of household-based assistance. It compared the effects of the minimum-standards housing allowance program with the major established housing programs in existence at the time, namely public housing, Section 236, and Section 23. The results of some of this research are reported earlier in this paper.

In the Integrated Analysis, the Urban Institute helped to design all of the experiments and used data from all of the experiments to analyze many of the same questions considered by the contractors operating the experiments. The Administrative Agency Experiment conducted by Abt Associates focused on the behavior of local administrative agencies in operating an allowance program. Unlike the Demand Experiment, it was not a controlled experiment.

The best introductions to this vast literature are the final reports of the Supply Experiment, the Demand Experiment, and the Integrated Analysis (Lowry 1983; Kennedy 1980; Struyk and Bendick 1981), an edited volume containing summaries of the findings by the major contributors to EHAP research (Friedman and Weinberg 1983), an edited volume containing evaluations of this research by outside scholars (Bradbury and Downs 1981), a monograph containing some of the more technical results on consumer behavior from the Demand Experiment (Friedman and Weinberg 1982), and HUD's 1980 summary report (HUD 1980).

Although it is impossible to present a detailed review of the findings here, it is possible to state a few of the most important results for housing policy. Since the only type of tenant-based housing assistance studied in EHAP that has been used in an established program is the cash grant conditional on occupying a dwelling meeting certain housing standards, and both the Supply and the Demand experiments studied this type of program, the summary below will focus on it.[52]

The experiments revealed that many unsubsidized low-income households live in housing meeting reasonable standards. About half of the eligible families in the Supply Experiment occupied housing meeting its standards, and about a fourth of the eligible families in the Demand Experiment sites occupied housing meeting its more stringent standards prior to receiving assistance. Even at the lowest income levels, many households occupied units meeting the standards of the Demand Experiment, which suggests the importance of preferences in determining whether poor households meet housing standards. Not surprisingly, households whose units met the standards prior to the program were much more likely to participate in the minimum-standards housing allowance program. They could receive a subsidy without moving or getting their landlords to improve their apartments.

In estimating the cost of an entitlement housing assistance program, it is often assumed that all eligible households would participate. The Supply Experiment revealed that this assumption could be far from the mark. Although the entitlement housing allowance programs in Green Bay and South Bend were heavily publicized, the participation rate leveled off at about a third after three years. It was about 41 percent for eligible renters and 27 percent for eligible homeowners. The primary reasons for the low participation rates are easy to understand. Since the subsidy declines linearly with income until the upper income limit is reached and the density of eligible households increases with income, many eligible households were entitled to small subsidies. Many others who were eligible for somewhat larger subsidies had to move to get them because their apartments were substantially below the program's minimum standards. Many house-

52. The Section 8 Voucher Program implemented in 1983 and currently being phased out is a program of this type. (See figure 6.4.) Since this program does not have the same specific parameters (housing standards, real guarantee, and benefit reduction rate) as the programs studied in the experiments, and since participation in the Section 8 Voucher Program depends importantly on administrative selection, it should not be expected to have the same quantitative effects as the experimental programs. The best sources of information about the effects of the Voucher Program are the detailed studies commissioned by HUD (Leger and Kennedy 1990; Kennedy and Finkel 1994).

holds eligible at a point in time were only briefly eligible. Finally, despite the heavy publicity, 17 percent of eligible households had not learned about the program by the end of its third year. Obviously, we should not conclude that the participation rate in any entitlement minimum-standards housing allowance program would be a third. This is heavily dependent on the generosity of the subsidy and the minimum standards. It is possible to have an expensive entitlement housing allowance program serving a large number of households or an inexpensive program serving a small number.

The minimum-standards housing allowance program tested in the Supply and Demand experiments resulted in modest increases in overall housing consumption as measured by the mean market rent of the units occupied and a substantial effect in terms of the fraction of eligible households meeting the program's minimum standards. Recipients in the Supply Experiment devoted 80 percent of their increased spending to goods other than housing. For a slight majority of recipients, the minimum housing standards were non-binding constraints. So the effect of the program on the consumption patterns of these households was an income effect alone. For many others, only modest improvements in their current housing were necessary to meet the standards. Indeed, the required improvements were so modest that many renters made them without involving their landlords.

Evidence from the Supply Experiment shows beyond a reasonable doubt that an entitlement housing allowance program similar to the one tested will have no significant effects on rents of units with specified characteristics even in the short run. Reasons for the program's small effect on rental housing prices are easy to find. Eligible families account for only a small fraction of the demand for housing services in a given housing market, and many of these families choose not to participate. So even a large increase in demand by participants will have a small effect on aggregate demand for housing services, and this small increase occurs gradually over time because not all families respond instantly to an offer of assistance.[53] Furthermore, the Supply Experiment revealed that even over short periods suppliers are willing to make many changes in existing units in response to small changes in the profitability of housing with different characteristics.

6.5   Reform Options

The major options for reform of the system of housing subsidies to low-income households are answers to the following questions. Should housing

53. The response to an offer of housing assistance with minimum housing standards is surely slower than the response to an offer of assistance for most other goods because many households must substantially renovate their current housing or move in order to receive assistance. Despite this drawback of tenant-based housing assistance of this form, it still gets households into satisfactory housing much faster than any form of new construction. The lag between authorization of funds and occupancy under all construction programs is much greater than the lag under this form of tenant-based assistance.

assistance be an entitlement? Should housing subsidies be delivered to additional households by building new projects under some type of construction or substantial rehabilitation program or by giving them housing vouchers? Should we require households currently living in subsidized projects for which future federal expenditure is discretionary to live in these projects to receive a subsidy and should their owners be given a sufficient subsidy to induce them to continue to serve these households, or should these households be given housing vouchers? This section will consider each of these questions.

Unlike other major means-tested transfer programs, housing assistance is not an entitlement, despite its stated goal of "a decent home and suitable living environment for every American family" (Housing Act of 1949). No coherent justification for this feature of the system of housing subsidies has been offered. That is, no one has attempted to explain why we should offer assistance to some but not other households with the same characteristics.

It is difficult to reconcile these features of the Section 8 Existing Housing Program and all other low-income housing programs with plausible taxpayer preferences. In thinking about whether housing assistance should be an entitlement, it is helpful to think about how a nonrecipient who pays the taxes to support housing programs feels about dividing a fixed amount of assistance between two families that are identical in his or her eyes. At one extreme, we could give one of the families all of the money. At the other extreme, we could divide it equally between them. The former is inconsistent, and the latter consistent, with the usual assumptions about preferences, namely, that the amount that a person is willing to sacrifice for an additional unit of anything of value decreases as its quantity increases. To say that two potential recipients are the same in the eyes of a taxpayer is to say that the taxpayer is willing to sacrifice the same amount for the same change in the consumption pattern of either family. If all housing assistance goes to one potential recipient, the value to the taxpayer of the change in the consumption bundle resulting from the last dollar of housing assistance received by this recipient will be less than that resulting from the first dollar of housing assistance to the other recipient. Therefore, the taxpayer's well-being can be increased by reallocating housing assistance until both potential recipients receive the same assistance. Although each recipient would like to have more than half of the total, this obviously provides no guidance for policy.

The usual argument against making housing assistance an entitlement is that it would be too expensive. Those who make this argument seem to have in mind delivering housing assistance to all currently eligible households using the current mix of housing programs and the current rules for the tenant's contribution to rent. This would indeed increase the amount spent on housing assistance greatly, although this magnitude has not been estimated. However, we do not have to make more than 40 percent of the population eligible for housing assistance; we can reduce the fraction of housing assistance delivered through programs that are cost-ineffective, and we can reduce subsidies at every income level. Indeed, U.S. housing policy has been moving in this direction as a result of, first, a series of amendments of the 1937 Housing Act that required an increasing percentage of households served by tenant-based assistance to be the poorest of the currently eligible households; second, the introduction and rapid expansion of the cost-effective tenant-based Section 8 Program authorized by the 1974 Housing Act; and, third, the increase in the tenant contribution to rent mandated by the Housing and Community Development Amendments of 1981. Each of these reforms moved us in the direction of an entitlement program.

Furthermore, it is easy to develop an entitlement housing assistance program with any cost desired. For example, we could have an entitlement housing assistance program without spending any additional money by a simple change in the Section 8 Voucher Program, namely reducing the subsidy available to each eligible household by the same amount. This will effectively eliminate from the program all households currently eligible for subsidies smaller than this amount. These are the currently eligible households with the largest incomes. This would free up money to provide vouchers to poorer households who want to participate. The reduction in subsidies to those who continue to participate would free up money to provide vouchers to households with identical characteristics who had not previously been served. At current subsidy levels, many more people want to participate than can be served with the existing budget. As we reduced the subsidy at each income level, the number of households that are eligible for a subsidy and willing to participate would decline until we reached a point where all households who wanted to participate in the program were participating. So without any change in the program's budget, we could create an entitlement housing assistance program serving the poorest of the currently eligible households. If reductions in the subsidies received by current participants seem too draconian, we could phase in the new system by freezing subsidies at current levels and allowing inflation to erode real subsidy levels.

In discussions of housing policy, a common objection to this proposal is that no one would be able to find housing meeting the program's standards with the lower subsidies. Obviously, this objection is logically flawed. We start from a position where many more people want to participate than can be served with the existing budget. If we reduce subsidy levels slightly, it will still be the case that more people want to participate than can be served. If we decrease the subsidy levels so much that no one wants to participate, we have decreased them more than the proposed amounts.

A more sophisticated argument against the proposal is that the poorest households will be unable to participate in the proposed program. The simple proposal above calls for reducing the guarantee under the Voucher

Program (called the Payment Standard). This is the subsidy received by a household with no income. If the Payment Standard is less than the rent required to occupy a unit meeting the program's minimum housing standards, then a household whose income and assistance from other sources is just sufficient to buy subsistence quantities of other goods would be unable to participate in the proposed Voucher Program. Previous studies (Olsen and Reeder 1983; Cutts and Olsen 2002) have shown that the Payment Standard exceeds the market rent of units just meeting the program's minimum housing standards in all of the many metropolitan areas and bedroom sizes studied. The median excess varied between 33 and 80 percent between 1975 and 1993. So a considerable reduction in the payment standard could occur almost everywhere without precluding participation by the poorest of the poor. However, the preceding proposal might lead to a particularly low participation rate by these households. This could be counteracted by a smaller reduction in the guarantee combined with a greater benefit reduction rate. For a given program budget, this would yield a higher participation rate by the poorest of the poor and a lower participation rate by other eligible households.

Another objection to the proposed program is that participants in the revised Section 8 Voucher Program would receive much smaller subsidies than the majority of identical households receiving project-based assistance, thereby introducing additional inequities into the system of housing subsidies. This objection could be overcome by increasing the tenant contribution under the programs of project-based assistance and using the savings from the reduced subsidies under these programs to increase the budget of the Voucher Program. If this were done, subsidies under the Voucher Program would not have to be reduced as much to make it an entitlement program, and hence the program's participation rate would be higher.

Should housing subsidies be delivered to additional households by building new projects under some type of construction or substantial rehabilitation program or by giving them housing vouchers?

The unanimity of the evidence on the cost-effectiveness of tenant-based vouchers compared with any form of project-based assistance studied is a strong argument for providing vouchers to all additional households receiving housing assistance, especially because the parameters of a voucher plan can be altered to change many of its other effects without affecting its cost-effectiveness or its total cost to taxpayers. For example, if we want to increase the participation rate of the poorest households at the expense of other eligible households, we can increase the program's guarantee (that is, the Payment Standard) and benefit reduction rate (that is, the tenant contribution as a fraction of adjusted income). Changes in the minimum housing standards, the payment standard, the benefit reduction rate, and the upper limit on housing expenditure will also lead to changes in consumption of housing and other goods.

Two main objections have been raised to exclusive reliance on tenant-based assistance.[54] Specifically, it has been argued that tenant-based assistance will not work in markets with the lowest vacancy rates and that new construction programs have an advantage compared with tenant-based assistance that offsets their cost-ineffectiveness: Namely, they promote neighborhood revitalization to a much greater extent.

Taken literally, the first argument is clearly incorrect in that Section 8 certificates and vouchers have been used continuously in all housing markets for more than two decades. It is true that some households who are offered vouchers do not find such housing within their housing authority's time limits. However, other eligible households use these vouchers. For many years, public housing authorities have over-issued vouchers and thereby achieved high usage rates despite low success rates. In recent years, they have had a reserve fund for this purpose, and current regulations call for penalties on authorities with usage rates below 95 percent. The national average usage rate is high (about 92 percent). So the overwhelming majority of certificates and vouchers are in use at each point in time. Local housing authorities rarely, if ever, return certificates and vouchers to HUD.

The real issue is not whether tenant-based vouchers can be used in all market conditions but whether it would be better to use new construction or substantial rehabilitation programs in some circumstances. In this regard, two questions seem especially important. Will construction programs get eligible households into satisfactory housing faster than tenant-based vouchers in some market conditions? Are construction programs more cost-effective than tenant-based vouchers under some circumstances? Although careful studies of these two questions have not been done, we can be very confident about the answer to the first questions.

Based on existing evidence, there can be little doubt that tenant-based vouchers get households into satisfactory housing much faster than any construction program even in the areas where the highest fraction of vouchers are returned unused. Two major studies of success rates under the tenant-based Section 8 program have been completed over the past fifteen years (Leger and Kennedy 1990a; Kennedy and Finkel 1994). These studies collected data on more than fifty local housing authorities selected at random. The lowest success rate observed was 33 percent for New York City in the mid-1980s.[55] If a housing authority with this success rate issued only the vouchers available at each point in time and allowed recipients up

---

54. See Weicher (1990) for a more extended discussion of the voucher/production debate.

55. The success rate is the percentage of the households authorized to search for a unit who occupy a unit meeting the program's standards within the housing authority's time limit. The success rate in New York City in the mid-1980s was much lower than the second lowest (47 percent in Boston in the mid-1980s) and much lower than in New York City in 1993 (65 percent). An earlier study based on data from the late 1970s found lower success rates. However, at that time housing authorities were still figuring out how to administer this new program, so these success rates are of no relevance for predicting the effects of expanding the program today.

to three months to find a unit meeting the program's standards, about 80 percent of the vouchers would be in use within a year. If they followed the current practice of authorizing more households to search for units than the number of vouchers available, almost all of the vouchers would be in use in much less than a year.

Based on data on a large stratified random sample of 800 projects built between 1975 and 1979, Schnare et al. (1982) found the mean time from application for project approval to completion of the project ranged from twenty-three months for Section 236 to fifty-three months for conventional public housing. Mean times ranged from twenty-six to thirty-one months for the variants of the Section 8 New Construction and Substantial Rehabilitation Program. Occupancy of the completed units required additional time. Although the authors did not report results separately for different markets, it seems reasonable to believe that these times were greater in the tightest housing markets because the demand for unsubsidized construction would be greatest in these locations. So if Congress were to simultaneously authorize an equal number of tenant-based vouchers and units under any construction program, it is clear that all of the vouchers would be in use long before the first newly built unit was occupied no matter what the condition of the local housing market at the time that the money is appropriated.

Although the cost-effectiveness studies discussed in section 6.4 are based on data for projects built in twenty-five cities at many different times and these studies are unanimous in finding that it costs significantly more than a dollar to provide a dollar's worth of housing under construction programs such as public housing, Section 236, and Section 8 New Construction, they do not report results that enable us to determine how the cost-effectiveness of these programs vary with market conditions. Therefore, we cannot be certain that vouchers are more cost-effective than construction programs in all circumstances. Whether there are any market conditions under which construction programs are more cost-effective than vouchers is one of the most important unanswered questions in housing policy analysis.

The second major objection to the exclusive reliance on tenant-based assistance is that new construction promotes neighborhood revitalization to a much greater extent than tenant-based assistance. The evidence from EHAP is that even an entitlement housing voucher program will have modest effects on neighborhoods, and the small literature on the Section 8 Voucher Program confirms these findings for a similar nonentitlement program (Lowry 1983, 205–17; Galster, Tatian, and Smith 1999). These programs result in the upgrading of many existing dwellings, but this is concentrated on their interiors. It is plausible to believe that a new subsidized project built at low density in a neighborhood with the worst housing and poorest households would make that neighborhood a more attractive place to live for some years after its construction. The issue is not, however, whether some construction projects lead to neighborhood upgrading. The issues are the magnitude of neighborhood upgrading across all projects under a program over the life of these projects, who benefits from this upgrading, and the extent to which upgrading of one neighborhood leads to the deterioration of other neighborhoods.

Economic theory suggests that the primary beneficiaries of neighborhood upgrading will be the owners of nearby properties. Since the overwhelming majority of the poorest households are renters, it is plausible to believe that most of the housing surrounding housing projects located in the poorest neighborhoods is rental. Therefore, if a newly built subsidized project makes the neighborhood a more attractive place to live, the owners of this rental housing will charge higher rents and the value of their property will be greater. Since the occupants of this rental housing could have lived in a nicer neighborhood prior to the project by paying a higher rent, they are hurt by its construction. The poor will benefit from the neighborhood upgrading only to the extent that they own the property surrounding the project.

Housing programs involving new construction may primarily shift the location of the worst neighborhoods. With the passage of time, the initial residents will leave the neighborhood in response to the projects, and others who value a better neighborhood more highly will replace them. The desirability of the neighborhoods into which the original residents move will decline in response to their weaker demand for neighborhood amenities. The possibility of a shifting of the locations of the worst neighborhoods has not even been recognized in discussions of housing policy, let alone studied.

What has been studied is the extent to which projects under various housing programs affect neighborhood property values. The existing studies find small positive effects on average for some programs and small negative effects for others (Lee, Culhane, and Wachter 1999; Galster, Tatian, and Smith 1999). No study finds substantial positive effects on average for any program.

Should we require households currently living in subsidized projects for which future federal expenditure is discretionary to live in these projects to receive a subsidy and their owners to be given a sufficient subsidy to induce them to continue to serve these households, or should these households be given housing vouchers?

HUD devotes a substantial fraction of its budget for housing assistance to discretionary expenditures that provide additional subsidies to public housing authorities and the owners of privately owned subsidized projects in an attempt to insure that their projects provide satisfactory housing without charging rents that are regarded as excessive. For example, more than $6 billion annually is spent on operating and modernization subsidies for public housing. Many units under all major construction programs that have been in existence for more than twenty years receive similar subsidies. Given the evidence on the cost-effectiveness of different methods of delivering housing assistance, an obvious policy reform is to replace these discretionary expenditures with tenant-based vouchers.

In the case of public housing, this reform would involve using the money currently devoted to operating and modernization subsidies to offer public housing tenants vouchers that can be used in private or public housing.[56] At present, if tenants leave public housing, they lose their subsidies, so housing authorities have a captive audience. Under the proposed reform, housing authorities would be forced to compete with the private sector for tenants, albeit with the considerable advantage of having been given their projects.

To offset this large reduction in revenue and enable housing authorities to raise the money to continue to provide housing that meets program standards, they could be allowed to charge market rents for the units vacated after the implementation of the reform. Households with tenant-based vouchers would occupy many of these units. Other households eligible for housing assistance would occupy the rest. Public housing tenants who rejected vouchers would be able to remain in their apartments on the previous terms.

Housing authorities could raise additional money by taking advantage of the current regulation that allows them to sell projects. At present, they have little incentive to do it. Without guaranteed federal operating and modernization subsidies, many of the larger authorities may well decide to sell their worst projects. These are projects that will be largely abandoned by tenants with vouchers, and they are the most expensive to operate. If they are sold to the highest bidders, some of these buildings will undoubtedly be torn down and the land put to some better use.

In general, if vouchers are the most cost-effective method of providing housing assistance to additional households, they are also the most cost-effective way to serve households currently living in housing projects. However, two other objections to vouchering out public housing warrant consideration.

One objection to this proposal is that it will force some tenants who prefer to stay in their current units to move. This objection applies equally to the current initiatives within the public housing program involving the demolition or major rehabilitation of projects. When these activities occur, displaced tenants are provided with tenant-based vouchers. It also applies equally to similar activities in the unsubsidized housing market. Legal prohibitions against this displacement are rare.

---

56. During its first term, the Clinton administration proposed this reform (HUD 1995). Robert Dole made a similar proposal during his presidential campaign.

Another objection to the proposal is that it will reduce the number of affordable housing units. The meaning of this objection is not entirely clear. Since any dwelling is affordable with sufficient subsidy, vouchering out public housing does not change the number of affordable units unless it leads to a smaller housing stock. Even if vouchering out public housing led to the demolition of more public housing units than pursuing current policies, it does not follow that the total housing stock will be smaller on that account. When vacancy rates fall, private unsubsidized construction increases. Finally, this objection might refer to a reduction in the number of apartments reserved for occupancy by subsidized households. However, the advantages to assisted households or taxpayers of requiring subsidized households to live in particular units in order to receive a subsidy have not been explained. Among the disadvantages are the cost-ineffectiveness of project-based assistance and the severe limitation on the tenant's ability to adjust his or her housing in response to changes in circumstances such as job location.

Under all programs that provide substantial project-based assistance to private parties who build or rehabilitate housing for low-income households, these parties agreed to provide housing meeting certain standards to households with particular characteristics for a specified number of years. At the end of the use agreement, the government must decide whether to change the terms of the agreement, and the private parties must decide whether to participate on these terms. Since the government provides mortgage insurance for the overwhelming majority of these projects, it must also decide whether to provide additional subsidies to these projects when the private parties default on their loans or to sell these projects without subsidies. When use agreements are not renewed, current occupants are always provided with other housing assistance, usually tenant-based vouchers.[57] Up to this point, housing policy has leaned heavily in the direction of providing owners with a sufficient subsidy to induce them to continue to serve the low-income households in their projects.

Given the evidence on the cost-effectiveness of different methods of delivering housing assistance, an obvious policy reform is not to renew any use agreement and to provide the subsidized occupants of these projects with tenant-based vouchers. The issues involved in this decision are the same as those involved in the decision to voucher out public housing. However, it should be pointed out that for-profit sponsors will not agree to extend the use agreement unless this provides higher profits over the remaining life of the project than operating in the unsubsidized market. Since these subsidies are provided to selected private suppliers, the market mechanism

57. Indeed, they have normally been given the option of staying in their current apartment with the government paying the difference between the market rent of the unit and the standard tenant contribution or receiving the regular voucher that would be offered to any household with the same characteristics.

does not insure that profits under the new use agreement will be driven down to market levels. If this does not happen, it will be more cost-effective to provide the occupants of these units with tenant-based vouchers.

6.6   Summary and Conclusions

The primary justification for housing subsidies to low-income households seems to be a desire on the part of many citizens to help these households combined with the view that many low-income households undervalue housing. To provide assistance consistent with this justification, an incredibly complicated system of housing programs has been developed, involving much larger indirect subsidies than is common for means-tested transfer programs. The total cost of this system exceeds the cost of other better-known parts of the welfare system. Only Medicaid is larger. The evidence on the major effects of housing programs is sparse or old or both. Based on this evidence, the effects of low-income housing programs can be summarized as follows.

In aggregate, all major housing programs increase housing consumption substantially, and almost all significantly increase consumption of other goods. The increase in housing consumption is especially marked for new construction programs in their early years. However, well before they reach the midpoint of their useful lives these projects have provided less desirable housing than the housing occupied by voucher recipients. All programs increase aggregate housing consumption more than would occur if each participant were given a cash grant equal to his or her housing subsidy.

The net effect of these changes in consumption patterns is that housing programs typically provide large benefits to their recipients. Although mean benefit is large compared with their mean income, it is small compared with the cost to taxpayers. The mean benefit is about 75 percent of the mean subsidy for construction programs and about 80 percent for vouchers. For vouchers the cost to taxpayers exceeds the subsidy by the modest administrative cost. For construction programs, the cost to taxpayers is much larger than the sum of the subsidy and administrative cost. The mean benefit of each program varies inversely with income and directly with family size, but the variance in real benefits among similar households is large under most programs.

For the entire system of housing subsidies, the participation rate among eligible households is far below 50 percent for each combination of income and family size. For each family size, the participation rate first rises and then falls as income increases. The poorest households of each size have very low participation rates. Within each income class, participation rates are highest for one-person households, reflecting the strong preference received by the elderly in housing programs.

Evidence on the effect of housing programs on the characteristics of the neighborhoods in which recipients live is particularly meager. It suggests that public housing tenants live in noticeably worse neighborhoods than in the absence of the program and that the program contributes to racial segregation in housing. Section 8 New Construction/Substantial Rehabilitation and Section 8 certificates and vouchers appear to have modest effects in the opposite direction. The existing studies find small positive effects on neighboring property values on average for some programs and small negative effects for others. No study finds substantial positive effects on average for any program.

Housing programs appear to have small work disincentive effects. They also have miniscule effects on the prices of unsubsidized units that are not located near subsidized units.

The most important finding of the empirical literature from the viewpoint of housing policy is that tenant-based vouchers and certificates provide equally good housing at a much lower cost than any type of project-based assistance that has been studied. This finding implies that a shift of all discretionary resources from programs of project-based assistance to tenant-based vouchers would enable us to provide several million additional households with adequate housing at an affordable rent without any increase in government expenditure.

The major issues in housing policy for low-income households are (a) whether housing assistance should be an entitlement, (b) whether housing subsidies should be delivered to additional households by building new projects under some type of construction or substantial rehabilitation program or by giving them housing vouchers, and (c) whether we should require households currently living in subsidized projects for which future federal expenditure is discretionary to live in these projects to receive a subsidy and should give their owners a sufficient subsidy to induce them to continue to serve these households, or give these households housing vouchers. The available empirical evidence has much to contribute to the policy debate over these important questions. However, the magnitude of the public expenditures involved argues for producing better information on which to base these decisions. This evidence should be based on recent data on the full range of major housing programs for low-income households.

References

Barnett, C. L., and Lowry, Ira S. 1979. *How housing allowances affect housing prices.* Santa Monica, Calif.: The RAND Corporation, October.
Bradbury, Katherine, and Anthony Downs. 1981. *Do housing allowances work?* Washington, D.C.: Brookings Institution.

Buron, Larry, Sandra Nolden, Kathleen Heintz, and Julie Stewart. 2000. *Assessment of the economic and social characteristics of LIHTC residents and neighborhoods.* Final report. Cambridge, Mass.: Abt Associates, August.

Carliner, Michael S. 1998. Development of federal homeownership "policy." *Housing Policy Debate* 9:299–321.

Clemmer, Richard B. 1984. Measuring welfare effects of in-kind transfers. *Journal of Urban Economics* 15:46–65.

Crews, Amy D. 1995. Self-selection, administrative selection, and aggregation bias in the estimation of the effects of in-kind transfers. Ph.D. diss., University of Virginia.

Cummings, Jean L., and Denise DiPasquale. 1999. The Low-Income Housing Tax Credit: An analysis of the first ten years. *Housing Policy Debate* 10:251–307.

Currie, Janet, and Aaron Yelowitz. 2000. Are public housing projects good for kids? *Journal of Public Economics* 75:99–124.

Cutts, Amy Crews, and Edgar O. Olsen. 2002. Are Section 8 housing subsidies too high? *Journal of Housing Economics* 11:214–43.

De Leeuw, Frank, and Raymond J. Struyk. 1975. *The web of urban housing.* Washington, D.C.: Urban Institute.

Early, Dirk W. 1998. The role of subsidized housing in reducing homelessness: An empirical investigation using micro-data. *Journal of Policy Analysis and Management* 17:687–96.

Friedman, Joseph, and Daniel H. Weinberg. 1982. *The economics of housing vouchers.* New York: Academic Press.

———. 1983. *The great housing experiment.* Beverly Hills, Calif.: Sage Press.

Galster, George C., Peter Tatian, and Robin Smith. 1999. The impact of neighbors who use Section 8 certificates on property value. *Housing Policy Debate* 10:879–917.

Hammond, Claire H. 1987. *The benefits of subsidized housing programs: An intertemporal approach.* Cambridge: Cambridge University Press.

Kain, John F. 1981. A universal housing allowance program. In *Do housing allowances work?* ed. Katherine Bradbury and Anthony Downs, 339–65. Washington, D.C.: Brookings Institution.

Katz, Lawrence F., Jeffrey R. Kling, and Jeffrey B. Liebman. 2001. Moving to opportunity in Boston: Early results of a randomized mobility experiment. *Quarterly Journal of Economics* 116 (May): 607–54.

Keane, Michael, and Robert Moffitt. 1998. A structural model of multiple welfare program participation and labor supply. *International Economic Review* 39 (August): 553–89.

Kennedy, Stephen D. 1980. *Housing allowance demand experiment: Final report.* Cambridge, Mass.: Abt Associates, June.

Kennedy, Stephen D., and Meryl Finkel. 1994. *Section 8 rental voucher and rental certificate utilization study.* Cambridge, Mass.: Abt Associates.

Kraft, John and Edgar O. Olsen. 1977. The distribution of benefits from public housing. In *The distribution of economic well-being,* ed. F. T. Juster, 51–65. New York: National Bureau of Economic Research.

Lee, Chang-Moo, Dennis P. Culhane, and Susan M. Wachter. 1999. The differential impacts of federally assisted housing programs on nearby property values: A Philadelphia case study. *Housing Policy Debate* 10:75–93.

Leger, Mireille L., and Stephen D. Kennedy. 1990a. *Final comprehensive report of the Freestanding Housing Voucher Demonstration.* Vols. 1 and 2. Cambridge, Mass.: Abt Associates, May.

———. 1990b. *Recipient housing in the housing voucher and certificate programs.* Cambridge, Mass.: Abt Associates, May.

Lowry, Ira S., ed. 1983. *Experimenting with housing allowances: The final report of the Housing Assistance Supply Experiment.* Cambridge, Mass.: Oelgeschlager, Gunn, & Hain.

Ludwig, Jens, Greg J. Duncan, and Joshua C. Pinkston. 2001. Urban poverty and juvenile crime: Evidence from a randomized housing-mobility experiment. *Quarterly Journal of Economics* 116 (May): 655–79.

Ludwig, Jens, Helen F. Ladd, and Greg J. Duncan. 2001. Urban poverty and educational outcomes. In *Brookings-Wharton papers on urban affairs,* ed. William G. Gale and Janet Rothenberg. Washington, D.C.: Brookings Institution.

Mayo, Stephen K. 1986. Sources of inefficiency in subsidized housing programs: A comparison of U.S. and German experience. *Journal of Urban Economics* 20 (September): 229–49.

Mayo, Stephen K., Shirley Mansfield, David Warner, and Richard Zwetchkenbaum. 1980a. *Housing allowances and other rental assistance programs—A comparison based on the Housing Allowance Demand Experiment, part 1: Participation, housing consumption, location, and satisfaction.* Cambridge, Mass.: Abt Associates.

———. 1980b. *Housing allowances and other rental assistance programs—A comparison based on the Housing Allowance Demand Experiment, part 2: Costs and efficiency.* Cambridge, Mass.: Abt Associates.

Mikesell, James J., Linda M. Ghelfi, Priscilla Salant, George Wallace, and Leslie A. Whitener. 1999. *Meeting the housing needs of rural residents: Results of the 1998 survey of USDA's Single Family Direct Loan Program.* Rural Development Research Report no. 91. Washington, D.C.: United States Department of Agriculture, Economic Research Service, December.

Mills, Edwin S., and Arthur Sullivan. 1981. Market effects. In *Do housing allowances work?* ed. Katherine Bradbury and Anthony Downs, 247–76. Washington, D.C.: Brookings Institution.

Murray, Michael. 1975. The distribution of tenant benefits in public housing. *Econometrica* 43 (July): 771–88.

———. 1980. A reinterpretation of the traditional income-leisure model, with application to in-kind subsidy programs. *Journal of Public Economics* 14:69–81.

———. 1983. Subsidized and unsubsidized housing starts: 1961–1977. *Review of Economics and Statistics* 65 (November): 590–97.

———. 1999. Subsidized and unsubsidized housing stocks 1935 to 1987: Crowding out and cointegration. *Journal of Real Estate Economics and Finance* 18:107–24.

Newman, Sandra J., and Joseph M. Harkness. 2002. The long-term effects of public housing on self-sufficiency. *Journal of Policy Analysis and Management* 21 (Winter): 21–43.

Newman, Sandra J., and Ann B. Schnare. 1997. ". . . And a suitable living environment": The failure of housing programs to deliver on neighborhood quality. *Housing Policy Debate* 8:703–41.

Nolden, Sandra, Jessica Bonjorni, Carissa Climaco, Naomi Michlin, and Karen Rich. 2002. *Updating the Low Income Housing Tax Credit (LIHTC) Database: Projects Placed in Service Through 1999.* Final report. Contract C-OPC-21293. Cambridge, Mass.: Abt Associates.

Olsen, Edgar O. 1981. The simple analytics of the externality argument for redistribution. In *Economic perspectives: An annual survey of economics,* ed. M. B. Ballabon, 155–73. Vol. 2. New York: Harwood Academic Publishers.

———. 1983. The implications of the Experimental Housing Allowance Program for housing policy. In *The great housing experiments,* ed. Joseph Friedman and Daniel Weinberg. Beverly Hills, Calif.: Sage Publications.

————. 2000. The cost-effectiveness of alternative methods of delivering housing subsidies. Working Paper no. 351. University of Virginia, Thomas Jefferson Center for Political Economy, December.

Olsen, Edgar O., and David M. Barton. 1983. The Benefits and Costs of Public Housing in New York City." *Journal of Public Economics* 20 (April): 299–332.

Olsen, Edgar O., and William Reeder. 1983. Misdirected rental subsidies. *Journal of Policy Analysis and Management* 2 (Summer): 614–20.

Painter, Gary. 1997. Does variation in public housing waiting lists induce intra-urban mobility? *Journal of Housing Economics* 6:248–76.

Reeder, William J. 1985. The benefits and costs of the Section 8 Existing housing program. *Journal of Public Economics* 26 (April): 349–77.

Reid, William J. 1989. A benefit-cost analysis of Section 23 leased public housing. Ph.D. diss., University of Virginia.

Rydell, C. Peter, Kevin Neels, and C. Lance Barnett. 1982. *Price effects of a housing allowance program.* Report no. R-2720. Santa Monica, Calif.: RAND Corporation.

Schnare, Ann, Carla Pedone, William Moss, and Kathleen Heintz. 1982. *The costs of HUD multifamily housing programs: A comparison of the development, financing, and life cycle costs of Section 8, public housing, and other major HUD programs.* Vols. 1 and 2. Cambridge, Mass.: Urban Systems Research and Engineering.

Schone, Barbara Steinberg. 1992. Do means tested transfers reduce labor supply? *Economics Letters* 40:353–58.

————. 1994. Estimating the distribution of taste parameters of households facing complex budget spaces: The effects of in-kind transfers. Agency for Health Care Policy and Research. Unpublished manuscript.

Schwab, Robert M. 1985. The benefits of in-kind government programs. *Journal of Public Economics* 27 (July): 195–210.

Stegman, Michael A. 1991. The excessive costs of creative finance: Growing inefficiencies in the production of low-income housing. *Housing Policy Debate* 2:357–73.

Struyk, Raymond J., and Marc Bendick, eds. 1981. *Housing vouchers for the poor: Lessons from a national experiment.* Washington, D.C.: The Urban Institute Press.

Susin, Scott. 2002. Rent vouchers and the price of low-income housing. *Journal of Public Economics* 83 (January): 109–52.

U.S. Department of Commerce, Bureau of the Census. 1991. *American housing survey for the United States in 1989.* Current Housing Reports. Series H150/89. Washington, D.C.: Government Printing Office.

U.S. Department of Housing and Urban Development (HUD). 1974. *Housing in the seventies.* Washington, D.C.: Government Printing Office.

————. 1980. *Experimental Housing Allowance Program: The 1980 report.* Washington, D.C.: Government Printing Office, February.

————. 1992. *Characteristics of HUD-assisted renters and their units in 1989.* Washington, D.C.: Government Printing Office.

————. 1995. *HUD reinvention: From blueprint to action.* Washington, D.C.: Government Printing Office, March.

————. 1997. *Characteristics of HUD-assisted renters and their units in 1993.* Washington, D.C.: Government Printing Office, May.

————. 2000. *Rental housing assistance—the worsening crisis: A report to Congress on worst case housing needs.* Washington, D.C.: Government Printing Office.

U.S. General Accounting Office (GAO). 1997. *Tax credits: Opportunities to improve oversight of the low-income housing programs.* GAO/GGD/RCED-97-55. Washington, D.C.: U.S. GAO.

———. 2001. *Federal housing programs: What they cost and what they provide.* GAO-01-901R. Washington, D.C.: U.S. GAO.

———. 2002. *Federal housing assistance: Comparing the characteristics and costs of housing programs.* GAO-02-76. Washington, D.C.: U.S. GAO.

U.S. House of Representatives, Committee on Ways and Means. 1998. *1998 green book: Background material and data on programs within the jurisdiction of the Committee on Ways and Means.* Washington, D.C.: Government Printing Office.

Wallace, James E. 1995. Financing affordable housing in the United States. *Housing Policy Debate* 6:785–814.

Wallace, James E., Susan Philipson Bloom, William L. Holshouser, Shirley Mansfield, and Daniel H. Weinberg. 1981. *Participation and benefits in the urban Section 8 Program: New construction and existing housing.* Vols. 1 and 2. Cambridge, Mass.: Abt Associates.

Weicher, John C. 1979. Urban housing policy. In *Current issues in urban economics,* ed. P. Miezkowski and M. Straszheim, 469–508. Baltimore, Md.: John Hopkins University Press.

———. 1990. The voucher/production debate. In *Building foundations: Housing and federal policy,* ed. Denise DiPasquale and Langley C. Keyes, 263–92. Philadelphia: University of Pennsylvania Press.

Weinberg, Daniel H. 1982. Housing benefits from the Section 8 Program. *Evaluation Review* 6 (February): 5–24.

7

Child Care Subsidy Programs

David M. Blau

7.1 Introduction

Child care and early education subsidies for low-income families make up a relatively small but growing share of the portfolio of government means-tested transfer programs in the United States. The federal and state governments are estimated to have spent at least 18 billion dollars on such subsidies in fiscal year 1999. Many different government programs have provided means-tested child care and early education subsidies. Several of the major programs were consolidated into a single block grant as part of the welfare reform of 1996, but a number of major programs and many minor programs remain separate. Child care and early education subsidies are an important part of public efforts to help low-income families support themselves by work rather than welfare. They are also an important part of efforts to improve child outcomes for low-income families.

Economic analysis of child care subsidies is important for at least four reasons. First, the monetary cost of child care is often cited as a major barrier to economic self-sufficiency for low-income families with young children. Child care subsidies reduce or eliminate this cost of employment, and parental employment is an eligibility requirement for many child care subsidy programs. But there are other approaches to encouraging low-income parents to be employed—for example, the Earned Income Tax Credit. The relative effectiveness of child care subsidies at increasing employment

David M. Blau is professor of economics at the University of North Carolina at Chapel Hill.

The author is grateful to Ronald Oertel for very helpful research assistance. He thanks Susan Averett, Barbara Bergmann, Dan Black, Janet Currie, Jonah Gelbach, Suzanne Helburn, Robert Moffitt, David Ribar, Philip Robins, and James Walker for useful comments. The author is responsible for errors and opinions.

compared to other possible approaches is an important issue. An economic analysis can clarify the conditions under which a child care subsidy is a relatively effective policy tool for increasing employment of low-income parents.

Second, the quality of child care in the United States is typically characterized as mediocre on average, particularly in comparison to child care in most European countries. Improving the quality of child care has been an explicit goal of several major child care subsidy programs in the United States. But recent federal child care programs emphasize freedom of choice and flexibility for parents, with few restrictions on the type or characteristics of child care arrangements eligible for subsidies. Economic analysis can demonstrate the conditions under which there is a trade-off in child care policy between increasing employment and improving the quality of care.

Third, early childhood education and intervention programs such as Head Start are intended to help low-income children overcome the developmental disadvantages of growing up in poverty. Such programs have different goals than child care subsidies, but they provide what is in effect subsidized child care of relatively high quality to large numbers of low-income children. A unified economic analysis of child care and early education subsidies can demonstrate the trade-offs between government expenditures on such programs.

Fourth, the legislation authorizing the major federal welfare reform of 1996 is up for reauthorization in 2002. The child care subsidy program created by the reform is also up for renewal, and there is considerable sentiment for increasing the level of funding for child care. Economic analysis of the effects of child care subsidies can and should be an important input in the debate over future child care policy.

This chapter describes child care and early education subsidy programs in the United States; discusses the rationale for such programs and the economic issues raised by the existence and structure of the programs; reviews evidence on the effects of the programs on the behavior and outcomes of low-income families; and discusses proposals for reform of such programs. Section 7.2 summarizes the history and rules of the main programs, and section 7.3 tabulates information on expenditures, caseloads, and characteristics of subsidy recipients and child care users. Section 7.4 discusses the economic issues: Why does the government subsidize child care, what are the goals of such subsidies, what are the work incentives of the programs, and what are the incentives provided by the programs with respect to the quality of child care and the well-being of children? Empirical evidence on these issues is discussed in section 7.5, including evidence drawn from experimental demonstrations, evaluations of existing subsidies, and econometric analysis of price effects. Section 7.6 discusses a number of policy issues that have been prominent in recent discussions of child care subsidies and describes options for further reform of the child care subsidy system in the United States. Section 7.7 concludes by suggesting fruitful avenues for research.

7.2   Structure and Recent History of Child Care and Early Education Subsidy Programs

The programs considered in this chapter provide subsidies for non-parental child care and early education of children in low-income families. Some of the programs subsidize work-related child care expenses only, but others, such as Head Start, have no employment requirement for the parents. The goals and structure of work-related child care subsidy programs are typically quite different from those of early education programs, and it would simplify the discussion if only work-related child care subsidies were considered in this chapter. However, this would neglect an important issue that recurs throughout the chapter: the trade-off faced by policymakers between the goals of improving child well-being and increasing economic self-sufficiency. This trade-off is recognized as a fundamental issue in child care policy, and as such it should be discussed in this chapter. The structure of a subsidy for work-related child care expenses affects the quality of child care purchased, whether or not this is a goal of the subsidy program; and the structure of an early education program affects the work incentives of the parents, whether by design or not. Tax deductions and credits that provide unrestricted *child subsidies* (subsidies based on the presence of children that are not restricted in how parents can spend the funds) are not discussed in this chapter, although the related issue of "child allowances" is included in the discussion of reform options in section 7.6. The one major child care subsidy program not discussed here is the exclusion from taxable income of employer-provided dependent care expenses, because it is not means tested.[1]

The history, goals, and main provisions of the major child care and early education programs considered in this chapter are summarized in table 7.1.[2] The subsidy rate in the Dependent Care Tax Credit (DCTC) declines with the level of income, so this program is means tested in a sense, although the subsidy rate remains constant for Adjusted Gross Income (AGI) above $28,000. More importantly, because the credit is not *refundable* the amount of credit available to low-income families is relatively small. A nonrefundable credit is limited to the amount of income tax lia-

1. See U.S. House of Representatives, Committee on Ways and Means (1998, 838–39) for a description of this program. Another non-means-tested program not considered is military child care (U.S. General Accounting Office 1999a).
2. Some smaller programs omitted from the table are listed in U.S. General Accounting Office (1994b) and Robins (1991). A number of states have their own tax credits for child care, but they generally provide small benefits.

Table 7.1 Summary of the History, Goals, and Provisions of Major Federal Means-Tested Child Care and Early Education Programs

Program	Dependent Care Tax Credit	Aid to Families with Dependent Children Child Care	Transitional Child Care	At-Risk Child Care	Child Care and Development Block Grant	Title XX Social Services Block Grant	Head Start	Child and Adult Care Food Program[a]	Title I, Part A of the Elementary and Secondary Education Act
Acronym	DCTC	AFDC-CC	TCC	ARCC	CCDBG	TXX-CC	HS	CCFP	Title IA
Year began	1954	1988[b]	1988	1990	1990	1975[c]	1965	1968	1965
Goal	Subsidize employment-related dependent care expenses	Facilitate participation in the JOBS program	Help families who recently left AFDC for work maintain self-sufficiency	Help families who need child care in order to work and are at-risk of going on AFDC if child care is not provided	Provide child care services for low-income families and improve the overall supply and quality of child care	Help low-income families achieve self-sufficiency; prevent child neglect	Improve the social competence, learning skills, health, and nutrition of low-income children aged three to five	Improve nutrition of low-income children. Part of the National School Lunch Act	Provide programs and services for educationally disadvantaged children (children who are failing or at risk of failing student performance standards)
Original form	Tax deduction	Open-ended entitlement; vouchers, contracts, or reimbursement of expenses; no fee for recipients	Same as AFDC-CC; limited to one year; sliding fee for recipients	Capped entitlement; state match required; sliding fee for recipients; income limits set by states	Block grant to states; no state match; 75% of funds for direct subsidies (income <75% of SMI); 25% for quality improvement and consumer education	Capped entitlement; population-based distribution to states	Part-day preschool, health screening, nutrition and social services	Cash subsidies for meals and snacks in day care centers and family day care homes	Grants to states based on number of children from low income families and per-pupil education expenditures
Major changes	1976: credit replaced deduction; 1982: subsidy rate and maximum allowable expenses raised; 1983: added to short form 1040A; 1988: required SSN of provider	1996: PRWORA consolidated AFDC-CC, TCC, ARCC, and CCDBG into a single program, the Child Care and Development Fund (CCDF)				1981: converted to block grant; 1996: states allowed to transfer up to 10% of TANF funds to TXX	1995: extended to children aged 0–2	1981: reimbursement rates and age of eligibility reduced	1997: preschool programs must comply with Head Start performance standards

Current form	Nonrefundable tax credit	Combination discretionary and entitlement block grant; states must meet maintenance of effort and matching requirements for some of the entitlement funds; states may transfer up to 30% of their Temporary Assistance for Needy Families (TANF) block grant funds into the CCDF; states may also use TANF funds directly for child care, without transferring them to CCDF	Block grant to states that can be used for many social services; 15% of funds on average used for child care	Same as original	Same as original	Same as original
Current provisions	30% tax credit on expenses up to $4,800 for 2 children for AGI ≤ 10K; subsidy rate falls to 20% for AGI > 28K; effective 2003, 35% credit on expenses up to $6,000 for 2 children for AGI ≤ 15K	Sliding fee scale, but states may waive fees for families below the poverty line; at least 4% of funds must be spent on quality improvement and consumer education; child care must meet state licensing and regulatory standards; contracts or vouchers; relative care eligible if provider lives in a separate residence	Child care must meet state regulatory and licensing standards	Free	Child care must meet state regulatory standards; must serve mainly low-income children	A school or local education agency may operate a preschool program
Current eligibility criteria	Both parents (or only parent) employed	Family income no more than 85% of SMI, but states can (and most do) impose a lower income eligibility limit; children < 13; parents must be in work-related activities	States choose income eligibility; employment required	Kids 0–5 (mainly 3–5); 90% of enrollees must be below the poverty line; 10% of slots reserved for disabled children	Subsidy amount depends on whether income < 130% of poverty line, 130–185% of poverty line, or >185% of poverty line	Target funds to schools with the highest percentage of children from low-income families

Source: U.S. House of Representatives, Committee on Ways and Means (1998) and U.S. Department of Education (1996).

[a] Less than 2 percent of the funds in the food program go to adult care centers.

[b] Before explicit child care subsidies were added to the AFDC program in 1988, states could choose to disregard from earnings up to $200 per month in child care expenses incurred by employed AFDC recipients in determining AFDC eligibility and benefit amounts.

[c] Earlier provisions of the Social Security Act provided federal matching funds to the states for social services.

bility; many low-income families have no federal income tax liability and therefore cannot receive any tax credit. Data from the Internal Revenue Service indicate that 20.8 percent of the total amount of tax credit claimed in 1999 went to families with AGI of less than $30,000, but almost all of this amount was claimed by families with AGI between $15,000 and $30,000; only 0.7 percent of the total was claimed by families with AGI less than $15,000.[3] As noted in table 7.1, the DCTC is scheduled to become more generous in 2003, with the maximum subsidy rate increasing from 30 to 35 percent, the income limit for the maximum subsidy rate increasing from $10,000 to $15,000, and allowable expenses increasing form $4,800 to $6,000 for two children.

The 1988 Family Support Act (FSA) mandated two new programs, Aid to Families with Dependent Children Child Care (AFDC-CC) and Transitional Child Care (TCC). The AFDC-CC subsidy was intended to facilitate participation of welfare recipients in the Job Opportunities and Basic Skills (JOBS) program, an employment/training program mandated by the FSA to move families off welfare to economic self-sufficiency. The goal of the TCC program was to help maintain employment by providing subsidies to families who had recently moved off welfare, for up to one year after leaving welfare. The Omnibus Budget and Reconciliation Act (OBRA) of 1990 introduced two more new programs, At-Risk Child Care (ARCC) and the Child Care and Development Block Grant (CCDBG). The ARCC program provided child care subsidies to families who might otherwise not have been able to work and would as a result be at risk of going on welfare. The CCDBG had two goals: to provide more funds to subsidize employment-related child care expenses for low-income families, and to subsidize quality-improvement activities and consumer education. The quality-improvement activities that could be subsidized included resource and referral services, grants to providers to enable them to meet state child care regulations, improvements in monitoring and enforcement of regulations, and training programs for staff.

The proliferation of programs with different target populations, eligibility requirements, and subsidy rates following the passage of FSA and OBRA led to a fragmented system in which families would have to switch from one program to another as a result of changes in employment and welfare status, and some families would not be eligible for any subsidy despite having economic circumstances quite similar to those of eligible families. Examples of the consequences of this fragmentation are given in U.S.

3. Internal Revenue Service (2001). 31.2 percent of returns filed in 1999 had AGI of less than $15,000, but the number of these with children is unknown. Thirty-eight percent of returns with AGI under $15,000 owed income tax. In 1999, single household heads with gross income of at least $9,100 and married households with income of at least $12,700 were required to file a tax return. The number of low-income households that did not file a return is unknown.

Advisory Commission on Intergovernmental Relations (1994), U.S. General Accounting Office (1995), Ross (1996), and Long et al. (1998). For example, Long et al. (1998, 6–7) note that prior to welfare reform in California and Massachusetts the various child care programs were administered by different state agencies. Families had to apply separately for each of the programs and could incur significant time and hassle costs in changing from one program to another as a result of a change in family income or age of the child.[4]

In 1996 the Personal Responsibility and Work Opportunity Reconciliation Act (PRWORA) consolidated the four programs created by FSA and OBRA into a single child care block grant program called the Child Care and Development Fund (CCDF).[5] The main goal of the consolidated program is to facilitate the transition from welfare to work and help maintain employment of low-income parents. A minimum of 4 percent of funds must be used by states for quality-improvement and consumer education activities. Federal CCDF funds are provided to the states in three "streams": discretionary, mandatory, and matching. Discretionary and mandatory funds are distributed according to rules similar to those of the old programs, primarily based on the number of children and state income. These two streams do not require state matching funds. To receive funds from the matching stream, "a state must maintain its expenditure of state funds for child care programs at specified previous levels ('maintenance-of-effort' spending) and spend additional state funds above those levels" (U.S. General Accounting Office 1998, p. 5). One of the main goals of the consolidation of the four programs was to eliminate the fragmentation that existed under the previous system. Under the new system, states can (but are not required to) allow a family that moves from welfare to work to continue receiving a child care subsidy without changing programs. According to Long et al. (1998), states have made considerable progress in creating more seamless child care subsidy programs since the passage of PRWORA,

---

4. Most of the discussion of child care cost in this chapter refers to the monetary cost of care. There are other costs as well, such as the cost of establishing and maintaining eligibility for a subsidy, searching for care, arranging for substitute care when the regular provider is not available, and the disutility associated with using nonparental care. These nonmonetary costs are difficult to measure but may be quite important. The models described in section 7.4.2 incorporate a general form of nonmonetary child care cost.

5. Three of the previous programs (AFDC-CC, TCC, and ARCC) were authorized and funded by Social Security Title IV-A. They were replaced by the Temporary Assistance for Needy Families (TANF) Child Care Block Grant, funded by the Social Security Act. PRWORA also reauthorized and revised the existing CCDBG program with its own funding. Finally, it stipulated that both the new TANF Child Care Block Grant and the CCDBG be administered by the CCDBG program. The combined program is called the CCDF, and it consists of the two separately authorized funding streams, administered jointly and subject to the same rules (Pitegoff and Bream 1997). Many documents continue to refer to the joint program as the CCDGB, but the correct name of the combined program is now the CCDF. Most of the information on the CCDF provided here is from the Final Rule issued by U.S. Department of Health and Human Services (1998).

including single points of entry to the program, unified waiting lists, and consolidation of programs in a single agency (see also Adams, Snyder, and Sandfort 2002).

States can use CCDF funds to assist families with income up to 85 percent of state median income (SMI) but are free to use a lower income-eligibility criterion. Parents must be employed, in training, or in school, although some exceptions are permitted. In general, priority for CCDF funds is supposed to be given to families with very low incomes and children with special needs. Specifically, states must use at least 70 percent of their mandatory and matching funds to serve families on welfare, families in work activities who are moving off welfare, and families at risk of going on welfare. These correspond to the three groups previously served by the AFDC-CC, TCC, and ARCC programs, respectively. The CCDF also requires that a substantial portion of the discretionary funds and the other 30 percent of mandatory and matching funds be used to assist working poor families who are not current, recent, or likely future welfare recipients—the group previously served mainly by the CCDBG program. As part of the general increase in flexibility provided by PRWORA, states are permitted to transfer up to 30 percent of their TANF block grant funds to the CCDF to be used for child care, and they can also use TANF funds directly for child care services without transferring the funds to CCDF. States must use "certificates" (formerly called vouchers) that allow families to purchase care from any provider that meets state regulations and licensing standards or is legally exempt from licensing, including relatives (who do not live in the child's household) and babysitters. The regulations that govern health, safety, group size, training, and so forth are determined entirely at the state level with no federal requirements, and they vary widely across states.[6] States are permitted to impose more stringent requirements for child care services funded by CCDF, but any such additional requirements must be consistent with the strong provisions of the CCDF requiring flexibility in parental choice of child care (see U.S. Department of Health and Human Services 1998, p. 39986). States can also contract to purchase slots in day care centers and family day care homes and provide such slots to eligible families.

The other main subsidy program with an employment focus is the Title XX Social Services Block Grant (TXX). This program subsidizes a wide variety of social services and gives states flexibility in how the funds are allocated across the various eligible services. On average, about 15 percent of TXX funds have been spent on child care in recent years (U.S. House of Representatives, Committee on Ways and Means 1998, 720). Child care funded by Title XX must meet applicable state standards, and it is often

---

6. See the National Child Care Information Center (http://nccic.org) for information on state child care regulations.

provided through "slots" in centers and family day care homes purchased through grants and contracts with state or local agencies.

The last three programs listed in table 7.1, Head Start, the Child Care and Adult Food Program (CCFP), and Title I-A, are intended to improve child well-being, and these programs therefore have no employment or training requirement for the parents. Head Start programs must meet a set of federal standards that are more stringent and child development–oriented than most state regulations, and Title I-A programs must meet the Head Start standards as well. Head Start also requires parental involvement and provides nutrition and health services as well as early education. The CCFP provides subsidies for meals meeting federal nutrition requirements served in licensed day care centers and family day care homes serving low-income children. Subsidy rates depend on family income of the children served, with a maximum income of 185 percent of the poverty level. Most Title I-A funds go to schools serving K-12 students, but state and local education agencies may use such funds to serve preschool age children as well, in school-based or community-based programs.

7.3 Program Statistics

7.3.1 Expenditures, Caseloads, and Program Rules

Table 7.2 summarizes federal and state expenditures on child care subsidies in recent years and the numbers of children served by the subsidy programs. Assuming that 25 percent of DCTC expenditures went to low-income families and that fiscal year (FY) 1999 CCFP expenditures were the same as in FY 2000, a rough figure for total expenditure on means-tested child care subsidies in FY 1999 is $18 billion. A meaningful total for the number of children cannot be computed, because the DCTC lists only the number of families served, data are not available for TXX and Title I-A, and some children may be served by more than one program (for example, the DCTC and the CCFP). The CCDF is the biggest program in terms of expenditure, at about $9 billion. Much of the CCDF funding was transferred from TANF; the CCDF appropriation for 1999 was $5.285 billion. Head Start is the second largest program, with expenditure of $4.7 billion in 1999, $5.3 billion in 2000, and $6.2 in 2001. Head Start is the best-funded program per child served, with annual expenditure of $5,688 per child versus $5,189 per child in the CCDF, and a maximum of $720 per child in the DCTC.

The provisions of the DCTC, Head Start, the CCFP, and the Title I-A programs are determined at the federal level, with little discretion given to states. The main provisions of these programs are summarized in table 7.1. In contrast, states have substantial flexibility in designing their CCDF programs, including the income eligibility limit, copayments by families, and reimbursement rates to providers. These rules are summarized for each

Table 7.2   **Federal and State Expenditures and Children Served by Major Means-Tested Child Care Subsidy Programs**

	DCTC	HS	TXX-CC	CCFP	CCDF	Title I-A
	Federal + State Expenditures (billions of current dollars)					
FY 2001		6.200				
FY 2002		5.267	0.231	1.559		
FY 1999	2.675	4.968	0.285		9.132	2.015
FY 1998	2.649	4.347			6.399	
FY 1997	2.464	3.981	0.370	1.524	4.369	
FY 1996	2.663	3.569	0.352	1.580		
FY 1995	2.518	3.534	0.414	1.467	3.100	
	Children Served (millions)					
FY 2001		0.905				
FY 2000		0.857				
FY 1999	6.182	0.826			1.760	
FY 1998	6.120	0.822		2.6	1.515	
FY 1997	5.796	0.794		2.2	1.248	
FY 1996	6.003	0.752		2.4		
FY 1995	5.964	0.751		2.3	1.445	

Sources: Dependent Care Tax Credit (DCTC): U.S. House of Representatives, Committee on Ways and Means (2000, 816), except 1999: Internal Revenue Service (2001). Figures in the lower panel are number of returns filed claiming the credit, not the number of children. Head Start (HS): Administration for Children and Families (2002). Title XX Child Care (TXX-CC): Committee on Ways and Means (2000, pp. 600, 634): 15 percent of $1.9 billion for 1999; 13 percent of $1.775 billion for 2000; Committee on Ways and Means (1998, pp. 714, 720): 14.8 percent of $2.800, $2.381, $2.500 for FY 1995, 1996, 1997. Child Care Food Program (CCFP): expenditure: Committee on Ways and Means (2000, 600); Committee on Ways and Means (1998, pp. 714, 720); children served: U.S. Department of Agriculture (2001). Child Care and Development Fund (CCDF): Expenditure: 1997–99: I computed expenditure figures by summing all federal and state expenditures on the CCDF, either directly or through transfers to TANF, using data from the Annual TANF Reports to Congress (U.S. Department of Health and Human Services, various years) and reports from the Administration for Children and Families (various years). The latter source provides allocations to the CCDF for FY 2000 and 2001, but there are no data available on transfers from TANF for these years. Transfers to TANF constituted about half of CCDF spending in FY 1999. 1995: U.S. General Accounting Office (1998, 4); total funding for the four programs later consolidated in to the CCDF: AFDC-CC, TCC, ARCC, CCDBG. Children served: 1999: Administration for Children and Families (2000); 1998: Administration for Children and Families (2001b); 1997: Administration for Children and Families (1998); 1995: Administration for Children and Families (1995). Title I-A: U.S. General Accounting Office (1999b, 6): Department of Education programs: Title I part A, Individuals with Disabilities Education Act, Even Start, Twenty-First Century Learning Centers. U.S. General Accounting Office (2000) gives different figures and an estimate of 341,000 preschool children served by Title I-A and Even Start.

Notes: See table 7.1 for definition of the program acronyms. Expenditures are given in current dollars to facilitate checking with the original sources. To convert expenditures to 2001 dollars using the Consumer Price Index, multiply dollar figures for 1995–2000 by 1.162, 1.129, 1.103, 1.0865, 1.063, and 1.028, respectively. Blank cells indicate data not available.

state in table 7.3. Only nine states set income eligibility at the maximum allowed by law, 85 percent of SMI. Ten states set the income eligibility limit at less than 50 percent of SMI. States are permitted to waive fees (copayments) for families with income below the poverty line, and the fourth column of table 7.3 shows that there is substantial variation across states in use of this provision. Fees are determined in many different ways, including flat rates, percent of cost, percent of income, and combinations of these. States are required to have sliding scale fee structures, with fees that rise with family income. The minimum fee shown in the fifth column of the table is the copayment required of the lowest-income families, and the maximum fee shown in the sixth column is the copayment for the highest-income eligible families. The reimbursement rates listed in the last two columns represent the amount of the subsidy exclusive of the family copayment. States that provide relatively generous reimbursement also tend to have higher income eligibility limits: The correlation between the figures in columns (2) and (8) is .51, and between the figures in columns (3) and (8) is .25. Federal guidelines for implementation of the CCDF law require that the subsidy rate be set at the 75th percentile of the price distribution from a recent local market rate survey. In practice many states use out-of-date market rate surveys or set the subsidy rate lower than the 75th percentile of the price distribution (Adams, Schulman, and Ebb 1998, 23). There are no systematic data available on the difference between reimbursement rates and fees actually charged by providers. Anecdotal evidence compiled by the Children's Defense Fund indicates that "In many states, child care subsidy rates are so low that many providers are unwilling to accept children who have subsidies or limit the number of children with subsidies they are willing to accept. Some providers may take subsidies, but only if *parents* pay them the difference between what the subsidy rate will cover and the provider's actual rate (in addition to the copayment the parent is already required to pay)" (Adams, Schulman, and Ebb 1998, 20). This is inconsistent with the requirement of the CCDF that payment rates should be sufficient to ensure equal access for CCDF-eligible children to comparable child care services provided to children not eligible for child care assistance (U.S. Department of Health and Human Services 1998, p. 39985).

The only subsidy program that is an open-ended entitlement is the DCTC (in terms of number of children served, not expenditures per child), and as explained above this is one of the smaller low-income child care subsidy programs. The other programs are capped entitlements, with no obligation to serve all eligible families. It is estimated that the CCDF serves only 15 percent of eligible children (Administration for Children and Families, 1999).[7] There is no systematic information available on how CCDF

---

7. Many families who are eligible do not apply for a subsidy from the CCDF. See Besharov (2002) for a discussion of the possible reasons for low take-up of the subsidy.

Table 7.3   Characteristics of State Child Care and Development Fund Plans

State	Monthly Income Eligibility Level ($)	Income Eligibility as a % of SMI	Are families at or Below Poverty required to Pay a Fee?	Minimum Fee (full-time rate)	Maximum Family Fee (full-time rate)	Reimbursement Rate for Preschool Age Child[a]	Implied Weekly Reimbursement Rate ($)[b]
Alabama	1,504	45	Some	$2.00/week	$85/week	$94/week	94.00
Alaska	3,694	85	Some	3% of cost	100% of cost	$800/month	185.00
Arizona	1,909	58	Some	$1.00/day + $0.50 each additional c.	$10/day + $5. additional c.	$20/day	100.00
Arkansas	1,533	60	None	$0	100% of fee	$14.40/day	72.00
California	2,821	75	None	$0	$10.10/day	$35.90/day	287.20
Colorado	2,139	52	Some	$6/month	$237/month + $15 each additional c.	$18.18/day	90.90
Connecticut[c]	3,264	75	Some	No fee	$326.30/month	$115/week	115.00
District of Columbia	2,326	62	Some	$0		$23.55/day	117.75
Delaware	1,764	44	None	1% of cost	46% of cost	$81.40/week	81.40
Florida	1,706	54	All	$0.80/day + $0.40 each additional c.	$9.60/day + $4.80 each additional c.	$102/week	102.00
Georgia	2,817	85	Some	$5/week + $3 each additional c.	$52/week + $26. each additional c.	$75/week	75.00
Hawaii	2,874	75	None	$0	$75/month	$375/month	86.54
Idaho	1,706	54	Some	1% of cost	100% of cost	$434/month	100.15
Illinois	1,818	45	All	$4.33 (1 c.) or $8.67/month (2 c.)	$134.32 (1 c.) or $233.98/month (2 c.)	$23.75/day	118.75
Indiana	2,161	58	None	$0	10% of gross income	$30/day	150.00
Iowa	1,793	49	None	$0	$6/half-day	$9.50/half-day	95.00
Kansas	3,114	85	Some	$0	$243/month	$2.28/hour	91.20
Kentucky	1,851	57	Some	$0	$11.50 (1 c.) or $12.75/day (2+ c.)	$15/day	75.00

Louisiana	2,420	75	None	$0	100% of cost	$15/day	75.00
Maine	3,957	85	Some	2% of income	10% of income	$130/week	130.00
Maryland	1,870	40	Some	$4/month + $4 each additional c.	$161/month + $122. each additional c.	$407/month	93.92
Massachusetts	3,869	85	Some	$0.20/day	$22.80/day	$29/day	145.00
Michigan	2,172	55	Some	$0.125/hour	$1.75/hour	$2.50/hour	100.00
Minnesota	3,181	75	Some	$0	$636/month	$44/day	220.00
Mississippi	2,333	85	Some	$10.00 (1 c.) or $20/month (2 c.)	$155 (1 c.) or $165/month (2 c.)	$70/week	70.00
Missouri	1,482	45	Some	$1/year	$4.00/day	$10/day	50.00
Montana	1,735	57	Some	$5	$243	$16.50/day	82.50
Nebraska	2,105	66	Some	$0	$187 (1 c.) or $334/month (2 c.)	$16/day	80.00
Nevada	2,798	75	Some	10% of cost of care	100% of cost of care	$100/week	100.00
New Hampshire[c]	1,784	49	Some	$0	$0.50/week per c. + 34% of daily cost of care	$16.70/day	83.50
New Jersey	1,735	37	All	$9.10/month + $6.80 second c.	$294.90/month + $156.85 second c.	$21.76/day	108.80
New Mexico	2,313	83	Some	$11	$191.	$346.50/month	79.96
New York	2,338	60	Some	$1/week	$90/week	$30/day	150.00
North Carolina	2,719	75	Some	9% of countable monthly income	9% of countable monthly income	$368/month	84.92
North Dakota	2,445	85	Some	10% of cost of care	80% of cost of care	$100/week	100.00
Ohio	2,105	58	All	$0	$172/month	$100/week	100.00
Oklahoma	1,936	62	Some	$0	100% of cost of care	$12/day	60.00
Oregon	2,088	55	Some	$25	$612.	$372/month	85.85
Pennsylvania	2,139	57	Some	$5.00	$65.	$22.70/month	113.50
Puerto Rico	1,279	85	None	$5.00/month	$48/month	$160/month	36.92
Rhode Island	2,603	72	None	$0	$48.0	$100/week	100.00
South Carolina	1,446	42	All	$3/week	$11/week	$74/week	74.00
South Dakota	2,140	65	None	$10/month	20% copayment	$2.00/hour	80.00

(continued)

Table 7.3 (continued)

State	Monthly Income Eligibility Level ($)	Income Eligibility as a % of SMI	Are families at or Below Poverty required to Pay a Fee?	Minimum Fee (full-time rate)	Maximum Family Fee (full-time rate)	Reimbursement Rate for Preschool Age Child[a]	Implied Weekly Reimbursement Rate ($)[b]
Tennessee	2,027	60	Some	$5 (1 c.) or $9/week (2 c.)	$35 (1 c.) or $61/ week (2 c.)	$77/week	77.00
Texas	1,735	52	Some	9% (1 c.) or 11% (2+ c.) of gross monthly income	9% (1 c.) or 11% (2+ c.) of gross monthly income	$20.09/day	100.45
Utah	1,794	56	Some	$10 (1 c.) or $15 (2 c.)	$255 (1 c.) or $281 (2 c.)	$17.19/day	85.95
Vermont	2,586	83	None	$0	$17.03/day	$18.92/day	94.60
Virginia	3,394	85	Some	10% of gross monthly income	10% of gross monthly income	$42.69/day	213.45
Washington	2,024	54	Some	$10.00	$407.	$23.41/day	117.05
West Virginia	1,735	60	Some	$0	$3.75 (1 c.) or $4.50 (2 c.)	$17/day	85.00
Wisconsin	1,909		All	$5 (1 c.) or $9/week (2 c.)	$63 (1 c.) or $78/ week (2 c.)	$5.10/hour	204.00
Wyoming	1,539	45	All	$0.05 per hour per c.	$0.50 per hour per c.	$2.14/hour	85.60

Source: Administration for Children and Families (2001a).

Note: c. stands for "child" or "children."

[a]In most states reimbursement rates vary by location.

[b]Figures in the last column are calculated from figures in the next-to-last column, assuming 8 hours of care per day, 5 days per week, and 4 and 1/3 weeks per month.

[c]Connecticut and New Hampshire did not report information, so figures for these states are from an earlier report.

funds are allocated among eligible families. Head Start served 822,316 children in FY 1998, compared to 4.775 million children under age six in poverty in calendar year 1998 (U.S. Bureau of the Census 1999, table 2). However, 89 percent of children in Head Start are aged three to four.[8] Assuming that one-third of the children under age six are ages three to four yields about 50 percent of three-to-four-year-old children in poverty who are served by Head Start (see Currie 2001 for a similar estimate). No figures are available on the percentage of eligible children served by the other programs.

Family income is a determinant of eligibility in all of the programs listed in table 7.1 except for the DCTC, and in several of the programs income determines the subsidy rate or amount (DCTC, CCDF, CCFP). If cash or in-kind benefits from other means-tested programs were counted as part of income for determining eligibility and/or benefits from child care subsidy programs, there would be important interactions between child care programs and other means-tested subsidy programs. States are given discretion in determining which sources of income are counted in determining CCDF eligibility. All states include earned income (a few disregard a small share of earnings), the majority include TANF and child support income, and almost all exclude food stamps and EITC from the income definition (Ross 2002).

7.3.2   Recipient Characteristics

The Survey of Income and Program Participation (SIPP) panel of 1996 collected information about child care subsidies from a sample of households with at least one child under age fifteen in spring 1999. Respondents were asked "Did anyone help you pay for all or part of the cost of any child care arrangements for the child?" Respondents who replied affirmatively were asked whether the source of the assistance was a government agency. In another section of the survey respondents were asked if any of their children were enrolled in Head Start. Many respondents who reported having a child enrolled in Head Start did *not* report receiving a subsidy, so I reclassified them as receiving a subsidy. The tabulations reported in Panel A of table 7.4 show that only 2.1 percent of the sample reported receiving a government subsidy. This could be a substantial underestimate of subsidy receipt if respondents did not include arrangements that were subsidized by tax credits or direct government reimbursement to the provider through grants and contracts, which remains a common form of subsidy in several means-tested programs. The incidence of receipt of a subsidy was 4.0 percent for the lowest income group and 11.2 percent for families who were public assistance recipients.

---

8. An "Early Head Start" program was authorized in 1994 to serve children below age three. It is a small part of the overall Head Start program.

Table 7.4   **Incidence of Child Care Subsidy Receipt and Characteristics of Recipient, 1990**

	Proportion with Subsidy	Receives Public Assistance		Does Not Receive Public Assistance	
		Subsidy	No Subsidy	Subsidy	No Subsidy
A. Incidence					
Annual household income ($000)					
All	.021				
0–4.99	.040				
5.00–9.99	.053				
10.00–14.99	.042				
15.00–19.99	.029				
20.00–24.99	.033				
25.00–29.99	.025				
30.00–34.99	.029				
35.00–39.99	.013				
40.00+	.009				
Public assistance (PA) status					
Receives PA	.112				
Does not receive PA	.022				
B. Characteristics of households with annual income < $25,000					
Center		.45	.05	.41	.05
Nonrelative		.44	.10	.33	.11
Other nonparent		.10	.31	.20	.30
Pay for care		.42	.10	.46	.14
Cost/hour		2.55	1.76	2.81	3.07
Mother employed		.61	.28	.79	.49
Hours worked (if > 0)		39	33	37	37
Wage rate		6.62	6.58	6.71	7.10
Education > 12		.45	.18	.52	.32
Married, spouse present		.12	.12	.35	.51
Annual earnings (if > $0)		$10,760	$7,575	$11,053	$11,953
Other adults		.09	.28	.17	.21
Fewer than five children		1.09	.72	.84	.68
Black		.34	.40	.28	.21
Hispanic		.23	.29	.17	.24
White		.43	.25	.52	.50
N	15,747	89	762	88	3,875

Source: Tabulations from the Survey of Income and Program Participation (spring 1999).

Notes: Unit of analysis is one child. Figures are weighted by the child's sample weight. A child is coded as receiving a subsidy if the mother reports that a government agency helps pay for child care or that one of the child's arrangements is Head Start. Public assistance includes cash (TANF, GA, SSI) and food stamps. Center care includes nursery, preschool, and Head Start. Nonrelative includes family day care homes, nannies, babysitters, and other nonrelatives (except centers).

Panel B of table 7.4 restricts the sample to households with annual income under $25,000 and classifies them by whether they received public assistance and whether they received a child care subsidy. Subsidy recipients were much more likely to use a day care center than nonrecipients (this is true even if Head Start cases are excluded). This may reflect the fact that direct provider reimbursement is used mainly for day care centers. The mother was much more likely to be employed in households receiving a subsidy. This is a major change from ten years earlier, and it is consistent with the post-PRWORA emphasis on employment for welfare recipients. In the welfare group, subsidy recipients had higher average earnings and hours of work, and wages similar to those of nonrecipients. In the nonwelfare group, subsidy recipients had a lower wage, similar hours per week, and higher annual earnings than nonrecipients.[9] Some important questions about subsidies that cannot be answered based on these data are what fraction of nonrecipients were ineligible, what fraction of eligible families were aware of their eligibility, what fraction of those who were aware applied for a subsidy, and what fraction of applicants were awarded a subsidy. Information from site-specific surveys suggests that lack of awareness of subsidies among eligible families is widespread (Meyers and Heintze 1999; Fuller et al. 2000).

The only other information available on characteristics of child care subsidy recipients is fragmentary. Piecyk, Collins, and Kreader (1999) used data from administrative records in Illinois and Maryland for 1997 and 1998 to tabulate characteristics of children and families whose child care was subsidized by a voucher and who were current or former cash assistance recipients. Of those children who were current or recent welfare recipients and were receiving subsidized child care from a voucher, roughly half were current welfare recipients and half former recipients. Maryland subsidy recipients were much more likely to use center and family day care than Illinois voucher recipients. Voucher use increased substantially during 1997, and there was also a substantial amount of turnover in the voucher programs.[10]

9. An earlier study, the 1990 National Child Care Survey (NCCS), asked respondents whether they planned to claim a tax credit for child care expenses for 1989. Twenty-eight percent of respondents with family income under $25,000 planned to claim a credit, compared to 35 percent of families with income above this threshold. These figures cannot be compared to IRS data because the population covered in the NCCS includes only families with children under thirteen, and the IRS does not report the number of tax returns by age of children. Among the lower-income group in the NCCS, claimants had higher wages and earnings and were less likely to be married, Hispanic, and white than nonclaimants.

10. For additional information on characteristics of subsidy recipients in site-specific studies, see Schumacher and Greenberg (1999) and Fuller, Kagan, and Loeb (2002). Chipty et al. (1998), Fuller et al. (1999) and Meyers and Heintze (1999) use samples of low-income mothers to examine child care subsidy issues but do not report characteristics of subsidy recipients separately from other groups.

7.3.3   Types of Child Care and Payment for Care

An important feature of the child care market is the diversity of types of child care used. Table 7.5 shows the distribution of primary child care arrangements of children under age six of employed mothers in Spring 1999, using data from SIPP. In almost half of all primary child care arrangements for young children of employed mothers, the caregiver is the mother, the father, or another relative. About 30 percent of arrangements are in day care centers or preschools, 11 percent in family day care homes, and 9 percent in other nonrelative arrangements such as a babysitter or nanny. These figures are quite similar to the distribution in the Urban Institute's 1997 National Survey of America's Families (Capizzano, Adams,

Table 7.5   **Distribution of Children under Age Six of Employed Mothers by Primary Child Care Arrangement in the Survey of Income and Program Participation, Spring 1999**

	Father	Other Relative	Mother, while at work	Other Nonrelative	Family Day Care Home	Center or Preschool
All	17.1	28.4	3.0	9.5	11.1	30.9
White	18.4	23.4	3.3	9.3	13.8	31.8
Black	11.2	34.7	1.8	8.2	5.2	39.0
Hispanic	17.5	39.6	3.0	12.7	7.2	19.8
Married	20.3	24.0	3.5	9.7	11.7	30.6
Widowed, divorced, or separated	7.9	32.4	2.9	7.5	12.4	37.0
Never married	9.8	43.1	1.2	9.9	8.0	23.7
Child age						
0	24.3	33.1	3.0	9.4	11.0	17.1
1	19.1	31.6	3.1	13.5	13.6	19.1
2	17.4	30.1	5.4	10.5	12.5	24.2
3	18.0	33.3	2.1	7.9	12.0	26.8
4	12.9	24.7	1.6	8.7	10.4	41.8
5	13.4	19.1	1.7	7.2	7.4	51.4
Full-time	13.4	28.4	1.9	10.1	13.1	33.2
Part-time	25.5	28.9	5.0	8.4	7.8	24.5
Day shift	12.3	26.9	2.9	9.3	13.2	35.3
Nonday shift	30.1	32.4	3.3	10.0	5.4	19.0
Annual family income ($000)						
< 18.00	14.2	34.0	1.0	10.0	8.8	30.2
18.00–35.99	20.9	35.6	2.7	8.2	8.1	24.5
36.00–53.99	18.8	24.9	3.7	10.7	11.1	30.8
54.00+	14.8	24.0	2.9	9.5	13.7	36.1
Poor	12.9	36.2	3.7	11.0	6.7	29.7
Not poor	15.5	27.3	2.6	9.3	11.7	31.1

Source: Tabulations from the 1999 SIPP.

Note: Figures are weighted by the child's sample weight.

and Sonenstein 2000). The distribution varies considerably by family characteristics. Relative care is much more frequent in black and Hispanic families than in white families, with center care less common for Hispanics,
and father, nonrelative, and family day care less common for blacks. Families with a married mother are much more likely to use care by the father
than are families with an unmarried mother, whereas the latter are more
likely to use relative care. Center care is substituted for relative care, family day care, and other nonrelative care as children age. Father, mother, and
relative care together account for 44 percent of arrangements for mothers
who work full time, 60 percent for mothers who work part time, 42 percent
of arrangements for mothers who work a day shift, and 66 percent for
mothers who work nonday shifts. It is often asserted that there is a shortage of center care during evening and weekend work hours, but it is not
clear whether the heavier use of informal arrangements during nonday
shift hours reflects a shortage of more formal arrangements or greater
availability of another family member to provide care. The distribution
of types of care arrangements varies considerably by family income
and poverty status. Loosely speaking, center and family day care and babysitters appear to be normal goods, substituted for relative care as income rises. However, this pattern may also be the result of a substitution
effect: The opportunity cost of informal care is high in upper-income
housholds if all potential earners in such households have relatively high
wage rates.

One reason the distribution of child care by type is important is that it is
closely associated with whether a family pays for child care. Unpaid child
care arrangements are quite common and play an important role in the economic analysis of child care subsidies discussed in the next section. Table 7.6
describes the distribution of child care arrangements by payment status and
the amount paid. Panel A shows that of families with an employed mother
and at least one child under fifteen, the percentage who made any payment
for child care fluctuated between 31 and 44 percent from 1985 to 1999 with
an upward trend since 1991. Total weekly payments conditional on any payment showed a slight upward trend in real terms (1999 dollars) during the
second half of the 1980s, from $91 in 1985 to $97 in 1988. Expenditure appears to have declined on average since 1988 to a low of $76 in 1999. How-
ever, changes in survey design during the 1990s may have affected the comparability of the figures. The percent of family income spent on child care
increased slowly and steadily from 6.3 percent in 1986 to 7.5 percent in 1999.
Panel B shows that in 1999 56 percent of families with a child under age six
and an employed mother paid for child care. The incidence of payment and
the amount paid tend to increase with family income, while the amount paid
as a percentage of family income falls with the level of family income. Mothers working full time are much more likely to use paid care than mothers
working part time, but conditional on paying for care the amount paid is

Table 7.6   Family Child Care Expenditures

	% Paying	Weekly Expense, All Children (if pay; $1999)	% of Income
A. Families with Employed Mother, Children < 15			
Spring 1999	43.0	75.6	7.5
Spring 1997	44.1	74.7	7.4
Fall 1995	40.5	92.9	7.4
Fall 1993	35.5	85.1	7.3
Fall 1991	34.5	86.4	7.1
Fall 1990	38.0	87.6	6.9
Fall 1988	39.9	97.2	6.8
Fall 1987	33.3	94.7	6.6
Fall 1986	31.4	93.6	6.3
Winter 1985	33.7	90.6	n.a.
B. Spring 1999, Families with Employed Mother, Child < 6 Only			
All	56.1	88.9	9.0
Annual family income ($000)			
< 18.00	51.0	57.9	22.2
18.00–35.99	47.9	80.6	11.9
36.00–53.99	57.4	81.4	7.2
54.00+	62.2	105.8	5.0
Below poverty line	44.0	67.7	33.1
Above poverty line	57.3	90.5	7.5
Full-time employee	63.9	92.7	8.6
Part-time employee	41.1	77.0	5.7
Married	58.0	95.2	6.8
Widowed, divorced, or separated	62.0	77.0	14.0
Never married	48.4	69.3	12.5

Source: Tabulations from the 1997 and 1999 SIPP, and Smith (2002).
Note: N.a. indicates data not available.

only $15 higher for full-time than for part-time care. Married and previously married mothers are more likely to pay than never-married mothers.[11]

7.4   Economic Issues

This section discusses three important economic issues concerning child care subsidies for low-income families: First, why does the government

11. See Giannarelli and Barsimontov (2000) for comparable data from the 1997 National Survey of America's Families. Data from the 1990 NCCS show that paying for care is much less common when the mother is not employed and when the youngest child is school age (Hofferth et al. 1991). Relative care is least likely to be paid, with the largest percentage of relatives paid being 36 percent for employed mothers of children under five. For employed mothers, centers, babysitters, and family day care arrangements are almost always paid, but for nonemployed mothers unpaid arrangements of these types are quite common.

subsidize child care? Is there a market failure? If so, what is the source of market failure, and under what conditions can subsidies help to correct the failure and improve resource allocation? Or are child care subsidies merely a form of income redistribution? Second, what are the work incentives caused by child care subsidy programs? How does the availability of informal (unpaid) child care affect these incentives? How effective are child care subsidies compared to employment subsidies in achieving the goal of economic self-sufficiency? To what extent do child care subsidies crowd out private child care expenditures by mothers who would have worked anyway? Third, what are the effects of child care subsidies on the quality of child care and on child well-being? How are these effects influenced by the form of the subsidy? How do subsidies of different types affect incentives for parents to purchase high-quality care?

7.4.1 Why Subsidize Child Care?

Three main arguments have been used in support of government subsidies to child care. The arguments are based on attaining economic self-sufficiency, child care market imperfections, and distributional considerations.

Self-Sufficiency

Child care subsidies can help low-income families be economically self-sufficient. Self-sufficient in this context means employed and not enrolled in cash-assistance welfare programs. Self-sufficiency may be a desirable goal for noneconomic reasons, but it also may be considered desirable if it increases future self-sufficiency by inculcating a work ethic and generating human capital, thereby saving the government money in the long run (Robins 1991, 15). These arguments explain why many child care subsidies are conditioned on employment or other work-related activities such as education and training. Child care and other subsidies paid to employed low-income parents may cost the government more today than would cash assistance through TANF. But if the dynamic links suggested above are important, then these employment-related subsidies could result in increased future wages and hours worked and lower lifetime subsidies than the alternative of cash assistance both today and in the future. Note that this argument has nothing to do with the effects of child care on children, and there are few restrictions on the type and quality of child care that can be purchased with employment-related subsidies such as the CCDF and DCTC. There is little evidence either for or against the existence of strong enough dynamic links to make means-tested employment-conditioned child care subsidies cost-effective for the government in the long run.[12]

---

12. There is substantial evidence of positive serial correlation in employment. Whether this is due to "state dependence" (working today changes preferences or constraints in such a way

Walker (1996) has argued that difficulties in attaining economic self-sufficiency are caused by imperfections in the credit market, not the child care market. If the dynamic links suggested above are important, then a family could borrow against its future earnings in a perfect credit market to finance the child care needed in order to be employed today and gain the higher future earnings that result from employment today. Imperfection in the credit market caused by moral hazard and adverse selection prevent this, but the remedy according to Walker lies in government intervention in the credit market, not the child care market. Walker's proposal is discussed in section 7.6.

Market Imperfections

The second main argument in favor of government child care subsidies is imperfection in the child care market. The imperfections that are often cited as a basis for government intervention are imperfect information available to parents about the quality of care, and positive external benefits to society generated by high-quality child care.[13] These considerations can be used to argue for child care subsidies to all families, since the externalities and information problems are not necessarily income-specific.[14] Walker (1991) spells out these points in detail; the discussion here follows his arguments closely.[15] There is imperfect information in the child care market because consumers are not perfectly informed about the identity of all potential suppliers, and because the quality of care offered by any particular supplier identified by a consumer is not fully known. A potential remedy for the first problem is government subsidies to resource and referral (R&R) agencies to maintain comprehensive and accurate lists of suppliers. This may not solve the problem in practice because of very high turnover and unwillingness to reveal their identity among informal child care providers. The second information problem is that consumers know less about product quality than does the provider, and monitoring is costly. This can lead to moral hazard

---

as to make working in the future more attractive) or unobserved heterogeneity (working today does not affect the attractiveness of future work; some people find work more attractive than others in every period) is unclear. See Heckman (1981) for an early discussion and Hyslop (1999) for recent evidence. I am not aware of any evidence on this issue that is specific to the low-income population. Gladden and Taber (2000) analyze the effect of work experience on wage growth for less-skilled workers.

13. It is often claimed that there are shortages of child care of particular types such as center care for infants, night shift care, and care for sick children. Most of these claims are by non-economists who use the term "shortage" in the usual noneconomic sense that providers are not willing to supply much child care of these types at prices that most consumers are willing to pay. See Waller (1997) for an example.

14. Evidence summarized by Currie (2001) suggests that the benefits of high-quality preschool programs are larger for the most disadvantaged children than for other children. If the magnitude of the externalities and/or information problems are the source of market imperfections are proportional to the gains from high-quality care, then this would suggest that subsidies be targeted to disadvantaged children.

15. See also Council of Economic Advisors (1997), Magenheim (1995), Robins (1991), and U.S. Department of Health and Human Services (2001).

and/or adverse selection. Moral hazard is a plausible outcome in day care centers (e.g., changing diapers only before pick-up time). Adverse selection of providers is plausible in the more informal family day care sector: Family day care is a very low-wage occupation, so women with high wage offers in other occupations are less likely to choose to be care providers. If the outside wage offer is positively correlated with the quality of care provided, then adverse selection would result. Regulations are often suggested as a solution to this information problem, but Walker notes that the monitoring required to enforce regulations may be costlier for the government than for consumers. He also points out that the conditions under which regulations are beneficial to consumers are unlikely to be satisfied in the child care market.[16]

Some evidence suggests that parents do not obtain much information about the child care market before making a choice. Walker (1991) reports that 60–80 percent of child care arrangements made by low-income parents are located through referrals from friends and relatives or from direct acquaintance with the provider. This suggests that consumers may not be well-informed about potential providers, but it does not prove that a suboptimal amount of information is used by consumers. If consumers have strong preferences for acquaintance with the provider, then limited information may be optimal from the parents' perspective, although not necessarily from a social perspective if acquaintance is uncorrelated with quality of care. A referral from friends and relatives or direct acquaintance with the provider may serve as a signal of quality to parents, but it may not be a good signal of the developmental appropriateness of child care if parents are not good judges of the quality of child care. Cryer and Burchinal (1995) report a direct comparison of parent ratings of various aspects of the developmental appropriateness of their child's day care center classroom with trained observer ratings of the same aspects, using data from the Cost, Quality, and Outcomes study. The results show that parents give higher average ratings on every item than do trained observers, by about 1 standard deviation on average for preschool age classrooms and by about 2 standard deviations on average for infant and toddler rooms. The instrument containing these items is of demonstrated reliability when administered by trained observers, so this suggests that parents are not well-informed about the quality of care in the arrangements used by their children.[17] Child care

16. See Walker (1991, 68–69), which is based on applying Leland's (1979) model of regulations to the child care market. The conditions are low price elasticity of demand, relevance of quality to consumers, low marginal cost of quality, and consumers' placing a low value on low-quality care.

17. The instrument is the Early Childhood Environment Rating Scale (ECERS) and its counterpart for infants and toddlers, the Infant-Toddler Environment Rating Scale (ITERS). See Harms and Clifford (1980) and Harms, Cryer, and Clifford (1990) for discussion of the instruments. Helburn (1995) discusses their reliability in the Cost, Quality, and Outcomes study. The correlation between parent and observer scores was .21 for infant-toddler rooms and .29 for preschool rooms (Cryer and Burchinal 1995, 206). Thus parents do appear to have some ability to distinguish among programs of different quality. However, from a child development perspective it is the absolute level of quality that matters, not relative quality.

subsidies targeted at high-quality providers could induce parents to use higher quality care by reducing the relative price of such care. This would not necessarily remedy the information problem, but it would deal with a consequence of that problem, namely a level of child care quality that is suboptimal from the perspective of society.

The externality argument is a standard one and closely parallels the reasoning applied to education. High-quality child care may lead to improved intellectual and social development, which in turn increases school-readiness and completion and thereby reduces the cost to society of problems associated with low education: crime, drug use, teenage childbearing, and so forth. If parents do not account for the external benefits of high-quality child care, then they use child care of less than optimal quality. This argument could rationalize subsidies targeted to high-quality providers, such as Head Start. The evidence that child care quality affects child development is of two main types. The first is from randomized assignment studies that have evaluated the impact of high-quality preschool programs for disadvantaged children. A comprehensive review of early childhood interventions by Karoly et al. (1998; discussed in more detail in section 7.5) concludes that such programs can provide significant benefits to participating children and can reduce future expenditures on welfare, criminal justice, and related items. The second type of evidence is from observational studies of children placed by their parents in child care arrangements of varying quality. Such studies have generally not followed the children long enough to determine whether any observed developmental gains are long lasting and whether there are subsequent effects on school outcomes. Also, there have been few efforts to determine whether results are robust to controls for self-selection and unobserved heterogeneity. Love, Schochet, and Meckstroth (1996) review this literature and conclude that higher child care quality is associated with better social skills, cooperation, and language development, and fewer behavior problems. But they acknowledge the limitations of existing evidence. The evidence cited by Karoly et al. is compelling but is based mainly on very intensive and costly programs that are quite different even from Head Start. It is unclear whether child care of moderately high quality provides positive but proportionately smaller developmental benefits, or whether there exists a threshold of quality below which benefits are negligible.

Distributional Issues

The third argument for government child care subsidies is based on distributional considerations related both to cross-sectional equity at a given time and to the long-run benefits to children of high-quality child care. For example, Bergmann (1996) argues that high-quality child care can be thought of as a "merit good, something that in our ethical judgment everybody should have, whether or not they are willing or able to buy it" (p. 131).

This would justify in-kind subsidies aimed at low-income families, but also at middle- and upper-income families if positive social externalities of high-quality child care are prevalent throughout the income distribution. In its pure form this argument is based solely on the moral grounds that it is unethical to deprive any child of the optimum conditions for development if society has the resources to provide such conditions.

Bergmann argues that the usual economic considerations in favor of cash transfers over in-kind subsidies do not apply to merit goods. The main arguments she advances are that children have little or no say in how parents spend a cash grant; that society has a responsibility to ensure that children are well cared for while the parents work; and that high-quality child care has benefits to children that parents may not fully account for in their spending decisions. These arguments suggest an in-kind subsidy program for child care that is restricted to high-quality care, an issue discussed in depth below. There has apparently been no research on the implicit cash value of in-kind child care subsidies, or on the rate at which child care subsidies "crowd out" private child care expenditures.[18]

7.4.2 Work Incentives in Child Care Subsidy Programs

Child care subsidies generally increase a parent's incentive to be employed.[19] Most child care expenditures are made in order that a parent may work. A child care subsidy reduces this work-related expense and therefore increases the net return from employment. However, many parents have access to child care by relatives at no monetary cost. Subsidies will influence the trade-off between paid and unpaid child care, and this may affect the magnitude of the work incentive of a child care subsidy. Subsidies targeted at low-income families are usually phased out as income rises, and this will influence the work incentive of the subsidies. This subsection begins with a simple model that ignores these complications as well as issues involving the quality of care. This provides a baseline for subsequent consideration of the issues raised by unpaid care, phaseout, and the quality of child care.

A Simple Model

The canonical static one-person labor supply model (Pencavel 1986) augmented with assumptions about child care is a useful vehicle for analysis of work incentive effects of child care subsidies. The mother is assumed to be the caretaker of her children, so she is the agent in the model. Suppose that child care is homogeneous in quality and commands a mar-

18. Besharov and Samari (2000) discuss vouchers versus cash payments for child care subsidies. They note that some states are switching CCDF subsidies from vouchers to cash.

19. If a mother works only in order to afford to purchase high-quality child care, then a child care subsidy could reduce her incentive to work. See Gelbach (2002) for a discussion of this and related possibilities.

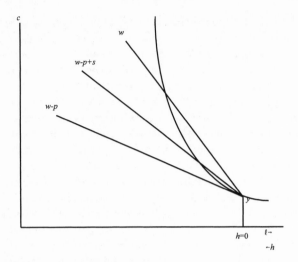

Fig. 7.1   Child care price and a linear subsidy

ket price of p dollars per hour of care per child, taken as given by the mother.[20] There is no informal unpaid care available and the mother cannot care for her children while she works, so paid child care is required for every hour the mother works. By assumption, the mother cares for her children during all hours in which she is not working. There are no fixed costs of work, and the wage rate w is the same for each hour of work. For simplicity, suppose there is only one child who needs care. The mother's budget constraint is $c = I = y + (w - p)h$, where c is consumption expenditure other than child care, I is income net of child care expenditure, y is nonwage income, and h is hours of work. The time constraint is $h + \ell = 1$, where ℓ is hours of leisure, and the utility function is $u(c, \ell)$ The monetary cost of child care reduces the net wage rate $(w - p)$, making the slope of the budget line in consumption-leisure space flatter than if child care was free, as illustrated in figure 7.1. A higher price of child care increases the likelihood that the net market wage is below the reservation wage (the slope of the indifference curve at $h = 0$), thereby reducing the likelihood of employment.

A *linear* child care subsidy of s dollars per hour changes the budget constraint to $c = y + (w - p + s)h$, raises the net wage, makes the budget line

20. Homogeneous quality means that we can ignore for now the possibility that the mother cares about child outcomes. Child outcomes in this model can be influenced by only two things: the quality of purchased care, which is fixed by assumption for now, and the quality of the mother's care, which in this very simple model we can think of as being a component of the marginal utility of leisure. This assumption will be relaxed below. A mother who perceives that she is a low-quality caregiver can be interpreted in this simple model as having a low marginal utility of leisure. She will be more likely to work, other things equal, in order to take advantage of the higher quality substitute care available in the market.

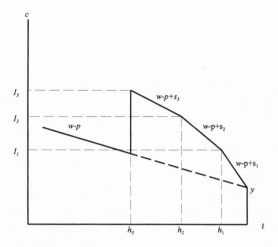

Fig. 7.2   A nonlinear child care subsidy

steeper, and thereby increases the likelihood of work. For the preferences and constraints shown in figure 7.1, the mother would not work in the absence of the subsidy, and the subsidy is large enough to induce her to work. The effect of such a subsidy on hours of work conditional on employment is indeterminate because the subsidy has a positive substitution effect and a negative income effect on hours of work. In this simple model, a wage subsidy such as provided by the EITC (which is linear in the phase-in region of the credit) is equivalent to a child care subsidy of the same amount and has the same incentives.

Nonlinear Subsidy

Most child care subsidies do not have the simple linear form described above. As shown in table 7.3, states typically structure their CCDF subsidies to have a declining subsidy rate as income rises, and a maximum income level for eligibility.[21] A generic example of such a structure is illustrated in figure 7.2. The subsidy rate declines from s_1 to s_2 at income level I_1, corresponding to hours of work h_1, and from s_2 to s_3 at income level I_2, corresponding to hours h_2. The subsidy rate remains constant at s_3 until the income eligibility cutoff I_3, corresponding to hours h_3, is reached, and then drops to zero, resulting in a "notch" or "cliff" in the budget constraint. A nonlinear subsidy of this type does not alter the qualitative result that a child care subsidy creates a work incentive. It does affect the incentive to locate at any particular positive level of h, compared to a linear subsidy,

---

21. This is also true of TXX child care subsidies and, except for the income eligibility limit, the DCTC as well. Averett, Peters, and Waldman (1997) analyze the impact on labor supply of the DCTC using nonlinear budget constraint methods.

and could induce some mothers to reduce hours from above h_3 to h_3 or less in order to qualify for a subsidy.[22]

Unpaid Child Care

Some families have access to care by a relative, including the father or another family member, at no monetary cost. But not all families with access to such care use it, because it has an opportunity cost: The father or other relative sacrifices leisure or earnings in order to provide care. The quality of such care compared to the quality of market care is also likely to influence the use of informal care, but consideration of quality is taken up below and ignored here. If the mother pools income with the father or relative or has preferences over the father or relative's leisure hours, then the mother will behave as if unpaid child care has an opportunity cost. To illustrate in the simplest possible setting, take as given that the relative who is the potential unpaid child care provider is not employed.[23] Let H represent hours of *paid* child care purchased in the market and U hours of *unpaid* child care provided by the relative.[24] Maintaining the assumption that the mother is the caregiver during all hours in which she is not employed, we have $h = H + U$, and $h \geq H$, $U \geq 0$. The budget constraint is $c = y + wh - pH$. The utility function is $u(c, \ell, \ell_r)$, where ℓ_r is leisure hours of the relative. The time constraints are $\ell + h = 1$ for the mother, and $\ell_r + U = 1$ for the relative. If U and H are both positive, then the shadow price of an hour of relative care is the marginal utility of the relative's leisure. In this case relative care is used for the number of hours U^* for which the marginal rate of substitution between consumption and leisure of the relative equals the market price of care: $u_{\ell_r}/u_c = p$; and paid care is used for the remaining $H^* = h - U^*$ hours for which child care is required.

In order to examine the work incentive effects of a child care subsidy in this model, classify outcomes as follows:

Outcome	Mother Employed	Unpaid Care Used	Paid Care used
1	no	no	no
2	yes	yes	no
3	yes	yes	yes
4	yes	no	yes

22. Another form of nonlinear subsidy is a subsidy for a fixed dollar amount or a fixed amount of care independent of the mother's hours of work and employment status. Head Start is an example of such a subsidy: Care is free for half the day. Public schools provide another example (Gelbach 2002). This type of subsidy is discussed below.

23. See Blau and Robins (1988) for a model in which the relative's employment status is a choice variable. This extension does not change the qualitative implications of the analysis.

24. The key distinction is paid versus unpaid, not relative versus nonrelative. Some relatives are in fact paid for child care. Paid care by a relative would be classified here as part of H, not U. Subsidies such as the DCTC and CCDF that allow paid care by a relative require that the relative not be coresident with the mother.

A linear child care subsidy reduces the effective price of market care from p to $p - s$ but does not affect the price of unpaid relative care, because no money changes hands for such care. A subsidy therefore increases the probability of choosing outcomes 3 and 4 and reduces the probability of choosing outcomes 1 and 2. Notice that in addition to providing a work incentive for the mother (outcome 1 is less likely) a subsidy also provides an incentive to use paid care conditional on the mother working (outcome 2 is less likely). So in the presence of an unpaid care option, a subsidy will induce some women who would have worked anyway to increase use of paid care and reduce use of unpaid care in order to qualify for the subsidy. Thus a subsidy to paid child care "crowds out" unpaid care.[25] A child care subsidy will have income effects on all goods, so the additional expenditure on child care by families who would have paid for care in the absence of a subsidy will be less than the amount of the subsidy. Private child care expenditures are crowded out.

Is a child care subsidy the most cost-effective way for the government to increase employment of low-income mothers of young children? An obvious alternative is a wage subsidy such as the Earned Income Tax Credit (EITC). Child care subsidies are available only if paid care is used, and some mothers will prefer to use unpaid care and pass up the subsidy. This could make a child care subsidy more effective at increasing employment per subsidy dollar spent than a wage subsidy. On the other hand, a child care subsidy will induce some mothers who would have worked anyway to switch from unpaid to paid care, causing an increase in government expenditure with no resulting increase in employment. Some insight can be gained by making a few simplifying assumptions. Suppose that hours worked per worker are not affected by wage or child care subsidies (income and substitution effects exactly offset); the wage and child care price are not affected by subsidies (no general equilibrium effects); all mothers who are induced to work by the subsidy use paid care; and both subsidies are additive (for analytic convenience). Under these assumptions, the number of additional hours of work per dollar spent by the government on a wage subsidy of e dollars per hour of work is $\eta_{Nw}/(w + e\eta_{Nw})$, where η_{Nw} is the elasticity of employment (N) with respect to the wage rate. The additional hours of work per dollar spent by the government on a child care subsidy of s dollars per hour of paid care is $-\eta_{Np}/(p\theta - \eta_{Np}s - \theta s\eta_{Pp})$, where η_{Np} is the elasticity of employment with respect to the price of paid care, θ is the proportion of working mothers who use paid care, and η_{Pp} is the elasticity of paid care use with respect to the price of care conditional on employment. For a wide range of plausible values of the parameters and variables,

25. A subsidy could induce a mother to pay for care by a relative that would have been unpaid in the absence of a subsidy. Allowing for this possibility would complicate the model but would not alter any of the results discussed here.

an additive child care subsidy that is a given proportion of the child care price generates many more additional hours worked per dollar of government expenditure than an additive wage subsidy of the same proportion of the wage.[26] This may seem surprising, because a wage subsidy appears to be a more direct instrument for increasing employment. But a wage subsidy provides benefits to all working mothers, including those who use unpaid child care, whereas a child care subsidy provides no benefit to the latter group. It is the reluctance of some mothers to use paid care that makes a child care subsidy a more cost-effective method of increasing employment. If all working mothers used paid care then there would be no difference in the cost effectiveness of the two subsidies if they were set at the same proportional level (see the appendix).

7.4.3   Quality of Child Care

If the quality of market child care is variable and if the quality of care affects child outcomes, then the mother will be concerned about the quality of care she purchases. The simplest case to consider is unidimensional quality: Quality is a single "thing." The price of an hour of child care is $p = \alpha + \beta q$, where q is the quality of care and α and β are parameters determined in the market. Think of this as a hedonic price function determined by the market supply of and demand for quality (a linear price function is not essential to the argument). The mother cares about the quality of child care because it affects her child's development outcome, d. Let the child development production function be $d = d(\ell q_m, hq)$, where q_m is the quality of the care provided by the mother. The effect of purchased child care on development depends on its quantity (h) and quality (q). For simplicity, no distinction is made between the mother's leisure and her time input to child development, and assume also for simplicity that no unpaid care is available. Relaxing these assumptions does not change the main implications of the model. Assume for the moment that child care subsidies are available only if the mother is employed. The utility function is $u(c, \ell, d)$ and the budget constraint is $c = y + [w - (\alpha + \beta q)]h$.

Most existing child care subsidies can be interpreted as affecting α but not β, because they are independent of the quality of care. Some subsidies, such as the DCTC, are explicitly independent of quality. Others, such as the CCDF, can be used only in arrangements that satisfy state licensing standards or are legally exempt from such standards. Such subsidies can be thought of as being subject to a quality threshold but independent of quality beyond the threshold. Thus they do not alter the effective marginal price of quality, βh, faced by the consumer (ignoring equilibrium effects). The two issues considered here are how child care subsidies affect the incentive to work and how they affect the demand for quality. A subsidy that reduces

26. See the appendix for the derivation of the formulas and illustrative calculations.

α or β increases the incentive to be employed because it reduces the monetary cost of child care when employed, and it has no impact on utility when not employed. One might expect that such a subsidy would also cause an increase in the level of quality demanded conditional on being employed, which raises the net price of an hour of child care. However, in a quality-quantity model the interaction between quality and quantity yields substitution effects of market prices that cannot be signed (Becker and Lewis 1973).

Nevertheless, the following two results from this model can be demonstrated (see the appendix for proofs). A subsidy that is independent of quality—call it an α-subsidy—has a bigger positive effect on employment than a subsidy that is quality-specific, a β-subsidy. So if the goal of a subsidy program is to facilitate employment, this is best accomplished by an α-subsidy. The second result is for the relative magnitude of the effect of α-subsidies and β-subsidies on the demand for quality. In a quality-quantity model the substitution effect of a change in price on the level of quality demanded is ambiguous, and this holds for changes in both α and β. But it can be shown that (a) if the substitution effects $\partial q/\partial\alpha|_{\bar{u}}$ and $\partial q/\partial\beta|_{\bar{u}}$ are both negative, then $\partial q/\partial\beta|_{\bar{u}}$ is larger in absolute value than $\partial q/\partial\alpha|_{\bar{u}}$; and (b) if $\partial q/\partial\alpha|_{\bar{u}} > 0$ then either $\partial q/\partial\beta|_{\bar{u}}$ is positive but smaller than $\partial q/\partial\alpha|_{\bar{u}}$ or $\partial q/\partial\beta|_{\bar{u}} < 0$. Thus a β-subsidy has a bigger positive effect or a smaller negative effect on the level of quality demanded than an α-subsidy. So if the goal of a subsidy program is to improve the level of quality of child care to which children are exposed, this is best accomplished by a β-subsidy. These results illustrate the policy trade-off described earlier: Policies that are most effective at accomplishing one goal will not be as useful in accomplishing the other goal of policy. The model is very simple, but this trade-off will hold in more general models as well.

Now consider the case in which paid child care can be used to enhance child development even when the mother is not employed. This allows us to consider the effects of a subsidy like the Head Start program on work and child care quality incentives. Maintain the assumption that no unpaid child care is available. Head Start provides h^* hours of child care of quality q^* at no monetary cost, where h^* and q^* are taken as given by the mother. If she works fewer than h^* hours then she does not incur any monetary child care cost. If she works more than h^* hours and less than h' hours, where h' is the number of hours at which her income exceeds the eligibility threshold for Head Start, then she incurs costs of $p(h - h^*)$ for child care, where as before $p = \alpha + \beta q$ and q is the quality of care purchased. For $h > h'$ she receives no subsidy. For a low-wage mother, it is reasonable to assume that $h^* < h'$. Assume for simplicity that child care in excess of the h^* hours provided by Head Start is used only for employment purposes, not for child development. Also assume that the Head Start subsidy is taken up if offered.

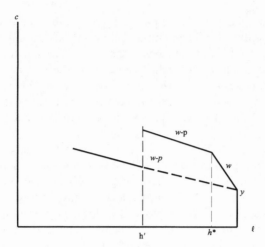

Fig. 7.3   Head Start

Ignoring quality for the moment, the budget constraint under Head Start is depicted in figure 7.3, with the subsidy rate along the first segment $s_1 = p$, the subsidy rate along the second and third segments zero, a kink at h^*, and a notch at h'. The subsidy clearly provides a work incentive for mothers who would not have worked in the absence of the subsidy, with $h = h^*$ a likely outcome given the kink in the budget constraint at h^*. The subsidy has offsetting substitution and income effects for mothers who would have worked $h^* \geq h > 0$ hours in the absence of the subsidy. The subsidy causes only an income effect for mothers who would have worked $h' > h > h^*$ hours in the absence of the subsidy, and it therefore causes a reduction in their hours worked.[27] The subsidy has a work disincentive effect for mothers who would have worked more than h' hours in the absence of the subsidy. A marginal change in the subsidy (i.e., a change in h^*) has no effect on work incentives for mothers who are not induced to work by the subsidy. Such mothers do not work because their wage rate is too low compared to their reservation wage even in the absence of monetary child care costs, so offering them additional hours of free child care does not change their incentives.

The effect of a Head Start subsidy on child development is uncertain because it depends on the quality of child care that would have been purchased in the absence of the subsidy, and on the quality of additional child care purchased beyond the subsidized hours of care. It seems likely that q^* is relatively high and that the average quality of care experienced by a child as a result of the Head Start subsidy will increase. If it is assumed that q^* is greater than or equal to the highest quality care available in the market,

27. Gelbach (2002) presents a similar analysis of the work incentives of free public school.

then the Head Start subsidy results in an improvement in child development. Marginal changes in $h*$ and $q*$ have ambiguous effects on the level
of quality demanded by mothers who purchase additional hours of care
beyond the $h*$ free hours provided by the subsidy. A comparison of the
effects on quality of Head Start and price subsidies (α and β-subsidies) also
yields ambiguous results.

7.5   Evidence

This section describes evidence on the employment and child care quality effects of means-tested child care subsidies. The evidence discussed is
from three types of studies: evaluations of experimental demonstration
projects, evaluations of actual child care subsidy programs, and studies of
the effects of the price of child care. The latter type of study does not directly measure subsidies and their impact but infers the impact of subsidies
from the estimated price effects. This type of study is the least direct but by
far the most common. The first three subsections focus on evidence pertaining to employment, and the fourth subsection discusses the much more
limited evidence available on child care quality and other outcomes.

7.5.1   Demonstrations

Several demonstration programs designed to help low-income families
achieve economic independence included child care subsidies along with
other benefits and services. These programs were evaluated using randomized assignment methods, so the average effects of the programs on outcomes of interest are estimated without bias by simple comparisons of
treatment and control group averages. However, in each case the child care
subsidy was only one of several services provided as part of the program,
so it is not possible to determine how much of the program impacts were
due to the child care subsidy.[28] I discuss one example of a demonstration
program in order to illustrate the nature of the evidence from such programs.

New Hope was a program intended to reduce poverty among the low-
income population in Milwaukee (Bos et al. 1999). It operated from 1994
through 1998 with broad eligibility rules that made virtually anyone with
low income eligible to enroll, regardless of employment and family status.
The program was voluntary and provided an earnings supplement, afford-

---

28. A 1989 randomized experiment in Mecklenberg County, North Carolina offered a
treatment group of 300 AFDC mothers guaranteed access to subsidized child care for up to
one year within two weeks of taking a full-time job, while a control group of 302 AFDC mothers had access to subsidized child care only through a long waiting list with an average wait
of six to ten months. However, the offer was made by mail with no telephone or personal contacts, and the take-up rate was very low: Only one-sixth of the treatment group applied for
and received a subsidy. The treatment had no significant impact on welfare participation or
expenditure. See Bowen and Neenan (1993) for details.

able health insurance, a child care subsidy, and a full-time community service job if no other employment was available. The program required full-time employment (thirty hours per week) and provided benefits for up to three years. Participants made their own child care arrangements and were reimbursed for most of the expenses, with a copayment that increased with family income. Thirty-nine percent of participants with children used child care at an average subsidy of $2,376 over two years. An early evaluation based on two years of data from the program found that among individuals who were not employed at entry to the program, participation in the program increased employment by 7 percentage points, boosted earnings by about $700 per year (13 percent), raised income by 12 percent, and had no impact on welfare participation. The program had no statistically significant effects on employment and earnings for those who were employed for at least thirty hours per week at entry, although the sample size was small (the point estimate of the earnings impact was –$571 per year), and reduced AFDC and food stamp participation by 7–10 percent in year two. The program increased use of formal child care by 7.4 percent for boys and 12.5 percent for girls, and it resulted in improved academic performance, study skills, social competence, and behavior among boys but not girls.[29]

7.5.2 Actual Subsidy Programs

Four studies have estimated the impact of actual child care subsidies on employment. Two evaluate means-tested state subsidies for low-income families funded by federal programs prior to the 1996 welfare reform. A third study evaluates the labor supply effects of the implicit child care subsidy provided by free public school. This is not a means-tested subsidy (and is not usually thought of as a child care subsidy at all), but information about its impact could be useful for evaluating the effects of means-tested child care subsidies with a similar structure. The fourth evaluates the impact of subsidies in a sample of thirteen states in 1997. In each of these studies the subsidy recipients are self-selected, and the studies recognize and attempt to deal with the possibility of selectivity bias.

---

29. Other demonstrations and experiments that included child care subsidies were the Teenage Parent Demonstration (Kisker, Rangarajan, and Boller 1998), New Chance (Quint, Bos, and Polit 1997), GAIN in California (Riccio, Friedlander, and Freedman 1994), the National Evaluation of Welfare-to-Work Strategies, formerly known as the JOBS program (Hamilton et al. 1997), the Minnesota Family Investment Program (Miller et al. 1997), the Florida Family Transition Program (Bloom et al. 1999), and the Gary, Seattle, and Denver Income Maintenance Experiments. The GAIN demonstration excluded children under age six. Granger and Cytron (1999) report that the effects of the Teenage Parent Demonstration and New Chance (which was also targeted at teenage mothers) on use of center-based child care were smaller than in New Hope and often statistically insignificant. Robins and Spiegelman (1978) estimate that eligibility for a SIME-DIME child care subsidy increased use of market child care by 18 percentage points in Seattle and 14 percentage points in Denver. Results for child care use in the other demonstrations are not available. See Hamilton, Freedman, and McGroder (2000) for a summary of the effects of all the recent demonstration programs.

Berger and Black (1992; hereafter BB) evaluate the employment impact of two Kentucky child care subsidy programs funded by Title XX in 1989. Both programs subsidized slots in licensed day care centers only and imposed a work requirement of at least twenty hours per week. One program reimbursed day care centers directly for up to $40 per week, depending on family income, and had an income eligibility limit of 60 percent of state median income; the corresponding figures for the other program were $50 and 80 percent. The two programs are treated by BB as a single program. BB administered a telephone survey to single mothers who were either subsidy recipients or on the wait list for a subsidy. The employment status of subsidy recipients was ascertained for periods both before and after they entered the wait list. In addition, a sample of single mothers in Kentucky was drawn from the May 1988 Current Population Survey (CPS).

BB recognize that if program administrators select subsidy recipients on the basis of characteristics not observed by the investigators, then the wait list would not be a valid control group for the subsidy recipients. Furthermore, the wait list itself may be self-selected if women who are more motivated to work are more likely both to seek a subsidy and to be employed even in the absence of a subsidy. BB pool the before and after observations from subsidy recipients and the wait list with the CPS sample in a regression model with the following specification: $EMP = \alpha_0 + \alpha_1 WL_{t-1} + \alpha_2 WL_t + \alpha_3 SUB_{t-1} + \alpha_4 SUB_t + \beta X + u$, where EMP is an indicator for being employed, WL is an indicator for the wait list group, SUB is an indicator for subsidy recipients, $t - 1$ is the "before" observation (before beginning to receive a subsidy for the subsidy recipients, and before entering the wait list for the wait list group), t is the "after" observation, the CPS sample is the reference group, X is a vector of control variables, and u is a disturbance. BB refer to α_1 as the "sign-up effect" (self-selection into the wait list), $\alpha_2 - \alpha_1$ as the "wait list effect" (the employment effect of entering the wait list), $\alpha_3 - \alpha_2$ as the "creaming effect" (selection of recipients from the wait list by administrators on the basis of unobservables), and $\alpha_4 - \alpha_3$ as the "subsidy effect" (the before-after difference in employment of eventual recipients).

The estimates show a sign-up effect of 22.6 percentage points, a wait list effect of 16.9 percentage points, a creaming effect of 4.0 percentage points, and a subsidy effect of 8.4 points, all significantly different from zero except the creaming effect. BB view the sign-up and creaming effects as selection effects that are not part of the true subsidy effect. However, they suggest that the wait list effect could be either a selection effect (i.e., the employment rate of the wait list group would have increased even if they had not applied to the program) or part of the impact of the subsidy as mothers go to work in anticipation of needing to meet the work requirement upon being selected for a subsidy from the wait list.

If the 16.9 point wait list effect is treated as part of the impact of the subsidy, then the full subsidy effect is $16.9 + 8.4 = 25.3$ percentage points from an average weekly subsidy of $45.62. Assuming this was a 100 percent subsidy and noting that the employment rate of subsidy recipients while receiving the subsidy was 97.5 percent, this implies an employment rate of 72.2 percent in the absence of the subsidy, yielding an employment effect of 35 percent and an elasticity of 0.35. If the 16.9 is treated as being due entirely to selection effects, then the corresponding elasticity estimate is 0.094 [$= 8.4/(97.5 - 8.4)$]. One drawback to generalizing from the study is that the subsidy was available only for use in day care centers, whereas most current programs provide vouchers that can be used in any paid arrangement. It is also not clear whether Kentucky is reasonably representative of the United States.

Meyers, Heintze, and Wolf (2002; hereafter MHW) use data from a sample of California AFDC recipients in four counties to analyze the determinants of receipt of a child care subsidy and the impact of subsidy receipt on employment. Individuals were randomly selected from AFDC administrative records in November 1992, interviewed about eighteen months later, and interviewed again eighteen months after the first interview. By the time of the second interview, 25 percent were no longer receiving welfare. Those still receiving welfare were eligible for subsidies under a variety of different programs, and assuming that the nonrecipients still had relatively low income they were also likely to have been categorically eligible for a subsidy under various California programs. MHW use a subsample of 903 single mothers who responded to the second interview to estimate probit models explaining whether a mother used any nonparental child care at the time of the survey and whether the mother received a child care subsidy conditional on using nonparental child care. These probits are estimated jointly in order to allow for the possibility that the unobserved determinants of subsidy receipt are correlated with the unobserved determinants of child care use. The predicted probability of subsidy receipt was computed from the estimated subsidy receipt probit for all mothers in the sample and was used as a regressor in an employment probit. One variable was excluded from the employment probit and included in the subsidy probit in order to identify the effect of subsidy receipt: an ordinal measure of the mother's knowledge of child care subsidy rules. The predicted subsidy probability has a positive coefficient in the employment probit with a t-ratio of 2.31. Simulations indicate that changing the probability of subsidy receipt from 0.0 to 0.5 would cause the employment probability to increase from .210 to .727 at the sample means of the other regressors. No information on the subsidy amounts or child care expenditures are provided, so an elasticity cannot be computed.

A potential problem with the evidence from this study is that there is no natural control or comparison group available. The implicit assumption is that mothers with little knowledge of child care subsidy rules are a valid comparison group for mothers with greater knowledge. Although this could be true, no evidence is presented to support the assumption. Mothers who are more motivated to work might also be more likely to seek information about subsidy programs. If such motivation is not captured by observed regressors, then the instrument is not valid and the comparison group is not comparable to the treatment group.[30]

Gelbach (2002) estimates the impact on employment of the implicit child care subsidy provided by free public kindergarten for five-year-old children. The structure of the subsidy is like Head Start: Free child care of a given quality is provided for a fixed number of hours, and child care outside school hours must be purchased by the family or supplied by informal providers. Gelbach notes the likely possibility that mothers with stronger unobserved tastes for work will be more likely to enroll a child in school at the earliest possible age, making subsidy receipt endogenous. To identify the effect of the subsidy, Gelbach exploits variation in quarter of birth of children and the fact that all states impose a date-of-birth requirement for entry to kindergarten. For example, if a child must have his fifth birthday by December 31 in order to enter kindergarten in the year in which he turns five, a mother whose child was born in the fourth quarter of the year will have access to the subsidy for that school year, whereas a mother whose child was born in the first quarter of the next calendar year will not, independent of labor supply preferences (assuming quarter of birth is exogenous). Gelbach uses quarter-of-birth dummies as instrumental variables for enrollment in public school. He uses data from the Public Use sample of the 1980 census (quarter of birth was not collected in the 1990 census) on 10,932 single mothers and 53,163 married mothers whose youngest child was aged five at the time of the census on 1 April 1980.[31] Gelbach's instrumental variable estimates indicate that access to free public school increased the employment probability of single mothers whose youngest child was aged five by 5 percentage points at the interview date and by 4 percentage points during calendar year 1979. He also finds positive effects of about 3 on hours of work per week, 3.6 on weeks worked per year, $932 on wage-salary income in 1979, and a 4 percentage point lower probability of receiving public assistance in 1979. All the estimates are significantly different from zero. The corresponding effects for married mothers whose youngest child was aged five were very similar for employment status and smaller for the other outcomes, compared to single mothers. Gelbach was not able to estimate the value of the subsidy, so the elasticity of employment with respect to the subsidy could not be computed.

30. A related but distinct conceptual issue is that the natural specification for the employment equation would include the actual subsidy receipt indicator, as in BB, not the predicted probability of subsidy receipt.

31. Gelbach reports that his instrumental variables (IV) strategy performed poorly for single mothers with a five-year-old child and another child younger than five.

Gelbach's approach is creative and provides credible evidence of the impact of a child care subsidy on employment of mothers whose youngest child is five years old. However, it is unclear whether his results can be generalized to children younger than five.[32] Gelbach cites evidence that employment *responsiveness* to the price of child care does not differ by age of the child, although there are of course differences in the *level* of employment by child age. He presents an extensive discussion and analysis of whether his results can be generalized to younger children and concludes that "While the estimates are not directly comparable to those for five-year-olds, they do make the case that large child care subsidies for parents of younger children are likely to have significant effects on maternal labor supply" (p. 320).

A final point about these three studies is that the drastic nature of the 1996 welfare reform may make the prereform results of these studies less relevant for predicting responses to current and future subsidies. Less emphasis was placed on moving welfare participants into employment before PRWORA. A mother might have been able to turn down a child care subsidy offer before PRWORA and remain out of the labor force without losing her welfare benefit. A mother who turned down a child care subsidy today would be more likely to lose eligibility for welfare. It seems plausible that a mother who is going to lose her welfare eligibility in any case would be likely to accept a subsidy offer and join the labor force. So the results of studies conducted in the pre-PRWORA environment will not necessarily be a good guide to behavior in the post-PRWORA era.[33]

Blau and Tekin (2002) use data from thirteen states in the 1997 National Survey of America's Families (NSAF) to estimate the impact of receiving a child care subsidy on employment, welfare participation, and other outcomes of single mothers with children under age thirteen. Subsidy receipt is measured by the respondent's report that a welfare or social service agency pays all or part of the monetary cost of child care for the family. Identification of the effect of subsidy receipt comes from the assumption that subsidies are rationed at the county level. Information on the county of residence is available for thirteen states that were oversampled in the NSAF. The employment and other outcome equations include the subsidy receipt indicator, state dummies, twenty-one county characteristics, lagged welfare and child care subsidy receipt, and demographic variables. A first-

32. There is also the issue of whether results from a universal subsidy are a reliable guide to the effects of a means-tested subsidy. Thirty-four percent of Gelbach's sample of single mothers whose youngest child was five years old received public assistance in 1979, and average 1979 wage-salary earnings of workers were $5,193. Thus this is a relatively low-income sample that is likely to have been representative of mothers eligible for means-tested subsidies in 1980, so his results do seem useful for predicting the impact of a similarly structured means-tested subsidy.

33. I thank Dan Black and Barbara Bergmann for emphasizing this point to me.

stage equation for subsidy receipt includes county dummies, the lagged dependent variables, and demographic variables. Thus the identifying assumption is that there are no unobserved county-level determinants of employment; that is, county dummies can be excluded from the outcome equations. Ordinary least squares estimates show effects of subsidy receipt of 10.7 percentage points on employment, 8.0 points on school enrollment, and –1.4 points on welfare participation, with the first two significantly different from zero. Two-stage least squares (2SLS) estimates show effects of 4.6 percentage points on employment, 5.3 points on school enrollment, and 5.5 points on welfare participation, but none of the estimates are significantly different from zero. The standard errors are two to three times larger in the 2SLS estimates, making it difficult to draw any reliable conclusions from these estimates.

The data used by Blau and Tekin are more recent than in the other studies, but the identification strategy is problematic. They cannot determine whether any given family in their sample is eligible for a child care subsidy. Thus the differences in subsidy receipt by county may in fact reflect differences in eligibility and take-up behavior, as well as rationing by county agencies. The twenty-one county characteristics may help alleviate this problem, but there is no guarantee that the remaining county differences in subsidy receipt are exogenous. As in the MHW study, there is no natural comparison or control group.

7.5.3   Inferences Based on Effects of the Price of Child Care

More than a dozen studies have estimated the effect of the price of purchased child care on the employment of mothers. One of the motivations for this literature is to infer how child care price subsidies would affect employment decisions. Whether inferences about the effects of subsidies drawn from this literature are useful depends on several factors. First, if there are substantial costs to taking up a subsidy, either in the form of time costs required to negotiate the subsidy bureaucracy or psychic costs ("stigma") of participating in a means-tested program, then price effects on employment may not be a reliable guide to subsidy effects. Second, the price effects estimated in this literature are generally assumed to be linear, whereas most subsidies are nonlinear. As noted in section 7.4, nonlinearity of a subsidy does not affect the qualitative result that a child care price subsidy increases the incentive to be employed, but it could affect the magnitude of the employment effect. Thus estimates of linear price effects could be an unreliable guide to the effects of typical nonlinear subsidies. Third, issues of specification and estimation of econometric models of price effects could affect the inferences drawn from such effects. There is little basis for evaluating whether the first two issues are important in practice, so most of this subsection focuses on specification and estimation issues.[34] The two key specification and estimation issues concern identification of the price effect and accounting for unpaid child care.

Table 7.7 summarizes results from studies of the effect of the price of child care on employment of mothers in the United States.[35] Estimated price elasticities reported by the authors of the studies range from 0.06 to −1.26. The studies differ in the data sources used and in sample composition by marital status, age of children, and income. Sample composition does not explain much of the variation in the elasticity estimates; the range of estimates is large within studies using the same sample composition. Differences in the data sources also do not appear to account for much variation in the estimates. There is substantial variation in estimates from studies using the same source of data (for example, Connelly 1992 versus Ribar 1992). Hence specification and estimation issues most likely play an important role in producing variation in the estimates.

The eleven studies listed in the upper panel of the table use very similar methods and are discussed as a group. These studies estimate a binomial discrete choice model of employment by probit or logit. The price of child care is measured by the fitted value from a child care *expenditure* equation estimated by linear regression on the subsample of employed mothers who paid for care. The expenditure equation is corrected for selectivity on employment and paying for care using either a standard approach (Heckman 1979) or a reduced-form bivariate probit model of employment and paying for care, following Maddala (1983) and Tunali (1986). In order to avoid relying exclusively on functional form for identification, some variables that are included in the child care expenditure equation are excluded from the employment probit in which the fitted value from the expenditure equation appears as a regressor. Also, some variables that are included in the probit selection equations are excluded from the child care price equation in order to help identify the selectivity effects. A Heckman (1979) selectivity-

34. The limited evidence on take-up of child care subsidies is discussed in section 7.5.4. Averett, Peters, and Waldman (1997) estimate a labor supply model that incorporates the DCTC by IV and a full information maximum likelihood (FIML) method that accounts for the kinks induced by the DCTC. The FIML estimate of the net wage effect on hours worked is about 50 percent larger than the IV estimate.

35. Other reviews of this literature can be found in Anderson and Levine (2000), Connelly (1991), and Ross (1998). Chaplin et al. (1999) review the literature on the effect of the price of child care on child care mode choice. Some studies are not included in the table because the elasticity of employment with respect to the price of child care was not estimated or reported. Some of the latter studies estimated an hours of work (or a marginal rate of substitution) equation instead of an employment equation (Averett, Peters, and Waldman 1997; Heckman 1974; Michalopolous, Robins and Garfinkel 1992). Others did not report enough information to determine the method of estimation or the elasticity (Connelly 1990; Kimmel, 1995). Michalopoulos and Robins (2000) use a pooled sample of Canadian and U.S. families, and Powell (1997) analyzes Canadian data. Michalopoulos and Robins report an elasticity of employment with respect to the price of child care of −.156, and Powell's estimated elasticity is −.38. See also Michalopoulos and Robins (2002) for a pooled analysis of Canadian and U.S. single mothers.

Table 7.7 Summary of Studies of the Effect of the Price of Child Care on Employment of Mothers

Study	Data	Population	Employment	Price	Method	Elasticity
Anderson and Levine (2000)	SIPP 1990–93	Child <13	Binary: LFP	Total child care expenses per mother's hours worked	Probit; standard	Married, <13: −0.30; single, <13: −0.47; married, <6: −0.46; single, <6: −0.58
Baum (2002)	NLSY 1988–94	Women who gave birth 1988–94	Month of return to work following birth	Total child care expenditure per hour worked	Discrete time logit hazard	low income: −0.59; others: −0.02[a] (one year after birth)
Blau and Robins (1991)	NLSY 1982–86	Child <6	Binary: employed in last 4 weeks	Total child care expenses per hour of care	Probit; standard	0.04[a]
Connelly (1992)	SIPP 1984	Married, child <13	Binary: LFP	Total child care expenses per mother's hours worked	Probit; standard	−0.20
Connelly and Kimmel (2000)	SIPP 1992–93 (data for 1994)	Child <6	FT, PT, OLF	Expenditure per hour on primary arrangement of youngest child	Ordered probit on FT, PT, OLF	Married: FT: −0.71, PT: −0.08; single: FT: −1.22, PT: −0.37
Connelly and Kimmel (2001)	SIPP 1992–93 (data for 1994)	Single, child <6	Binary: LFP	Expenditure per hour on primary arrangement of youngest child	Probit; standard	−1.03

(continued)

Table 7.7 (continued)

Study	Data	Population	Employment	Price	Method	Elasticity
U.S. GAO (1994a)	NCCS 1990	Child <13	Binary: LFP	Total weekly child care expenses	Probit; standard	Poor: −0.50; near poor: −0.34; not poor: −0.19
Han and Waldfogel (2001)	CPS 1991–94	Child <6	Binary: employed	Total child care expenses per mother's hours worked (from SIPP)	Probit; standard	Married: −0.30; single: −0.50
Hotz and Kilburn (1994)	NLS72, 1986	Child <6	Binary: employed	Total child care expenses per hour of care	Probit	−1.26
Kimmel (1998)	SIPP 1987	Child <13	Binary: worked last month	Total child care expenses per mother's hours worked	Probit; standard	Married: −0.92; single: −0.22
Ribar (1992)	SIPP 1984	Child <15	Employed	Total child care expenses per hour of care	Probit	−0.74
Blau and Hagy (1998)	NCCS 1990	Child <6	Employed	Quality-adjusted location-specific price from provider survey	Multinomial logit	−0.20

Study	Data	Population	Labor supply	Price variable	Method	Price elasticity
Blau and Robins (1988)	EOPP 1980	Married, child <14	Employed	Average location-specific weekly child care expenditure	Multinomial logit	−0.34
Fronstin and Wissoker (1995)	NCCS 1990	Child <6	Employed	Average location-specific price from child care provider survey	Binary logit	Low-income area: −0.45; high-income area: 0.06[a]
Ribar (1995)	SIPP 1984	Married, child <15	Employed FT, employed PT	Total child care expenses per hour of care	Structural multinomial choice	Child <15: −0.09; child <6: −0.09
Tekin (2002)	NSAF 1997	Single, child <13	Employed FT, employed PT	Total child care expenses per hour of care	Multinomial logit	Full time: −0.15; part time: −0.07

Notes: SIPP = Survey of Income and Program Participation. NLSY = National Longitudinal Survey of Youth. NCCS = National Child Care Survey. CPS = Current Population Survey. NLS72 = National Longitudinal Survey of the Class of 1972. EOPP = Employment Opportunity Pilot Projects. FT = full-time. PT = part-time. OLF = out of the labor force.

[a]Underlying coefficient estimate on the price of care was *insignificantly* different from zero at the 10 percent level.

corrected wage equation is used to generate fitted values for the wage rate, which are included in the employment model.[36]

In order to provide a context for evaluating this empirical approach, it is useful to combine and extend the models developed in the analysis of informal care and quality in section 7.4. Recall that H is hours of paid child care purchased in the market, U is hours of unpaid child care provided by a relative, and child care is assumed to be required for every hour in which the mother works and for none of the hours in which she does not work, so $h = H + U$. The time constraints are $\ell + h = 1$ for the mother, and $\ell_r + U = 1$ for the relative. The child development production function is respecified as $d = d(\ell q_m, Hq, Uq_r : \mathbf{X_1})$, where $q_m(q_r)$ is the quality of child care provided by the mother (relative), $\mathbf{X_1}$ is a vector of family and child characteristics that affect child development, and for simplicity q_m and q_r are assumed to be fixed. The utility function is $u(c, \ell, \ell_r, d; \mathbf{X_2})$, where $\mathbf{X_2}$ is a vector of utility determinants. The budget constraint is $c = y + wh - pH$, where $p = \alpha + \beta q + f(\mathbf{X_3}) + \varepsilon_p$, $\mathbf{X_3}$ is a vector of price determinants other than quality, and ε_p is a disturbance.

We are interested in estimating the effect of p on the probability of employment, denoted $P(E)$. As noted in the previous section, there are several different outcomes (corner solutions) of the model in which the mother is employed. They differ by whether paid child care is used and whether unpaid child care is used. The price of child care affects the employment decision by its effect on the utility of these outcomes compared to the utility of not being employed. The general form of the conditional indirect utility functions (IUF) for each of the outcomes in the model is as follows:

Outcome	Mother Employed	Relative Care Used	Paid Care Used	Indirect Utility Function (V_i)
1	no	no	no	$V_1(y, q_m, X_1, X_2) + \varepsilon_1$
2	yes	yes	no	$V_2(y, q_m, w, q_r, X_1, X_2) + \varepsilon_2$
3	yes	yes	yes	$V_3(y, q_m, w, q_r, p, X_1, X_2) + \varepsilon_3$
4	yes	no	yes	$V_4(y, q_m, w, p, X_1, X_2) + \varepsilon_4$

The εs are disturbances representing variables unobserved by the investigator and are specified as additive for simplicity. The effect of interest $\partial P(E)/$

36. Exceptions to this general approach among the eleven studies include the following. Baum (2002) specifies the employment equation as a discrete-time monthly hazard model of return to work following birth of a child. Blau and Robins (1991) estimate the employment probit jointly with equations for the presence of a preschool age child and use of nonrelative care. Connelly and Kimmel (2000) estimate an ordered probit model for full-time employment, part-time employment, and nonemployment. Ribar (1992) estimates the employment equation jointly with equations for hours of paid and unpaid care. Hotz and Kilburn (1994) estimate their binary employment equation jointly with equations for use and hours of paid child care, child care price, and the wage rate. The wage, price, and nonwage income variables are not adjusted for taxes and subsidies in any of the studies listed in the table.

∂p is derived from the model as $\partial[1 - P(1)]/\partial p$, where $P(1)$ is the probability of choosing outcome 1. To estimate this effect, a multinomial discrete choice model can be specified with functional form assumptions for the IUFs and disturbances, and empirical measures of the arguments of each IUF included as specified above. Depending on assumptions about the joint distribution of the disturbances, the model can be estimated by multinomial probit or logit, and the desired probability derivative can be computed. Two issues raised by this model are the interpretation and specification of a binomial employment equation and specification of the price p.[37]

In the multinomial choice model the probability of not being employed is

$$P(1) = \mathrm{pr}(V_1 > V_2, V_1 > V_3, V_1 > V_4),$$

and the desired effect $\partial[1 - P(1)]/\partial p$ is derived by substituting the expressions for the V_is and computing the derivative. An equivalent expression for the probability of not being employed that could serve as a basis for a binary employment equation is

$$P(1) = \mathrm{pr}(V_1 > \max\{V_2, V_3, V_4\}) = pr\left(V_1 > \sum_{i=2}^{4} D_i V_i\right),$$

where $D_i = 1$ if $V_i > V_j$, $i, j = 2, 3, 4$, $i \neq j$, and $D_i = 0$ otherwise. The binary variables D_i "dummy out" regressors that are not relevant to the mother's employment decision. For example, if the mother's highest-utility employment outcome ($\max\{V_2, V_3, V_4\}$) does not involve paid care, then the V_i functions on the right-hand side of the inequality that include p will be dummied out. Thus, estimating a binomial employment equation based on this model requires knowing which of the employment outcomes 2, 3, and 4 provides the highest utility for each mother. For mothers who choose not to be employed, we do not know which of the employment options would have provided her the highest utility (i.e. we do not observe the values of D_i). For employed mothers we observe these outcomes, but whether the best employment option involves paid care, relative care, or both is a choice made by the mother. Consistent estimates of the parameters of the employment equation cannot be obtained without accounting for this choice, regardless of the distribution of the disturbances. The multinomial choice model accounts for this choice, but the binomial model does not.

37. Another issue is determining whether a mother has the option of unpaid child care by a relative. If we observe a mother using unpaid relative care then we know this option was part of her choice set. If she does not use unpaid relative care, it is possible to ask her whether such care was available, and some surveys have done this (e.g., the National Child Care Survey). The reliability of responses to such questions is unknown, but they could be used to determine the choice set: If a mother indicates that relative care is unavailable, options 2 and 3 can be eliminated from her choice set. Alternatively, it can be *assumed* that unpaid relative care is available to every mother, with a "relative" of last resort being self-care by the child, an option with presumably very low quality.

To illustrate this point, suppose the disturbances are independently and identically distributed as Type I Extreme Value, yielding the multinomial logit functional form for the choice probabilities. Suppose we assume that the best employment option for all mothers is number 4, in which only paid child care is used. The likelihood function contribution for a mother who chooses option 1 (not employed) under this assumption would be

$$P(1 \mid 1 \text{ or } 4) = \frac{e^{\overline{V}_1}}{e^{\overline{V}_1} + e^{\overline{V}_4}},$$

where $\overline{V}_i = V_i - \varepsilon_i$. The correct likelihood contribution for a mother for whom option 4 is in fact the best employment alternative is

$$P(1) = P(1 \mid 1 \text{ or } 4)P(1 \text{ or } 4) = \frac{e^{\overline{V}_1}}{e^{\overline{V}_1} + e^{\overline{V}_4}} \cdot \frac{e^{\overline{V}_1} + e^{\overline{V}_4}}{\sum_{i=1}^{4} e^{\overline{V}_i}} = \frac{e^{\overline{V}_1}}{\sum_{i=1}^{4} e^{\overline{V}_i}}.$$

If option 4 was in fact the best employment option for every mother, then without loss of generality we can set $\overline{V}_2 = \overline{V}_3 = -\infty$. In this case the second term in the expression following the second equality sign is equal to one, and $P(1 \mid 1 \text{ or } 4)$ is the correct likelihood contribution. If not, then the wrong likelihood contribution is used, resulting in inconsistent estimates. For a mother for whom option 4 is not the best employment choice, $P(1 \mid 1 \text{ or } 4)$ is obviously not the correct likelihood contribution. It is not possible to determine the nature of the bias caused by this misspecification, since the model is nonlinear and there is no analytic expression for the estimator. If unpaid care was an infrequent choice, ignoring it might cause little bias. But the data show that unpaid care is a common choice, particularly among low-income mothers and mothers with young children (see table 7.6). Specifying an employment model under the assumption that paid care is always the relevant nonmaternal child care option is thus a potentially serious error, leading to inconsistent parameter estimates. This was noted by Heckman (1974) in one of the earliest economic studies of child care but has been ignored in many recent analyses.

The other main issue is how to measure the price of child care. The first eleven studies listed in table 7.7 all use the fitted value from a selection-corrected child care expenditure[38] equation estimated on the subsample of employed mothers who use paid care. This approach is intended to deal with the facts that expenditure on child care is not observed for mothers who do not pay for care, and observed expenditure for mothers who pay is endogenous if the quality of paid care affects price and if quality is a choice variable. The demand function for the quality of paid care can be derived by solving the first order conditions conditional on paying for care:

---

38. Expenditure is measured per hour of paid care or per hour of the mother's work, except in U.S. General Accounting Office (1994a), in which it is expenditure per week.

$$q = q(X_1, X_2, y, q_m, w, q_r, p, \varepsilon_i).^{39}$$

Substitute this quality demand function into the price equation $p = \alpha + \beta q + f(X_3) + \varepsilon_p$, and solve to obtain a reduced-form price function

$$p = p(X_1, X_2, X_3, y, q_m, w, q_r, \alpha, \beta) + \varepsilon_p^*,$$

where ε_p^* is a function of ε_p and ε_i.[40] For simplicity ignore the issues discussed in the preceding paragraphs, and specify a binomial employment equation of the form

$$P(E) = P(p, X_1, X_2, y, q_m, w, q_r, \varepsilon_i).$$

The employment equation includes p and excludes X_3, α, and β, and the latter three variables appear in the reduced-form price equation. If X_3 contains at least one variable not also included in X_1 or X_2, or if α or β varies across mothers and can be measured, then the price effect in the employment equation is identified by exclusion restrictions. Researchers have typically used child care regulations, average wages of child care workers, and other factors that vary across geographic locations as identifying variables in X_3, under the assumption that such variables affect household behavior only insofar as they affect the price of child care. Some studies have also used variables such as the number of children by age for identification.

If the unobserved factors that influence employment and child care behavior (ε_i) are correlated with the unobserved determinants of the price of care (ε_p), then estimating the reduced-form price equation on a sample of mothers who are employed and pay for care yields biased estimates. Most researchers who use this approach have recognized this problem and as noted above have specified reduced-form employment and pay-for-care equations that are used to correct the child care price equation for selection effects in a two-stage estimation. However, the model implies that *there are no theoretically justified exclusion restrictions* to identify the selection effects: the price function is a reduced form, so it contains all of the exogenous variables in the model. Substitute the reduced-form price equation into the employment equation and solve to obtain

$$P(E) = P^*(X_1, X_2, X_3, y, q_m, w, q_r, \alpha, \beta, \varepsilon_i, \varepsilon_p),$$

Where P^* denotes the reduced-form employment equation. This has the same determinants as the price equation. The same result holds when a reduced-form pay-for-care equation is derived, conditional on employment. Hence the only basis for identification of a child care price equation using

---

39. This must be done separately for each outcome in which paid care is used. If unpaid care is not used jointly with paid care (outcome 4), then q_r is omitted from the demand function.

40. If the mother's wage is thought to be endogenous, its determinants can be substituted, since we are not particularly interested in the wage effects in this equation.

consumer expenditure data in a manner consistent with economic theory would be functional form or covariance restrictions (i.e., assume that the unobserved factors that influence employment and child care behavior are uncorrelated with the unobserved determinants of the price of care).

The estimated elasticity of employment with respect to the price of child care ranges from 0.04 to –1.26 in the first eleven studies listed in table 7.7. Without a detailed examination of specification and estimation differences across the studies along the lines of Mroz (1987), it is difficult to explain why these estimates are so varied. It is possible that some of this variation is due to the two problems discussed here: treating paid child care as if it were the best option for all mothers, and inappropriate exclusion restrictions to identify the child care price equation. Different identification restrictions are used in each study, possibly leading to different degrees of bias. Different data sources containing different proportions of mothers who use paid care are used in each study, and the bias caused by treating paid child care as if it were the best option for all mothers is likely to depend on this proportion.

Of the five studies in the lower part of the table, Fronstin and Wissoker (1995) differ from the standard approach in measuring the price of care from a survey of child care providers rather than from consumer expenditure. This approach will be discussed below. They specify a binary employment equation, estimated by logit, based on the standard implicit assumption that paid care is always the best option.

The other four studies in the lower panel of table 7.7 use variants of the multinomial choice framework discussed above. Ribar (1995) specifies a structural multinomial choice model with a quadratic utility function in consumption, hours of work, and hours of paid care. The discrete outcomes are full-time employment with unpaid care, full-time employment with paid care, part-time employment with unpaid care, part-time employment with paid care, and no employment. The standard approach of imposing arbitrary exclusion restrictions on reduced-form employment and payment equations is used.[41] However, paid child care is *not* treated as if it was the best option for all mothers: The price of child care influences behavior by affecting the utility of the two options in which paid care is used, consistent with the theory described above. Two disturbances are incorporated, allowing the unobserved determinants of employment and child care to be correlated.

Tekin (2002) estimates a discrete choice model with outcomes defined by cross-classifying employment status (full-time, part-time, not employed) with indicators for use of paid child care conditional on employment and

41. Ribar specifies an equation for total expenditure rather than expenditure per hour and allows it to be nonlinear in hours of care and to contain a fixed component. These equations are estimated jointly with the child care expenditure equation by FIML instead of by the usual two-stage approach.

receipt of a child care subsidy conditional on employment and use of paid care. A multinomial logit model with a discrete random effect accounts for the possibility of correlation in the disturbances across the discrete choices (Mroz 1999). A child care expenditure equation identified by state dummies (which are excluded from the discrete choice model) is estimated jointly with the discrete choice model. Similar to Ribar, Tekin's approach does not impose the assumption that paid care is always the best option for an employed mother. Like the studies in the upper panel of table 7.7, Tekin uses consumer expenditure data to measure the price of child care, but unlike those studies he does not impose arbitrary identification restrictions to identify selection models of child care payers. Rather, he imposes a covariance restriction: The unobserved determinants of the price of care are assumed to be independent of the unobserved determinants of employment and child care decisions.

Blau and Hagy (1998) specify a multinomial choice model with categories defined by cross-classifying binary indicators of employment and paying for care with a four-way classification of mode of care (center, family day care, other nonparental, and parent). As in Ribar (1995) and Tekin (2002), the price of child care affects behavior only by affecting the utility of outcomes involving paid care, so paid child care is not treated as if it was the best option for all mothers. The model is estimated by multinomial logit jointly with equations for hours of work, hours of child care, and several other continuous outcomes. A discrete random effect is incorporated to account for the possibility of correlation in the disturbances across the discrete choices and between the disturbances in the discrete and continuous outcomes.

As in Fronstin and Wissoker (1995), the price of child care is derived from a survey of day care centers and licensed family providers, conducted in the same geographic locations as the survey of consumers. Blau and Hagy use these data to estimate regressions of the form

$$p_{ik} = \alpha_j + \beta q_{ij} + \gamma X_{3ij} + \varepsilon_{pij},$$

for provider i in site j. These are estimated separately for centers and family day care homes. Quality is measured by factors thought to influence the quality of care, such as group size, teacher qualifications, provider goals, and staff turnover. Other provider characteristics such as age, race, and hours of operation are included in X_{3ij}. The slope coefficients (β and γ) are restricted to be the same across sites, but the intercepts (α_j) are allowed to be site-specific. The price assigned to each household in site j for a given mode of care is $\hat{p}_j = \hat{\alpha}_j + \hat{\beta}\bar{q} + \hat{\gamma}\bar{X}_3$, where a hat indicates an estimated parameter and a bar indicates the overall sample mean. Hence the only source of variation used is geographic variation in the intercept of the price function. This can be thought of as a quality-adjusted price, where the sample mean quality has been assigned to all observations. This approach avoids selection and identification problems inherent in the use of consumer child care expenditure data to measure the price of care, and allows for observed differences across locations in quality and other factors.[42] However, it does not allow for the possibility of unobserved heterogeneity across locations in the average quality of child care. If such unobserved heterogeneity is present (after controlling for a large number of observed factors in q and X), then $\hat{\alpha}_j$ (and therefore $\hat{p}_j$) would be correlated with the disturbances in the multinomial choice model, since those disturbances incorporate unobserved preferences for quality. Fronstin and Wissoker's approach to measuring the price of child care can be though of as a special case of this approach in which the restrictions $\beta = \gamma = 0$ are imposed.

Blau and Robins (1988) estimate a multinomial choice model derived from the framework described above, with two modifications: They assume that paid and unpaid care cannot be used simultaneously, and they allow the employment status of the relative to be a choice variable. The model was estimated by multinomial logit, but the price of child care was included in all of the outcomes in which the mother is employed instead of only those in which paid care is used. This is inconsistent with the theory described above and is equivalent to assuming that paid care is always the best option. Blau and Robins used the site-specific average weekly child care expenditure as a measure of the price of care for all families in a given site. This is equivalent to the Fronstin-Wissoker approach, using weekly instead of hourly price, and using consumer expenditure instead of provider price.

The studies that are most consistent with an underlying framework in which informal care is dealt with appropriately are Blau and Hagy (1998), Ribar (1995), and Tekin (2002). These studies produce estimates of the elasticity of employment with respect to the price of child care at the lower end of the range (in absolute value) in table 7.7: –0.09 in Ribar, –0.15 in Tekin, and –0.20 in Blau and Hagy. Blau and Hagy repeated their analysis using consumer expenditure data to measure the price of child care in place of the provider survey data, and they estimated an elasticity of –0.06 in this case. This could explain why Ribar's and Tekin's estimates are smaller than those of Blau and Hagy, since Ribar and Tekin used consumer expenditure data to measure price. It is risky to generalize from only three studies, but the fact that the studies that accounted for informal care in ways consistent with economic theory produced small elasticities suggests that the true elasticity may be small.

The elasticity of employment with respect to the price of child care may

42. This approach could not be used to assign prices for other nonparental care. Such care consists mainly of babysitters, small unlicensed family day care, and relatives, and providers of this type were not sampled in the provider survey. The consumer expenditure data were used to estimate a price equation for this mode, not corrected for selection.

differ across groups. Ribar (1995) uses a sample of married mothers and Blau and Hagy use a sample with married and single mothers, dominated by the former. If the elasticity of employment with respect to the price of child care is different for married and single mothers, then the evidence from these two studies would not be a good guide to price effects for single mothers. However, Tekin's estimates for single mothers are similar to those of Ribar and Blau and Hagy. Kimmel's (1998) results indicate quite different elasticities for married and single mothers, but Anderson and Levine (2000) and Connelly and Kimmel (2000) produce estimates that are closer for the two groups. If the elasticities differ substantially by income, then estimates for random samples of the population, as in Blau and Hagy (1998), Ribar (1995), and Tekin (2002), could be misleading if applied to the low-income population. Estimates produced by Anderson and Levine (disaggregated by education of the mother; not shown in table 7.7), Baum (2002), Fronstin and Wissoker (1995), and U.S. General Accounting Office (1994a) all show larger elasticities for low-income groups. This suggests that the true elasticity for low-income mothers could be larger than the estimates from Blau and Hagy, Ribar, and Tekin.

Four studies provide estimates of the effect of the price of child care on hours of work by the mother, conditional on employment. Averett, Peters, and Waldman (1997) report an uncompensated labor supply elasticity with respect to the price of child care of $-.78$ from their kinked budget constraint model for annual hours of work. Blau and Hagy (1998) estimate the price effect on weekly hours of work separately by the mode of child care used and find uncompensated effects of 1.3, 2.0, and -1.8 respectively for users of centers, family day care, and other nonparental care. These imply elasticities at the sample means of 0.06, 0.08, and -0.05, respectively. Michalopoulos, Robins, and Garfinkel (1992) report an elasticity of annual hours worked with respect to the price of child care of essentially zero based on a structural model with a Stone-Geary utility function. Baum (2002) also finds small elasticities, not significantly different from zero. The large elasticity estimated by Averett, Peters, and Waldman (1997) compared to the much smaller estimates of the other studies could be a result of the use of the kinked budget constraint method, which imposes a substitution effect with a sign consistent with economic theory whether or not this is consistent with the data (MaCurdy, Green, and Paarsch 1990).

7.5.4 Evidence on Other Effects of Subsidies and Price of Child Care

Quality of Child Care

As discussed in section 7.4, economic theory does not predict the sign of the effect of the price of child care on the quality of care demanded. The literature contains only two studies of the effect of the price of child care on demand for quality: Blau and Hagy (1998) and Hagy (1998).[43] Blau and Hagy estimate consumer demand functions for inputs to the production of quality: staff-child ratio and group size in the child care arrangement, and whether the provider has received any training in early childhood care and education. Hagy focuses exclusively on staff-child ratio. Developmental psychologists argue that the quality of a child care arrangement is best measured by the nature of the interactions between the provider and child and aspects of the curriculum, as measured by instruments such as the ECERS-ITERS described above (see note 17). Staff-child ratio and so forth are inputs to producing quality, although some recent evidence suggests that the productivity of these inputs is modest at best (Blau 1997, 1999, 2000). So these are not the best measures of quality, but they are the only ones available that can be matched to a price.

Blau and Hagy use the price measure described above, $\hat{p}_j = \hat{\alpha}_j + \hat{\beta}\overline{q} + \hat{\gamma}\overline{X}_3$. Price effects on demand for the inputs were estimated separately for users of centers and family day care, and separately by whether the mother was employed, accounting for self-selection into these groups. The results for users of day care centers show a negative effect of $\hat{p}_j$ on group size, essentially zero impact on staff-child ratio, and a positive effect on the probability of having a trained provider. These results imply that α-subsidies that reduce $\hat{p}_j$ would lead to demand for *larger* groups and *less* provider training by center users, leading to lower quality of child care. Price effects on hours of care demanded per week were negative, indicating that when price falls consumers substitute toward quantity and away from quality. As the quality-constant price falls, consumers purchase more hours of care, raising the implicit price of quality. This leads to a decrease in demand for quality. For users of family day care, the price effects were positive on group size, negative on staff-child ratio, and positive on training. In this case α-subsidies that reduce $\hat{p}_j$ would lead to demand for *smaller* groups, a larger ratio of staff to children, and less provider training, producing an uncertain effect on quality depending on the relative productivities and elasticities of demand for the inputs.

Hagy (1998) specifies a price regression of the form $p_{ij} = \alpha + \beta_{1j}q_{ij} + \beta_{2j}q_{ij}^2 + \gamma X_{3ij} + \varepsilon_{pij}$ for provider i in site j, where quality q is measured by the staff-child ratio. The model is quadratic in quality and allows β to vary by site instead of α as in Blau and Hagy. The implicit marginal price of staff-child ratio facing a consumer in site j is $\partial p_{ij}/\partial q_{ij} = \beta_{1j} + 2\beta_{2j}q$, where q is the staff-child ratio in the arrangement used by the consumer. This implicit marginal price is included as a regressor in a model to explain consumer demand for staff-child ratio. Recognizing that the marginal price depends on

43. Some studies have estimated price or subsidy effects on other attributes of child care such as choice of mode, hours of care, and travel time to the arrangement. These are interesting, but of less policy relevance than effects on employment and child care quality, and they are not discussed here. See Blau and Hagy (1998) and Chaplin et al. (1999) for examples and references to other studies.

quality, Hagy instruments the marginal price with a set of site dummies, thus using only geographic variation to identify the price effect, as in Blau and Hagy. The demand for staff-child ratio is estimated only for users of day care centers, accounting for self-selection into this mode of care. The effect of the price is positive and significantly different from zero, but very small in magnitude, with an implied price elasticity of .017.

Child Development

There are no studies of the effect of the price of child care or child care subsidies on child development outcomes. However, there is a substantial literature that evaluates the child development effects of Head Start and other early intervention programs.[44] Since these programs can be interpreted as child care subsidies, their effects on child development are discussed here. This large literature has been reviewed by Karoly et al. (1998), Barnett (1992, 1995), Currie (2001), and Waldfogel (2002) among others, and is summarized briefly here. Karoly et al. (1998, p. xiii) conclude that "in some situations, carefully targeted early childhood interventions *can* yield measurable benefits in the short run and that some of those benefits persist long after the program has ended." This conclusion is based on evaluations of nine early intervention programs with randomized assignment to treatment, including the well-known Perry Preschool, Carolina Abecedarian, and Infant Health and Development projects. Most of the programs produced short-run gains in IQ, but few have produced IQ gains that have lasted past age twelve. However, short-run improvements in academic achievement caused by the programs did persist in most of the programs through the latest age at which achievement was measured (age twenty-one in the Abecedarian project[45]). The Perry Preschool evaluation followed the children longer than any of the other intervention evaluations and has found substantial improvements through age twenty-seven in high school graduation, crime and delinquency, income, and welfare participation. No effects on grade repetition and teen pregnancy were found. The mechanisms through which these effects occur are not well understood, because it seems clear that they are not a result of long-run improvements in IQ.

There have been many evaluations of Head Start, but they have been hampered by two factors: None have been based on randomized assignment, and Head Start is not a single program but is rather an umbrella for a large number of programs that vary in design and quality while presumably meeting the main requirements for a Head Start program (Karoly et al. 1998).[46]

44. I am not aware of any studies of the effects of Head Start or other early education programs on maternal employment.

45. See Campbell et al. (2001, 2002) for age twenty-one results in the Abecedarian study.

46. A recent report of the Advisory Committee on Head Start Research and Evaluation (1999) strongly recommended a randomized assignment evaluation of Head Start. A random assignment evaluation of Head Start is now under way, with field work having begun in 2002.

Evaluations of Head Start have almost uniformly found substantial positive short-run impacts on IQ that have subsequently faded out within a few years after exit from the program. About half of the Head Start evaluations found short-run positive effects on reading and mathematics achievement that faded out within a few years, and the others found no short-run effects. However, Head Start evaluations that have examined effects on grade retention (seven), special education (four), and high school graduation (one study) have sometimes found positive effects on these outcomes (Barnett 1995).

The only Head Start evaluation that has found effects on cognitive ability that have *not* faded out over time is Currie and Thomas (1995), who found this result for white children but not black children. Like other Head Start evaluations, theirs was not based on a randomized design. But unlike other evaluations they were able to control for at least some potentially confounding unobserved factors by exploiting the facts that the National Longitudinal Survey of Youth (NLSY) contains data on multiple children in the same families, and there are substantial numbers of families in which at least one child attended a Head Start program and at least one child did not. Using a fixed effects estimator that identifies the effect of Head Start only by within-family differences between siblings who did and did not attend Head Start, Currie and Thomas find substantial positive short-run effects on cognitive ability (the Peabody Picture Vocabulary Test) for whites and blacks that do not fade out for whites but do for blacks; no short- or long-run effects on grade retention for blacks, but a substantial positive effect for whites that fades only a bit over time; and positive short-run effects on measles immunization that fade out for both races. Currie and Thomas note that their method relies on the assumptions that assignment of children to Head Start within families is uncorrelated with child-specific unobservables and that there are no spillover effects of Head Start attendance by one child on other children in the family. The first assumption would be valid if, for example, Head Start slots were rationed by some randomized method that did not favor the siblings of children who had already attended Head Start, or if family income changed over time in a way that was unrelated to child-specific factors and led to one child in the family being eligible for the program and another not being eligible. They argue and present evidence that if child-specific unobservables and spillover effects matter, they will tend to bias the fixed effects estimates of the effect of Head Start toward zero.[47]

---

47. Garces, Thomas, and Currie (2002) report positive long-run effects of Head Start for both races using a within-family estimator with data from the Panel Study of Income Dynamics. Currie and Thomas (2000) present evidence that the fade-out effects observed for blacks may be due to the fact that black children attend lower-quality schools than whites. Currie and Thomas (1999) find positive effects of Head Start on cognitive outcomes for children of native-born Hispanic mothers but not for children of foreign-born Hispanic mothers. They do not examine fade-out in this paper.

An important issue concerning early childhood interventions that involve a child care component is whether the benefits of the intervention exceed the costs. The interventions tend to be expensive relative to typical market child care because they are designed to provide very high-quality services to help overcome the developmental disadvantages faced by low-income children. But the benefits are potentially large as well, if academic achievement, higher earnings, and lower welfare participation are permanent results of the intervention. The data needed to perform a credible and thorough benefit-cost analysis of Head Start and other early intervention programs do not exist. Cost data are readily available, but many of the benefits are intangible, and others that could in principle be quantified are spread over long time periods and require data that have not been collected. Karoly et al. used data from an analysis by Barnett (1993a, 1995) to perform a cost savings analysis of one early intervention program, the Perry Preschool Project. This analysis does not attempt to measure all of the benefits of the program to the participants or society, but rather tries to determine whether the program results in direct savings to the government that (in present value terms) exceed the cost of the program to the government. If the answer is yes, government funding of the program can be justified purely as a way for the government to reduce net expenditures without even considering other possible benefits of the program. This is a conservative approach to evaluating a program, but Karoly et al. argue that it is the only approach available given data limitations, and even for this approach the data needed are available for only one program. If savings to the government do not exceed the cost of the program, this does *not* necessarily mean that funding the program is not worthwhile.

The following figures illustrate the calculations by Karoly et al., based on Barnett's figures using data through age twenty-seven of the participants, expressed in 1996 dollars discounted at 4 percent to the date of birth of the child:

		Government Savings	
Item	Program Cost	Through Age 27	Projected, Ages 28–65
Cost of preschool, ages 3–4	$12,148		
Reduced special education costs		$6,365	
Increased taxes on earnings		$3,451	$3,115
Decreased welfare payments		$1,968	$341
Decrease in criminal justice cost		$7,378	$2,817
Total	$12,148	$19,162	$6,273

These calculations do not place any value on the decrease in tangible and intangible losses to crime victims, or the increased earnings of the program participant. Even this very conservative approach that prices out only tangible cost savings to the government leads to the conclusion that the Perry Preschool Project was a highly worthwhile investment.

Subsidy Take-Up

Meyers and Heintze (1999) examine the use of child care subsidies in a sample of current and former welfare recipients in four counties of California in 1995. In their sample, 16 percent of employed mothers received a child care subsidy, 30 percent of mothers enrolled in education or training programs received a subsidy, and 34 percent of mothers in neither activity received a subsidy (including Head Start). The public subsidy system for child care in California was quite complex prior to PRWORA, with at least seven different subsidy programs. When mothers were asked why they did not receive subsidies from the programs for which they appeared to be eligible, the majority response for all three employment-related subsidy programs, one out of two education-and-training-related subsidies, and one out of two child-education subsidies was that they were not aware of the program. The majority response for the other two subsidy programs was "aware of the program but did not apply." The acceptance rate for mothers who applied averaged 72 percent across all programs.

Fuller et al. (1999) estimate a model of the child care subsidy take-up decision of mothers enrolled in TANF using data collected in San Francisco, San Jose, and Tampa in 1998.[48] Of the women in their sample who used any nonmaternal child care, 37–44 percent received a subsidy, depending on the site. Presumably, all of the women in this sample were categorically eligible for a child care subsidy, but there is no way to determine whether the mothers not receiving a subsidy were rationed out or did not take up the subsidy offer. A regression analysis showed that a woman's knowledge of child care subsidy rules and participation in a TANF-sponsored job search class were positively associated with receiving a subsidy.

Welfare Receipt

Connelly and Kimmel (2001) use 1994 data on single mothers from the SIPP to estimate the impact of the price of child care on AFDC participation. Using the standard approach to measuring price, they find an elasticity of AFDC participation of .55 with respect to the price of child care from an ordinary probit model, and an elasticity of .28 from a probit model estimated jointly with an employment probit.

Tekin (2001) estimated the effect of the price of child care on enrollment in TANF using data on single mothers with children aged zero to thirteen from the 1997 NSAF. He specified a multinomial model of employment, welfare participation, and payment for child care. Using the estimation ap-

---

48. See Fuller et al. (2000) for a complete description of the data.

proach in Tekin (2002) described above, the estimated elasticity of TANF enrollment with respect to the price of child care was .098.

7.6   Current Policy Issues and Reform Options

7.6.1   Current Policy Issues

Three issues arise frequently in recent discussions of child care policy: insufficient funding for subsidies to meet welfare reform goals, inequitable distribution of subsidies, and concern about the quality of child care purchased with subsidies.

Insufficient Funding

It is estimated that despite spending all of the available federal and required state matching CCDF funds, as well as using up to a billion dollars of their TANF block grants on child care, states provided subsidies to only 15 percent of eligible children in 1998 (Administration for Children and Families 1999). States face considerable pressure and incentives from the federal government to reduce welfare rolls, and it is likely that the majority of subsidy recipients are current or former welfare participants.[49] It is unclear whether the current level of child care subsidy funding is sufficient to help states meet their specific welfare reform targets for employment, but it seems likely that demand for subsidies by eligible low-income families who are not connected to the welfare system exceeds the supply of subsidies available to such families with the current level of funding.[50]

Inequity

Before the welfare reform of 1996, the existence of many different child care subsidy programs with varying eligibility rules and fee schedules created considerable horizontal inequity in the distribution of subsidies. Many observers noted the fragmentation and lack of coordination that resulted from the proliferation of subsidy programs with varying goals and

49. Piecyk, Collins, and Kreader (1999, 11) report that 68 percent of children receiving child care subsidies through state-administered programs in Maryland in January 1998 were current or former welfare recipients, and the corresponding figure for Illinois was 84 percent. National data on the characteristics of subsidy recipients are not available. CCDF regulations require states to stipulate a plan for spending 70 percent of subsidy funds on current and former welfare recipients.

50. See Besharov (2002) and Mezey et al. (2002) for alternative views of the adequacy of current child care subsidy funding. It would be useful to know how much additional funding would be required in order to serve all eligible children. A naïve estimate would be about $36 billion (1998 dollars) = (6.399/.15) − 6.399: the 1998 level of CCDF funding divided by the estimated proportion of eligible children served, minus the 1998 level of funding. However, this ignores issues such as whether all eligible families would want a subsidy, whether the average expenditure per child would change if all eligible children were served, and whether states would change their subsidy rules if more funding was available.

rules (Barnett 1993b; Gomby et al. 1996). The consolidation of subsidy programs mandated by PRWORA helped to reduce this problem but did not eliminate it (Adams, Snyder, and Sandfort 2002). For example, there is often little coordination at the local level between Head Start and other child care subsidy programs, so some families may receive both a Head Start and a CCDF subsidy and others receive neither. Many observers call for closer coordination between Head Start and other child care subsidy programs (Schumacher, Greenberg, and Lombardi 2001).

Child Care Quality

Most of the child care subsidies provided under the CCDF are in the form of certificates (vouchers) that can be used for any legal child care arrangement. Some observers are concerned that subsidies of this form provide no direct incentive to purchase high-quality care and that parents may be too willing to purchase child care of mediocre quality (Blau 2001, ch. 10; Hayes, Palmer, and Zaslow 1990, p. 241).[51] Subsidies that are disbursed directly to providers, including Head Start, Title I-A, and some CCDF and TXX funds, can be tied more closely to meeting standards that are associated with high quality. Child development advocates push for increased attention to the quality of child care subsidized by the CCDF and other employment-related subsidies. Some would prefer to see an entirely child development–oriented public subsidy system for child care. In contrast, welfare reform advocates concerned mainly with increasing employment focus on the flexibility and freedom of choice provided by vouchers that are not tied to quality standards.

7.6.2   Reform Options

Proposals for reform of child care and early education subsidy programs fall into two broad groups. One set of proposals, mainly by economists, is focused on the low-income population, emphasizes freedom of choice for parents, and is typically although not always more employment-oriented than child development–oriented. These include Barnett (1993b), Blau (2001), Helburn and Bergmann (2002), Robins (1990), and Walker (1996). The other set of proposals is advocated mainly by child development experts and emphasizes universal coverage and supply-side subsidies that are tied closely to the quality of care rather than to employment. Examples include Kagan and Cohen (1996) and Finn-Stevenson and Zigler (1999).[52]

51. See Besharov and Samari (2000) for a detailed discussion of child care vouchers and the quality of child care.
52. Other authors have discussed general principles for reform of child care policy but have not made specific reform proposals. See Committee for Economic Development (2002); Hayes, Palmer, and Zaslow (1990, ch. 10); Gomby et al. (1996); Kahn and Kamerman (1995); and Vandell and Wolfe (2000). Hayes, Palmer, and Zaslow do offer some specific recommendations, including expansion of Head Start. Gormley (1995) makes a number of child care policy recommendations that are generally similar in style and intent to those of the economists.

Barnett (1993b) calls for a unified federal child care subsidy program for preschool-age children that would replace all other child care subsidies except Head Start. A baseline subsidy would be available to all families, with a supplemental subsidy for families in which the mother is employed. The subsidy would be universal but would decline in value from $6,000 per child plus $2,000 if the mother works for the poorest 25 percent of families, to $3,500 plus $4,500 for the next poorest quarter of families, to $1,000 per child plus $1,000 if the mother works for the upper half of the family income distribution. The subsidy could take the form of vouchers, contracts, or "credit accounts," the latter envisioned as a child care credit card. Barnett states that his proposal explicitly relies on parents to monitor quality and on the market to respond to increased demand for high-quality care by supplying more such care. He is willing, however, to consider limiting use of the subsidy to child care providers who meet high quality standards (p. 549). He estimated the cost of his proposal at about $60 billion after accounting for elimination of funding for subsidies that would be replaced by his program. The goals of Barnett's proposal are to make high-quality child care affordable for all families and to increase the financial rewards from employment for women.[53]

Blau (2001) proposes a child care subsidy in the form of a voucher that is worth more if higher-quality care is used. For families below the poverty line, the voucher would be worth $6,000 per child aged zero to five for care of "excellent" quality, $4,000 for care of "good" quality, and $2,000 for care of "other" quality. Quality would be determined by accreditation based on the developmental appropriateness of the care offered. The value of the voucher would decline with family income, and families with income over four times the poverty line would be ineligible. The voucher would be worth less for children aged six to twelve, and a family could qualify for vouchers for two children at most. Eligibility for the voucher would not depend on employment; the aim of the subsidy is to improve child development, not encourage employment. The proposed voucher plan would replace all other child care subsidies (including Head Start, which would be integrated into the voucher scheme), at an estimated net annual cost of $54 billion.[54]

Helburn and Bergmann (2002) propose a subsidy for child care in the form of a voucher that would cover the full cost of child care for families below the poverty line. Families with income above the poverty line would incur a copayment of 20 percent of the excess of family income over the

53. Other elements of his overall strategy to achieve these goals include paid parental leave and support for increased accreditation and professionalization of child care.
54. Other elements of the reform proposed by Blau (2001) include a child allowance, subsidies to providers for the cost of the accreditation process, and an educational campaign to disseminate information about the quality of child care. The cost of these additional elements is not included in the $54 billion.

poverty line. The value of the voucher would be higher if higher-quality child care is used, where quality is based on accreditation or staff qualifications. The voucher could be used only at licensed facilities, including family day care, babysitters, nannies, and relatives if they choose to become licensed. Helburn and Bergmann would also earmark $2.25 billion per year for activities to improve quality and increase market efficiency. These activities include tightening state regulations and increasing monitoring, standardizing the accreditation system, overhauling the training of care providers, and improving dissemination of information. The total annual cost of the proposed program, after accounting for elimination of existing child care subsidies, is estimated to be $29 billion. The proposed program would provide subsidies only for families in which both parents (or the single parent) are employed.

Robins (1990) advocates making the DCTC refundable, more progressive, and more generous. Refundability would make the tax credit of value to low-income families by paying a credit to families with no tax liability. His proposed schedule for the DCTC would have an 80 percent subsidy rate (instead of the current 30 percent) for families with AGI under $10,000, phased down gradually to zero for AGI over $60,000. He would also increase the maximum amount of child care expenses for which a credit could be claimed from $2,400 to $3,600 for one child and $4,800 to $7,200 for two or more. He estimates that making the credit refundable would increase its cost by about 20 percent, and making it more generous and progressive would increase cost by another 55 percent. He also proposes a safety net system of publicly funded day care centers for poor families who cannot take advantage of the DCTC for some reason.

Walker (1996) would replace several existing programs with an unconditional (on employment) child allowance for low-income families, and expanded parental leave. The amount of the child allowance would depend on income and the number and ages of children, but would not require the mother to be employed. The maximum allowance per family would be $7,600 for a family with three children under six years old and income less than 150 percent of the poverty line, and about half that level for three children over age six. The subsidy would be cut in half for families with income between 150 percent and 175 percent of the poverty line, and eliminated for income in excess of 175 percent of poverty. The estimated cost of $45 billion per year would be financed without raising taxes by eliminating the DCTC, AFDC, all other child care subsidies (except Head Start), and the income tax exemption for children. Eliminating the DCTC and the income tax exemption for children would significantly redistribute benefits from higher- to lower-income families.[55]

55. The other part of Walker's plan is a Parental Leave Account (PLA), funded by an additional payroll tax on employees of 3.5 percent. Parents could draw funds from their PLA to finance a leave from work for up to one year after the birth of a child, with the right to their old job back.

Finn-Stevenson and Zigler (1999) propose a "Schools of the 21st Century" plan that would use public schools as a setting to provide care for children aged three to five and before and after-school care for children aged six to twelve.[56] The child care provided in the schools would be of high quality and available to all families regardless of income. By providing child care in schools, Finn-Stevenson and Zigler also hope to professionalize the child care occupation and raise pay for providers.[57] Child care in the schools would be financed mainly by sliding scale parent fees. They argue that the fee for high-quality child care in the schools need be no higher than the fee for average-quality care in other settings because administrative, occupancy, and utility costs would be absorbed by the school system, leaving only staff and materials costs to be financed by parent fees. Start-up costs such as building renovation and expansion would be financed by a combination of federal, state, and local government funding and private foundations. They do not provide estimates of the total cost of their proposal. They suggest that funding come from a variety of sources and mainly be new funding rather than funding reallocated from existing programs (they do propose to reallocate funding for existing pre-K programs). Given the large scope of the program, it seems likely that it would be at least as costly as the Barnett, Blau, and Helburn-Bergmann proposals.

Kagan and Cohen (1996) discuss a "vision" for reinventing the early care and education system in the United States. Their discussion emphasizes the principles of a new system but does not propose a specific program. However, they do make some specific proposals related to licensing. They propose that individual staff who care for children in centers and family day care homes be required to hold a license that can be obtained only by completing a high level of education and training and demonstrating competency. All education and training would be provided in a setting in which academic credit would be earned. They also propose eliminating most existing licensing exemptions, such as those for church-sponsored day care centers in some states and for small family day care homes. They do not provide an estimate of the cost of their proposals, and they propose funding them mainly through new revenue.

The key element of the plans proposed by economists is allowing parental choice of child care. These proposals rely on parents to use subsidies to purchase child care of high quality. The very limited evidence on the price elasticity of demand for child care quality suggests that the elasticity is small (Blau and Hagy 1998; Hagy 1998). Recall that this evidence per-

56. Kahn and Kamerman (1987) also propose a school-based child care system, in less detail than Zigler and Finn-Stevenson.

57. They propose a network of support and outreach services for family day care providers who care for children up to age three, but this is not a major or well-developed part of their proposal. They recognize that their plan does not specifically provide for the care of children before age three, and they state that care for such children can be addressed by paid parental leave.

tains only to demand for specific attributes of child care such as group size, staff-child ratio, and staff training, not to the process-oriented measures of quality that are the best predictors of child development. There is no direct evidence either for or against the proposition that reducing the effective price of child care to consumers will result in a substantial increase in the quality of care demanded, as measured by child development–oriented instruments such as ECERS. Thus, Barnett, Blau, and Helburn-Bergmann would provide differential reimbursement for high-quality care as an additional incentive. With the exception of Blau and Walker, facilitating employment of mothers is another important goal of the proposals by economists. Allowing parents flexibility in using the subsidies is likely to be helpful in achieving this goal. The child allowances proposed by Blau and Walker allow additional flexibility to parents who wish to use the allowance to purchase child care.

Congress is currently debating reauthorization of PRWORA, including the CCDF. The Bush administration has proposed increasing the work requirement for TANF recipients from thirty to forty hours per week, and this has led to discussion of increasing the level of funding for the CCDF and for giving states increased discretion to shift funds from the TANF block grant to the CCDF. Changes to the key feature of the CCDF subsidy program—vouchers that can be used for any licensed or legally exempt child care arrangement—have not been prominent in the reauthorization debate.

The key features of proposals by developmental psychologists are supply-side subsidies and regulations that are tied to the quality of care. Finn-Stevenson and Zigler would attempt to ensure high quality by locating child care in schools, where the environment and pay would promote high-quality care. Kagan and Cohen are less specific about location and funding issues, but they do emphasize much tougher licensing standards and enforcement as a way of raising the quality of child care. It seems likely that these approaches could be successful in improving the average quality of child care supplied in the United States. However, the emphasis on public supply of child care raises the possibility that problems that are thought to be prevalent in many public schools could affect child care as well. These include absence of incentives for efficient use of resources, resulting in high cost and low productivity. Standard economic analysis of regulations that restrict entry to a service occupation suggest that such regulations will raise the cost of the service, reduce the supply, and increase the "underground" supply of the service. This seems especially likely in the case of family day care, in which the proportion of providers who are unlicensed is estimated to be as high as 90 percent (Hayes, Palmer, and Zaslow 1990, 151).

7.7   Conclusions

Child care policy can be used to facilitate employment of mothers and enhance the development of young children. The tension between these alternative goals ensures that debate and discussion of child care policy issues will continue for the foreseeable future. There is not a consensus on the goals of child care policy or on the means to achieve those goals. This is due in part to conflicting views on the proper role of the government in a domain that was mainly left to families as recently as a generation ago. But it is also a reflection of lack of knowledge about the magnitudes of important parameters that affect the costs and benefits of alternative policies. Economists could make significant contributions to knowledge by careful empirical studies that produce reliable estimates of such parameters. The following issues seem important and well suited to analysis by economists.

- Despite a large number of studies, there is considerable uncertainty about the magnitude of the elasticity of maternal employment with respect to the price of child care. A careful sensitivity analysis along the lines of Mroz's (1987) analysis of the labor supply of married women could be a major contribution to resolving this uncertainty. Many of the studies of this issue include some sensitivity testing, but none have systematically examined all of the main specification and estimation issues using a single data set and a common framework. Research on the price-responsiveness of low-income mothers would be especially useful.
- Consumer demand for quality in child care is not well understood, and additional research could make useful contributions to knowledge. It is important to go beyond studying consumer demand for inputs to the production of quality in child care (group size, etc.). The demand function for quality itself, as measured by ECERS and related instruments, should be estimated. This will require data containing such measures of quality as well as the price and other arguments of the demand function from a representative sample of families. Such data are beginning to be made available in the on going National Institute of Child Health and Human Development's Study of Early Child Care.[58]
- Research on the subsidy take-up decisions of families eligible for child care subsidies would be very useful in order to determine the likely effectiveness of different forms of subsidies. The possibility for research along these lines will be enhanced by including questions on child care subsidies in large nationally representative surveys, as in the Urban Institute's NSAF and recent waves of the SIPP. However, to be useful for this issue, such surveys must explicitly ask respondents who are not receiving a subsidy whether they applied for and were offered a subsidy.
- New research on the supply of child care would be useful. Subsidies to consumers may bid up the price of child care, and it is important to be able to quantify such effects. It would also be useful to examine the

58. See NICHD (2002) for information about the Study of Early Child Care.

quality supply decisions of providers, in order to determine how responsive the supply of high-quality care might be to subsidies (Blau and Mocan 2002). Evidence on the supply of child care for low-income families would be especially useful.

- Finally, despite the fact that a number of welfare-to-work demonstration programs included child care subsidies, it has not been possible to determine the effects of such subsidies because they have almost always been included as part of a package of services provided. A random-assignment demonstration program that focused exclusively on child care could provide valuable information about the impact of child care subsidies on employment of low-income mothers.

Appendix

Cost-Effectiveness Formulas

Under the assumptions stated in the text, the cost of the wage subsidy is $(N + \Delta N)he = hNe(w + e\eta_{Nw})/w$, where ΔN is the additional employment generated by the subsidy. The gain in hours worked is $h\Delta N = hNe\eta_{Nw}/w$. The cost of the child care subsidy is $Phs + \Delta Nhs + \Delta Phs$, where P is the number of working mothers who use paid care. The first term is the cost of subsidizing the paid hours of care that would have been used in the absence of the subsidy; the second term is the cost of subsidizing the paid care hours of the mothers induced to enter the labor force as a result of the subsidy; and the third term is the cost of subsidizing the paid care hours of mothers who would have worked and used unpaid care in the absence of the subsidy and are induced to switch to paid care as a result of the subsidy. This expression can be written as $Nhs(\theta p - \eta_{Np}s - \theta s\eta_{Pp})/p$. The change in hours worked induced by the subsidy is $h\Delta N = -\eta_{Np}hNs/p$.

The figures in table 7A.1 illustrate the cost-effectiveness of wage and price subsidies for alternative values of the elasticities and the proportion of employed mothers who use paid care. The price per hour of child care was fixed at \$2.00 in all of the calculations, and the wage rate was fixed at \$6.00. Let $CE_e = \eta_{Nw}/(w + e\eta_{Nw})$ represent the cost-effectiveness of the wage subsidy, and let $CE_s = -\eta_{Np}/(p\theta - \eta_{Np}s - \theta s\eta_{Pp})$ represent the cost-effectiveness of the price subsidy. The last column shows the ratio of the cost effectiveness figures. The subsidies are assumed to be additive, but in order to compare them I specify each subsidy as a given proportion of the wage or price. The calculations use a subsidy rate of 0.2, so the subsidies are, $e = \$1.20$ and $s = \$0.40$. Using a higher wage rate increases the ratio CE_s/CE_e by a large amount, and using a higher subsidy rate decreases it by a small amount.

Table 7A.1   **Cost-Effectiveness of Wage and Price Subsidies (alternative values of the elasticities) and Proportion of Employed Mothers Using Paid Care**

η_{Nw}	η_{Np}	η_{Pp}	θ	CE_e	CE_s	CE_s/CE_e
0.2000	−0.2000	−0.2000	0.4000	0.0321	0.2193	6.8421
0.2000	−0.2000	−0.2000	0.7000	0.0321	0.1302	4.0625
0.2000	−0.2000	−0.5000	0.4000	0.0321	0.2083	6.5000
0.2000	−0.2000	−0.5000	0.7000	0.0321	0.1235	3.8519
0.2000	−0.5000	−0.2000	0.4000	0.0321	0.4845	15.1163
0.2000	−0.5000	−0.2000	0.7000	0.0321	0.3019	9.4203
0.2000	−0.5000	−0.5000	0.4000	0.0321	0.4630	14.4444
0.2000	−0.5000	−0.5000	0.7000	0.0321	0.2874	8.9655
0.5000	−0.2000	−0.2000	0.4000	0.0758	0.2193	2.8947
0.5000	−0.2000	−0.2000	0.7000	0.0758	0.1302	1.7188
0.5000	−0.2000	−0.5000	0.4000	0.0758	0.2083	2.7500
0.5000	−0.2000	−0.5000	0.7000	0.0758	0.1235	1.6296
0.5000	−0.5000	−0.2000	0.4000	0.0758	0.4845	6.3953
0.5000	−0.5000	−0.2000	0.7000	0.0758	0.3019	3.9855
0.5000	−0.5000	−0.5000	0.4000	0.0758	0.4630	6.1111
0.5000	−0.5000	−0.5000	0.7000	0.0758	0.2874	3.7931

If everyone uses paid care then $\theta = 1$, $\eta_{Np} = -\eta_{Nw}$, and $\eta_{Pp} = 0$. Let $s = e$ and use $w^* = w - p$ as the base for computing the proportional magnitudes of both subsidies, that is, replace both w and p in the formulas with w^*. Making the substitutions, the number of additional hours worked per dollar spent on the child subsidy becomes $\eta_{Nw}/(w^* + e\eta_{Nw})$. The number of additional hours worked per dollar spent on the wage subsidy is $\eta_{Nw}/(w + e\eta_{Nw})$. Substitute w^* for w and the two formulas are identical.

Subsidy Effects in the Quality Model

Without loss of generality, let quality be restricted to the unit interval: $0 \le q \le 1$. Since quality has no natural units, any measure of quality can be rescaled to the unit interval, with α, β, and the child development production function rescaled accordingly. Let V_e denote the value of being employed and V_n the value of not being employed. The price parameters α and β do not affect V_n, so the employment effects of child care price subsidies depend only on their effects on V_e. Solve for the demand functions for ℓ and q conditional on employment, substitute these functions into the budget constraint and production function, and substitute the latter two equations into the utility function. This defines V_e. It is then simple to show that $\partial V_e/\partial\alpha = -u_c h$ and $\partial V_e/\partial\beta = -u_c hq$, where u_c is the marginal utility of consumption and h and q are understood to be the values that satisfy the first order conditions. Since $0 \le q \le 1$, this shows that an α-subsidy has a (weakly) bigger impact on employment than a β-subsidy.

Totally differentiating the first-order conditions and solving for the substitution effects of α and β on quality yields

$$\left.\frac{dq}{d\alpha}\right|_{\bar{u}} = \frac{\lambda D_{\ell q}}{D} \qquad \left.\frac{dq}{d\beta}\right|_{\bar{u}} = \frac{\lambda(D_{\ell q} + D_{qq})}{D},$$

where $\lambda > 0$ is a multiplier, $D_{\ell q}$ is the minor of element $\ell - q$ of the Bordered Hessian, D_{qq} is the minor of element $q - q$, and D is the determinant of the Bordered Hessian. $D_{\ell q}/D$ is indeterminate in sign but D_{qq}/D is unambiguously negative by the second-order conditions. Thus if $D_{\ell q}/D < 0$ then $(dq/d\beta)|_{\bar{u}}$ is more negative than $(dq/d\alpha)|_{\bar{u}}$ and if $D_{\ell q}/D > 0$ then $(dq/d\beta)|_{\bar{u}}$ is either negative or is a smaller positive than $(dq/d\alpha)|_{\bar{u}}$.

References

Adams, Gina, Karen Schulman, and Nancy Ebb. 1998. Locked doors: States struggling to meet the child care needs of low-income working families. Washington, D.C.: Children's Defense Fund, March.

Adams, Gina, Kathleen Snyder, and Jodi R. Sandfort. 2002. Getting and retaining child care assistance: How policy and practice influence parents' experiences. Urban Institute Occasional Paper no. 55. Washington, D.C.: Urban Institute, March. Available at [http://www.urban.org/UploadedPDF/310451.pdf].

Administration for Children and Families. 1995. Federal child care programs in FY1995. Washington, D.C.: Administration for Children and Families. Available at [http://www.acf.dhhs.gov/programs/ccb/research/1995.htm].

———. 1998. HHS fact sheet: State spending under the child care block grant. Washington, D.C.: Administration for Children and Families, November. Available at [http://www.acf.dhhs.gov/news/press/1998/cc97fund.htm].

———. 1999. Access to child care for low-income working families. Washington, D.C.: Administration for Children and Families, October. Available at [http://www.acf.dhhs.gov/programs/ccb/research/ccreport/ccreprt.htm].

———. 2000. New statistics show only small percentage of eligible families receive child care help. Washington, D.C.: Administration for Children and Families, December. Available at [http://www.acf.dhhs.gov/news/press/2000/ccstudy.htm].

———. 2001a. Child Care and Development Fund: Report of state plans for the period 10/01/99 to 9/30/01. Washington, D.C.: Administration for Children and Families. Available at [http://nccic.org/pubs/CCDFStat.pdf].

———. 2001b. Final 1998 state data tables and charts. Washington, D.C.: Administration for Children and Families, February. Available at [http://www.acf.dhhs.gov/programs/ccb/research/archive/98acf800/index.htm].

———. 2002. 2002 Head Start fact sheet. Washington, D.C.: Administration for Children and Families. Available at [http://www2.acf.dhhs.gov/programs/hsb/research/02_hsfs.htm].

———. Various years. CCDF final allocations and earmarks. Washington, D.C.: Administration for Children and Families. Available at [http://www.acf.dhhs.gov/programs/ccb/policy1/statlist.htm].

Advisory Committee on Head Start Research and Evaluation. 1999. A recommended framework for studying the impact of Head Start programs. Washington, D.C.: U.S. Department of Health and Human Services, October. Available at [http://www2.acf.dhhs.gov/programs/hsb/hsreac/octrep.htm].

Anderson, Patricia M., and Philip B. Levine. 2000. Child care and mothers' employment decisions. In *Finding jobs: Work and welfare reform,* ed. Rebecca M. Blank and David Card, 420–62. New York: Russell Sage Foundation.

Averett, Susan L., H. Elizabeth Peters, and Donald M. Waldman. 1997. Tax credits, labor supply, and child care. *Review of Economics and Statistics* 79 (1): 125–35.

Barnett, W. Steven. 1992. Benefits of compensatory preschool education. *Journal of Human Resources* 27 (2): 279–312.

———. 1993a. Benefit-cost analysis of preschool education: Findings from a 25-year followup. *American Journal of Orthopsychiatry* 64 (4): 500–08.

———. 1993b. New wine in old bottles: Increasing coherence in early childhood care and education policy. *Early Childhood Research Quarterly* 8 (4): 519–58.

———. 1995. Long-term effects of early childhood programs on cognitive and school outcomes. *The Future of Children* 5 (3): 25–50.

Baum, Charles L. 2002. Child care costs and work decisions of low-income mothers. *Demography* 39 (1): 139–64.

Becker, Gary S., and H. Greg Lewis. 1973. Interaction between quantity and quality of children. *Journal of Political Economy* 81, part 2 (2): S279–88.

Berger, Mark C., and Dan A. Black. 1992. Child care subsidies, quality of care, and the labor supply of low-income single mothers. *Review of Economics and Statistics* 74 (4): 635–42.

Bergmann, Barbara. 1996. *Saving our children from poverty: What the United States can learn from France.* New York: Russell Sage Foundation.

Besharov, Douglas J. 2002. Testimony before the Subcommittee on 21st century competitiveness. Washington, D.C.: U.S. House of Representatives, Committee on Education and the Work Force. 27 February.

Besharov, Douglas J., and Nazanin Samari. 2000. Child-care vouchers and cash payments. In *Vouchers and the provision of public services,* ed. Eugene Steuerle, Robert Reischauer, Van Doorn Ooms, and George Peterson, 195–223. Washington, D.C.: Brookings Institution Press, Committee for Economic Development, and Urban Institute Press.

Blau, David M. 1997. The production of quality in child care centers. *Journal of Human Resources* 32 (2): 354–87.

———. 1999. The effect of child care characteristics on child development. *Journal of Human Resources* 34 (4): 786–822.

———. 2000. The production of quality in child care centers: Another look. *Applied Developmental Science,* 4 (3): 136–48.

———. 2001. *The child care problem: An economic analysis.* New York: Russell Sage Foundation.

Blau, David M., and Alison P. Hagy. 1998. The demand for quality in child care. *Journal of Political Economy* 106 (1): 104–46.

Blau, David M., and H. Naci Mocan. 2002. The supply of quality in child care centers. *Review of Economics and Statistics* 84 (3): 483–96.

Blau, David M., and Philip K. Robins. 1988. Child care costs and family labor supply. *Review of Economics and Statistics* 70 (3): 374–81.

———. 1991. Child care demand and labor supply of young mothers over time. *Demography* 28 (3): 333–52.

Blau, David M., and Erdal Tekin. 2002. The determinants and consequences of child care subsidies for single mothers. University of North Carolina–Chapel Hill, Department of Economics. Working paper, January.

Bloom, Dan, Mary Farrell, James J. Kemple, and Nandita Verma. 1999. The family transition program: Implementation and three-year impacts of Florida's initial time-limited welfare program. New York: Manpower Demonstration Research Corporation, April.

Bos, Johannes M., Aletha C. Huston, Robert C. Granger, Greg J. Duncan, Thomas W. Brock, and Vonnie C. McCloyd. 1999. New hope for people with low incomes: Two-year results of a program to reduce poverty and reform welfare. New York: Manpower Demonstration Research Corporation, August.

Bowen, Gary L., and Peter A. Neenan. 1993. Does subsidized child care availability promote welfare independence of mothers on AFDC: An experimental analysis. *Research on Social Work Practice* 3 (4): 363–84.

Campbell, F. A., E. P. Pungello, S. Miller-Johnson, M. Burchinal, and C. T. Ramey. 2001. The development of cognitive and academic abilities: Growth curves from an early childhood educational experiment. *Developmental Psychology* 37 (2): 231–42.

Campbell, F. A., C. T. Ramey, E. P. Pungello, J. Sparling, and S. Miller-Johnson. 2002. Early childhood education: Young adult outcomes from the Abecedarian Project. *Applied Developmental Science* 6 (1): 42–57.

Capizzano, Jeffrey, Gina Adams, and Freya Sonenstein. 2000. Child care arrangements for children under five: Variation across states. Assessing the New Federalism Working Paper Series B, no. B-7. Washington, D.C.: Urban Institute, March. Available at [http://www.urban.org/UploadedPDF/anf_b7.pdf].

Chaplin, Duncan D., Philip K. Robins, Sandra L. Hofferth, Douglas A. Wissoker, and Paul Fronstin. 1999. The price elasticity of child care demand: A sensitivity analysis. Washington, D.C.: The Urban Institute. Working Paper.

Chipty, Tasneem, Ann Dryden Witte, Magaly Queralt, and Harriet Griesenger. 1998. What is happening to families receiving cash assistance? A longitudinal study of the early stages of welfare reform. Ohio State University, Department of Economics. Working Paper, November.

Committee for Economic Development. 2002. Preschool for all: Investing in a productive and just society. New York: Committee for Economic Development. Available at [http://www.ced.org/docs/report/report_preschool.pdf].

Connelly, Rachel. 1990. The cost of child care and single mothers: Its effect on labor force participation and AFDC participation. Bowdoin College, Department of Economics. Working Paper.

———. 1991. The importance of child care costs to women's decision making. In *The economics of child care,* ed. David Blau, 87–118. New York: Russell Sage Foundation.

———. 1992. The effects of child care costs on married women's labor force participation. *Review of Economics and Statistics* 74 (1): 83–90.

Connelly, Rachel, and Jean Kimmel. 2000. Marital status and full-time/part-time work status in child care choices. Working Paper no. 99-58. Kalamazoo, Mich.: Upjohn Institute, March. Available at [http://www.upjohninstitute.org/publications/wp/99-58.pdf].

———. 2001. The effect of child care costs on the labor force participation and welfare recipiency of single mothers: Implications for welfare reform. Working Paper no. 01-69. Kalamazoo, Mich.: Upjohn Institute, March. Available at [http://www.upjohninstitute.org/publications/wp/01-69.pdf].

Council of Economic Advisors. 1997. The economics of child care. Washington, D.C.: Council of Economic Advisors, December.

Cryer, Debbie, and Margaret Burchinal. 1995. Parents as child care consumers. In Cost, quality, and child outcomes in child care centers: Technical report, ed. Suzanne W. Helburn, 203–20. University of Colorado–Denver, Department of Economics, Center for Research in Economic and Social Policy, June.

Currie, Janet. 2001. Early childhood intervention programs: What do we know? *Journal of Economic Perspectives* 15 (2): 213–38.

Currie, Janet, and Duncan Thomas. 1995. Does Head Start make a difference? *American Economic Review* 85 (3): 341–64.

———. 1999. Does Head Start help Hispanic children? *Journal of Public Economics* 74 (2): 235–62.

———. 2000. School quality and the longer-term effects of Head Start. *Journal of Human Resources* 35 (4): 755–74.

Finn-Stevenson, Matia, and Edward Zigler. 1999. *Schools of the twenty-first century: Linking child care and education.* Boulder, Colo.: Westview Press.

Fronstin, Paul, and Doug Wissoker. 1995. The effects of the availability of low-cost child care on the labor-supply of low-income women. Working Paper. Washington, D.C.: Urban Institute, January.

Fuller, Bruce, Sharon L. Kagan, Gretchen Caspary, Nancy Cohen, Desiree French, Laura Gascue, Africa Hands, James Mensing, Jan McCarthy, Gege Kreischer, Jude Carroll, and Kristen Cool. 2000. Remember the children: Mothers balance work and child care under welfare reform. University of California–Berkeley, Policy Analysis for California Education. Available at [http://pace.berkeley.edu/remthechild_exsum.pdf].

Fuller, Bruce, Sharon L. Kagan, and Susanna Loeb. 2002. New lives for poor families? Mothers and young children move through welfare reform. The Growing Up in Poverty Project: Wave 2 findings, Technical Report. University of California–Berkeley. Available at [http://www-gse.berkeley.edu/research/PACE/gup_tech_rpt.pdf].

Fuller, Bruce, Sharon L. Kagan, Jan McCarthy, Gretchen Caspary, Darren Lubotsky, and Laura Gascue. 1999. Who selects formal child care? The role of subsidies as low-income mothers negotiate welfare reform. Paper presented at the Society for Research in Child Development Meeting. April, Albuquerque, New Mexico.

Garces, Eliana, Duncan Thomas, and Janet Currie. 2002. Longer-term effects of Head Start. *American Economic Review* 92 (4): 999–1012.

Gelbach, Jonah. 2002. Public schooling for young children and maternal labor supply. *American Economic Review* 92 (1): 307–22.

Giannarelli, Linda, and James Barsimontov. 2000. Child care expenses of America's families. Washington, D.C.: The Urban Institute. Occasional Paper no. 40, December. Available at [http://www.urban.org/UploadedPDF/310028_occa40.pdf].

Gladden, Tricia, and Christopher Taber. 2000. Wage progression among less skilled workers. In *Finding jobs: Work and welfare reform,* ed. Rebecca M. Blank and David Card, 160–92. New York: Russell Sage Foundation.

Gomby, Deanna S., Nora Krantzler, Mary B. Larner, Carol S. Stevenson, Donna L. Terman, and Richard E. Behrman. 1996. Financing child care: Analysis and recommendations. *The Future of Children* 6 (2): 5–25. Available at [http://www.futureofchildren.org/information2826/information_show.htm?doc_id=73244].

Gormley, William T. 1995. *Everybody's children: Child care as a public problem.* Washington, D.C.: The Brookings Institution.

Granger, Robert C., and Rachel Cytron. 1999. Teenage parent programs: A synthesis of the long-term effects of the New Chance demonstration, Ohio's Learning, Earning, and Parenting program, and the Teenage Parent demonstration. *Evaluation Review* 23 (2): 107–45.

Hagy, Alison P. 1998. The demand for child care quality: An hedonic price theory approach. *Journal of Human Resources* 33 (3): 683–710.

Hamilton, Gayle, Thomas Brock, Mary Farrell, Daniel Friedlander, and Kristen Harknett. 1997. The national evaluation of welfare-to-work strategies. Evaluating two welfare-to-work approaches: Two-year findings on the Labor Force Attachment and Human Capital Development programs in three sites. New York: Manpower Demonstration Research Corporation, December.

Hamilton, Gayle, Stephen Freedman, and Sharon M. McGroder. 2000. Do mandatory welfare-to-work programs affect the well-being of children? A synthesis of child research conducted as part of the national evaluation of welfare-to-work. New York: Manpower Demonstration Research Corporation, June.

Han, Wen-Jui, and Jane Waldfogel. 2001. The effect of child care costs on the employment of single and married mothers. *Social Science Quarterly* 82 (3): 552–68.

Harms, Thelma, and Richard Clifford. 1980. *Early childhood environment rating scale.* New York: Teachers College Press.

Harms, Thelma, Deborah Cryer, and Richard Clifford. 1990. *Infant/toddler environment rating scale.* New York: Teachers College Press.

Hayes, Cheryl, John Palmer, and Martha Zaslow. 1990. *Who cares for America's children? Child care policy for the 1990s.* Washington, D.C.: The National Academy of Sciences Press.

Heckman, James J. 1974. Effects of child-care programs on women's work effort. *Journal of Political Economy* 82, part 2, (2): S136–63.

———. 1979. Sample selection bias as a specification error. *Econometrica* 47 (1): 153–62.

———. 1981. Heterogeneity and state dependence. In *Studies in labor markets,* ed. Sherwin Rosen, 91–139. Chicago: University of Chicago Press.

Helburn, Suzanne W., ed. 1995. Cost, quality, and child outcomes in child care centers. Technical Report. University of Colorado–Denver, Department of Economics, Center for Research in Economic and Social Policy, June.

Helburn, Suzanne W., and Barbara R. Bergmann. 2002. *America's child care problem: The way out.* New York: Palgrave, for St. Martin's Press.

Hofferth, Sandra, L., April Brayfield, Sharon Deich, and Pamela Holcomb. 1991. National child care survey, 1990. Report no. 91-5. Washington, D.C.: Urban Institute.

Hotz, V. Joseph, and M. Rebecca Kilburn. 1994. Regulating child care: The effects of state regulations on child care demand and its costs. Santa Monica, Calif.: RAND. Working Paper, August.

Hyslop, Dean. 1999. State dependence, serial correlation, and heterogeneity in intertemporal labor force participation of married women. *Econometrica* 67 (6): 1255–94.

Internal Revenue Service. 2001. Individual tax statistics, complete report publications, tax year 1999. Available at [http://www.irs.gov/taxstats/display/0,,i1%3D40%26genericId%3D16840,00.htm].

Kagan, Sharon L., and Nancy Cohen. 1996. A vision for a quality early care and education system. In *Reinventing early care and education: A vision for a quality system,* ed. Sharon Kagan and Nancy Cohen, 304–32. San Francisco, Calif.: Jossey-Bass.

Kahn, Alfred J., and Shiela B. Kamerman. 1987. *Child care: Facing the hard choices.* Dover, Mass.: Auburn House.

———. 1995. *Starting right: How America neglects Its youngest children and what we can do about it.* New York: Oxford University Press.

Karoly, Lynn A., Peter W. Greenwood, Susan S. Everingham, Jill Houbé, M. Rebecca Kilburn, C. Peter Rydell, Matthew Sanders, and James Chiesa. 1998. Investing in our children: What we know and don't know about the costs and benefits of early childhood interventions. Report no. MR-898-TCWF. Santa Monica, Calif.: RAND. Available at [http://www.rand.org/publications/MR/MR898/].

Kimmel, Jean. 1995. The effectiveness of child care subsidies in encouraging the welfare-to-work transition of low-income single mothers. *American Economic Review Papers and Proceedings* 85 (2): 271–75.

———. 1998. Child care costs as a barrier to employment for single and married mothers. *Review of Economics and Statistics* 80 (2): 287–99.

Kisker, Ellen E., Anu Rangarajan, and Kimberly Boller. 1998. Moving into adulthood: Were the impacts of mandatory programs for welfare-dependent teenage parents sustained after the programs ended? Princeton, N.J.: Mathematica Policy Research, February.

Leland, Hayne. 1979. Quacks, lemons, and licensing: A theory of minimum quality standards. *Journal of Political Economy* 87:1328–46.

Long, Sharon K., Gretchen G. Kirby, Robin Kurka, and Shelley Waters. 1998. Child care assistance under welfare reform: Early responses by the states. Washington, D.C.: Urban Institute. Assessing the New Federalism Occasional Paper no. 15. Available at [http://www.urban.org/UploadedPDF/occa15.pdf].

Love, John M., Peter Z. Schochet, and Alicia L. Meckstroth. 1996. Are they in any real danger? What research does—and doesn't—tell us about child care quality and children's well-being. Princeton, N.J.: Mathematica Policy Research, May.

MaCurdy, Thomas, David Green, and Harry Paarsch. 1990. Assessing empirical approaches for analyzing taxes and labor supply. *Journal of Human Resources* 25 (3): 415–90.

Maddala, G. S. 1983. *Limited and qualitative dependent variables in econometrics.* New York: Cambridge University Press.

Magenheim, Ellen B. 1995. Information, prices, and competition in the child care market: What role should government play? In *Readings in public policy,* ed. J. M. Pogodzinksi, 269–307. Cambridge, Mass.: Blackwell.

Meyers, Marcia K., and Theresa Heintze. 1999. The performance of the child care subsidy system: Target efficiency, coverage adequacy, and equity. *Social Service Review* 73 (1): 37–64.

Meyers, Marcia K., Theresa Heintze, and Douglas A. Wolf. 2002. Child care subsidies and employment of welfare recipients. *Demography* 39 (1): 165–80.

Mezey, Jennifer, Rachel Schumacher, Mark H. Greenberg, Joan Lombardi, and John Hutchins. 2002. Unfinished agenda: Child care for low-income families since 1996: Implications for federal and state policy. Policy Brief. Washington, D.C.: Center for Law and Social Policy, March. Available at [http://www.clasp.org/pubs/childcare/child_care.htm].

Michalopoulos, Charles, and Philip K. Robins. 2000. Employment and child care choices in the United States and Canada. *Canadian Journal of Economics* 33 (2): 435–70.

———. 2002. Employment and child care choices of single parent families in Canada and the United States. *Journal of Population Economics* 3: 465–95.

Michalopoulos, Charles, Philip K. Robins, and Irwin Garfinkel. 1992. A structural model of labor supply and child care demand. *Journal of Human Resources* 27 (1): 166–203.

Miller, Cynthia, Virginia Knox, Patricia Auspos, Jo Anna Hunter-Means, and Alan Orenstein. 1997. Making welfare work and work pay: Implementation and 18-month impacts of the Minnesota Family Investment Program. New York: Manpower Demonstration Research Corporation, September.

Mroz, Thomas A. 1987. The sensitivity of an empirical model of married women's hours of work to economic and statistical assumptions. *Econometrica* 55 (3): 765–99.

———. 1999. Discrete factor approximations in simultaneous equation models: Estimating the impact of a dummy endogenous variable on a continuous outcome. *Journal of Econometrics* 92:233–74.

National Institute of Child Health and Human Development. (NICHD). 2002. The NICHD study of early child care and youth development. Bethesda, Md.: NICHD. Available at [http://public.rti.org/secc/home.cfm].

Pencavel, John. 1986. Labor supply of men: A survey. In *Handbook of labor economics,* vol. 1, ed. Orley Ashenfelter and Richard Layard, 3–102. Amsterdam: North Holland.

Piecyk, Jessica B., Ann Collins, and J. Lee Kreader. 1999. Patterns and growth of child care voucher use by families connected to cash assistance in Illinois and Maryland. Columbia University, National Center for Children in Poverty, May. Available at [http://cpmcnet.columbia.edu/dept/nccp/ccrp2.pdf].

Pitegoff, Peter, and Lauren Bream. 1997. Child care policy and the Welfare Reform Act. *Journal of Affordable Housing and Community Development Law* 6 (2): 113–30.

Powell, Lisa M. 1997. The impact of child care costs on the labour supply of married mothers: Evidence from Canada. *Canadian Journal of Economics* 30 (3): 577–94.

Quint, Janet C., Johannes M. Bos, and Denise F. Polit. 1997. New chance: Final report on a comprehensive program for young mothers in poverty and their children. New York: Manpower Demonstration Research Corporation, October.

Ribar, David. 1992. Child care and the labor supply of married women: Reduced from evidence. *Journal of Human Resources* 27 (1): 134–65.

———. 1995. A structural model of child care and the labor supply of married women. *Journal of Labor Economics* 13 (3): 558–97.

Riccio, James, Daniel Friedlander, and Stephen Freedman. 1994. GAIN: Benefits, costs, and three-year impacts of a welfare-to-work program. New York: Manpower Demonstration Research Corporation, September.

Robins, Philip K. 1990. Federal financing of child care: Alternative approaches and economic implications. *Population and Policy Review* 9 (1): 65–90.

———. 1991. Child care policy and research: An economist's perspective. In *The economics of child care,* ed. David Blau, 11–42. New York: Russell Sage Foundation.

Robins, Philip K., and Robert Spiegelman. 1978. An econometric model of the demand for child care. *Economic Inquiry* 16 (January): 83–94.

Ross, Christine. 1996. State child care assistance programs for low-income families. Washington, D.C.: Mathematica Policy Research, April.

———. 1998. Sustaining employment among low-income parents: The role of child care costs and subsidies. Washington, D.C.: Mathematica Policy Research, December.

———. 2002. E-mail to author, based on a forthcoming report on characteristics of state CCDF plans, not yet released to the public, 2 May.

Schumacher, Rachel, and Mark H. Greenberg. 1999. Child care after leaving welfare: Early evidence from state studies. Washington, D.C.: Center for Law and Social Policy, October. Available at [http://www.clasp.org/pubs/childcare/child_care.htm].

Schumacher, Rachel, Mark H. Greenberg, and Joan Lombardi. 2001. State initiatives to promote early learning. Washington, D.C.: Center for Law and Social

Policy. Policy Brief, April. Available at [http://www.clasp.org/pubs/childcare/child_care.htm].

Smith, Kristin. 2002. Who's minding the kids? Child care arrangements, spring 1997. Current Population Reports no. P70–86. Washington, D.C.: U.S. Census Bureau, July. Available at [http://www.census.gov/population/www/socdemo/childcare.html].

Tekin, Erdal. 2001. *The responses of single mothers to welfare and child care subsidy programs under the new Welfare Reform Act.* Ph.D. diss., University of North Carolina–Chapel Hill.

———. 2002. Child care subsidies, wages, and employment of single mothers. Georgia State University, Department of Economics. Working Paper, May.

Tunali, Insan. 1986. A general structure for models of double-selection and an application to a joint earnings/migration process with remigration. *Research in Labor Economics* 8, part B:235–82.

U.S. Advisory Commission on Intergovernmental Relations. 1994. Child care: The need for federal-state-local coordination. Report no. A-128. Washington, D.C.: U.S. Advisory Commission on Intergovernmental Relations, March.

U.S. Bureau of the Census. 1999. Poverty in the United States, 1998. Current Population Report P60-207. Washington, D.C.: U.S. Bureau of the Census, September. Available at [http://www.census.gov/prod/99pubs/p60-207.pdf].

U.S. Department of Agriculture. 2001. Child and adult care food program. [http://www.fns.usda.gov/cnd/Care/CACFP/cacfpfaqs.htm].

U.S. Department of Education. 1996. Serving preschool children. Washington, D.C.: U.S. Department of Education, April. Available at [http://www.ed.gov/legislation/ESEA/Title_I/preschoo.html].

U.S. Department of Health and Human Services. 1998. Final rule. Federal Register, 24 July 1998, 39935–98. Available at [http://www.acf.dhhs.gov/programs/ccb/policy/fr072498.pdf].

———. 2001. The economic rationale for investing in children: A focus on child care. Washington, D.C.: U.S. Department of Health and Human Services, Office of the Assistant Secretary for Planning and Evaluation, December.

———. Various years. Temporary Assistance for Needy Families (TANF) Program, annual report to Congress. Washington, D.C.: U.S. Department of Health and Human Services. Available at [http://www.acf.dhhs.gov/programs/opre/director.htm#annual].

U.S. General Accounting Office. 1994a. Child care subsidies increase the likelihood that low-income mothers will work. Report GAO/HEHS-95-20. Washington, D.C.: U.S. GAO, December. Available at [http://www.gpo.gov].

———. 1994b. Early childhood programs: Multiple programs and overlapping target groups. Report GAO/HEHS-95-4FS. Washington, D.C.: U.S. GAO, October. Available at [http://www.gpo.gov].

———. 1995. Welfare to work: Child care assistance limited; welfare reform may expand needs. Report GAO/HEHS-95-220. Washington, D.C.: U.S. GAO, September. Available at [http://www.gpo.gov].

———. 1998. Welfare reform: States' efforts to expand child care programs. Report GAO/HEHS-98-27. Washington, D.C.: U.S. GAO, January. Available at [http://www.gpo.gov].

———. 1999a. Child care: How do military and civilian center costs compare? Report GAO/HEHS-00-7. Washington, D.C.: U.S. GAO. October. Available at [http://www.gpo.gov].

———. 1999b. Early education and care: Early childhood programs and services for low-income families. Report GAO/HEHS-00-11. Washington, D.C.: U.S. GAO, November. Available at [http://www.gpo.gov].

————. 2000. Title I preschool education: More children served, but gauging effect on preschool readiness difficult. Report GAO/HEHS-00-171. Washington, D.C.: U.S. GAO, September. Available at [http://www.gpo.gov].

U.S. House of Representatives, Committee on Ways and Means. 1998. 1998 green book. Washington, D.C.: U.S. House of Representatives. Available at [http://www.access.gpo.gov/congress/wm001.html].

————. 2000. 2000 green book. Washington, D.C.: U.S. House of Representatives. Available at [http://www.access.gpo.gov/congress/wm001.html].

Vandell, Deborah Lowe, and Barbara Wolfe. 2000. Child care quality: Does it matter and does it need to be improved? Special Report no. 78. Madison, Wis.: Institute for Research on Poverty, November. Available at [http://www.ssc.wisc.edu/irp/sr/sr78.pdf].

Waldfogel, Jane. 2002. Child care, women's employment, and child outcomes. *Journal of Population Economics* 3: 527–48.

Walker, James. 1991. Public policy and the supply of child care services. In *The economics of child care,* ed. David Blau, 51–77. New York: Russell Sage Foundation.

————. 1996. Funding child rearing: Child allowance and parental leave. *The Future of Children* 6 (2): 122–36. Available at [http://www.futureofchildren.org/information2826/information_show.htm?doc_id=73300].

Waller, Margy. 1997. Welfare-to-work and child care: A survey of the ten big states. Washington, D.C.: Progressive Policy Institute, September. Available at [http://www.ppionline.org/documents/welfare_childcare.pdf].

8

Employment and Training Programs

Robert J. LaLonde

8.1 Introduction

The passage of the Area Redevelopment Act in 1961 started a prolonged effort by U.S. policymakers to reshape and upgrade the skills and employment prospects of the nation's low-income and displaced workers through publicly subsidized job training programs. These programs began with the goal of providing vocational training to dislocated workers, but they soon shifted to cover persons in poverty, many of whom were receiving public aid and who were especially economically disadvantaged with poor employment histories.

During the 1960s the menu of services provided to these groups expanded, but since that time their variety and content has not changed very much. Nevertheless, the orientation and goals of U.S. training policy have shifted frequently. During the last forty years, policymakers have varied their emphasis on low-cost compared with high-cost services; the degree to which they serve the economically disadvantaged or the unemployed; the amount of emphasis on serving adults compared with youths, especially young high school dropouts; and the extent to which these programs encourage participants to acquire new skills or help them to quickly find regular jobs.

A closer look at these programs indicates that it is sometimes incorrect to characterize individuals' participation in them as training. Relatively few participants enroll in publicly subsidized vocational courses long

Robert J. LaLonde is a professor at the Irving B. Harris Graduate School of Public Policy Studies, University of Chicago, and a research associate of the National Bureau of Economic Research.

The author thanks Jill Corcoran for her excellent research assistance.

518 **Robert J. LaLonde**

enough to acquire some kind of credential. Participants who enroll in programs that place them in a subsidized job with a private employer often receive little or no training other than employment experience. Many participants receive services whose stated objective is simply to facilitate their search for a job. These features of government training programs underscore their dual purpose: skill development and job placement. Policymakers have designed programs that conform with the latter objective to make participants more productive job searchers and produce better "job matches," but they are not intended to raise vocational skills. For this reason it is more accurate to refer to the existing menu of services as employment and training programs.

Compared with other means-tested programs summarized in this volume, the United States spends relatively little on these programs each year. Expenditures amount to approximately 0.1 to 0.2 percent of gross domestic product (GDP), depending on which programs are counted. Further, these expenditures amount to approximately 3 to 6 percent of the annual cost of training by private employers. As a share of GDP nearly all other Organization for Economic Cooperation and Development (OECD) countries spend substantially more on such programs (Heckman, LaLonde, and Smith 1999). Given the size of this investment in these programs compared to the levels of poverty and the amount of wage inequality, it is not hard to understand why U.S. employment and training programs have not had a very large impact on output or the structure of wages.[1]

By design these programs should not dramatically affect the well-being of the average participant. The evaluation research makes clear that existing programs do not integrate their participants into the economic mainstream. When employment and training programs are effective they make economically disadvantaged persons less poor, but they do not substantially reduce poverty. This finding should not be surprising, because the vast majority of these services are provided at relatively low cost per participant, much less than the cost of a year of formal schooling. For example, during program year 1997, programs operated under the Job Training Partnership Act (JTPA) spent on average about $3,000 per participant.[2] To expect such programs to raise participants' subsequent productivity enough so that their annual earnings rise by, say, several thousand dollars would imply that these social investments have an extraordinary internal rate of return.

Although expenditures on these programs are relatively small, they have been as carefully evaluated as any social program in the United States (and probably the world for that matter). These studies have produced many im-

---

1. See Heckman, Roselius, and Smith (1994) for an instructive calculation of how large the public commitment to these programs would have to be to affect these outcomes.
2. Unless otherwise indicated, costs and expenditures figures presented in this chapter are expressed in 1999 dollars.

portant methodological advances for the field of program evaluation more generally. Further, there are few areas in the social sciences in which there exists such a large mix of both conventional nonexperimental evaluations and social experiments. Indeed, many of the methodological advances have occurred because of the opportunity to directly compare evaluations that use nonexperimental methods to those that rely on experimental methods.

Despite the relatively modest public expenditures on these programs, the evidence indicates that these services have consistently improved the employment prospects of economically disadvantaged adults. The findings for displaced workers are unclear. Under plausible assumptions about the welfare cost of taxation and the duration of these programs' impacts, the internal rates of return from these programs are quite large (Heckman, LaLonde, and Smith 1999). Indeed, a case can be made that time in these programs may be more efficient than time in formal school. The reason that their impacts on the economy and on the individuals themselves are small is that the investment is small (LaLonde 1995).

By contrast, among economically disadvantaged youths, these programs generally fail to produce any employment or earnings gains. As will be shown, this result has been confirmed in many nonexperimental evaluations and in several social experiments of alternative program models. The one exception to this finding is the Job Corps program. Some evaluations, including one experimental evaluation, report that these services modestly increase participants' employment rates and earnings. That this program works is instructive because, unlike most services received by government training participants, these services are comprehensive and expensive. At the same time it is important to acknowledge that some studies of this program and of services like it come to a different conclusion. Moreover, depending on how long the program's earnings impacts last, cost-benefit analyses suggest that the earnings impacts from Job Corps may not be sufficient to justify the program's high costs. Indeed, a case can be made that on the margin, society would have been better off if employment and training resources were shifted from Job Corps youths to adults.

The primary purpose of this chapter is to describe employment and training policy in the United States and to follow the key developments in this policy during the last forty years. It touches briefly on some of the methodological developments that the evaluations of these policies have produced. Finally, it surveys some of the principal empirical findings in the literature on the effectiveness of these programs. As this chapter is written, the nation is in the midst of a major overhaul and consolidation of its employment and training services; therefore we will not discuss proposed reforms, as has been done in other chapters in this volume. Instead, in the next section we describe these changes and what they imply about U.S. policy.

8.2   History of U.S. Employment and Training Policy

8.2.1   The Menu of Employment and Training Services

During the last four decades, federal policymakers have authorized an array of employment and training services targeted toward a variety of different groups in the population. These services have targeted mostly the economically disadvantaged, displaced workers, and the disabled, but some components have specifically targeted particular groups such as Native Americans, senior citizens, farmers, homemakers, and migrant workers. Although these programs have primarily served low-income persons, they have never been entitlements, nor has access to them always been means-tested. Policy has consistently required that program operators provide employment and training services only to eligible applicants who they believe would benefit from the program.

In the next subsection of this chapter, we examine in greater detail the changes in employment and training policy during the last forty years and how these changes have affected the eligibility for training programs. Although there have been several significant policy changes during this period, with one exception, the mix of government employment and training services has remained largely the same. Presently, there are likely to be three broad categories of services available to participants. During the 1970s this mix of services also included public service employment opportunities.

As shown by table 8.1, the first of these service categories features programs designed to increase participants' human capital or skills. Within this category policymakers have emphasized two approaches with varying intensity over the years. The first approach is to provide participants with vocational training in a classroom or institutional setting (known as classroom training, or CT). In addition to vocational training, participants in CT also may receive a range of remedial skills. These include courses that provide basic education, literacy training, preparation for the (GED), instruction in English for non-native speakers, and some school-to-work activities.

The second approach to skill development takes place outside the classroom in subsidized on-the-job training (OJT) positions. This program provides participants with a subsidized job in the private sector with the expectation that the private-sector employer will retain the worker after the training period ends. Employers receive a 50 percent wage subsidy for up to six months. The content of the training—indeed, the extent to which participants even receive any formal training—varies substantially among both participating employers and locales.

The second category of services is designed to introduce participants to the world of work and to provide them with an employment experience.

Table 8.1   A Classification of U.S. Government Employment and
                   Training Programs

  I. Skill Development
     A. Classroom Training (CT)
        1. Basic Education: Toward goal of attaining high school certification (e.g., a
           diploma or GED).
        2. Vocational Skills Training: General skills for specific occupation or industry.
           Duration usually less than twenty weeks.
     B. On-the-Job Training (OJT)
        Jobs in private sector. Subsidies paid to employer to hire targeted group. When
        subsidy ends after six months to one year, employer may retain trainee as a regular
        employee. Training content varies from little to some. Occasionally coordinated with
        off-the-job training.
 II. Work Experience
        Similar to OJT, but provides temporary experience in a job in the public or nonprofit
        sector. Targeted to youth and economically disadvantaged with little past
        employment. Meant to introduce participant to the world of work and to provide
        very general work skills. Not designed to provide vocational skills.
III. Employability Development
     A. Job Search Assistance
        Provides job search training skills, counseling, workshops, job clubs, and resource
        centers. Career counseling and assessment includes testing to determine if individual
        is job-ready and to design appropriate job search strategies. Program staff may
        recommend training.
     B. The Public Labor Exchange
        Available to all persons, including the employed and individuals who are out of the
        labor force. Focus is on matching existing skills to attributes listed by employers.
        Participants receive job "referrals" that may lead to job placements.
IV. Job Development
        Public-Sector Employment: creates temporary public-sector jobs for the
        unemployed, especially the long-term unemployed, in areas with relatively high
        unemployment.

Source: Butler (1976).

Work experience programs (WE) create temporary jobs in public and nonprofit employment. The jobs are of limited duration and participants are
expected to find regular jobs when they leave the program.

Although work experience potentially raises participants' human capital, program operators do not expect participating employers to provide
any vocational skills. In practice, the distinction between WE and OJT may
not be very great, except that in the latter case officials anticipate that the
private employer will retain the trainee. By contrast, the purpose of WE is
to ease participants' transition into the labor market. These programs usually are targeted toward economically disadvantaged youths and welfare
recipients who have had little recent labor market experience.

Policymakers have designed a third category of services to enhance participants' job search and job matching skills (job search assistance, or JSA).
Participants may receive career counseling, skill assessments, information

about the labor market, job referrals, and sometimes job placements. In addition, they may participate in classes that teach job search skills, including interviewing skills expected by employers. Under this category of services, participants also receive referrals to other supportive social services that provide subsidies for child care and transportation, or substance abuse counseling. The employment service (operated by the states under the Wagner-Peyser Act of 1933) provides many of the services in this category, but authorities also may subcontract for them from other sources.

This third category of employment services also highlights the dual goals of U.S. employment and training policy. Policymakers provide CT and OJT to help individuals develop new skills; these programs are like formal school. By contrast, they provide WE and especially JSA services to facilitate rapid placement into a regular job; the function of these services is like those provided by the employment service. In the first case models of human capital investment seem to motivate these programs' existence, whereas in the second case these programs seem to be motivated by models of job search. As we show below, over time policymakers have alternatively emphasized one goal over the other. But there also is reason to believe that in practice CT and especially OJT are to some extent facilitating job placement and are not simply designed to improve participants' vocational skills (Heckman, LaLonde, and Smith 1999).

The final category of employment and training services shown in table 8.1 is not a part of current U.S. policy. But during the 1970s a substantial portion of federal expenditures on these programs was on public-sector employment (PSE). These government-created jobs reflected a policy that emphasized job placement instead of skill development. Under this approach, the government was the employer of last resort. Participants in PSE jobs were either (a) the long-term unemployed or (b) more economically disadvantaged persons who could not find a job on their own or be placed in an OJT position.

8.2.2   History, Rules, and Shifting Goals

The Area Redevelopment Act

Active federal involvement in employment and training policy began with the passage of the Area Redevelopment Act (ARA) in 1961.[3] Con-

---

3. Much of current U.S. employment and training policy evolved during the 1960s. There are several sources that provide details of this history and of the subsequent changes in these policies since that time. Levitan and Mangum (1969) provide a detailed description of the programs that were created during the 1960s. Taggart (1981) does the same for training policy during the 1970s. The history of these programs during the 1980s and 1990s is covered in various reports of the National Commission for Employment Policy (see, e.g., National Commission for Employment Policy 1987, 1995). Another resource is various volumes of the Manpower Report of the President and the Employment and Training Report of the Secretary of Labor; see the references for examples.

gress enacted this legislation in response to the rise in unemployment that followed the start of the 1958 recession. They perceived that technological change had permanently dislocated workers and that its consequences were especially geographically concentrated. The primary purpose of this legislation was to bring "economic prosperity to depressed areas," designated as "redevelopment areas" because of their persistently high unemployment rates. It intended to stimulate economic growth by providing financial and technical assistance for business expansion in these areas.

Another component of ARA foreshadowed much larger future federal involvement in the development of the nation's human resources. The legislation provided for subsidized training to unemployed or underemployed persons in redevelopment areas. Local officials in state departments of employment security selected and referred eligible participants to training centers and other training providers. Participants received a training allowance or stipend for up to sixteen weeks while they were enrolled in occupational training. Because the funding and geographical coverage of the ARA's training component were limited, its overall impact was small. But the policy provided a model for subsequent training legislation.

Manpower Development and Training Act

In 1962, Congress expanded both the scope and quantity of training services when it enacted the Manpower Development and Training Act (MDTA). It also sought to provide these services in the context of broader human resource strategy for the country. The act required "the federal government to appraise the manpower requirements and resources of the nation, and to develop and apply information and methods needed to deal with the problems of unemployment resulting from automation and technological changes and other types of persistent unemployment" (Manpower 1964, 1). This objective of U.S. employment and training policy continues to the present and is at the heart of current policy under the Workforce Investment Act (WIA).

Like the ARA, this legislation targeted laid-off workers who could not "reasonably be expected to secure full-time employment without such training." In addition, the legislation also provided for training to "qualified persons for new and improved skills." This component of the legislation required the Department of Labor to monitor occupational trends and to estimate those occupations where it expected skill shortages to arise. Authorities were supposed to use these estimates to select the types of vocational training provided to participants. In addition, the act also instructed the Labor Department to use this more detailed labor market information to expand counseling and placement services for the unemployed in order to improve the job matching function of the employment service.

An important distinction between MDTA programs and those that came before or after them is that the government not only subsidized the direct costs of training, but also provided participants with training allowances or stipends that lasted a relatively long time. Under the act, participants could receive a training stipend for up to fifty-two weeks paid by the Department of Labor through state departments of employment security. Believing that longer training was necessary, Congress amended the act and extended the stipends to seventy-two weeks. In 1965, Congress again extended the duration of these stipends to 104 weeks.

During its first four years, MDTA maintained the same objective as the ARA by serving unemployed workers who had been laid off because of technological change. More than one-third of the early cohorts of trainees had been unemployed for more than twenty-six weeks prior to enrolling in MDTA. The primary recipients of the program's training stipends were household heads who had worked for at least three years. Relatively few participants under MDTA were youths.

The MDTA provided two types of training that continue to be among the most important categories of services available today. First, the program subsidized vocational and technical training in private and public educational institutions, usually in classroom settings. Early cohorts of male participants were trained for blue-collar occupations such as semiskilled machine shop workers, skilled motor vehicle mechanics, or welding. Female participants received training for clerical occupations. The former Department of Health, Education, and Welfare programs administered these services. The second type of training, administered by the Department of Labor, provided OJT training, usually with a private employer. OJT participants were selected through the employment service. After training was complete, participants in both CT and OJT could receive counseling and job placement services.

During the 1960s the composition of MDTA training slots shifted from being primarily CT to being a mix of CT and OJT as policymakers grew concerned that CT training was not providing skills demanded by employers. During the first three years of the program, approximately 80 percent of participants were approved for CT. By 1968, nearly one-half of participants received OJT (Manpower 1969, 4). In addition, the fraction of participants who received a combination of CT and OJT rose to about 15 percent by 1967, with about one-third of all OJT participants receiving these "coupled" services. In most instances, recipients of these coupled services received basic education rather than vocational instruction.

The 1966 MDTA Amendments

Congress amended MDTA frequently, but the 1966 amendments constituted a substantial change in the program's policy objectives. Motivated partly by a strong economic expansion that had driven the unemployment rate below 4 percent, Congress decided to target the programs' services toward the economically disadvantaged and to "rectify skill shortages."

Table 8.2   Characteristics of MDTZ Participants in Classroom Training and On-the-Job Training Programs (percentages for fiscal year 1966)

Characteristics	Classroom Training		On-the-Job Training	
	Male	Female	Male	Female
Percent of total	57	43	77	23
Black	31	42	12	19
Age > 34	26	33	20	38
High school dropout	59	42	34	47
Some college	5	8	11	8
10+ years prior experience[a]	33	16	30	22
Unemployed > 26 weeks	23	43	13	42
Unemployment insurance claimant	19	8	9	4
Public assistance	9	16	1	2

Source: Manpower (1997, 278).

Notes: Among 87 percent of participants who were unemployed prior to MDTA, the percentage whose ongoing spell was at least twenty-six weeks long. Expenditures are in 1999 dollars. n.a. = not available.

[a]Persons with ten or more years of employment experience prior to MDTA.

Until this point, the program targeted what today we refer to as displaced workers. The act now required authorities to use 65 percent of its resources to train persons whose skills were such that they were "not ready for competitive employment" (Manpower 1969). Because these participants faced greater barriers to employment, program operators had to provide them with more services and longer training than had been the case for previous MDTA cohorts. This meant that the cost of enrolling these participants was higher than the cost of enrolling dislocated workers.

As a result of these policy changes, later MDTA cohorts consisted of a larger fraction of economically disadvantaged persons than did the early program cohorts. As shown by table 8.2, in 1966, more than one-half of the male CT participants and more than one-third of male OJT participants were high school dropouts. Relatively few participants were unemployment insurance claimants when they participated. The figures for women, shown in columns (2) and (4) of table 8.2 are similar. This shift in the composition of MDTA trainees is important to keep in mind when comparing evaluations of this program on successive cohorts (e.g., Ashenfelter 1978, 1979; Cooley, McGuire, and Prescott 1979; Kiefer 1978, 1979). Ashenfelter's study evaluated a more advantaged group than did the studies by Cooley, McGuire, and Prescott and by Kiefer.

As shown by table 8.3, during the mid-1960s, the cost of MTDA services averaged approximately $6,500 per participant. These costs included the direct cost of training, the training stipends, and the costs of transportation. Classroom training was approximately four times as expensive as the cost of OJT. During fiscal year (FY) 1967, CT cost per trainee averaged

Table 8.3   Participants and Costs of MDTA Training, 1963 to 1968

| | Total Participants | | | | |
	In Thousands	% Classroom Training	% Classroom Training and On-the-Job Training	Expenditures ($ thousands)	Expenditures per Participant ($)
1963	59	96	0	290	4,900
1964	126	89	0	790	6,300
1965	231	72	8	1,500	6,500
1966	273	58	7	1,860	6,800
1967	298	48	15	1,490	5,000
1968	296	52	n.a.	1,590	5,400

Source: See table 8.2.
Notes: See table 8.2.

nearly $10,000.[4] This total was larger than per-pupil expenditures on a year of primary or secondary schooling.

Part of the reason for the difference between CT's and OJT's costs was that about one-half of CT's costs consisted of the training stipend (Levitan and Mangum 1969, 78). By contrast, during the early days of OJT, the program paid for materials but did not subsidize trainees' wages. The value of these CT training stipends averaged somewhat less than $3,500 per trainee. A formal cost-benefit analysis of training considers only the resources spent on training as a cost, whereas the stipend is a transfer from taxpayers to trainees. This amount of the stipend implies that during the mid-1960s the direct cost of CT averaged about $3,000 per participant. The total social cost of training includes this latter figure plus the trainees' opportunity costs of participating in training.

Historically, the cost of OJT services has been substantially lower than CT. This difference is not because trainees' wages were unsubsidized: In later years, the federal government paid such a subsidy. However, in a formal cost-benefit analysis, such a subsidy constitutes a transfer between taxpayers and employers. To be sure, the costs of OJT are understated somewhat because they do not include the formal and informal training costs incurred by employers when they employ MDTA participants. Such information is not available.

Other 1960s Employment and Training Programs

As discussed above, federal employment and training programs have been delivered through a complex array of programs administered in sev-

---

4. These training costs varied depending on the skills that were being provided. During fiscal year 1964, the direct costs of training nurse's aides, not including stipends, averaged $937, compared with the direct costs of training a licensed nurse, which averaged nearly $6,000.

eral different government agencies. A general pattern that has emerged is that the policymakers consolidate these programs and then, over time, add additional components and disperse control over them (e.g., Taggart 1981, 13–15). After a period has passed, they step in to consolidate the programs and the process begins again. This pattern emerged from the very beginning. Not long after creating MDTA, Congress not only repeatedly amended the original legislation—sometimes substantially changing its focus—but also created many entirely new and separate programs.

By the time Congress amended MDTA to shift the program's emphasis toward the economically disadvantaged, it had already created an array of educational and training services that targeted this group. Much of the emphasis of these other programs was to increase school completion rates and to ease the school-to-work transition of low-income youths. Under the Economic Opportunity Act (EOA) of 1964, Congress established several programs that have remained part of the nation's training strategy to the present day.

The Job Corps. The best known of the former EOA programs is Job Corps. This program provides a "structured residential environment for learning and development" for up to two years to low-income youths. It has three features that distinguish it from other employment and training services. First, the federal government continues to administer and operate the program. Funds for this $1.4 billion program are not distributed to the states or to the local Workforce Investment Boards. Instead, the Department of Labor directly hires subcontractors to operate approximately 120 training centers. During the 1960s, well-known firms such as General Electric and Westinghouse operated Job Corps centers.

A second distinctive feature of the Job Corps is its services. Participants receive a comprehensive set of counseling, education, training, work experience, health care, and job placement services. The assumption underlying Job Corps's design is that many youths from impoverished environments need many services to address a range of deficiencies but that these services can only be effective when participants are removed from their home environment. Their neighborhoods constitute a barrier to acquiring the educational, social, and vocational skills necessary to integrate these young people into the labor market. Accordingly, Job Corps centers usually are located outside participants' neighborhoods, sometimes in remote rural settings.

Finally, a third distinctive feature of Job Corps is its residential training centers. Participants usually live in dormitory settings and usually receive most of their education and vocational training on site. These services often are not integrated with the existing educational establishment.

The program has adopted several types of models for these centers. Among two early models was the Civilian Conservation centers, which were loosely modeled on the Civilian Conservation Corps created during the Great Depression and were located in remote rural areas. These centers housed 100 to 250 persons. Unlike other Job Corps centers, these centers have been operated by the Departments of Agriculture and Interior.

The second model was misleadingly referred to as an "urban center." During the early years of the program, these centers often were located on federally owned, abandoned military installations near urban labor markets, although usually not in them. These centers were large, usually housing between 600 and 3,000 Corps members, and offered a much wider menu of vocational training options than would be offered in the Civilian Conservation centers. Indeed, participants in the urban centers have tended to be relatively more "job-ready" and able to benefit from vocational training than their counterparts assigned to the Civilian Conservation centers.

Because of the high costs of operating these two types of centers, Congress scaled back their number during the early 1970s and introduced two additional residential models. Residential Manpower Centers were located close to urban centers from which participants resided, and were close enough that it was practical to allow participants to go home on weekends. They included both resident and nonresident training participants. Further, when possible, these centers used existing vocational training institutions to provide training, rather than providing the training on site. These sites were approximately the same size as the Civilian Conservation centers. At the same time, a fourth residential model provided living and support services, but all education and training services were provided off site. These Residential Support Centers have tended to be small, housing approximately thirty persons.

Given that a criterion for being admitted to a residential Job Corps center is that applicants with children show that arrangements have been made for child care, it is not surprising that during the program's history approximately two-thirds of Job Corps participants have been males. Females have been disproportionately assigned to nonresidential centers. Overall, about 10 percent (and 1993 amendments to JTPA allowed up to 20 percent) of Job Corps participants have been assigned to these centers. These centers offer the same comprehensive set of services, except for the living quarters, and are located near participants' homes. Females with children are disproportionately assigned to them, because the residential centers do not accommodate children. In addition, twenty- to twenty-four-year-old Job Corps participants, especially those who are parents, are also more likely to be assigned to the nonresidential centers.

Because of the cost of the residential component of Job Corps (about 15 to 20 percent of program costs) and because this component has been assumed to be essential for the program to be effective, policymakers have been interested in assessing its value. During the late 1980s, the Department of Labor financed a social experiment, known as the JOBSTART demonstration, based roughly on the nonresidential center model (Cave and Doolittle 1991). More recently, in another social experiment, the National Job Corps Study, researchers compared the effectiveness of Job Corps services for participants in residential and nonresidential settings (Schochet, Burghardt, and Glazerman 2000).

When it first began, Job Corps served fourteen- to twenty-one-year-old youths from economically disadvantaged families. During the 1980s the target group shifted to sixteen- to twenty-four-year-olds (U.S. Department of Labor 1988). In addition, administrators must select applicants who have the need, ability, and temperament to benefit from the education, training, and supportive services provided by the program. Participants must also be free from behavioral and medical problems and must have arranged for adequate child care when necessary. Since 1995, the program has had a zero-tolerance policy toward illegal substances. In practice, however, any youth who satisfied the age and income eligibility requirements for the program and who persisted in wanting to participate in Job Corps has been admitted into the program (Schochet, Burghardt, and Glazerman 2000).

Today the Job Corps enrolls approximately 70,000 youths and young adults annually. As shown by table 8.4, this figure is substantially larger than the number served during the 1970s, the program's first full decade, and is up somewhat from enrollments during the 1980s. As a consequence of the shifting demographics and increased real expenditures, there are more Job Corps slots per person in the sixteen- to twenty-four-year-old population than at any time in the program's history.

Table 8.4   **Job Corps Enrollments and Appropriations (selected years 1966–2000)**

Year	Enrollees	Enrollees per 16- to 24-year-Olds	Appropriations (nominal in $000s)	Appropriations (1999 in $000s)	Real Appropriations per Enrollee ($)
1966	18,146	0.63	310,000	1,606,000	88,504
1970	42,600	1.31	169,782	740,249	17,376
1975	45,800	1.25	210,499	665,176	14,523
1980	70,851	1.82	415,700	881,284	12,438
1985	63,020	1.72	617,000	962,520	15,273
1990	61,423	1.81	803,000	1,035,870	16,864
1995	68,540	1.83	1,089,000	1,197,900	17,478
1998	67,425	2.02	1,246,000	1,270,920	18,849
2000	70,400	2.04	1,358,000	1,325,408	18,826

Source: The 2000 enrollee figures are from the U.S. Department of Labor requested fiscal year 2000 appropriation.

Notes: Enrollees are for program years, not fiscal years. Enrollees per sixteen- to twenty-four-year-olds figures are multiplied by 1,000. Appropriations are for fiscal years.

As a result of its eligibility criteria, Job Corps has served youths who have had great difficulty finding steady employment, even in tight labor markets. During the 1960s about one-half of its entering participants read at the fifth-grade level or below; even during the 1980s about one-half of participants read only at the sixth-grade level or below (Levitan & Mangum 1969; U.S. Department of Labor 1988). Approximately 80 percent of participants do not have high school degrees, and about 60 percent are from families receiving public assistance. Younger Job Corps participants appear to be more economically disadvantaged; they are more likely to have been arrested and are more likely to be from single-parent homes.

Because Job Corps provides such a comprehensive array of services, it is an expensive program to operate. During FY 1967, a year of Job Corps cost nearly $40,000 per participant (Levitan and Mangum 1969). This high cost lead Congress, starting in 1968, to cut back on the number of centers, especially the more expensive Civilian Conservation centers, and on services. Accordingly, by FY 1971 public expenditures for a year of Job Corps had fallen to about $27,000 per participant year (O'Neill 1973). This figure was in line with the expenditures for a year of MDTA institutional (CT) training.

As shown by table 8.4, real expenditures per Job Corps enrollee have remained relatively high and have increased substantially since 1980. Part of the increase is due to longer stays in Job Corps. The average time spent in the program averages about eight months. This duration measure implies that Job Corps costs approximately $25,000 per participant year. These expenditures are more than double those for a year of formal schooling and substantially larger than those for other programs serving economically disadvantaged youths.

The foregoing cost figures overstate the social cost of Job Corps or the size of the skill investments made by policymakers. First, many of the program expenditures constitute transfers between taxpayers and Corps members. During much of its history, participants have received a modest living allowance, and even today they may receive performance bonuses and a "readjustment allowance" when they leave the program. In addition, Corps members receive in-kind transfers such as food, clothing, and medical care; even if they did not value these items as cash, they would likely have received these services through some other aid program had they not participated in Job Corps. Estimates that take these factors into account suggest that the social cost of a year of Job Corps is about three-fifths the total expenditures (O'Neill 1973). This estimate implies that the social cost of a year of Job Corps is approximately $16,000.

A second reason that program costs understate social costs is that, unlike CT program participants, Job Corp participants often produce output that is potentially socially valuable while they are in the program. Participants in the Civilian Conservation centers build or renovate facilities in national parks and on federal lands, and part of the training for participants in urban centers is to renovate Job Corps facilities or provide unpaid work experience to nonprofit community organizations. In one evaluation of the program this output was valued at more than $2,000 per participant (Mallar et al. 1982).

Neighborhood Youth Corps/Summer Youth Program. Another enduring EOA program has been the Neighborhood Youth Corps (NYC). This program enrolled nearly 1.6 million youths from low-income families between 1964 and 1968. When Congress first created this program its two purposes were to provide fourteen- to twenty-one-year-old economically disadvantaged youths with incentives to stay in school, and to either encourage those who had dropped out of school to return or facilitate their transition into the labor force. Perhaps the best-known component of this program, which was later added after the original legislation passed, has provided eligible youths with full-time summer jobs. Because the vast majority of the program's participants do not have a high school degree, the program evolved to include a modest educational component designed to improve participants' basic educational skills.

Although this program was targeted to a population similar to that of Job Corps, it provided different and fewer services and was much less expensive to operate on a per-person basis. Program participants mostly received work experience positions, but some supportive social services have been available. Program operators design these services to help participants complete school or find a regular job. In-school participants received part-time jobs, while out-of-school participants received full-time positions. During the 1960s, these jobs paid approximately $6.50 per hour (in 1999 dollars).

Serving the out-of-school participants has been more expensive than serving the in-school and summer participants, who were either part-time or part-year workers. During the 1960s, the cost of a yearlong slot for an out-of-school youth was about $14,000 of which 70 percent of this amount was accounted for by participants' wages. The cost for the other program enrollees amounted to about $3,000 per participant (Levitan and Mangum 1969, 213). Most of these resources were spent on participants' wages in jobs that provided little or no vocational training. Therefore, this expenditure largely constituted a transfer between taxpayers and participants and not a social cost of the program.

At its peak during the late 1960s, this program served about 450,000 participants at a cost of approximately $1.8 billion (Levitan and Mangum 1969, 212). In subsequent years, policymakers consolidated the NYC program into MDTA's successors. Until recently, this program model accounted for a significant fraction of the total resources spent on employment and training policy. As shown by table 8.5, during the 1980s and 1990s total expenditures averaged nearly $1 billion annually, approximately the

Table 8.5   Participants and Expenditures for the Summer Youth Program 1984–98
                   (under JTPA Title IIB)

Year	Participants (000s)	Expenditures ($000,000s)	Outlay/Participant ($)
1984	672	942	1,400
1985	768	1,210	1,560
1986	785	1,134	1,440
1987	634	1,068	1,670
1988	723	1,004	1,380
1989	607	944	1,550
1990	585	902	1,520
1991	555	855	1,530
1992	782	1,176	1,460
1993	647	1,067	1,620
1994	574	953	1,640
1995	489	984	1,960
1996	521	1,122	2,153
1997	492	972	1,976
1998	495	829	1,675

Source: U.S. House of Representatives, Committee on Ways and Means (1996, 2000).

Notes: The Summer Youth Program ended with JTPA. Under WIA localities are to provide these services as part of their "Youth Activities." Starting in fiscal year 1996, states could apply some funds from the summer youth program to full-year youth programs under Title IIC of JTPA. Dollar figures are expressed in 1999 dollars.

same amount that has been spent on Job Corps. But the NYC/Summer Youth Programs serve somewhat more than 500,000 participants annually, far more than the number served by Job Corps. These figures imply an average expenditure of about $2,000 per participant. Under existing policy, this program has formally ended, although the statute requires local program operators to provide these services as part of their youth activities.

Despite the size of the investment and the policy's durability, the NYC and the summer youth program have received relatively little attention from program evaluators. One notable exception came with the passage of the Youth Employment and Demonstration Projects Act of 1978, when Congress authorized that this program model be formally evaluated. The resulting Youth Incentive Entitlement Pilot Project tested the effect of a guaranteed job on high school reenrollment, retention, and completion rates for 30,000 economically disadvantaged youths in select cities.

Work-Welfare Programs: WIN and JOBS.[5] Despite the sharp decline in unemployment rates during the long economic expansion of the 1960s, wel-

5. The JOBS program under the Family Support Act of 1988 is different from the Job Opportunities in the Business Sector program established by Congress in 1968. Policymakers created the earlier JOBS program to encourage private-sector employers to voluntarily provide more on-the-job training slots to economically disadvantaged persons.

fare case loads grew rapidly. Alarmed by this trend, Congress amended Title IV of the Social Security Act in 1967 to establish the Work Incentive Program (WIN; Manpower 1974). This program's goal was to reduce dependency on the welfare system by helping AFDC applicants and recipients find regular employment. (The chapter in this volume by Robert Moffitt provides a detailed description of the AFDC program.)

The WIN program followed two earlier programs that Congress created during the 1960s to require employable fathers to work rather than to receive public aid. In 1962 Congress amended the Social Security Act to allow those states with AFDC-UP programs to use their (50 percent) share of federal funds to create jobs and require employable fathers to "work off" their public assistance. These Community Work and Training Programs were essentially work experience programs with no training component. The number of hours that participants were required to work was equal to their aid divided by the prevailing wage. Two years later, Congress expanded the coverage of this model when it created the Work Experience and Training Program as part of the EOA. This program provided states with 100 percent federal funding to establish WE and training slots not only for fathers on AFDC-UP, but for poor fathers and single persons not eligible for such aid. This program also covered women, but the Johnson Administration discouraged states from providing WE to single women with children (Levitan and Mangum 1969).

With WIN the federal government began a prolonged thirty-year shift in policy toward the idea that even poor single women with children should work. WIN participants received a variety of usually low-cost employment and training and supportive social services (U.S. Department of Labor 1974; Butler 1976). During the program's first few years welfare recipients' participation was voluntary. The WIN program simply made these resources available as an incentive for aid recipients to seek economic independence on their own.

Starting with the Talmadge amendments in 1971, WIN participation became mandatory for "employable" AFDC recipients. These persons consisted of aid recipients whose children were six years of age or older, excluding persons who were disabled or ill or those who were already working more than thirty hours per week. "WIN II" required eligible AFDC recipients to register with the employment service. At this point registrants were to be apprised as to whether they would benefit from WIN services. Those found likely to benefit were placed in a WIN funded program.

Once AFDC participants were placed in WIN, program operators' goal was to place the participant into a regular job as quickly as possible. To achieve this objective WIN first provided participants with job search assistance and then with training or supportive social services such as child care or counseling if they were needed. The program also provided participants with supportive services during their first ninety days on the job.

The WIN program's emphasis on job placement instead of human capital development marked another programmatic change that resulted from the Talmadge amendments. In the last year of WIN, as originally authorized under the 1967 legislation, more than 20 percent of participants received skill training. During the first year of WIN II, this percentage fell below 10 percent (Manpower 1974, chart 19). Offsetting this change was an expansion of subsidized OJT positions and public service employment (PSE). The program subsidized these jobs for six months. To accommodate participants who could not be placed in an OJT position, WIN also established a limited number of PSE positions. These fully subsidized jobs usually lasted for one year, with the intention that the public-sector employer would then pay the participants' wages when the subsidy ended.[6]

This legislation also marked the start of a thirty-year change in policy toward impoverished children. Prior to WIN, policymakers intended that poor single mothers would receive aid under the assumption that they would remain at home and care for their children (see Moffitt, chap. 5 in this volume). But with the enactment of WIN II, policy clearly shifted and was based on a new assumption that employable aid recipients with school-age children should work. In principle, parents who refused an appropriate WIN placement, whether into a regular or subsidized job, could be refused welfare.

In practice, WIN II never evolved into a "Workfare" program, because of inadequate funding. First, there was never funding to ensure a slot for each WIN participant, and in addition there were not enough resources to ensure, as the legislation required, that "adequate child care be available" for WIN placements (Levitan and Mangum 1969). Appropriations were sufficient to provide job search assistance and training to less than 10 percent of potentially eligible participants (Manpower 1969). As the population eligible for the program grew throughout the 1970s, funding did not increase substantially, and as a result most eligible AFDC recipients were not assigned WIN slots. As shown by table 8.6, in 1969 about 100,000 persons received WIN employment and training services. This total amounted to approximately one-eighth of the total population of WIN participants.

Although most WIN participants received little from the program, during the 1970s a substantial minority did receive substantial amounts of training. Approximately one-half of these received CT, about one-quarter received OJT, and about one-tenth received PSE. Note that the budgetary

6. To foster the placement of WIN participants in private-sector jobs, Congress also instituted a tax credit that amounted to 20 percent of the first year's wages as long as the WIN recipient was retained for two years. Another example of this shift in policy is seen in the 1967 legislation, when Congress recognized that existing AFDC rules created strong disincentives for work. To address this problem they allowed AFDC recipients to keep the first $30 in earnings per month (or about $150 in 1999 dollars) before additional earnings caused their monthly benefits to drop.

Table 8.6   **WIN and JOBS Participation and Expenditures, Selected Years**

	Expenditures[a] ($000,000s)	Participants Receiving Services
Work Experience and Training		
1965	590	51
1966	580	58
1967	500	67
WIN		
1969	540	100
1973	1,100	354
1975	833	n.a.
1977	673	n.a.
1980	790	277[b]
1981	700	276[b]
JOBS		
1993	1,000	545
1996	1,500	665

Sources: Levitan and Mangum (1969, 258–59); Manpower (1969, 9); Manpower (1974, 131); Butler (1976); NCEP (1995, xvi); Congressional Research Service (1999); U.S. Department of Labor (1982, 43).

Note: n.a. indicates not available. Dollar figures are expressed in 1999 dollars.

[a]Some figures include both employment and training expenditures and expenditures on supportive social services.

[b]In 1980, 778,000 AFDC recipients received appraisal interviews; in 1981 the figure was 808,000.

cost of providing PSE to 9,100 WIN participants in 1975 was more than $28,000 per person. The cost of OJT was more than $11,000. These "investments" are far more than what is currently spent on adult employment and training activities. At the same time, these cost figures underscore the substantial costs associated with a mandatory workfare program that guarantees a slot for all employable recipients on public aid.

During the late 1970s the coverage of the WIN program increased, but the cost of the services provided declined. In fiscal year 1981 the percentage of AFDC recipients that received training or subsidized employment rose to more than one-third. Significantly, about two-thirds of this group also received job search assistance, and many received nothing more than this service. As a result, the cost of WIN services per participant fell sharply from its levels in the mid-1970s as the program shifted to serving a larger population with low-cost employment services. (In addition, 317,000 persons received various forms of counseling and another 166,000 persons received subsidized child care.)

After 1981, Congress expanded state welfare agencies' authority over WIN and allowed many states to experiment with the program by adding a short-term work experience component to WIN. Significantly, states now could use their AFDC funds to create temporary work experience positions in the public or nonprivate sector (Community Work Experience) or to fund jobs in the nonprofit sector (Work Supplementation Program). In these work experience positions states set the maximum number of required work hours in public and nonprofit organizations to be equal to participants' annual AFDC benefits divided by the minimum wage. For the first time authorities could require AFDC participants to work in return for their welfare benefits. In addition, this legislation also expanded the work requirement for aid recipients by requiring parents with children between the ages of three and five to participate in WIN when child care was available (U.S. Department of Labor 1982; Gueron 1986).

One result of these legislative changes was that policymakers in several states agreed to randomly assign WIN participants into scarce work experience slots. This practice led to a proliferation of social experiments whose results were influential in the debate surrounding the Family Support Act of 1988 and to some extent the Personal Responsibility and Work Opportunity Reconciliation Act (PRWORA) of 1996 (see Moffitt, chap. 5 in this volume).

As part of the Family Support Act of 1988, Congress repealed WIN and replaced it with a more comprehensive program entitled the Job Opportunities and Basic Skills Program (JOBS). This program combined the elements of WIN with those of the work-welfare initiatives of the 1980s and added an education and training component. The legislation also expanded the population required to participate in the program to include (a) cash recipients between sixteen and fifty-nine with children over three (or over one at the discretion of the state); (b) teen parents over sixteen with a child of any age; and (c) nonparents in families receiving cash assistance who were not in school.

During its history JOBS operated as a federal-state-local partnership. At the federal level, the Department of Health and Human Services administered the program. States had considerable flexibility to design their own JOBS programs but were limited by some federally imposed constraints. The legislation required that each JOBS program include an assessment and develop a customized employment plan for each participant. It also stipulated that each program make available a wide array of employment and training services, and guarantee child care when needed.

At the local level, JOBS was administered jointly with MDTA's successor JTPA. In practice JOBS funds could be spent on JTPA participants and JTPA participants could be supported by JOBS funds.[7] Neither program was required to keep track of the services provided by other programs. By the mid-1990s, JOBS and JTPA together were the largest programs that provided employment and training services to the economically disadvantaged (National Commission for Employment Policy 1995).

---

7. Title V of JTPA explicitly provides for closer coordination between JTPA and WIN and, later, JOBS than was the case under CETA and prior programs.

The federal government never fully funded JOBS. Instead, it capped its commitment to match state resources.[8] Nonetheless, during the mid-1990s, federal and state expenditures on the program exceeded $1 billion, with the federal government covering about 60 percent of the total. To get states to provide JOBS's services to long-term AFDC recipients and other recipients with "barriers to employment," the federal government reduced its "match" if states failed to meet predetermined participation rates and to spend a certain percentage of their resources on particular groups. Several states operated JOBS demonstrations testing various program components using an experimental design. Also starting in the mid-1980s, there were several social experiments that tested the effectiveness of JOBS-like services.

The workfare component of WIN and its successor, JOBS, is an important feature of these programs that should be kept in mind when comparing the effectiveness of these services to other employment and training programs. This workfare component implies that evaluations of its impacts on earnings and welfare dependence assess these services in an environment in which participants were compelled to participate. An implication of the joint operation of JOBS and JTPA for program evaluation is that after 1988 some JTPA participants have been required to participate in the program as a result of having to participate in JOBS. By contrast, evaluations of most other employment and training programs occur in a context in which participation is voluntary. All other things being equal, we expect that the returns from a program that mandates participation would be less than for a program in which individuals participate voluntarily.

Public-Sector Employment. Through the 1960s, U.S. employment and training programs targeted the disadvantaged and structurally unemployed. In 1971 the scope of these programs increased. In response to the recession of that year, Congress passed the Emergency Employment Act. This act set up the first countercyclical employment program since the New Deal. The legislation provided for funds to go to local governments in order to create jobs for unemployed workers. Although the legislation singled out workers living below the poverty level, younger and older workers, women, and Vietnam veterans, the participants in these programs typically were more skilled than were participants in MDTA.

In the mid-1970s, additional legislation expanded the size of these countercyclical employment programs. The program's funding came to depend on locales' unemployment rates; during the 1975 recession more than 300,000 persons worked in public employment jobs. Despite a stronger economy, by 1979 this total had grown to 790,000 at a cost of about $8 bil-

8. But under Title IVA of the Social Security Act, the Family Support Act provided for an unlimited commitment to match state expenditures for child care for its JOBS participants.

lion. After reaching this peak, these programs and the nation's experiment with PSE abruptly ended with the JTPA in 1982.

The objective of this PSE program was different from the PSE services funded under WIN. In the case of WIN-PSE, policymakers intended that the government be the employer of last resort for persons whose skills made it unlikely that they would find regular jobs in any economic environment. By contrast, policymakers intended that PSE created by the Emergency Employment Act address the problem of cyclical unemployment. PSE slots expanded during the 1974–75 recession. As a result, participants in these programs were more job-ready and employable than WIN-PSE participants or other employment and training participants. During the mid-1970s, Congress recognized this dual purpose of PSE and incorporated this concept into MDTA's successor, the Comprehensive Employment and Training Act (Taggart 1981).

Comprehensive Employment and Training Act of 1973

During the 1970s, Congress embarked on an ambitious effort to consolidate the wide array of employment and training services that had emerged during the 1970s and to decentralize their operations. The Comprehensive Employment and Training Act (CETA) replaced MDTA and consolidated most of the existing 1960s programs under one statute. The CT and OJT programs under MDTA were authorized under Titles IIB and IIC of the act; work experience slots under Title IID; Job Corps under Title IV; and the NYC summer youth employment program under Title IV.

More importantly, CETA brought the concept of "revenue sharing" to national employment and training policy. It authorized the federal government to provide block grants to states so that they could customize and administer their own programs. The rationale underlying these changes was (and this continues to be current policy) that local officials knew better their own labor market and could customize a more effective array of services for participants.

This trend toward a greater local role in determining how federal employment and training dollars are spent has continued. However, the federal government retains substantial control over how these block grants are spent (Taggart 1981). Various formulas have constrained locales by dictating how funds could be allocated among different demographic groups and for different program categories. CETA required locales to submit plans each fiscal year to the Department of Labor for approval of their program activities. The federal government also retained direct control over several important elements of the program, such as Job Corps. In addition, an array of nationally run programs was gradually added to the program including those for older workers, Native Americans, ex-offenders, and youths.

Although CETA began a movement toward greater local control over employment and training policy, it did not create any additional programs or tools for carrying out these policies. What distinguishes the CETA era from those that came both before and after is that (a) policymakers spent substantially more on employment and training services for low-income persons and the unemployed, and (b) a relatively large fraction of program expenditures were on WE and PSE programs.

At its peak during the Carter administration, CETA expenditures on all program components amounted to nearly $25 billion. Even excluding the costly PSE program, real expenditures on CETA programs were approximately 50 percent greater than those for similar MDTA and EOA programs during the late 1960s, and nearly double the real expenditures during the early 1990s on similar services under JTPA. Despite the trend toward higher training expenditures shown in table 8.7, under CETA outlays per trainee were lower than they were under MDTA. This change reflects a policy shift toward making smaller public investments in a larger number of low-income persons. This decline occurred as program operators emphasized services of shorter duration and placed greater emphasis on programs that provided job search assistance, job placement, and job creation. These services sought to place participants in jobs quickly rather than to increase their vocational skills.

Job Training Partnership Act of 1982

In 1982, Congress reduced the size and narrowed the focus of U.S. employment and training programs. Interestingly, job creation programs, which had been scaled back as the national unemployment rate rose during the early 1980s, were eliminated under JTPA during the height of the 1982–83 recession. Besides eliminating PSE programs, the JTPA refocused the nation's employment and training effort on hard-to-employ, economically disadvantaged persons. As with CETA, the basic menu of services remained the same. But as time passed, amendments to the act led operators to spend a larger share of resources providing training opportunities, especially CT, and less resources on employment-related services, as was the case under CETA.

An important difference between JTPA and its predecessors involved the manner in which training services were delivered and administered. The legislation continued the principle embodied in CETA that local officials were in a better position to administer and determine the type of training to be provided to participants. To implement this goal the legislation required that each of approximately 600 training jurisdictions—known as service delivery areas (SDAs)—establish a private industry council (PIC) consisting of representatives from local businesses, labor organizations, and political and community officials. The intent behind having business representation on these councils was to address policymakers' long-standing concern that government training programs were not providing skills that employers wanted.

Table 8.7   CETA and JTPA Participation and Expenditures, Select Years

Participants	Total (000s)	% Classroom Training	% On-the-Job Training	Expenditures (in $000,000s)	Expenditures per Participant ($)
A. CETA Title II B, C: CT and OJT Activities Only[a]					
1975	364	80	20	1,200	3,300
1976	663	78	22	2,270	3,400
1977	707	76	24	2,604	3,700
1978	774	75	25	2,900	3,700
1979	726	78	22	2,670	3,700
1980	626	79	21	2,913	4,600
B. Total Participants and Expenditures Under CETA Title IIB, C and JTPA-Title IIA, C					
1975	1,122	26	7	3,998	3,563
1976	1,731		9	4,870	2,813
1977	1,416	30	12	4,690	3,312
1978	1,332	38	15	5,969	4,481
1979	1,194	44	13	5,870	4,916
1980	1,114	48	12	6,712	6,025
1981	1,011	44	n.a.	6,396	6,326
1982	n.a.	n.a.	n.a.	4,008	n.a.
1983	n.a.	n.a.	n.a.	3,857	n.a.
1984	935	n.a.	n.a.	2,153	2,303
1985	1,077	n.a.	n.a.	2,665	2,474
1986	1,100	n.a.	n.a.	2,905	2,640
1987	1,336	n.a.	n.a.	2,779	2,080
1988	1,246	n.a.	n.a.	2,699	2,142
1989	1,187	n.a.	n.a.	2,530	2,131
1990	1,096	n.a.	n.a.	2,326	2,122
1991	1,022	n.a.	n.a.	2,162	2,115
1992	955	n.a.	n.a.	2,105	2,204
1993	636	n.a.	n.a.	2,038	3,450
1994	635	n.a.	n.a.	1,935	3,047
1995	536	n.a.	n.a.	1,709	3,188
1996	480	n.a.	n.a.	1,116	2,325
1997	483	n.a.	n.a.	1,011	2,093
1998	452	n.a.	n.a.	1,110	2,456

Sources: Taggart (1981, pp. 25, 46); NCEP (1995, appendix pp. 1–8); U.S. House of Representatives, Committee on Ways and Means (1996, 2000).

Notes: n.a. indicates not available. Participation figures prior to 1995 are the number of enrollees. Expenditures and dollar figures are in 1999 dollars.

[a]CETA Title IIB, C provides full range of activities to the economically disadvantaged and to the unemployed. JTPA Title A, C provide services to the economically disadvantaged.

The amount of money that states and PICs could spend depended on a statutory formula that gave one-third weight to the number of economically disadvantaged persons in the state; one-third weight to the difference between the number of unemployed persons in the state and the number of unemployed persons when the state unemployment rate is 4.5 percent; and one-third weight to the relative number of unemployed persons in areas determined to have substantial unemployment (National Commission for Employment Policy [NCEP] 1987).

As shown by table 8.8, like CETA, the act also imposed constraints on who among the low-income population could receive JTPA services. The legislation required that 90 percent of participants in the CT and OJT programs under Title IIA (and later Title IIC for youths) be economically disadvantaged. Locales could reserve 10 percent of their training slots for persons who were not economically disadvantaged, but who had poor English skills, were high school dropouts, were teenage parents, or were determined by local officials to be likely to benefit from the program. The statute required that 40 percent of program funds be spent on training economically disadvantaged youths; it also required that AFDC recipients and high school dropouts be served equally depending on their proportions in the local population.

The JTPA also formalized a system of performance management that had evolved under CETA (Taggart 1981). Under this system, PICs, local training providers, and the U.S. Department of Labor (DOL) were to use a set of outcome-based performance standards to monitor the effectiveness of SDAs and their training services. As shown by table 8.9, these standards included JTPA trainees' "entered employment rate" or the percentage of trainees who were employed when officials terminated them from the program, and their hourly wage rate in that first job. Later, a thirteen-week follow-up employment rate was added as a new standard. The DOL adjusted these standards for each locale in order to account for differences in demographics and economic conditions.[9]

Policymakers anticipated that this system of performance management would improve net impact measures for these programs. The legislation sets aside some funds to reward sites that exceeded these standards or to provide "technical assistance" to those that fell short. In principle, poorly performing sites could be sanctioned.

Although policymakers designed JTPA performance standards to improve their programs, they also created incentives that potentially undermined their intent to concentrate resources on the hard-to-employ. Under JTPA, as with its predecessors, employment and training services have never been an entitlement for the economically disadvantaged or the unemployed. Program operators have considerable discretion over who they admit into their programs: They are only required to provide these services to persons who they believe will benefit from them. JTPA performance management gave operators incentives to "cream-skim" the most job-

---

9. See Barnow (1992, 2000) and Heckman, Smith, and Taber (1996) for more detailed descriptions of the JTPA performance standards system. Similar outcome-based performance measures are now a part of other U.S. training programs and are accepted among education policymakers. Also see these papers and Gay and Borus (1980) for evidence that such performance measures are not highly correlated with program impacts.

Table 8.8   Comparison of Eligibility Requirements for Major Categories of Program Services under CETA, JTPA and the Workforce Investment Act (WIA)

	Adults	Youths (1)	Youths (2)	Youths (3)	Displaced Worker
			CETA, 1973–82		
Programs	CETA Title IIBC	CETA Title IV (YETP)	CETA Title IV (Summer Jobs)	CETA Title IV (Job Corps)	Covered under CETA Title BC or CETA Title D, if economically dis advantaged
Eligibility	22 years and older Economically disadvan- taged or unemployed; 6.5% funds for under- employed	14 to 21 years old Economically disadvan- taged, but eligible if fam- ily income is < 85% of BLS (LLS)	Same as YETP	Same as under Economic Opportunity Act	Eligible for Title VI, Public Service Emp., if unemployed 10 of 12 weeks and income < 100 BLS LLS for 3 months
			JTPA, 1982–2000		
Programs	JTPA Title II-a	JTPA Title II-C (Year Round)	JTPA Title II-B (Summer Youth)	JTPA Title IV (Job Corps)	JTPA Title II[d]
Eligibility	22 years and older Economically disadvan- taged;[a] 10% need not be economically disadvan- taged	14- to 21-year-olds Economically disadvan- taged, or eligible for free school meals, or Chapter 1 participant;[b] 10% need not be economically dis- advantaged	14- to 21-year-olds Economically disadvan- taged or eligible for free school meals[c]	16- to 24-year-olds Economically disadvan- taged and residing in a "disorienting environ- ment"; 80% are < 21 years	Laid off and either ex- hausted or ineligible for UI benefits; laid off b/c of mass layoff or plant closing; or long-term unemployed; or dis- placed farmer or home- maker
Appropriations FY 1998	$955 million	$130 million	$871 million	$1.2 billion	$1.0 billion

Program	WIA Title I.B.5 (Adult Activities)	WIA Title I.B.4 (Youth Activities)	WIA Title I.C (Job Corps)	Covered under WIA Title B
		WIA 2000–present		
Eligibility	18 years and older; no income test; priority given to cash benefit recipients	Low income,[e] but not free lunch participants	16–24 years old; low income; and low literacy, homeless, dropout, foster child, parent, or requiring additional assistance to complete school	Repealed, but states must provide summer youth services under WIA Title I.B.4
Appropriations FY 2001 (2001$)	$950 million	$1.4 billion	$1.4 billion	$1.4 billion

Sources: Taggart (1981); National Commission for Employment Policy (1987); Congressional Research Service (1999); DOL (2002).

Notes: BLS = U.S. Bureau of Labor Statistics. LLS = lower living standard. YETP = Youth Employment Training Programs.

[a]Under JTPA an individual was defined as "economically disadvantaged" if he or she (a) received or is a member of a family who receives cash welfare payments under a federal, state, or local program; (b) is a member of a family that receives food stamps or received food stamps during the previous six months; (c) has family income, excluding unemployment insurance, child support, and welfare payments, during the previous six months that is no higher than the official poverty level or is no higher than 70 percent of the U.S. Bureau of Labor Statistics lower living standard; (d) is a foster child living in a family receiving payments from a state or local government; or is a handicapped adult whose income meets the eligibility standards, even if his or her family income exceeds it. There were no as-set rules determining eligibility.

[b]Participant in a Chapter 1 compensatory education program under the Elementary and Secondary Education Act.

[c]The family income threshold that determines eligibility for school lunches under the National School Lunch Act is 130 percent of the poverty level.

[d]The statute allowed states to limit or extend these eligibility requirements.

[e]Under WIA the term "low-income" is defined similarly to the JTPA definition of "economically disadvantaged."

Table 8.9   National Performance Standards under JTPA Program Years
                 (July 1 to June 30)

	1984–85	1986–87	1998–99
Adults under Title IIA			
Entered employment rate (all participants; %)	55	62	60[a]
Entered employment rate (welfare participants; %)	39	51	52[a]
Placement wage ($)	4.91	4.91	289[b]
Cost per placement ($)	5,704	4,374	n.a.
Youths under Title IIC			
Entered employment rate (all participants; %)	41	43	45
Positive termination rate ($)[c]	82	75	72
Cost per positive termination ($)	4,900	4,900	n.a.

Sources: NCEP (1987, 12, table 2); DOL, Employment and Training Administration website: wdr.do-leta.gov/opr/performance/overview.asp.

Note: n.a. indicates not applicable.

[a]In program years 1998–99 the standard is the "follow-up employment rate."

[b]In program years 1998–99, the standard is the "follow-up weekly earnings."

[c]Includes enrollment in school, the military, or other non-Title II training, or completion of an educational degree.

ready applicants. These individuals would tend to have high postprogram employment rates and wages, even if the program itself had little impact on these outcomes. However, research on this issue indicates that (a) even if this shift had occurred it probably would not have lowered estimates of the effectiveness of JTPA, and (b) program operators did not appear to substantially cream-skim in response to these incentives (Heckman and Smith 1997b; Heckman, Smith, and Taber 1996).

JTPA has served an economically disadvantaged population. As was shown by table 8.7, JTPA provided employment and training services to approximately 800,000 economically disadvantaged persons each year. In 1985, more than one-half of its participants had not worked in the six months prior to their application to the program, 40 percent were receiving public assistance, 41 percent were high school dropouts, and 92 percent were from families in poverty.

The program did succeed in providing training opportunities to a large share of its participants. During program year 1985, approximately 35 to 40 percent of enrollees participated in CT, and about 20 to 25 percent of enrollees were placed in an OJT slot. Because few people received both services, this figure indicates that during any given year as many as 65 percent of JTPA participants received some skill training. This emphasis on CT remained strong and even grew as the program evolved. This growth in CT occurred as the share of OJT participants declined. During JTPA's early years the median CT participant received instruction for approximately eighteen weeks, but this measure increased during the 1990s (NCEP 1987; Social Policy Research Associates [SPR] 1999).

Despite JTPA's emphasis on serving the most economically disadvantaged, Title III of the act did provide explicitly for job search and training services for displaced workers. (These persons are defined when we described the WIA program.) Because they tended to have substantial employment histories, participants under this title of the act were more skilled than other JTPA participants. In addition, they have tended to be more skilled than the unemployed who received PSE under Title VI of CETA (NCEP 1987). Despite the large numbers of displaced workers in the 1980s, Congress initially appropriated little funding for this group. During the mid-1980s, expenditures were no more than $350 million per year (NCEP 1987; Barnow and Aron 1989).

During JTPA's existence Congress made two significant policy changes that affected services to displaced workers. First, the Omnibus Trade and Competitiveness Act (1988) underscored policymakers' desire to shift away from providing low-cost job search skills to training participants and instead emphasize more expensive training activities. Under these amendments 50 percent of local funds for displaced workers were to be spent on training activities instead of job search assistance. Further, persons receiving assistance under the Trade Act (1974) now had to participate in CT or OJT as a condition for receiving extended unemployment insurance benefits.[10]

The second change occurred during the mid-1990s when the Clinton Administration proposed expanding funding of employment and training services for displaced workers. As was shown by table 8.8, by program year 1997 expenditures exceeded $1 billion per year despite the strong economic expansion. This increase foreshadowed the policy change reflected the following year in the Workforce Investment Act, in which policymakers appear to have refocused low-cost employment and training services away from the most economically disadvantaged and toward a broader segment of the population.

Toward the end of JTPA, these policy changes also affected economically disadvantaged youth. The original legislation instructed locales to spend at least 40 percent of their funds (under Title A, C) on youths. As recently as 1993, these expenditures totaled more than 600 million and the program served 280,000 youths (DOL 1996). During the mid-1990s Congress sharply cut expenditures on youth services. By program year 1997, expenditures for these low-intensity services (under Title IIC) had fallen to only $130 million. One important reason for this change was research from

---

10. Congress established the Trade Adjustment Assistance program (TAA) in the early 1960s to provide supplemental unemployment benefits to workers who lost their jobs as a result of trade liberalization. In 1974, Congress expanded the program's scope to cover workers who had lost their jobs as a result of increased foreign trade.

the nonprofit and academic community showing that low-intensity non-comprehensive training services were not effective for youths. The final blow for these services came with the results of the National JTPA Study, a social experiment conducted starting in the late 1980s, which showed that even after four years neither youth participants nor society benefited from these services (Orr et al 1994; Bloom et al. 1997; U.S. GAO 1996).

8.2.3   The Workforce Investment Act of 1998

Policy Goals of the Workforce Investment Act

Today, a large portion of current federal policy is governed by the Workforce Investment Act of 1998 (WIA), which took effect in July 2000. The passage of WIA signaled policymakers' intent to consolidate the assortment of existing federal and state education and training programs and to coordinate them with existing social services. To this end, the act folds JTPA and other employment and training and work-welfare programs into a broader system designed to manage and develop the nation's human resources. Besides these programs, other programs covered under WIA include those formerly under the Adult Education and Family Literacy Act, employment services under the Wagner-Peyser Act, and the Rehabilitation Act. In addition, the legislation also allows states to design programs that incorporate appropriate resources available under the Food Stamp Act of 1977, the Trade Act of 1974, certain programs under the Social Security Act, and the training activities of the Department of Housing and Urban Development.

Although WIA increases states' ability to use several sources of federal dollars to develop their own employment and training policies, the federal government still maintains some control over their programs. The statute requires each state to submit a "training plan" for approval to the DOL. As part of the plan governors must establish Workforce Investment Areas within their states. Within these areas Workforce Investment Boards, consisting of representatives from business, labor, the community, and of elected local officials, govern these programs. Within the constraints set in the statute, they decide whom to service, what kinds of services to provide, and who should provide the services. However, the programs developed by the local boards must include the range of employment and training services previously described (in table 8.1) and offered to specific groups within the eligible population.[11] Further, federal authorities must approve the aggregate performance of the state's training providers.

11. WIA requires local programs to include the following elements: (a) tutoring, study skills, instruction to complete secondary school or GED, dropout prevention strategies; (b) summer employment opportunities for youths; (c) work experience; (d) OJT and CT; (e) supportive social services such as child care and transportation; (f) follow-up services; and (g) comprehensive services, such as counseling, substance abuse referrals, mentoring, and leadership development.

An important goal of WIA is that participants should be able to attain access to the array of employment and training and supportive services, including educational services in one location. Accordingly, WIA requires that each Workforce Investment Board establish at least one "one-stop career center" within its jurisdiction.[12] All labor exchange services that have been provided through the employment service (under the Wagner-Peyser Act) must be delivered through these centers.[13] Policymakers designed the one-stop centers so that all groups in the population have access in one physical location to information about employment and training services as well as other supportive social services. State employment service agencies not only are a partner in these one-stop centers and serve on local boards, as required by the statute, but in practice they operate these centers.

Although WIA makes several potential important changes in the administration of U.S. employment and training policy, it does not substantially alter the menu of services available to participants. Instead, policymakers intend that two components of the legislation operating together will improve the effectiveness of these services. Consequently, policymakers intend that even though the mix of services probably will not change much under WIA, these administrative changes will enable local authorities to better serve their clients and will cause WIA-sponsored programs to have larger impacts than prior training initiatives. A premise of the act is that greater "customer" choice will lead to better use of training resources. By contrast to past practices in which local authorities sent participants to pre-subcontracted training providers, under WIA, adult participants are given voucherlike individual training accounts that they may use to purchase training services from previously certified training providers.

To facilitate "customer" choice, the legislation encourages local boards to increase the number of certified training providers. In addition, the act expands reporting requirements for training providers. WIA participants are to have access to information that compares alternate providers' program completion rates, entered employment rates, and wage rates for their former participants. The intention underlying these reporting requirements is that by using this information, WIA participants should be able to make more informed decisions about the quality of training providers and to use their vouchers to "buy" training from providers with better programs.

12. The DOL began to experiment with one-stop centers starting in 1994 when it awarded grants to six states—Connecticut, Iowa, Maryland, Massachusetts, Texas, and Wisconsin—to develop and implement one-stop systems.
13. Unlike the use of Section 7(a) funds, WIA does not require all Wagner-Peyser funds to be used as part of the one-stop centers. For example, Section 7(b) funds, known as the "Governor's reserve," are excluded from this requirement.

Who Is Served by WIA?

As summarized by table 8.8, under WIA there is no requirement that eligible adults be from low-income families. Instead, the legislation simply states that operators give priority to persons receiving cash assistance. This distinction in eligibility criteria for youths and adults is a departure from the policy under WIA's predecessor, JTPA. During the tenure of JTPA, most adult and youth participants had to be classified as "economically disadvantaged." The legislation defined such individuals as meeting one of several criteria: They (a) received or were a member of a family who received cash welfare payments under a federal, state, or local program; (b) were a member of a family that received food stamps or received food stamps during the previous six months; (c) had family income, excluding unemployment insurance, child support, and welfare payments, during the previous six months that was no higher than the official poverty level or no higher than 70 percent of the U.S. Bureau of Labor Statistics lower living standard; (d) were a foster child living in a family receiving payments from a state or local government, or were a handicapped adult whose income met the eligibility standards, even if their family income exceeded it.

By contrast, under WIA, eligible fourteen- to twenty-one-year-olds generally must be from low-income families. In addition, the statute requires that they also possess one of the following "barriers" to employment: They must be deficient in basic skills, a high school dropout, homeless or a foster child, pregnant or a parent, an offender, or in need of additional assistance in order to complete school. This low-income eligibility standard for youths is similar to the economically disadvantaged concept used under JTPA.

For adults, WIA essentially combines adult services previously provided under two different sections of JTPA that had different eligibility criteria. "Adult Activities" now encompass services previously targeted to economically disadvantaged persons aged twenty-two and over (under JTPA Title IIA) and services targeted toward unemployed adults (under JTPA Title III). Many participants in this later group have not been from low-income backgrounds.[14] As shown in the last column of table 8.8, under JTPA such unemployed adults were eligible for services and classified as displaced workers if they had been (a) laid off and either were ineligible for or had exhausted their unemployment insurance benefits, and were unlikely to return to their previous industry or occupation; (b) terminated because of a plant closing or a mass layoff;[15] or (c) unemployed for a long period and had had limited opportunities for finding work. Further, the act

14. WIA also lowers the age threshold to qualify for Adult Activities to eighteen years.

15. Individuals whose former employer had to provide them with sixty days' advance notice of a layoff or plant closing under the Worker Adjustment and Retraining Act (1988) were eligible for JTPA services.

gave states considerable authority to identify persons that fit these definitions of a displaced worker. Because of these eligibility criteria, many of JTPA's displaced workers have been relatively skilled. For example, during the 1997 program year, 35 percent of such participants had earned more than $15 per hour in their previous jobs (SPR 1999). Consequently, policy changes under WIA probably enable authorities to provide employment and training services to a less economically disadvantaged adult population than they could under JTPA.

WIA Expenditures and Participation

Because WIA has just begun operating, there are no statistics available on participation and relatively little information on expenditures for each of the service categories summarized in table 8.1. Statistics for FY 2001 indicate that the federal government spent about $2.4 billion on "Adult Activities," including 1.4 billion for "dislocated workers employment and training activities." In addition, the federal government spent $1.4 billion each for "Youth Activities" and the Job Corps and $500 million for an array of small national programs. Because of the role of the employment service (ES) in operating the program's one-stop centers, some of the $1 billion spent on the ES should be considered part of the WIA policy. Accordingly, a rough but reasonable estimate of current federal expenditures on employment and training programs for the economically disadvantaged and the unemployed is about $6 billion (DOL 2002).

Recent statistics for program year 1997 under JTPA likely depict the participation and expenditure patterns that will manifest themselves during the early years of WIA. As shown by table 8.10, federal policymakers allocated approximately $2 billion to fund services for economically disadvantaged adults and for displaced workers. By contrast, expenditures on services for full-year services for youths amounted to only about $130 million. During this period a combined total of more than 450,000 adults and approximately 88,000 youths left the program. The second row of the table also indicates that a sizable share (25 percent) of economically disadvantaged adults who left the program received no services other than an assessment by program officials.[16]

As suggested by the differing eligibility criteria for its services, JTPA programs attracted a diverse group of participants. Services for which eligibility is means-tested have been provided for the intended economically disadvantaged population. Youth participants have been particularly disadvantaged, which might be expected as their eligibility criteria includes a

---

16. These figures do not include youth participants in Job Corps (under Title IV) or the Summer Youth Programs (under Title IIB). These programs are discussed above. Under WIA Job Corps remains intact and continues to be operated at the federal level. The Summer Youth Programs are no longer funded as a separate item, but the statute requires local authorities to provide these services as part of their youth activities.

Table 8.10   Participation, Expenditures, and Characteristics of JTPA Terminees ($ in group for program year 1997)

	Title II-A Adult Services	JTPA Program Title II-C Youth Full-Year Services	Title III Displaced Workers
Terminated	198,033	88,438	266,112
Number who received services	147,717	74,816	n.a.
Allotments	$0.89 billion	$0.13 billion	$1.03 billion
Sex			
Female	68	59	54
Male	32	41	46
Age			
18–21	n.a.	57	n.a.
20–29	41	n.a.	18
30–44	47	n.a.	46
45+	12	n.a.	35
Ethnic background			
White	45	38	65
Black	34	33	19
Hispanic	17	24	12
Education level			
Less than high school	21	71	12
High school graduate	57	26	50
Post-high school	21	3	38
Single parent	47	20	15
Reading level			
Less than 7th grade	13	28	9
7th or 8th grade	16	23	10
9th grade+	71	50	81
No job in prior 26 weeks	51	74	17
Unemployment insurance claimant	12	7	69
Food stamps	53	39	7

Sources: Social Policy Research Associates (1999, p. II-2, table II-1; p. 8, table II-4; p. III-2, table III-1; p. III-6, table 3; p. V-2, table V-2; p. V-2, table V-1; p. VI-4, table VI-2).

Note: n.a. indicates not applicable.

barriers-to-employment test in addition to an income test. The vast majority of youth participants have not had a job in the previous six months, even though most of these participants were aged eighteen years or older. One-half of them read at the eighth-grade level or less, and only somewhat more than a quarter of them had a high school degree.

Adult participants under Title IIA of JTPA are somewhat less disadvantaged than the youths. Nevertheless, about one-half had not had a job in more than six months, slightly more than one-half received food stamps, about 30 percent of participants read at the eighth-grade level or below, and about one-fifth were high school dropouts. As shown by contrasting the figures in the first and third columns of table 8.10, the adult displaced workers who received JTPA services under Title III were more skilled. They had a larger percentage of workers with post–high school education, higher reading levels, and better work histories. Because unemployment is an eligibility criterion for these services, it is not surprising that more than two-thirds had received or were receiving unemployment insurance benefits, and relatively few of these participants were receiving food stamps.

JTPA participants have several other characteristics that are worth noting. First, the majority of adult and youth participants are women. Even among Title III participants whose eligibility depends on having been displaced, 54 percent of participants are women. Second, adult participants in both Title II-A programs for the economically disadvantaged and Title III programs for the unemployed are not especially young. The typical recipient of both service categories is aged between thirty and forty-four years. Among those receiving Title III services, more than one-third of participants are over forty-five. Finally, the majority of adult participants, even those receiving Title II-A services, are not single parents, but are from two-parent households or are single.

The recent JTPA program statistics also help portray the likely distribution of participants among the broad categories of services depicted in table 8.1 during the early years of WIA. These statistics suggest that CT will be the most important adult activity under WIA, but that youths will receive a more diverse set of services. As shown by table 8.11, the most common service received by adult JTPA participants during program year

Table 8.11 Distribution of Program Services for JTPA Terminees (% receiving service for program year 1997)

Workers	Title II-A Adult Services		Title II-C Youth Full-Year Services		Title III Displaced	
	Females	Males	Females	Males	Females	Males
Service received (%)						
Basic skills	21	16	44	50	13	10
CT	68	59	39	26	51	48
OJT	8	15	2	2	4	5
WE	5	5	25	32	n.a.	n.a.
Other	13	14	32	37	n.a.	n.a.
Two or more	19	15	37	41	8	7
Time receiving training						
% with zero hours	8	10	6	6	40	42
Average hours	440	329	372	321	289	268

Sources: Social Policy Research Associates (1999, p. II-14, table II-6; p. III-14, table III-8; p. V-15, table V-6).

Notes: n.a. indicates not applicable. The figures for the Title II-A and Title II-C programs exclude 25 percent and 15 percent, respectively, of all terminees who did not receive any services beyond a formal assessment. Information on eligibility for these programs is found in table 8.7.

1997 was vocational classroom training. More than two-thirds of the female participants received this service. The percentages of displaced male and female workers receiving this service are smaller, but these differences largely reflect the different ways these measures are reported for the two groups. The figures calculated for the economically disadvantaged participants exclude those participants who received only an "objective assessment" by program officials.

Turning to the other figures in the table, much smaller percentages of male and female participants received OJT, although among disadvantaged participants, about one-sixth of the males received this service. Among adults, between 10 and 20 percent received basic skills training; this percentage was larger for economically disadvantaged men and women than it was for displaced workers, as was expected based on differences between the two groups' baseline characteristics.

Finally, as shown by the sixth row in the table, nearly one-fifth of the female participants and nearly one-sixth of the male participants received services from two or more of the categories listed in the table. This result is not surprising because policy encourages program operators to customize a package of services for each participant. When program operators assess a potential participant they devise a training plan. This plan often recommends that the participant receive a sequence of services. Any of these services alone might lead to improved outcomes. Consequently, a consideration when evaluating the effectiveness of one category of services is that participants also may have received services from other categories.

The distribution of Title II-C youth participants among the service categories differs from the adults in several respects. First, youths are more likely than adult participants to receive two or more of the services described in the table. Second, nearly one-half received basic skills training, while 39 percent of the males and 26 percent of the females received CT. Third, more than one-quarter received WE, whereas only very small percentages of adults received this service. Finally, by contrast to the adults, few youths received OJT.

WIA's Place among Other Active and Passive Labor Market Policies

The foregoing description of recent expenditures and participation patterns in employment and training programs is for just one of several federal programs that have been providing these services. For some time, U.S. employment and training policy has manifested itself as a complex patchwork of federal education and training programs. Each program has its own goals and rules governing eligibility. Although JTPA and its successor, WIA, have been the most prominent of these programs, taken together these other federal programs have cost as much to operate and, if anything, serve more people.

Each of these employment and training programs operates in a policy environment in which there are substantial federal, state, and local subsidies for postsecondary schooling as well as vocational education in secondary schools. Depending on the program, these subsidies are received both by the individual and by the institutions providing the schooling or training. The program rules governing which individuals receive these subsidies also differ from those of JTPA. Yet JTPA's CT often takes place in a community college, and sometimes JTPA participants receive this training in the same classroom as other non-JTPA participants. Many of these non-JTPA students are likely from low-income households or are recently unemployed. As a result, figures on the resources spent on programs like JTPA and how they are distributed among service categories provide information on only a portion of U.S. employment and training policy.

The listing of alternative employment and training programs in table 8.12

Table 8.12   Expenditures and Participants in Employment and Training Programs

Program	Department	Expenditures ($000,000s)	Participants (000s)
Unemployment insurance	Labor	21,900	7,800
Employment service	Labor	811	21,346[a]
Postsecondary education			
Pell grants	Education	5,788	3,743
Family Education Loan Program	Education	5,825	5,326
Supplemental opportunity grants	Education	583	991
Perkins Loan Program	Education	166	697
Work study	Education	617	713
Postsecondary employment and training			
JTPA			
Adult	Labor	1,015	389
Youth Summer	Labor	677	648
Youth	Labor	651	360
Dislocated Workers	Labor	571	312
Job Corps	Labor	966	101
JOBS	HHS	1,000	545
Other employment and training programs			
Vocational rehabilitation	Education	1,873	1,049
Vocational rehabilitation projects	Education	29	24
Rehabilitation employment services	Education	32	24
Trade Adjustment Assistance	Labor	75	27
Food Stamp Employment and Training Program	Agriculture	135	1,400
Senior Community Service Employment Program	Labor	396	97
Disabled Veterans Outreach Program	Labor	79	932
Targeted Jobs Tax Credit	Treasury	n.a.	632[b]

Source: NCEP (1995, pp. xii–xvi).

Notes: HHS = U.S. Department of Health and Human Services. N.a. indicates not available. Figures are for FY 1993.

[a]Number of unduplicated registrants, see note 17 in text.

[b]The figure is the number of vouchers.

is not complete, but the most important ones are included. For comparison purposes, the first two rows of the table report the expenditures and number of participants in the Unemployment Insurance Program and the ES (i.e., Wagner-Peyser Act). The first of these comparisons reflects the degree of policy emphasis on active versus passive labor market policy. Compared to European countries, expenditures in the United States on active policies, which encompass employment and training services, compared to passive policies, which encompass unemployment insurance benefits, are relatively small (Heckman, LaLonde, and Smith 1999).

The second row of table 8.12 provides a glimpse of the number of persons that potentially enter the system each year. Most recipients of unemployment insurance and most social welfare recipients are required by law to register with the employment service. But any job seeker, whether unemployed or not, may register to use the ES services.

During the 1990s, approximately 16 to 20 million (different) persons registered annually with the ES. By registering or applying, these individuals gained access to the job matching and training referral services offered by the program.[17] In a typical year, 20 to 30 percent of these persons received a referral, and somewhat less than one-third of those with referrals obtained a job placement. Only a small fraction of the ES's referrals have gone to employment and training participants. However, such persons are more likely to receive JSA and referrals to training.

Table 8.12 also reveals that expenditures and participation in meanstested grant and loan programs for higher education are also greater than for the entire array of employment and training programs. A complete accounting of employment and training programs would in principle attempt to sort out the extent that these other programs constitute substitute services to those offered under JTPA and similar programs.

8.3   Economic and Evaluation Issues

8.3.1   Economic Rationale

The policy rationale underlying employment and training programs is not precise but often turns on one of several arguments. First, joblessness is costly because of the effects it has on state and federal budgets. Consequently, to reduce dependency on various social welfare programs, governments have an incentive to provide job training so that jobless persons become economically self-sufficient. Second, joblessness is costly to the nation not only in terms of lost output and tax revenues, but also in terms

17. This figure is intended to be the number of unduplicated registrants. Persons would be double-counted if they registered with the employment service in two different states. The most recent figure for the number of annual registrants is approximately 16 million. This information is available from the DOL, Employment and Training Administration.

of the social costs associated with a rising incidence of substance abuse, crime, and broken homes, as well as costs associated with the loss of individuals' self-esteem that is thought to come from work. To reduce these costs the government invests in job training programs (NCEP 1987).[18] Moreover, low-income persons lack the resources to invest on their own in job training. Further, because low-income persons face capital constraints, there are social benefits associated with subsidizing training. Despite the intuitive appeal of the last of these rationales, there is little evidence that capital constraints can explain the low skill levels among persons likely to participate in government training programs (Heckman and Smith 1998).

The rationale for subsidizing employment and training programs depends on the reasons that motivate individuals to participate in them in the first place. In most studies of these programs, the determinants of program participation receive attention only because they provide input into econometric procedures that deal with selection bias when estimating the impact of training. However, recent research suggests that study of the determinants of program participation also helps us to understand why individuals participate in these programs and what rationale may motivate public subsidies for these activities (Heckman and Smith 1997; Jacobson, LaLonde, and Sullivan 2002).

As we have discussed, nearly 1 million people enrolled annually in programs operated under JTPA. The vast majority of these persons participated voluntarily. A common view is that these individuals participated for the same reasons that they might have gone to school. If we adopt a schooling model to characterize this process, individuals take training if they expect that the private benefits exceed the private costs. The private benefit includes the subsequent earnings gains associated with training. The total cost of training includes earnings forgone during training and the costs of tuition and supplies, as well as any psychological costs associated with learning in a classroom setting. This model assumes that when in training, individuals forgo labor market opportunities. In the case of government-sponsored training, these costs are sometimes partially or completely subsidized.

More formally, if training takes one period to complete, credit markets operate perfectly, individuals' remaining work lives are N periods, and earnings are zero during training, then individuals seeking to maximize their discounted lifetime earnings participate in training when

(1)
$$\frac{\beta_i}{r}\left[1 - \left(\frac{1}{1+r}\right)^N\right] - Y_{is} - c_i > 0.$$

18. This is the view expressed by the NCEP. The Commission was an independent federal agency established by Congress under Title IV, Section F of the JTPA. Its purpose is to advise Congress and the president on broad employment policy as well as to evaluate JTPA programs.

In equation (1), β_i is the impact of training on earnings for an individual during each period after training is complete. The term $\beta_i/r[1 - 1/(1 + r)^N]$ is the discounted gain from participating in training during the remaining N periods of an individual's work life. The term Y_{is} denotes forgone earnings during the training period s, and c denotes the (private) direct costs of training, such as tuition. We can modify this specification to account for skill depreciation and part-time work during training.

In the foregoing model, individuals participate in training when the impact, β_i, is large. But they also tend to participate when the direct costs of training, c_i, are low, when they are young (so N is large), when they have low earnings, or if they experience an adverse earnings shock during or prior to the training period.

Government training programs affect participation by reducing the private costs of participation. Under programs such as WIA and JTPA, the public sector subsidizes the direct costs of training, c_i. The government has also sometimes subsidized a portion of the forgone earnings costs of training, Y_{is}. Under MDTA and CETA, stipends were often paid to trainees. Today some states allow unemployment insurance recipients to satisfy the "work test" if they participate in an approved training program. Similarly, persons displaced because of imports, including those deemed to have been affected by NAFTA, are eligible to receive extended unemployment insurance benefits if they are enrolled in a training program.

By subsidizing the costs of training, the government increases participation in training. Under some circumstances, this policy also might lead to increased participation among individuals who expect to derive relatively small benefits from training. Consider that the impact of training, β_i, likely varies among individuals. Individuals who expect to derive small gains from training participate only when the private costs of training are low.

The foregoing model provides the theoretical basis for much of the evaluation research on training programs. In particular, it motivates a variety of longitudinal strategies for evaluating these programs, discussed in Ashenfelter (1978); Heckman and Robb (1985a,b), and Heckman, LaLonde, and Smith (1999). A strength of this model is that it corresponds with one of the most consistent empirical findings in this literature. Starting with Ashenfelter's (1978) study of 1964 participants in the MDTA program, many analysts have reported that the earnings of training participants decline just prior to their participation in the program. A nearly universal feature of the data from job training programs is that training participants (a) have low pretraining earnings and (b) experience a decline in their mean earnings prior to their enrollment. For the vast majority of demographic groups and programs, there is a decline in participants' average earnings just prior to the date they enter the program. The drop is most pronounced for white males. (For a fuller discussion of this finding and some examples, see Heckman and Smith 1999; Heckman, LaLonde, and Smith 1999).[19]

Despite the appeal of the schooling model for characterizing participation in government training programs, it may not be the right model. In section 8.2, we observed that many employment and training services could be better characterized as having a job placement rather than a training motive. These programs provide individuals with information about the labor market, employers, and their own set of skills so that they can better match themselves to an appropriate job. In practice, even OJT may offer very little training, but may instead provide a subsidy to employers to learn about prospective low-income hires.

This characterization of employment and training programs is consistent with the view that individuals participate in training to find a job. It also is consistent with the emphasis on job placement in employment and training policy. Studies indicate that people enroll in training programs when they are unemployed, and that transitions into unemployment—whether from employment or from out of the labor force—are strong predictors of participation (Sandell and Rupp 1988; Heckman and Smith 1997). Earnings dynamics that appear so important in predicting program participation appear likely to be explained by dynamics in employment rates. Card and Sullivan (1988) find that the quarterly employment rates of CETA participants dip prior to participation, and Ham and LaLonde (1990) report the same pattern in semimonthly employment rates of very disadvantaged AFDC participants in the National Supported Work Demonstration. Indeed, Heckman and Smith (1997) characterize the participation process as being one motivated by "displacement" from employment and from out of the labor force.

Therefore, an important reason that individuals enroll in employment and training programs is to facilitate their job search. In the context of a job search model, they enter training (a) to increase the arrival rate of job offers and (b) to improve their wage (offer) distribution. However, given that the literature reveals little evidence of wage impacts of these programs, no matter what the motive for participation, it is reasonable to focus on the

19. Several institutional features of most training programs suggest that the participation rule is more complex than that characterized by this simple schooling model. Eligibility for training is partly based on a set of objective criteria, such as family income being below some threshold. For example, under JTPA, single household heads can enroll in publicly subsidized training in Title II programs only if they have had low earnings. Therefore, it is possible that Ashenfelter's dip results from the operation of program eligibility rules that condition on recent earnings (Heckman and Smith 1999). Such rules may select individuals with particular types of earnings patterns into the eligible population. Devine and Heckman (1996) demonstrate that certain family income processes can generate such dips. However, they also show that the substantial difference between the mean earnings patterns of JTPA participants and persons eligible for JTPA implies that Ashenfelter's dip does not result from the mechanical operation of program eligibility rules.

first reason why individuals enroll in these programs. Individuals enroll in training because the expected increase in arrival rates of job offers increases the value of unemployment.

This job search view of training participation also is consistent with the relatively short durations of participants' stays in CT. If there is an important networking component to CT, then people would use CT to facilitate finding a job and would leave the program when they are employed and before training is completed. Indeed, some of the literature reports substantial variation in the duration of training spells even among participants who are observationally similar (Heckman, LaLonde, and Smith 1999).

If the schooling model is not the best way to characterize the participation process, rationales for public support of these activities that are based on the idea that training programs are like schooling are weakened. The idea that targeted individuals face capital constraints becomes a weaker rationale for subsidizing training absent a strong schooling motive. Further, much of CT already takes place in heavily subsidized community or junior colleges.

Instead, the evidence on individuals' participation decisions suggests that individuals may enroll in these programs to learn more about the labor market and themselves. The rationale behind subsidizing these services is in this case similar to that for subsidizing the employment service. By providing information about the world of work, policymakers facilitate the creation of productive job matches. The establishment of one-stop centers in each Workforce Investment Area (under WIA) underscores policymakers' intent to better link the employment and training industry with the job matching responsibilities of the employment service.

8.3.2 Methods Used to Evaluate Training Programs

During the 1970s, evaluations of government employment and training programs began to accumulate. The question most often asked by evaluators was the following: "What is the difference between participants' postprogram earnings and the earnings that they would have received had they not participated in training?" Although other outcomes are of interest, most evaluations of U.S. programs have focused on the impact of training on subsequent earnings.

One argument for this focus is that the impact of training on earnings includes its impact on employment rates, hours paid for among the employed, and hourly or weekly wage rates (Ashenfelter 1974). Another reason so many evaluations focus on earnings is that these studies often use administrative data to estimate the impact of training. These data usually contain only measures of quarterly or annual earnings, or social welfare receipts. Wage data, which is important for assessing whether training raises worker productivity, has rarely been available for U.S. studies.

Despite the seeming simplicity of the central question in these studies, the impact of these programs remains a controversial topic (Heckman et al. 1999). Besides providing information on these programs' effectiveness, an important contribution of the literature on the evaluation of public-sector employment and training programs has been the attention given by researchers in this field to the empirical methods used to identify and to estimate impacts. Most of these methodological studies have been concerned with estimating the impact of government-sponsored training programs in the United States. However, the same issues underlie studies of not only similar programs abroad and of training in the private sector, but also more generally the impact of any policy intervention—whether means tested or not—on individuals.

There have been several influential papers that have contributed to the development of methods used to evaluate these programs. These papers include those by Goldberger (1972); Heckman (1978); Ashenfelter (1978); Barnow, Cain, and Goldberger (1980); Ashenfelter and Card (1985); and Card and Sullivan (1988). The papers by Heckman and Robb (1985a,b) constitute the classic reference for this literature. They describe these alternative methods in detail and introduce a variety of new approaches. More recent surveys by Moffitt (1991) and Heckman, LaLonde, and Smith (1999) provide extensive summaries of this literature. Because of the wealth of existing material on the methods used to evaluate employment and training programs, this chapter provides only a brief summary of some of the key issues.

The Evaluation Problem

The central problem underlying empirical studies of employment and training programs is that it is impossible to observe the same person experiencing two different states at the same time. For individuals who received training, we cannot observe what they would have experienced had they never been trained.[20] If we could observe this counterfactual state, we could measure the impact of training for each individual.

Because it is impossible to observe this counterfactual, evaluators have usually sought to define the conditions under which it is possible to estimate the mean impact of training either for (a) a sample of trainees or (b) a population of eligible persons. Most program evaluations have one of these two goals. The first and most common objective has been to estimate the conditional mean impact of training on those who actually participated: $E(\Delta_i | D_i = 1)$, where Δ_i is the impact of training for individual i, and $D_i = 1$ denotes whether the individual received training. This measure is known as the impact of the "treatment on the treated."

A second and less common objective of program evaluations has been to estimate the unconditional mean impact or $E(\Delta_i)$, which measures the average impact of training for a randomly selected sample of individuals

20. For potential exceptions, see Holland (1986).

from the eligible or target population. When training has the same impact on all potential participants, these two measures of the impact of training are identical. However, when training affects people differently and individuals self-select into training partly based on their expected gains from the program, these measures are not the same.

Econometric work usually seeks to estimate structural parameters, such as the "unconditional" mean impact of training. But when evaluating employment and training programs, this conventional parameter is not very useful for policy purposes. Participation in training is voluntary. But knowing what amounts to the weighted average of the effect of the treatment on the treated and the impact of training on those who were not trained should not be of much interest to policymakers. In the context of U.S. programs, this point is strengthened by the observation that only a very small percentage of eligible persons receive these services each year (Devine and Heckman 1996). An interesting alternative to this parameter is the impact of training on the "marginal" participants (Heckman, LaLonde, and Smith 1999; Aakvik, Heckman, and Vytlacil 1999).

To estimate the impact of training on earnings for those who received training, we need to estimate trainees' earnings had they not been trained. In nonexperimental settings, there are two common solutions to this problem. The first approach is to estimate the counterfactual outcome using the trainees' preprogram outcomes. This approach relies on a before-after comparison.

The second approach is to use the earnings of a comparison group of nontrainees or "no-shows" to the program. The impact of training is then measured as the (regression-adjusted) difference between the mean earnings of training participants and nonparticipants. This approach produces unbiased estimates of training if those who self-select into employment and training programs would have had the same (regression-adjusted) mean outcomes in the absence of training as those individuals in the comparison group. As discussed below, this premise generally is unlikely to hold. If participants selected themselves into training because they had poorer labor market prospects than nonparticipants, the estimated impact of training would be downward biased. The most challenging task for program evaluators is to provide a rationale for why their econometric methodology eliminates selection bias.

Nonexperimental Methods

The nonexperimental approaches to the evaluation problem can be sorted in three categories: (a) method of matching, (b) cross-sectional methods that formally model the selection process, and (c) longitudinal methods.

Methods of Matching. Many program evaluations done by social science consulting firms have identified the impact of employment and training programs using one of several forms of matching. To be sure, most program evaluations use a type of matching when they adopt the practice of screening out of the comparison group individuals who did not satisfy the program eligibility criteria.

The premise underlying the method of matching is that the selection process into the program is captured by observed variables (Rubin 1973). Accordingly, the difference between the outcomes of observationally similar trainees and comparisons produces an unbiased estimate of the training effect. More formally, let X_i be a vector of observed characteristics for individual i, and Y_{i11} equal the outcome if the individual participated and received training; Y_{i10} equal the outcome had the individual who did not participate receive training; Y_{i01} equal the outcome had the individual participated but been denied training; and Y_{i00} equal the outcome if the individual did not participate and did not receive training. The crux of the evaluation problem is that we can not observe $Y_{i11} - Y_{i01}$ for any individual. Instead, we observe Y_{i11} for each of the trainees and Y_{i00} for each of the comparison group members. Both theory and empirical evidence indicate that the selection process into training causes the mean difference between these two outcomes to be a biased estimate of the effect of the treatment on the treated.

The method of matching assumes that once we condition on the vector of observed characteristics, the mean outcome for the trainees had they not received training would equal the mean outcome of the comparisons: $E(Y_{i01}|X) = E(Y_{i00}|X)$. Conditional on the observed characteristics, an unbiased estimate of the training effect, X, is the difference between the conditional mean outcome for the trainees and the conditional mean outcome for the comparisons: $\Delta(X) = E(Y_{i11}|X) - E(Y_{i00}|X)$. An estimate of the mean treatment effect is $\Delta = \Sigma w(X)\Delta(X)$, where the weight, $w(X)$, is the share of trainees with values of $X = x$.

There have been three variants of this method used in the evaluation literature. One approach is known as "cell matching." This procedure is especially practical when there are few available observed characteristics and they are discrete. In this case, it is straightforward to divide the samples of treatments and comparisons into cells—for example, (a) high school dropout and single; (b) high school dropout and married; (c) high school graduate and single; and (d) high school graduate and married. Analysts then compute the difference between mean outcomes within each cell. Card and Sullivan (1988) present an intuitively appealing application of this approach when estimating the impact of training on the employment rates of the 1976 CETA cohort. In their study, they match trainees to comparison group members who had exactly the same employment history during the years leading up to the training year.

A second approach to matching is used when there are many available characteristics, especially when some are continuous. The idea underlying statistical matching is to find an exact match or "nearest neighbor" for each person in the training group from among a sample of nontrainees (Rubin 1979; Dickinson, Johnson, and West 1986; Heckman, LaLonde, and Smith 1999). The Mahalanobis distance has been one of the most common metrics used to select an appropriate comparison group. Predicted earnings is another potential metric, but this approach appears to produce comparison groups whose members have significantly different baseline characteristics from those of the trainees (Fraker and Maynard 1987).

Finally, a third approach has matched trainees and comparisons with the same or similar "propensity scores" (Rosenbaum and Rubin 1983). In this context, the propensity score is the predicted probability that a person in the training group or the comparison group would participate in training given his or her observed characteristics. An advantage of this approach is that it reduces the "dimensionality" of the matching problem by enabling the analyst to match on a single value, the propensity score $P(X)$, instead of matching on many values of X.

To implement this approach, evaluators first estimate a logit model to obtain estimates of $P(Z)$, where Z is a vector of individual characteristics and their interactions thought to be correlated with individuals' participation in training. Then, using one of a variety of different procedures, evaluators match trainees and comparisons with similar $P(Z)$ (Heckman, Ichimura, and Todd 1998; Dehejia and Wahba 1999). Some important recent work using a sample of JTPA-eligible individuals has shown that it can be difficult to find comparisons from economically disadvantaged populations whose characteristics imply that they have a high probability of participating in the program (Heckman et al. 1998).

Cross-Sectional Methods and Selection on Unobservables. The basic model used in cross-sectional methods is derived from the dummy endogenous variable model developed in an influential paper by Heckman (1978). In most work adopting this approach, analysts assume that the outcome of interest, usually quarterly or annual earnings, is a function of a set of individual characteristics, X_i, a dummy variable indicating whether an individual participated in training, D_i, and a residual denoting unobserved characteristics, ε_i:

$$(2) \qquad Y_i = \beta X_i + \delta D_i + \varepsilon_i.$$

In addition, these models specify a participation equation with a latent dependent variable that isolates the determinants of an individual's decision to participate in training:

$$(3) \qquad D_i^* = \gamma Z_i + \eta_i, \text{ where } D_i = 1 \text{ if } D_i^* < 0.$$

In equation (3), Z_i is a vector of observed characteristics that affect whether individuals participate in training, and η_i is a residual denoting unobserved determinants of participation. Ideally, the vector $\mathbf{Z}_i$ includes characteristics that affect whether someone participates in training that are not included in $\mathbf{X}_i$ because they do not affect earnings. An example of such a characteristic might be the distance between a person's residence and a training center.

Evaluations that rely on cross-sectional methods generally adopt one of three approaches to identify the impact of training. First, the simplest approach requires imposing the strong assumption that the errors in the outcome and participation equations are uncorrelated: $E(e_i, \eta_i) = 0$. In this case, the training effects can be estimated simply by regressing the outcome, Y_i, on all observed characteristics, including those in $\mathbf{Z}$. This approach assumes that the trainees are selected into training based on some known characteristics (Barnow, Cain, and Goldberger 1980).

In the second approach, analysts relax the assumption that the errors in the outcome and participation equations are uncorrelated. Now it is assumed that there is selection on the unobservables. In this case, the training effect is usually identified from a combination of distributional assumptions about e_i and η_i and one or more restrictions on the vector of observed characteristics, $\mathbf{X}$. Less parametric methods have been proposed for identifying the training effect, although they have yet to be adapted in a significant amount of research (Heckman 1990; Powell 1994).

By far the most widely used method that follows this second approach is Heckman's two-stage estimator (Heckman 1979; Björklund and Moffitt 1987). Use of this estimator is especially common in evaluations of European employment and training programs. It has been used less frequently in U.S. evaluations, largely because these studies have relied less on cross-sectional data (Heckman, LaLonde, and Smith 1999). However, one of the most influential U.S. evaluations, Mathematica's evaluation of the 1977 Job Corps cohort, adopts this approach (Mallar 1978; Mallar et al. 1982).

A third approach to identifying the training effect uses the method of instrumental variables. This approach has been used rarely in conventional nonexperimental evaluations of training programs. In nearly all such studies, analysts have had difficulty producing a plausible instrument. Usually the available data have not been sufficiently rich to include any variables that might serve as an instrument. More fundamentally, the design of these programs creates an environment in which it is hard to construct a natural experiment.

Longitudinal Methods. The availability of federal and especially state administrative earnings records has fostered reliance on longitudinal methods to evaluate many U.S. employment and training programs. This practice has been heavily influenced by Ashenfelter's study of the 1964 MDTA cohort that relied on individuals' annual earnings records from the U.S. Social Security Administration (Ashenfelter 1978). A strength of administrative data like those used by Ashenfelter is that they contain long earnings histories, both prior to and after training. Their shortcoming, however, is that they often contain little information about individuals' demographic characteristics.

Evaluations that use longitudinal methods identify the impact of training by assuming that the program does not affect earnings prior to individuals' participation in the program. They often rely on a model that assumes the following structure of earnings:

$$(4) \qquad Y_{it} = \delta D_{it} + b_i + \lambda_t + \varepsilon_{it},$$

where b_i is an individual fixed effect, λ_t is a common time effect, and ε_{it} is a random disturbance denoting individuals' unobserved characteristics that vary through time. A key assumption in these analyses concerns whether the residual is serially correlated. If movement in ε_{it} represents "transitory" movements in individuals' earnings, then a natural estimator of the impact of training is the least squares estimate of d in the following:

$$(5) \qquad Y_{it} - Y_{is-1} = \delta D_{it} + (\lambda_t - \lambda_{s-1}) + (\varepsilon_{it} - \varepsilon_{is-1}).$$

In equation (5), period $s - 1$ is the period before training. Indeed, in the model depicted in equation (4), earnings in any pretraining period are sufficient to identify the impact of training. If no time-varying observed characteristics are available, the least squares estimate, also known as the difference-in-differences estimator, is simply the difference between the mean change in the trainees' earnings and the mean change in the comparisons' earnings.[21] If time-varying variables such as age are available, it is straightforward to include them in the model and estimate the training effect, δ, using least squares.

In practice, the problem with estimates based on equation (5) is that they overstate the impact of training (Ashenfelter 1978; LaLonde 1986; Heckman, Hotz, and Dabos 1987; Heckman and Hotz 1989; Heckman, LaLonde, and Smith 1999). The reason for this result is that movements in the residual, ε_{it}, are not necessarily transitory and are serially correlated. Changes in this component of earnings, $(\varepsilon_{it} - \varepsilon_{is-1})$, likely motivated the unemployed to participate in training. Empirical work indicates that this time-varying component of earnings is serially correlated. Trainees' earnings are not unexpectedly low simply during the training period; they tend to be unexpectedly low in prior periods as well. This tendency produces the phenomenon described earlier as Ashenfelter's dip. Under these circumstances it matters which pretraining year analysts use as the base year in the

---

21. To implement this estimator it is not necessary to have longitudinal data. If analysts have samples from repeated cross-sections of the same populations of trainees and controls, it is not necessary that the trainees and comparisons in the posttraining period be the same persons as the trainees and comparisons in the pretraining period (Heckman and Robb 1985a, b; Heckman, LaLonde, and Smith 1999).

difference-in-differences estimator. More refined evaluations of employment and training programs have used the availability of longitudinal histories to estimate the covariance structure of earnings (see Ashenfelter and Card 1985). Such analyses suggest among other things that the earnings model in equation (4) should also include an individual-specific time trend.

The Experimental Solution

A seemingly simpler approach to the evaluation problem is to adopt an experimental design. Randomization applied to the sample of individuals who apply for and are admitted into training solves the evaluation problem by creating a comparison group consisting of individuals who selected into training the same way as the trainees.[22] As a result of randomization, the distributions of the treatments' and controls' observed and unobserved baseline characteristics should be similar.

Another way of characterizing the experimental solution is that randomization solves the evaluation problem because it creates an instrumental variable that leads to variation in the receipt of training among training participants (Heckman 1996). The control group members are participants who were randomly denied services. Under these conditions, the impact of training can be estimated from the difference between the treatments' and controls' mean earnings.

Despite the advantage of simplicity, these social experiments have important limitations (Heckman 1992). Many of the complications that arise in experimental evaluations, such as sample attrition, also arise in nonexperimental studies (Kornfeld and Bloom 1996). However, some limitations are unique to social experiments. First, given the decentralized operation of many U.S. employment and training programs, the integrity of the experimental design depends on the cooperation of many local officials and administrators. In such a policy setting, the experience with the National JTPA Study is illustrative of how difficult it is to conduct a social experiment of an ongoing program (Doolittle and Traeger 1990; Hotz 1992). By contrast, the National Job Corps Study appears to have been more successful because this experiment evaluated a program that is under the control of federal authorities (Schochet, Burghardt, and Glazerman 2000, 2001).

A second problem that arises in social experiments is that members of the control group may obtain the same services through another community organization or sometimes even the same provider. This phenomenon, known as "control group substitution," has been substantial in many social experiments (Heckman, LaLonde, and Smith 1999). A related problem oc-

---

22. Randomization eliminates selection bias as a source of bias in the estimated impacts of training. However, the selection problem is usually not eliminated. Participants continue to self-select into training from the population. Random assignment creates a comparison group in which the selection from the population is the same as for the trainees.

curs with the treatment group members because participation is voluntary. In practice, many persons assigned to the treatment group do not show up to receive services or drop out after a short stay in the program.

Social experiments most often estimate the effect of receiving an offer to participate in training, "the intention to treat," and not the impact of training itself. When there are many no-shows among the treatments and there is control group substitution, the evaluation of the training effect requires the analysts to rely on one of the nonexperimental methods described above.[23] In practice, social experiments work better when they test the impact of services that are valued by participants and difficult to obtain elsewhere in the community. An example of such a study was the National Supported Work Demonstration (Hollister, Kemper, and Maynard 1984). Its high-cost services were not otherwise available. Consequently, this program had high rates of participation among the treatment group members and low levels of control group substitution.

A third limitation of social experiments arises because many questions about the impacts of employment and training programs are not easily evaluated with an experimental design. These questions include the effects of training on program participation, on the earnings of those who complete training, on hourly wages, or on the duration of subsequent employment spells (see Moffitt 1992; Ham and LaLonde 1996; Eberwein, Ham, and LaLonde 1997). In order to examine these questions analysts must rely on the same nonexperimental methods previously described. In addition, experimental evaluations are also infeasible when evaluators are asked to assess the impact of a program on individuals who participated in it in the past. The classic study by Ashenfelter (1974, 1978) of the 1964 MDTA cohort and the influential CETA studies of the 1976 cohort are examples of such studies (Barnow 1987). In instances such as these, researchers have no choice but to rely on nonexperimental methods.

8.4 Survey of Program Impacts

8.4.1 The Influence of Social Experiments

As explained above, an unusual characteristic of the empirical literature in this field compared with other areas in the social sciences is the frequent use of social experiments, mainly in the United States. Part of the reason for the proliferation of experimental evaluations in this field has been the skepticism expressed by both the academic and policy-making communities about the results of nonexperimental studies (see Ashenfelter and Card

23. When experimental data are available, a nonexperimental estimator of the training effect uses the variable indicating whether an individual was randomly assigned into the treatment group as an instrument (Imbens and Angrist 1994).

1985; Burtless and Orr 1986; Burtless 1995). Particularly important in heightening this skepticism were the results of six major evaluations of the 1976 CETA cohort (Barnow 1987). Although studies of different training cohorts have generated a considerable range of estimated impacts, these studies examined the same group of trainees and used essentially the same data. Yet the estimated impacts in these studies ranged from $1,210 to $1,350 for male participants and from $20 to $2,200 for female participants. Not surprisingly, one group of CETA evaluators concluded that

> [a]lthough these evaluations have all been based on the same data sets, they have produced an extremely wide range of estimated program impacts. In fact, depending on the particular study chosen, one could conclude that CETA programs were quite effective in improving the post-program earnings of participants or, alternatively, that CETA programs reduced the post-program earnings of participants relative to comparable nonparticipants. (Dickinson, Johnson, and West 1987, 452–53)

In the mid-1980s an advisory panel created by the DOL reviewed this and related evidence and recommended that policymakers rely more on experimental designs to evaluate their programs (Stromsdorfer et al. 1985).

To be sure, prior to this report, social experiments, such as the National Supported Work Demonstration, the Louisville WIN Laboratory, and the first Work-Welfare demonstrations, were already underway or completed. But this recommendation influenced the mix of experimental and nonexperimental studies. It motivated the DOL to fund the large experimental studies such as the JOBSTART Demonstration, the National JTPA Study, and the National Job Corps Study.

Social experiments have also been used to test alternative nonexperimental strategies to address the evaluation problem. A modest literature has accumulated that attempts to use alternative nonexperimental methods to replicate the results of experiments.[24] One approach has been to use the treatment group from the experimental study and then examine whether an analyst would have been able to replicate the experimental results using alternative comparisons groups and econometric methods. A second approach compares the control group to alternative comparison groups. This approach has the advantage of focusing analysts' attention on the selection problem.

These studies have generally concluded that nonexperimental methods have a difficult time replicating experimental results. But they do suggest that nonexperimental methods are likely to perform significantly better when comparisons group members are drawn from the same labor market

---

24. See, for example, LaLonde (1984, 1986); Fraker and Maynard (1987); Heckman, Hotz, and Dabos (1987); LaLonde and Maynard (1987); Heckman and Hotz (1989); Friedlander and Robbins (1995); Heckman et al. (1998); Dehejia and Wahba (1999); Smith and Todd (2003); Wilde and Hollister (2001); and Zhao (2001).

as the program participants. It also appears to be important that information on treatments' and controls' desired outcomes be drawn from the same instrument. This finding suggests the shortcomings of nonexperimental evaluations that begin with rich survey and baseline data on a group of program participants and then attempt afterward to construct a comparison group from administrative records.

The evidence from this literature on whether richer data or more sophisticated econometric methods are more important for overcoming the evaluation problem is yet to generate a consensus. The study by Heckman et al. (1998) demonstrates just how difficult and costly it is to collect enough covariates to solve the selection program, even when comparison group members are from the same labor market. Some studies suggest that less parametric methods, such as propensity score matching, perform better than more conventional econometric approaches (Dehejia and Wahba 1999). But other studies, such as the one by Smith and Todd (2000), which uses the same data, disagree. They conclude that in the absence of better data, these less parametric methods do not generate substantially improved nonexperimental impact estimates.

8.4.2   The Impact of Employment and Training Programs

The empirical literature on the impact of employment and training programs contains a relatively large number of both experimental and nonexperimental studies. However, experimental and nonexperimental evaluations often report estimates of different parameters. Because treatment no-shows and control group substitution can be substantial in social experiments, the impact parameter measured in experimental evaluations is often the impact of the intention to treat and not the effect of training on the trained. Nonexperimental studies usually report the impact of training on those who actually received the services. Estimates of the comparable parameter in most experimental studies would generally be larger than the estimate reported in these evaluations.

The point that experimental and nonexperimental studies often report different impact parameters is now widely recognized. Many recent experimental evaluations report estimates of both the intention-to-treat parameter and a training-on-trained parameter (Bloom et al. 1997; Schochet, Burghardt, and Glazerman 2000, 2001). The later estimator, known as the "Bloom estimator," is usually formed by simply dividing the "intention to treat" estimate by the fraction of treatments that enrolled and received program services (Bloom 1984; Heckman, Smith, and Taber 1998).

Experimental Evidence

Starting in the mid-1970s, some U.S. training evaluators began to use experimental designs to evaluate employment and training programs. Today a sizable body of evidence exists on the impact of relatively low-cost services on economically disadvantaged persons, especially for adult single women. These studies have been surveyed elsewhere by many other authors (see, e.g., Friedlander and Gueron 1990; LaLonde 1995; and Heckman, LaLonde, and Smith 1999). Here we summarize some of the key findings using as examples evidence from a few programs.

The experimental evaluations indicate that a variety of employment and training services can raise the postprogram earnings of disadvantaged adult women but that such programs have mixed impacts on disadvantaged adult men and usually no effects on the earnings of youth. As shown by table 8.13, when adult women participate in these programs these earnings gains usually (a) are modest in size, (b) persist for several years, (c) arise from a variety of treatments, and (d) sometimes are achieved at remarkably little expense.[25] Further, although job search assistance is generally the most cost-effective treatment, more expensive services such as work experience and OJT often produce modestly larger earnings gains.

The experimental evidence indicates that very low-cost strategies, such as job search training, can significantly raise adult women's postprogram earnings. For example, the Arkansas WORK program tested the value of mandated job search assistance (and the threat of sanctions) by requiring a randomly selected group of AFDC applicants and recipients to participate in two weeks of group job search assistance followed by sixty days of individual job search.[26] As shown by table 8.13, the Arkansas WORK program was remarkably cost-effective. The cost of the job search assistance services amounted to $183 per participant. Yet even though participation was mandatory, AFDC applicants and recipients who participated in these services had earnings that were $287 higher in the first year following the baseline into the program than were controls' earnings. By the third year following their assignment those earnings gains had grown to $535. In addition, in results not shown in the table the program reduced welfare payments by about $250 in the first year and in the third year after the baseline. Therefore, not only did the program pay for itself, but it also led to (small) long-term earnings gains for AFDC participants.[27] Similar, if somewhat less striking, results were reported for job search assistance in the Louisville WIN Laboratory experiments and in other work-welfare demonstrations (Wolfhagen and Goldman 1983).

Experimental studies have also tested the effectiveness of job search

25. In recent work, Black et al. (2001) use data on unemployed workers in Kentucky to explore the question of whether the "threat of training is more effective than training itself."

26. See Friedlander et al. (1985). Women whose children were less than three years old and who volunteered for WORK were also randomly assigned into either the treatment or the control group.

27. The cost-benefit analysis indicates that taxpayers derived considerable benefit from the Arkansas WORK Program. The participants appear not to have benefited financially from the program. The earnings gains were "offset by reductions in AFDC and Medicaid payments" (see Friedlander et al. 1985, 21–22).

Table 8.13   **Impacts of Selected Experimental Evaluations of Employment and Training Services for Economically Disadvantaged Adult Women**

		Impacts on Employment Rates and Earnings[a]			
Study	Costs ($)[b]	Last Quarter (%)[c]	Year 1/2 ($)	Year 3/4/5 ($)	Earnings (%)
Job Search Assistance					
Arkansas WORK	244	6.2*	339*	487*	31
Louisville (WIN-1)	206	5.3*	425*	643*	18
Cook County, IL	231	1.2	12	n.a.	1
Louisville (WIN-2)	340	14.2*	679*	n.a.	43
San Diego—CWEP	891	-0.7	402*	n.a.	8
Food Stamp E & T	180	-2.5	-90	n.a.	-3
Minnesota—MFIP[d]	n.a.	14.5*	921*	n.a.	30
Job Search Assistance and Work Experience					
West Virginia	388	-1.0	25	n.a.	4
Virginia ES	631	4.6*	106	387*	11
San Diego—CWEP	690	3.8*	1,120*	n.a.	23
Baltimore Options	1,407	0.4	231	764*	17
Job Search Assistance and CT or OJT Services					
Maine TOP	2,972	1.1	433*	1,720*	36
San Diego SWIM	964	0.3	509*	180	15
New Jersey	1,165	n.a.	874*	n.a.	14
GAIN (JOBS):	3,757	5.9*	339*	740*	25
Alameda (Oakland)	6,036	6.0*	266	901*	37
Los Angeles	6,356	1.9	-5	178	9
Riverside	1,753	7.5*	1,173*	1,176*	40
San Diego	2,099	2.7*	445*	830*	23
MFSP San Jose (CETP	5,132	8.6*	1,470*	n.a.	25
MFSP other sites	4,525	1.2	400	n.a.	6
Florida PI (JOBS)	1,339	0.4	93	n.a.	3
Work Experience and Training					
National Supported Work	8,614	7.1	657	1,062	43
AFDC Homemaker	8,371	n.a.	2,135*	n.a.	n.a.
NJS (JTPA)	1,028	n.a.	691*	441*	7
Recommended for CT	1,690	n.a.	359	n.a.	n.a.
Recommended for OJT	643	n.a.	747*	n.a.	n.a.

Source: LaLonde (1995) and Heckman, LaLonde, and Smith (1999).

Notes: All dollar figures are in 1997 dollars. N.a. indicates not available. CWEP = California Work Experience Program. MFIP = Minnesota Family Investment Program. E&T = Employment and Training. TOPS = Training Opportunities in the Private Sector Program. SWIM = Saturation Work and Initiative Model. GAIN = Greater Avenues for Independence Program. MFSP = Minority Family Single Parent Demonstration. PI = Project Independence. NJS = National JTPA Study.

[a]The earnings' impacts are annual (or annualized) difference between the treatments' and controls' mean earnings during the first or second year (Year 1/2) and during the third, fourth, or fifth year (Year 3/4/5).

[b]Average net costs are the incremental costs of providing services to the members of the treatment group.

[c]"Employment rate last quarter" refers to the difference between treatments' and controls' employment rates during the last quarter of the follow-up period for which data were available.

[d]Figures are for long-term welfare recipients only. Two other components of this program included threats of sanctions and financial incentives for welfare recipients to find work.

*Impact is statistically significant at the 10 percent level.

training coupled with mandated work experience. An interesting feature of these experiments was that welfare applicants and recipients were required to participate in employment and training services as a condition for receiving welfare benefits. This requirement enabled policymakers to evaluate the effect of these services on a wider segment of the disadvantaged population, instead of the narrower subset of program "volunteers." Another important feature of these experiments was that the design allowed policymakers to assess the separate effects of job search assistance and work experience on participants' earnings. In the San Diego studies, when women applied for AFDC, they were randomly assigned to one of three groups. Those assigned to the control group were not required to participate in work-welfare programs.[28] The second group was required to participate in job search assistance in order to receive cash benefits. Finally, the third group not only had to participate in job search assistance but, if they remained unemployed, also had to participate in WE.

As shown by table 8.13, the earnings of AFDC applicants who were assigned to either of the treatment groups in the San Diego-I experiment were $600 higher than those who were assigned to the control group. Although the cost-benefit calculations were less impressive than those for the Arkansas WORK program, they indicate, nonetheless, that the program benefited taxpayers (see Goldman, Friedlander, and Long 1986, xxv–xxxix and 165–84). Breaking down the result by program component, the studies indicated that job search assistance raised women's short-term earnings, whereas mandated WE raised women's long-term earnings.

Perhaps the most persuasive evidence that economically disadvantaged women can benefit from employment and training programs comes from the National Supported Work (NSW) Demonstration. The most significant finding from this study is that WE modestly raised long-term AFDC participants' earnings for at least seven years after the end of the program. In 1986, seven years after the NSW program had ended, the treatments' annual earnings exceeded the controls' earnings by about $1,000 (Couch 1992). Although these gains from the NSW program are among the most substantial and long-lasting documented, this program was also relatively expensive to operate. The social cost of NSW was approximately $7,000 per participant (Kemper, Long, and Thornton 1984). But if the program-induced earnings gains persisted throughout a woman's work life, the real social rate of return from training would be about 15 percent. This gain appears to constitute very productive social investment.

The National JTPA Study provides additional support that government training programs can raise the earnings of adult women. The thirty-month evaluation found that access to Title IIA programs raised adult women's earnings by approximately $700 during the twelve-month period

---

28. This group was required to participate in the preexisting WIN program. However, in practice this program placed few constraints on the controls' behavior.

prior to the thirty-month follow-up interview. This gain amounted to 10 percent of the control groups' earnings. The (incremental) social cost of JTPA services provided the trainees was less than $2,000. Therefore, should these earnings gains persist, the social rate of return from JTPA is likely to be substantial (Heckman, LaLonde, and Smith 1999). Indeed, a U.S. Government Accounting Office (GAO) study that used U.S. Social Security Administration earnings data reported that among adult women in the 1988 training cohort, the treatments had significantly higher earnings than the controls during four of the five postbaseline years (GAO 1996).

In contrast to what is known from social experiments about the effects of employment and training programs on economically disadvantaged women, much less is known from social experiments about their effects on adult males and youths. What is known indicates that although these programs sometimes raise males' earnings, they also sometimes have no effect. The NSW demonstration found that guaranteed work experience did raise the earnings of disadvantaged ex-criminal offenders and ex-drug addicts, but this impact was not statistically significant. The work-welfare demonstrations indicated that the job search and work experience services increase the postprogram earnings only for the minority of men who had a prior history of receiving welfare. The National JTPA Study (NJS) found that adult men experienced gains from JTPA services similar to their female counterparts. These earnings gains were approximately $650 per year or 7 percent of the controls' earnings (Orr et al. 1994, 82). A follow-up study using Social Security earnings data suggests that these impacts are smaller during the fifth year after the baseline (GAO 1996).

Findings for Youths and the National Job Corps Study

The findings from the few social experiments that study disadvantaged youths are less encouraging than the findings for disadvantaged adults. For example, more than seven years of follow-up data indicate that the prolonged WE provided to disadvantaged high school dropouts in the NSW demonstration had no effect on their subsequent earnings (Couch 1992). Similarly, the JOBSTART demonstration, which provided disadvantaged youths with services similar to those of Job Corps but without the residential living centers, did not generate significantly higher earnings for its participants during the four postprogram years followed in the evaluation (Cave and Doolittle 1991). Finally, the National JTPA Study finds no evidence that disadvantaged youths benefited from this program's relatively low-cost services (Orr et al. 1994).

The National Job Corps Study presents the most recent opportunity to use an experimental design to assess whether there are employment and training services that can improve the employment prospects of economically disadvantaged youths. As previously discussed, Job Corps is much more comprehensive and expensive than the services tested in previous so-

Table 8.14   **Impacts of Selected Experimental and Nonexperimental Studies of Job Corps on Post-Program Annual Earnings**

Authors	Program Cohort	Earnings Impact
O'Neill (1973)	1969	$504
Gay and Borus (1980)	1969–1972	–$273/$188[a]
Mallar et al. (1982)	1977	$2,032*/$1,016*[b]
JOBSTART	1986	–$260
National Job Corps Study	1995	
Year 1		–$2,093*/$1,212*[b]
Year 2		$1/–$188[b]
Year 3		$1,183*/$943*[b]
Year 4		$1,362*/$1,178*[b]
Residential		$1,235*/$1,218[b]
Nonresidential		$3,169*/–$1,076[b]
16–17-year-olds		$983*
18–19-year-olds		$323
20–24-year-olds		$2,871*

Sources: O'Neill (1973, 43); Cave and Doolittle (1991, 175); LaLonde (1995, 157); Schochet, Burghardt, and Glazerman (2001, pp.D.5–D.24, D.28).

Notes: Impacts are expressed in 1999 dollars. Annual earnings equal the estimated impact on weekly earnings times 52.

[a]Separate estimates for whites and minorities.

[b]Separate estimates for males and females; the female figures when evaluating Job Corps members assigned to residential and nonresidential centers in the National Job Corps Study are for females without children.

*Statistically significant at the 10 percent level.

cial experiments. Evidence that Job Corps is effective would underscore the importance of its comprehensive treatment for this population and, in light of the JOBSTART results, also suggest the importance of its residential model.

As shown by tables 8.14 and 8.15, previous studies of Job Corps report mixed results. Collectively the experimental and nonexperimental studies do not provide consistent evidence that Job Corps improves participants' employment prospects. Until now the most influential of these studies has been the Mathematica evaluation of the 1977 Job Corps cohort (Mallar 1978; Mallar et al. 1982; Long, Mallar, and Thornton 1981). As shown in the tables, this (nonexperimental) analysis of four years of postprogram earnings data indicates that Job Corps increased male participants' subsequent earnings by about $2,000 per year. Although this impact is large, because Job Corps is such an expensive program—the social costs net the value of in-program output amounted to about $12,000 per participant—they would have had to continue for more than two additional years to justify the costs of the program. However, if these four-year earnings impacts did persist throughout a participant's working life, Job Corps would prove to be a remarkably productive social investment.

Table 8.15   National Job Corps Study, 1995 Cohort, Impacts by Ethnicity and Age

	Ethnicity		
Age/Center Type	White	Black	Hispanic
16–17	$3,146*	$572	–$743
18–19	–$572	$744	$0
20–24	$5,872*	$3,432*	–$1,945
Hispanic center	–$343	$744	–$1,400

Sources: O'Neill (1973, 43); Cave and Doolittle (1991, 175); LaLonde (1995, 157); Schochet, Burghardt, and Glazerman (2001, pp. D.5–D.24, D.28).

Notes: Increase in participants' annual earnings during fourth year after the baseline; annual earnings equal estimated impact on weekly earnings times 52. Impacts are expressed in 1999 dollars.

*Statistically significant at the 10 percent level.

It is in this context that policymakers and analysts have awaited the results of the National Job Corps Study. As shown by table 8.15, the last year of earnings data collected during the forty-eight-month interview indicates that the opportunity to participate in Job Corps raised treatments' earnings by $1,258 or 12 percent. This impact held for both males and females and is comparable to, if not somewhat larger than, the impact of a year of formal schooling. Further, unlike the experience with JOBSTART, this impact is not clearly liked to differing effectiveness of the residential and non-residential centers.

One important implication of the National Job Corps Study is that it demonstrates that comprehensive employment and training services can improve the earnings and employment history of disadvantaged youths and young adults. Another implication of the study is that if the earnings impacts persist throughout a participant's career, the program generates substantial net social benefits. Under these circumstances, the study indicates that society receives $2 for every $1 spent on Job Corps (McConnell and Glazerman 2001).

A closer look at the evaluation reveals considerable heterogeneity in the estimated impacts of Job Corps. The impacts for sixteen- to seventeen-year-old participants, who tend to come from the most economically disadvantaged backgrounds, are substantially larger than the average impact for eighteen- to nineteen-year-olds, but smaller than the impact for the twenty- to twenty-four-year-old participants. For the former group, the estimated impact is $983 per year.[29] Should the magnitude of this impact persist, and given the benefits associated with the reported reduction in the treatments' use of the criminal justice system, which are concentrated

29. Author's calculation based on Schochet, Burghardt, and Glazerman (2000, pp. D15–D23).

in this age group, the longer-term cost-benefit analysis for this especially hard-to-serve group may turn out to be very impressive.

The foregoing results for Job Corps youths do not provide as much evidence that the program works for disadvantaged youths as first appears. As shown by table 8.15, the positive impacts for youths under twenty are concentrated among sixteen- to seventeen-year-old white participants who did not enroll at centers with relatively large concentrations of Hispanics. For other Job Corps youths the results look more like other studies of youth participants in employment and training programs for which it has been difficult to find evidence that these programs work. This assessment is especially true for the Hispanic youths in Job Corps.

Indeed, the most striking results reported in the National Job Corps study indicate that the gains from the program are concentrated among white and black twenty- to twenty-four-year-olds. As shown by the table, the estimated impacts for these two groups are extremely large, even given the size of the investment. These results support policymakers' decision during the 1980s to expand eligibility for Job Corps to young adults.

Nonexperimental Evaluations

Despite the controversy sometimes associated with nonexperimental evaluations of employment and training programs, a pattern of results has emerged that is broadly consistent with and reinforces the findings from the experimental literature. Studies of different cohorts of adult women spanning a three-decade period find that government employment and training programs consistently raise their subsequent earnings. As shown by table 8.16, annual impacts of $1,000 or more are common. As a rule, when the earnings impacts are positive for both adult men and adult women, the impacts tend to be larger for women than for men. For example, Ashenfelter's (1978) study of the 1964 MDTA cohort found that training raised minority males' earnings by $675 and minority females' earnings by $2,000. These impacts are larger than usually reported, but they are not usual in this literature. The direct costs of MDTA's CT were nearly $10,000 (see Ashenfelter 1978, 56), but about one-half of these costs included a stipend paid to the trainee. If these estimated impacts persisted for the remainder of trainees' work lives, the real rate of return to training would be 7 percent per year for men, but a substantial 20 percent per year for women. These cost figures do not include forgone earnings, which are smaller for female participants, especially economically disadvantaged female participants. Consequently, although the social rates of return of CT training are smaller than indicated here, these estimates imply that the returns from training women are substantial.

As was discussed in section 8.2, the direct costs of training services usually amount to only a few thousand dollars per participant. Given the magnitude of the estimated impacts in nonexperimental studies, it is essential

Table 8.16   Selected Impacts of Nonexperimental Evaluations of Employment and Training Programs under MDTA and CETA (increase in postprogram annual earnings)

Study	Training Cohort	Men (whites/minorities; $)	Women (whites/minorities; $)
A. Nonexperimental Estimates for Economically Disadvantaged Adult Participants			
Ashenfelter (1978)	1964 MDTA	945/$655	2,191/$1,939
Kiefer (1979)	1969 MDTA	–2,103/–2,329	1,977/2,721
Gay and Borus (1980)	1969–72 MDTA	158/167	1,425/391
Cooley, McGuire and Prescott (1979)	1969–71 MDTA	1,448	2,115
Westat (1984)	1976 CETA	–12/264	1,020/831
Bassi (1983)	1976 CETA	63/–1,095	1,335/2,770
Dickinson, Johnson, and West (1986)	1976 CETA	–1,612	25
Geraci (1984)	1976 CETA	0	2,103
Bloom and McLaughlin (1982)	1976 CETA	378	1,914
Ashenfelter and Card (1985)	1976 CETA	1,700	2,304
Dickinson, Johnson, and West (1986)	1/76–6/76 CETA	–1,070	567
Westat (1984)	1977 CETA	1,171/1,536	1,247/1,776
Bassi et al. (1984)	Welfare 1977 CETA	1,473/–239	2,091/1,587
Bassi et al. (1984)	Nonwelfare 1977 CETA	176/566	1,712/1,851
B. Nonexperimental Estimates for Economically Disadvantaged Youth Participants			
Cooley, McGuire and Prescott (1979)	1969–71 MDTA	1,549	756
Gay and Borus (1980)	1969–72 Job Corps	–273/188	–1,614/–409
Mallar et al. (1982)	1977 Job Corps	2,443/2,710	1,016
Dickinson, Johnson, and West (1986)	1976 CETA	–1,398	466
Westat et al. (1984)	1976 CETA-WE	69 (males and females)	
Westat et al. (1987)	1977 CETA-WE	1,305 (males and females)	
Bassi et al. (1984)	1977 CETA	–1,272/–1,675	100,326

Sources: See Barnow (1987), LaLonde (1995), and Heckman, LaLonde, and Smith (1999, table 24, p. 2065).

Notes: All dollar figures are in 1999 dollars. MDTA refers to programs funded under the Manpower Development and Training Act, 1962; CETA refers to programs funded under the Comprehensive Employment and Training Act, 1973. The sets of estimates for each gender refer to the training effect for whites and minorities, respectively.

for cost-benefit analyses of these programs to know how long these impacts persist. Ashenfelter's study was one of the first, and for a long time one of the relatively few, that assessed the impact of government training services beyond a year or two after participants left the program. Although evidence on these programs' long-term effects is scarce, there is some evidence that these impacts last several years and do not dissipate at pronounced rates (McConnell and Glazerman 2001). Accordingly, as suggested by some of the experimental studies, the internal rates of return to these programs may be very large. Indeed, it is not unreasonable to assert that when targeted toward adult women, the federal government's employment and training programs constitute a more productive social investment than a year of formal schooling.

The case in support of these programs is less strong when they are targeted toward adult males. As shown by table 8.16, the nonexperimental studies suggest that these programs produce smaller and less consistently positive impacts on males. But this is not always the case (Heckman, LaLonde, and Smith 1999). It is possible that the evaluation problem is more difficult to address for male than for female training participants (see Bassi 1984). This possibility might explain the greater uncertainty about the impacts of these programs on males.

8.5 Conclusions

During the last four decades policymakers have made modest investments in a variety of employment and training services designed to improve the skills and employment prospects of the economically disadvantaged and unemployed. Compared to other programs surveyed in this volume, expenditures on such services are relatively small. During FY 1998, the federal government spent about as much on JTPA as it did on programs like WIC, Head Start, child care and development block grants, and the school lunch program (Congressional Research Service 1999).

Government training programs under WIA, JTPA, and CETA differ from other programs covered in this volume, because (a) they are not necessarily limited to low-income people and (b) low-income persons are not necessarily entitled to receive these services. As shown above, many JTPA participants had previously held jobs in which their average wages were above the (national) average hourly earnings for production and non-supervisory workers. Under WIA, program operators must give priority to low-income persons, especially those receiving public assistance, but they are not required to limit participation to the economically disadvantaged.

This ambiguity in the groups targeted to receive assistance from federal employment and training programs is not surprising, given the frequent policy shifts on this issue during the last forty years. During this period, policymakers have targeted their programs alternately toward the most economically disadvantaged and toward otherwise moderately skilled displaced workers. Current policy calls for devoting a relatively larger share of WIA resources to more employable adult participants. This emphasis constitutes a significant shift away from policy during the early years under JTPA.

These policy changes mirror those that have occurred under PRWORA. The policy changes embodied in this legislation adversely affect potential long-term welfare recipients. But compared with AFDC as it operated after 1981, the current program is a more generous one for more employable welfare recipients who are prone to short spells on welfare. Because of expanded earnings disregards and child care subsidies, and the greater flexibility granted states to use resources to provide supportive social services, it is easier for these persons to work and still receive cash benefits. By contrast, the changes to the AFDC program in 1981 adversely affected this group by making it more difficult to work and collect benefits.

During the last four decades, policymakers have also changed their emphasis on services that provide vocational training and on those designed to help participants quickly find new jobs. In the early years, the emphasis was on vocational training in classroom settings. Starting in the mid-sixties, policymakers sought to provide more training on the job in private firms. By the 1970s the emphasis had moved to job placement as more resources were spent on providing job search skills, work experience, and public-sector employment. Under JTPA greater emphasis was placed on CT, especially as the program evolved. During these early years of WIA it seems likely that the emphasis will continue to be on CT with some attention given to better coordination between this service and other supportive social services.

During the last three decades, policymakers have sought to determine the effectiveness of their employment and training programs. Per dollar spent on these programs, it is likely that they have been as carefully evaluated as any social program in the United States—and probably in the world, for that matter. Although controversy persists about their impacts, several patterns have emerged from the many experimental and nonexperimental evaluations. First, these programs do not have a substantial effect on poverty rates. This finding occurs because the magnitudes of the investments are generally small. The investments are a lot less than a year of formal schooling. Consequently, it would be surprising, perhaps implausible, for them to have a dramatic impact on the living standards of their participants.

Despite the modest size of the investments in employment and training services, the impacts for economically disadvantaged adult women have been consistently positive. Although too little is known about the long-term impacts of these programs, what we do know suggests that, for this population at least, they may generate a substantial social rate of return. Indeed, depending on the assumptions about how long the impacts persist, a reasonable case could be made that on the margin it would be socially beneficial to raise taxes to finance more of these services for this particular population.

By contrast to the results for adult women, the results for economically disadvantaged youths are discouraging. With the possible exception of Job Corps, there is little evidence that these programs produce earnings gains for youths. Consequently, policies such as the one that required local administrators during the early years of JTPA to spend 40 percent of their resources on youths were probably wasteful. In the absence of other proven low-cost services for this group, the substantial reduction in JTPA expenditures on youths that occurred starting in the mid-1990s appears to be a reasonable policy response to the empirical evidence. The evidence on the impacts of Job Corps is less clear, but a much stronger case can be made that this program, which provides high-cost comprehensive services, might constitute a very productive social investment.

References

Aakvik, A., J. Heckman, and E. Vytlacil. 1999. Local instrumental variables and latent variable models for estimating treatment effects. University of Chicago, Department of Economics. Mimeograph.

Ashenfelter, O. 1974. The effect of manpower training on earnings: Preliminary results. In *Proceedings of the 27th Annual Meeting of the Industrial Relations Research Association*, ed. J. Stern and B. Dennis, 252–60. Madison, Wis.: Industrial Relations Research Association.

———. 1978. Estimating the effect of training programs on earnings. *Review of Economics and Statistics* 60:47–57.

———. 1979. Estimating the effects of training programs on earnings with longitudinal data. In *Evaluating manpower training programs,* ed. F. Bloch. Greenwich, Conn.: JAI Press.

Ashenfelter, O., and D. Card. 1985. Using the longitudinal structure of earnings to estimate the effect of training programs. *Review of Economics and Statistics* 67 (3): 648–60.

Barnow, B. 1987. The impact of CETA programs on earnings: A review of the literature. *Journal of Human Resources* 22 (Spring): 157–93.

———. 1992. The effects of performance standards on state and local programs. In *Evaluating welfare and training programs,* ed. Charles Manski and Irwin Garfinkel, 277–309. Cambridge: Harvard University Press.

———. 2000. Exploring the relationship between performance management and program impact: A case study of the Job Training Partnership Act. *Journal of Policy Analysis and Management* 19 (1): 118–41.

Barnow, B., and L. Aron. 1989. Survey of government-provided training programs. In *Investing in people: A strategy to address America's workforce crisis,* Background Papers, vol. 1, Commission on Workforce Quality and Labor Market Efficiency. Washington, D.C.: U.S. Department of Labor.

Barnow, B., G. Cain, and A. Goldberger. 1980. Issues in the analysis of selectivity bias. In *Evaluation studies,* vol. 5, ed. E. Stromsdorfer and G. Farkas, 43–59. Beverly Hills, Calif.: Sage Publications.

Bassi, L. 1983. The effect of CETA on the post-program earnings of participants. *Journal of Human Resources* 18 (fall): 539–56.

———. 1984. Estimating the effect of training programs with non-random selection. *Review of Economics and Statistics* 66 (1): 36–43.

Bassi, L., M. Simms, L. Burnbridge, and C. Betsey. 1984. Measuring the effect of

CETA on youth and the economically disadvantaged. Final report prepared for U.S. Department of Labor, Employment and Training Administration. Washington, D.C.

Björklund, A., and R. Moffitt. 1987. Estimation of wage gains and welfare gains in self-selection models. *Review of Economics and Statistics* 69 (1): 42–49.

Black, D., J. Smith, M. Berger, and B. Noel. 2001. Is the threat of reemployment services more effective than the services themselves? Experimental evidence from the UI system. University of Maryland, Department of Economics. Working Paper.

Bloom, H. 1984. Accounting for no-shows in experimental evaluation designs. *Evaluation Review* 82 (2): 225–46.

Bloom, H., and M. McLaughlin. 1982. CETA training programs: Do they work for adults? Joint report of Congressional Budget Office and National Commission for Employment Policy. Washington, D.C.

Bloom, H., L. Orr, S. Bell, G. Cave, F. Doolittle, W. Lin, and J. Bos. 1997. The benefits and costs of JTPA Title II-A programs. *Journal of Human Resources* 32 (3): 547–76.

Burtless, G. 1995. The case for randomized field trials in economic policy research. *Journal of Economic Perspectives* 9 (spring): 61–84.

Burtless, G., and L. Orr. 1986. Are classical experiments needed for manpower policy? *Journal of Human Resources* 21 (4): 606–39.

Butler, W. 1976. Employment and training programs. Staff Working Paper. Washington, D.C.: Congressional Budget Office, May.

Card, D., and D. Sullivan. 1988. Measuring the effects of CETA participation on movements in and out of employment. *Econometrica* 56 (3): 497–530.

Cave, G., and F. Doolittle. 1991. *Assessing JOBSTART: Interim impacts of a program for school dropouts.* New York: Manpower Demonstration Research Corporation.

Congressional Research Service (CRS). 1999. Cash and non-cash benefits for persons with limited income: Eligibility rules, recipient and expenditure data, FY 1996–FY 1998. In *CRS report for Congress.* Washington, D.C.: Congressional Research Service, The Library of Congress, December.

Cooley, T., T. McGuire, and E. Prescott. 1979. Earnings and employment dynamics of manpower trainees: An exploratory econometric analysis. In *Research in labor economics,* vol. 4, suppl. 2, ed. R. Ehrenberg, 119–47. Greenwich, Conn.: JAI Press.

Couch, K. 1992. New evidence on the long-term effects of employment and training programs. *Journal of Labor Economics* 10 (October): 380–88.

Dehejia, R., and S. Wahba. 1999. Causal effects in non-experimental studies: Reevaluating the evaluation of training programs. *Journal of the American Statistical Association* 94 (448): 1053–62.

Devine, T., and J. Heckman. 1996. The structure and consequences of eligibility rules for a social program. In *Research in labor economics,* vol. 15, ed. S. Polachek, 111–70. Greenwich, Conn.: JAI Press.

Dickinson, K., T. Johnson, and R. West. 1986. An analysis of the impact of CETA on participants' earnings. *Journal of Human Resources* 21 (Winter): 64–91.

———. 1987. An analysis of the sensitivity of quasi-experimental net estimates of CETA programs. *Evaluation Review* 11 (August): 452–72.

Doolittle, F., and L. Traeger. 1990. *Implementing the National JTPA Study.* New York: Manpower Demonstration Research Corporation.

Eberwein, C., J. Ham, and R. LaLonde. 1997. The impact of classroom training on the employment histories of disadvantaged women: Evidence from experimental data. *Review of Economic Studies* 64 (4): 655–82.

Fraker, T., and R. Maynard. 1987. The adequacy of comparison group designs for evaluations of employment-related programs. *Journal of Human Resources* 22 (2): 194–227.

Friedlander, D., and J. Gueron. 1990. *Are high-cost services more effective than low-cost services? Evidence from experimental evaluations of welfare-to-work programs.* New York: Manpower Demonstration Research Corporation.

Friedlander, D., G. Hoerz, J. Quint, and J. Riccio. 1985. *Arkansas, the demonstration of state work/welfare initiatives: Final report on the WORK Program in two counties.* New York: Manpower Demonstration Research Corporation, September.

Friedlander, D., and P. Robbins. 1995. Evaluating program evaluations: New evidence on commonly used nonexperimental methods. *American Economic Review* 85 (4): 923–37.

Gay, R., and M. Borus. 1980. Validating performance indicators for employment and training programs. *Journal of Human Resources* 15 (Winter): 29–48.

Geraci, V. 1984. Short-term indicators of job training program effects on long-term participants' earnings. Report to the U.S. Department of Labor, Employment and Training Administration. Washington, D.C.

Goldberger, A. 1972. Selection bias in evaluating treatment effects. Discussion Paper no. 123–172. University of Wisconsin: Institute for Research on Poverty.

Goldman, B., D. Friedlander, and D. Long. 1986. *California, the demonstration of state work/welfare initiatives: Final report on the San Diego Job Search and Work Experience Demonstration.* New York: Manpower Demonstration Research Corporation, February.

Gueron, J. 1986. *Work initiatives for welfare recipients: Lessons from a multi-state experiment.* New York: Manpower Demonstration Research Corporation, March.

Ham, J., and R. LaLonde. 1990. Using social experiments to estimate the effect of training on transition rates. In *Panel data and labor market studies,* ed. J. Hartog, J. Theeuwes, and G. Ridder, 157–72. Amsterdam: North Holland.

———. 1996. The effect of sample selection and initial conditions in duration models: Evidence from experimental data. *Econometrica* 64 (1): 175–205.

Heckman, J. 1978. Dummy endogenous variables in a simultaneous equations system. *Econometrica* 46:931–61.

———. 1979. Sample selection bias as a specification error. *Econometrica* 47:153–61.

———. 1990. Varieties of selection bias. *American Economic Review* 80 (2): 313–18.

———. 1992. Randomization and social policy evaluation. In *Evaluating welfare and training programs,* ed. Charles Manski and Irwin Garfinkel. Cambridge: Harvard University Press.

———. 1996. Randomization as an instrumental variable. *Review of Economics and Statistics* 73:336–40.

Heckman, J., and J. Hotz. 1989. Choosing among alternative methods of estimating the impact of social programs: The case of manpower training. *Journal of the American Statistical Association* 84 (December): 862–74.

Heckman, J., J. Hotz, and M. Dabos. 1987. Do we need experimental data to evaluate the impact of manpower training on earnings? *Evaluation Review* 11 (4): 395–427.

Heckman, J., H. Ichimura, J. Smith, and P. Todd. 1998. Characterizing selection bias using experimental data. *Econometrica* 66 (October): 1017–98.

582   **Robert J. LaLonde**

Heckman, J., H. Ichimura, and P. Todd. 1998. Matching as an econometric evaluation estimator. *Review of Economic Studies* 65 (2): 261–94.
Heckman, J., R. LaLonde, and J. Smith. 1999. The economics and econometrics of active labor market policy. In *Handbook of labor economics,* vol. 3C, ed. O. Ashenfelter and D. Card, 1865–2097. Amsterdam: North Holland.
Heckman, J., and R. Robb. 1985a. Alternative methods for evaluating the impact of interventions. *Journal of Econometrics* 30:239–67.
———. 1985b. Alternative methods for evaluating the impact of interventions: An overview. In *Longitudinal analysis of labor market data,* Econometric Society monograph series, ed. J. Heckman and B. Singer, 156–245. New York: Cambridge University Press.
Heckman, J., R. Roselius, and J. Smith. 1994. U.S. education and training policy: A re-evaluation of the underlying assumptions behind the "new consensus." In *Labor markets, employment policy, and job creation,* ed. L. Soloman and A. Levenson, 83–121. Boulder, Colo.: Westview Press.
Heckman, J., and J. Smith. 1997. The determinants of participation in a social program: Evidence from the Job Training Partnership Act. University of Chicago, Department of Economics. Unpublished manuscript.
———. 1998. Evaluating the welfare state. In *Econometrics and economic theory in the twentieth century: The Ragnar Frisch Centennial Symposium,* ed. S. Storm, 241–318. Cambridge: Cambridge University Press.
———. 1999. The pre-programme earnings dip and the determinants of participation in a social programme: Implications for simple programme evaluation strategies. *Economic Journal* 109 (457): 313–48.
Heckman, J., J. Smith, and C. Taber. 1996. What do bureaucrats do? The effects of performance standards and bureaucratic preferences on acceptance into the JTPA Program. In *Reinventing government and the problem of bureaucracy,* vol. 7 of *Advances in the study of entrepreneurship, innovation, and economic growth,* ed. G. Libecap, 191–217. Greenwich, Conn.: JAI Press.
———. 1998. Accounting for dropouts in evaluations of social programs. *Review of Economics and Statistics* 80 (1): 1–14.
Holland, P. 1986. Statistics and causal inference. *Journal of the American Statistical Association* 81 (December): 945–60.
Hollister, R., P. Kemper, and R. Maynard. 1984. *The National Supported Work Demonstration.* Madison, Wis.: University of Wisconsin Press.
Hotz, V. J. 1992. Designing an evaluation of the Job Training Partnership Act. In *Evaluating welfare and training programs,* ed. C. Manski and I. Garfinkel, 76–114. Cambridge: Harvard University Press.
Imbens, G., and J. Angrist. 1994. Identification and estimation of local average treatment effects. *Econometrica* 62 (4): 467–76.
Jacobson, L., R. LaLonde, and D. Sullivan. 1993. Earnings losses for displaced workers. *American Economic Review* 83 (4): 685–709.
———. 2002. Measures of program performance and the training choices of displaced workers. In *Targeting employment services,* ed. R. Eberts, C. O'Leary, and S. Wandner, 187–214. Kalamazoo, Mich.: W. E. Upjohn Institute for Employment Research.
Kemper, P., D. Long, and C. Thornton. 1984. A benefit-cost analysis of the Supported Work Experiment. In *The National Supported Work Demonstration,* ed. R. Hollister, P. Kemper, and R. Maynard, 239–85. Madison, Wis.: University of Wisconsin Press.
Kiefer, N. 1978. Federally subsidized occupational training and the employment and earnings of male trainees. *Journal of Econometrics* 8:111–15.

————. 1979. Population heterogeneity and inference from panel data on the effects of vocational training and education. *Journal of Political Economy* 81 (October): S213–26.

Kornfeld, R., and H. Bloom. 1996. Measuring the impacts of social programs on the earnings and employment of low-income persons: Do UI wage record and surveys agree? Abt Associates, Unpublished manuscript.

LaLonde, R. 1984. Evaluating the econometric evaluations of training programs with experimental data. Industrial Relations Section Working Paper no. 183. Princeton University.

————. 1986. Evaluating the econometric evaluations of training programs with experimental data. *American Economic Review* 76 (September): 604–20.

————. 1995. The promise of public sector-sponsored training programs. *Journal of Economic Perspectives* 9 (2): 149–69.

LaLonde, R., and R. Maynard. 1987. How precise are the evaluations of employment and training programs: Evidence from a field experiment. *Evaluation Review* 11 (August): 428–51.

Levitan, S., and G. Mangum. 1969. *Federal training and work programs in the sixties.* Ann Arbor, Mich.: Institute of Labor and Industrial Relations.

Long, D., C. Mallar, and C. Thornton. 1981. Evaluating the benefits and costs of the job corps. *Journal of Policy Analysis and Management* 1 (1): 55–76.

Mallar, C. 1978. Alternative econometric procedures for program evaluations: Illustrations from an evaluation of Job Corps. *Proceedings of the American Statistical Association,* 317–21. Alexandria, Va.: American Statistical Association.

Mallar, C., T. Good, K. Lai, and G. Labovich. 1982. *Evaluation of the economic impact of the Job Corps Program: Third follow-up report.* Princeton, N.J.: Mathematica Policy, September.

Manpower report of the president, U.S. Department of Labor. 1964. Washington, D.C.: U.S. Government Printing Office.

————. 1969. Washington, D.C.: U.S. Government Printing Office.

————. 1974. Washington, D.C.: U.S. Government Printing Office.

————. 1997. Washington, D.C.: U.S. Government Printing Office.

McConnell, S., and S. Glazerman. 2001. National Job Corps study: The benefits and costs of Job Corps. Prepared for the U.S. Department of Labor Employment and Training Administration. Princeton, N.J.: Mathematica Policy Research, June.

Moffitt, R. 1991. Program evaluation with nonexperimental data. *Evaluation review* 15 (3): 291–314.

————. 1992. Evaluation methods for program entry effects. In *Evaluating welfare and training programs,* ed. C. Manski and I. Garfinkel. Cambridge: Harvard University Press.

National Commission for Employment Policy (NCEP). 1987. *The Job Training Partnership Act.* Washington, D.C.: NCEP.

————. 1995. *Understanding federal training and employment programs.* Washington, D.C.: NCEP.

O'Neill, D. 1973. *The federal government and manpower: A critical look at the MDTA-Institutional and Job Corps programs.* Washington, D.C.: American Enterprise Institute for Public Policy Research.

Orr, L., H. Bloom, S. Bell, W. Lin, G. Cave, and F. Doolittle. 1994. The National JTPA Study: Impacts, benefits, and costs of Title II-A. Report to the U.S. Department of Labor. Cambridge, Mass.: Abt Associates, March.

Powell, J. 1994. Estimation of semi-parametric models. In *Handbook of econometrics,* vol. 4, ed. R. Engle and D. McFadden, 2443–521. Amsterdam: North Holland.

Rosenbaum, R., and D. Rubin. 1983. The central role of the propensity score in observational studies for causal effects. *Biometrika* 70 (1): 41–55.

Rubin, D. 1973. Matching to remove bias in observational studies. *Biometrics* 29:159–83.

———. 1979. Using multivariate matched sampling and regression adjustment to control bias in observational studies. *Journal of the American Statistical Association* 74:318–28.

Sandell, S., and K. Rupp. 1988. Who is served in JTPA Programs: Patterns of participation and intergroup equity. Washington, D.C.: U.S. National Commission for Employment Policy.

Schochet, P., J. Burghardt, and S. Glazerman. 2000. *National Job Corps study: The short-term impacts of Job Corps on participants' employment and related outcomes: Final report.* Prepared for the U.S. Department of Labor Employment and Training Administration. Princeton, N.J.: Mathematica Policy Research, Inc.

———. 2001. *National Job Corps study: The impacts of Job Corps on participants' employment and related outcomes.* Prepared for the U.S. Department of Labor Employment and Training Administration. Mathematica Policy Research, Inc., (June).

Smith, J., and P. Todd. 2003. Does matching overcome LaLonde's critique of non-experimental estimators? *Journal of Econometrics,* forthcoming.

Social Policy Research Associates (SPR). 1999. PY 97 SPIR data book. Prepared for Office of Policy and Research, Employment and Training Administration, U.S. Department of Labor. Washington, D.C.: SPR, June.

Stromsdorfer, E., R. Boruch, H. Bloom, J. Gueron, and F. Stafford. 1985. *Recommendations of the Job Training Longitudinal Survey Research Advisory Panel to the Office of Strategic Planning and Policy Development.* Washington, D.C.: U.S. Department of Labor. Unpublished manuscript.

Taggart, R. 1981. *A fisherman's guide: An assessment of training and remediation strategies.* Kalamazoo, Mich.: W. E. Upjohn Institute for Employment Research.

U.S. Department of Labor (DOL). 1974. *Manpower Report of the President, U.S. Department of Labor.* Washington, D.C.: Government Printing Office.

———. 1982. *Employment and training report to the president.* Washington, D.C.: U.S. Government Printing Office.

———. 1988. *Employment and training report of the secretary of labor.* Washington, D.C.: U.S. Government Printing Office.

———. 1996. *Employment and training report of the secretary of labor.* Washington, D.C.: U.S. Government Printing Office.

———. 2002. Summary of budget authority, fiscal years 2001–2002. Washington, D.C.: DOL, Employment and Training Administration.

U.S. General Accounting Office (GAO). 1996. Job Training Partnership Act: Long-term earnings and employment outcomes. Report no. GAO/HERE 96-40. Washington, D.C.: GAO.

U.S. House of Representatives, Committee on Ways and Means. 1996. *1996 green book: Background material and data on programs within the jurisdiction of the Committee on Ways and Means.* Washington, D.C.: U.S. Government Printing Office.

———. 2000. *2000 green book: Background materials and data on programs within the jurisdiction of the Committee on Ways and Means.* Washington, D.C.: U.S. Government Printing Office.

Westat, Inc. 1984. Summary of net impact results. Report prepared for U.S. Department of Labor, Employment and Training Administration. Washington, D.C.

Wilde, E., and R. Hollister. 2001. How close is close enough? Swarthmore College, Department of Economics. Mimeograph.

Wolfhagen, C., and B. Goldman. 1983. *Job search strategies: Lessons from the Louisville WIN laboratory.* New York: Manpower Demonstration Research Corporation.

Zhao, Z. 2001. *Two essays in social program evaluation.* Ph.D. diss., Johns Hopkins University.

Child Support
Interactions between Private and Public Transfers

Robert I. Lerman and Elaine Sorensen

9.1 Introduction

Child support is a private transfer, typically from the noncustodial parent to a custodial parent. Although it is neither public transfer nor means-tested, child support is integral to the means-tested public transfer system. Governments have come to play a major role in enforcing private support obligations. Traditionally, in the United States, state governments and courts exercised authority over laws governing divorce and parental financial obligations, including decisions about how much parents owe and how to make sure parents pay their obligations. As the welfare rolls and the number of one-parent families soared in the late 1960s and early 1970s, several members of Congress began looking for ways both to reinstate the financial responsibility of parents and to reduce welfare costs. In 1974, Senator Russell Long, the powerful chair of the Senate Finance Committee, convinced Congress that establishing a federally funded child support enforcement program was part of the solution.

The Child Support Enforcement (CSE) program was established in 1975 as part D of the Social Security Act. The statute authorized federal matching grants to states to collect support obligations, to establish paternity, and to obtain support awards. In turn, states had to provide child support enforcement services to welfare recipients (Aid to Families with Dependent Children, or AFDC) and any nonwelfare family who requested them. Furthermore, it decreed that, as a condition of receiving cash benefits, AFDC families had to assign their rights to collect child support to the

Robert I. Lerman is professor of economics at American University and director of the Labor and Social Policy Center at the Urban Institute. Elaine Sorensen is a principal research associate at the Urban Institute.

state to compensate it for the cost of providing aid to the family, and they had to cooperate with the CSE agency in establishing paternity and securing support. Thus, Congress created two functions for the child support enforcement programs that remain today: to increase child support and reduce welfare costs.

CSE helps set and enforce the terms of private transfers, directing the flow from a responsible donor (the noncustodial parent) to a deserving recipient (the child). In contrast, standard transfer programs establish no direct link between an individual taxpayer and a recipient. Instead, the source of the transfer is from taxpayers as a whole and the payments go to recipients as a whole. In practice, the case of CSE varies with the welfare status of the family. For nonwelfare families, CSE ensures that individual donors meet their responsibility to individual recipients. For welfare families, CSE establishes a link between payments by a responsible donor and dollar savings by taxpayers.

Child support's direct effect upon noncustodial parents is central to understanding how its incentive and distributional effects differ from those of standard income transfer programs. We must explicitly take account of not only the recipient's utility function, incentives, and income level, but the donor's as well. One implication is that the effects on the distribution across income groups are less clear than those of standard income transfer programs. Since the incomes of the donors can be lower than the incomes of recipients, raising support payments could yield little reduction in inequality or poverty, especially if the relevant policies themselves create costly disincentives. Some noncustodial parents view their payments as nothing more than a tax, either because they gain little or no utility from raising their child's living standard or because their support payments simply offset government benefits. In such cases, child support payments clearly exert a direct effect on the incentives of the donor as well as of the recipient.

In addition, CSE provides a set of open-ended services that are not means-tested as are other transfer programs. For all custodial parents, the state CSE agency will assist in establishing support awards and collecting them. Even in the absence of formal income testing in CSE programs, the program ends up targeting low-income families because so many custodial families are poor. In 1997, 37 percent of custodial parent families were poor and only 20 percent had incomes greater than 300 percent of the poverty threshold. Nonetheless, the involvement of moderate-income parents influences the perception, operations, and political debate over CSE in ways that are not present for other means-tested programs. On one hand, the role of CSE becomes less controversial when seeking support for moderate-income parents because noncustodial parents usually have the capacity, if not the will, to pay. On the other hand, middle-income fathers subject to higher support awards and more rigorous collection strategies have increasingly sought assistance in claiming their visitation rights.

The dramatic reductions in welfare caseloads illustrate the changing interplay between child support and income transfer programs. When the majority of low-income, one-parent families received AFDC, custodial parents eligible for child support often faced weak incentives to seek support, and noncustodial parents saw little gain for their children by making support payments. Today, as fewer families receive cash welfare assistance, support payments can become more of a supplement to the incomes of low-income families and less of a substitute for government benefits. For low-income families, this means that child support can raise the living standards of their children. For states, however, this means that their CSE programs have less ability to reduce welfare costs.

The purpose of this paper is to examine child support policies, especially the activities of the Child Support Enforcement Program, and how they interact with transfer policies and affect the low-income population. Section 9.2 reviews the history of the CSE program, its rules, and objectives. Next, in section 9.3, we review the economic rationale for government's role in child support. In section 9.4, we describe trends in child support awards and payments. In section 9.5, we discuss the importance of child support to low-income families. The next section, 9.6, examines the capacity of noncustodial parents to pay child support. Section 9.7 discusses the trends in costs and effectiveness of the child support program. Section 9.8 reviews the financing of this program. In section 9.9, we examine the effects of child support incentives on behavior. Section 9.10 discusses remaining equity issues within child support. In section 9.11, we consider several reform proposals. The final section draws conclusions about directions for the future of child support policies.

9.2   Program History, Rules, and Goals

State family law has traditionally governed marriage, divorce, child custody and support, adoption, and child welfare.[1] Under state statutes, mothers[2] were able to go to local and state courts to request payments and custody as part of a divorce, separation, or paternity proceeding. When the parents could not agree, judges used a great deal of discretion to decide how much noncustodial parents were to pay as child support and/or alimony. This approach was problematic in several respects. First, low-income parents too often had little access to the system because of the high expense of going to court. Second, judicial discretion led to wide variations in child support obligations, even among divorce or paternity cases involving similar circumstances. Third, the only recourse for the nonpay-

1. For an interesting discussion of the early antecedents of modern child support, see Hanson (1999).
2. Since custodial parents are nearly always mothers and noncustodial parents are nearly always fathers, we will sometimes use gender-specific language.

ment of child support was going back to court, which had proven ineffective.

When the federal government began to intervene in 1950, its focus was on children receiving public assistance because of abandonment or desertion by parents.[3] The 1950 amendments to the Social Security Act required state welfare agencies to notify law enforcement officials so that the legal responsibilities of the parent could be enforced and thus allow welfare programs to count support payments as resources available to the family (Solomon 1989).

The Social Security Amendments of 1974 marked the first significant involvement of the federal government in making child support policy (Solomon 1989). As table 9.1 notes, the 1974 amendments established the federal Office of Child Support Enforcement (OCSE) to oversee the state child support enforcement programs but left the basic responsibility for administering the programs to the states. The federal government agreed to reimburse 75 percent of the administrative costs of running the program (which has since declined to 66 percent). In turn, each state had to establish a child support enforcement program that assisted AFDC families and any other non-AFDC family who requested such services in establishing paternity and child support obligations, and enforcing those obligations.

Since then, virtually every Congress has passed federal laws to expand enforcement tools, alter the incentive formulas for states, and limit the ability of noncustodial parents to escape their obligations. Indeed, with new provisions becoming law in 1981, 1982, 1984, 1986, 1987, 1988, 1989, 1990, 1992, 1993, 1994, 1995, 1996, 1997, 1998, and 1999, Congress has clearly found a popular area for legislation. The most important laws enacted are described below.

9.2.1   Establishing Paternity

Legal paternity is rarely an issue for children born to married parents, but it is always an issue for children born outside of marriage. As nonmarital childbearing has risen, so has the concern regarding paternity establishment. For CSE, it is a critical first step; without it, additional child support services cannot be pursued. The federal government's role in this area significantly increased in 1988, when it set numeric goals for states to meet with regard to paternity establishment and financial penalties for not meeting these goals. By that time, DNA testing could identify a father with near certainty, and the federal government mandated that all parties in a contested paternity case submit to genetic testing if requested by any party. It also gave greater financial responsibility to the federal government for genetic testing and established time limits for processing paternity cases.

---

3. See Brito (2000) for a discussion of the interaction between family law and welfare law as governing child support cases.

Table 9.1	Major Changes in Federal Laws Affecting Child Support Enforcement
1950	The first federal child support enforcement legislation was Section 402(a)(11) of the Social Security Act, which required state welfare agencies to notify law enforcement officials upon providing Aid to Families with Dependent Children (AFDC) to a child who was abandoned or deserted by a parent.
1975	PL 93-647, The Social Security Amendments of 1974 created Part D to Title IV of the Social Security Act, providing federal matching funds to states for child support enforcement for AFDC cases and creating a separate unit (the Office of Child Support Enforcement) within the federal Department of Health, Education, and Welfare (now Health and Human Services) to establish standards for states, provide them with technical assistance, evaluate and review state plans and program operations, and certify cases for referral to the federal courts and the Internal Revenue Service (IRS) for enforcement and collection. Each recipient of AFDC was required to assign support rights to the state and cooperate in establishing paternity and securing support. A disregard policy was established, and an audit division was created within the program.
1980–82	These years saw federal laws extending and strengthening the information-gathering and enforcement powers of state child support agencies under Title IV-D. In 1980, PL 96-272 amended Title IV-D to provide incentive payments to the states for child support collections they made in all AFDC cases and made federal matching funds available for serving non-AFDC families on a permanent basis. In 1981, PL 97-35 added provisions to IV-D programs authorizing the IRS to withhold all or part of federal income tax refunds from nonpaying parents. It also required states to withhold a portion of unemployment benefits from absent parents delinquent on their support payments. In 1982, three new public laws reduced federal financial participation in child support enforcement but also allowed for members of the armed forces to have their wages garnished for nonpayment of child support and provided for disclosure of information obtained under the Food Stamp Act of 1977.
1984	The Child Support Enforcement Amendments (PL 98-378) mandated that the states establish improved enforcement mechanisms, including expedited procedures for establishing orders and collecting support. They required that states provide equal services for welfare and nonwelfare families, revised federal auditing procedures and incentive payments, and required states to implement mandatory wage withholding for delinquent cases. New funding was made available for developing automated systems, including those for interstate enforcement.
1988	The Family Support Act (PL 100-485) contained several provisions to strengthen enforcement on AFDC cases. The act required judges and other officials to use state guidelines for child support awards, and mandated three-year reviews for AFDC cases. It set standards for state establishment of paternity and allowed for federal reimbursement for the costs of paternity testing. It required immediate wage withholding for all new or modified orders, beginning in January 1994, and even earlier (November 1990) for cases enforced by the CSE program. All states were required to develop and put in place statewide automated tracking and monitoring systems by October 1995 or face federal penalties.
1989–90; 1992–94	Each year saw expanded state mandates or penalties on individuals for noncompliance. For example, PL 102-521 (1992) imposed criminal penalties for willful failure to pay past-due child support obligations. PL 103-66 (1993) increased the percentage of children for whom a state must establish paternity and required states to adopt laws mandating civil procedures for the voluntary acknowledgement of paternity.

(continued)

Table 9.1   (continued)

1996	The Personal Responsibility and Work Opportunity Reconciliation Act (PL 104-193) required that states operate a child support program that met federal mandates in order to be eligible for block grants under Temporary Assistance for Needy Families (TANF). States were required to expand their efforts in income withholding, paternity establishment, enforcement of orders, and the use of central registries. The act provided for uniform rules, procedures, and forms for interstate cases. It established a Federal Case Registry and National Directory of New Hires to track delinquent parents across state lines. The act altered the federal and state shared of the $50 disregard to families receiving public assistance on whose behalf child support payments were made and eliminated the mandate on the states to provide for a disregard.
1998	The Deadbeat Parents Punishment Act (PL 105-187) toughened the 1992 law creating federal criminal penalties for willful failure to pay past-due child support by creating two new categories of federal felonies with penalties of up to two years in prison.

Sources: U.S. Department of Health and Human Services (1997a); Institute for Research on Poverty (2000).

It wasn't until 1993, however, that the federal government required states to establish voluntary procedures for acknowledging paternity in the hospital. Since then, every state has adopted an in-hospital paternity acknowledgment program, and federal rules in this area have been strengthened and broadened. Today, if a father signs a paternity acknowledgment form in the hospital, he will be considered the legal father of the child unless it is rescinded within sixty days, except in limited circumstances of fraud, duress, or material mistake of fact. Genetic testing is not required to sign these forms; nor is it necessarily sufficient evidence to overturn the legal requirements of being a father once a paternity acknowledgment form is signed.

9.2.2 Establishing Child Support Awards

Setting child support awards has historically been the responsibility of the courts. Child support orders were typically set on a case-by-case basis, in accordance with broadly enunciated principles of family law. Over time, confidence waned in the ability of judges to use discretion wisely, as judges appeared to mandate widely different support obligations to families in similar circumstances.

States responded to this perceived unfairness of judicial discretion by developing numeric guidelines for judges to follow when establishing child support awards. State initiatives started as early as 1975, but most states did not establish child support guidelines until Congress mandated that they do so in 1984. At that time, Congress required the states to adopt numeric child support guidelines and to make them available to those responsible for setting child support awards. These guidelines were not binding; they were "advisory." It was not until 1988 that Congress required that state child support guidelines be binding on judges (unless a written finding was issued).

Today, federal law dictates that child support orders must be set in accordance with state child support guidelines, unless the judge writes a justification, or "finding," that explains why the application of the guidelines is inappropriate. In other words, the presumption is that judges will follow state child support guidelines. The principle rationale of judges for deviating from the guidelines is that such deviations will be in the best interests of the child.

States are expected to develop their own child support guidelines within broad parameters set by the federal government. All of the states have developed guidelines that ultimately make payments a function of the income of the noncustodial parent, at least on a marginal basis. Two models dominate state child support guidelines: percentage of income and income shares (Williams 1994).

Currently, thirteen states set payments equal to a percentage of before-tax or after-tax income of the noncustodial parent, with the percentage varying with the number of children (Rothe and Meyer 2000). According to the well-known Wisconsin standard, the percentages vary from 17 percent of gross income for one child to 25 percent for two, 29 percent for three, and 34 percent for four or more. Minnesota requires fathers of four children with net incomes of over $1,000 per month to pay 39 percent of net income.

Under the income-shares approach used in almost all other states, the noncustodial parent pays some percentage of the combined income of the two parents. In fourteen income-share states, the percentage of income paid for child support decreases with the level of combined parental income; in sixteen states, the percentage increases and then decreases. When the percentage of income allocated to children is a fixed percentage of income, the child support obligation rises proportionately with income. For example, assuming the two parents must provide 20 percent for the child, a $100 rise in income of the noncustodial parent raises his support order by $20. However, as Bassi and Barnow (1993) show, when the percentage allocated to child support increases or decreases with joint income, some odd impacts occur. An increase in the custodial parent's income can raise support obligations of the noncustodial parent even if his income remains constant. In some cases where the percentage of income paid decreases with combined income, an increase in the noncustodial parent's income can lower his contribution.

Child support guidelines typically use current income to determine the amount of a child support order, but a parent's current income may not reflect his or her earnings potential. In particular, a parent may be voluntarily underemployed or unemployed. In these cases, judges may impute income based on a parent's earnings potential. Determining whether a parent is voluntarily underemployed or unemployed is not straightforward. For example, some judges have ruled that imprisonment is voluntary and thus their child support order should reflect earnings potential; others have ruled that imprisonment is involuntary and thus their order should reflect current earnings (Morgan 1998). Staying home to take care of a child is another example in which what is deemed voluntary varies with the judge and the state. Some states and most judges do not impute an income to a parent if she had been staying home prior to the marital separation, but staying home to care for subsequent children is generally considered voluntary.

In addition, current income is not typically used in determining default child support orders, which are issued whenever noncustodial parents do not appear at the time the order is set. In these situations, there is often no income information for the noncustodial parent. Noncustodial parents are informed of the hearing, often through first class mail, but many still do not appear. States have established different procedures to respond to this situation, and judges are usually given discretion in this matter. Furthermore, some states do not base a default order on ability to pay, but base it on a minimum standard of care for a child (Sorensen 1999).

A third issue arises when parents share physical custody. As children spend increasing amounts of time under the care of the parent legally designated as noncustodial, the notion of custodial and noncustodial parents as fixed categories becomes less appropriate. In principle, child support formulas should alter the payment obligations to reflect the extent to which both parents are caring for and paying the expenses of children. However, making equitable adjustments is difficult to implement. Determining the actual time and expense each parent incurs and making appropriate adjustments would require frequent updating of support obligations. Some costs, such as the need for a room for the child, are fixed and largely independent of the amount of visitation by a noncustodial parent. Currently, few state formulas take account of the costs incurred by the noncustodial parent by lowering support obligations. Some formulas make adjustments, but only when the noncustodial parent has the child for more than 20 percent of the time.[4] An exception is California, where the noncustodial parent's obligations peak when no sharing of physical responsibility takes place and then decline as the shared component of physical responsibility increases.

9.2.3   Collecting Child Support

The primary means by which CSE collects child support is wage withholding. Congress first mandated this tool in 1984, and it has since been

---

4. Apparently, the perception arose that widely used guidelines incorporate the costs of shared custody up to a threshold of 20 percent and thus require no downward adjustment for noncustodial parents providing 20 percent of the child's care and possibly an upward adjustment for noncustodial parents providing no care at all. But according to Robert G. Williams (1996), the primary author of the guidelines used in many states, guidelines in Ohio (and presumably similar states) do not presume a 20 percent sharing arrangement and make no adjustment for costs incurred in visitation or shared custody. Also see Henry (1999).

strengthened numerous times. At first, wage withholding was only mandatory for child support obligors who were at least one month behind in their
child support orders. This approach gave way to "immediate wage withholding," which states began to implement in the late 1980s. Immediate
wage withholding means that as soon as an order is established, child support is taken directly from wages (no delinquency is needed to initiate wage
withholding). Since 1994, the federal government has required that all new
child support orders include an immediate wage assignment. The only exceptions are for cases of good cause (for example, a fear that withholding
will lead to domestic violence) or cases in which the parties mutually agree
to an alternate agreement.

Although state agencies now have authority and responsibility to establish immediate wage withholding on all new child support orders, their primary difficulty is maintaining contact with the noncustodial parents' employers over time. To deal with this administrative problem, Congress
required in 1996 that all employers report every new hire within twenty
days of hire to the CSE agency. The data from these reports are, in turn,
matched against child support obligors. If a match is found, a wage withholding form is sent to the employer to begin immediate wage withholding.
The new hire reports are sent to the federal government, which, in turn, has
built a new data file called the National Directory of New Hires that can be
used for interstate child support collections efforts.

9.2.4   Distribution of Support Payments to the Government and Custodial Parents

Once collected, child support payments go to the custodial parent unless
the custodial parent is receiving or has received cash welfare benefits. In
these cases, the distribution of child support is extremely complicated.
Custodial parents on welfare are required to assign their rights to child
support to the government. Thus, the government can retain any current
or past child support paid while the custodial parent is on welfare. Half of
this amount paid is typically distributed to the federal government; the
other half is retained by the state government. On one hand, these sums
simply reimburse the government for its costs of providing cash assistance
to the custodial family. However, to the extent the government captures
past as well as current child support, the custodial parent not only faces a
$1 benefit reduction for each $1 of current child support income, but also
loses a portion of an asset (accumulated debts owed to the custodial parent from the noncustodial parent).

Prior to PRWORA, Congress mandated that states pass through and
disregard the first $50 per month of child support paid on behalf of welfare
families. Under PRWORA, Congress eliminated this mandate and replaced it with an option for states to pass through any amount of child support collected on behalf of the custodial parent to the family and disregard

that amount in determining cash assistance, but they were still required to pay the federal government their half of any support collected. Despite this onerous payment requirement, many states, especially the larger ones, chose to continue their $50 child support pass-through and disregard policy, but most did not.

Once the custodial parent leaves welfare, any current support paid by the noncustodial parent goes directly to the custodial parent and is counted as income for other government programs (Barnow et al. 2000). If past support is due, then who receives those payments depends on the method of collection. If it is collected via wage withholding, which most arrears are, then the custodial parent receives it. On the other hand, if it is collected via intercept programs, then the government receives it.

Many child support advocates and administrators have argued for simplification of the distribution rules, and the House of Representatives passed legislation in 2000 that would have simplified them, but this legislation died in the Senate. Similar legislation will probably be reintroduced because the distribution rules are so complicated.

9.2.5   Retroactive Support

In divorce cases, child support orders typically start at the time of the divorce settlement, but courts may go back to the date of separation. Thus, most divorce cases do not start out with large arrearages. In nonmarital cases, on the other hand, states can go back as far as the child's birth if they wish, even though the order may have been requested much later. Thus, nonmarital cases often start with large arrearages as the result of retroactive support, arrearages owed both to the government and to the custodial parent. Retroactive support amounts depend on what would have been owed on the noncustodial parent's actual or imputed income in prior years. Some states also include the birthing costs of a Medicaid birth as part of the retroactive support.

9.3   Economic Rationale for Government's Role in Child Support

The work of Weiss and Willis (1985) provided the first formal analysis of the inefficiencies that arise in divorce because of the collective-good character of expenditures on children. Since both the custodial and noncustodial parents derive utility from their children, children are a couple-specific public or collective good. While the parents live together, proximity, altruism, and mutual trust serve to overcome the "free-rider" problem associated with the provision of public goods. However, once the parents live apart, these positive attributes tend to weaken. The noncustodial parent can no longer influence or monitor the allocation of resources between public and private goods; child support is paid to the custodial parent, who, in turn, decides how it will be allocated. This loss of control leads to a less efficient allocation of resources; in particular, the amount that non-custodial parents spend on supporting their children declines. Weiss and Willis (1993) estimate that expenditures on children when their parents are divorced are only half the amount provided during marriage. Graham and Beller (forthcoming) provide a simple model showing how non-cooperation among parents reduces children's consumption. Both parents gain utility from their own and from their child's consumption, but, especially when they are apart, each parent would prefer to maximize the cost of the child's consumption borne by the other parent. Using reaction functions, Graham and Beller find that the Cournot-Nash and Stackelberg solutions of these non-cooperative games yield lower expenditures on children than when the parents cooperate.

Government interventions to determine custody and visitation, specify support obligations, and collect payments are ways to raise spending by noncustodial parents closer to efficient levels. However, such policies do not resolve the underlying collective-goods problem because custodial parents are able to allocate support payments in ways that are suboptimal from the point of view of noncustodial parents. The added collections of child support from noncustodial parents may be partly offset by reduced spending on children by custodial parents. As a result, noncustodial parents may begin to view their payments as an involuntary tax not going to support their children.

One direct and compelling incentive for noncustodial parents to pay support arises with the link between visitation and support payments. Ribero (1994) argues that negotiations between parents lead to a joint visitation–child support outcome in which noncustodial fathers trade income for visitations allowed by mothers. Although estimates do not entirely confirm the theoretical model involving negotiations for child time and parental consumption, Ribero maintains that the level of child support paid by noncustodial fathers may not be "too low" but, rather, the amount that yields an optimal visitation-payment outcome.

These models highlight a key difference between child support and other transfer programs. Unlike standard welfare programs, child support transfers link an individual donor with an individual recipient. Because the value of the transfer to the donor can depend on the behavior and circumstances of the recipient, child support directly alters the incentives of donors as well as recipients. In some ways, the interest in taking account of the incentive effects on donors is similar to the recognition that transfers require taxes that may induce distortions and impose real social costs. (We are referring to the literature on the marginal efficiency costs of public funds.) However, in the case of child support, the clear expectation is that the utility of the donor depends directly and strongly on the income of the recipient (his child).

Another critical government role is to establish paternity and support awards. As Willis (1999) shows in a recent theoretical paper, relying on the unfettered incentives of men and women can lead to an equilibrium in which out-of-wedlock childbearing is widespread. According to the model, when women outnumber men or women's incomes are high relative to those of men, some share of low-income men will choose to father children outside marriage and some low-income women will voluntarily bear and raise children outside marriage. As a result, marriage as an institution for raising children is undermined, and children receive lower resources than would be the case if all fathers married. Willis points out that effective paternity establishment and collection of child support can reduce the attractiveness of nonmarital fatherhood and lower the fraction of children born and raised outside marriage. Since high rates of nonmarital births impose a variety of costs on taxpayers—from direct welfare support to compensatory payments aimed at helping children born and raised outside of marriage to overcome educational and other problems associated with having fewer economic and social resources—lowering the nonmarital birth rate is very much in their interests. Studies noted later find evidence to support the connection between government efforts to establish paternity and reduced out-of-wedlock childbearing.

Averting the direct and indirect costs to third parties that result from divorce provides another justification for government intervention in child support enforcement. However, the theoretical impact of strict enforcement is unclear. Higher support payments raise the ability of custodial parents to raise children outside marriage while increasing the costs of divorce to noncustodial parents. Here is another instance in which child support policies interact with welfare programs. Child support should reduce divorce most among the lowest-income families, since child support primarily substitutes for welfare payments and does little to increase the independence of custodial parents. In moderate-income families, both the independence effect for potential custodial parents and the support costs facing potential noncustodial parents come into play. Several empirical studies noted later examine which effect appears to predominate.

9.4   Trends in Child Support Awards and Payments

Collecting formal child support requires several steps, as illustrated with the following equation showing the average payment per child living with a custodial parent as the product of four key quantities.

$$C = LF\left(\frac{A}{LF}\right)S\left(\frac{P}{S}\right),$$

where C is the amount collected per child living with a custodial parent, LF is the percent of children with a legal noncustodial parent, A is the percent of children for whom a support award is present and due, S is the average size of the award, and P is the amount paid on the award.

Initially, soon after the federal government began playing an active role in child support, most of the emphasis was on the fourth component: collecting a high share of the amount owed. The movement to create child support guidelines was partly prompted by the recognition of the importance of the third component: the average size of awards. In recent years, administrators have started putting resources behind raising LF and A. Note that even were the government to insure a perfect collection record ($P/S = 1$), collections could erode if LF declined over time.

The Census Bureau has compiled data on some of these components (with custodial mothers as the unit of analysis) since the late 1970s, using the April Current Population Survey-Child Support Supplement (CPS-CSS). Unfortunately, we cannot determine LF and thus the impact of a low paternity establishment rate on collections. However, table 9.2 presents trends in the product of components one and two, which equals the share due an award.

Note that despite massive changes in federal and state laws regarding

Table 9.2   **Trends in Child Support Awards and Payments: 1978–97**

	All Custodial Mothers				Poor Custodial Mothers		
	% Received Child Support	% with an Award	% Received among Those Due	Payments Received perMother (1997 $)	% Received Child Support	% with an Award	% Received among Those Due
1978	34.6	59.1	71.6	1,532	17.8	38.1	58.8
1981	34.6	59.2	71.7	1,286	19.3	39.6	61.4
1983	34.9	57.7	76.0	1,317	19.6	42.4	62.0
1985	36.8	61.2	74.0	1,216	21.3	40.4	65.7
1987	38.5	58.0	76.1	1,469	27.3	43.4	72.0
1989	37.4	57.7	75.2	1,449	25.4	42.3	68.3
1991	37.6	55.8	76.3	1,334	24.1	38.9	70.4
1993	36.4	59.7	70.9	1,305	27.5	51.9	64.9
1995	37.4	61.2	69.8	1,484	26.5	51.1	61.9
1997	36.4	59.5	68.5	1,331	24.8	53.0	55.0

Sources: U.S. House of Representatives, Committee on Ways and Means (2000), U.S. Bureau of the Census at http://www.census.gov/hhes/www.chldsupt.html, various tables. Dollar figures are adjusted to reflect 1997 dollars using the CPI-U as the inflation adjustment.

Notes: Data for 1993, 1995, and 1997 are not directly comparable to earlier years because of major changes in the April Current Population Survey–Child Support Supplement. In particular, the percentage of amounts due to custodial parents that were actually received may appear lower in the 1993–97 data than in earlier periods because the recent data include amounts of "back payments due" whereas the pre-1993 data included only current amounts due in the denominator. Note also that in the CPS-CSS, "child support awards" and "child support due" are not the same. "Child support awards" measures the existence of an award at the time of the survey (April); "child support due" indicates whether child support income was expected last calendar year. Thus, multiplying the second and third columns does not necessarily equal the first column, as our simple formula in the text might suggest.

child support and billions of dollars spent on child support enforcement, trends in child support awards and real payments are disturbingly unchanged or have declined according to the CPS-CSS. Table 9.2 shows that the percent of custodial mothers who received child support has increased only slightly since 1978, from 35 percent in 1978 to 36 percent in 1997. Furthermore, table 9.2 shows a remarkable constancy since the late 1970s not only in the percentage of custodial mothers receiving child support, but also in the percentage of custodial mothers with an award, receiving support among those with an award, and the amount of child support received per custodial mother. Moreover, the ability of the CSE system to collect on the amounts actually due to custodial mothers improved after 1981, but it appears to have stagnated ever since. In 1978, the CPS reports indicate that 72 percent of the total amounts due were actually collected; this figure rose to 76 percent in 1983, then remained near that level through 1991. The data in table 9.2 show a decline to 68–69 percent in 1993 through 1997, but these figures are not exactly comparable to earlier years since they include amounts due to custodial parents that are owed on unpaid support from prior years.

These data also show, however, that poor custodial mothers are much more likely to receive child support in 1997 than they were in 1978. In 1997, 25 percent of poor custodial mothers received child support, up from 18 percent in 1978. As table 9.2 shows, most of this gain is due to increased award rates among poor custodial mothers, rather than increased collections on existing awards. In 1997, 53 percent of poor custodial mothers had a child support award, up from 38 percent in 1978.

Underlying these disparate results for custodial mothers and poor custodial mothers is a dramatic shift in the marital status composition of custodial mothers, away from divorced and separated mothers toward never-married mothers, which affected all custodial mothers more than it affected poor custodial mothers. Table 9.3 shows that never-married mothers increased from 20 percent to 32 percent of all custodial mothers between 1981 and 1997. Over the same period, the share of never-married mothers with awards more than tripled from 14 percent to 47 percent and the share receiving a payment also tripled from 7 percent from 22 percent. Still, even had the composition of custodial mothers remained at 1981 levels, the overall improvement in awards and collections would have been modest. The proportion with support awards would have increased from 59 percent to 62 percent, and the proportion receiving a payment would have risen from 35 percent to 39 percent.

It is important to note that the success or failure in the collection of child support depends, in part, on the interest of the custodial parent in collecting support and on the income of the noncustodial parent. To better understand why so many custodial parents did not receive child support, the Census Bureau has asked custodial parents to indicate their reasons for not

Table 9.3   **Changes in Awards and Payments by Marital Status of Custodial Mothers: 1981 and 1997**

	% Distribution of Custodial Mothers		% of Custodial Mothers with Support Awards		% of Custodial Mothers Receiving a Payment	
	1981	1997	1981	1997	1981	1997
Married	26.2	21.9	77.8	65.3	39.3	45.0
Divorced	34.1	30.9	80.5	70.4	52.5	47.3
Separated	18.5	13.1	42.8	56.2	26.7	32.4
Widowed	0.8	1.9	68.8	54.3	14.1	27.0
Never married	20.4	32.2	14.3	46.7	6.6	22.3
Total	100.0	100.0	59.2	59.5	34.6	36.4
1997 levels, using 1981 marital status distribution				61.4		38.7

Source: U.S. Bureau of the Census publications and tabulations by authors.
Note: See table 9.2.

having a legal child support award. Many custodial parents gave multiple responses, but the most common responses in 1996 were "did not feel the need to have a legal agreement" and "other parent could not afford to pay" (U.S. Bureau of the Census 1999). In addition, nearly one in four (23 percent) custodial mothers without awards stated they did not want to have contact with the other parent. Recent studies of nonmarital births indicate that about half of unmarried parents are living together at the time of the birth, vitiating the interest in and collection of child support (Garfinkel, McLanahan, and Harknett 1999).

The most recent detailed profile of families who do and do not receive child support comes from the analysis by Sorensen and Zibman (2000) of the 1997 National Survey of America's Families (NSAF). According to the 1997 NSAF, only about 52 percent of children with a nonresident father had a court-ordered child support award. This award percentage among children is 8 percentage points lower than the 60 percent figure observed in the 1997 CPS among mothers, presumably because the CPS figure includes all written agreements, not only those ratified by courts. However, the NSAF figure for the proportion with an award and a payment is 34 percent, nearly as high as the 36 percent figure for the CPS. Tabulations from the NSAF provide information on the receipt of financial support from noncustodial fathers who do not have a formal support order. Fully 36 percent of children lacking awards still receive some support from their father. Overall, Sorensen and Zibman estimate that 53 percent of noncustodial fathers provided assistance within the prior twelve months.

One striking finding from the Sorensen-Zibman study is the large variation across states in the receipt of child support. Among the thirteen states with large samples, the proportion of children with a noncustodial parent, with a child support order, and receiving the full amount due ranges from 14 percent and 15 percent in California and New York to 29 percent and 30 percent in Minnesota and Wisconsin.

9.5   Importance of Child Support For Low-Income Families

Several recent studies have examined the extent to which child support reduces welfare dependency and child poverty and whether it contributes to self-sufficiency and income equality (Meyer and Hu 1999; Wheaton and Sorensen 1998a; Sorensen and Zibman 2000). In general, these studies find that child support reduces welfare dependency and child poverty, but only slightly, and contributes to self-sufficiency and income equality, but only slightly. One of the reasons that child support has such limited redistributional effects is that the government keeps essentially all of the child support paid on behalf of children who are on public assistance.

Most recently, Sorensen and Zibman (2000) estimate that child support payments lift nearly half a million children out of poverty, reducing poverty among children eligible to receive child support by 5 percent. They also estimate that child support reduces these children's poverty gap by 8 percent. They also find that child support payments reduce the Gini coefficient among custodial families, but only slightly, suggesting that child support contributes to income equality among those eligible for it.

Sorensen and Zibman also show that child support appears relatively unimportant to the average child, representing a mere 2 percent of family income, but that child support is an important source of income for children who receive it, especially among low-income children. Table 9.4 shows that only 39 percent of children eligible for child support received it

Table 9.4   Child Support Characteristics of Children with a Noncustodial Parent by Their Poverty Status: 1996

Poverty Status (%)	% of Children with a Noncustodial Parent Whose Family Received Child Support	Among Families Receiving Child Support	
		Average Amount Received ($)	As % of Family Income
Less than 100	29	1,979	26
100–199	40	3,265	15
200–299	45	4,373	12
300 or more	50	5,764	9
All	39	3,795	16

Source: 1997 National Survey of America's Families.

in 1996, but the average amount received by these families was $3,795, representing, on average, 16 percent of their family income. Among poor children eligible for child support, only 29 percent of their families received child support in 1996, and the average amount received was $1,979, but it represented, on average, 26 percent of their family income.

The NSAF data also show that receipt of child support among poor children differs substantially by welfare status. Among poor children, child support went to only 22 percent of children on welfare in the prior year but to 36 percent of children not on welfare. Of the poor children whose family had left welfare, 42 percent received child support, averaging $2,562 per year or 30 percent of family income. In contrast, child support paid to children on welfare amounted to only $816 per year for those receiving a payment. Child support can be an important supplement to income, but rarely is the payment of support enough to make up for a lack of earnings or other income sources. Sorensen and Zibman show that among poor children not on AFDC, nearly half of the family income comes from earnings.

Compared to other benefit programs, child support plays a sizable role in moving poor single-mother families above the poverty line (Meyer and Hu 1999). In 1995, about 6–7 percent of poor mother-only families became nonpoor as a result of child support payments. This outflow was higher than those moved out of poverty by social insurance programs and was about the same as those removed from poverty through welfare programs. However, part of the reason is that those receiving child support had pretransfer incomes closer to the poverty line than did welfare recipients. Welfare removed 28.5 percent of the poverty gap of the pretransfer poor, while child support filled only about 6 percent of the gap.

Evidence that improvements in child support collections are responsible for some of the recent reductions in welfare caseloads comes from a recent work by Huang, Garfinkel, and Waldfogel (1999). The two-stage least squares model used by the authors includes a first stage that predicts child support collections as a function of political variables and other factors and a second stage that predicts welfare caseloads (logged) as a function of predicted child support collections as well as welfare benefit levels; fixed state and year effects; and state demographic, political, and economic variables. The findings indicate that effective child support enforcement reduces welfare caseloads both by reducing the proportion of single mothers receiving welfare and by reducing the number of single mothers. Simulations indicate that child support improvements accounted for about one-quarter of the decline in welfare caseloads between 1994 and 1996.

9.6   Capacity of Noncustodial Parents to Pay Child Support

Although census household surveys have collected child support data from custodial mothers since the late 1970s, few surveys have collected similar information from noncustodial fathers. Household surveys have had problems identifying noncustodial fathers because of reporting and coverage problems. Research shows that male fertility is underreported in household surveys and that noncustodial fathers' fertility is particularly underreported (Cherlin, Griffith, and McCarthy 1983; Clarke, Cooksey, and Verropoulou 1998). Two groups outside of the sampling frame of household surveys that are particularly relevant to identifying noncustodial fathers are the institutionalized and those in the military (Sorensen 1997). In addition, household surveys undercount certain groups, especially young minority males in their late twenties and early thirties, a group that disproportionately consists of noncustodial fathers (Sorensen 1997).

Given the lack of household survey data on noncustodial fathers and the policy interest in their ability to pay, Garfinkel and Oellerich (1989) developed an indirect method of imputing noncustodial fathers' income using the characteristics of custodial mothers. Initially, this method used the relationship between married fathers' earnings and their wives' characteristics to estimate the relationship between noncustodial fathers' earnings and the characteristics of the mothers of their children. More recent updates have used divorced couples' earnings and characteristics and the earnings of unwed men to predict the earnings of noncustodial fathers (Miller, Garfinkel, and McLanahan 1997). Although these updates have reduced the distortion that occurs because of unobserved variables and/or self-selection, it is still expected that this approach will yield upwardly biased earnings estimates. Nonetheless, using this method, Miller et al. estimated noncustodial fathers' average income by marital status, which, in 1990, ranged from $13,621 for never-married fathers to $28,226 for remarried fathers.

The focus of this research was to ascertain the potential amount of child support that noncustodial fathers could pay. Garfinkel and Oellerich found that noncustodial fathers paid $7 billion in 1983, but they could have paid between $24 and $30 billion that year (1989). These latter results were derived by applying the child support guidelines in Wisconsin, Colorado, and Delaware to the imputed incomes of noncustodial fathers in 1983. In other words, if noncustodial fathers had paid child support according to these state child support guidelines, they would have paid three to four times what they actually paid that year. Of course, this does not mean that noncustodial fathers legally owed $24 to $30 billion. Garfinkel and Oellerich note that they legally owed only $10 billion that year.

More recently, Sorensen used the 1990 Survey of Income and Program Participation and the 1987 National Survey of Families and Households (NSFH) to identify noncustodial fathers and measure their ability to pay child support (Sorensen 1997). Since these surveys suffer from reporting and coverage problems, she develops a range of estimates regarding noncustodial fathers' ability to pay child support. Using the Wisconsin child support guidelines, she found that noncustodial fathers paid around $17 billion in 1996, but they could have paid between $37 and $51 billion that year.

It is also worth noting that Sorensen (1997) finds that a sizable minority of noncustodial fathers are poor, possibly as many as 25 percent. Furthermore, she reports that as many as 35 percent of noncustodial fathers are not working at all or are working intermittently in 1990. These figures are considerably higher than those found among resident fathers, about 8 percent of whom were poor during the same time period and 15 percent of whom did not work year-round in 1990. Using a slightly different method of adjusting the 1987 NSFH for underreporting and coverage problems, Garfinkel, McLanahan, and Hanson (1998) report that 20 percent of noncustodial fathers earn less than $6,000 year.

Further details of the lives of poor noncustodial fathers can be found in several recent ethnographic studies (Edin, Lein, and Nelson 1998; Johnson, Levine, and Doolittle 1999; Waller and Plotnick 1999; Pate and Johnson 2000) and in descriptive information from a recent demonstration project called Parents' Fair Share (PFS), which provided employment-related services to unemployed noncustodial fathers who were behind in their child support payments and had children receiving welfare (Martinez and Miller 2000). These studies find that poor noncustodial fathers face severe employment barriers, including limited education, limited work experience, criminal records, housing instability, and poor health. For example, the PFS demonstration found that nearly 70 percent of its participants had a criminal record and nearly one-third had been arrested and charged with a crime during their participation in the program.

Other researchers have used the 1979 National Longitudinal Survey of Youth (NLSY79) to examine the characteristics of young noncustodial fathers. In an analysis of the earnings and employment patterns of young unwed fathers over time, Lerman (1993) found that the earnings of young unwed fathers were similar to the earnings of other young men around the time they fathered their children and that their earnings increased over time, but their earnings did not grow at the same rate as their peers. Pirog-Good and Good (1995) used the same data and found similar results.

Some studies have used data that include information on *both* the custodial mother and the noncustodial father (Nichols-Casebolt 1986; Sonenstein and Calhoun 1990; Peters et al. 1993; Bianchi, Subaiya, and Kahn 1999). Nearly all of these studies examine divorcing couples at or around the time of the divorce and approximately one year later. They typically report that shortly after divorce, custodial mothers and children experience a sharp decline in their economic well-being, whereas noncustodial fathers do not. Duncan and Hoffman (1985) examined the incomes of divorcing couples one year and five years after divorce. Their estimates show that, even after five years, women's incomes still lag behind those of their ex-husbands but return to approximately their predivorce levels.[5] These latter increases, however, are often the result of a new spouse.

9.7   Trends in Costs and Effectiveness of the Child Support System

One indicator of cost-effectiveness of programs aimed at helping low-income families is the resource cost of raising the incomes of low-income families by $1. Making this judgment in the child support arena is more complicated than doing so with the typical transfer program. It requires examining the balance between administrative costs, economic distortions, positive incentive effects, and distributional shifts between low-income families. A review of CSE's performance should also take account of the investment component of CSE spending. Put another way, some of the administrative outlays go for computerization, for establishing paternity, and for helping establish support orders. Because these investments may yield a flow of direct benefits in the future in higher support payments, these outlays should be amortized over the life of the investment and not treated as current expenses. Finally, the entire CSE system may generate long-term indirect benefits by reducing the number of never-married, separated, and divorced parents.

In judging the role of the child support system, both the trend in overall payments reported to the census and the trend in the amounts collected through the CSE program are relevant indicators. Figure 9.1 shows the trend in the percent of single mothers by marital status and welfare status receiving child support based on the March CPS. Note that while the overall percentage of single mothers reporting at least some child support has remained remarkably constant (at about 30 percent), the numbers receiving child support have increased sharply within groups of never-married mothers and the welfare recipients who have ever been married. However, the rise in the share of never-married mothers—the group for whom child support is the exception, not the rule—is making collections harder to obtain.

A recent study has examined the impact of state enforcement policies on the receipt of child support payments (Sorensen and Hill, forthcoming). This study strongly suggests that CSE programs raised support payments above what they would have been. Among the never-married mothers, who typically live in very low-income families, receipt of child support went from about 4 percent of families in 1976 to 17.5 percent in 1997. Sorensen and Hill find about half of the gains are associated with the child support system. About one-third of the much smaller increases among previously married mothers resulted from CSE activities. Still, attaining these signifi-

---

5. Duncan and Hoffman (1985) examine divorcing couples regardless of the presence of children, and thus these findings may not hold for divorcing couples with children.

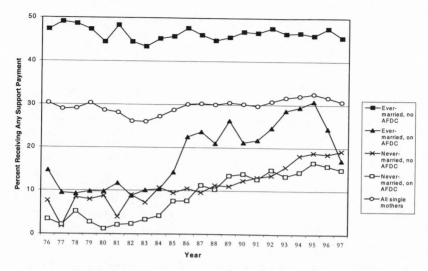

Fig. 9.1   Percent of single mothers receiving child support, by marital and AFDC status: 1976–97.

Source: Sorensen and Hill (forthcoming).

cant and large impacts apparently required substantial outlays for CSE programs.

Trends in the amounts collected through the CSE program appear in table 9.5. Note that CSE collections have increased rapidly over the period but collections per case have remained constant. Thus, the growth in overall collections is a result of more cases flowing through the CSE program, not higher average real payments per case. Between 1978 and 1997, the proportion of total child support that was collected through CSE programs rose from 23 percent to 85 percent (U.S. House of Representatives, Committee on Ways and Means 2000, 529).

At the same time, CSE administrative expenditures have been rising rapidly in real terms. In fact, total administrative outlays per custodial mother tripled in real terms between 1983 and 1997; as of 1997, they amounted to nearly 22 percent of total payments (see table 9.6). Since much of the child support payments would have taken place without CSE, the administrative cost per additional payment is no doubt well above 20 percent. For example, if we attribute all of the $4.4 billion growth in aggregate payments between 1978 and 1997 to CSE, the added CSE cost would amount to 57 percent of each additional $1 of child support. But it is unlikely that in the absence of the CSE program aggregate support payments would have remained constant in the face of the 50 percent growth in the number of custodial mothers. In an analysis of the effect of AFDC and non-AFDC administrative expenditures on collections for AFDC and non-AFDC cases over the 1979 to 1991 period, Nixon (1996) estimates that each dollar spent

Table 9.5   Aggregate Child Support Collections Through the CSE Program and
                 Child Support Amounts per Case: 1978–98 ($1996)

	Aggregate Collections ($000)	CSE Cases with Payment by Type (in 000s)			Child Support Per case ($)
		On AFDC	Not on AFDC	Total Cases	
1978	2,555	458	249	707	3,614
1980	2,882	503	243	746	3,863
1982	2,885	597	448	1,045	2,761
1984	3,591	647	547	1,194	3,008
1986	4,609	582	786	1,368	3,369
1988	6,125	621	1,083	1,704	3,594
1990	7,272	701	1,363	2,064	3,523
1991	7,919	755	1,555	2,310	3,428
1992	8,921	836	1,749	2,585	3,451
1993	9,620	879	1,958	2,837	3,391
1994	10,441	926	2,169	3,095	3,374
1995	11,152	976	2,409	3,385	3,295
1996	12,019	940	2,564	3,504	3,430
1997	13,364	865	2,850	3,715	3,517
1998	13,811	789	3,070	3,859	3,579

Source: Office of Child Support Enforcement.

Table 9.6   Performance Indicators of CSE Program Based on CPS and CSE Data: 1978–97

	Aggregate Receipts (CPS) ($1995 billions)	Custodial Mothers (CPS) (in millions)	Total CSE Costs (CSE data) ($1995 millions)	CSE Costs per Custodial Mother (CSE data)	CSE Costs as % of Payments (CSE data)
1978	10.6	7.1	729	103	6.9
1981	10.3	8.4	882	105	8.6
1983	10.8	8.7	1,057	122	9.8
1985	10.2	8.8	1,153	131	11.3
1987	13.4	9.4	1,430	152	10.7
1989	13.7	10.0	1,675	168	12.2
1991	13.2	9.9	2,019	204	15.3
1993	13.8	11.5	2,364	206	17.1
1995	16.4	11.6	3,012	260	18.4
1997	15.0	11.9	3,255	274	21.7

Sources: U.S. Bureau of the Census, *Child Support and Alimony* (various years); U.S. Bureau of the Census, *Child Support for Custodial Mothers and Fathers* (various years); U.S. Department of Health and Human Services (various years).

on AFDC cases yielded only an additional $0.10 in child support but that a dollar spent on non-AFDC cases increased collections by $3.30.

Not surprisingly, the impact of money spent on administration is highly sensitive to the activities undertaken with the added dollars. A demonstration project in four states tested whether reviewing and updating child support awards would yield added support payments (Bishop 1992). Cases that were not modified for the last three years were reviewed and, where appropriate, modified in about 15 percent of AFDC cases reviewed and 6 percent of non-AFDC cases. The total cost of the effort amounted to about $1.5 million, while the added government savings from offsetting benefits against the higher support payments reached about $4.6 million.

In examining the high and rising cost of the CSE program in relation to support payments, one must bear in mind that, as noted above, the mix of custodial mothers has shifted from married and divorced mothers toward never-married mothers, the latter of whom are more costly to serve than the former.

Finally, the collections data overlook the CSE program's most impressive achievement—the sharp rise in the establishment of paternity. As of the mid-1980s, births to unmarried women amounted to about 850,000, and only about 240,000 paternities were being established that year, resulting in one paternity establishment for every three and a half nonmarital births.[6] Fortunately, the CSE system has made such enormous progress in paternity establishment that as of 1997, there were slightly more paternities established or acknowledged (1.29 million) than births to unmarried women (1.28 million).[7] Since paternities can be established for children born outside marriage in past years and since the accumulated stock of potential paternity cases is far higher than annual nonmarital births, annual paternities can easily exceed annual nonmarital births for several years to come.

9.8   Trends in State and Federal Financing of Administrative Costs

Together with providing enforcement tools and mandating policies, the federal government contributed substantially to the funding of state child support programs. The administrative matching incentive payments are complex, but states typically receive 66 percent of the normal administrative costs as well as 90 percent of the costs of laboratory blood testing. A second component of state funds comes from the recovered child support payments made on behalf of welfare recipients that are kept by the government to recoup its costs of providing welfare. The recovered payments are divided between the federal and state government based on the matching percent-

6. Our estimate of births to unmarried mothers is from Vital Statistics, which collects its data from the states. A few states identify nonmarital births by comparing the mother's last name to that of the father's last name. If they are different or there is no last name for the father, the state assumes that the mother is unmarried, which overstates the number of unwed births.

7. There may be double-counting of paternities established because both hospitals and child support offices count paternities and child support offices do not necessarily eliminate the overlap between these two sources before submitting their reports to the state child support agency.

age used for Medicaid, which had been the AFDC matching rate before the block grant was introduced. Low-income states like Mississippi, which received an 80 percent federal match, must return 80 percent of collections to the federal government. High-payment states split the collections on a fifty-fifty basis. A third source is federal incentive payments that provide states with additional funds that can add up to as much as 10 percent of collections. Congress recently changed the basis on which these funds are distributed (U.S. Department of Health and Human Services 1997b).

In fiscal year 1996, states received from the federal government a combined sum of about $2 billion in direct administrative matching payments and $400 million in incentive payments. Total administrative expenses, including the $600 million net contribution by states, amounted to about $3 billion. Since states claimed about $1 billion of the collections, they ended up netting about $400 million under CSE. In table 9.7, we can see the trends in the size of the administrative costs and of the amounts recovered and retained by the state and federal governments. Note that the real dollar gains of states from CSE have remained constant despite much more rapid increases in total administrative costs than in recovered contributions. Through 1984, combined (federal and state) recovered collections actually exceeded combined administrative costs. By 1996, the balance had shifted to the point at which combined administrative costs exceeded recovered collections by about $1.1 billion. In that year, the federal govern-

Table 9.7   **Federal and State Spending on Administrative Costs and Federal and State Collections Recovered: 1978–98 ($1996 millions)**

	Net Federal Administrative Outlays	Federal Share of Collected Child Support	Net Federal Government Cost	Net State Administrative Outlays	State Share of Collected Child Support	Net State Government Cost
1978	708	759	−51	54	361	−307
1980	821	480	341	88	534	−447
1982	923	507	416	75	577	−502
1984	968	607	361	124	677	−553
1986	1,123	524	599	213	602	−389
1988	1,365	597	767	192	698	−507
1990	1,603	645	958	340	750	−410
1991	1,714	720	994	362	805	−443
1992	1,839	827	1,013	395	881	−486
1993	2,005	839	1,165	416	915	−499
1994	2,277	808	1,469	434	944	−511
1995	2,570	846	1,724	533	967	−435
1996	2,449	888	1,561	606	1,013	−407
1997	2,675	1,023	1,652	676	1,132	457
1998	2,677	924	1,753	773	1,048	275

Source: U.S. House of Representatives, Committee on Ways and Means (2000).

Note: The net federal outlays include incentive payments to state governments; the net state outlays equal state administrative expenditures less federal incentive payments.

ment bore not only this $1.1 billion net cost, but also another $400 million in net state receipts.

These state surpluses, however, may be a thing of the past as incentive funding shifts and welfare caseloads decline (Turetsky 1998). By 1998, net federal costs had increased to $1.8 billion, while the dollar gain to states had declined $275 million. Since the fall of 2000, incentive funding has been capped, and states have been competing for a limited amount of money. In addition, the amount of income generated from cost recovery has stagnated as welfare caseloads have fallen. Just as revenue is stagnating, demand for child support services continues to increase and may well accelerate now that welfare is time-limited. This tension in the financial structure of the child support system is clearly evident on Capitol Hill as well as across the country.

9.9   Effects of Child Support Incentives on Behavior

The empirical evidence documents the role of the CSE system in raising child support payments. Given the fact that the CSE program is not a paper tiger and actually adds to collections, we might expect to observe behavioral effects on such outcomes as the labor supply of custodial parents and noncustodial parents, welfare use, nonmarital childbearing, divorce and remarriage, and the involvement of noncustodial parents in raising their children. In general, theory does not yield firm predictions on how child support enforcement affects each of these behaviors. Moreover, incentive effects on one behavior may be offset or reinforced by effects on another behavior. If, for example, stricter CSE enforcement were to encourage custodial mothers on welfare to go to work, the increased independence of single mothers might reduce their probability of marriage or remarriage (Hu 1999, 78).

Although the empirical strategies naturally vary depending on the behavior examined, several authors identify policy impacts by regressing variations across states and over time in CSE policies on a behavioral outcome. The first problem is obtaining accurate measures of the implementation of policies. For example, states whose guidelines require unusually high child support awards may find that judges define income less comprehensively than in other states. A second problem is the simultaneity of policies and behavioral outcomes. If, for example, high nonmarital birth rates stimulate stronger paternity establishment efforts, then estimates may show paternity establishment effort increasing rather than reducing the rate of nonmarital births. Untangling the short-run and long-run effects of policies poses another serious estimation problem. Policies that increase the state's effectiveness in establishing paternity may reduce nonmarital childbearing, but only after expectations of potential mothers and fathers change.

Ideally, one would like to follow how CSE changes the constraints faced by each individual, which, in turn, change child support payments or receipts as well as other behaviors. Since problems arise in identifying impacts of CSE from state and over time variation, the focus is sometimes on the effects of actual child support payments or receipts by individuals on their work, welfare status, marital status, and parental involvement. This strategy would be appropriate if actual payments or receipts were better indicators of the impact of CSE than estimates derived from cross-section and time series estimates. Unfortunately, it is not easy to isolate the effect of child support on an individual basis because unmeasured characteristics plausibly affect child support payments and other outcomes. A noncustodial father who cares for his children and trusts their mother is more likely to both work hard and make support payments than another father with the identical observable characteristics.

Several strategies have emerged to deal with these issues. One is to use a comparison group methodology. The idea is that variation and changes in state CSE policies should only affect groups potentially affected by such policies. For example, by examining how state policy variables affect the work effort of noncustodial fathers compared to the work effort of custodial fathers (or single nonfathers), Freeman and Waldfogel (1998) attempt to take account of any spurious relationship between state policies and the supply of labor. Nixon (1996) uses estimates of CSE variables on married women without children as a quasi–control group in an analysis of CSE's effects on divorce. This approach is worthwhile but fails to capture the potential simultaneity between the child support situation and state policies. If low work effort and low support payments by noncustodial fathers stimulated states to adopt tough collection policies, then CSE policies might appear to be reducing work effort even in the absence of such an impact. To deal with this problem, some researchers model the state policies as a function of factors exogenous to the child support situation in the state. Using a two-stage least squares procedure, Case (1998) estimates a first-stage equation of paternity enforcement policies as a function of the gender composition of the state legislature, on the grounds that women legislators will have a deeper interest in effective child support enforcement. The second stage involves regressing state paternity policies on out-of-wedlock childbearing.

Still another approach is to use state policies as instrumental variables in equations estimating the effects of individual child support receipts or payments on behavior. This method bases estimates on the indirect effects of policy operating through individual payments or receipts. Such an approach is particularly useful when the child support effects operate through complex budget constraints. Finally, a few social experiments have tested interventions to increase child support payments.

9.9.1 Effects of Child Support Incentives and Employment Services on Child Support Collections

Policymakers have funded experiments to test the impacts of efforts to improve the weak incentives and limited capacity of noncustodial fathers to pay child support. In the W-2 Child Support Demonstration in Wisconsin, parents on welfare and in the treatment group were allowed to retain the full amount of child support paid on behalf of their children while control group parents could only keep the higher of $50 per month or 41 percent of the support paid by noncustodial parents. Meyer and Cancian (2001) found that the enhanced incentives raised the share of fathers paying support by 2–3 percentage points (from a base of about 50 percent) and the level of total support payments by about 5 percent. The effects varied substantially among subgroups, with the largest impacts taking place among fathers divorced from their children's mothers, fathers with a recent history of paying child support, and mothers with no recent history on welfare. Although the increased incentive to pay and to receive child support stimulated support payments, the treatment induced no significant effects on the work effort of noncustodial fathers, their involvement with their children, or the earnings of mothers.

The PFS demonstration used employment services, peer support groups, mediation, and improved linkages with the child support system to increase child support payments by noncustodial fathers as well as to raise their earnings and involvement with their children. The participants were men whose children were on AFDC, who were behind in their support payments, and who were unemployed or underemployed. Although the PFS intervention raised formal child support payments by about 25 percent (from $313 to $397 over a six-month period), 44 percent of the increase came from reductions in informal support (Knox and Redcross 2000). Estimates of the effects of PFS on fathers' earnings vary with the sample and data set. Using the full sample and information from unemployment insurance wage records, one finds little evidence of PFS-induced gain in earnings. However, data from a sample of fathers interviewed for the study suggest positive PFS impacts on earnings of over 20 percent (Martinez and Miller 2000).

The experimental results show that incentives and services can affect both the ability and the willingness of low-income noncustodial parents to pay child support. However, determining the size of the effects and which interventions work best will require additional research and demonstration activity.

9.9.2   Child Support and Work Effort by Custodial and Noncustodial Parents

Economic theory predicts that child support income, like other nonemployment income, should have a negative impact on the work effort of custodial parents. However, as the labor-leisure budget constraint in figure 9.2 illustrates, the interaction between child support and welfare programs complicates the analysis. In the absence of any welfare benefits, the presence of child support income simply raises nonemployment income and plausibly exerts a negative income effect on work. But when the custodial

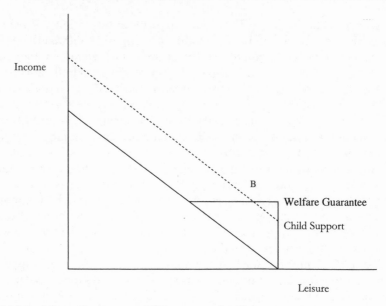

Fig. 9.2   Interaction between child support and welfare

parent is eligible for welfare benefits that exceed child support, the receipt of child support has no effect on the amount of nonemployment. As long as welfare payments are positive (net of child support), child support income should have no income or substitution effect. Child support can become a factor encouraging work effort over some ranges because it lowers the point at which custodial parents leave welfare and thus are no longer subject to the high marginal tax rates from welfare programs. A custodial parent choosing whether not to work or to work enough to move beyond point B will be more likely to work if child support is available. The presence of child support thus raises the net return to work for custodial parents, at least in a segment of earnings, and should reduce the size of welfare payments and the amount of welfare received.

In a recent paper, Hu (1999) finds that, as predicted, increases in child support payments reduce welfare participation and reduce work effort among nonwelfare mothers but raise labor force participation among all divorced mothers. Added child support also slows the rate of remarriage. Hu develops an elaborate six-equation model estimated with joint maximum likelihood techniques. The first three equations estimate how child support and other factors affect hours of work while on welfare, hours of work off welfare, and whether the custodial parent works while off welfare. A fourth equation determines whether the custodial mother chooses to participate on welfare. The fifth is a hazard function yielding potential impacts of child support on remarriage, and the sixth is a child support equation that embodies the role of child support policies as well as other variables presumably exogenous to the mother's work and marriage behavior. Hu uses five years of data from the Panel Study of Income Dynamics (PSID) on women with children under eighteen who divorced or separated and became heads of households between 1969 and 1987.

Hu's findings show that the additional work stimulated by child support comes about through its impact on reducing AFDC use. Both for those who remain on AFDC and for those not on AFDC, child support lowers labor supply. The impact of additional child support varies depending on which mothers receive the money. One simulation raises amounts paid to mothers already receiving support and assumes modest payments to mothers not receiving any support. This change would raise child support income from $2,516 to $4,221, reduce welfare participation from 20 to 15 percent, increase the proportion working from 76 to 79 percent, and raise average hours worked from 1,311 to 1,403.

In an earlier analysis, Graham and Beller (1989) found that the total effect of child support payments on labor force participation of divorced mothers was negative, but exceedingly small. They estimated that a $1,000 increase in child support reduced work by just two hours. Their estimated effect of child support on welfare participation was similar to that of Hu (1999).

Evidence from the New York Child Assistant Program (CAP) reinforces the idea that substituting child support or a child support–like payment for welfare can raise the earnings of single mothers (Hamilton et al. 1996). The CAP payment went to mothers who had support orders but could not collect from noncustodial fathers. The payment declined only at a 10 percent rate on earnings up to the poverty line, but it fell at a sharp 67 percent on earnings above the poverty line. Using a random assignment experimental design, the evaluators found that CAP raised earnings by 20 percent over five years, increasing both hours worked and the proportion working. The gain in the share working was about 3 percentage points, as the share that was working rose from 26 percent among controls to 29 percent among the treatment group.

In addition, it should be noted that work incentives for custodial parents are further complicated in states that use income-shares guidelines. In general, the custodial parent faces no decrease in the marginal gain from working, but in states that have an income-share model of determining child support awards that declines with income, additional earnings to the custodial parent will, by placing the income in a lower rate bracket, reduce the amount owed by the noncustodial parent. Consider an income-share state in which the required contribution starts at 25 percent of joint income through $40,000 and then drops by 1 percentage point per $5,000 until joint income reaches $80,000. Suppose further that the income of the noncustodial parents is constant at $30,000 per year. As the custodial parent raises her income from $10,000 per year to $20,000, she loses $600, for an implicit tax rate of 3 percent. Income share formulas in which the rate applied to joint income increases with income will work in the opposite direction.

For noncustodial parents, most guidelines embody rules that raise payment obligations as income increases. If the noncustodial parent does not benefit at all from these additional payments (say, by gaining utility from the knowledge that his child has more resources because of his contributions), then payments under a percentage of income or income-shares guideline act like an income tax, with offsetting income and substitution effects on work.

However, although most awards are set as a nominal dollar amount that reflects the noncustodial parent's ability to pay child support at that time, only about one-quarter of the orders are ever modified to reflect changes in income or circumstances. Thus, changes in obligations do not materialize immediately after an income change, and since they sometimes take a long time, a noncustodial parent may view his or her payment as a fixed sum, a sum that exerts an income but no substitution effect. But, as Freeman and Waldfolgel (1998) point out, if the noncustodial parent can avoid this levy by engaging in self-employment, casual work, or off-the-books work, or by "disappearing" to some other locale, there may be a huge substitution effect in work activity, away from wage and salary employment to less readily observable activities.

Freeman and Waldfolgel (1998) find that child support policies had little, if any, effect on noncustodial fathers' labor supply, which is consistent with the general finding in male labor supply studies that male labor supply is relatively unresponsive to variations in wages. As best as they could tell, noncustodial fathers in states with stronger CSE policies were slightly more likely to be working relative to custodial fathers and slightly less likely to be working off the books. Their findings come from regressions in which state CSE policies are determinants of work effort by noncustodial parents. By interacting the CSE policy variables with the probability that a man is a noncustodial father, the coefficients reflect the difference between CSE effects on noncustodial fathers and the potentially spurious effects of CSE on custodial fathers and/or men with no children. The data come from the 1986 and 1991 Surveys of Income and Program Participation (SIPP). Although CSE was not as rigorous in those years as it is today, especially among low-income noncustodial fathers, Freeman and Waldfogel do find large positive effects of wage-withholding on the payments of never-married fathers. Thus, at this point, there is no evidence that CSE reduces the amount worked by noncustodial parents.

Noncustodial parents with children on welfare have even less to gain from paying child support. With their payments simply offsetting government aid, noncustodial parents may well perceive no benefit from paying support. As noted above, in this case, the income-conditioned support obligations become akin to a tax on the parent's income. The cumulative reduction to the net wage can easily become substantial: A noncustodial parent with two children and earning $18,000 per year will owe over $5,000 per year (about 29 percent of income) in child support in the median state (Pirog, Klotz, and Byers 1998). Add payroll taxes (7 percent) and the lowest income tax class (15 percent), and you have a marginal tax rate of 52 percent.

Even when mothers leave welfare, noncustodial fathers may still pay most of their support to the government for back welfare or Medicaid costs or for arrearages built up during the period in which their children received welfare. At the moment, there are no studies that provide an analysis of the marginal tax rates that noncustodial parents face with respect to child support alone or with respect to cumulative rates that incorporate child support, taxes, and transfers.

9.9.3   Child Support Impacts on Nonmarital Births, Divorce, Remarriage, Father Involvement

Several studies have examined the impact of child support enforcement on nonmarital child bearing, divorce, remarriage, and father involvement. In general, policies that require noncustodial parents to assume greater financial responsibility for raising their children potentially increase the independence of custodial parents, but they also increase the cost of family formation and dissolution for noncustodial parents.

Recent research on the impact of child support on divorce suggests that child support enforcement discourages divorce, especially among mothers most likely to be eligible for welfare assistance. Nixon (1997) finds robust evidence that tighter child support enforcement lowers the rate of divorce. Apparently, the CSE-induced disincentive for fathers was enough to outweigh the CSE impact on independence. Using marital history information from the 1988 and 1990 March/April Current Population Surveys, Nixon estimates the probability of divorce within a five-year period, given that a marriage had taken place by the survey year. The key independent variables are five state child support enforcement variables representing the policy climate and state effectiveness in collections. As noted, Nixon takes account of spurious relationships between policies and outcomes by using married mothers with no children as a quasi–control group. The CSE variables exert no effect on these women, making the negative CSE impacts on divorce among mothers more convincing. The effects are larger among low-income mothers, perhaps because the existence of welfare programs means that CSE provides little additional independence but does create disincentives for fathers.

With regard to remarriage, it appears that increased child support enforcement has resulted in lower remarriage rates among custodial and noncustodial parents. Increased child support leads to greater independence for custodial parents, which, in turn, results in lower remarriage rates for them (Beller and Graham 1993; Yun 1992; and Hu 1999). On the other hand, Bloom, Conrad, and Miller (1998) find that increased child support enforcement leads to increased costs to noncustodial parents, which, in turn, reduces their likelihood of remarriage. This analysis compares the impact of CSE variables on the rate of remarriage among divorced men with children as compared to divorced men without children. Using the SIPP and the NLSY79, the authors estimate that an increase in the collection rate from the thirtieth to the tenth ranked state reduces the yearly hazard of remarriage by 28–31 percent. Extending the time to remarriage does not, however, appear to improve the quality of marital matches. Bloom, Conrad, and Miller also investigate the potential impacts of CSE on the entry into first marriage among men who fathered nonmarital children and on the probability of a second nonmarital birth. The results suggest little or no impact of CSE on these behaviors.

Several recent studies have examined the relationship between child support enforcement and nonmarital childbearing. As mentioned earlier, the expected effect of increased child support on nonmarital childbearing is ambiguous—stronger child support enforcement increases the cost of nonmarital fatherhood, but it also increases the independence of nonmarital motherhood. In general, results from these studies suggest that increased child support enforcement reduces nonmarital childbearing. Case (1998) provides a two-stage model in which state paternity enforcement policies are determinants of nonmarital births but are endogenous and are identified using the number of women in the state legislatures and other exogenous state characteristics. The estimates cover variations across states and over time from 1978 through 1991. The two-stage approach turns out to make a major difference in outcomes. The simple ordinary least squares regressions of state policies on nonmarital childbearing yield no negative impacts, but in the two-stage model, CSE policies consistently exert significant, negative impacts.

An analysis by Plotnick et al. (1999) attempts to determine whether strict CSE enforcement influenced the likelihood that women had a premarital birth as a teenager. The authors follow the fertility and marital history through age twenty of a sample of 2,153 women, ages fourteen to sixteen in 1979, drawn from the NLSY. Controlling for an array of individual and area characteristics, the regressions relate state rates of paternity establishment, state collections per case, and state collections per administrative dollar to the probability of teen premarital childbearing. Although paternity establishment rates do exert a negative impact, the main specification shows only statistically significant effects on white women, none for black women. Still, the authors project that raising state performance on paternity establishment from existing levels to the rates achieved by the most successful states would lower the proportion who have premarital births by more than 50 percent, from 11.5 to 5.5 percent.

The connection between child support payments and visitation by noncustodial parents is often a contentious issue. Some fathers' rights groups claim that although public agencies go to great lengths to enforce the payment obligations of noncustodial parents, the government shows little interest in making sure that the visitation rights of noncustodial parents are upheld (Pearson and Thoennes 1998). One worry is that strict CSE policies, by driving fathers to work longer hours or to leave the state to avoid making payments, could weaken contact between noncustodial parents and their children. On the other hand, as effective policies push noncustodial parents to make payments, these parents may see themselves as having more of a stake in their child's life and more of an earned right to participate in raising the child. Seltzer, McLanahan, and Hanson (1998) examine the effect of child support on the involvement of fathers and on the conflict between parents using data from the 1987–88 and the 1992–94 NSFH. The authors use a sample of 1,300 families with a child eligible for child support as of 1987 and a small longitudinal sample of children whose parents were married in wave 1 and separated or divorced between waves 1 and 2. The raw data show that child support payments are positively associated with both visitations and with conflict between parents. To test for CSE effects, the authors regress state CSE variables on visitation and conflict and also use state CSE variables as instruments in regressions of child support payments on outcomes. Some CSE practices raised the extent of visitation by fathers, although the effects were not statistically significant in the instrumental variable analyses. At the same time, higher child support payments, including payments induced by tighter enforcement, heightened parental conflict in the analyses using instrumental variables.

The fact that welfare programs cause support payments to go to the government instead of one's child could well add to the disincentive associated with family splitting. A noncustodial parent could realize that if he separates from his children and they go on welfare, he will have to pay child support and little, if any, of his support will benefit his children, which may cause him to be marginalized in his children's lives. Of course, given the disincentives of both parents to channel money through the formal system and report payments to welfare programs, noncustodial parents could make payments informally and custodial parents could avoid reporting them (Edin and Lein 1997). In this case, the support would end up raising the child's family income (Bassi and Lerman 1996). However, noncustodial parents would have to bear the penalty of limiting their job choices to the informal sector indefinitely or would face the prospect of having to make back payments; custodial parents would have to commit welfare fraud by not cooperating with CSE agencies.

9.10   Equity Issues in Child Support

Certainly, several equity issues are involved in the setting of child support awards. Betson, Evenhouse, and Reilly (1992) examine the trade-off between equity and incentives embedded in alternative methods of setting awards. They find that, when the incomes of noncustodial parents are substantially higher than the incomes of custodial parents, the standard approaches used in state guidelines cause the custodial parent and children to suffer large declines in living standards relative to the predivorce incomes, whereas noncustodial parents living alone typically gain. However, moving to formulas that do more to equalize living standards raises marginal tax rates on noncustodial parents substantially.

Custody and visitation issues complicate considerations of the equity of child support. A parent may willingly trade the loss of income in order to retain custody of his or her child. In this context, making the parent who is not granted custody pay child support punishes the loser and thus may weaken the equity case for large support payments, especially since payments to the custodial parent cannot be monitored to assure that they mainly benefit the child. Another complication arises when parents who provide partial custody do not receive credit for their in-kind contributions.

A frequent complaint of noncustodial parents is the state's lack of interest in enforcing their visitation rights with the same vigor as their efforts to collect child support. Congress recently acknowledged the problem when it enacted in 1996 a small grant program under the Personal Responsibility and Work Opportunity Reconciliation Act (PRWORA) to facilitate access and visitation by noncustodial parents, through such mechanisms as mediation, counseling, education, parenting plans, and monitoring and supervision of visits. Although most states received only about $50,000–200,000 under the program in 1997, they established 131 programs and served about 20,000 people (U.S. Department of Health and Human Services 1999).

Finally, there are the inequities in the establishment of payment obligations for low-income fathers (Sorensen and Lerman 1998). To an unknown extent, judges set support obligations on the basis of expectations of a custodial parent's income, even when such income is out of reach. In addition, some states charge fathers for the cost of the delivery of the child and for welfare payments, even when these charges are much higher than the noncustodial parent would owe if the guidelines were followed. Low-income fathers often lack the knowledge of how to have their payments adjusted during periods of unemployment and incarceration. Once the orders are established, the federal Bradley amendment of 1986 prohibits judges from forgiving past-due support, called arrearages. Moreover, arrearages cannot be discharged in a bankruptcy proceeding, even when the amounts owed would go to the state. Fathers often claim they are making in-kind contributions to their children that are not taken into account when they face legal proceedings. According to Waller and Plotnick (1999), the in-kind contributions are accepted by the community and the custodial parent but are ignored by the CSE system. In some cases, fathers must even pay back child support for periods in which they were living with and supporting their children.

The inflexibility of the CSE system in dealing with low-income fathers may contribute to driving many such fathers into the underground economy. Although one quantitative analysis finds little evidence of a child support–induced decline in legitimate earnings of nonresident fathers (Freeman and Waldfogel 1998), the data were far from ideal and effects on underground earnings are consistently reported in the qualitative literature (Johnson, Levine, and Doolittle 1999; Waller and Plotnick 1999).

The differences between tax and transfer policies in the treatment of child support also weaken the noncustodial parent's incentive to make payments. The tax system does not permit the noncustodial parent to deduct child support, but it does exclude child support from the mother's income (Wheaton and Sorensen 1998b). In contrast, child support is typically counted as income to the recipient in determining transfer benefits, but at least in the case of food stamps, noncustodial parents can deduct support payments from countable income. The problem arises when the custodial parent receives welfare benefits while the noncustodial parent does not and is subject to income taxes. In this case, the payer (noncustodial parent) cannot take the payments as deductions, yet the receiver must count the payments as income.

One can look at child support's treatment in the transfer system from two perspectives. Some policymakers have argued for exempting all or part of child support from income counted in transfer programs. Such a policy would face the problem of horizontal equity because families with similar incomes but different income sources (say, one with earnings and one with child support income) would be treated differently. On the other hand, since the individual earning the income to pay child support would already have been taxed on the receipt of that income, counting payments in the income of recipients would amount to a kind of double taxation.

9.11   Critical Reform Options

In one sense, child support should have a bright future. The CSE programs have all the tools they need to establish paternity, establish appropriate support awards, and collect payments. The declining welfare caseloads are reducing the number of families exposed to perverse incentives under which noncustodial parents see their hard-earned payments going, not to their children, but to reimbursing the government, and neither parent has a stake in having support payments flow through official channels. For many parents, these trends do augur well for the future. But for the many low-income fathers with large arrearages, too many of the familiar disincentives remain in place. Some may face past obligations that loom so large as to discourage all but the most motivated.

Although no national reports are available that document the distributional impact of arrearages, there is enough state-specific evidence to stimulate calls for reforms (Roberts 2001). The federal government has made it clear that states can forgive arrears owed to the government. Some states are now forgiving arrears owed to them in exchange for full compliance with present and future obligations. However, the underlying causes of the large arrearages owed to the government are not fully understood and need to be identified.

Child Support Assurance (CSA), a widely discussed reform proposed by Irwin Garfinkel and others, would require that noncustodial parents make payments according to specified guidelines (Garfinkel, McLanahan, and Robins 1992; Roberts 1994).[8] In cases where the noncustodial parent was unable to pay or the government was unable to collect the payments, the government would provide an assured payment not conditioned on the income of the custodial parent. If the nonresident parent paid some amount less than the assured benefit, the program would pay the difference. Given the very low incomes of many noncustodial parents, many custodial parents are bound to receive minimal or highly varying support payments. Such instability weakens the ability of single parents to package enough income through earnings and other sources outside welfare to make ends meet. The CSA could smooth the payments custodial parents are due from the contribution of the other parent. Counting CSA benefits as income would lower the welfare break-even point and thus raise the likelihood that families earn their way off income-tested public assistance. From Garfinkel's (1994) perspective, CSA would extend the social insurance concept now embodied in Survivors Insurance to children who suffer income losses due to the absence of a parent.

Although an assured benefit is appealing, the program would extend to other groups the disincentive problem in welfare under which support payments do very little to raise the living standard of the children. As in the welfare case, the presence of assured benefits would reduce the incentives for many noncustodial parents to make payments and for many custodial parents to pursue delinquent parents.

The costs and impacts of a CSA program would vary substantially with

8. The National Commission on Children (1991) recommended adopting a child support assurance program. Federal legislation has been introduced several times to implement some form of child support assurance, but these efforts have never been enacted. Several states, such as California, are currently experimenting with the concept. Several European countries implement the CSA concept under Advanced Maintenance programs.

the level of the assured benefit and the group of custodial parents covered. According to Sorensen and Clark (1994), a payment of $1,500 per year per child in 1989 limited to families with a support award would have cost about $1.6 billion and reduced child poverty by 0.6 percent. Extending the CSA to all custodial families would have quadrupled the cost to $7 billion and would have lifted 3 percent of poor children out of poverty. Meyer et al. (1994) make estimates for 1985 of alternative CSA plans that take account of labor supply responses by custodial parents. They find the costs, antipoverty effects, and labor supply effects are modest for low payment plans limited to families with awards. Only if the CSA stimulated improvements in award levels and in the proportion receiving an award would the CSA approach substantially increase the labor supply of recipients of Temporary Assistance for Needy Families and reduce the poverty gap.

One experimental program similar to a CSA, New York's CAP, was available in seven counties to custodial parents eligible to receive AFDC in the late 1980s and early 1990s. The assured benefit under CAP was set below the AFDC guarantee but above the average level of actual child support payments. However, because payments under CAP declined only by 10 percent of income up to the poverty line and by 67 percent of income above the poverty line, CAP dominated AFDC for mothers with earnings of $350 or more per month. At the same time, CAP was income-tested and limited to welfare-eligible families, unlike proposals for CSA. Another difference was CAP's provision of case management and employment services outside of AFDC. To determine the impacts of CAP, researchers studied the child support, employment, and welfare use of families randomly assigned to the CAP treatment and to a control group (Burstein and Werner 1994). They found that CAP generated a significant increase in child support awards (rising from 7.6 to 12 percent of participants) but not actual support payments, and significant increases in employment and earnings, but only modest gains in family income. Still, the changes in work incentives induced enough increased earnings to raise family incomes and save government resources at the same time. Family income rose by a modest $850 over five years while government spending saved $2,366 over the same period (Hamilton et al. 1996).

9.12   Conclusions

Child support enforcement has become an increasingly important function of our income support system for low-income families. Although the real costs of the CSE program are substantial—federal and state governments spend over $4 billion in administrative costs—so are the benefits. Already, nearly 30 percent of poor unmarried mothers receive a child support payment. As fewer low-income single parents remain on welfare, the incentives for custodial parents to receive support and for noncustodial parents to pay will rise substantially. Although it is not enough to provide basic support for families, child support can play a critical role in supplementing the incomes of low-income single parents and their children. Child support payments can be part of an income packaging strategy that includes earnings, the Earned Income Tax Credit, food stamps, child care subsidies, and Medicaid or subsidized health insurance. Until recently, low rates of paternity establishment (below 30 percent of nonmarital births) limited collections on behalf of the poorest group of single mothers, never-married mothers. But in the last few years, the CSE system has made great strides in raising rates of paternity establishment. The increase in paternity establishment not only is critical for expanding child support payments to the lowest-income families, but may even be discouraging nonmarital births.

Still, child support enforcement has a long way to go. One major problem is how to deal with arrearages facing low-income fathers subject to child support obligations. Without changes in policy, many low-income fathers will see their support payments going to the state for arrearages instead of helping raise living standards of their children. Parents will find themselves with the same disincentives experienced under the welfare system. In addition, the CSE system must find fairer ways to take account of the low income levels and high income instability of many noncustodial parents. Finally, given the greater acceptance of an expanded CSE, Congress should consider expanding the federal government's role in resolving the critical equity issues of visitation and access.

References

Barnow, B., T. Dall, M. Nowak, and B. Dannhausen. 2000. *The potential of the Child Support Enforcement Program to avoid costs to public programs: A review and synthesis of the literature.* Washington, D.C.: U.S. Department of Health and Human Services, April.

Bassi, L., and B. Barnow. 1993. Expenditures on children and child support guidelines. *Journal of Policy Analysis and Management* 12 (summer): 478–97.

Bassi, L., and R. Lerman. 1996. Reducing the child welfare disincentive problem. *Journal of Policy Analysis and Management* 15 (winter): 89–96.

Beller, A., and J. Graham. 1993. *Small change: The economics of child support.* New Haven, Conn.: Yale University Press.

Betson, D., E. Evenhouse, and S. Reilly. 1992. Trade-offs implicit in child support guidelines. *Journal of Policy Analysis and Management* 11 (Winter): 1–20.

Bianchi, S., L. Subaiya, and J. Kahn. 1999. The gender gap in the economic well-being of nonresident fathers and custodial mothers. *Demography* 36 (2): 195–203.

Bishop, S. 1992. *Evaluation of child support review and modification demonstration projects in four states.* Final report. Fairfax, Va.: Caliber Associates.

Bloom, D., C. Conrad, and C. Miller. 1998. Child support and fathers' remarriage and fertility. In *Fathers under fire: The revolution in child support enforcement,* ed. I. Garfinkel, S. McLanahan, D. Meyer, and J. Seltzer, 128–56. New York: Russell Sage Foundation.

Brito, T. 2000. The welfarization of family law: The case of child support. *Focus* 21 (spring): 67–71.

Burstein, N., and A. Werner. 1994. The New York State Child Assistance Program: Design, operation, and early impacts. In *Child support and child well-being,* ed. I. Garfinkel, S. McLanahan, and P. K. Robins, 207–36. Washington, D.C.: Urban Institute Press.

Case, A. 1998. The effects of stronger child support enforcement on nonmarital fertility. In *Fathers under fire: The revolution in child support enforcement,* ed. I. Garfinkel, S. McLanahan, D. Meyer, and J. Seltzer, 191–215. New York: Russell Sage Foundation.

Cherlin, A., J. Griffith, and J. McCarthy. 1983. A note on martially-disrupted men's reports of child support in the June 1980 Current Population Survey. *Demography* 20 (3): 385–89.

Clarke, L., E. Cooksey, and G. Verropoulou. 1998. Fathers and absent fathers: Sociodemographic similarities in Britain and the United States. *Demography* 35 (2): 217–28.

Duncan, G., and S. Hoffman. 1985. A reconsideration of the economic consequences of marital dissolution. *Demography* 22 (4): 485–97.

Edin, K., and L. Lein. 1997. *Making ends meet: How single mothers survive welfare and low-wage work.* New York: Russell Sage Foundation.

Edin, K., L. Lein, and T. Nelson. 1998. Low-income, non-residential fathers: Off-balance in a competitive economy, an initial analysis. Available at [http://aspe.hhs.gov/fathers/eln/eln98.htm].

Freeman, R., and J. Waldfogel. 1998. Does child support enforcement policy affect male labor supply? In *Fathers under fire: The revolution in child support enforcement,* ed. I. Garfinkel, S. McLanahan, D. Meyer, and J. Seltzer, 94–127. New York: Russell Sage Foundation.

Garfinkel, I. 1994. *Assuring child support: An extension of Social Security.* New York: Russell Sage Foundation.

Garfinkel, I., S. McLanahan, and T. Hanson. 1998. A patchwork portrait of nonresident fathers. In *Fathers under fire: The revolution in child support enforcement,* ed. I. Garfinkel, S. McLanahan, D. Meyer, and J. Seltzer, 31–60. New York: Russell Sage Foundation.

Garfinkel, I., S. McLanahan, and K. Harknett. 1999. Fragile families and welfare reform. Paper prepared for the conference "For Better and For Worse: State Welfare Reform and the Well-Being of Low-Income Families and Children," sponsored by the Joint Center for Poverty Research. 16–17 September, Washington, D.C.

Garfinkel, I., S. McLanahan, and P. Robins. 1992. Child support assurance: Design issues, expected impacts, and political barriers as seen from Wisconsin. Washington, D.C.: Urban Institute Press.

Garfinkel, I., and D. Oellerich. 1989. Noncustodial fathers' ability to pay child support. *Demography* 26 (2): 219–33.

Graham, J., and A. Beller. 1989. The effect of child support payments on the labor supply of female family heads: An econometric analysis. *Journal of Human Resources* 24:664–88.

———. Forthcoming. Nonresident fathers and their children: Child support and visitation from an economic perspective. In *Handbook of father involvement: Multidisciplinary perspectives,* ed. S. Tamis-LeMonda and N. Cabera.

Hamilton, W., N. Burstein, A. Baker, A. Earle, S. Gluckman, L. Peck, and A.

White. 1996. *The New York State Child Assistance Program: Five year impacts, costs, and benefits.* Cambridge, Mass.: Abt Associates, October.

Hanson, D. 1999. The American invention of child support: Dependency and punishment in Early American child support law. *Yale Law Journal* 108 (5): 1123–53.

Henry, R. 1999. Child support at a crossroads: When the real world intrudes upon academics and advocates. *Family Law Quarterly* 33 (1): 235–64.

Hu, W. 1999. Child support, welfare dependency, and women's labor supply. *Journal of Human Resources* 34 (winter): 71–103.

Huang, C., I. Garfinkel, and J. Waldfogel. 1999. Child support and welfare caseloads. Columbia University School of Social Work. Unpublished manuscript.

Institute for Research on Poverty. 2000. Child support enforcement policy and low-income families. *Focus* 21 (1): 3.

Johnson, E., A. Levine, and F. Doolittle. 1999. *Father's fair share: Helping poor men manage child support and fatherhood.* New York: Russell Sage Foundation.

Knox, V., and C. Redcross. 2000. *Parenting and providing: The impact of Parents' Fair Share on paternal involvement.* New York: Manpower Demonstration Research Corporation. October.

Lerman, R. 1993. A national profile of young unwed fathers. In *Young unwed fathers: Changing roles and emerging policies,* ed. R. Lerman and T. Ooms, 52–73. Philadelphia: Temple University.

Martinez, J., and C. Miller. 2000. The effects of Parents' Fair Share on the employment and earnings of low-income, noncustodial fathers. *Focus* 21 (1): 23–26.

Meyer, D., and M. Cancian. 2001. *W-2 Child Support Demonstration Evaluation, phase 1: Final report.* Vol. 1, *Effects of the experiment.* University of Wisconsin-Madison, Institute for Research on Poverty, April.

Meyer, D., I. Garfinkel, D. T. Oellerich, and P. K. Robins. 1994. Who should be eligible for an assured child support benefit? In *Child support and child well-being,* ed. I. Garfinkel, S. McLanahan, and P. K. Robins, 175–205. Washington, D.C.: Urban Institute Press.

Meyer, D., and M. Hu. 1999. A note on the antipoverty effectiveness of child support among mother-only families. *Journal of Human Resources* 34 (winter): 225–34.

Miller, C., I. Garfinkel, and S. McLanahan. 1997. Child support in the U.S.: Can fathers afford to pay more? *Review of Income and Wealth* 43 (3): 261–81.

Morgan, L. 1998. *Child support guidelines: Interpretation and application.* New York: Aspen Law and Business.

National Commission on Children. 1991. *Beyond rhetoric.* Washington, D.C.: U.S. Government Printing Office.

Nichols-Casebolt, A. 1986. The economic impact of child support on the poverty status of custodial and noncustodial families. *Journal of Marriage and the Family* 48 (4): 875–80.

Nixon, L. 1996. *Child support enforcement and welfare reform.* Washington, D.C.: Mathematica Policy Research, August.

———. 1997. The effect of child support enforcement on marital dissolution. *Journal of Human Resources* 32 (1): 159–81.

Pate, D., and E. Johnson. 2000. The ethnographic study for the W-2 Child Support Demonstration evaluation: Some preliminary findings. *Focus* 21 (1): 18–22.

Pearson, J., and N. Thoennes. 1998. Programs to increase fathers' access to their children. In *Fathers under fire: The revolution in child support enforcement,* ed. I. Garfinkel, S. McLanahan, D. Meyer, and J. Seltzer, 220–52. New York: Russell Sage Foundation.

Peters, E., L. Argys, E. Maccoby, and R. Mnookin. 1993. Enforcing divorce settlements: Evidence for child support compliance and award modifications. *Demography* 30 (4): 719–35.

Pirog, M., M. Klotz, and K. Byers. 1998. Interstate comparisons of child support orders using state guidelines. *Family Relations* 47 (July): 289–95.

Pirog-Good, M., and D. Good. 1995. Child support enforcement for teenage fathers: Problems and prospects. *Journal of Policy Analysis and Management* 14 (1): 25–42.

Plotnick, R., I. Garfinkel, D. Gaylin, S. McLanahan, and I. Ku. 1999. Better child support enforcement: Can it reduce teenage childbearing? Paper presented at the Association for Public Policy and Management. November, Washington, D.C.

Ribero, R. 1994. Visitations and child support transfers: A competitive equilibrium approach. New York University, Department of Economics. Mimeograph.

Roberts, P. 1994. *Ending poverty as we know it: The case for child support enforcement and assurance.* Washington, D.C.: Center for Law and Social Policy.

―――. 2001. *An ounce of prevention and a pound of cure: Developing state policy on the payment of child support arrears by low-income parents.* Washington, D.C.: Center for Law and Social Policy.

Rothe, I., and D. Meyer. 2000. Setting child support orders: Historical approaches and ongoing struggles. *Focus* 21 (1): 58–63.

Seltzer, A., S. McLanahan, and T. Hanson. 1998. Will child support enforcement increase father-child contact and parental conflict after separation? In *Fathers under fire: The revolution in child support enforcement,* ed. I. Garfinkel, S. McLanahan, D. Meyer, and J. Seltzer, 91–215. New York: Russell Sage Foundation.

Solomon, C. 1989. *The Child Support Enforcement Program: Policy and Practice.* Congressional Research Service report to Congress. Washington, D.C.: Congressional Research Service.

Sonenstein, F., and C. Calhoun. 1990. Determinants of child support: A pilot survey of absent parents. *Contemporary Policy Issues* 8 (January): 75–94.

Sorensen, E. 1997. A national profile of nonresident fathers and their ability to pay child support. *Journal of Marriage and the Family* 59 (November): 785–97.

―――. 1999. Obligating dads: Helping low-income non-custodial fathers do more for their children. Strengthening Families Brief Series. Washington, D.C.: Urban Institute, March.

Sorensen, E., and S. Clark. 1994. A child support assurance program: How much will it reduce child poverty, and at what cost? *American Economic Review* 84 (May): 114–19.

Sorensen, E., and A. Hill. Forthcoming. Single mothers and their child support receipt: How well is child support enforcement doing? *Journal of Human Resources.*

Sorensen, E., and R. Lerman. 1998. Welfare reform and low-income noncustodial fathers: Sanctions alone will not work. *Challenge: The Magazine of Economic Affairs* 41 (4): 101–16.

Sorensen, E., and C. Zibman. 2000. To what extent do children benefit from child support? Assessing the New Federalism: Discussion Paper no. 19. Washington, D.C.: The Urban Institute.

Turetsky, V. 1998. You get what you pay for: How federal and state investment decisions affect child support performance. Washington, D.C.: Center for Law and Social Policy. Working paper, December.

U.S. Bureau of the Census. 1999. *Child support for custodial mothers and fathers: 1995.* Current Population Reports, Series P60, no. 196. Washington, D.C.: U.S. Government Printing Office.

————. Various years. *Child support and alimony.* Washington, D.C.: U.S. Government Printing Office.

————. Various years. Child support for custodial mothers and fathers. Washington, D.C.: U.S. Government Printing Office.

U.S. Department of Health and Human Services. 1997a. *22nd annual report to Congress.* Washington, D.C.: U.S. Department of Health and Human Services.

————. 1997b. *Child support enforcement incentive funding.* Washington, D.C.: U.S. Department of Health and Human Services.

————. 1999. *State child access and visitation programs: A preliminary report for fiscal year 1997 funding.* Washington, D.C.: U.S. Department of Health and Human Services.

————. Various years. *Child support enforcement annual report to Congress.* Washington, D.C.: U.S. Department of Health and Human Services.

U.S. House of Representatives, Committee on Ways and Means. 1998. *1998 green book: Background material and data on programs within the jurisdiction of the Committee on Ways and Means.* Washington, D.C.: U.S. Government Printing Office.

————. 2000. *2000 green book: Background material and data on programs within the jurisdiction of the Committee on Ways and Means.* Washington, D.C.: U.S. Government Printing Office.

Waller, M., and R. Plotnick. 1999. *Child support and low-income families: Perceptions, practices, and policy.* San Francisco, Calif.: Public Policy Institute of California.

Weiss, Y., and R. Willis. 1985. Children as collective goods and divorce settlements. *Journal of Labor Economics* 3 (3): 268–92.

————. 1993. Transfers among divorced couples: Evidence and interpretation. *Journal of Labor Economics* 11 (4): 629–79.

Wheaton, L., and E. Sorensen. 1998a. Reducing welfare costs and dependency: How much bang for the child support buck? *Georgetown Public Policy Review* 4 (1): 23–37.

————. 1998b. Tax relief for low-income fathers who pay child support. In *Proceedings: Ninetieth annual conference on taxation.* Washington, D.C.: National Tax Association.

Williams, R. 1994. An overview of child support guidelines in the United States. In *Child support guidelines: The next generation,* ed. M. Haynes. Washington, D.C.: U.S. Department of Health and Human Services, Office of Child Support Enforcement, April.

————. 1996. Letter to the assistant deputy director of the Ohio Office of Child Support Enforcement, November.

Willis, R. 1999. A theory of out-of-wedlock childbearing. *Journal of Political Economy* 107 (6): S33–64.

Yun, K. 1992. Effects of child support on remarriage of single mothers. In *Child support assurance: Design issues, expected impacts, and political barriers as seen from Wisconsin,* ed. I. Garfinkel, S. McLanahan, and P. Robins, 315–38. Washington, D.C.: Urban Institute Press.

Contributors

David M. Blau
Department of Economics
Gardner Hall
University of North Carolina
Chapel Hill, NC 27599-3305

Richard V. Burkhauser
Department of Policy Analysis and
 Management
Cornell University
N134 Martha Van Rensselaer Hall
Ithaca, NY 14853

Janet Currie
Economics Department
University of California, Los Angeles
405 Hilgard Avenue
Los Angeles, CA 90095-1477

Mary C. Daly
Federal Reserve Bank of San
 Francisco
101 Market Street, Mail Stop 1130
San Francisco, CA 94105

Jonathan Gruber
Department of Economics, E52–355
Massachusetts Institute of
 Technology
Cambridge, MA 02142-1347

V. Joseph Hotz
Department of Economics
University of California, Los Angeles
Box 951477
Los Angeles, CA 90095-1477

Robert J. LaLonde
Harris Graduate School of Public
 Policy
University of Chicago
1155 East 60th Street, #145
Chicago, IL 60637

Robert I. Lerman
Department of Economics
Roper 117
American University
4400 Massachusetts Avenue, NW
Washington, DC 20016-8029

Robert A. Moffitt
Department of Economics
Johns Hopkins University
Baltimore, MD 21218

Edgar O. Olsen
Department of Economics
University of Virginia
PO Box 400182
Charlottesville, VA 22904-4182

John Karl Scholz
Department of Economics
University of Wisconsin–Madison
1180 Observatory Drive
Madison, WI 53706

Elaine Sorensen
The Urban Institute
2100 M Street, NW
Washington, DC 20037

Author Index

Subject Index

639